Ed

Enjoy This Book —

Thanks For All your Support in

2006 —

Semper Fi

Bruce

JUNGLE RULES

JUNGLE RULES

A True Story of Marine Justice in Vietnam

Charles W. Henderson

BERKLEY CALIBER
NEW YORK

THE BERKLEY PUBLISHING GROUP
Published by the Penguin Group
Penguin Group (USA) Inc.
375 Hudson Street, New York, New York 10014, USA
Penguin Group (Canada), 90 Eglinton Avenue East, Suite 700, Toronto, Ontario M4P 2Y3, Canada
(a division of Pearson Penguin Canada Inc.)
Penguin Books Ltd., 80 Strand, London WC2R 0RL, England
Penguin Group Ireland, 25 St. Stephen's Green, Dublin 2, Ireland (a division of Penguin Books Ltd.)
Penguin Group (Australia), 250 Camberwell Road, Camberwell, Victoria 3124, Australia
(a division of Pearson Australia Group Pty. Ltd.)
Penguin Books India Pvt. Ltd., 11 Community Centre, Panchsheel Park, New Delhi—110 017, India
Penguin Group (NZ), Cnr. Airborne and Rosedale Roads, Albany, Auckland 1310, New Zealand
(a division of Pearson New Zealand Ltd.)
Penguin Books (South Africa) (Pty.) Ltd., 24 Sturdee Avenue, Rosebank, Johannesburg 2196, South Africa

Penguin Books Ltd., Registered Offices: 80 Strand, London WC2R 0RL, England

While the author has made every effort to provide accurate telephone numbers and Internet addresses at the time of publication, neither the publisher nor the author assumes any responsibility for errors, or for changes that occur after publication. Further, publisher does not have any control over and does not assume any responsibility for author or third-party websites or their content.

This book is an original publication of The Berkley Publishing Group.

First edition: November 2006

Library of Congress Cataloging-in-Publication Data

Henderson, Charles, 1948–
   Jungle rules : a true story of Marine justice in Vietnam / by Charles
Henderson.
       p. cm.
   Includes index.
   ISBN 0-425-21186-X (alk. paper)
   1. Trials (Military offenses)—Vietnam.   2. Courts-martial and courts
of inquiry—United States—History.   3. United States. Marine Corps
—History—Vietnam War, 1961–1975.   4. Vietnam War, 1961–1975
—United States.   I. Title.
KF7654.3.H46 2006
959.704'3—dc22

2006023917

PRINTED IN THE UNITED STATES OF AMERICA

10   9   8   7   6   5   4   3   2   1

For my friends Geoff Lyon and John Reynolds,
Marine Corps lawyers,
and for my pal John Britt,
the Mustard King

Young man, the secret of my success is that at an early age I discovered that I was not God.

—Oliver Wendell Holmes, Jr.

FOREWORD

MOST MEN AND women who served in the U.S. Marine Corps, or who have lived in the company of a Marine, will quickly recognize the meaning of this book's title, *Jungle Rules*. Unlike its literary derivative, Robert Service's poem "Law of the Yukon," the term, "Jungle Rules" has little to do with rules that apply to life in a jungle setting and nothing at all to do with a jungle itself. In fact, if the truth were known, the term more likely came from some Stateside origin quite remote from any tropical rain forest and more likely in a sandlot.

"Jungle Rules" is a sports term describing a method loosely governing the play of a game. In other words, when observing Jungle Rules one overlooks many of a sport's fouls or penalties that seem petty and that get in the way of the game's fun, such as allowing tackling in flag football, or hockey-style body checking under the boards when battling for rebounds in a basketball game. Marines use Jungle Rules when playing unorganized contests of baseball, football, basketball, soccer, or any other team sport encumbered by too many rules that tend to overly slow down play. So they just don't bother to call most fouls or penalties, unless the infraction is so harsh or blatant that it stops the game itself. Then they may step off five yards or allow two free throws, while they drag the victim of the penalty to the sidelines for resuscitation and medical care.

Jungle Rules, therefore, are very flexible standards that are open to broad interpretations. Playing a game by Jungle Rules is usually rough, and adherence to any specific rules of a sport depends purely on the participants' senses of fair play and sportsmanship. Generally, there are no referees.

Throughout much of the history of the armed services of the United States, military regulations and the administration of justice also had broad interpretations and varying applications. Justice itself relied mainly on the sensibilities of the officer who held command over the individual who broke the rules.

For more than a hundred years, U.S. military law was based on the 1774 British Articles of War. Until 1951, nearly four years following the creation of the Department of Defense, unifying the military services, each armed force branch had its own separate regulations, system of justice, and application of existing military law.

The need to create a single, uniform system of military justice became clear during World War II. Until then, the United States had only a small standing army and navy, and the "Rocks and Shoals," a popular term that described the 1774 British Articles of War, along with a few updated amendments pertinent to the navy or the army at the time, seemed to suffice, although some legal historians may successfully argue that the Rocks and Shoals denied justice and constitutional guarantees to those tried under them.

However, the need for a major retooling of the military justice system became clear during World War II, when the United States put more than sixteen million men and women in uniform, and conducted more than two million courts-martial during the war years. Throughout the nearly four years of U.S. participation in World War II, the military obtained on average sixty general courts-martial convictions each day of the war, and totaled more than eighty thousand felony convictions. Many of the courts-martial involved infractions that dealt with rules governing good order and discipline, and outside the military community the committed acts would not have violated any civilian laws.

America's first secretary of defense, James V. Forrestal, who assumed his newly created office on September 17, 1947, realized that the same logic that required unifying the armed forces under the Department of Defense also required a uniform code of justice for the military consistent with the U.S. Constitution and the command authority of the president.

Thus, in 1950, Congress enacted Title 10 of the U.S. Code, Sections 801 through 946, known as the Uniform Code of Military Justice and the

Manual for Courts-Martial. The UCMJ and MCM embodied a full system of laws and directives for the administration of justice pertaining to those laws. The UCMJ and MCM went into effect the following year.

By the mid-1960s, with the advent of the conflict in South Vietnam, many federal lawmakers began to recognize various shortcomings within that version of the UCMJ and MCM, many of which dealt with the qualifications of defense counsel, trial judges, and who might hold authority over these judges and lawyers. Accordingly, Congress made a number of sweeping revisions to the UCMJ and MCM. As a result of those changes, during 1967 and 1968 military lawyers found themselves struggling through a period of uncertain transition from the old UCMJ and MCM to the newer version. Understanding was often nebulous at best. Interpretation of the rules frequently depended on who read them.

That period in South Vietnam left the judges and lawyers tasked to defend and prosecute cases in an often frustrating state, trying to adapt order from an unsettled system. It took several years for the military judges and lawyers to finally settle on some consistent interpretations of the new UCMJ and MCM. In the meantime, the application of justice took on the nature of playing the game by Jungle Rules.

The events described in *Jungle Rules* are taken from actual transcripts of trials and investigations, primarily conducted by military lawyers assigned to the Office of the Staff Judge Advocate, First Marine Aircraft Wing, during 1967 and 1968. Therefore, the stories told in *Jungle Rules* are true, at least inasmuch as the court transcripts, investigation records, and testimony reflect.

However, except for those people of obvious prominence or historic importance, such as Lieutenant General Robert E. Cushman, Jr., the commanding general of the III Marine Amphibious Force in Da Nang, or President Lyndon B. Johnson, the names, and backgrounds of many of the characters in *Jungle Rules* have been altered.

The Marines who committed most of the offenses described in *Jungle Rules* paid their penalties decades ago. Dredging up these people's sometimes painful pasts could possibly cause harm to some who today may live respectable lives. They deserve to be left alone. The lawyers and some of the other Marines in *Jungle Rules* may prefer to be left alone, too. The true identities of any of these people would contribute little to the stories in this book.

However, the events surrounding the people in *Jungle Rules* are true.

Lastly, the idea that gave birth to this book came to me from a friend who deserves a great deal of thanks and rightful acknowledgment for his contributions. That friend is John C. Reynolds, an attorney who served as a Marine captain in South Vietnam in 1967 and 1968, assigned as a lawyer to the Office of the Staff Judge Advocate, First Marine Aircraft Wing in Da Nang.

I came to know John Reynolds in New York City in 1986 while I lived and worked there. We became good friends. During that time he told me many stories about cases that he and others tried in Da Nang, and about a riot that took place in the brig on Freedom Hill in August 1968.

As those war stories amassed and grew more interesting, before long the idea for *Jungle Rules* began to take hold. In 1987, as I drafted the first outline for the *Jungle Rules* project, first envisioning it primarily as a motion picture screenplay, John Reynolds answered my questions and clarified issues about the circa 1968 military justice system, and the way things were done at First MAW Law.

Although we had fun developing the outline, and sometimes argued over trivial ideas, the project never really got anywhere. John Reynolds even went to the trouble of registering the outline with the Writers' Guild in New York in 1987, as a potential motion picture, but nobody at that time expressed any interest in a project about a brig riot and lawyers in Vietnam. In time, our interests in the project also waned, and the outline soon took residence in my file drawer for nearly twenty years.

I left New York in 1990, and that is the last time I saw or heard from John Reynolds. In the summer of 2004, when at long last I knew that *Jungle Rules* would finally be a book, I tried to find my old friend and tell him the good news. Despite my repeated efforts through every means I could imagine, as of publication of the book I have not been able to locate him.

I feel bad that we did not stay in touch after I moved from New York City. I hope that today John Reynolds is well and happy.

Charles Henderson

Chapter 1

FIRST LOOK

DOGPATCH.

To get there from anyplace in Da Nang, just follow the smell.

Rusted tin, cardboard, broken stucco, discarded cars, mud and thatch. All of it pinned, nailed, or wired together by desperate hands of humankind's abandoned. A patchwork blanket of crap that spreads a square mile. Shacks, hovels, junk piles, hardly any of them providing real shelter, but all of them representing the overcrowded homes for the slum's wretched inhabitants. Mostly shoved wall against wall, their roofs overlapping, these haphazard dins offer just enough space out front for a bicycle pushed by a skinny person to squeeze past.

Slime-caked trenches carry a constant trickle of sewer water running alongside the narrow, hard-pac pathways that meander through the ramshackle maze. Flowing over or through the decaying body of a dead cat here, a dead rat there, spilling out of the ditch into big puddles that gather at every turn, the pestilent runoff wreaks a foul stench that adds a pronounced flavor to the dank, smoke-enriched air that wafts across Da Nang.

Pigs, chickens, half-naked kids dart about the dark alleys of Dogpatch. A black-toothed old grandma tosses out a pan full of liquid, feeding the putrid trench in front of her home, while inside the dismal little warren where she had emerged, another black-toothed woman squats on the dirt floor by a charcoal fire, stirring with a stick a boiling concoction of catch-as-catch-can stew. Tromping in the shadows, a dog with mangy blotched skin stretched over rib bones, spine, and hips looks warily for a handout. Dusty and sad, he may try to steal a grab-and-run meal while dodging a fate that could land him in a soup kettle. Like everyone else in Dogpatch, luck of the moment is all he has.

Poverty, filth, and disease live in Dogpatch. So does corruption.

Crime bosses stockpile heroin, guns, and black-market booze here, often in the backs of dope-den bordellos that overlook galleries surrounding blood-spattered plyboard arenas where around-the-clock gambling takes place: dog and cock fights, pitched battles between snakes and mongooses, and once in a while a death match between human combatants, kick-boxing to the finish. Whatever the game, here they play for keeps.

In Dogpatch, it's all for sale. Flesh, lives, homicide, oblivion.

Need a matchbox, lid, or kilo of pot or something stronger? Hash or opium? Something more refined? Pills perhaps? Blues, yellow jackets, reds, uppers, downers? How about some LSD? Perhaps an ounce or two of H? Take your pick, China rock, Burma white, or regular old brown shit, dealers have ample stocks. Little shops with lots of incense burning in their fronts to attract hungry clients, sell the dope both retail and wholesale from under the counter. Out back, the storekeeper may just be finishing bagging out a fresh batch of Buddha, opium-soaked marijuana, a particular favorite among American GIs. A few tokes of a pin joint and the blue bus cruises into Wonderland.

Need a man dead? Hits for hire come cheap in Dogpatch. Just ask one of the cowboys leaning in a shanty door with his opium stare and a gun stuffed in his waistband, under his shirt.

Tucked within the slum, large villa-style houses surrounded by high, concrete walls with razor wire on top lay hidden here and there, obscured from most prying eyes. Quiet little whore farms. Ranches, they call them in Dogpatch-savvy American lingo. Prostitutes raised, trained, and put on the streets from these urban spreads. A steady flow of girl children bought or snatched from hungry, displaced families keeps the flesh trade fueled with a fresh array of new talent, made ready in Dogpatch for the street hustle in Da Nang.

Guarded by a crew of armed cowboys, the rancher, usually a crime boss, dope-dealing, Murder, Inc., pimp, lives here in luxury with his harem. He dictates the rules. He writes the laws. He makes it worthwhile for the local constabulary to leave his territory alone. Not even the Communists bother him.

That's because people come here to get lost. To avoid. To disappear beneath the putrid tide. They don't come here to fight anybody's war. If anything, they come here to escape it.

Dogpatch is the Deadwood of Da Nang. A haven for outlaws, addicts, and misfits desperate to get away.

IN THE LATE fall of 1967, James Harris ran to Dogpatch after slipping off the leash of a dimwitted brig chaser. The indolent fatso guard had flopped into the jeep's front seat, and casually left his prisoner to bounce on the back cargo floor, unwatched, sitting on his cuffed hands, while they drove from the Freedom Hill lockup to a preliminary hearing at the First Marine Aircraft Wing head shed, for Harris to face charges of dope peddling and insubordination.

Before his jeep ride that morning, the ratty-looking Marine lance corporal had managed to grab a shower and a shave with a dull, donated razor, but still wore his same old oil-stained and dirt-encrusted utility trousers, and sleeveless, green T-shirt from the Da Nang Air Base flight line, where two days ago a pair of narcs from CID had stung him in a fake buy. They nailed him dead to rights with three dozen pin joints of Buddha, a couple more loose ounces of the stuff twisted in a plastic bag, a dozen packets of Zig-Zag regulars and big Bambu' rolling papers, a hash pipe, some roach clips, and a thick pile of cash.

As the undercover narcotics cops hustled him from the flight line, Harris mouthed off to his squadron's adjutant, a first lieutenant from Freeport, Texas, named Clyde Brazwell, who had sicced the rat dogs from the Criminal Investigation Division of the III Marine Amphibious Force Provost Marshal's Office on the troublesome Marine. They had wasted no time sending two shaggy-haired dirtbags to make the buy and bust.

Various rumors about Harris peddling dope had surfaced off and on among the senior enlisted and junior officers since he had landed in the squadron. Then this morning, while sipping coffee and gazing out his office window, thoughtlessly watching the flight-line mechanic who idled away most days smearing epoxy goo and paint over minor bullet and shrapnel damage on airplanes parked between sorties just outside the squadron's hangar, the lieutenant saw two other lowlife dregs take up residence by Harris's big gray tool chest. There in broad daylight, in plain sight, squatting in the shade of the airplane wing, the trio exchanged a handful of cash for a handful of dope that Harris took from a cigar box he kept stashed inside the big gray chest.

4   CHARLES HENDERSON

The former Marine sergeant who had fought his way out of the enlisted ranks by going to college at nights and earning a regular officer's
commission, despite the blatant prejudices stacked against men of his
color, had never liked the ditty-bopping shit bird in the first place. Nor did
he like the man's bushed-out, Jimi Hendrix–style Afro hair or his insolent,
mouthy, big-city attitude. First Lieutenant Clyde Brazwell didn't even
bother going to the squadron commander first. He saw what he saw, and
needed no guidance, nor did he need anyone's permission to finally burn
this waste of skin. The middle-aged mustang officer called CID on the
spot, then told his boss.

In less than an hour, two shaggy dudes wearing dirty, sleeveless
T-shirts, scuffed-up boots, bleached-out, fluff-dried utility trousers, and
their long, bare hair blowing in the breeze, ambled to the airplane where
James Harris had resumed his piddle, wiping more epoxy goo on a bullet
hole. Seeing the likely duo, he jumped down to his toolbox and flipped up
the lid. While one dirtbag held out a handful of cash, and Harris thumbed
open the cigar box, the other dirtbag snatched the cool lance corporal by
the free hand and stepped behind him, twisting his arm like a rag and
nearly breaking off his thumb as he doubled his wrist backward. The other
dirtbag snatched the cigar box, and took that hand as their new prisoner
dropped to his knees. Just like that, the CID narcs had their man, and
cuffed him clean. No struggle.

Brazwell stood in the shade of the squadron headquarters hangar, his
arms folded and a big smile on his face as the two undercover CID Marines
led their prisoner away.

"Fucking Oreo brother motherfucker," James Harris said to Brazwell,
seeing the lieutenant standing there so cool, so smug, and so very satisfied.
"You're black on the outside but white through your middle."

"That's disrespect to a commissioned officer," the senior CID Marine
said to Harris, lifting him by his handcuffs, raising him to his tiptoes.
"Keep it up, clown, and we'll write even more charges."

The jailers took possession of James Harris's two-inch-long, hand-
carved ebony fist that he wore on a leather thong, dangling around his
neck, along with his blue bandanna that he kept tied around his head, and
his wallet, a pocket knife, and loose change. The cigar box full of dope and
cash went into a large brown envelope, marked "evidence," and he knew
he would never see it again. He figured that the narc rats working inside
CID would quickly absorb the cash, and smoke all but a few representative joints.

"Fucking wingers with your long hair, sideburns, and big-ass Afro hairdos. What are you trying to be, a Navajo tying that rag around your head? Fucking hippies, all of you air wing shit birds. You get back from your court hearing, and get formally charged, we're going to have ourselves a party, shaving that nappy scruff off your skull," a staff sergeant guard said to Harris as they walked him to his cage. "What do you think about that, Slick?"

Harris stared coldly at the white Marine MP, and said nothing as the heavy-gauge expanded-steel-mesh door slammed shut. He vowed to say nothing more to anyone. From here on out, they would have to read his mind. Last time he had stood before a judge, his fast mouth had jumped him onto a new set of tracks that led him to where he was today.

Back then, two years ago, the Chicago magistrate told the young, Blackstone Rangers gang lord from the Windy City's South Side that he had a choice between going to prison and continuing on a path of personal destruction, or seizing hold of a new beginning by enlisting in the Marine Corps. That day Harris talked way too smart and way too much, he later discovered, playing on the old white man's sympathies toward the underprivileged black youths of his city. With no lawyer to beat the assault charges, stemming from a street fight, he talked smart enough to get the offer of four years' military service rather than six months in jail. He felt so wise at the time. Beat the system. Yes, sir! he thought.

James Harris snapped at the chance to avoid hard labor behind bars, but quickly discovered at Marine Corps Recruit Depot Parris Island, South Carolina, that dragging chain in Cook County Jail would have been a cakewalk compared to the life into which he fell. Harsh discipline meted out by brutal drill instructors put the fear of God in him for a while. At least until a week after graduation. Then his old, salty self came slowly back to life. His attitude seemed to grow with the thickness of his hair. He smarted his way into airframe mechanics' school and slid downhill from there.

"White man's world, white man's rules, white man's war," he had reminded himself as he sat in his cage for two days, waiting for his initial hearing. Then the fat chaser cuffed him extra tight, and threw him in the back of the jeep. While his wrists ached with the pain that the manacles brought, their hard, sharp edges twisting into his flesh, James Harris kept a steely face and told himself that one day he would even the score.

A pothole on a sharp turn sent the handcuffed prisoner airborne. Seizing the opportunity that the slack-minded driver handed him, Harris bailed over the spare tire and hit the street, running like a wide receiver dashing for the goal line. He never looked back.

The chaser slung two full magazines of .45-caliber lead at him but never got close. Fat, lazy, and disheveled, the shit-bird guard was a bad shot, too. In seconds, the fleeing prisoner had ducked through a hedge and disappeared.

Through most of that first night, the Marine provost marshal in Da Nang had his men search the area into which Harris had fled. The MPs even brought in dogs. They sniffed a trail that wound through alleys, across roofs, and then down to the little shit creek that spilled out of Dog-patch. That's where they stopped.

James Harris managed to get his cuffed hands from behind his back by wriggling them under his butt and stepping through, but he could not work the steel bracelets off either wrist. He spent his first night in Dog-patch sleeping under a slab of concrete, sharing the space with a mangy brown mutt starved to skin and bones. The lumpy mongrel with gaping patches of bare skin across his back followed Harris throughout the next morning as the escaped prisoner searched for more suitable shelter, a hack-saw, a new set of clothes, and something to eat. The filthy dog kept fol-lowing him even after two cowboys had caught him blind-sided, and led him at gunpoint to the ranch of their boss, a Marine deserter named Brian Thomas Pitts.

"Sing out your fucking name, ass-wipe," Pitts said, sitting on a green leather sofa chair, sipping a tall glass of iced tea, and looking at the hand-cuffed bag of rags in front of him, and the tattered dog that crouched, head down, behind the prisoner's heels.

"Fuck you," Harris said.

The cowboy standing to Harris's right slapped the prisoner on the back of his head with the cocked, U.S. government-issue Colt .45-caliber pistol that he had held pointed in the young man's ear. Just as the blow sent the Marine's head forward, the cowboy on the left laid a hard backhand across Harris's mouth.

"No," Pitts said, taking a sip of tea, "you're the one who will be fucked if you don't lose that street nigger attitude in about one heartbeat. My man Huong, standing to your right, will simply put a round in your stupid skull and feed your ass to a pen of hogs we keep out back to dis-pose of garbage like you."

The prisoner flashed a bloody smile at Brian T. Pitts and said, "Now that you put it that way, my name's James Harris. My peas down on the flight line, though, they all call me Mau Mau."

"What's your claim to fame, Mau Mau, waltzing into my world with those government irons on your wrists?" Pitts said.

"Got busted selling reefer, and mouthed off to the squadron adjutant," Harris said. "Coon called CID on my ass. The motherfucker."

"You obviously live a charmed life," Pitts said, "to slip their grip and land on my doorstep."

"And who the fuck are you?" Harris snarled, glaring at his new captor.

"I could be your judge, jury, and executioner," Pitts retorted, "or your new best friend. It's pretty much up to you."

"I'll be your friend if you get these handcuffs off my wrists," Harris said, and showed Pitts his most encouraging smile.

THE MOST MEMORABLE thing that greeted Captains Jonathan Charles Kirkwood and Terence Boyd O'Connor when they landed in Da Nang was the stink. Nearly inescapable. The wretched, rotten air smothered and choked them and made their eyes burn. When the wind is right, even a tough guy fights back a gag reflex as he steps down the ladder off the freedom bird and samples his first taste of South Vietnam. For the two new First Marine Aircraft Wing lawyers, the dank, smoky, rotten-egg-smelling air left an indelible imprint in both their minds.

"Fuck me to tears!" Kirkwood exclaimed as he took his first step down the ladder from the Flying Tigers Airlines Boeing 707. The middle-aged blond flight attendant who stood on the landing next to the plane's open hatch, bidding farewell to the departing American servicemen, smiled kindly at the dark-eyed, dark-haired, six-foot-tall, youthful-looking Marine captain and simply shook her head at his comment.

"Watch your fucking mouth, Jon," O'Connor, a five-foot-ten-inch-tall, reddish-brown-haired, blue-eyed Philadelphia Irishman said, smiling his dimples at the woman, "there's ladies present."

"Sorry, ma'am," Kirkwood mumbled in a serious tone. Then he looked at his mischievous, freckle-faced buddy whom he first met at Officer Candidates' School, sleeping in the rack above him, now more than a year ago, and had been his classmate for six months through the Basic School at Quantico, and his best friend and study partner for ten months through Naval Justice School at Newport, Rhode Island. "Terry, you watch your mouth, too."

"I hope it's not like this every day," O'Connor said, now bounding down the stairs behind a sometimes clumsy Kirkwood. "I get some really serious sinus headaches. The New York City pollution nearly wiped me out while I went to college and law school there. Now the slightest bit of crap in the air makes me crazy."

"My college and law school days didn't do my sinuses any favors either. I thought the smog in Los Angeles was the world's worst until I got here," Kirkwood said, now holding his handkerchief over his mouth and nose, and squinting at a burly, bald-headed staff sergeant waiting at the bottom of the ladder.

"Captain Kirkwood, Captain O'Connor, my name is Staff Sergeant Derek Pride. Welcome to Da Nang, Republic of South Vietnam," the robust Marine said cheerfully, snapping a quick salute to both officers. "It's a pressure inversion, little wind, and what flow we do have is from the east, so it is like a lid on a jar here. All the shit bottled up. Sorry you came on such a bad day, but you'll get used to it."

"What is it?" Kirkwood then asked the sergeant. "Is there a paper mill or something nearby to cause such a terrible smell?"

"No, sir," Pride said, leading the men across the tarmac, "that's Dogpatch."

"Dogpatch?" Kirkwood said. "Like from the Lil' Abner cartoons?"

"Sort of," Pride said, walking abreast the two captains. "It's the slum. Bad area. Nobody righteous goes there. At least nobody with any brains. We leave it alone because it's far enough from any of our forces to not be a factor for them, and frankly, we just don't need another headache. We have our hands full with Charlie and the NVA, out there on the ridges. Nothing but dopers and deadbeats in Dogpatch anyway. Maybe a few deserters, too, but I'd rather be in jail than that place. Believe me."

"Where do we go from here?" O'Connor said, pulling his handkerchief over his nose and mouth, too.

"Just inside," the sergeant said. "Receiving will endorse your orders and get you started on the happy road to check-in. From here, however, we will go directly to billeting, and get you into your quarters."

"I could use a nap," Kirkwood said, now ambling a pace behind O'Connor and Staff Sergeant Pride. "Terry, aren't you tired?"

"A little punchy, Jon, but I'm making it," O'Connor said.

"If you're smart, sir, you'll grab a nap, too," Pride said, opening the door to the Da Nang Air Base passenger terminal, and then leading the two officers toward a high counter where a round-faced gunnery sergeant sat like a Buddha behind a desk placard that said: *Officer and Staff NCO Check-in*. "The wing staff judge advocate, Lieutenant Colonel Lewis Prunella, always hosts a hail-and-farewell party for the staff on the last Friday of each month, and gentlemen, that's tonight. While he may not say anything, should you sleep in, the military justice officer, Major Dudley

Dickinson, will most certainly. Since both of you gentlemen will be joining the defense team, you're already on the negative with him."

"How's that? He's never met us," O'Connor said, stuffing his handkerchief into his trousers pocket and picking up a pen and signing his name on a log sheet latched down on a clipboard overseen by the silent, round-faced gunny who rubber-stamped both officers' travel orders.

"Yeah," Kirkwood chimed in, now signing his name, "that's right. How can he start us on the negative when he knows nothing about us?"

"You'll find out when you check in with him," the staff sergeant said, escorting the duo back out the screen door and leading them to a jeep with a red plate emblazoned with the letters S-J-A stenciled in yellow fastened on its front bumper. "First we'll get you billeted, and then we'll go meet Major Dickinson. Just don't let him wear through your skin right off on your first day."

"Terry?" Kirkwood said, climbing onto the backseat of the jeep, his lanky frame adjusting uncomfortably to the perch.

"Yeah, Jon," O'Connor said, tossing his seabag on top of Kirkwood's duffel in the back floorboard, and then sliding himself comfortably onto the front seat.

"I think I know about this Major Dickinson," Kirkwood said. "They call him Dicky Doo and the Don'ts."

Staff Sergeant Pride laughed. "That's him, sir."

"Remember that good-looking lawyer we met back on Okinawa, at the Officers' Club at Kadina?" Kirkwood added.

"Manley Tufts," O'Connor said. "Sure, I recall the guy. Very fit. Good-looking. Like six-foot-two and some couple-hundred pounds. He walked with his arms out so he wouldn't wrinkle the inside creases on his shirtsleeves. From New Orleans, very aristocratic. Strange fellow."

"Right," Kirkwood said as the jeep now dodged between trucks and other traffic, making its way around the flight line and then down a street to a series of Quonset huts and concrete block buildings all painted tan. "His older brother, Stanley, is also a lawyer, both of them Tulane Law graduates. At any rate, Stanley is here as a prosecutor. So that's how Manley Tufts came to know about Major Dickinson, and his nickname."

"Yeah," O'Connor said, stepping out of the jeep. "I can hardly wait to meet the Mojo now. Dicky Doo, and I can only imagine how the Don'ts fit in."

"Gentlemen," Staff Sergeant Pride said with a smile, walking to the big red Staff Judge Advocate sign in front of the headquarters, "welcome to First MAW Law."

Kirkwood looked at the sergeant, flashed him a goofy grin, and began mimicking rocker Jim Morrison, singing a familiar tune by The Doors, "I got my Mojo working! I got my Mojo working!"

HAD BRIAN THOMAS Pitts not gone native six months into his tour, he might have gotten to attend his father's funeral a year ago. By now he would have long since left South Vietnam and have gotten an honorable discharge from the Marine Corps, too. Going on his third season in country, the sandy-haired cowboy from Olathe, Kansas, had come to dismiss nearly any chance of ever seeing home again.

At random times through the year, he used the telephone of an expatriate American building contractor in Da Nang who had a taste for young girls, reefer, and high-stakes poker. In return for laying off some of the man's always increasing gambling debt, along with giving him an attractive smoker's discount, and free visitation one night each month for a romp at the ranch with a farm-fresh virgin, the contractor let Pitts use his company telephone to call his Aunt Winnie Russell, the matronly older sister of his late mother, back home in Olathe.

Aunt Winnie brought him up to date on family news regarding what little of their kin who now remained aboveground. She tearfully told how they had found his poor father sitting there stone dead in a living room chair, the TV still running and a half-full whiskey bottle on the floor. It was a lovely funeral. An amazing array of flowers surrounded the casket. Nearly all the people at the Calvary Baptist Church came, too. They laid Dad to rest next to Mom, who had died of a brain hemorrhage when Brian was only ten years old. That's when life got hard for the boy.

His dad, Roy Pitts, drank more and worked less after his beloved wife, Bess, died. Then Brian moved into a room above Aunt Winnie's garage, which sat behind her house, just off East Cedar Street, near Highway 50, one of the main routes from Olathe into nearby Kansas City, and trouble.

Within a few years, the sweet little boy from the Calvary Baptist Sunday school in Olathe became a street-savvy cynic after a tough curriculum of life's hard lessons taught to him in late-night Kansas City pool halls and backroom gaming dens. By age sixteen, Brian Pitts had already learned that a hooker with a heart of gold will always rob a John cold, cut his throat, and leave him for dead if she thought she could get away with it. Likewise, gamblers and junkies were no better, but sometimes proved easy pickings with a sucker's game of eight-ball.

The guys at Robbie's Pool Hall on the southwestern edge of Kansas

City, where Brian spent his time after dropping out of high school, took to calling him Small Change, because he would start a mark off with a two-bit bet on his eight-ball game and let the sucker win. After each loss, he would throw another quarter on the table, and rack again and again, letting the chump build up a large head of superiority. He would pal right up to his prey, asking him for tips on how to shoot a better game. A seemingly innocent boy just learning a seasoned man's sport.

After dropping a couple of dollars in small change, luring the fish onto his line, Brian would then start to shoot a little better, and rave on and on about what an amazing shot he had just somehow accidentally made. What a streak of luck!

"Thanks for the help with my game. How about a dollar bet?" he would then ask the sucker, who nearly always laughed and confidently threw down a bill.

"Hate to take your money, kid," the mark often said.

"My dad's a dentist over in Shawnee," Brian would then lie. "I get fifty bucks a week allowance, so a dollar is nothing. Don't sweat the small shit."

"Make it five bucks then, rich boy," the sucker would many times follow through.

"How about ten?" Brian would come back with a cocky grin, and throw a Hamilton greenback on the table.

Sometimes the mark backed down, and begged off on a five-dollar bet. Most often, however, the sucker took the ten-dollar bait and played for blood.

Although he could have easily done it, Brian Pitts never ran the table, but barely won each folding-cash game. Just by a hair. Close enough to keep the sucker wanting to get back on his winning streak, and confident that he could play to even money with his next rack. Losers love to bet big, and ironically the more most of the marks lost, the greater each one bet, doubling his stakes as the hole got deeper from ten to twenty dollars, and sometimes even fifty.

With often a hundred dollars or more wadded in his jeans pockets, while letting the mark rack one more last game, Pitts would finally excuse himself to the can, and then duck out the backdoor. He would never let the sucker see him leave. It took only one ass whipping to teach him that rule of pool hustle life.

He learned the hard lesson after a sore loser had followed him out of Robbie's front door and caught him as he stepped around the corner to where he had parked Aunt Winnie's car. It took six stitches across his right eyebrow to close the gash after the angry mark had slammed the boy's head against the front bumper of the 1958 Ford Fairlane coupe.

If Brian ever saw a hustled player again, he would lie a tale of getting sick with the squirts, and heading out the backdoor, embarrassed, because he had accidently crapped his pants. Then with his clean-faced innocent smile, the boyish shark would offer the guy a fresh chance to play him and get even. This time Brian would win a few and lose a few, and leave his victim only a little short, but never quite even, certainly never on the plus side. The youngster the old Kansas City pool hall pros called Small Change always finished out ahead with at least a few newly won bills folded in his front pocket.

In the summer of 1963, Brian Pitts turned eighteen years old, and dutifully registered for the draft with the Johnson County, Kansas, U.S. Selective Service Board. A few weeks later he got his official Selective Service registration card in the mail that had the letters 1-A typed next to classification, just below his name. Three months later, he got a letter from the Johnson County draft board that began "Greetings," and ordered him to the U.S. Armed Forces Induction Center in Kansas City to take a physical examination to determine his fitness for service in the armed forces of the United States.

Since he didn't have flat feet or wear a dress, he knew that his life of nights at Robbie's Pool Hall and days relaxing in his room above Aunt Winnie's garage had ended. Considering that he had always liked the look of the Marine uniform over any of the other services' outfits, and that he had also heard that the Corps would get a guy in good shape and teach him some useful hand-to-hand combat skills, too, rather than punching a two-year draft ticket in the army, Brian joined the Marines for double the time.

Standing six feet tall and a trim 175 pounds, the Kansas cowboy had little trouble adapting to the physical stress that the Marines demanded of him. His sandy hair cut in a flattop flattered his golden face. Ruggedly attractive, he looked like a poster model in his uniform.

Aunt Winnie kept his dress-blues photograph in a large frame on the mantel, next to the portrait of her late husband, Joe, who in 1956 had driven his pipe truck off a cliff on Raton Pass rather than crash head-on into a carload of Trinidad, Colorado, teens, boozed out of their brains after a Friday night football game. With no children of her own, Winnie Russell regarded Brian as more her son than a nephew. He had her sister's pale blue eyes and dimpled smile, and his father's easy-to-like personality. She boasted about her Marine often, and kept her friends thoroughly briefed on his weekly letters.

When Brian came home on leave, several of the old widow's church friends brought their daughters to meet the handsome young man. The girls and their mothers all swooned at the sight of him looking so tall, fit, and dashing in his well-tailored green serge uniform. He fully enjoyed and took every advantage of the attention and fringe benefits that his good looks now bought.

Back at Marine Corps Air Station, El Toro, California, the young Marine could always count on two or three letters from admiring Olathe debutantes in each day's mail call. He laughed with his buddies, letting them sniff the perfume on many of the envelopes. Dutifully, he replied to each letter, too, and kept the mail flowing his way. Brian felt good about himself and liked his job. He even finished high school, taking off-duty courses, and planned next to enroll in a nearby Orange County community college.

Then in March 1965, President Johnson announced that he was sending in the Marines to end the Viet Cong rebellion in South Vietnam. Corporal Brian Pitts, assigned as an aviation ordnance technician to the First Marine Aircraft Wing, soon joined that first bunch of Vietnam veterans in country, racking bombs under the wings of F-4 Phantom jets at Da Nang.

Until the day that Corporal Pitts arrived in South Vietnam, he had kept his nose clean, except for a minor skirmish in the barracks at El Toro, where he paid penance by washing windows on Saturdays, but got no page 11 entry in his Service Record Book. His pro-con marks, with a possible top rating of 5.0, ran from a 4.9 high in proficiency to a 4.3 low in conduct. Overall, a good Marine. Yet three months into his combat tour, something finally snapped.

Gunnery Sergeant Clifford Goss headed the aviation ordnance section where Pitts now worked, arming the growing number of Marine attack planes based at Da Nang Air Base. Built like a bullet with legs, Goss had the mentality of a rock. By what measure he failed to know about his job or leadership he made up with loud profanity, doing his best to intimidate his Marines into conforming to his warped ideas of discipline and submissive respect. Like oil and water, Cliff Goss and Brian Pitts did not mix at all.

"That concrete-for-brains son of a bitch finally sent me over the edge," the deserter turned crime lord said to James Harris as he gnawed the last bit of meat off a barbecued pork rib and tossed the bone into a growing pile in a big bowl set between the two fugitives, who now feasted on what remained of a roast pig from a whorehouse luau Pitts had hosted for his best customers two nights ago. "The cocksucker would not let up, ever. No matter what I did, he fucked with me. Even in my hooch, on my own time.

I finally reached the point that I would have killed the motherfucker. Not a doubt in my mind. So I just grabbed a few duds, threw some shit in a pack that I needed for survival, along with my personal mementos, and I left."

"I should have done that," Harris said, wiping his mouth with a paper napkin. "Lifers down on my shit all the time, day in and day out. You were smart ducking out like you done, before they push you into something bad, so they can throw you in the slammer."

"Sometimes, I wonder if I could have hung on for seven more months and rotated home," Pitts said, setting the bowl of bones on the floor, by the table, and snapping his fingers for the skinny dog to come help himself to them. "Then I think about that bullethead son of a bitch Gunny Goss, and I know better. He did his best to push me into doing something stupid, to give him an excuse to bust my ass and shit-can me.

"First day I see the guy, he told me he didn't like my candy ass. He hated me because I knew my job, and all the guys came to me to figure shit out, instead of him. He fucked everything up that he touched. Seriously. Shit, he even had live ordnance hung on the pylons and wired ass-backward to the planes half the time. It's a wonder he didn't blow something up and kill a bunch of people."

"How did he get to be a gunny then?" Harris asked, watching the mangy dog that wouldn't leave his side chomp on the pork bones.

"Fucking lateral move, that's how," Pitts said. "Reenlisted to get an option out of the grunts, because he knew he would die in the bush, sure as shit. Dumbest fucking son of a bitch that ever walked, and they let him reup for aviation ordnance because they needed staff NCOs. I'll never understand Marine Corps thinking. Why didn't they just promote some of the sergeants who had their shit together?"

"Fucking crotch, that's why," Harris said. "There's the right way, the wrong way, and the Marine Corps way."

"So, did you think about what I said?" Pitts asked.

"Fuck, like I have any choice?" Harris answered.

"My man, there's always a choice. You can join my crew here, or take a shot at life on your own dime, like I did," Pitts said. "Benny Lam and his cowboys might let you live, but I doubt it. Then I know Major Tran Van Toan, one seriously bad motherfucker with the biggest operation in the northern provinces, would drop you on the spot, and not even say please. However, I managed to get past those two, and survived."

"You're a white man, though, and you got lucky," Harris said, "falling into all this good shit."

"Lucky my ass!" Pitts said and laughed. "I earned every bit of all this good shit. You've got a point about the advantage of my being white, because these guys don't cotton to any soul brother. Even you staying here, you still have to watch your back. But all this good shit, I didn't just fall into it. Every damned dope connection I got supplying all you assholes here in Da Nang and down at Chu Lai, I set up myself. The stupid motherfucker I killed to get this house, he didn't have a clue of what he had at his fingertips, until I appeared on his doorstep, damned near like you showed up on mine, Huong holding his .45 in my ear. Only I wasn't in cuffs.

"Things with old Tommy Nguyen might have worked out fine, too, if he hadn't gotten so fucking greedy. I had to kill him. No choice. The whole operation would have collapsed otherwise. All these cowboys knew it, too, and stuck with me. If he'd been straight with the gang, as soon as I drew down on him, right here in the patio, they would have capped my young ass and fed me to the hogs. But he fucked them, too, just like me, and they were glad to see him gone.

"Old Nguyen, the sorry bastard, didn't have a clue that his cowboys and I had finally turned on his ass. Not until none of the house girls would suck his dick anymore. The fat sack of shit couldn't get it up, so the girls had to blow him to get him off. Shit, they finally just told him no. Then, when none of the cowboys would enforce his law, he knew it was up. That's the day I shot him."

Refilling the two Marines' glasses with iced tea, playing the polite host, Pitts smiled casually at Harris, who sat staring blankly at his new boss, marveling at the coolness of this young man, so casually describing his bloody ascent to power.

"He had good ties with both the Viet Cong and the Da Nang police, due to our dope business and hookers," Pitts said, sipping tea and looking at the dog now flopped behind Harris's chair. "I knew that once he had figured out that he had lost the boys' and my loyalty, he would have had either the Cong or the cops take us down. They would have shot my ass in either case. So I popped the motherfucker first."

"Why wouldn't you think I might take over like that?" Harris asked, and smiled as he said it.

"Because Huong and his two brothers, along with about a dozen other cowboys that they supervise, adore my young ass," Pitts said. "I gave them the same deal I offered to you. Work for me, and I pay you a share of the profits at year's end, above all salaries and other benefits. I run it just like a business back in the States, and give the workers a respectable taste of the pie along with damned fine wages. These guys never had it so good, and they damned sure wouldn't get it this good from anyone else around here in this business, especially not from the likes of Benny Lam and Major Toan. These cowboys know it, too. They would drop you in your tracks the second they smelled any crossways shit coming from you. I'm their golden goose."

"So what I gotta do?" Harris said.

"First thing, you and that filthy mutt gotta go take a run through the rain closet," Pitts said. "You're pretty foul, and that dog, maybe a quart of motor oil after a lye-soap bath would kill that creeping crud on his back.

"Next, you will get a haircut. High and tight, just like mine. I want you looking squared away, like a 5.0 jarhead. That's a rule. No compromise. We go out in the ville. We're in uniform. Nobody questions a squared-away Marine who looks like he's taking care of official business. Come on and I'll show you something."

The two men left the table in the villa's shaded, courtyard patio, and walked back inside the house and into a large master bedroom. Pitts slid open a closet door to reveal a rack of starched and perfectly ironed Marine Corps utility uniforms. Silver first lieutenant bars gleamed on the collars. Then he slid a wallet from his back pocket and pulled out a green, Marine Corps identification card with his picture in the center of it and the name First Lieutenant Joseph A. Russell typed on it, along with Pitts's appropriate physical description, blood type, and a phony service number.

"Take a look here," Pitts said, and pulled out a set of dog tags hanging on a chain around his neck. "As far as anyone who checks me is concerned, I am First Lieutenant Joe Russell. That's really my Uncle Joe. He got the Silver Star on Iwo Jima."

Then Pitts looked at James Harris and said, "No offense, but we will have to make you a corporal or something. If I put lieutenant bars on your collar, people would notice. Dark green Marine officers are rare. Our objective is to go out in the ville, do our business, and not draw attention. We can maybe let you be a sergeant, but that is pushing it. If you're with me, it'll look righteous to anyone."

Harris smiled. "I wouldn't even want to fucking pretend to be any candy-ass officer anyway. I got my pride. I like sergeant, though. Where you get all this shit, anyway?"

"Fuck, man," Pitts said, "this is Vietnam! Shit, they print ID cards easy here. Once laminated, you can't tell them from the real thing, unless you run the number, and that takes a week at least. These gooners can make uniforms that look way better than any you can buy at cash sales Stateside.

We even have jump boots, traded to us by the doggies with the Americal division down at Chu Lai."

"So what's the story, if anybody asks while you're in the ville impersonating an officer?" Harris said.

"Some days I am a public information officer out on a mission for the Da Nang press center," Pitts said. "Other days I am a staff judge advocate, doing my lawyer thing for First MAW Law. Either way, some hardcharging grunt brass asks a question, he doesn't go much farther when he thinks he's talking to some kind of rear-echelon commando who he thinks doesn't rate to kiss his royal ass."

"So I take the identity of one of those pogge dudes, too?" Harris asked.

"You got it," Pitts said. "These two types just seem to be able to roam anywhere they want, and nobody really cares. So it works for what we need to do. Just keep a low profile, avoid crowds, and don't linger at any one place too long."

"You sure I gotta cut my hair, though?" Harris said, rubbing his hand on his head, feeling his Afro's thickness, and thinking about how much trouble he had endured from the officers and senior enlisted Marines who had always harassed him about it.

"No," Pitts said. "You can leave it like it is, and keep wearing that shit you got on, but you can't stay here if you do. And you won't last two days out there if you leave. It's up to you. If you stay, you play by my rules."

"That's cool," Harris said.

"As for this ragged-ass dog," Pitts said, "how did you latch on to him?"

"You got that part backward, bro. I never latched on to him. He just started following me and wouldn't go away," Harris said, looking at the ugly beast at his feet, wagging its scraggly tail at him.

"Maybe he deserves a break then, too," Pitts said, considering how he liked most dogs, even ugly ones. "So, Mau Mau, you got a name for the mutt?"

"Yeah, man, I do," Harris said, and grinned as he spoke. "I call him Turd."

Chapter 2

DICKY DOO AND THE DON'TS

"QUESTION FOR YOU, Staff Sergeant Pride," Jon Kirkwood said to the defense section's administrative chief and senior legal clerk.

"What's that, Skipper?" Derek Pride answered as he led the pair of newly arrived lawyers from the bachelor officers' quarters, where they had dropped their baggage on two open bunks. The staff sergeant casually walked with Kirkwood and O'Connor toward the legal office headquarters and an impatiently waiting Major Dudley L. Dickinson, the military justice officer and the staff judge advocate's second in command.

"Today some kind of holiday?" Kirkwood asked, looking at an attractive, middle-aged gentleman with dark hair and an exquisite tan, dressed in white shorts, shoes, and polo shirt. Violently swinging his racquet, alternating forehand and backhand strokes, the fellow relentlessly pounded a tennis ball off a large sheet of plywood wired against the court fence. With each loud whop of the racquet striking the ball, the man let out a deep grunt that echoed off the concrete and the nearby buildings.

Just outside the high chain-link enclosure where the tanned, middle-aged man in white toiled at trying to blast a hole in the plywood panel with his tennis ball, a much younger man relaxed quietly on a chaise lounge. He, too, sported white athletic shorts but wore no shirt. With black plastic sunglasses resting on the bridge of his deeply tanned nose, hiding his eyes, the fellow intently studied the fold-out feature photograph of an issue of *Penthouse* magazine.

A few feet from the man lying on the web-mesh reclining chair, an immaculately cleaned and polished jeep sat with a portable radio on its hood, tuned to Da Nang's American Forces, Vietnam, broadcast station. The comedic toot of a steam calliope playing Henry Mancini's popular hit "Baby Elephant Walk" drifted from the speakers, adding a tranquil accent to the placid afternoon scene.

"Oh, that's just the boss, Lieutenant Colonel Lewis Prunella, there on the tennis court, and his driver, Lance Corporal Dean, adhering to their regular afternoon physical training schedule," Staff Sergeant Pride said and cracked a wry smile.

"We should stop and introduce ourselves, then," Terry O'Connor said, stepping toward where the man reclined on the lounge chair, soaking up sun and now turning the *Penthouse* centerfold in various directions, examining every detail of the photo.

"Sirs," Pride said, and hastily stepped in front of the two captains, "we don't have a lot of time right now. I can see Major Dickinson watching us from his window. He can get very contentious when you keep him waiting."

"Contentious, eh? Guess that means pissed off in legal parlance. Don't want to piss off the Mojo, Jon, do we?" O'Connor said, looking toward the complex housing the First MAW staff judge advocate's offices, where he could clearly see the silhouette of the military justice officer standing in a side window. "At least not until he knows us better. Not in the first five minutes, anyway."

"You get a good look at that jeep?" Kirkwood said, following behind his pal Terry O'Connor and Staff Sergeant Pride, zagging at an angle across the grass, back to the gravel path and resuming their trek from the BOQ to the legal offices.

"Yeah," O'Connor said, "you could eat off the tires. Even the wheel nuts were shiny. Like chrome. Did you catch that?"

"Whole thing glistens like a diamond in a black goat's ass. How about that red license plate on the front with the bolt-on chrome letters S-J-A mounted on it," Kirkwood said. "At first I thought it was General Cushman's jeep, and the metal letters were three silver stars."

"From a distance, the colonel's jeep can mislead a person, unless you've been around here for a while and know it's just our boss," Pride said.

"He play tennis like that every afternoon?" O'Connor said, glancing a last look over his shoulder.

"Every morning, too," Pride said. "From about seven to nine he sharpens his game, then works in the office until noon, takes a jog with Lance Corporal Dean for lunch, then at three o'clock he has his afternoon P-T session. Almost daily, unless he has to preside over a trial or attend a staff meeting."

"Must be pretty laid back here then," Kirkwood said, cracking a hopeful smile at the apparent prospect of ample free time.

"Hardly that, sir," Pride said. "We stay quite busy. The colonel just keeps out of our way, unless we need his advice or help with something. Major Dickinson makes sure that rarely happens."

"So the major really runs the show at First MAW Law," O'Connor said.

"Colonel Prunella runs the show," Pride quickly spoke. "Don't let his hands-off style mislead you. Lewis Prunella is nobody's fool, and is quite the gifted defense counsel or prosecutor. Take your pick. He's worked both sides of trials, and is as sharp as they come."

"So, what's this?" Kirkwood said. "Retirement on active duty?"

"Some people might say that, more or less, in some respects," Pride said. "But everyone here likes him, especially at III MAF. The colonel expertly plays the political game, gentlemen, and as a result, he keeps us well fixed. For example, we have six people assigned to us from Marine Wing Headquarters Squadron-1 administrative section, just to do typing. Normally, any other SJA would only get a couple of regular oh-one-five-ones. In fact, during my six-year career I've seen JAG sections where we had just one clerk-typist. Talk about getting backed up!

"Here in Da Nang, though, the colonel gets just about anything he wants. Take his driver, for instance. On loan from Lieutenant General Robert E. Cushman Jr., personally. Pulled directly from the III Marine Amphibious Force command section's pool of drivers normally reserved for the senior staff. Some of the MAF bird colonels don't even have personal drivers assigned specifically to them, but Lieutenant Colonel Prunella does."

"That's good to know," Jon Kirkwood said, appreciating the genuine respect and obvious loyalty that Pride held toward Colonel Prunella.

"Now, if you ask me, that driver has the choicest job of anyone I've seen so far," O'Connor said, looking back at the tall, tan Marine who now bent over an ice chest and took out two cold sodas. He then turned and handed one of the canned pops to the SJA, who had just walked out the tennis court gate, mopping his face with a white towel and smiling at the man like they were best friends.

"Lance Corporal James Dean from Malibu, California," Staff Sergeant Pride said. "The authentic beach boy. All he does is drive Colonel Prunella, and do whatever the boss needs him to get done. Otherwise, between runs, when he's not polishing his jeep, he lifts weights, or works on his tan while improving his reading skills, as you may have observed."

"Yeah, right," Kirkwood snorted, picking up on the staff sergeant's subtle sarcasm. "Think he ever gets much past the pictures?"

"No shit," O'Connor said, and laughed. "James Dean. That fits, too. As soon as I laid eyes on him, he struck me as a regular Joe Hollywood sort—tall, good-looking, sporting that tan and those Foster Grants. Even has that Troy Donahue sun-bleached hair going for him. The name, James Dean, though, just seems a little too ironic. That's for real?"

"Yes, sir, that's one of the reasons why most people around here call him Movie Star," Pride said, arching one eyebrow and cracking a wise smile. "That and his background. Supposedly his family has money. That's why the Malibu address. His dad's some kind of big-time Hollywood studio executive. So typical of those people, the boy went maverick on the old man and joined the Marine Corps. You know, just to piss off the parents.

"However, Lance Corporal James 'Movie Star' Dean is no great gift, and certainly no loss to Hollywood. I would say that he has the mentality of a plate of noodles and the personality of a department store mannequin. I think they invented the term 'shallow-minded' just for him. He will screw up anything more complicated than wiping mud off his jeep or picking up the colonel's laundry. That's why nobody hassles Movie Star to do anything except piddly stuff. And that's not much. Big, good-looking and d-u-m-b, dumb. Colonel Prunella loves him, though. Mostly because he keeps that jeep absolutely spotless and is always right there, handy."

"Movie Star, huh?" O'Connor said.

"Yes, sir, Movie Star," Pride said, opening the front door to the headquarters and leading the two captains inside.

"I GET PAID to be the royal asshole here," Major Dudley L. Dickinson said, casting a patronizing, fake smile at the pair of officers as he stepped from behind his desk while offering his hand for Captains O'Connor and Kirkwood to shake. "I like my work, too."

"So I've heard, sir," O'Connor said, giving the major a one-pump shake and then letting go.

"Jonathan C. Kirkwood, sir, UCLA Law School class of '64," Kirkwood said, giving the major a dutiful, multipump handshake.

"Very good, Captain," Dickinson said, and then turned back to O'Connor, who stood staring up at the large, posterboard sign thumbtacked on the wall adjacent to the major's desk. On it someone had carefully handwritten in bold, inch-long, black-marker-ink letters a list of a dozen sentences, each beginning with the word "Don't" written in red marker ink and underlined with black. "You're Terence B. O'Connor, then."

"Yes, sir," O'Connor said, still reading the sign.

"The initial B in your name comes from Boyd, your mother's maiden name," Dickinson said.

"Correct again, sir," O'Connor said, now looking at the major.

"Let's see, Columbia University Law School, also class of 1964," Dickinson said. "Editor of the *Columbia Law Review*. Very impressive. You passed the New York Bar, and did it on the first try. Not bad at all. Father, a Marine sergeant, World War II, awarded the Navy Cross for valor on Iwo Jima. Don't be so modest, Captain O'Connor. I have read all about both of you, including the special note from the Federal Bureau of Investigation regarding a minor hiccup with your secret clearance background check, relating to the fact that your fiancée is a Communist."

"Girlfriend, sir," O'Connor said, now looking squarely at the major's narrowed eyes. "Vibeke Ahlquist is my girlfriend. She's a very strongminded liberal, a Social Democrat from Sweden, and a journalism graduate student at Columbia University. She freelances articles and commentaries from time to time for the *Daily Worker*, a newspaper established by the American Communist Party in 1924, which they publish and distribute in the neighborhood just outside Columbia University. Not on campus. She's just a stupid student with no real-world experience. Does that make me a Communist?"

"Apparently not," Dickinson said, sitting behind his desk and opening O'Connor's Officer Qualification Record. "They still gave you a secret clearance, in spite of this relationship."

"My relationship with Miss Ahlquist is my business in the first place," O'Connor said, now realizing that he had just allowed Major Dicky Doo to push his one easy button.

"It's my business when you are fraternizing with an agent from a socialist country that is sympathetic to the enemy," Dickinson retorted.

Jon Kirkwood stepped away from O'Connor and began reading the sign on the wall, knowing that any comment he might add would only muddy the situation.

"Sir, with all due respect, Sweden is a friendly power to the United

States," O'Connor fumed. "Applying your logic would make Canada our enemy, too."

"I didn't say 'enemy,' Captain," Dickinson said, tossing O'Connor's OQR on his desk. "Sympathetic. Just like Canada."

"Canada is one of America's closest allies, sir!" O'Connor said. "I cannot believe you would regard them as anything less than a friendly nation."

"They allow draft dodgers to run there; they give them refuge and refuse to honor our requests for extradition. That is not the conduct of an ally," Dickinson huffed.

"Sweden is a social democracy, much like Canada. They are our friends. Just like us, they fear the Russians. They simply have a long-held tradition of neutrality," O'Connor said. "My girlfriend, a Swede, writes for a Communist newspaper from time to time, big deal. She's no Bolshevik!"

"Captain, I just pointed out that I was aware of the issue," Dickinson said, now trying to defuse the young lawyer's tirade.

"Major, sir, I happen to be a Republican. I cast the first presidential vote of my lifetime for Senator Barry M. Goldwater, for Pete sake!" O'Connor said. "If you look closer at my background check, you will also see notes regarding my stormy and often verbally combative relationship with Miss Ahlquist. All of our conflicts specifically centered on our divergent political perspectives. Although my father is a Marine veteran of World War II and recipient of the Navy Cross, he is today a history professor at the University of Pennsylvania, and a very liberal-thinking Democrat. He nearly always agrees with Vibeke in our political arguments. Does that make him a Communist, too?"

"Relax, Captain O'Connor," Dickinson said. "Nobody has called you a Communist."

"Agreed, sir," O'Connor said, taking hold of his temper and now trying to extinguish the flames of his anger.

"Captain Kirkwood," Dickinson said, looking at the quiet officer who had taken several steps toward the wall and busily read the posterboard sign attached to it.

"Yes, sir," Kirkwood responded, wheeling on his toes and striding quickly back to the major's desk.

"I see your wife has gotten herself a job teaching junior high social studies at the Department of Defense School System on Okinawa," Dickinson said, looking at a yellow note paper-clipped to the manila cover of Kirkwood's Officer Qualification Record.

"Correct, sir," Kirkwood said. "Her father knew some people with the DOD school system, and they made some arrangements for her to work there. Hopefully, occasions will arise where I may have cases that take me to Okinawa, and might afford us the opportunity to be together for a day or two during my thirteen months here in 'Nam. Just a hope, sir. You know."

"Any Okinawa junkets are plums that I award to only our stellar performers, Captain," Dickinson said. "Defense section has yet to show me any stellar performances, so you will have a precedent to set if you hope to get to Okinawa anytime soon."

"I think I understand, sir," Kirkwood said, choosing to keep any potential for argument to himself while trying not to show his stirring emotions and his immediate dislike for the major.

"Like I said," Dickinson said, and faked a laugh, "I get paid to be the asshole at this office."

"I understand, sir," Kirkwood repeated.

"Your father-in-law is quite the man, isn't he, Captain Kirkwood?" Dickinson said, running his finger down the note and then looking up at the flush-faced captain.

"Sir?" Kirkwood said carefully.

"Political power broker in California, Captain," Dickinson bellowed. "He and Governor Pat Brown are like Frank and Jesse James. They run the California Democrat machine. Bernice Layne Brown, the state's first lady, is your wife's godmother. Don't play so coy with me, Captain, you're quite well connected."

"Sir," Kirkwood said, "as you obviously know, Governor Ronald Reagan, a Republican, succeeded Edmund G. Brown this very year. So that California Democrat machine does not appear to have as great a head of steam as you might regard. Besides, if I have such clout, what am I doing in Vietnam?"

"Good question, Captain," Dickinson said. "I'm all ears."

"Sir, I got drafted," Kirkwood began to explain. "Rather than face two years as a private in the army, I opted to join the Marine Corps."

"Right, right, right," Major Dickinson said, waving his hand as he looked back at the folder, turning off what might develop into a long-winded explanation that he cared nothing to hear. Then the major rocked back on his chair and looked up from his desk at both captains. "Gentlemen, to get along here I ask only that you keep out of trouble, and abide by my rules, posted on yon wall."

"Your infamous list of Don'ts," O'Connor said.

"Correct, Captain," Dickinson said in a hot voice, "the infamous Don'ts. Read them, make notes of them, learn to recite them by heart if needed, but above all, abide by them. I'm not here to get you to like me, and I am not your buddy. Ever. Don't make the mistake of believing something otherwise."

"You don't have to worry about that, sir," Kirkwood said, now grabbing the opportunity to mouth off before O'Connor took it.

"Don't leave our offices without first checking out," Dickinson said. "Rule number one. Don't use the overseas telephone without obtaining a chit from me first. That's rule number two. Most importantly, don't ever, and I mean ever, take the colonel's jeep. Colonel Prunella's vehicle and his driver are exclusively off-limits to all hands. We have a staff jeep. Use the staff jeep. No exceptions. No excuses. Period!"

"What if it's out and we have an emergency?" O'Connor said.

"Nothing in our profession requires that kind of urgency, Captain," Dickinson snubbed. "If the staff jeep is out, then call the command taxi service or request a vehicle and driver from the motor pool. However, and another rule: Don't request a vehicle without getting my authorization first."

"How about a do?" O'Connor said smartly. "You have any of those? A do this or a do that?"

Yes, I have a do for you, Captain O'Connor," Dickinson said wryly. "Do not piss me off!"

"Sir, ah, that's not a do," Kirkwood said, gesturing with his index finger raised, trying to appear innocent but feeling good with adding his smart, two cents' worth. "You see, don't is simply a contraction of do not. That's another don't, sir."

"You just pissed me off!" Dickinson said, standing from his six-wheeled swivel chair and sending it banging into the government-gray steel credenza behind him. "Smart-ass behavior like that will only buy you beaucoup trouble around here, bub. Given your attitudes, you two clowns ought to fit in very nicely with the rest of the misfits in the defense section."

"No serious swimmers, then, I take it, sir, in the defense pool?" O'Connor said, smiling, seeing the major's anger and reaching for a fresh nerve to grate raw.

"Not a one, Captain," Dickinson hissed through his clenched teeth. "Not a one."

*   *   *

THE AFTERNOON SUN blazed across the steel matting, concrete, and hard-packed dirt at the infantry base and air facility at Chu Lai. The bustling aviation and ground complex occupied by the U.S. Army's Twenty-third Infantry "Americal" Division headquarters along with other elements of Task Force Oregon, and Marine Corps aviation and ground units of the First Wing and First Division sat smack in the middle of a stretch of nasty sand hills and hamlets that teamed with Viet Cong, just an hour's drive south of Da Nang on Highway One. While the South China Sea washed its clear blue tide along Chu Lai's east-side beaches, hostile rice paddies, canals, and thickly forested hedgerows, broken by a hillock here or a streambed there, stretched north, south, and west from the American forces' compound. Farther west, the dangerous lands that the grunts had come to call Indian country, places such as Happy Valley, Dodge City, and Charlie Ridge, lay in the mountains and steep terrain that overlooked the Chu Lai rice flats. Closer by, equally enemy rich haunts such as the Riviera and Que Son Hills loomed just outside Chu Lai's fences.

Celestine Anderson had spent the past nine days pounding holes in his boots, walking patrol in those dangerous suburbs with catchy names. Now, as his chopper descended onto home turf, he couldn't remember the last time he had closed his eyes and really slept. Slept with a good dream ending. Slept like a Saturday night cold beer and hot steak dinner.

Chu Lai looked awfully good to him as his tired eyes gazed out the back hatchway of the long, green grasshopper-shaped twin-rotor CH-46 Sea Knight helicopter when it finally set down at the Marines' base, letting off his bedraggled security platoon. He thought of how satisfying a real meal would taste as he bounded down the rear ramp. So instead of going straight to his hooch and crashing for a long and badly needed sleep, he ambled up the dusty jeep road that led to the headquarters complex's dining facility.

He had stood listening post duty the last night on patrol, so he hadn't even gotten to shut his eyes in two days. As the afternoon sun baked his shaved head and bare arms, he kept his face turned down, following the tracks in the road, shielding his bloodshot, sandpaper-feeling eyes. Just something warm in his stomach. Something to make him sleep good. That's all he needed now.

"Yo, bro," a familiar voice called from ahead. Celestine cupped his hands along his forehead, shading his eyes, and squinted to see which of his few friends shouted at him.

"Hey, blood," Celestine called back when he saw the Marine, a buddy named Wendell Carter, from Houston, his own hometown. He hadn't known the guy there, but knew of his neighborhood. Just a bit south on Jensen Drive from Celestine's own set of blocks. Since they lived so close to each other back there, both on Houston's rough North Side, they called each other "homey."

Carter stood in a cluster with two other Marines whom Celestine also knew well. The four of them worked at the wing's communications section, a unit in Marine Wing Support Group 17.

Although fully trained at coordinating air and ground communications, and performing basic maintenance and repair on a variety of radio and telephone equipment, Anderson and these three other air wing Marines of African heritage had found themselves mostly relegated out to security patrols, humping the backache PRC-25 radios and carrying rifles.

"Celestine, my man," Wendell called to his pal, and put out his right fist.

Anderson put out his right fist, too, and rapped it first on the top of Carter's, then he tapped the bottom, and after that knocked each side, and finished the greeting by butting his knuckles against those of his friend. To complete the ritual, each man then took his clenched fist and struck it across his own heart, and lastly raised it defiantly above his head.

Dapping, they called it. Its meaning mimicked that of the African Masai warriors' ritual greeting of his fellow Moran, and symbolized that neither man held status above or below the other, that both were equal, side by side, brothers in spirit and in blood. For Celestine, the greeting represented solidarity among his cohorts who shared his African roots, and his heritage of slavery in America from which his people still struggled to emerge today, even though the chains had been legally broken now for 102 years.

"Look at those fucking niggers," a skinny, darkly tanned Marine named Leonard Cross said to three of his buddies standing with him in a small circle near the chow hall. The surly crew of four had spent the better part of the day filling sandbags and burning shitters downwind from Chu Lai's population.

Laddie, as Cross preferred that his friends call him, wore no shirt, and had on scuffed-white combat boots and a pair of filthy utility trousers with the seat ripped out, but showed a failed attempt at a ragged patch job on the pants ass-end and at both knees. As he spoke, he let fly a stream of tobacco-brown spit that landed between his feet, making a small, dark lump in the dust.

"Fucking niggers," two other shirtless grunts wearing similarly ragged, dirty trousers and scuffed-white boots mumbled in agreement with him.

Harold Rein, the fourth man in the group, who also dressed in the same filthy, disheveled fashion, said nothing, but visibly fumed, staring hotly at the quartet of dark green Marines dapping a dozen yards away from him, also waiting for the chow hall to open for early supper.

Although his mother in Dothan, Alabama, had named him Harold, after her father, nobody here called him by that handle. If they did, he generally let the offender quickly know his dislike for it in verbally harsh and sometimes physically brutal terms. Officers and senior enlisted he let slide, but still set them straight with some strongly worded slurs between "sirs." People who didn't want a hard kick in the nuts from Private Rein, or at the very least an earful of profanity, called him Buster.

The nineteen-year-old, already twice promoted to private first class, and likewise twice demoted back to buck private, sported a cartoon bulldog wearing a Marine campaign hat tilted over his eyes and then understruck in a crescent below the bulldog's jowls the letters USMC tattooed on his right forearm. On his left shoulder he had a rebel flag tattooed above a poker hand that held three aces and two eights.

Like his father, Buster Rein's skin didn't tan. It just burned. Then it mostly freckled and peeled. Constantly peeled. Even his scalp pealed beneath his brush-cut red hair.

Rein sported a brawler's knuckles—dry and hard and heavily calloused. Black grease filled the many cracks that laced over his hands' thick skin, and embedded deeply under and around the fingernails on both of his meaty, pink, and freckled paws.

"Who the fuck do those porch monkeys think they are, standing there all high and fucking mighty, beating their nigger fists and shoving their black power, Mau Mau bullshit down my throat?" Buster finally bellowed, making sure his voice carried to the group that offended him.

"Fuck you niggers, you motherfuckers," Laddie Cross then called to them, not to have Buster outdo his racist zeal.

With his thumbs hooked in his waistband and his chin jutting upward, Buster Rein bellowed, "Jigass coons. Think they own the whole fucking world since Lyndon Johnson freed 'em all!"

Then Rein laughed hard and looked over his shoulder for agreement from his buddies. They nervously cackled and flashed toothy grins to show him that they supported his bravado. He took another step forward, scuffing through the dust, and growled, "Fucking black power! I ain't scared of no black power bullshit."

"Hey, man, don't let those peckerhead chuck motherfuckers mess in your head," Wendell Carter said to Celestine Anderson, seeing the anger immediately flush bright red across his normally deep honey-gold cheeks. "Don't let those fucked-up slices of white bread get to you, man. I mean it!"

"Shut the fuck up, and leave me to it," Anderson growled in a low voice, pulling his arm out of the sudden grasp of his hometown buddy who wanted to stop any trouble before it broke out.

"It's no good, man. Not here. Not right now. We can get those motherfuckers later on," Carter said, again grabbing for Celestine's arm as Anderson now stepped toward the redneck quartet and glared. He dared any of them to lock onto his eyes.

"Leave me the fuck alone!" Anderson said to Carter, yanking his arm again from his buddy's grasp, and now exchanging napalm stares straight on with Buster Rein.

"Watch this," Rein said to his now silent cohorts as he cockwalked arrogantly toward Anderson.

Wendell Carter stepped in front of Celestine Anderson, and looked at him nose to nose and whispered, "You got to walk away from this shit, man. Right now! These fuckups is all bad news. Bad all around, and not even any of the other white boys around this camp likes any of them either. Let it go, man. Let it go!"

"Hey!" Buster Rein called out, seeing Carter trying to block off his buddy from a certain fight. He clenched a cigarette in his teeth and bit down on its filter while smiling widely as he spoke. "Hey, hey, you coons! You boys hear me? Any you niggers got a light?"

"Sho!" Celestine called back, and shoved Carter out of his way. Then under his breath he said to himself, "You dead motherfucker."

"What's that, boy?" Buster called back.

"I said, sho, man," Anderson bellowed. "I gots a light."

While Buster Rein spread a wide smile, clenching the cigarette in his teeth, rolling in a spring step off the balls of his feet, his fists both clenched ready for battle, Celestine Anderson bounded straight at the cocky redneck.

Reaching in his left trouser pocket, the shaved bald Houston Marine pulled out his Zippo lighter and flicked open the lid. He thrust it toward Buster Rein's nose and struck a spark that licked out an orange fireball that leaped into the white boy's nostrils.

Rein automatically blinked his eyes shut and yanked his head backward, putting the tip of his cigarette into the four-inch flame, and then sucked hard on the filter.

In the same fluid motion that Celestine Anderson had brought out the flashing chrome lighter and ignited it with his left hand, he had reached behind his back with his right hand and found where his field ax dangled from its pouch on his utility belt. His thumb popped open the snap that closed the pouch over the ax head, and his fingers lightly lifted the knife-sharp blade from the pouch and found the tool's short, curved handle.

While Buster Rein sucked happily on his cigarette, satisfied that he had humiliated this uppity coon, and had shown everyone standing around the chow hall's entrance, watching the exhibition of his white superiority over black power, his courage and his boldness over what he regarded as black rebellion, Celestine Anderson dropped the ax head toward the ground, letting it slide down his palm, along the side of his leg, until his fingers slipped down the grip where they took a firm hold at the end of the handle's curved hilt.

Then in one long, arching swing, the African-American Marine brought down his field ax onto the top, front, center of the Alabama Marine's skull, and split it open clear past his eyebrows.

Buster Rein never felt a thing. Then, or ever after.

Chapter 3

RAYMOND THE WEASEL

"IN THE NAME of the Father, the Son, and the Holy Spirit, amen," the tall, skinny Marine, built like a man wearing stilts, said in a solemn voice, kneeling at the foot of his single-level military bunk, his mantislike arms folded beneath long, tendril fingers reverently interlaced under his chin, his elbows resting on top of a green, wooden footlocker. Seven other similar beds, each flanked by two gray steel wall lockers, alternating to the left and right sides, formed an open cubicle around each pair of beds, with an olive drab storage box at the end of every rack. With a center aisle extending from the front door to the back, the two-bunk billeting spaces lined each side of the all but deserted squad bay that housed First MAW Law's defense section.

The gangly captain had just finished praying while looking up at a crucifix centered high on the bulkhead at the head of his bed, a few inches above a color photograph of Pope Paul VI, hooked on a nail an inch beneath the cross on the left, and a black-and-white photograph of President John F. Kennedy, draped with black bunting, fastened on the wall to the right of the pope. As he teetered clumsily to his feet, rising like a dizzy stork, while turning away from his bed, he moved his long and bony right forefinger from the center of his forehead to the center of his chest, then to his left shoulder and to his right, blessing himself.

"Spectacles, testicles, wallet, and watch," Terry O'Connor mumbled with a smirk to Jon Kirkwood. "I swear I knew this guy back in Philly when I was a kid in Catholic school. Just a little bit on the creepy side, if you catch my drift."

"Oh!" the man gasped, seeing the pair of newly joined lawyers standing at the main entrance to the barracks, holding ajar the inwardly opening, double-wide screen doors so they would not bang shut, waiting respectfully for him to finish his devotionals before invading his sanctum.

"Sorry, Mack," O'Connor said, letting go of the screen, allowing it to slam against the frame, and then striding forward to where the man stood and thrusting out his right hand. "We just barged through the doors and there you were on your knees, talking to God, so we thought we ought to give you a moment before we imposed our company on you. I'm Terry O'Connor, and this steely-eyed devil here on the port side is my all-around best friend and cohort in sin, Jon Kirkwood."

"I am totally embarrassed," the lanky captain said, taking O'Connor's hand and shaking it, and then grabbing Kirkwood's, too. "You must think I am some kind of a religious freak."

"Not at all," O'Connor said, unconsciously wiping the clammy sweat from the handshake on the seat of his trousers. "You have my utmost respect."

"Mine, too," Kirkwood said, pulling his hand from the damp and cold-as-death grip. "Didn't catch your name, though."

"I am so sorry," the ghostly complected man said, his long, narrow face immediately flushing red, causing the shaggy blond tangle of thinning hair atop his head, fanning in every direction above his close-cropped temples like the fronds on a coconut palm, to take on a pink cast from the reflection of the blush glowing off his scalp. "I am in such a fluster this afternoon, totally out of sorts. Michael Carter here, Harvard Law, class of 1962."

"Glad to know you, Mike," Kirkwood said, offering a friendly smile to the strange-looking man.

"Same here, Mickey," O'Connor said, chopping out the words with his rapid-fire, Philadelphia-born-and-raised manner of speech.

The man beamed a wide smile filled with tartar-caked yellow teeth spreading from puffy, pink gums and said, "I am equally glad to know you both."

Jon Kirkwood suddenly took two steps to one side and pretended to look for his bunk, where he had left his seabag and valise. The full brunt of Michael Carter's breath had assaulted him.

Not losing a beat, Terry O'Connor pulled a roll of peppermint Certs from his pocket and popped one in his mouth. Then he tore back the paper and motioned for Michael Carter to take one.

"Oh, thank you," Carter said, fingering the mint from the pack.

"Ah, here's my gear, right where I left it," Kirkwood said, thinking that the last time he had smelled anything so foul as Carter's breath, he had stumbled on the carcass of a dead goat at the mouth of a drainage run while hiking at Big Sur in August.

"Harvard Law, no shit," O'Connor said, sucking on the peppermint lozenge.

"My undergraduate work was at Haverford College, in Pennsylvania, where I graduated summa cum laude," Carter said proudly. "I applied for Harvard just on a lark, and what do you know!"

"I was Columbia all the way, both undergrad and law school," O'Connor said. "Jon did the same at UCLA. Nothing like Harvard, but not exactly community college either."

"I had also applied at Cornell, and was accepted," Carter then beamed, "but who can turn down Harvard if you get in?"

"Very true," Jon Kirkwood said. "While Terry and I will end up scraping nickels from the gutters, you'll be up there in some Park Avenue high-rise stacking the long green."

"Not at all," Carter said, frowning. "I have dedicated myself to the poor. I intend to do legal aid in Boston when I finish my military service. The plight of the poor is no laughing matter, gentlemen. Money does not interest me at all. Justice is my cause, and my reward shall be the satisfaction of righting the injustices heaped upon our brothers and sisters who struggle against poverty."

"Politics, I get it," O'Connor said with a smile. "You'd really get along with this Swedish lady I know back in New York. I think she's read some of the same crap that you did."

"No, I am not political," Carter said, stiffening and then looking back at the photograph of JFK on his wall, after seeing Terry O'Connor's gaze travel to the pictures of the pope and the dead president.

"So you have Kennedy up there, draped with black bunting, for sentimental reasons?" O'Connor said, a tone of sarcasm lilting from his voice.

"Exactly!" Carter said. "I have ties with the Kennedy clan."

"You're related?" Kirkwood said, pulling a khaki uniform from the suitcase he had unfolded on his bunk, and then neatly hanging the garment in the wall locker.

"Philosophically related, if you will," Carter said. "I greatly admired the president, and I subscribe to his philosophy of asking not what my country can do for me, but what I can do for my country."

"You didn't even get a draft notice then, did you?" O'Connor said.

"No," Carter said. "I joined the Marines straight out of school. My duty to my country."

"Your family must have a lot of money, pal," O'Connor then said, grabbing his seabag and dumping its contents on his bunk, spilling half of it across the floor.

"Why would you say that?" Carter said, surprised.

"Guys like you are either completely crazy or filthy rich," O'Connor said. "Crazy people don't make it through Harvard. Don't even get an interview to get in Harvard, or Yale, at that matter. Rich does. I peg you as filthy fucking rich, with a capital F."

"Filthy or fucking?" Kirkwood asked, laughing.

"Take your pick," O'Connor said, throwing his boots into the bottom of his wall locker. "Don't get me wrong, Mickey, I like filthy fucking rich. I want to be filthy fucking rich one day. I admire filthy fucking rich. I'll take the corner office with the big leather chair any day of the week over camping in a slum with a soap box as a desk."

"Rich is not all it's cracked up to be," Carter said, walking back to his bunk and sitting on it, resting his chin on his hands, and staring at the floor.

"See?" O'Connor said to Kirkwood. "Can I pick 'em or can I pick 'em?"

"Carter, you are filthy fucking rich, aren't you," Kirkwood said.

"Yes," Carter mumbled. "I hate it, too."

"My wife is well-to-do," Kirkwood then admitted as he shoved his empty suitcase under the end of his bunk, hiding it behind his footlocker. "She has her emotional problems with the money and all, sounds a lot like you, too, when she bemoans the problems of having loads of cash, but given the choice of having wealth or living out of a soup can, she will choose to suffer in the lap of luxury every time."

"I intend to do good," Carter said. "I refuse to be another rich, Boston elitist tossing crumbs to the poor from my Bentley on my regular weekend sojourns to Martha's Vineyard."

"You drive a Bentley?" O'Connor said, kicking his suitcase under his rack. "I would have taken you for a Rolls-Royce purist."

"Very funny," Carter said, still brooding with his face in his hands.

"Hey, pal," O'Connor said, "don't take it so hard. Hell, you can give me a couple of your millions, and then you won't be so rich. How's that?"

"Fuck off. You wouldn't take it if I did give it to you," Carter said.

"Good judge of character," Kirkwood said, leaning against his wall locker, "but I know this Irishman a lot better than that. I think that if you put a million bucks under Terry O'Connor's nose, he would grovel for it like a hungry dog."

"Fuck-an-a, Jack," O'Connor laughed, wadding his empty seabag and stuffing it in his footlocker. "Like I said, nothing wrong with money. It greases the axle for the proverbial wheel of life to keep right on spinning round and round. I'm a lawyer, for crying out loud. A law whore. Pay me a fee and I am all yours, baby."

"They don't put guys like that on the defense team," Carter said. "You're a weenie just like the rest of us, trying to exact a little humanity and justice out of this fucked-up system. Now tell me the truth."

"I guess you saw the Nathan's Hotdogs sign stenciled on my shorts," O'Connor said and laughed, letting go of his footlocker's lid, allowing it to bang shut. "Yeah, I really do give a shit what happens to these poor bastards. I also get good and pissed off seeing them railroaded by the likes of Dicky Fucking Doo and his Fabulous Don'ts."

"Dicky Doo is nothing," Carter said. "You have not yet met the consummate evil, Captain Charles E. Heyster."

"As in shyster?" Kirkwood chimed with a laugh.

"Heyster the shyster," Carter said. "That's good but not original, yet quite apropos. You're not the first to call him that, nor will you be the last."

"So he is the shining star in Dicky Doo's galaxy?" O'Connor said, pulling off his sweat-stained shirt.

"He *is* Dicky Doo's galaxy," Carter said with a sigh, still sitting on his bunk resting his chin on the heels of his hands and his elbows propped on his bony knees. "His foremost champion for injustice. This morning in court, Charlie the shyster handed me my head yet again. This time he not only humiliated me, but my client, too, and he pissed squarely in the face of justice, railroading a completely innocent man, simply from the way he looks and a dirty little name that people called him behind his back. How can a human being be so cruel as to knowingly send an innocent man to prison?"

"They do it every day," Kirkwood said, noticing O'Connor stripping down to his T-shirt and boxer shorts, and following suit.

"I know," Carter said, and began choking on his words, his emotions now starting to overwhelm him. "I am such a failure at stopping it, too. That's what I was praying about."

Jon Kirkwood could say nothing, seeing the stick figure of a man shuddering as grief from his loss took full charge and sent tears coursing from his pink-rimmed blue eyes.

"Suck it up, pal," O'Connor then muttered, tossing his dirty socks in his laundry bag and dropping it on the floor by the foot of his rack.

"Yeah, right, suck it up," Carter said, sobbing and wiping his wet face on his khaki shirt's shoulder and upper sleeve. "I keep sucking it up, and Charlie Heyster keeps cheating and winning."

"What the hell did he do?" O'Connor said.

"Subliminal influence and mind games for the jury," Carter said, pulling out a yellow stained handkerchief and blowing his nose. "He cheats, and the judges let him get away with it. I object, and even when the judge sustains it, the jury is still influenced by the sideshow. He gets what he wants."

"You're driving me crazy with your rhetoric," O'Connor said, lying on his bunk and propping himself on his elbows. "Start at the point where you are in court, and give us a clue of what went on."

"Sorry," Carter said, dabbing his eyes. "We began at nine o'clock this morning. My client, Lance Corporal Raymond Zelinski, rather former lance corporal, now private, was railroaded on false charges of possession of narcotics with intent to distribute, and the whole raft of typical misconduct charges they tie to such a case. None of it true."

"Kingfish, all my clients is innocent, don't you know," O'Connor said, rolling his eyes and grinning at Kirkwood, who lay on the neighboring bunk. "That's why we'uns gots jobs as defense counsels."

"Calhoun the lawyer from *Amos 'n' Andy*," Kirkwood laughed, turning on his side and looking at O'Connor. "I loved that old show. That and *The Honeymooners*."

"It's not funny, gentlemen," Carter said with a frown at the racial bend of O'Connor's wisecrack. "You'll have your turns in the tub with Heyster, and then you won't be so jovial about it."

"Oh, now wait a minute there, Sapphire," O'Connor said, his eyes still open wide as he shifted his smile to Carter.

"You want to hear this or not?" Carter fumed, now towering over O'Connor, whose bunk sat directly across the center aisle from Carter's.

"Shoot, Luke," O'Connor said, lying back. "I'm all ears."

"We're a little punchy after flying twenty-three hours straight from California to Okinawa, then no sleep, and catching the predawn flight from Kadina to Da Nang," Kirkwood said, relaxed on his bed, propped on his elbows.

"I did the same thing," Carter said, now taking off his uniform shirt, revealing his dingy T-shirt with yellow sweat rings staining the garment's armpits. "I know how you feel. Wednesday departure from Norton Air Force Base, landing in Okinawa, and then Friday morning the predawn freedom bird to Da Nang."

"It will rot out your brain," O'Connor said.

"At any rate," Carter continued, pulling off his shoes and sitting on his bed, "Raymond Zelinski is not your poster-type Marine. Like yours truly, when God passed out good looks, we were someplace else."

"I can count at least a dozen not so pretty Marines I saw just getting off the plane and checking in today," O'Connor said. "Take that guy at supply who issued us our helmets, flak jackets, and other duce gear, or even the guy at the armory that gave us our .45s. Somebody should have spanked their mamas! I doubt looks had really that much influence on the jury. They see ugly daily."

"*Au contraire,*" Carter said. "There is ugly, which I agree is quite common. Then there is repulsive. Lance Corporal Zelinski stands about five feet, ten inches tall and weighs all of 135 pounds at best. He has very dark eyes that are quite large and bug out. His brows are black as coal. His skin is a translucent pasty gray, and the tissue surrounding his eyes looks fragile and bruised, but it's not. That's just the color. Gray circles around very large brown eyes overhung with thick, black brows."

"Sounds beautiful so far," O'Connor said and mimicked gagging, putting his finger down his throat. "He might look more natural with a hooded black cape and a scythe. Now that I think about it, I'll bet that was his sister I took on a blind date once, just after I enrolled at Columbia. The dark circles and thick eyebrows bring back those old freshman nightmares. She originally came from Hell's Kitchen. I think she kills ducks for a living nowadays, out on Long Island."

"Very possibly his sister," Carter said, offering a cheesy grin. "Zelinski happens to come from Hell's Kitchen in New York."

"No shit?" O'Connor said, dropping his head back and letting out a laugh, and then looking back at Carter. "Doesn't sound very Irish, though."

"No, I think Raymond is Polish," Carter said, still showing his yellow teeth. "He has a very strong New York brogue, though, a voice that sounds like Muggs McGinnis from the Bowery Boys."

"Oh, good, I like that," O'Connor said, propping himself back on his elbows. "Them and *The Three Stooges* were my favorites."

"That was *The East Side Kids*, though," Kirkwood said, looking at

Carter and then at O'Connor. "Leo Gorcey played Muggs in *The East Side Kids* movies. In *The Bowery Boys* he portrayed Terrence Aloysius 'Slip' Mahoney. Huntz Hall had the roll of Horace Debussy Jones, better known as 'Sach.' They're some of my favorites, too, but for that era of comedies, I always liked Abbott and Costello best."

"What about *The Dead End Kids*?" O'Connor asked, looking at Kirkwood. "Leo Gorcey and Huntz Hall played in those too, right?"

"Yeah," Kirkwood said, "*The Dead End Kids* were the first movies with Huntz Hall and Leo Gorcey, in the late 1930s, then came *The East Side Kids* in the early 40s, and then *The Bowery Boys* later in the 40s and through most of the 50s. Same bunch, just different names. Gorcey's father, Bernard, played Louie Dumbroski, the old man with Louie's Sweet Shop, and Leo's younger brother, David Gorcey, played Chuck."

"Carter, the man is a walking encyclopedia," O'Connor said, pointing his thumb at Kirkwood. "Hell of a library between his ears. He can tell you anything about anything, and right down to the gnat's ass, too."

"At any rate, gentlemen," Carter interjected, standing up from his bunk and starting to pace, as though he now addressed a jury, "getting back to the subject: Zelinski, with his voice like Leo Gorcey, not only has these horrid eyes, but his hair is jet-black, well oiled, and combed straight back from his high-pitched forehead, like Dracula. The poor boy has thick blue lips and a nose that is at least four inches from its tip to his face. Beneath that prominent schnozzola, hugging his top lip and in the center making right-angle turns upward to each nostril, almost like it was drawn on with an eyebrow pencil, he has this sharply edged snit of a mustache, also very black and vividly contrasting his pale skin. If that's not pathetic enough, his shoulders slope forward from a pronounced stooped back, slumping so badly that he looks like he's slouching even when he stands straight. Just having him seated at the defense table was bad enough. He would have been a disaster on the witness stand. He looked and sounded like some two-bit hood from a B-class gangster movie."

"Sounds more like that character Gomez, from *The Addams Family* cartoons, you know the one that Charles Addams draws in *The New Yorker* magazine. Not so much like the Gomez Addams that John Astin plays on the television series, but the cartoon guy," O'Connor said, leaning on his side and training his eyes at Kirkwood on the bunk next to him.

"That or Peter Lorre, you know from the 1942 movie *Casablanca*, with Claude Rains, Ingrid Bergman, and Humphrey Bogart," Kirkwood said, looking back at O'Connor.

"Yeah, Rick's Café Américain, the usual suspects, and play it again,

Sam," O'Connor said, focused on his pal and completely ignoring Carter, who now stopped pacing and stood with his arms folded, glaring impatiently at the two fellow captains.

"But Peter Lorre didn't have a mustache," O'Connor continued, not giving Carter a glance. "He had the creepy eyes, but clean above the lip. Granted that Lorre would have made a better-looking Gomez, though, than John Astin. You know, more like the Addams cartoon guy, but he's not the comedian that Astin is, so I guess it's a wash. John Astin's eyes and smile, though, as Gomez, kill me. The way Astin went after Carolyn Jones all the time, you know, Morticia Addams, kissing her up the arm, that's classic stuff."

"Well, think of a skinny Peter Lorre, quite a bit taller, with a very narrow Gomez Addams mustache and slicked-back, ink-black hair, and you have Raymond Zelinski," Carter said, once again steering the attention of his two colleagues back to the discussion of his case.

"Little Richard has a mustache like that!" Kirkwood said, smiling at O'Connor and then at Carter. "Just hit me. You sure this character isn't a little light in the loafers?"

"No. 'This character,' as you call him," Carter said, now getting frustrated with the trivial interruptions, "got railroaded today, purely on those odd looks."

"How so?" O'Connor said, returning his focus to Carter. "I know that prejudice played a part, but come on. Even the most bonehead Marine grunts would need more than looks to convict."

"Oh, there was quite a bit more, thanks to Heyster," Carter said, again pacing as he spoke. "If I wasn't up against a wall with Zelinski's looks and demeanor, leave it to Charlie the shyster to put the whipped cream and cherry on top."

"This has got to be good, the way you've bled me on this," O'Connor said, lying back on his bunk.

"Well, Zelinski has his odd looks, and as such has absolutely no friends," Carter said, now stopped between O'Connor's and Kirkwood's racks, his hands resting on his hips. "I can sympathize with him, because I have endured similar prejudices. At any rate, Zelinski is walking guard duty at Da Nang Air Base, and the corporal of the guard checks his post, gives him a shot of coffee from his thermos, and shoots the breeze with Zelinski while he drinks it. Just before he leaves he asks Raymond if he smoked pot. Zelinski tells him that he has never tried it, so the corporal offers him a single marijuana cigarette. Wanting to be cooperative, cool, and one of the guys, the dumb lance corporal accepts the joint."

"Guilty as charged," Kirkwood said, looking up at Carter. "Possession, whether you like it or not."

"Not so fast," Carter said. "The corporal of the guard had no more than driven from the scene, and Zelinski still had the joint in his hand when the military police swooped down on him from nowhere with three jeeps, and Zelinski's gunny in tow."

"I smell a rat," O'Connor said, sitting up. "Zelinski's gunny does not like our boy Raymond, does he."

"Precisely," Carter said. "When they took Zelinski in custody, and the military police wanted to check out his story with the corporal of the guard, the gunny intervened. Clearly protecting the corporal. If you ask me, that gunny sent the joint out with the corporal of the guard, just to burn Zelinski. That's entrapment."

"So you have the word of the lance corporal against the word of the corporal, and the gunny vouches for the corporal," Kirkwood said.

"Correct," Carter said, again pacing the aisle at the foot of the two captains' racks. "The corporal and the gunny both lied on the stand, denying knowing anything about planting the joint on Zelinski. Also, like a bolt from the blue, the prosecution brought in the testimony of three other Marines from Zelinski's squadron who were caught and arrested that same night smoking marijuana behind a hangar. Our only saving grace was the fact that all that the military police confiscated from Zelinski was the single joint of marijuana, and nothing else. Not even a book of matches or a cigarette lighter with which to light the joint, since Zelinski doesn't even smoke."

"Well, that should have thrown some doubt the jury's way," O'Connor said, putting his feet on the floor, now sitting on the side of his bed. "The kid's got a roll of dope, but no way to light it."

"Oh, but Charlie the shyster neutralized any reasonable doubt we had managed to put forth with his so-called character witness, Private First Class John White," Carter said, pacing the floor faster. "He was not charged, nor was he ever listed as a material witness."

"Since when does the prosecution bring in character witnesses?" Kirkwood said, falling back on his bunk.

"He had totally nothing to do with the case!" Carter exclaimed, waving his arms, punctuating his words with their frantic movement. "Yet the judge allowed him to testify. This is what killed us.

"I had pretty much discredited the gunny and the corporal of the guard, and tied them together in their conspiracy. The military police who arrested my client testified as to the contents of Zelinski's pockets, and the

lack of any kind of lighter or matches. Plus the three other culprits they arrested smoking dope in the hangar were nowhere near Zelinski at any time
that evening.

"Then the judge called the next witness. The doors in the back of the
courtroom swing open and in walks the largest, blackest Marine I have
ever seen: Private First Class John White."

"Oh, shit," O'Connor said, falling back on his bunk, laughing. "Big,
very black, and the name White. Oh, that is good. Sleazy but good."

"Charlie Heyster had this Marine state his name not once but twice for
the jury," Carter said, waving his arms faster. "And in all, three times!"

"You objected?" Kirkwood said, leaning on his elbows.

"Of course I did, right after the second time Heyster had him say his
name, but the judge let it slide," Carter said, again pacing hard. "I tried to
approach the bench, but the judge stopped me in my tracks before I could
even take two steps toward him, and told us to move on. I think that the
judge just didn't want me near his face."

"I wonder why," O'Connor said, and then flashed a quick, eyebrows-
raised grin at Kirkwood. "So what did Private White have to offer in the
way of evidence?"

"Nothing of relevance," Carter said, stopping again between the two
racks. "However, his nonevidence nailed the coffin lid shut on Lance Corporal Zelinski.

"Picture this very black Marine private sitting in the witness box,
wearing a khaki uniform, which is a sharp contrast to his skin color. The
eyes of all six jurors fixate on him. His presence quite literally mesmerized
the whole court after Heyster had him state his name for a third time, right
after my objection. A disgusting racial trick, and I know that even Private
White did not like it."

"So the jury is hypnotized on Private White," O'Connor said. "What
did he have to say?"

"Heyster asks him, 'Do you know the accused, Lance Corporal Raymond Zelinski?' " Carter said, mimicking the prosecutor, putting his
hands backward on his hips as he spoke. "Poor Private White cannot even
say Zelinski, and stutters and stumbles trying to repeat the name.

"Then I see it. I see Heyster smile that dirty, I-got-you-now smile of
his. He looked at me, looked at the jury, all of whom sat transfixed on
White, and then with his back to the jury, I see Heyster raise his eyebrows
and give PFC White the nod to now finish his statement.

"White looks right at the jury, just the way Charlie told him to do, and
says, 'I don't rightly know him as Lance Corporal Zuh, whatever you said

his last name was. All us guys down on the flight line, we just calls him Raymond the Weasel!'

"At that moment, White looked at Zelinski and smiled, and every eye in the court then followed White's cue and looked at my client, sitting there with his pointed little face, bug eyes, pencil-thin mustache, slicked-down black hair, and poor posture. It was as though the whole trial focused on that moment. That name. At that instant he became guilty. He turned to slime. In their minds he was no longer Lance Corporal Zelinski, but a street item named Raymond the Weasel."

Carter then screamed, standing on his tiptoes and swinging his arms as he now ranted nearly uncontrollably, "Raymond the Weasel! My God! Everyone in the courtroom, including the jury and the judge himself, laughed out loud!

"The jurors' eyes immediately shifted from the very black Private White to my client, who could only slink down in his chair with his ratty little paws curled under his chin, looking very much like Raymond the Weasel! They convicted that boy purely on his looks!"

"That and a joint of marijuana that he held in his hand, planted or not," Kirkwood added, sitting on the side of his bunk.

"Well, yes," Carter said, standing with his arms folded at the end of Kirkwood's rack. "But he was set up, and everyone knew it."

"Possession is possession," O'Connor said, now sitting, too.

"The judge, no doubt duly influenced by my client's weasel looks, sentenced Raymond to, you guys just guess what," Carter said.

"Oh, crap, how should I know?" O'Connor said. "Thirty days in the brig. A little harsh, but for a weasel, a month in the cooler."

"Typically, a guy would get some restriction, a fine, but you said Raymond was no longer a lance corporal, so he must have gotten a bust," Kirkwood said.

"Wrong on nearly all counts," Carter said. "The three others who were charged with possession, who the military police caught red-handed smoking the pot in the hangar, each got off with a fine and thirty days' confinement. For having a single marijuana joint in his hands, not smoking it, nor having even a match with which to light it, and not even time to put it in his pocket, Lance Corporal Raymond the Weasel got busted to private, received six months in the brig, a fine of six months' pay, and a bad-conduct discharge. For possession of one stinking joint, he's ruined for life."

"Six, six, and a kick," O'Connor said, "That is harsh."

"Get used to it, gentlemen," Carter said, walking back to his bunk. "Dicky Doo believes in harshness. He even told me once that every enlisted

Marine is guilty of something, and should be lashed at the mast. He claims that a little brig time for them just balances the scales of justice."

"Oh, he is definitely a flogging kind of a guy," O'Connor said. "I got that right off."

"Gentlemen," Kirkwood said, looking at his wristwatch and sliding his toes between the thong straps of his green rubber shower shoes, "I am off to clean up before the big hail-and-farewell bash tonight. Just a couple of hours away. No time to snooze, but a long shower and a shave might restore my soul at least for a little while anyway."

"I'm with you, my man," O'Connor said, rolling off the bunk, and grabbing a towel and toiletry kit, and trotting barefooted after Kirkwood.

JAPANESE LANTERNS TIED on communications line stretched between tent poles decorated the lawn behind the Officers' Club that night. Vietnamese chefs stood in front of flaming grills, turning giant prawns and porterhouse steaks over the fires and dropping the surf 'n' turf fare on the plates of First MAW Law's attorneys, staff, and their many guests, who outnumbered the lawyers three to one.

Country music from a Filipino group with a Japanese lead singer blared from two batteries of six-foot-tall loudspeaker cabinets that flanked the foot-high riser of plywood laid on concrete blocks that served as a stage. Electric cords buried between two-by-fours stretched to the back of the club, where an octopus of outlets fed the band's amplifiers and microphones.

"How'd ya like ole Yamaguchi Ritter and his Angeles City Cowboys?" a Marine nearly a size too large for his tiger-stripe pattern jungle-camouflage utility uniform said to Terry O'Connor, slapping a paw the size of a beef chuck roast on the lawyer's shoulder, knocking him off balance, and causing beer to slosh out of his glass.

"Not bad at all," the five-foot, ten-inch O'Connor said, looking up at the Marine, who towered a foot above his head.

"He kind of fucks up the L sounds, but after a while, over here, a guy stops noticing it," the gigantic Marine said, craning his neck over his shoulder, looking at the band playing at the opposite end of the lawn, where much of the crowd had gathered, near the bar and the barbecue grills.

"Terry O'Connor," the lawyer said, and extended his hand to the huge man.

"Archie Gunn," the hulk said, returning the shake, wrapping his mitt around O'Connor's almost like a man taking a child by the hand. "Just call me Lobo. My old Basic School roommate over yonder, T. D. McKay, is in your outfit, and always invites me to your cross burnings and beefsteak sacrifices."

O'Connor glanced past Lobo, and noticed Jon Kirkwood walking toward him, a half smile on his face.

"Here comes my TBS roommate," O'Connor said, "Jonathan Kirkwood."

"Oh, yeah, I met him a while ago," Gunn said, letting go of O'Connor's hand and offering Kirkwood a wave. "He was cornered by old Stanley the shithead Tufts and the Brothers B."

"I know who Tufts is; I met his brother Manley at staging on Okinawa. He came on our plane today, and I think he got assigned to one of the grunt battalions for a couple of months before he goes to work at First Marine Division Legal, but the Brothers B? I haven't met them," O'Connor said.

"Phillip Edward Bailey-Brown and Miles Christopher Bushwick. Charming fellows from New England," Jon Kirkwood said as he joined Lobo and O'Connor.

"Yeah, that's the names," Gunn said and grinned. "Their shit don't stink, either. I don't think they even fart."

"They're not related I gather from the different names," O'Connor said, seeing the two men talking and laughing with Major Dickinson, Stanley Tufts, and Charlie Heyster.

"Naw, they just call them the Brothers B because of the same initial on their last names, which also stands for Boondoggle, which we have assigned them as their unofficial last name. Plus, those two are joined at the hip most of the time," Lobo said. "You don't see one without the other. From up in New England someplace."

"Old money, and well connected," Kirkwood added. "According to Mike Carter, our noble Mojo, Dicky Doo, cannot kiss their asses enough. He's always worming around that pair, and ironically, they treat him like a poor relation."

"Dicky Doo takes it up the ass," Lobo said, and gulped down a mouthful of beer from a can that he crushed with his hand as he sucked it empty. "Speaking of taking it up the ass, I've gotta get a closer look at this crew of L-B-F-Ms that Yamaguchi Ritter has dancing on the sidelines. See you gents later."

"What did he call those Filipino go-go girls?" O'Connor asked, laughing while watching Lobo walk through the crowd of cocktail-sipping officers clustered across the lawn, parting them as he pushed through like Moses did with the Red Sea.

"L-B-F-Ms," a major now standing by Kirkwood said. "Little brown fucking machines."

The dark-haired and olive-complected Marine stood an inch or two shorter than O'Connor. He wore a khaki garrison cap cocked to one side, and a dark green flight suit with zippered pockets and vents on his legs and sleeves, and a white with red and blue embroidered, circular McDonald-Douglas F4 Phantom patch on his left shoulder. He had a brown leather rectangle attached to the flight suit on his left breast, above a slanted zipper-closed pocket. In gold letters it said "Buck Taylor, Major, USMCR."

"Terry, here is a guy you have to meet," Kirkwood said as O'Connor made eye contact with the major.

"Monahan S. Taylor," the Marine said, extending his hand to O'Connor, "but call me Buck. Everyone does. I drive Fox-Four Phantoms when I'm not acting as my aircraft group's legal officer."

"Major Taylor is a Yale Law School graduate," Kirkwood said.

"And you fly Phantoms?" O'Connor asked, surprised. "I thought a Yale Law degree guaranteed you body and soul to the Staff Judge Advocate Corps."

"Usually it does," Taylor said, pulling two cans of beer from a six-pack he held under his arm, and handed one each to Kirkwood and O'Connor, along with a fold-up beer-can-opener he pulled from his pocket. "However, I graduated first in my class at the Basic School. So I had my pick of where I wanted to go. Most dive into the ought-three profession, commanding grunts on the charge, but I had my head in the clouds. I wanted to fly jets. Always did, ever since I saw the Blue Angels perform at South Weymouth when I was a kid. So I went to flight school, down at Beeville, Texas. Got my wings, and here I am."

"A naval aviator who graduated TBS," O'Connor chirped. "That's pretty rare. Most, I hear, miss that evolution."

"There are a few of us with some ground training. Captain Archie Gunn, over there, is another TBS graduate pilot," Taylor said. "I expect the crotch to eventually get away from the Marine Corps option out of the navy's flight officers' candidate school, and make all their pilots go to Quantico for both Officer Candidates' School and the Basic School. I think it's a good idea. It certainly helps my perspective when laying snake and nape for a gaggle of grunts under fire."

"I'm sorry. Snake and nape?" Kirkwood said, popping a triangular hole in his beer can with the opener and handing it to O'Connor.

"Snake eyes, your standard five-hundred-pound, mark-eighty-two general-purpose bomb, and nape is napalm," Taylor said.

"Lobo's a pilot?" O'Connor said, taking a sip from his beer and handing the opener back to Major Taylor.

The three men then turned and watched as the massive Marine in the camouflage uniform now grabbed the asses of two Filipino dancing girls.

"Observation planes," Taylor answered, dropping the opener back in his pocket and turning toward O'Connor and Kirkwood. "He came to Beeville a month or so before I graduated there and went on to Yuma, where I got my follow-on, F-4 fighter pilot training. Damned good pilot, but way too big. A Martin-Baker seat in a Fox-Four is just not that accommodating, plus if he ever managed to get strapped in he'd rip off his kneecaps if he had to punch out. Never had a prayer to fly jets, so they trained him in Broncos, which is still a mighty tight fit for his big ass. I think that's why he prefers to fly that J-2 Cub. He's got room for his butt, and he can throw a friend in the backseat, too. Not that I would ever want to go riding with that crazy son of a bitch."

"Why's that?" Kirkwood asked, finishing his beer as the major handed him another one.

Buck Taylor looked at the two lawyers and laughed.

"That fucking monster killer over there wrestling with those girls," Taylor said, pointing to Lobo who now had a Filipino go-go dancer kicking and screaming under each of his arms, "he has a genuine death wish. He keeps a case of hand grenades on the floor of his plane, in the space behind his feet, some other odds and ends explosives stashed here and there, an M79 grenade launcher and a sackful of blooper rounds hanging on the right-hand door, and an arsenal of assorted small arms and ammo in the backseat. The boy spends entirely too much time trimming treetops with his landing gear hunting Charlie. Gentlemen, I get pretty ice-cold up there flying my Phantom, but to be honest with you, Lobo scares the shit out of me. I do like living."

"No shit," O'Connor said, looking at the hulk tossing around the girls like rag dolls.

"Don't get me wrong," Taylor added. "I love that goon like my own flesh and blood. He, Tommy McKay, Wayne Ebberhardt, and me, we're asshole tight as family. I just won't fly with that insane Doctor Death because I would spend all my time talking to God instead of enjoying the ride. McKay and Ebberhardt, on the other hand, they go with Lobo all the time. But then they don't know any better, because they're both nearly as crazy as he is, even if they are lawyers."

"I've only just met First Lieutenant McKay, and have not yet met First Lieutenant Ebberhardt," Kirkwood admitted to the major. "I don't believe that Terry has yet met either gentleman."

"We'll fix that," Buck Taylor said, and then he put his fingers in his mouth and whistled an ear-splitting call to the two men, who stood across the crowded lawn, laughing at Lobo now with a go-go girl riding atop his shoulders and her miniskirt bunched over the top of his partially bald head. Archie Gunn immediately wheeled toward the signal, and offered a wide grin while pointing to the girl's legs wrapped around his neck. Then he turned and pulled up the back of the girl's miniskirt to reveal that she no longer wore any panties. McKay and Ebberhardt waved, and the major then motioned with his hand for them to come to him.

"I think that Archie is terminal as a captain," Taylor said, opening the last beer in the six-pack after handing O'Connor one, and then dropping the opener in the lawyer's palm. "He doesn't give a shit about it, either. Great entertainment, but then look over there with Dicky Doo and Colonel Prunella, along with the Wing chief of staff. I'll bet that those three have their assholes puckered equally as tight as they have their jaws locked right now, watching ole Lobo having fun with these girls. You couldn't get a broom straw up any of them."

"He burned out or what?" O'Connor said, punching a triangular hole in his beer can and handing the opener back to Major Taylor.

"Probably, burned to his boot laces, but nearly anyone who sees a lot of the enemy has that syndrome going on," Taylor said, swigging beer and dropping the opener back in his pocket. "I think his shit-bird attitude comes from the Miss Goody Two Shoes he married and then discovered she was a slut."

Terry O'Connor laughed. "I should have guessed it. Behind the misery of every good man lurks some form of skanky psycho bitch ready to perform a hose job on his ass."

"Archie got hosed pretty good by this one," Taylor said. "During his senior year at the University of New Mexico, where he played noseguard for the Lobos, hence the nickname, he ran into this girl one night sitting on the tailgate of some cowboy's pickup truck outside a bloody bucket, rod and gun club honky-tonk on the north side of Albuquerque, crying her eyes out. Melted ole Archie's gigantic heart right off. Her boyfriend was inside dancing with another girl, and she needed a ride home.

"Leave it to Archie Gunn to quickly oblige. When he dropped her off at her mother's front door, she invited him to go to church with her the next morning. A good Baptist girl, just like big boy's mama. Lobo fell in

love. One thing leads to another, and he is head over heels, kissing his little buttercup's ass, eating the peanuts out of her turds. Meanwhile, back at
the ranch, she and her dear whore of a mother can't get over their luck,
having mister big-time New Mexico football star dangling by his sweet testicles on their little puppet strings.

"Right after graduation, Archie and this hog get married. Lobo gets his
draft notice and joins the Marines, like about half of the people here
tonight did. All during OCS and TBS, and all the while he is off at Naval
Flight School, our little Baptist princess, named Bunny, and her mother,
Mandy, are painting Albuquerque and Santa Fe red, white, and blue in
Lobo's little tricked-out Pontiac GTO, spending Archie's money and fucking every truck driver and cowboy with a hard dick.

"I was still at Beeville when Archie got the letter from no less than his
defensive line coach at UNM. Somebody had to finally tell him. The coach
loves Lobo to this day like his own son, so he did the dirty job. Devastated
the poor guy.

"Archie started to file for divorce, but then changed his mind. He decided on cold revenge. Then he couldn't get to Vietnam fast enough.
While he was still at El Toro, though, he started trying to fuck every
skanky hole that looked like it could breed the clap or anything worse. He
seriously wanted to catch every kind of VD known to man so he could go
home on leave, before he shipped out to 'Nam, and give the creeping crud
to Bunny. To this day, he still wants to give her the worst shit that he can
catch, so that she can pass it around to these assholes fucking her behind
his back."

"He's never gotten divorced from her?" Kirkwood said, surprised.

"Fuck no, because he found out that as long as he is in Vietnam, the
Soldiers and Sailors Civil Relief Act prohibits her from taking any sort of
legal action against him, like divorce. So he keeps extending over here, just
to fuck with her," T. D. McKay said, slapping Buck Taylor across the
shoulder and putting out his hand to Terry O'Connor.

"You're McKay?" O'Connor said, shaking the hand. "Right, and this
skinny degenerate in my hip pocket here, helping me carry all these fresh
beers for you lowlives, is Wayne Carolina Ebberhardt. He's out of Duke
University School of Law, and I am a University of Texas lawyer, through
and through. Born in Dalhart, raised in Dumas, educated in Austin."

"And you guys go flying with that maniac?" O'Connor said, tilting his
head toward Lobo, who now headed their way, still holding the go-go girl
on his shoulders while guzzling beer.

"Lobo's a damned good pilot," Ebberhardt said, shaking hands with

Kirkwood. "Glad to meet you, Captain Kirkwood. And you, too, Captain O'Connor.

"As the man said, I'm Wayne Ebberhardt, born and bred in Boone, North Carolina. Home of the world's best moonshine whiskey. If you're real good, ole Tommy McKay and I might let you sample our little secret stash of homemade lightning that we have bottled up for most any special occasion. Some guys we know with the amtrac battalion have a nifty little still set up. Even has a copper boiler and condenser coils. I gave those boys a few pointers on preparing the corn mash, along with an old family recipe, and they went to work and made a pretty fair-sized batch before they ran out of corn. It tastes a lot like Jack Daniels, only better."

"You two are on the defense team, right?" McKay said and smiled. "Otherwise I would swear that Wayne's a liar."

"We moved in today," O'Connor said, drinking down the last of his beer. "Already met Mike Carter, and now with you two that makes up our whole section, doesn't it?"

"You guys, me and Wayne, and our lead attorney, His Holiness, Father Michael Carter, Esquire," McKay said, taking out a beer from a six-pack that he carried and handing it to O'Connor. "That's it. We're the defense that never rests."

"However, Major Taylor does lend us moral support, and will moonlight a little homework and legal research for us when we can use a helping hand," Ebberhardt offered, handing Kirkwood a fresh beer from the six-pack he had under his arm. "He's our secret sixth man, if you want to count him, too. It pisses Dicky Doo the fuck off, though, to have him doing any legal work. The lifer prosecutors hate Buck because he betrayed the juristic cause to fly jets. However, the Right Honorable Major Monahan S. Taylor, after graduating Yale Law, passed both the New York and Massachusetts bars, and is a member in good standing of those fine fraternities. So fuck those tight assholes if they don't like a jet jockey helping us with some case preparation."

"Speaking of preparing a case," Taylor said, handing Kirkwood the opener and looking at Lobo, now smiling with the rim of a cocktail glass firmly held in his teeth, "time for Archie Gunn to say good night. His alcohol consumption gauge just hit too much. When he starts to eat glass to impress everyone, it's time to put him back in the cage."

"He doesn't have to do that to impress me. He did that at hello," O'Connor said, cringing and offering a hopeful smile at Lobo, who then bit off half the side of the highball tumbler and started chewing.

"Archie, time to hit the rack," Taylor said in a commanding voice, seeing Lobo crunch the broken glass. "You want to spit that crap in this napkin?"

"That's okay, Buck," Lobo slurred, the go-go girl still sitting atop his shoulders. "I'll go spit it in that shit can by the bar."

"Good, and while you're at it, leave the girl there, too. She may be tired of playing horsey," Taylor said.

"She's going to the barracks with me," Lobo said with a broad grin, showing a mouthful of red teeth and blood trickling from his lips where the broken glass had cut him.

"I bet that Yamaguchi Ritter might not want you to do that with his go-go girl," Taylor suggested.

"I'll ask him if I can fuck her," Lobo said, still grinning and bleeding. "If he says no, I'll put her down."

"Good man," Taylor said, and shook his head as McKay, Ebberhardt, O'Connor, and Kirkwood watched the hulking giant amble to the bar, spit the broken glass in the trash can, and then walk to the stage, where he began talking to the Japanese-born country-western singer, who immediately began shaking an emphatic no at a pleading Lobo, his out-of-shape, straw cowboy hat nearly bobbing off his head.

"Gentlemen, having a good time this evening?" Michael Carter chirped as he approached the small group of friends. He held a red-colored drink that had a wad of maraschino cherries and some lime slices floating on top of a berg of shaved ice.

"What's that, a cherry limeade?" O'Connor asked, eyeing the drink.

"Sort of my own concoction of one, yes," Carter said. "With a healthy double shot of gin."

"Bet that'd be good with a hamburger and french fries," McKay said. "I know that cherry-lime drink would be a big hit at the Tastee-Freez back in Dumas."

"Where have you been hiding all evening, Mike?" Kirkwood asked, sipping his beer.

"Before the party, I had to catch up on some paperwork back at the office, wrapping up today's disaster, and I ran into Major Dickinson. He gave me a heads up on assignments for you two," Carter answered.

"We're not even checked in," O'Connor said, making a basketball toss at a trash barrel with his empty beer can and missing. "We're supposed to have five days."

"You can check in, but Major Dickinson expects you to get started on these cases while you're at it," Carter said, sipping from the top of the gin-spiked limeade. "Staff Sergeant Pride will take care of most of the check-in for you anyway. He'll get your pay records and OQRs to headquarters and service squadron first thing Monday morning. You'll have to see medical, dental, and the chaplain on your own, but the rest he can get handled."

Carter then furrowed his pale brow and deepened his voice to sound authoritarian. "First of all, Captain O'Connor, you will be defending a Private First Class Celestine Anderson, a radioman with Marine Wing Support Group 17. He was taken into custody at Chu Lai this evening after planting his field ax in the head of another Marine private who was apparently touting Private Anderson outside the mess hall."

"We talking about a battery or a murder?" O'Connor said.

"Murder," Carter said. "Major Dickinson has assigned Charlie Heyster to prosecute for murder in the first degree, along with a raft of mindless misconduct charges so that the man will be sure to serve a good deal of brig time after they hang him. Your client is a black Marine; the victim was, of course, white. Racism will be at issue."

"Oh, I imagine Dicky Doo is delighted," O'Connor said, shoving his hands in his pockets. "A lawyer fresh off the boat, no real practical experience, and suddenly I am the defense attorney on a murder-one rap. I am sure we have a whole host of eyewitnesses to this crime, too."

"About a hundred fifty or so Marines saw the entire spectacle, all of them crowded outside the main dining facility just moments before it opened for early evening chow," Carter said.

"Fucking great," O'Connor said. "My client has a hundred fifty witnesses see him kill a guy."

"Captain Kirkwood," Carter said, "your case is also at Chu Lai. Your client is Lance Corporal Nathan L. Todd, an American Indian who I believe is a native of the Cheyenne nation in Colorado. Lance Corporal Todd is accused of homosexual conduct and sexual assault on a fellow Marine. Apparently Lance Corporal Todd tried to suck the dick of a black Marine who was sleeping in the rack above the accused. Todd protests his innocence, claiming that he never got near the man and that the whole thing is a lie."

"At least its not murder," Kirkwood said, smiling.

"Gentlemen, good evening," Major Dudley Dickinson said, joining the slowly growing cluster of Marines. "You give them the good news, Captain Carter?"

"Yes, sir, Major Dickinson," Carter said, stepping back to allow the Mojo to shoulder his way into the ongoing conversation.

"What do you think, gents?" Dickinson said.

"Welcome to First MAW Law?" O'Connor offered, taking a fresh beer from T. D. McKay.

The crack drew a few smirks, and Dickinson faked a good chuckle.

"I have the paperwork in my office," the assistant staff judge advocate and military justice officer said. "Both of these ass wipes are in custody, locked tight in the Chu Lai cage. Not a real brig. A couple of steel container boxes with windows cut in the sides and bars welded across the openings. A tad bit hot at midday."

"Sounds a little on the harsh side, Major," Kirkwood said. "These cages conform to code?"

"Code?" Dickinson laughed. "What code? We're just fine with how we handle these dirt bags we clear out of here. You two gentlemen need to focus more on getting these two knuckleheads processed and in the brig, and quit worrying about where they cool their heels tonight."

"Processed, sir?" Kirkwood said, raising his eyebrows.

"Adjudicated. How's that, Captain?" Dickinson said, and sucked down a gulp of beer.

"How about tried, sir?" O'Connor said, clenching his teeth. "We adjudicate a property settlement. People are brought to trial by courts-martial, last time I checked. Innocent until proven guilty, and treated as such."

"Get off your fucking soapbox, Captain. You sound like Missus Carter there, pleading for the huddled masses," Dickinson snarled, locking his eyes on O'Connor's. "Most of these lamebrains we process through our system joined the Marine Corps to avoid jail in the first place. It's just a matter of time before they fuck up here, too, and we toss them in the brig, where they belonged from the get-go. Don't be such a bleeding heart. It doesn't become you."

Terry O'Connor held his rapidly heating stare at the major's eyes, started to speak, but then said nothing.

"What time, sir?" Kirkwood said, seizing the opportunity to head off his best friend from finally letting his temper boil past his quickly eroding self-control and saying something regrettable.

"Time?" Dickinson said, slurping his beer.

"Yes, sir," Kirkwood replied. "You said you had the paperwork on our two clients, and I just wanted to know what time to be in your office to formally get assigned the cases and receive the paperwork from you. We do have to plan a defense."

"Tomorrow morning. Zero seven hundred, sharp, Captains," Dickinson said, finishing his beer. "Captain Carter, why don't you get me a refill when you freshen up that Shirley Temple you're nursing."

Carter nodded to the Mojo, took his empty can, and headed to the bar, thankful for the excuse to depart his presence.

"You two better get this straight on these cases, and all others, for that matter," Dickinson said, pressing his thin lips back, showing his tightly clenched teeth. "Don't fuck around with me. I want this shit off our docket and these people processed and in the brig without any holdups. If they'll plead guilty, let them do it. Go straight to sentencing. The cocksucker is easy, anyway. The ax murderer may take a few more steps, given the mandatory procedures, but I want them both out of my hair, fast."

"We'll do our best, sir," Kirkwood said, and flashed a hard look at O'Connor to keep his mouth shut. "Terry and I will excuse ourselves now. No sleep for a couple of days, and we're both a little edgy and not clearheaded."

"Understood, Captain," Dickinson said, and offered his best disingenuous smile at O'Connor. "Get some rest, boys. I'll see you in the morning at seven sharp. The daily logistics chopper to Chu Lai launches at nine, should you want to see your clients and perhaps get them moved to the Freedom Hill brig for pretrial confinement."

Kirkwood and O'Connor quickly turned on their heels and hurried toward their quarters, following the gravel path that led past the tennis courts where Lieutenant Colonel Prunella had volleyed his ball off the plywood backstop earlier that day. The batteries of mercury vapor lamps posted at each corner of the concrete square created an island of light in the surrounding darkness. Ahead they could see the single yellow bulb hanging in the receptacle beneath the white and green metal reflector suspended above the squad bay door on the old two-story French barracks where they now lived.

"Hey, before you guys disappear, can I get a favor?" T. D. McKay said, running to Kirkwood and O'Connor after they had walked well outside earshot of Major Dickinson and the others.

"Depends," O'Connor said, both captains stopping in the light from the tennis court. "If I don't catch the clap or go to jail for it, I might consider it."

McKay laughed.

"No, just cover for me if Dicky Doo goes snooping this weekend," McKay said. "Just because its Saturday doesn't stop him when he wants something."

"We just learned that lesson," Kirkwood said. "I wanted to lay in the rack and read tomorrow morning. Now Terry and I have to stand tall for Dicky Doo at zero-seven, and then catch a chopper to Chu Lai at nine."

"Oh, yeah, that's right," McKay said. "Sorry, guys. I can hit up Mike Carter. He's usually good for a cover story."

"What's going on tomorrow that you've got to have the alibi?" O'Connor said, his curiosity hard at work.

"I've got a pal in the grunts, First Lieutenant Jimmy Sanchez," McKay said, hanging his thumbs in his belt. "The two of us graduated Texas together. We both got our B.A.'s in history. He wants to teach; I went into law school. To make a long story short, Sanchez has a platoon with Third Reconnaissance Battalion, based up by Dong Ha. They run regular patrols along the length of Highway Nine, clear out past the Rock Pile, snooping and pooping, calling in air and arty, that sort of thing. Lots of fun and games. He lets me tag along with his guys."

"Sounds a little risky to me," Kirkwood said. "You get into the shit, and Dicky Doo will want your head. Patrolling with the grunts is one of the Don'ts near the top of his list."

"What the fuck is he going to do about it?" McKay asked. "Shave my head and send me to the grunts in Vietnam? I'm sick of his shit anyway. In a way, I hope he does nail my ass, and fire me off to the grunts. That's where I want to go anyway."

"That or hunting VC with Lobo, I hear," O'Connor said with a smile.

McKay laughed and shook his head.

"You guys know all my dirty little secrets," he said. "Wayne Ebberhardt is nearly as bad as I am, but I think a ton smarter. He doesn't get caught playing hooky with Archie. But if Lobo offers to drag you hunting with him, then take him up on it. What a trip! He's flying that plane, tossing grenades out the windows, you're in the back with a rifle, or that M60 chopping away. Treetops whipping under your feet. Many times we land and he's got branches stuck in the landing gear. Lobo loves to fly that plane with one hand and shoot the blooper out his window with the other. That's his big kick. Blowing up shit."

"So you're headed to Dong Ha in the morning?" Kirkwood said.

"Before daylight," McKay answered, walking away from the duo. "Archie's flying me up there, so I am crashing at his shack tonight. I'll be back sometime Monday or Tuesday."

"Stay safe, my friend," O'Connor said.

McKay trotted from the island of light where O'Connor and Kirkwood stood, and headed up the road to the line of hooches where Archie Gunn and the other animals of the observation squadron dwelled. The two exhausted and now half drunk Marine lawyers crunched their way along the gravel path that led to the double doorway of their barracks, and the two racks awaiting them inside for a few hours' sleep before they started work in the morning.

"Fuck it, Jon," O'Connor said, stripping down to his T-shirt and skivvy shorts. "I am a whipped puppy. You know, the only sleep we've had is the couple of hours shut-eye we caught on the Freedom Bird."

"That seems days ago, but you know, it was only this morning," Kirkwood said, draping his uniform over his wall locker door and tossing his socks inside a white laundry bag that he now tied back to the rail on the foot of his rack. "I dread tomorrow. Right off the top of the deck we're dealt a cocksucker and a murderer."

"Accused cocksucker and murderer, Jon," O'Connor muttered, throwing his blanket to one side and pulling the bunk's white cotton sheet across his lower legs.

"ONE OF THOSE poor bastards swallowed a chainsaw," First Lieutenant Michael Schuller whispered to Buck Taylor, who stood nearest to him. Wayne Ebberhardt, Michael Carter, Stanley Tufts, Charlie Heyster, and the Brothers B clustered close behind as the gaggle of late drinkers stood in the yellow light outside the defense section's barracks door.

Schuller, a newly assigned III MAF brig officer, had come to the party late, and missed meeting Kirkwood and O'Connor, so the officers who had remained until after midnight to close down the shindig decided to take care of that social oversight, and at the same time have a laugh at the two new lawyers' expense.

During some of their excursions with the infantry, playing hooky from legal duties, Wayne Ebberhardt and T. D. McKay had gotten to know Mike Schuller when he led a platoon of grunts from the Seventh Marine Regiment assigned to Fire Support Base Ross, west of Chu Lai. Schuller had devoted himself to his Marines. Any time one of them took a bullet or died in action, it devastated the lieutenant.

At the University of Vermont, where Schuller had initially entered the Marine Corps Platoon Leader Course, he had come to question the validity of the political reasons for American involvement in the Vietnam War. He had started to drop out of the course, and not enter the Marine Corps, but his adviser had appealed to him to reconsider.

Despite his misgivings about the war, Schuller showed himself as a vibrant and promising leader, intelligent, dogged, and fearless. He held fast to a strong set of principles and valued honor and integrity above all else, traits the Marine Corps reveres.

"My father, back home in Vermont, taught me that mankind can strip you of all that you may have, except for this one thing," Schuller had told T. D. McKay one night at Fire Base Ross, relaxing in his hooch after a day-long patrol that had netted them little but sore feet and salt rings on their uniforms. "Men can take all that you own, or ever will own. They can take your wealth, your family, your freedom, and even your life. Nearly everything that is yours in this world, men can rob from you, save for one thing. One thing in this stinking life. In this whole world, for that matter. And it's the most precious thing you have, too. My friend, that's your honor. No one can take that away. To lose it, you have to give it up yourself."

Schuller had then told McKay how, as a matter of honor, he had decided to drop out of the Platoon Leader Course and not join the Marine Corps. He felt wrong about the war, and could not support the political decisions that put America in South Vietnam and still maintain his integrity.

"I hated the idea of killing in a conflict I regarded unjustified," Schuller admitted to McKay that night in the hooch at Fire Base Ross, lying on their bunks in the dark. "I hate the killing. I hate seeing these boys, kids mostly, getting wounded and killed for something that I think is wrong. Yet, this PLC adviser was right when he told me that I needed to serve anyway, because these Marines need good leaders: an officer that cares so much for his men that he will lay his life on the line for any of them. Thinking about the war that way, I couldn't stay home. These Marines needed me, because I am an officer who cares that much. I will walk through fire for these guys. They know it, too. At the same time, they'll do anything I ask of them."

Because he cared so much for his Marines' lives, Mike Schuller sometimes found himself nose to nose with his company commander, arguing against what he regarded a bad tactic that could cost lives. His combative nature with his senior officers came to a head when three of his men died in action and five others suffered serious wounds in what he had called a boneheaded patrol for no good reason except to satisfy the battalion commander's itch. He had used those very words, and then spit tobacco juice on the battalion commander's right boot toe.

The lieutenant colonel rippled at the insult, but did not write insubordination or misconduct charges on the passionate young officer either. The battalion commander understood the pain of losing men, despite Schuller's opinion of him at the moment. The colonel wiped off his boot toe on the back of his pants leg and walked away. As he departed the platoon area, he whispered something to the captain who commanded the lieutenant's company. Two days later, First Lieutenant Mike Schuller found himself reassigned—temporary additional duty—to the Third Military Police Battalion, and sent to work at the III MAF brig on Freedom Hill.

"Charlie, you do it," Stanley Tufts whispered to Captain Heyster as the cluster of drunken officers did their best to keep quiet outside the screen doors.

"No, they wouldn't believe me, they'd know it's a prank," Heyster said, whispering in a strained voice. Then he looked at Michael Carter, who tottered on the barracks' concrete slab porch with a six-pack of beer under his arm and a bacchic yellow smile slashed sideways across his narrow face. "They'll believe Carter, though. He lives here, too."

Michael Carter blinked his half-shut, sleepy eyes at Charley Heyster and said, "Believe what?"

"The rocket attack, you nitwit," Heyster said.

"Right, right," Carter said, rocking on his unsteady feet and laughing out loud.

"Shush!" Buck Taylor said. "You'll wake them up."

"Oh, sorry," Carter said, and handed the major the package of beer from under his arm and gave Mike Schuller the half-full can that he had drank, and had spilled much of it down his shirt.

"Just run through the doors and yell 'Incoming!' " Taylor instructed. "Now go!"

While the audience found their places on each side of the walkway and the small slab of concrete that served as the porch in front of the barracks entrance, Michael Carter crashed open the two screens, letting them swing shut with a bang behind him. As the slamming doors echoed inside the barracks, the captain began to shout his alarm.

"Incoming! Incoming!" Carter screamed and ran toward the back of the barracks, where the two new officers' bunks sat across the center aisle from his. "Get out! Get out! Incoming rockets!"

Jon Kirkwood stopped his loud snoring and raised his head, hearing the commotion. He immediately looked across his cubicle at Terry O'Connor's empty bunk.

"Terry, where'd you go?" Kirkwood called, straining his sleepy eyes to see in the darkness.

Michael Carter looked at the empty bunk, too, and stopped yelling for the moment.

"Oh, yeah," Kirkwood said. "He kept waking me up, complaining about the snoring. I think he went up to the second deck to sleep, out of earshot."

"No time to look for him," Carter suddenly screamed, again resuming his panic. "We've got to get to the bunker right now!"

"Let me get my pants on," Kirkwood said, reaching up to the wall locker door and grabbing the back of his trousers hanging on it.

"No time!" Carter yelled, pulling the pants from Kirkwood's grasp. "They're shooting 122s at us. Didn't you hear the first volley?"

"No, I was sleeping," Kirkwood said, now grabbing his steel helmet off the top of his wall locker and slipping on his flak jacket.

"Come on, Jon, run for it!" Carter shouted, now jogging back toward the door and the stairs to the second deck. "Run to the bunker, and I will get Terry."

With the sleep finally clearing his head, sudden panic took hold of Jon Kirkwood and sent him dashing hard, clomping in his untied boots, his white skivvy shorts flapping in the wake of air he stirred from his strides. The steel helmet bobbed on his head, and the flak jacked slapped his sides as he passed the stairs for the second deck and came face to face with the double screen doors. The inwardly opening screen doors.

Kirkwood never lost a step as he burst through the entrance, sending the wooden frames that held the screens in place flying in pieces and the wire mesh falling in a limp wad that tangled under his feet. The mess sent the captain tumbling in a somersault that landed him flat on his back atop the remnants of the barracks screen doors.

Buck Taylor put his foot on Kirkwood's chest when the panicked Marine tried to bound to his feet. Then the lawyer saw the ring of cheery faces surrounding him, and he began to hear the laughter.

Seconds later, Terry O'Connor came charging out the destroyed barracks entrance, sucking wind as he ran barefoot, and wearing only his white skivvy shorts and T-shirt. From nowhere a foot and leg emerged from the sidelines and caught the captain just above the ankles. Seeing his friend sprawled on the walkway atop the remains of the splintered screen doors, O'Connor angled his fall to the side and slid across the dew-soaked grass.

"Here, this will cool you off, open your hatch," Taylor said to Kirkwood, still holding his foot on the captain's chest and now draining a can of beer into Jon's mouth.

Kirkwood jumped to his feet, coughing and spewing beer. Then Wayne Ebberhardt offered Terry O'Connor a hand, helping him to his feet, too.

"Hilarious!" Kirkwood said, catching his breath and kicking his way out of the pile of rubbish that used to be the barracks doors. "I'm glad you guys got a good laugh. What is it, 2:00 AM?"

"About that. Maybe later. Who knows. I'm too shit-faced to care," Carter said, and laughed in a high-pitched chirp. "Now you have officially joined our tribe."

Terry O'Connor kicked mud and sod from his naked feet, and pulled his brown-and green-streaked, wet T-shirt and shorts from his skin as he stepped on the better-feeling, smooth surface of the concrete porch.

"I'm not paying a cent toward fixing that door," O'Connor said, looking at Kirkwood and then laughing, too.

Jon Kirkwood never laughed, but did take a fresh beer from Buck Taylor's latest six-pack, popped it open, and drained the can down his throat in one chug a lug series of gulps.

At just a few minutes past four o'clock in the morning, several barrages of 122-millimeter Katusha rockets crashed on Da Nang Air Base. One of the salvos exploded on the bunkers across the road from First MAW Law's officer barracks, where all but three of the two buildings' inhabitants had sought shelter. While the sirens had sounded, and Marines shouted the alarm as they ran for cover, Terry O'Connor and Jon Kirkwood stayed on their bunks out of hardheaded rebelliousness. A drunken Michael Carter lay his rack, too, not from any act of stubbornness or defiance, but because throughout the commotion he never heard a thing.

Chapter 4

MAJOR DANGER

"HERE, SKIPPER, PUT this on," the tall, black Marine staff sergeant told Terry O'Connor. The helicopter crew chief had the name Toby Dixon embossed in gold beneath combat aircrew wings on the leather patch above the left breast pocket of his flight suit. He handed the lawyer a heavy, four-inch-wide nylon web belt that buckled in front with a large, metal latch riveted to a thick, six-inch-square piece of leather. Double-sewn to the center of the back, the apparatus had a two-inch-wide, six-foot-long adjustable strap that dangled in a pile on the ground and had a hook looped on the end of the tether with a spring-loaded safety catch that locked shut.

"What's this?" O'Connor said to the sergeant, who now handed Jon Kirkwood a similar-looking harness.

"Gunner's belt," the staff sergeant said, pulling from a metal box two green plastic headsets, each with a boom microphone extending from a bracket fastened to the right earpiece.

"Why do we need these?" Kirkwood asked, fastening the wide belt around his waist and pulling the leather adjustment tabs on either side of the buckle, drawing it tight around his middle.

"So you won't fall out," the crew chief said, handing each of the two captains a headset. "That long strap locks into the tie-down rings on the cargo deck. That way, if we get into some shit, you can maneuver around without involving yourselves in some short-term sky diving, if you know what I mean. You might dangle, but you won't splatter. I'll get your headsets hooked up to the intercom and the gunner's belts secured to the deck for you once we get aboard. Don't worry, you'll be fine."

"We're just catching a lift to Chu Lai," Kirkwood said, now helping O'Connor get his waist cinch tightened. "Can't we just use the seat belts?"

"If we had any seats," the staff sergeant said and laughed. "Mostly the grunts just pile in and sit on the floor, letting their feet hang out the sides with their rifles pointed between their toes. They don't wear shit. Since you guys are newbees, Captain Oliver, our pilot, told me to put gunner's belts on you two, in case we gotta dodge a few bullets."

"You're flying us over enemy territory en route to Chu Lai?" Kirkwood said, now feeling a lump tightening in his throat. He looked at O'Connor, who smiled wide. "Terry, this is no fucking joke, is it?"

"Hey, pal, I got here when you did. I had no chance to pull any pranks," O'Connor said, snugging the gunner's belt higher on his waist so it didn't interfere with his Colt .45 pistol hanging in its holster off his right hip.

"You didn't hear all about that shit, sir, when you went through orientation on Okinawa, before you shipped to Da Nang?" the staff sergeant said, helping Kirkwood and O'Connor get settled on the metal floor of the UH1E Huey utility helicopter.

"We only left Norton Air Force Base on Wednesday," Kirkwood replied. "As soon as we got to Okinawa, we got on a plane to Da Nang. Hell, we never got to sleep or even take a shower, much less go to any orientation briefings."

"Anyplace here can net you an enemy round," the staff sergeant said, snapping the tie-down straps from their gunner's belts to the cargo rings set in the chopper's floor panels. Then he looked at Terry O'Connor, who still worried with the adjustment of his sidearm. "Sir, you won't need that .45 at all, unless we get shot down and you survive the crash. We get in the shit, you're gonna open up with the two M14 rifles I'm fixing to hand to you."

The crew chief then flipped open the lid to a long, wooden box tied into the right rear cargo area, at the foot of one of the chopper's auxiliary fuel bladders. From it he drew out the two rifles and a large metal can of .30-caliber belted ammunition and set it between Kirkwood's legs.

"Hang on to those rounds for me, sir," the staff sergeant said, and pulled out an M60 machine gun and handed it to O'Connor. "Hold that up high for me when I stand in the door and pull down on those rubber straps. Once I got it hooked, then you can let go and it'll just hang in place. Then we'll feed a belt of that ammo up to it."

"You boys doing okay?" a voice spoke from the other side of the helicopter.

"That's Captain Jeff Oliver and First Lieutenant Bill Perry," Staff Sergeant Dixon said, pointing through the chopper's open cargo area, which had its center occupied by a large wooden crate, forcing any passengers to ride sitting on the outside edge of the floor.

Kirkwood and O'Connor both turned and waved to the helicopter's pilot and copilot and then offered thumbs-up signals.

"Toby, lets get rolling," the chopper pilot said, climbing in the left front seat, strapping himself in place, and plugging in his communications wire that dangled out of the back of his helmet.

"You guys hear me okay?" the pilot then added, now speaking through the headsets that Kirkwood and O'Connor wore, and through the crew chief's helmet phones. Tethered by a long coil of wire plugged into a gray metal control box overhead in the center of the helicopter's cargo area, Dixon also had connected Kirkwood's and O'Connor's lines from their headsets to the same communications terminal.

"Five by five," the staff sergeant spoke as he walked to the side of the helicopter, the black wire leading from his helmet coiled in his left hand. Once at his station, where he had eye contact with the pilot and a good view of the entire helicopter, he began rotating his right hand over his head, signaling Captain Oliver to start turning the blades and firing the chopper's turbine engine.

Terry O'Connor found the talk button for his microphone dangling against his chest on the wire that connected him to the overhead communications box. He then fastened the device to his shirt with the metal spring clip made on its back, and pressed the button.

"Roger, wilco, five by five," O'Connor said and laughed. "Kirkwood, can you hear me?"

"Yes!" the lawyer replied, shouting over the drone of the Huey's engine, now fired and spinning the rotor blade overhead, shaking the aircraft as it gained speed.

"If you'll push that button hanging in the middle of your chest, you won't have to yell," O'Connor said, pointing to the control device dangling on Kirkwood's wire.

"I keep forgetting that lawyer captains are like second lieutenants," Captain Oliver said, and laughed over the intercom. "This your first chopper ride?"

"We rode in them at TBS," O'Connor said, pushing the button. "Never had any headsets, though. Just rode in the belly of the beast and looked out the windows."

"First time in a Huey, though," Kirkwood said, finding his talk button and clipping it to his shirt. "We only rode in the troop transport helicopters, CH-34s and 46s."

As the skids lifted from the concrete flight line, Staff Sergeant Dixon stepped on the rail, and sat on the edge of the doorway beneath the M60 machine gun. A few feet above the ground, Oliver tilted the aircraft's nose down, lifting its tail high, and sped forward, slowly gaining altitude and barely clearing the buildings just past Da Nang Air Base's perimeter fences. Gaining only a few more feet of altitude, seeming to hug the treetops, the captain set the Huey's power to its cruise airspeed, leaving the world in a green blur beneath Kirkwood's and O'Connor's feet.

"Amazing! I love it," O'Connor said, holding tight to the M14 rifle that the crew chief had given him, and looking out at the vista of rice paddies and thatched-roof huts that suddenly appeared beneath the racing aircraft as it left the cityscape of Da Nang and entered the countryside.

"See the iron bridge crossing the river to the left?" Captain Oliver called on the intercom. "Then to the right of it, at our eleven o'clock, that big orange and green mountain with all the roads and crap around it?"

"Sure, I see it," Kirkwood said, holding fast to his rifle and sitting between O'Connor on his left and Staff Sergeant Dixon standing behind the machine gun on his right.

"Tallyho the iron bridge and the mountain," O'Connor said and laughed. "I always wanted to say that. Tallyho. That's pilot talk."

"Roger that," Oliver said and laughed. "That's Hill 55, home plate for the Seventh Marine Regiment. Straight south and just a tad west is Fire Support Base Ross, or as we call it, LZ Ross. It's a combat outpost on two low knolls in the middle of the Que Son Valley, between LZ Baldy to the east and LZ Ryder due west of it. Eleventh Marines has a mix of artillery batteries there, along with a fair-sized infantry task force detached from two battalions out of the Seventh Marines, not quite a regimental landing team but larger than a battalion landing team. They also have some elements from the First Tank Battalion and a few other supporting arms, along with a helicopter refueling station. Oh, and the army has some units from the First Cavalry Division there, too. So it's a pretty active plot on the map. We gotta set down there and drop off this box. Then we chop east to Chu Lai and get you guys to your destination. Should make it before noon chow."

"Terrific!" O'Connor said, beaming a smile.

"I'm not so sure it's all that terrific, Terry. I've heard stories about the Que Son Valley and Fire Base Ross, along with LZ Ryder and LZ Baldy. They call it Indian country for good reasons," Kirkwood said, frowning and now pointing his M14 out the door, wrapping his hand around the small of the stock and laying his finger on the side of the trigger ring.

"Wise fellow," Toby Dixon then offered, leaning his shoulder into the machine gun, angling his body out the door, behind the weapon, ready to fire. "We usually start picking up a little ground fire once we clear the southeastern finger of Hill 55. Sometimes before then. Charlie and his cousin, Luke the Gook from Hanoi, hang out in goodly numbers south of that iron bridge, thick as fleas around this Cam Ne hamlet area, and pretty much litter the countryside from there all the way to LZ Ross."

"What's this, piped-in music?" O'Connor said, suddenly hearing the broadcast of American Forces Vietnam Radio streaming through his headset.

"That's the ADF," Captain Oliver answered. "Automatic Direction Finder. We tune it to the broadcast from AFVN in Da Nang, and the little needle on this dial here in the middle of the instrument panel points a bearing to their transmitter tower. We use it as a backup navigation aid, plus we get to hear music on the intercom, if we want. Adds a little ambience to the setting, don't you think?"

"Gets me going," O'Connor said. "All we need now is coffee service."

"Got a thermos bottle full of it, and a jug of red Kool-Aid, too," Toby Dixon offered, and laughed. "But you gotta serve yourself."

"Gooooooooood morning, Vietnam!" the voice coming from the radio broadcast said. "Air Force Sergeant Dan Styers, live and in the grid with your special-request fire missions this fine Saturday on AFVN, simulcasting from beautiful downtown Da Nang and Hue City/Phu Bai. Spreading the gospel of rock and roll throughout Eye Corps. First in the breach: There's a bunch of jarheads up in Quang Tri Province, somewhere near Con Thien, filling sandbags today, and otherwise doing a little housekeeping and bunker mending along their DMZ home front. Staff Sergeant Ken Pettigrew, this one's for you and your weapons platoon widowmakers with Echo Company, Second Battalion, Ninth Marines.

"From their September 1965 album, *Animal Tracks*, a cut that seems to have become an anthem around these parts, Eric Burdon and the Animals. We gotta get outta this place! Yeah, baby."

"In this dirty old part of the city, where the sun refused to shine, people tell me there ain't no use in tryin'.

"Now my girl you're so young and pretty, and one thing I know is true, you'll be dead before your time is due, I know.

"Watch my daddy in bed a-dyin', watched his hair been turnin' gray, he's been workin' and slavin' his life away, oh, yes, I know it.

"(Yeah!) He's been workin' so hard. (Yeah!) I've been workin' too, baby. (Yeah!) Every night and day. (Yeah, yeah, yeah, yeah!)

"We gotta get out of this place. If it's the last thing we ever do. We gotta get out of this place, 'cause girl, there's a better life for me and you."

Just as the bass guitar soloed its heavy downbeat between the chorus and the next verse, Staff Sergeant Dixon opened fire with his .30-caliber machine gun, sending a trail of red tracers toward the edge of a clearing beneath the low-flying helicopter. Hot shell casings rained on Jon Kirkwood, who had zoned out listening to the music. The shock of the gunfire's sound and the heated brass and ammunition belt links dropping on his head and down his shirt collar sent him scrambling inside the chopper.

Terry O'Connor instinctively watched Dixon's glowing stream of red-phosphorus-tipped tracer rounds burning through the air, and followed their ruby streaks to a dozen running soldiers dressed in olive green uniforms with turtleshell-looking helmets on their heads. Most of the men had rifles with wooden stocks and banana-shaped magazines jutting from beneath the weapons. Two men had long, tubular weapons with a flanged opening at one terminal, and a bulbous, green object fixed to the opposite end.

"Fucking NVA," O'Connor said, and began firing his M14 rifle at the group of soldiers now running to cover.

"They've got a couple of B-40s," Dixon said, training his line of tracers toward the two soldiers with the rocket-propelled grenades. "We can deal with the small-arms stuff, but an RPG in the cockpit could ruin our day. Focus your fire on those two guys with the stovepipes."

Jon Kirkwood managed to stand, and snugged the rifle next to his cheek, shutting his off-side eye and looking down the top of the M14.

"Skipper! Don't bother trying to aim," Dixon said, seeing the captain struggling to gain his sight alignment before firing. "We've got them loaded with tracers. Just look at the target and guide your tracers to them. Like squirting a water hose."

Kirkwood and O'Connor both raised their heads from the cheek pieces of their rifles and began firing and watching the bright red glow of their tracers strike. Between the two lawyers and the helicopter crew chief, they managed to knock down four enemy soldiers, including one with a B-40 rocket launcher. However, the second man with the RPG had gotten to the cover of the trees.

Terry O'Connor saw the white smoke from the ascending rocket headed straight at the wide-open cargo door, just as Jeff Oliver turned the Huey hard right and dove. Suddenly all that Kirkwood and O'Connor saw was the sky and the rocket-propelled grenade climbing above them, narrowly missing the belly of the aircraft.

While Oliver maneuvered the helicopter away from the clearing, hugging the treetops and racing from the enemy force, Lieutenant Bill Perry radioed news of the sighting and map grid coordinates ahead to the air liaison in the operations section at LZ Ross, calling for an artillery fire mission from the two gun batteries based there. As the helicopter vectored west, to get out of the line of fire, the call of "shots out" came over the radio headsets. In minutes, columns of gray and brown smoke and debris blew skyward in the distance, as the salvo of 105-millimeter high-velocity explosive rounds crashed into the forest where the helicopter had encountered the North Vietnamese unit.

"Damn, that was fast. Besides the RPG, did they even get a shot off?" O'Connor said.

"They were shooting the whole time," Oliver answered. "You didn't see the fountain of tracers streaming up at us?"

"I only saw the rocket come at us," O'Connor said.

"I didn't see anything but our rounds going down," Kirkwood added.

"Take my word for it, guys," Oliver said, "they hosed us pretty good. I have two bullet holes in the windshield, and a third ding in the glass between Billy boy's feet and mine. When we get on the ground, we'll look for leaks. Hopefully, we just got a few fresh vents in the skin."

"Didn't hardly seem real," Kirkwood said, sitting back down, but not dangling his feet outside the door, crossing them under himself instead.

"Never does, sir," Dixon said, pinning a fresh belt of ammo into the M60 machine gun. "Only after it's over and you think about it a little while does it ever get a grip on you."

CHALKY ORANGE DUST billowed from the expeditionary airfield runway matting as the Marine UH1E Huey set down at the Fire Support Base Ross helicopter landing zone and refueling station, twenty minutes after the firefight. Guiding the chopper from the ground, a Marine wearing a hooded gas mask stood at the forward edge of the immense LZ made of steel planks crisscrossed with a series of two-inch- and four-inch-diameter holes. Two other hooded Marines holding on to man-size fire extinguishers mounted between two-foot-tall spoked steel wheels crouched at the front corners of the acre of metal decking.

Just as Toby Dixon stepped from the Huey and moved to his station at the side of the aircraft, a Marine major and a captain came running to the pilot's side window. Behind them a crew of six men ran to the chopper's opposite side and began hurriedly unlatching the tie-down straps on the wooden crate, and then dragged it out the open door.

"Captain!" the major shouted as the men worked, pulling the cargo off the helicopter landing pad. "I've got eight wounded, three in bad shape, just a few clicks east of us. Army can't help us. First Air Cav has its birds tied up west of here. Medevac helicopters from Marble Mountain will take half an hour to get to our guys, and you can be there in five mikes. You can have them at Charlie Med in the time it takes the two medevac choppers to get to their location. It might mean saving some lives."

"Jump in and guide me to them," Oliver said.

"My alpha, Captain Brown here, will go with you," the major said. "I'll radio ahead and get you cleared."

"Dixon, we dripping anywhere?" the pilot called to the crew chief.

After squatting to take a quick look under the chopper, and then above it, and along the tail section, the staff sergeant answered the captain, "Looks dry. No warning lights?"

"Not a one. I think we're intact. Jump back aboard and get on your gun," Oliver said. "Picking up eight, I'll need some room, so you two lawyers bail out for now. I'll pick you up back here once I get these wounded men to Charlie Med. You can grab some chow with these guys while you wait."

Kirkwood and O'Connor only had time to unlatch their gunner's belts from their waists and jump off the aircraft before it cleared the deck and sped away from them, leaving the two captains in a filthy cloud, still holding the M14 rifles and wearing the headsets that Dixon had issued them.

"Major Jack Hembee," the darkly tanned and weathered infantry operations officer said to Terry O'Connor and Jon Kirkwood as they followed the crew of Marines dragging the big wooden box from the landing site toward a line of heavily fortified bunkers and general-purpose tents with all of the wall flaps rolled up. As he said his name, the major put out his hand, rough and covered with thick calluses, and both lawyers took turns giving it a shake.

Nearby and in the distance, covering the fire base's two low hills, other rows of tents and hard-backed sea huts that Marines called hooches stood among a maze of bunkers and sandbagged emplacements ensconcing the two composite batteries of 105- and 155-millimeter howitzers based at LZ Ross from the Eleventh Marine Regiment, and a dozen or more 81-millimeter mortar positions from the Seventh Marine Regiment. Among the short barrels of the howitzers stood two long snouts jutting from a pair of eight-inch cannons capable of shooting quarter-ton projectiles more than thirty miles. Snuggled within the pattern of medium- and long-range artillery pieces, several M48 battle tanks sat in the shade of camouflage netting with their hatches open and Marines lounging near them. Along the perimeter of coiled razor wire and barbed-wire fencing stood half a dozen wooden observation towers fifty feet tall. For the two newcomers, the widespread fire-support base looked as much like a prison as it did a combat outpost.

"Welcome to LZ Ross," the major said, walking briskly to get away from the cloud of dust stirred by the departing helicopter.

"We're with wing legal," O'Connor offered nervously, trying to break friendly ice with the infantry officer, whose leathery look and tough demeanor had him intimidated. "On our way to Chu Lai to visit with clients."

"Hopefully, this won't delay you gentlemen much more than an hour," the major said, pulling a handful of chewing tobacco from a red-and-white striped pouch and stuffing the tobacco in his mouth. "Chew?"

"No, thanks," Kirkwood said.

"Don't mind if I do, sir," O'Connor said, and took a wad of the dark brown, sugary leaves and pushed them inside his cheek. The spicy tobacco immediately began to tingle and burn the soft tissue of the lawyer's mouth and caused saliva to gush.

"I didn't know you chewed," Kirkwood said.

"First time for everything," O'Connor said and spit.

"LIEUTENANT SANCHEZ, DON'T you guys want to take me and a machine-gun section and a mortar or two along with you?" a shirtless Marine standing atop a pile of dirt called to the reconnaissance platoon leader striding in the center of a string of twenty-three camouflage-clad men, First Lieutenant T. D. McKay walking among them.

"Staff Sergeant Pettigrew, I'd love to have you coming along, but I think you're better off filling those sandbags," First Lieutenant Jimmy Sanchez said, stopping to talk to the staff noncommissioned officer while his platoon from Third Reconnaissance Battalion ambled their way past him, spread at intervals thirty feet apart. "Besides, I hear that the beer fairy landed this morning, and I'm sure your guys wouldn't want to miss all of the doings this evening."

"Right on, sir," Ken Pettigrew said, "I heard that, too. Hey, you guys catch my song on the radio this morning?"

"Sure did," Sanchez said. "Had it blasting in the tents when my best bud here, Lieutenant Tommy McKay, blew in, riding aboard that beer-laden puddle jumper that landed out there on the cow trail."

"Yeah, I flew in with the beer fairy," McKay said, walking behind the unit's navy hospital corpsman and approaching the spot where the reconnaissance platoon commander now stood. "Along with my skinny ass, Lobo Gunn hauled in two hundred pounds of hamburger meat, and a dozen cases of Budweiser for you guys. Had a hell of a time taking off with that load, and then landing on that piss-poor excuse of a road you've got here, instead of at the airfield, had me pretty puckered, too. My fearless pilot didn't want the hassle of finding somebody to haul the beef and brews that last bit of yardage, so he set down right here, on your doorstep."

"I wondered why all the hubbub down there when you guys landed," Pettigrew said, leaning on a long-handled shovel by a perimeter bunker where his men dug the fighting trenches deeper and put the dirt inside the green mesh bags, building a wall along the ditch with them. "I thought somebody had got shot up or something, so you made a forced landing. Then I heard you had just delivered some burgers and beer. Pretty crazy. Where'd you guys find the loose goodies?"

"Shanghaied them off some army brass in Dong Ha," McKay said, stopping for a moment to chat with the staff sergeant alongside his pal Jimmy Sanchez. "They had a bunch of enlisted guys sweating their asses off, disembarking it from a C-117 into a truck for some wingding at the Officers' Club. My insane pilot pal Archie offered the doggies a hundred fifty bucks cold, hard cash for a dozen cases of the beer and four of their fifty-pound boxes of frozen beef paddies. These guys didn't even stutter step snatching the money, all too happy to screw their fearless leaders out of some of their bounty. They seemed delighted knowing that a bunch of Marine grunts out near Con Thien would get it."

"Doggies aren't such bad folks," Pettigrew said, slurring out the words in his Texas drawl. "It's their pansy-ass officers that could fuck up a wet dream."

"Lieutenant Sanchez tells me you're a Texas boy, too," McKay said, picking up on the accent in the staff sergeant's voice.

"I'm an eighter from Decatur," Pettigrew said, and smiled as he turned his right shoulder toward McKay to show off a lone-star flag he had tattooed there. "Done a couple of night operations with those rickie-recon cowboys you're strolling with today, back when we kicked off what used to be called Operation Kingfisher, now Operation Kentucky. Anyhow, that's where Lieutenant Sanchez and I got to knowing each other, fellow Texans and all."

"Texan here, too, grew up in Dumas," McKay said, beaming a proud smile for the staff sergeant. "Lieutenant Sanchez and I were classmates at Texas University in Austin. Played a little football there."

"Shit, I heard of you," Pettigrew said, and laughed. "Longhorns running back and a hell of a pass catcher, too, back in '63 and '64, when they damned near won back-to-back national championships. T. D. McKay, that's you! Well, shit a brick. Glad to meet you, sir."

"Now I'm a lawyer down in Da Nang, playing hooky for a few days with you guys," McKay said, smiling.

"Well, you fucked up, Skipper. I think I would play hooky down there," Pettigrew said and laughed. "Beer's cold and women hot. Up here, the beer's hot, if you can get any, and well, the women may trot, but they do it on four legs."

"Nervous sheep up here, Sergeant?" McKay said and laughed.

"Can't say as I've seen any ewes running loose in these parts," Pettigrew drawled, "but they'd be a durn sight prettier than some of these pigs I've seen a few of the boys chasing."

"We've gotta shove," Lieutenant Sanchez said, seeing his platoon sergeant giving him a high sign that he now brought up the rear of the line, and that all of his Marines had moved down the trail leading away from the compound and into the bush.

"Hook 'em horns," Pettigrew said, and held up his hand with his index and pinky fingers extended, signifying the University of Texas Longhorns hand gesture.

"We"ll catch you in the morning," Sanchez said, and with McKay made the same Texas Longhorns hand signs back at the staff sergeant.

"HERE, TRY SOME beef and rocks," Major Jack Hembee said to Jon Kirkwood, tossing him a box of C rations. "How you doing with that Beechnut, Skipper?"

"I think I've got it under control, now," O'Connor said, pushing the wad of chewing tobacco around his cheek with his tongue, and then spitting again in the dirt. The three officers squatted in the shade of one of the large green tents where the major dug through what remained of a cardboard case of C-ration meals.

"You got to slinging slobber pretty good for a while, like a kid with a mouthful of hair," Hembee said and laughed. "I fully expected you to barf up breakfast. Looked like your gills turned a little green back there, walking off the LZ."

"I have to admit, I felt a little queasy then, but I feel pretty good now. The stuff kind of lifts your spirits, like a little adrenaline charge," O'Connor said, smiling a brown-toothed grin at Kirkwood and letting fly a slug of Beechnut juice between his feet. "Got any more of those beef and rocks in that box? I'm feeling a little hungry too."

"I like you, Skipper," Hembee said, digging around the case of C rations, looking for another beef and potatoes meal. "You jump right in with both feet. Sorry, no more beef and rocks, but I have some ham and motherfuckers. They're pretty good. That's what I'm going to eat."

"Throw it here," O'Connor said, "I'll give ham and motherfuckers a whirl."

"There you go," Hembee said, tossing the box of canned rations to O'Connor. "Grab yourself one of those lawn chairs and kick back. Meanwhile, I'll scarf us up some bug juice from the vacuum jug down in the bunker."

The two Marines reclined in lounge chairs made of tubular aluminum with green and white plastic webbing while they took the cans of food from their meals' cardboard boxes. Kirkwood noticed on the white plastic armrest of his chair the words "Property of First MAW Officers' Club" stenciled in black.

"I thought these chairs looked familiar," he said, lifting the freshly cut lid from the can of his beef and potatoes and handing the thumb-size, P-7 can opener he had just used to O'Connor.

"Go ahead and string that John Wayne on your dog-tag chain, Terry," the major said, returning with a three-gallon thermos jug filled with Kool-Aid, and seeing Kirkwood handing off the can opener. Then he rummaged in the C-ration case and took out a small brown paper packet, tore it open, and removed a new P-7 from the package.

"One for you too, Kirkwood," Hembee said, and tossed the opener to the lawyer. "Like spare socks and boot laces, you need to have one of those with you at all times in the bush."

"Major Danger, sir," a lanky, blond-haired staff sergeant wearing a faded green T-shirt said, ducking under the tent where Kirkwood, O'Connor, and Hembee now sat, eating in the shade.

"What ya got, Goose?" Hembee said, looking up at the Marine who held a yellow slip of paper in his hand.

"Good news and bad news, sir," the staff NCO replied.

"Shoot," Hembee said, working the lid off his ham and motherfuckers.

"Good news first," the sergeant said. "All eight of our wounded got aboard the Huey, now inbound to Charlie Med. The three worst ones still have their eyes blinking and hearts pumping. Looks like they have a chance if that chopper doesn't go down first."

"Doesn't go down?" Hembee said, sitting up and looking at the staff sergeant he called Goose.

"That's the bad news, sir," the blond Marine said. "Inbound here, your luncheon guests took a few dings from the NVA. A hydraulic line or connection must have gotten creased or cracked by one of the rounds. At any rate, they sprung a leak. Got a warning light just after takeoff from the bush with the wounded aboard. If he makes it to Charlie Med, the pilot's shutting it down there for repairs. One way or the other, he sure as hell ain't gonna make it back here today. So your house guests may have to spend the night."

"Logistics bird usually drops on our doorstep about zero eight," Hembee said, looking at Kirkwood and O'Connor. "You can catch that to Chu Lai tomorrow, or you can try to ride out of here this afternoon on one of the supply trucks. They convoy to Chu Lai at about two o'clock, get you there by five or six this evening. I don't recommend going by truck, though, unless you like gunplay."

"Ambushes, you mean?" Kirkwood said.

"Lots of opportunity for them," Hembee said, now digging into his canned lunch with a spoon. "Mines and booby traps, too. We have guys clear them every day, but they still keep springing up like daisies each morning. Charlie's an industrious little bastard."

"We'll wait for the chopper," Kirkwood said, relaxing in his chair and focusing back on his meal.

"You're Hembee, right?" O'Connor said, spooning out ham and lima beans from his can.

"Right, Jack Hembee," the major said. "Born and raised on the family cattle ranch near Cody, Wyoming."

"That staff sergeant addressed you by another name," O'Connor said.

"You mean what Goose called me?" the major said and smiled. "Major Danger. That's the nickname my Marines assigned to me. Sooner or later, everybody gets one out here. Kind of a family thing. Could have gotten one like Major Disaster or Major Fuckup, just to name a couple that come to mind."

"Your men must think a lot of you," O'Connor said, smiling at the major.

"I hope so," Hembee said. "Even though I'm just the operations officer, they know I'd put my life on the line for any one of them. I trust they'd do the same for me, or any of the other guys in our battalion. Meanwhile, since you combat virgins will spend the night, we got to get you some accommodations."

The major sat up in his chair, looked in several directions, and then shouted, "Rat! Elvis! Henry! Front and center!"

In less than a minute a short, black Marine flanked by a tall, dark-haired man that looked strikingly like Elvis Presley, and a pug-nosed fellow with big ears whose shaved head glistened in the bright sunshine, looking like Henry from the Sunday newspaper comic strip, appeared under the tent.

"Yes, sir," the black Marine who answered to the name King Rat spoke to the major.

"This is Captain Kirkwood and Captain O'Connor," the major said to the three enlisted Marines. "They will remain overnight with us. Set up two cots in my hooch, and see if you can round up a canteen full of that raisin jack that your cannon-cocker buddies over at Golf battery cooked up last night. You might make sure that the sergeant major gets a taste, too; otherwise he'll go snooping."

"How did you know they made a batch last night?" King Rat said, grinning wide at the major.

"I've got a nose, Rat-man," Hembee said. "I'd have to have one bad sinus problem not to smell that shit cooking. You might bullshit the bull-shitter, but you can't snow the snowman."

"You know, that shit's illegal, sir," Rat said, offering a sarcastic smile to go with the reminder.

"We have no tax stamps in Vietnam, so its up to the commander's discretion," the major said. "Besides, I have my defense counsel sitting right here. Now disappear."

Quickly the three Marines ducked from the tent in three different directions.

"I think making distilled spirits does violate a few regulations, Major," Kirkwood said, finishing his can of beef and rocks.

"You tell on us, and I won't give you any," Hembee said, grinning at Kirkwood.

Terry O'Connor spit in the dust. "Hell, I'm game for a little rotgut raisin jack."

"You have any rounds to fit these rifles?" Kirkwood asked, picking up the M14 he had taken from the helicopter.

"One thing we have lots of, Skipper, that's rounds," Hembee said.

AT FIRST, TURD did not recognize James Harris as he stepped from the bathroom, showered, stinking of cologne and his hair cut slick on the sides and nearly to the scalp on top. The dog slouched under the coffee table and gave the man a second glance before finally seeing that his friend had merely changed his appearance and now smelled much differently. Turd blew his nose, sneezing the way dogs do, the new scent of his master irritating the membranes inside his nostrils.

"At least I look better than you do after a bath," Harris said to the dog, admiring himself in the full-length mirror and slipping on the brownish-green T-shirt and white boxer shorts that Brian T. Pitts had given him. He then forked his toes into a pair of yellow and white rubber shower shoes and flip-flopped out of his bedroom.

Turd, who had gotten his skin drenched in motor oil and then endured a fitful soap and water scrubbing in a metal tub on the patio, slunk in step behind Harris.

"That has got to be the ugliest fucking dog in the world," Brian Pitts proclaimed in a boisterous voice from the living room where he sat flanked by two young Vietnamese females, neither hardly more than sixteen years old. Huong and two other cowboys sat in chairs at the dining table, paying little attention to their new cohort and his companion beast whose tan skin was now shown in the hairless gaps where mangy scales used to exist.

"That dog look like shit now, but you wait," Huong spoke as he slammed mah-jongg tiles onto the tabletop, playing the game with his partners. "That dog he look pretty good, pretty soon. Don't worry. He plenty smart, too. He see thing come when we not see. We keep him. I think he good luck. So why you call him shit?"

"Turd," Harris said. "Not shit."

"Turd is shit," Huong said, throwing down another mah-jongg tile. "So why you name a good dog like this one such a bad name like that?"

"He brown like a turd, man," Harris said, and smiled, hoping to raise some sense of humor from Huong. "Then when I spend the night under that concrete with his nasty ass, he smell like a turd, too. His breath even smell like shit."

"Why not call him Joe?" Huong said, taking a sip of his tea and looking at the other two cowboys studying their game pieces. "I like name like Joe. Not like shit name."

"Man, he's Turd, and that's that," Harris said, flopping in a velvet upholstered sofa chair and spreading out his legs. The two girls cuddled next to Brian Pitts giggled as they looked at the view the black man had given them up his boxer shorts' legs.

Seeing the two young hookers taking notice of his somewhat exposed genitals, Mau Mau grabbed his crotch with his right hand and shook it hard as he spoke.

"You want some of this?" he said, pumping his hand back and forth and laughing at them. "You never go back to that slinky white thing once you had a taste of this Chicago black snake."

The two girls hid their faces in Brian Pitts's shoulders and giggled harder.

"You could wear a robe, you know," Pitts said, also noticing the billowing open legs of Harris's underwear and his exposed nether regions. "What I see is not a pretty sight."

"Then don't look, motherfucker," Harris retorted, and flopped his legs up and down, shaking what he had. Both girls giggled harder.

"With you beaming your ass in my face, it's hard not to get an eyeful," Pitts said. "What if I was queer? How would you feel then?"

Harris snapped his legs closed and then crossed them, tucking his shorts tight. "Don't even fucking joke like that, man," the suddenly shy Marine deserter said.

"You find that offensive?" Pitts asked.

"Fuck yeah, man," Harris said, and then carefully eyed the blond-haired fellow Marine deserter dressed only in a royal-blue silk calf-length afghan-style shirt with matching velvet slippers. "You ain't queer on anything. I see you with them bitches and all, but you dressed kinda sweet, too."

"No, not a faggot," Pitts said casually, lighting a cigarette. "However, I think that you should consider how you might offend other people by flashing your cock and balls. If you want to fuck one of the girls, just say so. Don't go trolling for it."

"Fuck you, man," Harris said, standing, angry. Turd jumped up from the floor, ready to beat a hasty retreat with his master. "I want pussy, I say it. I ain't like some pervert flashin' my dick an' all."

"Sit down then, and shut up," Pitts said, taking a long drag from his smoke. "We have some business."

"Like what?" Harris said, sitting. Turd laid back down at his feet.

"Tomorrow, while Huong and the boys make some distributions, we've got to attend Sunday Mass, and you're driving," Pitts said, looking at Harris and not showing any expression.

"I ain't no Catholic," Harris said.

"Nor am I," Pitts retorted. "We have some collections, and Sunday services have proved a good cover. Lots of Marines going and coming, nobody asking many questions, Sunday and all."

"Fuck, man, that's smart as shit," Harris said, and smiled at his new-found boss and friend.

"We go in uniform, and you're driving the jeep," Pitts said.

"That's cool." Harris nodded. "I feel best in uniform anyway, 'cause wearing something else, CID be asking all kind of questions, you know."

"Yes, I suspect so," Pitts said through a cloud of smoke that came from his mouth as he talked. "Tomorrow you will sit in the jeep, armed with a pistol and rifle. When I meet these people, you will watch me. Anything funny go down, you start taking down everyone around me."

"We on base, man?" Harris asked. "At chapel and all?"

"Yes," Pitts said, finishing his cigarette. "We're in a jeep with numbers that do not appear on any missing-vehicle report. I am dressed as a first lieutenant with an ID card and dog tags that match. You will dress as a sergeant, fully identified. Why would anyone question us?"

"Just gets me all scary and shit," Harris said, shaking his shoulders as he spoke. "You got giant-size balls do shit like that."

"We have more eyes looking for wrongdoing off-base than on-base," Pitts said, taking a sip from a tall glass of iced tea he had sitting on an end table by a tall, silk shaded lamp. "Besides, why would they even be looking for us?"

"They be looking for my ass," Harris said, shaking his head.

"They'll be looking for a dirt-bag nigger named James Harris who smelled like a pile of shit and looked worse, not a squared-away black Marine sergeant," Pitts said, and then added, "no offense."

James Harris looked cold-eyed at Brian Pitts, not liking the racial epithet but clearly understanding what he meant by it. He nodded and said nothing.

"You ever hear tell of a guy called the Snowman?" Pitts said, sipping his tea.

"A few times I hear guys say that name, but never knew nothin' about the dude," Harris said, flipping the lid open on a gold cigarette box and taking out a smoke. "They say he the big man out here. They mostly scared of him. Say he kill lots of guys, ship dope by the truckload back

Stateside. When I meet you I think about that, too. Maybe you the Snowman."

"Fair-complected, blond hair, rather snowy-looking, don't you think?" Pitts said, smiling.

"You be selling lots of shit, too. Snow, you know," Harris said, igniting his cigarette with a gold lighter that matched the case and gold ashtray. "This pad laid out with some heavy shit, too. Ain't no cheap stuff in this place. Ain't no brass. Anything yellow metal, it's gold. I checked it out. It's nice. Like a palace or Hollywood mansion."

"Then you understand where you are, then?" Pitts said. "What I expect of you. From my end you get loyalty and a fair cut of what we take. It's a commitment with your life."

"I done got that all clear in my head when old Huong there slap me on my ear with his .45," Harris said, smiling. "I be loyal with you. Honest, too. I don't tell no lie. Don't you go lyin' to me neither."

"We do not tolerate lies from anyone within my house," Pitts reaffirmed his American cohort. "I will never lie to you. Huong will never mislead you, either. No one will. Ever. Like betrayal, a lie reaps a bullet."

"Cool," Harris said, smiling nervously, thinking about the few times he had fibbed to his old supplier, Lance Corporal James Elmore, when he held back a little extra cash or skimmed a few grams of dope.

"Nanna has your uniforms nearly finished," Pitts said, speaking of the woman who ran his household, and bossed the intern hookers who lived there. "She'll have one of them ironed tonight so you'll have it for tomorrow. Huong picked up a pair of size 12 double-E Corcoran jump boots for you this morning and got them all spit-shined. Here's your new dog tags and an ID card to match, Sergeant Rufus Potter."

"Fuck, man," Harris said, sitting up, looking at the dog tags and identification card with his photograph on it that Pitts tossed to him. "Rufus Potter? What kind of fucked-up name you calling me? Man, that's the fucked-upest name I ever heard. Rufus fucking Potter! Man, you makin' fun of me!"

Huong suddenly swore a stream of Vietnamese profanity and looked at his two cowboys, and then with his left hand swept the mah-jongg tiles from the table onto the floor. As he stood from his chair, he pulled his .45-caliber pistol and put it to the forehead of the man sitting to his right.

"No, fuck, no!" Pitts screamed at Huong just as he pulled the trigger and sent the man's brains spraying from the back of his head, showering the mahogany dining chair and the oriental carpet below it with blood, bone, and pulverized gray matter.

The two girls screamed, fully terrified, and fled upstairs, wailing for Madam Nanna. Mau Mau said nothing, and sat motionless in his chair while Turd snuggled close to his feet. Such sudden, unbridled violence made him realize that the seemingly tranquil, family-style atmosphere that Pitts sought so hard to engender in his household offered but a very thin veil over raw brutality, explosive and lethal.

In junior high school, a teacher had given James Harris a copy of Jack London's, *Call of the Wild* to read. He had loved the book for many reasons. The dog and the black kid from the bad side of Chicago held much in common. Seeing Huong's deadly tantrum made him think of Buck's life as a sled dog, becoming leader and killing Spitz. He identified with the dog and his plight at surviving in a merciless place, akin to the nature of his own life back on his block in a neighborhood where life clashed with death daily.

"That man, he cheat me," Huong said. The other cowboy stood and nodded, affirming what Pitts's senior Vietnamese henchman told him. "He cheat at silly game. He do that, then he steal money, too. He sell us out too, if Benny Lam or Major Tran Van Toan pay him. He no good. I no like him long time."

"YOU GUYS KNOW Tommy Touchdown?" Jack Hembee said out of the blue, sitting up from his lawn chair and wiping out his canteen cup with a handkerchief. "He's a lawyer up at First MAW. I bet you guys know him."

"Not by that name. Only Tommy I've met there is First Lieutenant McKay," Kirkwood answered, holding out his canteen cup for Terry O'Connor to pour him some of the raisin jack from one of the two containers that King Rat and Elvis had brought them from Golf Company. "I heard a couple of guys call him Tommy, but mostly he goes by his initials, T. D."

"Same guy. I know for a fact he's at wing legal," Hembee said, stuffing a fresh wad of Beechnut chew inside his cheek and then offering the pouch to O'Connor. "Some of this cowboy candy goes good with that jack, Terry, if you've got the gut for it. Just tuck it to one side, and try not to swallow too much juice when you take a drink."

"Okay, I'm game," O'Connor said, taking some tobacco from the major's pouch and putting it in his mouth. "Chewing and drinking, I'm learning fast."

"Why Tommy Touchdown?" Kirkwood said as he handed the major the canteen full of raisin jack.

"Well, T. D.'s not his initials," Hembee said. "That stands for touchdown. If you followed college football during the past few years you'd know that McKay has a G for a middle initial. Gaylord. Thomas Gaylord McKay."

"No wonder he kept it a secret. Gaylord?" O'Connor yucked.

"Probably one of the best scatback, option-ball carriers the University of Texas has ever had play football," Hembee continued. "Next time you see him, check out his legs. They're like tree trunks. Your man grew up in Dumas, Texas, right?"

"That's him," O'Connor said. "He mentioned Dumas at the hail and farewell party last night. Never breathed a word about football."

"I know that's him," Hembee said. "He's a big reason why Texas won the national championship in 1963, T. D.'s junior year. They should have won it his senior year, too, back in '64, when they beat number-one Alabama in the Orange Bowl, 21 to 17. But since Arkansas upset the Longhorns in a game in October, beating them by a stinking point, 14 to 13, the AP and UPI polls did not consider Texas national-champion material, dropping them to number five. The Razorbacks just won on luck, one lousy point. When McKay and his class graduated they took the heart of the lineup with them, so Darrell Royal has not had a Longhorn team come close since. What's ironic, McKay got picked up by the Los Angeles Rams in the first round of the NFL draft, but went to law school instead. Talk about a bonehead move. Now he's a first lieutenant in Vietnam."

"He never let on, and I'll bet not many of the guys at the legal office know it either," O'Connor said, spitting. "Only football player they ever mentioned was that crazy observation pilot Lobo Gunn, who played at New Mexico."

"I'm sure Dicky Doo knows, and it probably explains the resentment that he holds for McKay," Kirkwood said as he took his first sip of the raisin liquor. "Wow! That tastes somewhere between a hundred ten and a hundred forty octane. Warm all the way down, like cognac."

"You know, Major Danger, this stuff is not all that bad," Terry O'Connor said with a satisfied purr as he reclined in the lawn chair and sipped more of the home-distilled raisin hooch. "Nice of them to give us two full quarts."

"A couple of canteens, I bet, didn't even make a dent in their supply," Hembee said, sipping from his cup. "Everybody writes home and asks for raisins, along with the cookies and other crap. Anytime somebody goes up to Da Nang or over to Chu Lai they bring back raisins. Didn't take long to figure out what they had going on, especially when I start getting people volunteering to burn the shitters. That's when they cook off a batch. Burning the shitters."

"Looks like the battalion commander or the sergeant major would start cracking down," Kirkwood said. "Last thing you need are drunks on watch."

"I've yet to see it," Hembee said. "Our CO doesn't go looking for trouble. We've got enough on our plate with the number of operational commitments out here. If a little UA raisin jack is all we've got in the line of personnel problems, then we're doing pretty good, I'd say. I hear stories about army troops up north and down south of us refusing to go on patrols, getting all doped up and shit. We haven't seen anything like that with our Marines."

"That you know about," O'Connor said, sipping his cup.

"True, Captain," Hembee said. "Then I know about their moonshine operation, don't I."

"First time I ever drank raisin jack," Kirkwood said, stretching out in the lounge chair alongside the two other officers reclining in theirs. The three Marines watched as the last light of the setting sun streaked across the sky, and gray dusk faded the distant rice paddies and grass huts into darkness.

"In New York, I tasted something very similar to this raisin jack," O'Connor said, sipping the aromatic liquor with its almost oily alcohol film that sheeted down the sides of his metal canteen cup as he swirled it, breathing the vapors. "Just like this stuff, it burned all the way down, and left a man feeling a nice, warm glow all over."

"Tastes like cognac to me," Kirkwood commented, now savoring the drink as he sipped it.

"This stuff I drank in New York is like cognac, but not aged in oak. A cousin to it, I guess," O'Connor said, looking at the twinkling fire lights among the peasant huts in the distance. "Aqua vitae, the French call it by one name, which translated means the water of life. They also call it eau de vie, or burning water. I think from the way it goes down the hatch. But a buddy of mine had another name for it that I think you'd appreciate."

Hembee laughed and said, "You sound as full of shit as a Christmas turkey, but go ahead. We've got all night."

"My dad, back in Philly, has a buddy in New York who was in the Marine Corps with him, out in the Pacific in World War II," O'Connor began. "Ben Finney is the guy's name. He was a major and worked with the war correspondents and stuff. Now he writes a column in the *New York Daily News.*

"A few years back, Major Finney introduced me to a young fellow from Germany, going to Columbia, same as me. This guy's dad was German ambassador to the United Nations, and supposedly he descended from Frederick the Great. He's got all kinds of Bavarian nobility in his family legacy. At any rate, his grandfather was an artillery captain for the kaiser in World War I, and fought the Marines at the Battle of Belleau Wood. During World War II, the same officer is now a German general, and oversees the occupation of France.

"According to my friend, and I have nothing to back me up on this except his word, his grandfather, because of his enduring respect for U.S. Marines from World War I, had German soldiers raise and lower the U.S. flag each day at the American national cemetery at Belleau, France. The site where they buried most of the Marines who died at the Battle of Belleau Wood, right by the battleground.

"This fellow said that his grandfather also got executed by the Gestapo for plotting to assassinate Hitler. So that makes his raising and lowering of the Stars and Stripes at Belleau more believable, too.

"Last year, I went home on leave during early November, and participated in a little Marine Corps birthday celebration of sorts in Manhattan at this guy's apartment. Now, even though he's a German and all, he idolizes Marines. He wanted to join the Corps, but his father raised hell, so he stayed in college at Columbia. However, here I am in the Marine Corps, so Major Finney insists that I go with him to this guy's apartment for the party.

"My boy's got a life-size oil painting portrait of Frederick the Great hanging inside the doorway. The face on Frederick the Great and the puss on this cat look identical. So I'm pretty impressed. Then he hands us drinks in these two-hundred-year-old, sterling silver goblets with all kinds of ornate little silver sculptures encrusting the sides of them, and serves them to us off a sterling silver tray that matches the cups, also made more than two hundred years ago. The stuff that he poured tasted damned near the same as this raisin jack."

"Stands to reason; raisins are grapes," Kirkwood said.

"Well, here's the good part. The story behind the liquor he served goes like this," O'Connor continued. "It seems that the Battle of Belleau Wood took place in French wine country. After the war the farmers went back to growing their grapes there and making wine. They do it to this day.

"My German friend goes to Belleau, France, every year with his father, as a family custom, to pay homage to his grandfather's memory, and to pay tribute to the Germans and Americans buried at the respective national cemeteries there. When he comes home he brings some of the wine and distilled spirits from the grapes these farmers grow at Belleau. The eau de vie or aqua vitae of Belleau Wood.

"Now, before we drank our toasts to the U.S. Marine Corps, the guy explains to us all this stuff about his grandfather, the German general, and his flag-raising, and how he admired the Marines at Belleau Wood. He also talks about how their blood soaked the land, and to this day mingles with the grapes that grow there. The eau de vie from Belleau he named Blood of Dead Marines. He has it bottled, and has even put on a private label: Blood of Dead Marines.

"Gentlemen, this raisin jack tastes like Blood of Dead Marines. So I propose that from this day hence, given the blood spilled by Marines in this far-off place, and given that this fine spirit came to life at the hands of good Marines, we should call it by that name: Blood of Dead Marines."

"Terry," Major Hembee said and laughed, "you're so full of shit that my eyes crossed five minutes ago, but I have to admit, that is a dandy story, and a noble tribute to some outstanding rotgut. Blood of Dead Marines it is, then. *Semper fi,* gentlemen."

"*Semper fi,* Major Danger," O'Connor said, and tapped his canteen cup with Hembee's and Kirkwood's.

"Ben Finney, he's still at the *Daily News,* right?" Kirkwood asked, sipping his drink. There's a Marine there that draws the sports-page cartoons. Is that him?"

"No, that's Bill Gallo," O'Connor said. "Gallo, Finney, and my dad are all buddies, though. They were on Iwo Jima together, when my dad won the Navy Cross."

"Hold up, one. He didn't win it. He *earned* it," Major Hembee said, correcting O'Connor. "You win a trophy for a footrace, but the Navy Cross, it's a major form of tribute for a great sacrifice. It's earned."

"My bust, Major," O'Connor said, blushing at his thoughtless choice of words. "Dad's a stark, raving Democrat, but I know he would like you. He's always pinging me on things like that, too. I called my trousers "pants" once, and he said, 'Girls and women wear pants; men wear trousers.' "

"Enlisted Marine?" Hembee asked and smiled.

"Yes, sir, a sergeant. How'd you guess?" O'Connor said.

"Just a hunch," the major said. "A sergeant with the Navy Cross from Iwo Jima impresses the hell out of me. I'd like to know your dad."

"Enroll in a history course at the University of Pennsylvania and you'll meet him," O'Connor said. "He's the professor. Now, you want to hear some long yardage on storytelling, just get my dad and Major Finney together with a pitcher of old Ben's famous mint juleps, and those two can keep you up all night."

"Mint juleps? Odd for a couple of Yankee gentlemen," Kirkwood said.

"Oh, you don't call Ben Finney a Yankee," O'Connor said and laughed. "That's as bad as me saying my dad won the Navy Cross. The good major is a classic southern gentleman, a Kentucky colonel, as a matter of fact, one of that state's favorite sons. Kentucky colonel is an honor only bestowed by the governor of that great state. Ben Finney is from Kentucky, and makes a classic mint julep. In fact, Major Finney even taught Ernest Hemingway the proper way to build a mint julep."

"Do tell," Hembee said and chuckled. "This Blood of Dead Marines has loosened your tongue, Captain O'Connor. Please continue."

"Just after the Second World War ended, old Ben got sent to France as a correspondent," O'Connor rambled as Kirkwood now began to snore in the cool darkness of the evening, having finished his canteen cup of ninety-proof liquor. "One weekend, he went off into the countryside, touring on a bicycle, and stopped at this pension house or inn someplace north of Paris. He said he had no more than sat down in the place when a glass came sailing across the room and shattered on the stone wall.

" 'Can't any of you frogs make a man a decent mint julep?' this heavy-set American guy with a salt-and-pepper beard bellowed from a table in the back. 'Doesn't anyone in this godforsaken country know how to make a mint julep?'

"Of course, Ben, coming from Kentucky, has always traveled with a quart bottle of Maker's Mark, Kentucky bourbon whiskey in his valise, just in case of snakebite or some other emergency that would lend a good excuse for him taking a drink. So he snatched out his trusty bottle of Maker's Mark and quickly ordered the barkeep to fetch some fresh-picked mint, along with a few other necessary ingredients, and he commenced to stir up a pitcher of genuine Kentucky mint juleps. The fellow was, of course, Ernest Hemingway."

"Gentlemen, with that, and taking Captain Kirkwood's snoring as a cue, I think that we need to ramble down to the hooch and hit the rack," Major Hembee said, pulling himself from the lawn chair. "Screw the lid on that canteen of Blood of Dead Marines, Terry. Otherwise it could start a fire."

Just as the major gave Kirkwood a slap across the sole of his boot, a flash as bright as daylight broke across the encampment, and a thunderous clap shook the air and the ground around the three officers.

"Incoming!" a voice shouted nearby.

Jon Kirkwood stood straight up, holding his M14, looking for an enemy target to engage.

"Slow down, Skipper," Hembee said in a calm voice, taking Kirkwood by the shoulder. "We'll just ease down to the operations bunker. Don't want to do any shooting just yet."

"What's this, mortars?" O'Connor said, grabbing his rifle and hurrying behind the major and Kirkwood as they followed a trail into a nearby dugout covered in sandbags.

"Yeah, rockets, mortars, you name it," Hembee said, calmly walking to a table where the staff sergeant he called Goose sat, his ear pressed to a field telephone as he quickly jotted notes on a legal pad.

"Sir," Goose said, looking at the major now, "looks like they're pretty much focused on the Americal positions. Could be they're trying to divert us so they can hit the fuel dump."

"Makes sense," Hembee said. "We've got the reaction force deploying along that arc, in case."

"What about the flank back this way?" Hembee asked.

"Pretty thin, but we still have some automatic weapons in place at two points that can cover it," Goose said.

Hembee looked at Kirkwood and O'Connor and thought a moment before speaking.

"Care to get your feet wet?" the major then asked the two captains.

"We got our cherries broke this morning, sir," Kirkwood said, "in case you're looking to take our combat virginity."

Hembee laughed loudly and put his arm around Jon Kirkwood.

"No, Captain," the major said, hugging him with his arm, "I'm not trying to fuck you. I just have a little job and thought you might want to help."

"Sure, Major Danger," O'Connor said, slipping the sling of his M14 rifle over his shoulder.

"If you need some help, that's a little different," Kirkwood said, shouldering his rifle, too.

"I wouldn't ask a couple of transient captains unless I felt that it was important," Hembee said, and walked to a map of the two knolls that made up the terrain of Fire Support Base Ross.

"Charlie has hit the army units posted over here on the southwest side," the major said, pointing on the chart with plastic overlays that showed gun and unit positions. "We're back here, and pretty much out of danger. We've got our reserves, the reaction team, going hi-diddle-diddle to where the enemy seems to have hit hardest, what seems to be his main force. I'm just thinking we have a soft spot on this flank, and we have two machine guns at the corners, but not much in between. You game for sitting in a fighting hole, watching for Charlie to try to hit the wire down there?"

Kirkwood looked at the map and hesitated, but O'Connor snapped at the chance.

"Sure, Major, no sweat," O'Connor said. He reached for a pouch of Beechnut laying on the field desk in the bunker and stuffed his mouth full.

"Good," Hembee said, and then turned and shouted, "Rat, Elvis, Henry, get up here!"

Like mice dashing from a woodpile, the three men appeared within seconds, emerging from the busy corners of the combat command and operations bunker where operations, communications, and other associated Marines, jammed inside the subterranean confine, strived to get a handle on the attack.

"Get flak jackets and helmets for the two captains and then join them out on the flank," Hembee said. "Kirkwood, you and O'Connor will man the fighting hole a few yards right of King Rat, Elvis, and Henry, who'll haul out another M60 chopper. That'll give us three .30-caliber machine guns along with individual weapons to cover that spot. We've got a field phone down in that hole. All you've got to do is pick it up and talk. You see anything start moving, get Goose on the horn. If you see any sappers going for the wire, start shooting. We'll come running."

While the two lawyers slipped on the helmets and flak jackets that Rat had brought them, Kirkwood took a long look at the three enlisted Marines already geared and ready, entrusted to the leadership of two green, boot officers. Then he glanced at O'Connor, beaming with his cheek bulging with tobacco and the straps on his steel helmet dangling like John Wayne playing Sergeant John M. Stryker on *The Sands of Iwo Jima*. He wondered if his partner and best friend had yet fully realized the risks and realities of stepping onto a combat line.

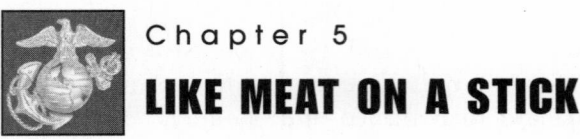

Chapter 5

LIKE MEAT ON A STICK

AN EERIE YELLOW daylight settled over LZ Ross as a dozen glowing flares danced beneath miniature parachutes that drifted across the night sky, leaving contrails of white smoke above them. Just beyond the bristle of big guns where the Eleventh Marine Regiment's artillery lay quiet, awaiting their inevitable fire missions once the American counterattack ensued and where the Seventh Marine Regiment's 81-millimeter mortars busily thunked out a mixture of high-explosive, white phosphorus, and illumination rounds, the flickering lightning and ceaseless thunder from the incoming enemy 122-millimeter rockets and 60-millimeter mortars flashed and echoed across the encampment. Red and green tracers crisscrossed inbound and outbound paths on the fringes as the infantry companies hurriedly prepared to launch their retaliation, designed foremost to protect the support base's helicopter refueling station. On the quieter side of LZ Ross, through the surrealistic nighttime's amber luminance, the silhouettes of five men dashed from the ground and hurried down a trail toward a pair of unmanned supplementary fighting positions that overlooked an untroubled section of the base's perimeter wire.

"You gentlemen going to make it okay?" King Rat said as he led the pair of lawyers to the first of the two holes covered by a low, plywood roof layered with sandbags and ringed with more sandbags for a parapet. "Just crawl down that opening in the back here, and settle down. I doubt we see shit. I hope so anyway."

"That your foxhole over there?" O'Connor said, seeing a similar-looking emplacement.

"Yeah," Rat said, squatting and helping Kirkwood unload the luggage he carried. "You got a field phone right there on that dirt shelf in the front, between you two. Just pick it up and mash the button on the handset to talk. Goose come right back at you."

"How long you think we'll sit out here tonight, Sergeant?" Kirkwood then asked the black Marine who now sported a set of sergeant chevrons but who had not worn any rank insignia when he saw him earlier in the day.

"Probably till daylight," King Rat said. "You got ample room in this position so's one of you can kinda kick back and sleep. Me and Henry and Elvis, we be sittin' up mostly. Packed pretty tight. Back a few weeks ago, when we still had old Houndog with us, it be me and Henry over there an Houndog and Elvis over here."

O'Connor laughed. "I knew Elvis had to have a hound dog around here someplace."

"Yeah, old Houndog, he was a pretty cool guy," King Rat said sullenly, shifting his eyes down as he spoke.

"He rotate back Stateside?" asked O'Connor cheerily.

"Naw, we lost old Houndog about two weeks ago," the sergeant said, looking at the ground. "He and Elvis, they got put on one of these cooks 'n' bakers patrols, you know, just a close-in security check around the fringes. Anyway, some damned gook got lucky and just picked him off. Shot him through the heart, where he had his flak jacket opened up. You know, hot and all. Had it unzipped. He died just about the time he hit the ground. Old Elvis over there, he ain't said hardly shit since then. Maybe two words in two weeks."

Kirkwood and O'Connor squatted and looked at the dirt, too.

"Shit don't mean nothing, no way," King Rat said, looking up. "We take it as it come. You know. That's all a man can do."

"Sorry about old Houndog, Elvis," Kirkwood said, and put his hand on the Marine's shoulder.

"You a couple of nice guys for officers," Henry then spoke, having not uttered a word through the entire day and night that the two captains had seen him.

"Thanks, Henry," O'Connor said, and smiled at the three Marines. "All we know is what we learned at Quantico, at the Basic School. So don't be shy about setting us straight if we need it. I'll do my best by you. Like Major Danger said, we gotta depend on each other, Marines first."

"Good to know, Captain," Elvis then said.

"Yeah, Skipper," King Rat said, nodding his head. "Good to know. You gentlemen need anything, just give us a whistle."

Squatting on their heels, the two captains watched the three enlisted Marines scramble to the other fighting position, twenty yards to their left, dragging the M60 machine gun, several cans of ammunition, and their individual rifles with them.

FIRST LIEUTENANT JIMMY Sanchez had divided his reconnaissance platoon into a quartet of four-man sections, leaving seven men in his command element, including Tommy McKay, the platoon's navy hospital corpsman, Petty Officer First Class Ted Hamilton, and his radio operator, Lance Corporal Bobby Sneed, and a four-man fire team. His platoon sergeant, Staff Sergeant Paul Rhodes, had the first of the four-man reconnaissance teams, and responded on the radio net with the call sign Cobra. Sergeant Lionel McCoy had team two, answering to the call sign Mamba. Corporal Kenny Price had team three, answering to the call sign Bushmaster. Corporal Floyd Bennett headed team four, answering to the call sign Rattler. Jimmy Sanchez had the call sign Snake Charmer.

Sanchez, T. D. McKay, and the twenty-two-man reconnaissance platoon had spent the greater part of the day moving westward from the base camp southwest of Con Thien. During Operation Kingfisher, they had reconnoitered this same area that took them to the eastern fringe of a territory patrolled by elements of the Third Marine Regiment. That territorial limit now marked the boundary of their new operational theater, overseen by the Ninth Marine Regiment, which had the name Kentucky. West in the Third Marines' tactical area of responsibility, the region had the name Lancaster. Two simultaneous operations took place, and Jimmy Sanchez carefully positioned his Marines so they did not mistakenly walk from Kentucky into Lancaster, and fall under fire from otherwise friendly forces.

Once in position, the lieutenant scattered out his four mobile teams along a line running east and west more than five kilometers long, patrolling in a northerly direction. With their exposed skin painted various shades of green, and moving swiftly and silently, each of the reconnaissance sections worked their way toward the Demilitarized Zone. Sanchez and his command element set their position near the crest of a mountain in the center of the five-kilometer fan. From there he sent out his command section's four-man team, led by Corporal Lynn Sanders, call sign Viper, forward of his position to scout.

Throughout the night, as each team reached mandatory reporting points, based on time and position triggers, the respective section leaders radioed Sanchez with short-range, VHF walkie-talkies, giving him a fix on their locations. From his station he plotted his map, showing each team's advance through their mission objectives. Hour by hour, as he kept track of his platoon's progress, scouting the region, searching for enemy activity, the reconnaissance lieutenant kept note of how the various positions related to a series of rally points and helicopter landing sites he also had plotted on his map.

The rally points served as locations where his force could consolidate, establish their best defense, and make a hasty departure by air, should the enemy make contact with them and pursue in force. As part of his patrol briefing, prior to their leaving the Con Thien base camp that morning, he made sure that not only did his platoon sergeant and noncommissioned officers have the rally points and associated landing sites marked on their maps, but also that T. D. McKay had a clear idea of their locations, call signs, and emergency radio codes. A thorough leader, Sanchez always planned for the worst cases while he sought the best results.

"Cobra, Snake Charmer," the radio squawked into the handset that Bobby Sneed, a six-foot, three-inch-tall, 265-pound communications Marine with curly yellow hair, held to his ear.

"Go ahead, Cobra," the radioman, who had the nickname Baby Huey, said in a low murmur, holding his mouth close to the handset and cupping his fingers over his lips while he spoke.

"Checkpoint Bravo, no joy," Staff Sergeant Rhodes, a medium-sized man who occasionally smoked a pipe and wore military-issue, black plastic framed glasses, spoke softly.

As the signal came to the radio, Jimmy Sanchez, a small-framed but solid man whose black hair and dark eyes spoke of his Latino heritage, had instinctively leaned his head next to the handset, too, so he could hear the report. Then he glanced at his buddy, Tommy McKay, a brown-haired, stockily built man with a bull neck and barrel chest. Although of average height, standing an inch and a half shy of six feet tall, the lawyer carried nearly 225 pounds of fat-free muscle on his frame. He quietly sat staring into the darkness with his AR15 carbine, a cut-down version of an M16, resting across his unusually massive thighs.

"Pretty boring stuff," Sanchez whispered to McKay. "More often than not, we spend most nights doing the same thing. No joy. Just empty terrain. Life in recon is said to be ninety percent boredom punctuated by ten percent sheer terror."

"Nothing in between?" McKay breathed, smiling pearly teeth through dark and light green face paint.

"We get in the shit, it is the shits," Sanchez said, letting go a whispered laugh. "Unless we're part of a major sweep, which puts a company or battalion at our backs, we end up meat on a stick. Nobody out here to back us up, so we have to depend on remaining unseen to stay alive. We carry weapons, but a good recon team should never have to use them."

"Snake Charmer, Rattler," a call sounded on the radio.

"Uh-oh," Jimmy Sanchez said, and leaned his head next to his communicator's and listened. "They're between reporting points."

"Go ahead, Rattler, Snake Charmer actual," Jimmy Sanchez spoke, taking the handset from the radioman.

"Bandits crossing our front, grid coordinate three-two-five-six-seven-niner, moving eastward, and drifting slightly south toward your position," Corporal Bennett said. "November, victor, alpha, confirmed. Company size unit with some hand-drawn rolling stock and heavy weapons. Count six one-hundred-twenty-millimeter mortar tubes. Sir, be on guard at your location. Confirm sighting two rifle-squad size patrols scouting ahead of the main body, moving along their flanks."

"Roger, Rattler, confirm November-victor-alpha company moving east southeast, present grid three-two-five-six-seven-niner, heavy weapons, six one-twenty-mike-mike mortar tubes, advancing with at least two satellite patrols scouting their flanks," Sanchez repeated back to Corporal Bennett.

"Snake Charmer actual, Rattler. Roger the information," Bennett responded.

"Snake Team, Snake Charmer actual," Sanchez called, sending a blanket signal to all five recon sections. "Copy the last?"

"Cobra, copy," Staff Sergeant Rhodes answered.

"Viper, copy. Mamba, copy. Bushmaster, copy," the other teams responded.

"Snake Team, Snake Charmer actual," Sanchez then radioed to all five of the four-man teams. "Withdraw, rally point Tango."

"Roger, withdrawing to rally point Tango, Bushmaster out," came the first response. Systematically, each of the other four teams answered, acknowledging the platoon commander's order to move as quickly as possible to the rally point, where they would consolidate their force and move away from the area where Rattler had spotted the NVA company.

"Red Rider, Red Rider, Snake Charmer actual, over," the lieutenant spoke sharply in a different handset's mouthpiece, calling the operations monitor at the Ninth Marine Regiment's combat command and operations center at Con Thien on the long-range radio that his reconnaissance platoon's communicator had strapped to his back.

After a moment of silence, Sanchez repeated the signal again and again until finally a static-riddled response crackled through the earpiece. In the same quick, shorthanded language that he had used with his teams, the lieutenant relayed the sighting to the regiment's operations officer, who then repeated the data to the platoon leader for confirmation.

"Roger, your copy is correct," Sanchez said, and then listened again while the regimental S-3 spoke to him.

"We heading back to Con Thien?" McKay whispered as he, Sanchez, the radio operator, and the corpsman now began to work their way south from the crest of the hill, where they had lain hidden, moving toward the platoon's primary rally point.

"Eventually," Sanchez replied, whispering over his shoulder at McKay. "Operations wants us to drift a tad west, and then get in position to the rear of these guys, along the flank of the track they took. We'd like to know if that NVA company represents an advance element leading a main force, or if that bunch is alone, just in transit to link up with a force already down here. Did you happen to get a look at the aerial photos they had at the CCOC this morning?"

"No, I didn't," McKay whispered, trying to walk softly as they descended the slope of the hill.

"The pictures show all along the DMZ the NVA has begun massing a hell of a lot of forces. They're getting ready for something big. Real big. We've now identified elements from the 320th NVA Division, the 325C Division, and the 308th and the 341st divisions. They're on the move from Laos, all across our front. Could be headed down to Camp Carroll or over to Khe Sanh, take your pick. Two good targets. Intelligence suspects that we have additional units crossing the DMZ to bolster the 304th NVA Division, who we have confirmed already in this area. Probably where that company is headed. Hopefully, for us, they're just in transit, headed to the 304th, and not a recon in force looking to engage lost souls in the darkness."

"Company size unit seems awfully big for a recon in force," McKay said, squatting behind Jimmy Sanchez, who now took a reading off his compass and looked at his watch.

"Big, but not unusual for the NVA. However, given they're pulling carts and have several heavy weapons, I think they're in transit," Sanchez said, pulling out his canteen from the pouch next to his fanny pack and taking a drink. "Let's hang loose here a minute, let the Viper team catch up with us. Four more guns might come in handy. I'm a little worried about these bandits patrolling along the flanks. Hate to run into them."

"READ THE SIDE of this ammunition can, just so I know we didn't get ours mixed up with theirs," Jon Kirkwood told Terry O'Connor as he climbed behind his partner into the two-man foxhole less than a hundred yards from the operations bunker where they had left Major Jack Hembee and a platoon of command center Marines scurrying from radio to field telephone, reacting to incoming information from the units now engaging the enemy. "In this light, I can't quite make out what it says."

"Lake City Arsenal, lot 106, ammunition, M14, .30-caliber ball," O'Connor said as he read the label. Then he popped open the lid and looked inside the can. "See, got these canvas bandoleers with cardboard sleeves full of M14 ammo. Just like at the rifle range. Here, take a bunch of rounds and pile them right in front of you so you can reload your magazine fast."

"Leave them in the box; they'll get dirty and jam the rifles," Kirkwood said, picking up a handful of rifle shells that O'Connor had dropped on an earthen ledge in front of them.

"They won't jam the rifles," O'Connor said, slapping the back of Kirkwood's hand, causing him to drop the rounds onto the fighting hole's dirt floor and sump.

"Now you've really fucked them up, Terry," Jon Kirkwood moaned as he knelt into the bottom of the fighting hole and felt for the loose ammunition.

"Forget it, man, we have like five hundred rounds in this box," O'Connor said.

"I don't want to be stepping on them," Kirkwood growled, now on his hands and knees in the bowels of the hole, feeling for shell cases among the debris left by previous inhabitants of the outpost.

"You're like an old-maid schoolteacher, Jon," O'Connor said with a laugh, shaking his head and putting the binoculars to his eyes that Major Danger had given him as a last-minute thought so they could search for movement beyond the cleared area outside the wire. "Shit, you can really see good through these things. Amazing at night in just this artificial light. Here, take a look out there."

Jon Kirkwood stood and peered through the binoculars, studying the bushes and trees several hundred yards beyond the area cleared of vegetation and other cover outside the wire.

"Anything moving?" O'Connor said, now sighting down his rifle, and checking the right and left limiting stakes that designated the zone of responsibility that his rifle covered on his side of the fighting position.

"Nothing moving, just bushes," Kirkwood said, taking the binoculars from his eyes and looking at O'Connor checking his field of fire. Then he located the wooden stake on the right side of his position and laid his rifle in the center between it and the middle stake.

"Remember the last time we did this?" O'Connor said, smiling. "Cold as a son of a bitch. Remember? Not half bad here, though, considering the end of November and all. Gotta still be around sixty-five or seventy degrees at night. Not that bad."

"Well, that was the Basic School, and we had no one shooting live ammunition at us," Kirkwood said, looking out the binoculars again, searching the tree lines for movement.

"Remember how it started snowing that night, and we had water up past our shins? That truly was the shits," O'Connor said, looking over the top of his M14, checking his sight adjustments to be sure the major had properly moved his to a 200-yard battle zero, like he had done Kirkwood's rifle, and had shown the two lawyers how to double-check them.

"This isn't Quantico, Terry," Kirkwood said, working the focusing ring on the binoculars to bring a fuzzy object into sharp definition. "We're not playing some sort of game in the Virginia woods either."

"We didn't play games then," O'Connor said, defending his nostalgia. "I took it damned serious. I knew we'd be in Vietnam soon enough."

"I didn't mean a game like that," Kirkwood said, still turning the knob, trying to sharpen the distorted image. "I meant that was just training. Not for real. This, my friend, is as real as life gets."

"We're not going to see shit, anyway," O'Connor said, now laying over the top of his rifle, staring into the orange-lit night. The attack at the opposite end of the base had subsided to sporadic popping of rifle fire and an intermittent mortar explosion. "It's all dying down."

"We have a friendly patrol out there, among those trees?" Kirkwood said, fussing with the focus ring on the binoculars. "I see one, two, three, four, five, six, seven, eight. Eight people just ran past that open spot!"

"Here, give me those binoculars," O'Connor said, grabbing the field glasses and now looking straight out from the bunker.

"Goose, Goose, I got eight bodies running across a gap in the trees about three or four hundred yards straight out from our position!" Kirkwood spoke on the field phone.

Just as he had made the report, Terry O'Connor dropped the binoculars on the parapet shelf in front of him and opened fire with his M14.

"Tell Goose we got sappers running toward the wire!" O'Connor yelled as he emptied his magazine and snapped in a second one.

Just as his rifle had fired, King Rat, Elvis, and Henry opened fire from their hole, chopping grazing fire across the frontal area with the machine gun and their two M16 rifles.

Behind the trees ahead of them, five hundred yards away, the telltale flashes of mortars flickered as they belched several rounds toward the Americans. In a few seconds, the earth churned and exploded all around the five Marines.

On two small rises to their right and left, other machine guns opened fire, cutting across the wide, barren flats before the wire. As the automatic weapons churned across the wasteland, more enemy mortars rained onto the two flanking machine gun nests.

"Keep shooting!" Kirkwood yelled at O'Connor, who had ducked below the parapet of the fighting hole when a sixty-millimeter round exploded a few feet from his side of their sandbagged nest. "They're trying to suppress our fire with the mortars so they can overrun us."

"Something's wrong over there with King Rat and the boys," O'Connor said, noticing that now only one rifle fired sporadically from that position. "Keep shooting man, I gotta go take a look. We need that machine gun to stop the sappers."

Terry O'Connor rolled out the back of the small bunker and raced the twenty yards to the next hole on his belly. As he got closer, he could see smoke rolling out of a jumble of sandbags and broken lumber.

"Jon, keep shooting!" O'Connor yelled, climbing around the debris and pulling it from the hole. "They got hit bad over here!"

In the bottom of the hole, Henry lay moaning, blinded from the mortar blast. King Rat had fallen limp on top of the machine gun. Elvis had taken shrapnel across the right side of his face and neck. His skin, wet with blood, was speckled with black. He alone managed to fire his rifle.

"Rat, Henry, you guys need to sit tight," O'Connor said. "Jon's got help coming pronto. Meanwhile, Elvis, we need that machine gun. Help me get it over to the other hole."

"Rat might be dead," Elvis said as he pulled the limp body from atop the machine gun and shoved it out to O'Connor.

"Nothing we can do right now except pray," O'Connor told Elvis, pulling the heavy weapon to his side and grabbing two cans of belted ammunition for it. "Can you help me drag the rest of the ammo with the gun? We'll move it to our hole; that way Charlie may leave these guys alone."

"Yes, sir, I just can't hear very good and I can only see out my left eye, but I can hump ammo for you," Elvis said, climbing out of the debris of the fighting hole with three cans of ammunition in his clutches.

"Rat! You and Henry lay quiet! Help's coming!" O'Connor shouted down in the hole.

"Yeah, man, we cool," a voice from the bottom answered.

DOC HAMILTON SAW the movement first and nudged Jimmy Sanchez, who, seeing the silhouette figure easing toward him, sat up from where he had lain and waved.

"Viper made good time off that hill," Sanchez said, turning back toward where Tommy McKay and Doc Hamilton lay on their bellies next to their radioman, Lance Corporal Sneed.

Suddenly four other silhouettes broke through the thick undergrowth, and Doc Hamilton reached for Jimmy Sanchez, who still sat up with his back turned toward the oncoming dark figures. Before he could pull the lieutenant down, a burst of rifle fire snapped at them, throwing the reconnaissance platoon commander on his face.

As soon as he saw the muzzle flash from the enemy's weapon, Tommy the Touchdown McKay opened fire with his AR15, sending his first bullet into the head of the man who had just shot his best friend. Bobby Sneed took out two of the four other North Vietnamese soldiers who attacked from behind the leader whom McKay had killed. The remaining two fell back as the lawyer lieutenant emptied his rifle's magazine at them.

"Shit, man," Jimmy Sanchez said, coughing blood and gasping for air as he began to writhe on the ground. "I'm lung-shot."

"We'll have to carry him," Doc Hamilton said. "Can't do much for him sitting here. We've gotta get him on a med-evac chopper as fast as we can."

McKay looked at Sanchez, feeling his heart tie up in his chest as his friend gasped to breathe, trying to talk but only able to mouthe a few words as Doc Hamilton dosed him with morphine, and with a bloody finger drew an M on the lieutenant's forehead. Then the corpsman turned the officer on his stomach, and pulled up his blouse and T-shirt. Finding the three entries made by the bullets, he rolled wads of gauze bandages tight and stuffed them into the holes, plugging them so that air no longer sucked through the wounds.

"That's the best I can do for now, Snake Man," Doc Hamilton told the lieutenant as he eased him on his back and sat him up. "Plugging the holes should help you pull in air a little easier. I know it's not a fix. You're just going to have to deal with getting shallow breaths until the folks at Charlie Med can take care of you."

"Jimmy," T. D. said, "you know that gunfire's going to draw the rest of those NVA patrols, just like shit draws flies. We've got to get the hell out of Dodge right now. Me and Doc's going to lift you to your feet, and we're going to *di di mao.*"

Sanchez nodded his head and gritted his teeth as his college classmate and the platoon corpsman lifted him to his feet and draped his arms over their shoulders.

"Grab his shit," McKay told Lance Corporal Sneed, who had already begun calling Ninth Marines combat command and operations center.

"Red Rider, Red Rider, Snake Charmer, flash-flash, shark bait, repeat, shark bait. Kilo-zero, whiskey-one, actual, med-evac lifeguard, Lima-Zulu-Oscar," Sneed repeated again and again, but heard no response as he lugged his two backpacked radios and now the rifle and map case of his platoon commander, in addition to his own weapon and canteen belt. His coded message that he continued to repeat, with the key words, shark bait, alerted Ninth Marines operations and command center that the reconnaissance platoon had engaged the enemy, compromising their presence, and was now on the run to their primary rally point and its associated landing zone for emergency extraction. His additional information advised that the platoon had zero members killed, one man wounded, the commander, and that he suffered life-threatening wounds and needed immediate medical evacuation at Landing Zone Oscar.

"Only a couple of clicks past this little ridge, partner," McKay told Sanchez as the wounded lieutenant tried to help the two Marines carrying him by kicking his legs, trying to run with them.

"Sir, don't do that," Doc Hamilton said, now breathing hard. "Your lungs are full of blood. You can't get enough air to support yourself as it is. Relax, sir, let us carry you."

Moonlight flashed through the tree branches overhead as the three Marines ran, carrying the fourth. Ahead of them a broad clearing loomed, more than three football fields wide, scattered with low bushes and palmettos in the waist-high grass.

"Go around! Go around! Danger area!" Sanchez gasped. "Too dangerous!"

"What do you think, Doc?" McKay asked the corpsman. Both men knew that time meant everything for Sanchez's survival.

"We start moving in the open, with this moonlight, anyone can see us. No cover out there," Hamilton said, catching his breath.

"Why not call the choppers into this place?" McKay then asked.

"Lots of times these places get pretty boggy, might not be a good LZ. The lieutenant saw it on his map but chose not to use it as a rally point or a landing site. I'm sure he had his reasons," the corpsman said. "What do you think, Sneed?"

"I've jumped on a Huey in a rice paddy before. No big deal. Can't be much worse," the radioman said. "Problem is, I ain't got any signal down here. Nothing we can call out on. Rally Point Tango has good reception, on that little hilltop, can't be more than another kilometer or two, just over that next rise. If Red Rider heard any of my Maydays when I called them right after we got hit, they'll have choppers and a reaction force inbound to us."

"All our teams have already headed to Tango anyway," Hamilton added. "They'll be on the run to the rally point, radios off, after hearing the shooting."

"Okay. You guys skirt the clearing. Stay under cover. I'll take Lieutenant Sanchez and cut straight across," Mckay then said, streams of sweat streaking the smeared camouflage paint on his face. "I think I can move faster with him across my shoulders than trying to do this three-legged foot race with him in the middle. Grit your teeth, Jimmy. You're going for a ride."

The stockily built McKay with his tree-trunk legs squatted under Sanchez, and bent the lieutenant across his shoulders. When he stood up, he gave Doc Hamilton and Lance Corporal Sneed a nod and then took off jogging.

"Try to keep me in sight, but don't stop for anything," Tommy McKay called out. "Run like hell. Meet me at Tango."

Sweat poured off Tommy McKay's body, soaking his clothes as he ran. He tried not to think of the North Vietnamese patrols now searching for them. He tried not to think of how easily the NVA could pick off him and his best friend in the broad moonlight as he dashed across the wide clearing. He tried not to think of the bogs and quicksand, the sinkholes and the booby traps that possibly lay in his path as he ran. He tried not to think of those things, but he did. He thought of them all. He ran ahead anyway. His best friend lay dying across his shoulders.

"Hang on, partner," McKay said as he pumped his legs. "We're coming to the other side. Easy as pie. Another touchdown at the Cotton Bowl."

Just as he thought he had the clearing behind him, and could see the forest's edge standing less than a hundred yards away, loud snaps and pops cracked through the air, and the ground suddenly burst with geyserlike plumes of dirt and debris all around him.

"Hang on, buddy. Hang on!" the former Texas Longhorn football star turned Marine lawyer and unauthorized grunt told his best friend as he reached into his heart and shifted his legs and his stamina to another, more powerful gear. Digging deep inside himself, far beyond any point he had ever before gone, at a depth that Tommy McKay had never known even existed within himself, he tapped into the root of the fire that had all of his life made him a champion: a source of strength that now released a whole new man within himself. This newfound energy sent his legs pumping harder and faster than he had ever before pushed them.

At the edge of the clearing where McKay had begun his dash for his best friend's life, a full rifle platoon of North Vietnamese soldiers emerged. They had begun their pursuit at the onset of the shooting, and found the easily followed trail within minutes. Seeing the silhouette of the Marine running across the clearing with his comrade draped across his shoulders, the Communist troops began firing at the fleeing target. Like deer hunters with buck fever, they excitedly yanked and cranked rounds all around T. D. McKay and Jimmy Sanchez.

"O God, please help me," McKay prayed as he ran. "I know Mama talks to You every day about me, and I don't talk to You nearly enough, but please, dear Jesus, please be with me tonight. Keep their bullets wide, and keep my buddy alive. If You can just do that for us, I can do the rest."

Tommy Touchdown McKay crossed the more than three hundred-yard-wide clearing, carrying his 165-pound best friend, in less than sixty seconds. Although they lost sight of him as he dashed into the forest, the North Vietnamese never stopped firing. Overhead and all around, bullets snapped through the branches, popped through the brush, and burst into the ground, but none hit T. D. McKay or Jimmy Sanchez.

"YOU REMEMBER HOW to load one of these things?" Terry O'Connor said breathlessly as he pushed the M60 machine gun into the fighting hole and then helped Elvis to crawl inside the shelter.

"I'm kind of busy," Jon Kirkwood answered, firing his M14 at more than a dozen enemy soldiers who now ran toward the barbed-wire fence and coiled razor wire barrier that stood less than a hundred yards in front of him.

"Push down on that latch, there, sir," Elvis said, pointing to a catch on the side of the machine gun. "This deal here pops up, then you just lay the belt with the first round right here, and then slam her down. Pull the charging handle and cut loose."

"Watch out for hot brass, Jon," Terry O'Connor grunted as he shoved the snout of the machine gun over the parapet and began chopping down small men dressed in sandals and black pajamas who now ran at the wire, throwing bags of short-fused explosives at the barrier.

One after another, the Viet Cong guerrillas ran their suicide charges, hurling their satchels at the fence, trying to blow open a breach through which the North Vietnamese soldiers attacking behind them could infiltrate the camp and destroy the stores of ammunition and fuel that the Americans kept here. As each wave of sappers broke across the open ground, Terry O'Connor chopped them down with the machine gun.

With their automatic weapon now speaking terms that the enemy could understand, Jon Kirkwood focused his M14's work on uniformed soldiers who moved through the gaps in the trees, seeming to direct the charges and mortar barrage.

"Cut off the head, the snake dies," the dark-haired lawyer spoke as he put round after round into the dodging shapes of what he regarded as North Vietnamese officers.

Elvis, with his one good eye, took aim with the M14 that Terry O'Connor had used until he got his hands on the M60. He picked targets that the machine gun had missed.

Overhead, the Seventh Marines' eighty-one-millimeter mortar sections had rained high explosives and Willy Peter white phosphorus projectiles down the stacks of the North Vietnamese and Viet Cong firing the mortars and rockets into the camp. The counterbattery rapidly took effect and soon silenced the enemy tubes, enabling the Marines who defended the line to focus their fire most effectively against the sappers and raiders.

Before Major Jack Hembee and a hundred Marine grunts could swarm the gap where the two lawyers and three enlisted Marines fought the overwhelming enemy force, the trio of men left standing had managed to turn back the tide.

"Evening, Major Danger," Elvis said, smiling at Jack Hembee as the operations officer put his head inside the backdoor of the fighting hole.

All along the flank now, dozens of Marines from the reaction force that accompanied the major set up hasty firing positions and began shooting at the fleeing enemy. The mortars kept pushing the North Vietnamese and Viet Cong units farther out, and soon the Eleventh Marines artillery began launching their salvos at them.

"You're no worse for wear here," Hembee said in a relaxed voice. "How about Rat and Henry?"

"They're over yonder, sir," Elvis said, climbing out of the fighting hole and hustling toward the neighboring bunker where he had left his two buddies. "We took a sixty in the window. Blew shit out of everything. Rat got the bad end of it. Henry got it in both eyes. Sir, I gotta check on my two boys."

"I'll go with you," Hembee said, and followed Elvis to the neighboring hole, where two Marines and a corpsman had already put a wrap around Henry's eyes and had King Rat lying on the ground with his knees elevated.

Behind Major Danger and Elvis, Jon Kirkwood and Terry O'Connor joined them in a squat by the exploded fighting hole, watching King Rat and Henry getting first aid. Marines from the reaction force had moved them out of the supplementary position and had taken over the watch.

"What do we do now?" Kirkwood asked the major.

"I've got a busy night still," Hembee said. "Be nice to catch these guys. So we'll be working on that for a while, anyway. You two might hit the rack, though. Elvis needs a patch job, and I'm afraid my other two house mice are out of commission, but Goose can show you where to lay your heads."

"Sir, you don't mind we catch some sleep?" O'Connor said, half embarrassed, since the major had work left to do. "I don't think Jon and I have shut our eyes more than four or five hours since we left California on Wednesday."

Hembee laughed.

"I know how you feel," the major said. "Seems that way to me, too, and I've been here ten months. You boys catch some Zs. We'll get you up and fed before that chopper hits the deck mañana. Get you on your way to see your clients at Chu Lai."

"Sure you don't mind?" Kirkwood said, blinking his tired eyes.

"Not at all, I insist," Hembee said, stuffing more tobacco in his jaw. "Care for a bedtime chew, Terry?"

"I'll take a rain check on that, Major Danger," O'Connor answered with a smile. Then he looked at the operations officer and the debris and havoc that surrounded him. "I think I figured out why they call you that."

Hembee smiled. "Shit does seem to happen, doesn't it."

Elvis looked at the two lawyers with his one good eye while the corpsman wrapped a battle dressing over the bad one. He cracked a wide smile, glancing up at the major, and nodded.

*   *   *

"JIMMY, YOU STILL with me, partner?" T. D. McKay said to the wounded lieutenant as he gently slid his best friend off his shoulders and laid him on the ground.

Sanchez raised his hand to let his buddy know he had held on to consciousness, but when he tried to talk he could only whisper. He felt as though a truck had parked on his chest. No matter how hard he pulled with his lungs, he could hardly get air inside them.

"Relax, buddy," McKay said, propping Sanchez up with his back against a tree, trying to see if the upright position would ease his breathing. "We're at the rally point. I don't see anyone else, though."

"Quit talking so loud," a voice came from behind McKay, and he turned, surprised, to see Staff Sergeant Paul Rhodes, his black-framed glasses taped across their nose bridge. "That Lieutenant Sanchez you got there, wounded?"

"Yeah. He took three hits in the back. I think they got his lungs. He can't breathe very well," McKay spoke in quiet breaths. "We thought it was the Viper team coming back to us. Caught Jimmy off guard. We took down all but two of the enemy patrol, though. Those guys may be dead or wounded, too. I unloaded a magazine right at them, not twenty feet away. The damned NVA wore flop hats a lot like ours. Silhouettes in the dark. How could we tell?"

"Shit happens when you go slack. Nobody else hit?" Rhodes whispered.

"Not in our group," McKay answered. "You just get here?"

"Just ahead of you," Rhodes spoke in a voice no louder than his breathing. "We heard you breaking timber after that gunplay, sounded like an elephant stampede, so we took cover. Mamba team got here first. Sergeant McCoy set them out as security with my guys. Eight of us, and you make nine. Rattler, Bushmaster, and Viper haven't shown their faces yet. Where's Doc and Baby Huey?"

"Baby Huey?" McKay asked.

"Sneed, the radio guy," Rhodes said.

"He and Doc skirted around that big clearing back about a mile," McKay said in short breaths. "I had hoped choppers would already be inbound, so I cut across."

"You mean that you cut across that wide clearing about two clicks north of us?" Rhodes whispered, raising his eyebrows.

Sanchez bobbed his head trying to talk, and began shaking his finger at McKay. Staff Sergeant Rhodes put his head close to Sanchez's lips and listened.

"Lieutenant says I am to whip your ignorant ass for crossing that clearing like you did, when he told you to go around it," Rhodes said, and offered McKay a smile. "Dumb stunt, sir. In fact, borderline insane. Besides making yourself an easy target in this bright moonlight, we had that spot circled on our maps as a confirmed danger area. We spotted it about four or five days ago, the last time we were out here. Charlie's got it rigged with all sorts of interesting items, like mines, booby traps, and punji pits. They'll do that to a likely landing site, hoping to catch a helicopter full of Marines setting down, and blow the shit out of them. They'll hose a few rounds at incoming choppers, so that when our guys offload, they'll hit the ground running and trip booby traps or dive on punji stakes, you know, sharpened bamboo. Sails right through your boot, your body, you name it. I'd like to know how you made it through there without blowing yourselves up."

"I ran like hell, straight across," McKay said, now feeling his stomach tie in a knot. "No wonder those NVA that shot at me didn't give chase. I looked back once, when I got in the trees, and they still stood there in a bunch, blasting away."

"I'm sure they didn't quit on you. Bet they took the loop around right on the heels of Huey and Doc," Rhodes said softly, now checking his watch. "We could sure use that long-range radio right now to get a medevac in here for the lieutenant. He's looking awfully punk. These little fox-mike walkie-talkies work good close up, but are worthless as a brick trying to talk to anyone outside a few miles. Maybe an airplane might hear us, if he had his VHF tuned to our frequency. Sure need to get the lieutenant some help, though. Doc give him anything?"

"Morphine," McKay said, and pointed to an M drawn in blood on Sanchez's forehead. "He also plugged the bullet holes."

"Until Sneed gets here with Doc, all we can do is hang tight," Rhodes said.

"SSSSH," DOC HAMILTON mouthed to Bobby Sneed. Somewhere behind them a man coughed. Quietly, the corpsman and the Marine crawled into bushes and sat, holding their breaths, waiting to see if the cough belonged to anyone they knew.

One by one, North Vietnamese soldiers drifted past them, working in a fan, hoping to intercept the trail left by McKay carrying Sanchez. The men wore no helmets; most of them patrolled bareheaded, a few had on soft caps or flop hats. Most of the guerrillas wore high-topped canvas sneakers, while a few sported sandals. They moved through the forest with the assuredness of seasoned commandos.

Bobby Sneed had seen little combat, but Doc Hamilton had already finished his first thirteen-month tour in Vietnam in 1966, with First Force Reconnaissance Company, and less than a year later had returned for another voluntary tour, now into his third month with Third Reconnaissance Battalion.

Seeing the enemy soldiers left his heart jumping. He had the platoon's radio operator at his side, along with the unit's only viable means of communications beyond the hills that surrounded them. The forests now teamed with NVA prowling all around the two men. With his lungs most likely collapsed and unknown internal bleeding, the hospital corpsman first class, equivalent to a Marine staff sergeant, knew that Lieutenant Sanchez could not likely survive more than a few more hours without the aid of a field hospital and surgeon. Somehow he had to get help to Rally Point Tango.

One kilometer west of where Doc Hamilton and Lance Corporal Bobby Sneed huddled among thick bushes, watching North Vietnamese reconnaissance commandos circulating through the forest trying to find the track left by the Americans they had encountered, Corporal Lynn Sanders and his Viper Marines had traversed west and picked up Corporal Floyd Bennett and his Rattler team. The eight Marines now converged on a path they speculated that Corporal Kenny Price and his Bushmaster recon section most likely had taken. They hoped to consolidate their force to twelve guns, in case the enemy found them, too.

The two western teams and Sanders with the command section's forward recon team had heard both the first brief firefight and then later the volleys of machine gun and rifle fire. Judging from the locations of the skirmishes, they suspected that the lieutenant and his command element, and possibly another of the teams from the eastern side of their reconnaissance fan, had come under fire, with the enemy perhaps now in pursuit of them. For that reason they had silenced their radios, complying with the platoon's standing operating procedures.

Now adjusting their route to follow a wide arc to the rally point, instead of a direct bearing, they hoped to move into the site from the southwest. The new track reduced their risk of encountering the enemy force they placed, judging from the direction and sounds of the gunfire, approximately two or three kilometers north of Tango.

Given the distance and terrain that the Marines had to cover in their vector away from the firefight, and considering the threat presented by the two enemy platoons patrolling the area, likely now in pursuit of their cohorts with possibly an unknown number of reinforcements joining the chase, Corporal Sanders, a twenty-year-old lad from Enid, Oklahoma, the senior noncommissioned officer in the group of eight Marines, estimated that with luck they might arrive at Rally Point Tango in approximately three hours. None of the Marines knew that their platoon commander's life rested in this precarious balance of time.

"BABY HUEY AND Doc either missed the rally point or had to sit tight someplace," Paul Rhodes muttered in quiet breaths, rubbing the dark green tape flat on the broken nose bridge of his Marine Corps-issued black plastic framed glasses. He checked the rubber strap attached to the earpieces that held the spectacles tight on his face and looked at T. D. McKay, and then at Jimmy Sanchez. "You still with us, sir?"

First Lieutenant Sanchez blinked his eyes at the staff sergeant, and tried to raise his hand but managed only a slight movement. His desperate gasps had shallowed to desperate wheezes.

"Damn, I wish the Doc was here," Rhodes whispered, and looked at his watch. "Lieutenant, you hang in there. You're going to make it. We just got to get our boys in here."

Tommy McKay lay in the brush next to the tree where he had propped Jimmy Sanchez and draped some brush over him. Rhodes lay across from the platoon commander, covered as well.

"What if I took a look-see out west of the rally point and tried to work my way back north?" McKay asked Paul Rhodes. "I might be able to find Baby Huey and Doc."

"Bad idea, sir," Rhodes whispered back. "You'd run into the trouble that has them sitting tight. Doc Hamilton has lots of grass time and is not lost. Even Baby Huey has his shit wired pretty well, too, for a new guy. They went underground because the enemy probably overtook them. I'm willing to gamble that unless we hear gunfire from over yonder, they'll get here. So will the others."

"We've got to do something pretty soon, or Lieutenant Sanchez, you know," McKay said, and looked at his friend, who now had his eyes closed, panting for air. "He's got to see a doctor pretty quick."

"We'll head out of here before daylight, with or without Doc and Sneed," Rhodes said. "They know the drill. They'll know we've beat feet out of here and headed back to Con Thien on foot. They'll head there, too, if it gets close to morning. It's only a little more than six hours by foot, if we hump hard."

"Why not go now?" McKay asked, still looking at Sanchez.

"Huey and Doc could show up any second," Rhodes said, feeling on the side of his Alice pack and pulling out a canteen of water. "We get a decent signal here with the PRC twenty-five. Once Sneed makes the call, we can have choppers picking us up inside half an hour."

"Of course, you're right," McKay said, reaching to the side of his utility belt and pulling out one of his two canteens. "But worst case, we walk six hours. I hate to think about Lieutenant Sanchez having to endure that ordeal."

"Odds are he won't have to," Rhodes said, putting his water bottle back. "Price and Bennett and Sanders, they're all good leaders, good recon Marines. So're Doc and Baby Huey. They'll get here."

"Hungry?" McKay said to the staff sergeant, taking a flat can of cheese and another of crackers from his ass pack fastened to the center of his utility belt, and started knifing the spread open with his John Wayne P7 that he had strung on his dog-tag chain, along with two Danish coins he had as mementoes from a trip he had taken with his father and uncle to Jutland the year he graduated from law school, fishing for brown trout in streams near Viborg.

The strong, sharp smell of the hot Velveeta from the can made Paul Rhodes's head snap at attention. Carried on the slight breeze from the southwest, an alert NVA patrol might notice it.

He had heard the stories of the Viet Cong and NVA sniffing out Americans hiding in an ambush. Some of the old salt Marines had sworn as fact to him that even without a westerner wearing cologne or deodorant, their Asian enemy easily smelled an American in the bush, simply from an apparently distinctive Occidental body odor. Something to do with high fat and red meat protein diets.

For that reason, Rhodes and many members of his platoon ate a great deal of Vietnamese food, such as rice and bean sprouts with small portions of fish or chicken, and minimized their intake of fats and red meat. Whether or not the scuttlebutt had a basis of truth, it seemed sensible to him.

If he smelled the cheese upwind of where McKay now spread it across a cracker, then anyone downwind would smell it, too.

"Sir," Rhodes whispered, "try to finish that cheese and cracker snack pretty quick. Then bury the cans. That shit stinks to high heaven, and Charlie can smell it downwind if he's nearby."

Tommy McKay's stomach growled and rumbled as he now hurriedly jammed the small meal in his mouth and gulped water from his canteen.

"Sorry," he said, digging a hole with his K-Bar knife and stuffing the empty but smelly cans into it and covering them.

Sergeant Lionel McCoy, a small-framed, sinewy Marine whose very black skin lay like a shadow beneath the green camouflage streaks he had smeared on his face and hands, looked squarely at Staff Sergeant Rhodes, and motioned his hand and arm up and down, close to the ground. Then he formed a fist with his thumb pointed downward.

Rhodes and the other Marines lying in an arch past him flattened in their hides. The staff sergeant looked at McKay, and motioned his hand toward the ground and showed him a thumbs down.

The lawyer lieutenant's mind raced through his memory of hand and arm signals, and the signs for take cover, enemy present suddenly flashed clear for him. He took a last look at Jimmy Sanchez and then slowly and deliberately closed the brush around his friend.

"They smelled the cheese," McKay told himself in his mind. "My fault. All my fault! A lawyer has no business out here. Now I'm going to get some of these guys killed, along with my buddy."

Shafts of moonlight splashed among the black shadows beneath the trees and among the low-growing bushes and weeds where the eight reconnaissance Marines, McKay, and Sanchez lay hidden. To their front an open field barely fifty yards in diameter offered space only large enough to land a single helicopter. When the platoon commander picked this site as his primary rally point, he considered that in a pinch, a chopper could drop in and fly out quickly. His primary landing zone, a five-acre meadow, lay just beyond another small rise to their south.

While he lay still, his eyes searching the shadows, McKay's mind pictured the map. He saw the small, solid plot with RPT written by it in red grease pencil, and halfway down the adjoining thousand-meter grid square just below Tango, he envisioned the red circle with LZO written in its center. Sanchez had made him study the map section, every mark, every label. He glanced up at Staff Sergeant Rhodes and smiled just as a North Vietnamese soldier fell face down between them, his head nearly cut off.

Sergeant McCoy had done his quiet knifework on the now dead man, apparently a scout, part of a larger, nearby patrol.

McKay's heart pounded. He had never seen McCoy move, but somehow now he stood, hugging the backside of a tree as he watched two more NVA soldiers enter the moonlit meadow and work their way along the edges. Suddenly, from behind the trees, two more of McCoy's Mamba section took the pair of intruders from behind and silently cut their throats to their spines, and pulled the dead men into the shadows and underbrush.

Across the small clearing, from its southwest side, several more figures emerged into the moonlight for an instant, but immediately disappeared into the black cover provided by the trees and bushes. McKay wrapped his left hand around the fore end of his rifle, and his right hand around his K-Bar knife, ready to cut a throat or shoot his way through the enemy.

He looked ahead at Staff Sergeant Rhodes, but the man had disappeared. Only the body of the NVA scout lay there now.

"Anyone here?" Doc Hamilton whispered as he nearly stepped on the dead man next to McKay.

"Only us chickens," Staff Sergeant Rhodes answered, stepping from behind a tree, his knife in his hand, and then wrapping both arms around the navy hospital corpsman. "Where's Baby Huey and that radio?"

"Right behind me," Doc Hamilton whispered, and looked over his shoulder to see Lance Corporal Sneed embraced by Sergeant McCoy.

"You had three enemy scouts traveling with you," Rhodes whispered. "McCoy and his team took them out just ahead of you guys."

"That's okay. We've got a dozen Marines behind us," Hamilton said, smiling. "When we met up with our guys, we had just sat through watching forty or fifty NVA walking over the top of us, almost two clicks due north of us, off the west side of that big clearing. They're crisscrossing this terrain with a vengeance. Once Bobby and I got behind the bad guys, we hi-diddle-diddled, *di-di-mao,* on a bearing due west. Figured we would skirt the area wide, and enter the RP from the south. That's when we met up with Sanders and Bennett and Price and their teams. So we're all here."

"Let's call Shark Bait to Red Rider ASAP. We need some artillery fire missions, a reaction company, and a med-evac pretty pronto," Rhodes said, pulling branches away from Lieutenant Sanchez.

"Bobby already made the call. We did it once we got onto enough high ground to get a signal out," Hamilton said, now looking at Sanchez's eyes and feeling his cold skin. "Sneed asked for immediate withdrawal of our platoon, with one serious WIA. As far as any fire missions, that's your call to make."

Tommy McKay squatted next to Jimmy Sanchez, Doc Hamilton, and Paul Rhodes as the corpsman examined the wounded platoon commander.

"He's unconscious or damned near it. Not hardly responsive," Hamilton said, listening to the fading heartbeats of Jimmy Sanchez.

"We need to *hiako* on over to the LZ," Rhodes said, and then looked at McKay. "You're in charge, Lieutenant. What's your plan? I'll tell you if it's any good."

"Glad you asked, Sergeant," T. D. McKay whispered back without blinking. "According to Doc, we've got two platoons of NVA swarming on our north end, and we need to get into position for the incoming helicopters, just beyond that little knoll half a click south of us."

"My observations exactly," Rhodes said.

"We can't fight well and carry a wounded man, so we need to send Lieutenant Sanchez with Doc Hamilton and two-thirds of the platoon, along with either you or Sergeant McCoy in charge, on over to the landing zone and sit tight on the fringe, like we did here."

"Yes, sir," Rhodes said.

"You know what a rearguard withdrawal is, don't you?" McKay asked the staff sergeant.

"A-firm-a-titty," Rhodes said. "We drift around to the other side of the rally point, set up a base of fire. Engage the advancing point of the enemy here, where we choose. Get them focused on our guns, and then we fire and maneuver backward to the landing zone. Right?"

"My idea exactly, Sergeant," McKay said, showing his white teeth through his green face. "We basically act as decoys here, engage them in a fight, maneuver toward the LZ while the choppers land, get our Marines aboard, and depart. Ideally, we get on the last bird out."

"You're in charge, sir. Care to issue the order?" Rhodes said, and signaled the platoon's sergeant and three corporals to gather around the lawyer-lieutenant and him.

"We turn on the VHF radios?" Corporal Sanders asked after McKay issued his five-paragraph order, following the Basic School format verbatim: detailing by category situation, mission, execution, action, command, and signal.

"Might as well," Staff Sergeant Rhodes answered. "Turn them on, but don't key up unless you have to, and not until after the shooting starts."

Tommy McKay looked at the group of serious-faced Marines. Except for Paul Rhodes, McCoy, and Doc Hamilton, all of the men were barely twenty years old. McKay himself wasn't even thirty yet, but felt like an old man compared to them.

"You need to know that I'll give up my life for any one of you men, just like Lieutenant Sanchez would," McKay said to the small gathering of platoon leaders. "I expect you to give me something in return for that commitment. Your faith in me as a Marine, and your obedience to my orders."

Tommy McKay looked at each man and continued, "We have three frogs inbound right now. Hopefully they'll have a security force aboard to back us up, because that LZ is going to get hot fast. When those 46's get ready to launch out of here, you be on them. Doc, you make sure that Lieutenant Sanchez gets on the first one.

"Listen carefully: Do not wait for me. I repeat: Do not wait for me. Don't think about what's going on with us out here. As soon as those birds hit the deck and drop their ramps, you hustle your asses aboard and don't look back.

"Staff Sergeant Rhodes, Corporal Sanders, and his Viper team have volunteered to fight the rear guard with me. We're going to be shooting and running. We don't need anyone holding us up. Clear? When we hit the LZ, all hell will be breaking loose like a tidal wave on our backs. Count on it. We'll jump aboard that last frog out. At least that's the plan."

"Don't make me have to be getting on that frog and then find myself twiddling my thumbs, waiting on any of you heroes to get aboard. You had better be there ahead of me. That's all I've got to say about that," Rhodes added gruffly.

As the team leaders departed the briefing circle, the staff sergeant took aside Lionel McCoy and Bobby Sneed.

"Get the lieutenant and as many of the boys as you can on the first frog out of here," Rhodes said, "It's going to get ugly."

Then he looked at Lieutenant McKay for approval as he continued to speak: "You and Baby Huey hang back, make sure everybody else is aboard, and then get on the last bird. I want the radioman next to you so you can keep on top of communications with us, and with Red Rider. You're the relay.

"Both the lieutenant and I will have walkie-talkies, along with Corporal Sanders, who's got his own, and one of his boys who took Bushmaster's radio, call them Viper One and Viper Two.

"Make sure that the security team from those choppers and the pilots all know we are out there. We're going to come barreling into the LZ with guns ablazing, our hair on fire, and lots of company jumping up our asses. No doubt you'll hear us shooting long before you see us. Don't let that spook anybody. Make sure the security teams know we'll be coming in shooting, but the other way. I don't want to be dodging their bullets along with the NVA's, too.

"Try to hold the chopper on the ground until we get there, but don't get yourselves overrun. Charlie hits the circle first, you're going to boogie. Got that?

"We'll do our damnedest to get aboard. I sure as shit don't want to walk home. We may be dragging wounded or dead, too. I damned sure ain't leaving anybody, either. Just do the best you can for us. Got it?"

Tommy McKay nodded his approval, and Sergeant McCoy gave Staff Sergeant Rhodes a hug.

"We ain't leaving you," McCoy said, and looked at both the staff sergeant and the lieutenant without any expression on his gaunt, dark face.

While the two sergeants spoke, Tommy McKay had studied the platoon commander's sectional chart of the patrol area that he took from Jimmy Sanchez's map pouch.

"What about artillery?" McKay asked, looking at Rhodes and McCoy.

"What about it?" the staff sergeant responded.

"Lieutenant Sanchez has several on-call targets marked here on his map, including this rally point," McKay said.

"Security will probably have a few sixty-mike-mike mortars, but I don't want to sit between them and Charlie if they decide to lob a few. Furthermore, I'd rather have my ass someplace else besides here if you decided to launch a major fire mission into this rally point," Rhodes said. "We get a bunch of enemy congregated here, though, and then call it as a target, we get in desperate straits, it might buy us the time we need to get into the LZ and aboard the choppers. The pilots sure as hell won't like the idea of in-bound artillery, though."

"Coming from where?" McKay asked.

"Twelfth Marine Regiment has units scattered all along Highway Nine. Plus, they're augmented by a whole shitload of army batteries, from outfits like the Fortieth, Forty-fourth, the Ninety-fourth, Twenty-ninth and the Sixty-fifth artillery regiments, just to name a few off the top of my head. Damned bunch of army artillery up here," Rhodes said. "Pretty much any direction you want except north of us. That's Charlie on the other side of the DMZ with his long-range one-thirties and one-fifty-twos. We've got friendly artillery at the Rock Pile, southwest of us, but those guns will interfere with the choppers' flight pattern. Besides, a short round could take out the LZ. Camp Carroll's due south of us, but the same story with the helicopters as the Rock Pile. Only thing we can get outside our flight pattern that might keep the LZ out of play would have to come from the batteries based to the east of us at Con Thien."

"So we have an artillery option if we can use it?" McKay asked, folding the map and putting it back in the pouch.

"Correct, sir," Rhodes answered. Then he took the lieutenant by the arm and said, "Last resort, though. Think about this: It took us eight hours to hump that distance, and we move fast, so those guns aren't exactly next door. The farther out from the fire base, the greater the room for error. Half a minute of angle off at their end could drop a round on us. You call Tango as your target, then LZ Oscar could catch an errant round if someone doesn't line up the numbers exactly square. Inside a five-hundred-meter circle, I'd say, which includes the north tree line at the landing zone, is danger-close."

"But it is an option," McKay said.

"Yes, sir, it is. And don't be afraid to use it, if we need it," Rhodes said. "We'll definitely call in a pattern on Tango and Oscar when we depart the area."

"Sergeant McCoy," McKay said, now looking at the second senior NCO, "you got it? On my signal, on-call target echo-zulu-six."

"Yes, sir, on your signal," McCoy said.

"Launch a Willy Peter spotter round first," McKay added. "I'll give you adjustments if needed. Once the round hits the pocket, I'll give you a fire-for-effect order. Have them lay a spread two hundred yards right and left of target center. By the time it hits, I plan to be running across the LZ."

McCoy smiled and nodded approvingly.

"Sir, excuse me," Lance Corporal Sneed said, taking McKay by the arm. "Your call sign. In command and signal, you didn't tell us your call sign. Something easy, we can remember."

T. D. McKay thought for a moment. Football terms flashed through his mind, but then he considered that most of the reconnaissance Marines knew him only as that lawyer from Da Nang. He looked at Sneed and smiled.

"How about, 'Law Dog'?" McKay said.

STEALTHILY MANEUVERING THE five hundred meters south from Rally Point Tango to the landing zone in less than twenty minutes, seventeen of the twenty-four men on the reconnaissance patrol now lay hidden with their unconscious and barely breathing platoon commander. They disbursed among the trees along the far southern edge of the meadow designated on their maps as LZ Oscar. Already the sounds of whirling chopper wings beating through the still night air began to echo across the moonlit hills around the rally point and the nearby landing zone.

Hugging the terrain, three Marine Corps CH-46D Sea Knight helicopters dispatched from Con Thien with a thirty-six-man security force, split on the first and last birds, closed on LZ Oscar. The sounds of the inbound choppers' engines singing as their twin-rotor blades thumped through the air immediately captured the attention of the two now reinforced platoons of North Vietnamese soldiers. The noise drew them due south, at a full-out run from their cross-hatched search for the briefly encountered enemy north of Tango, and sent them to intercept the trio of aircrafts as they landed.

As the point of the enemy force broke through the north-side tree line at Rally Point Tango, several of the men tripping over the three dead scouts, Tommy McKay opened fire with his carbine from the south side of the clearing. Staff Sergeant Paul Rhodes and Corporal Lynn Sanders and his three Viper cohorts sent lead flying, too, as the first wave of NVA emerged into the open. Under the sudden hail of bullets, the enemy soldiers immediately fell behind cover where their three dead scouts lay, and returned the volley.

McKay had paired his men into three elements. He and Rhodes lay in the first position, centered, employing a frontal enfilade against the NVA, while Sanders and his three Marines made up the second and third units. The Viper team leader and his partner engaged the enemy in a left oblique class of fire as his other two Vipers took up a right oblique position. With the NVA now halted in a fight, each two-man section began to fall back fifty yards a jump, one pair at a time, while the other two teams provided covering fire for the displacing third, leapfrogging backward.

As they moved rearward, and their shooting became somewhat obscured by the forest, the North Vietnamese platoons began to advance forward, flowing around Tango's small clearing, also using fire-and-movement tactics.

"Law Dog, Law Dog, Snake Charmer, choppers on the ground, security team out," Baby Huey reported on his radio.

"Law Dog, copy," McKay said, fumbling with the bricklike handheld device and then stuffing it back inside the front of his blouse when he finished his response.

"Just reach in your shirt and key the talk button twice! You don't have to take it out and say anything!" Staff Sergeant Rhodes shouted to McKay while continuing to lay grazing cover fire for Sanders and his men as they moved, and seeing the lieutenant juggling the radio. "Sneed will hear it and know you copy."

McKay gave the staff sergeant a thumbs-up sign and then sprang to his feet and ran fifty yards rearward as Sanders and his men now provided the cover.

In the distance, three hundred yards in front of him, the forest seemed to come alive with the silhouettes of running men, dashing from cover to cover, firing as they ran. Muzzle flashes among the dark shadows of the undergrowth surrounding Rally Point Tango sparkled like sequins on black velvet. McKay quickly realized that many more than fifty North Vietnamese soldiers now pursued them.

"Fire mission!" McKay screamed in the handheld radio. "One Willy Peter, on-call target, echo-zulu-six."

"Roger, Law Dog," McCoy responded, "fire mission, one Willy Peter, on-call target, echo-zulu-six."

As McCoy repeated back the instructions, Lance Corporal Sneed relayed the fire mission to Red Rider, who had the Twelfth Marines fire-control liaison at his side. In seconds, the single shot launched out of the muzzle of a 175-millimeter howitzer.

For Tommy McKay, the minute it took for the fire mission to return with delivery seemed like a lifetime. Then from his right he heard the unmistakable oscillating rumble of the artillery projectile traveling inbound, sounding to him like an old diesel truck gearing down at the top of a steep grade.

Suddenly, like a blinding, bright fountain of fire, the white phosphorus sprang from the thundering impact, dead center in the rally point's clearing.

"Fire for effect!" McKay shouted as he kept firing his rifle at the swarms of Communist soldiers diving for cover.

As he issued the order, McCoy and Baby Huey responded and relayed to Red Rider. In a few seconds, the 175-millimeter howitzer battery came alive with their opening salvo of half a dozen high-velocity explosive rounds launching toward Rally Point Tango.

"Everybody run!" McKay then screamed over his radio, his voice so loud that all five of the reconnaissance Marines heard him clearly without needing their walkie-talkies.

This time, as the six Marines ran the last two hundred yards, shooting as they fled, the time from the fire mission's call to the first wave of impacts seemed nearly instantaneous. Behind them the world came alight with the flashes of the exploding artillery projectiles, and rumbled as the earth shook under their feet. Hot air and smoke washed over the fleeing Americans like a sudden desert wind, and it seemed to the half-dozen warriors as they ran that the incoming rounds impacted at their heels.

Before the second salvo had reached the target area, the exhilarated Marines dashed from the tree line into the open meadow of the landing zone, where one twin-rotor Sea Knight helicopter sat with its blades spinning, bouncing on its wheels. On its down-tilted rear ramp, a Marine in a bush hat stood next to another in a white aviator helmet, both men waving at these last six to hurry aboard.

SWEAT DRENCHED T. D. McKay as he fell in the red nylon webbing of the passenger bench that hung along the wall of the shuddering helicopter as it flew south and then banked to the east. The lawyer looked out the ramp and saw Landing Zone Oscar now come alight with incoming artillery. Then he stood up and looked along the seating made of crisscrossed straps tied to tubular aluminum rails. He counted eight Marines who wore steel helmets, and seven Marines wearing bush hats, one with a backpack radio piled at his feet. He looked for Sergeant McCoy and sat next to him.

"You got them on the first chopper out, right?" McKay asked the sergeant.

"Everybody got out of the zone, sir," McCoy said, and then looked down at the metal floor under his feet.

Tommy McKay truly felt alive. In his chest he felt a rush similar to the one he last recalled feeling as he had run a touchdown in the Cotton Bowl. The exhilaration did feel good.

"Lieutenant Sanchez," McKay then asked. "Doc got him aboard that first chopper okay?"

Lionel McCoy kept looking at the floor between his toes.

"Sergeant, what about the lieutenant?" McKay demanded. His heart suddenly pounded, not from exhilaration, but from panic.

"Sir, he died in the LZ," McCoy finally said, his lips quivering and his eyes filling with tears.

Chapter 6

"AIN'T ANY QUEER INDIANS"

JON KIRKWOOD AND Terry O'Connor looked at the handwritten letters that Major Jack Hembee had given them as they climbed aboard the Huey helicopter that now flew the pair of wayward lawyers to Chu Lai on Sunday morning. True to his word, the operations officer had awakened the duo early, fed them a breakfast of scrambled eggs from a can, and had put the two misplaced Marines on the day's first chopper out of LZ Ross. Both of the lawyers wore the green plastic headsets clamped over their ears, and the M14 rifles from their first Huey ride held between their knees as they sat on the gray nylon bench seat that ran across the aircraft's rear bulkhead.

In the letters, Major Danger had certified as witness that both officers had sustained combat with the enemy and had exchanged fire, thus warranting them the highly esteemed Marine Corps Combat Action Ribbon. Hembee had added in the letters that each of the two captains had displayed great courage under fire, demonstrated undaunted leadership, and had made a significant contribution toward repelling a determined enemy.

"I'm going to mention you both in my dispatches," Jack Hembee had told them as he shook each of their hands and slapped them across their backs. Neither of the pair had any idea of what the operations officer had meant by his parting words, mentioning them in his dispatches. O'Connor had suggested to Kirkwood that it had a classical, old-style military ring and that he felt honored by the comment.

"That can be a double-edged sword," Kirkwood said as the two lawyers walked from the flight line at Chu Lai, now searching for a ride or directions to military police headquarters and the holding facility, nicknamed the Chu Lai Cage, where their clients waited for them.

"Jon, if someone handed you a sack full of candy you'd complain about tooth decay," O'Connor responded, walking alongside his friend, both carrying the M14 rifles in one hand and the green plastic headsets in the other, making their way toward a group of buildings in front of which flew the American flag.

"I'm not complaining," Kirkwood said defensively, walking inside the headquarters with O'Connor. "I'm just saying we might do better if all of what happened yesterday and last night didn't get mentioned in dispatches. I would rather that Major Dickinson heard nothing of it. That's all."

"That asshole has you intimidated!" Terry O'Connor said, walking down the passageway toward a desk in the hallway where a burrheaded gunnery sergeant sat behind an open logbook.

"I'm not intimidated," Kirkwood huffed.

"Dicky Doo has you by the balls, admit it," O'Connor said, and then looked at the gunny. "We're lawyers from Da Nang looking for our clients that you have boxed up around here somewhere."

"That would be at PMO," the gunny said. "I can call over there and have them send someone here to pick you up."

"Would you do that for us?" O'Connor said, smiling.

"What's going on out there?" a voice boomed from an office behind the gunny's desk. In a moment a barrel-chested, cigar-chomping colonel wearing a flight suit stepped through the doorway and gave the two captains a quick up-and-down look.

"Sir," the gunny said, "these are lawyers for a couple of turds we've got locked up. I'm calling PMO to give them a ride."

"You boys look like you've been shot at and missed, and then shit at and hit," the colonel said in a loud, rasping voice, while clenching the stogie in his teeth and laughing. Then he glanced down at the gunny. "Go ahead and give the desk sergeant a call, and tell him I said to get his ass over here and pick up these two officers."

"Thanks, Colonel," Kirkwood and O'Connor said simultaneously.

"Care to come rest your butts in my office?" the commander of Marine Wing Support Group Seventeen said, sweeping his hand back in a gracious gesture for the pair of captains to come inside and sit. "I'm Jerry Sigenthaler, one of the stud ducks in this pond."

"Jon Kirkwood, sir, and this is my colleague Terry O'Connor," Kirkwood said, stepping through the doorway and following the senior officer, who then flopped on a brown leather couch and threw his feet across a stack of magazines piled on a coffee table.

"You boys ride down in the wheel wells, or did you get totally fucked up like that on purpose?" the colonel said and laughed.

"We spent the night at LZ Ross," O'Connor offered.

The colonel roared laughing, nearly choking, and then took a sip from a mug of coffee to clear his throat.

"Well, that explains it," Sigenthaler said, and pointed at two brown leather chairs where the captains then sat. "Hell of a fight down there last night I hear. I guess it would have anyone's knob looking a little bit frayed."

On the colonel's desk sat a monstrous, ornately carved wooden nameplate. Adorning its left side, pinned to a red patch of felt, a colonel's silver eagle rank insignia gleamed. On the right side of the gaudy, ornamental placard, a silver and gold Marine Corps officer's emblem sparkled. Decoratively cut into the Filipino monkey wood in two-inch-high English script the words Jerome W. Sigenthaler stood in a sweeping arch.

"I guess you two learned how the other half lives over here then," the colonel then beamed. "You don't look any worse for wear, though. You ain't leaking anyplace, are you?"

"No leaks, sir. Although a shower and a good night's sleep would do wonders for us both," Kirkwood offered.

"Gunny Purdue, the boy out front, said you're lawyers seeing clients," the colonel then purred.

"Yes, sir," O'Connor answered. "I am the defense counsel for Private Celestine Anderson, and Captain Kirkwood represents Corporal Nathan L. Todd."

"Since they're the only two prisoners in the cage right now, I know who you're talking about," Colonel Sigenthaler growled, biting down on his cigar. "Cold-blooded ax murderer. Hell, I was a cunt hair from just pulling out my pistol and shooting the son of a bitch on the spot. You should have seen what he did to that poor boy. Split his head half in two."

"I heard that the sight of the death was quite gruesome, sir," O'Connor said, carefully choosing his words.

"So, what do you want with the boy?" Sigenthaler said, sipping coffee, and then noticing the two lawyers watching him. "Shit, I'm sorry, boys, right over there on the sideboard, grab some cups and pour yourselves some coffee. Hell, relax."

"Thank you, sir," Kirkwood said, and walked to the table, where an urn filled with coffee sat next to a stack of white mugs, and a jar of sugar and instant creamer. Terry O'Connor followed his partner and filled a cup, too.

"What about that cocksucker?" the colonel then asked.

"Accused cocksucker," Kirkwood responded. "Corporal Todd stands accused."

"So does the fucking ax murderer," Sigenthaler retorted, "but that doesn't change the facts of what happened."

"That's why we have a trial, though, sir," Kirkwood then said, "to seek the truth of what actually happened. I'm sure that even the ax murder has a basis of explanation. No one just kills another man with an ax for no reason."

"Oh, shit, I'm sure he had his reasons," Sigenthaler said, chewing his unlit cigar. "But this guy's pulling out another Marine's dick while he's sleeping, and trying to suck it. I'd like to hear the explanation of what motivated that son of a bitch."

"Sir, that does raise a lot of interesting questions, doesn't it?" Kirkwood said, sitting back in the chair. "We have six black Marines accusing this nonblack outsider of trying to sexually assault one of their cohorts as he slept, and then they beat the hell out of him for it. Quite a few questions arise."

"Shit, the son of a bitch needed his ass whipped, trying to suck a good man's dick while he's asleep," Sigenthaler growled, biting the stogie hard. "Damned disgusting! Don't that make you boys want to puke?"

"What if the group of black Marines whipped my client's ass, just for the sport of it, and then made up the cocksucking business as a good excuse to cover themselves for the assault and battery that they committed?" Kirkwood offered.

"Those son of a bitches would be painting white stripes on the runways in midday heat they pull something as chicken shit as that," the colonel said.

"Sir, I have not yet talked to my client, but he did make a quite long and very detailed voluntary statement," Kirkwood said, sipping his coffee. "He claims that he simply went inside the barracks after getting off duty, and the six black Marines jumped him as he entered his cubicle. He emphatically refutes the accusation that he has any homosexual desires whatsoever."

"That's his word against six pretty good Marines, Captain," the colonel then said. "The boys who nailed his wicked ass, they all have good records. Never any trouble. Totally out of character for them to attack any fellow Marine, no matter his color. This kid, Todd, he's new here, so I don't know what winds his clock."

"That's why we have a trial, sir," Kirkwood said, and then sighed. "Although in this man's case, just having such a charge levied against him has taken its toll in damages already, and threatens his entire future. Did you read his statement?"

"No, not yet," the colonel said. "We alerted your office Friday morning, after the shit happened Thursday night. The ax murder has taken priority. I'll get it read tomorrow, before we ship them up to the brig at Da Nang."

"Sir, I hope that you will consider what Corporal Todd asks in his statement before you process it any higher," Kirkwood said, seeing the opportunity to plea his case before facing Charlie Heyster and any theatrical tricks he might pull in court against a man accused of homosexual conduct.

"So, tell me, Captain," the colonel said, now walking to the sideboard and refilling his coffee mug, "what is so damaging?"

"The man will never be able to go home," Kirkwood said. "His people will ostracize him, simply based on the charges, even if we exonerate him. Any record that he was ever accused of homosexuality can brand him with an ugly specter that will ruin him not only where he lives but among his own family, too. They'll disown him."

"That's a little hard to swallow," the colonel said, and then laughed as he sat down, "like that big black dick he tried to suck."

Kirkwood and O'Connor smiled politely at the jovial colonel with his poor taste in humor.

"Sir, are you at all aware of Corporal Todd's background?" Kirkwood said, now walking to the coffee mess to refill his cup, too.

"Like I told you," Sigenthaler blustered, "the boy's new here, I don't even know what he looks like."

"He's a full-blooded Cheyenne from a highly respected family, coming from a very tightly knit Indian community in Colorado," Kirkwood explained, sitting back in his chair. "According to Todd's voluntary statement, the Cheyenne people have strict social standards and customs. They don't even marry outside their nation, did you know that? That's why we have so few of them remaining today."

"That boy's a Cheyenne Indian?" Colonel Sigenthaler bellowed. "Shit, those lying bastards, accusing him of cocksucking. They beat this poor boy to a pulp, too. The sons a bitches made the queer story up just to cover their attack on this lad. By damn, I'll have them filling sandbags and burning shitters for the next six months if I don't keel haul them first."

"Sir?" Kirkwood said, perplexed at the 180-degree outburst. "Now you're suddenly convinced that the six black Marines accusing my client are lying?"

"Damned right they're lying!" the colonel growled. "Shit, boy, anybody knows that there ain't any queer Indians! That'd be like calling John Wayne a fruitcake. And he damned sure ain't any fruitcake. Neither is this Indian boy."

The colonel then walked to his desk and removed a tan manila folder from a tower of wooden trays. He pulled the charge sheet accusing Corporal Nathan L. Todd of homosexual conduct from it and started to tear the paper in half. Jon Kirkwood quickly stepped to the desk and put his hand on the document.

"Sir, you can't just tear it up," the lawyer said.

"Why the fuck not? It's a damned lie!" Sigenthaler bellowed.

"We need you to write an endorsement disapproving the charges, and ordering that the entire incident be expunged from Corporal Todd's record," Kirkwood explained. "Say the complaint lacked material and corroborating evidence to support the charges, because that is clearly the case. We have a group of assailants accusing my client with nothing to back them up, and circumstances suspiciously pointing to their culpability in the gang-style assault and battery of my client. Furthermore, Corporal Todd vehemently denies the charges, and we both know about Indians, don't we."

"Hell, yes," Sigenthaler said, jotting some notes on a yellow writing tablet. "Ain't any queer Indians."

Terry O'Connor got a fresh cup of coffee, and then looked at the colonel as he walked back to his chair.

"You care to discuss my client's case, sir?" the lawyer said.

"Skipper, with a dead body in a bag, I don't think we have much to say about your client's case," the colonel said, not looking up and still scrawling hurriedly on the notepad.

"What about Todd, sir?" Kirkwood then asked, hoping to resolve all questions about his client's incarceration status.

"We'll let him out of that cage right now. He can pack his trash, and fly to Da Nang with you this afternoon. The lad damned sure can't stay here. Not now," Colonel Sigenthaler said, lying back on the couch and crossing his legs on the coffee table once again. "By now, half the Marines in the barracks have heard about the charges. News like that travels fast. They've got him flagged as queer, and they'll have his ass. Not fair, but the damned facts of life in these parts. We'll just ship him up to Freedom Hill anyway, only he'll be working on the other side of the bars at the brig."

"Sir?" Kirkwood said, now confused.

"We've got a quota to fill for a chaser up there, and I just filled it," the colonel said with a satisfied smile, sipping his coffee.

MONDAY AFTERNOON, JON Kirkwood left the defense section's offices early. Terry O'Connor had just begun to peel the layers of misinformation off his client's murder charge and surrounding statements by witnesses and authorities, and already realized that extenuating circumstances might offer some real hope for a lighter sentence or a reduced charge of manslaughter.

Kirkwood had aptly pointed out that rather than making the prosecution prove his client killed Buster Rein, concede the fact. Anderson did kill Rein, but argue that the man needed killing. Doing so would open the door to the many extenuating issues that led to the final act, done without planning, committed in a rage of anger, provoked by the victim. O'Connor had angled on that same avenue of thought, but had worried about trying to defend against the charge rather than maneuvering to the why of it. Such a concession would also eliminate the long parade of eyewitnesses who had seen the killing at a distance but who knew nothing of the circumstances that led to it. Stanley Tufts, the lead prosecutor on the case, ably assisted by Philip Edward Bailey-Brown, half of the intellectual tandem of the Brothers B, would no doubt look to call as many eyewitnesses as possible, to reinforce the heinous nature of the killing, and let them paint the defendant as cold-blooded and mean.

Concession of the fact that Anderson did kill Rein would remove the need for the court to examine the details of the slaying itself. The trial could then focus on the issues that provoked the killing. It removed many of the tools with which Tufts and Bailey-Brown would use to bury Anderson.

With a pared-down agenda of jobs to get done, Terry O'Connor went to work looking for witnesses and testimony that would justify the killing of the racist thug. Dicky Doo had told O'Connor that he could have First Lieutenant Wayne Ebberhardt to assist him in the defense, but no one had talked to the lieutenant since Friday night. Rumor speculated he might have gone flying with Lobo early that morning. Others reported sightings of him in the ville with a flight attendant, and that he had a tall, shapely white woman shacked in a Da Nang hotel. No one knew for sure where Ebberhardt had disappeared, but they didn't let the mojo know about it either.

With his own case now dropped and having nothing better to do, Jon Kirkwood took up the slack left by Wayne Ebberhardt and spent the day helping his buddy, Terry O'Connor, weed through a multitude of witness statements, and research a long list of legal precedents. Kirkwood also did not bother telling Major Dickinson that the wing support group commander at Chu Lai had dropped the charges against his client.

Shortly after he and O'Connor had returned to their office from lunch, Staff Sergeant Derek Pride came back from a summons by the military justice officer with a worried look on his moon-shaped face, holding a copy of the paper dismissing the charges against Corporal Nathan L. Todd, and a note from Dicky Doo to Jon Kirkwood that simply read, "See me."

"I'm gone for the day," Kirkwood told O'Connor and Pride.

"You will see the major first, though," the staff sergeant asked with a wishful tone.

"On my way now," Kirkwood beamed happily, picking up his khaki garrison cap and walking out the defense section's office door.

"Careful, sir," Pride cautioned. "Major Dickinson has had First Lieutenant McKay on the front burner most of the day. He's as angry as I have ever seen him."

An hour later, Kirkwood kicked open the barracks screen doors and walked straight to his bunk, where he threw down his cap and kicked the door of his wall locker.

"I see you've talked with the major," Michael Carter said, spreading a scrambled-egg smile as he peeked around the corner from where the lockers stood.

"Yes, I listened to him," Kirkwood snapped, wheeling on his toes and eyeballing Carter with a grimace that curled into a snarl. "I only said, 'yes, sir' and 'no, sir,' and 'three bags full, sir.' The son of a bitch."

"Join the club. He keeps me pissed off all the time," Carter beamed, showing Kirkwood his caked-up, yellow teeth.

"Fuck him, and his horse, too," Kirkwood said and pulled off his shirt. "Like I give a shit. I'm doing my time and going back to California. My wife owns a nice set of office spaces overlooking the Presidio. I just need to roll with it like the rest of you guys do, Mike."

"You know," Carter said, taking an uninvited seat on the corner of

Kirkwood's bunk, "Major Dickinson, with his unabashed bias against any accused, perhaps offers greater justice for these men that we defend than any other mojo might. So while you deal with his gross unfairness and featherbedding of the prosecution, think about it this way. Because he hates the defense section so much that he staffs it with lawyers he despises and leaves them with nothing to lose, the major ignorantly relinquishes his one means of manipulating them: his power over our fitness reports. None of us gives a shit what he does to us careerwise, do we?"

"You have a point, my friend," Kirkwood said, and now smiled.

"Everyone else is so worried about fitness reports and promotions, they will do whatever it takes to get ahead, including compromising their cases," Carter explained. "We don't have that problem. We keep Dicky Doo pissed off, and it entertains us. It's more his problem than ours."

"You ought to be a defense lawyer, Michael," Jon Kirkwood said, stripping off his trousers, underwear, and T-shirt and wrapping a towel around his waist. "Turning the negative to positive is a real talent. Thanks. You made me feel better."

"So the group commander dropped the charges, I hear," Carter said, now bubbling from the friendship that Kirkwood had shown him.

"On Corporal Todd? Yeah, he did," Kirkwood said, and laughed. "Indians can't be queer. Didn't you know?"

Carter tilted his head to one side and cocked an eyebrow.

"The group commander," Kirkwood explained, "has this notion that American Indians cannot be queer. Like calling John Wayne a homosexual, he told me. Todd's a Cheyenne from Colorado, ipso facto, not homosexually inclined."

Carter fell back on Kirkwood's bed and laughed.

"You're one lucky son of a gun," Carter said. "Charlie Heyster had his bonnet all set for prosecuting a homo, you know."

"Oh, I knew it Saturday morning when Dicky Doo took such enjoyment in letting slip that tidbit of news as he handed me the package on Todd," Kirkwood said, forking his toes through the rubber thongs on his shower shoes. "I thought of Heyster when Colonel Sigenthaler dropped the charges, too. One part of me wanted to sit in that courtroom just to see what kind of evil tricks Charlie the shyster would pull out of his hat. So in a sense, purely from a jurist's curiosity, I felt a little disappointed. It lasted about a millisecond before the jubilation for my client took hold."

"Don't worry," Carter said, ambling his long, stick-figure body back to his feet, "you'll have lots more opportunities to see Heyster in action. Don't feel too disappointed. I'm happy for your client."

"Yeah, me, too," Kirkwood said, flip-flopping down the center aisle of the barracks, his shower shoes slapping his heels as he walked.

As he passed the last cubicle before reaching the entrance to the toilet and shower facilities, a figure moved in the corner of his eye, catching his attention. First Lieutenant T. D. McKay sat at a small writing desk beneath an open window. He had his head resting on his arm as he wrote a letter.

"Speaking of the devil," Kirkwood called to him, "does anyone know you've returned from the far north jungles?"

Tommy McKay turned in the straight-back chair, resting his arm over the back, and looked at Jon Kirkwood. His face appeared puffy, and his eyes peeked through slits between swollen red lids.

"Allergy," McKay said, noticing that the captain had immediately focused on the condition of his face.

"I see," Kirkwood answered, walking to where the lieutenant sat and pulled over Wayne Ebberhardt's straight-back chair from across the cubicle and sat down. The captain glanced at the writing paper and the envelope, and McKay quickly laid his arm across it, as though he hid it for shame.

"Letter home?" Kirkwood asked.

"Sort of, I guess," McKay said, and turned over the page he had written.

"What's going on with you, Tommy?" the captain finally asked the sullen lieutenant.

"Nothing," McKay responded defensively. "I've got an allergic reaction to some vegetation or pollen from the bush up north. Got my sinus all plugged, my eyes irritated. Just like a cold, that's all."

"Staff Sergeant Pride told me that he got word that your buddy Lieutenant Sanchez died in action up there," Kirkwood said, and locked eyes with the lieutenant. "He added that the scuttlebutt from Ninth Marines and Third Recon puts a laurel wreath on your head for taking charge and saving the platoon."

McKay looked at Kirkwood and tears trickled from his eyes as he gulped back more of his grief.

"I didn't do a fucking thing, sir," McKay said and turned to the window.

"Maybe not, but the enlisted Marines here have a whole other story going around," Kirkwood offered, and sat still on Ebberhardt's chair.

"You know how the troops get, anytime someone gets into some shit," McKay answered.

"Yeah, I know," Kirkwood agreed, still sitting on the chair, holding his toiletry kit in his lap. The two Marines sat for a full minute, and neither spoke until the captain cleared his throat uncomfortably.

"I lost my best friend when I was seventeen," Kirkwood began. "He was a boy who lived next door to me in San Luis Obispo, where I grew up. We started first grade together there, and he remained my very best pal in the whole wide world right up until two weeks before our high school graduation, when he killed himself. My dad and his found him hanging from a tree in this grove behind our houses, where we had built a hideout. We played war out there, you know, as ten- and twelve-year-old boys do. Ironically, his name was Jimmy, too. Jimmy Sandoval.

"My dad carried his body home. My dad and Mister Sandoval cut him down off that tree where he had hanged himself. They took him home, and then called the police. They didn't want Jimmy left hanging out there while all the cops mulled around, drank their coffee, and investigated.

"Dad came home crying. That's how I found out about it. I had never seen my father cry until that day.

"He and Jimmy's dad were buddies, too. They took us fishing, up at Big Sur, and hunting out west near Paso Robles, where Jimmy's uncle ran a sheep ranch. They use these majestic, white Great Pyrenees dogs to shepherd the flocks out there.

"Jimmy's father never has gotten past his son's suicide. Destroyed both him and Jimmy's mom. They barely muddle through, still, mourning their poor son. I saw Mister Sandoval just before I shipped out, a few weeks ago, and he still talked about what if Jimmy hadn't hanged himself.

"I damned near didn't graduate high school because of my best friend committing suicide. You know, I blamed myself for it. I should have known. I should have seen his unhappiness. I even thought of killing myself, too.

"My dad never left me alone after that. I think he was scared I'd hang myself. I didn't go to school, and he didn't go to work. He stuck to me like glue until I finally broke down one day and let it all go with him. That's the second time I saw my father cry. He cried for me.

"Tommy, I know what you're feeling."

"I'm sorry about your friend, Jon," McKay said, snuffing his nose and now looking at Kirkwood.

"I'm sorry about yours, too," the captain said, and put his hand on the lieutenant's shoulder.

"You know, growing up in the Texas Panhandle, coming from a respected family, playing football at Dumas High School, and getting a full-ride scholarship at the University of Texas, I had it pretty good," McKay said, turning a black ballpoint pen in his fingers and looking at it as he spoke. "Like most boys from out there in that High Plains ranch country, I had my ample share of prejudices, even though I had not taken account of them.

"We didn't have a lot of black folks living up there: a few, but not many. However, we did have a whole shitload of Mexicans. Mostly they worked on the ranches, or did the really dirty jobs out in the oil fields. To us white boys, they were all worthless wetbacks. We called them taco benders and bean balers. Greasy spics. Right to their faces. And we'd laugh about it.

"I look back, and I feel ashamed of myself. Those folks lived as poor as people can ever imagine. They heated their shacks with wood stoves, if they were lucky enough to have a stove or wood. Some had to cook on grass twists and dried cow flops. Most of them didn't have running water or a toilet. They worked like dogs, and we treated them worse. And we thought ourselves better for it. While those people starved and survived a wretched life, we went to church on Sunday and sang praises to Jesus as though they didn't exist.

"I met Jimmy Sanchez the day I checked in the dormitory in Austin. They had the gall to put him in my room!

"When I walked through the door and saw this Mexican sitting in there, I had a fit. My dad and I marched down to the housing office, and told them what they could do with this fart blossom they put in my room. Hell, the idea of a white boy sharing space with a wetback insulted the white right out of us.

"The lady who made the assignment, a sweet old blue-haired gal I later came to adore named Isabelle Brown, very politely told me and my dad that we could kiss her bright, rosy pink, Tyler, Texas, ass, and she used those very words. She said that I would take the room assigned, or that my dad could pay tuition, room, and board for me elsewhere. We went to the athletic director after that, and made an even a bigger mistake showing our prejudices to him. I damned near lost my scholarship over it.

"So I stomped back to the dormitory and took up residence with this brown kid from South Texas with dead koodies dripping off his hair and the smell of DDT fresh in his clothes. My tilted perspective at that moment.

"I hated life, the University of Texas, and especially him. After about a month of suffocating in silence, I finally spoke up and told him that since I had to share space with his stinking ass, I might as well get to know him. That's when he put out his hand, and I swallowed my pride and shook it.

"Of course, living in Austin, training with the freshmen team, and coming in contact with all sorts of different types of people, pretty soon Jimmy Sanchez seemed to develop lighter skin. He didn't talk like a Mexican. He showered daily, kept his hair cut short and clean, too.

"By the time that first semester had ended, and we went our separate ways for Christmas holidays, we had become friends. I got home and told my dad it wasn't so bad sharing a room with a Mexican. In no time, during the spring semester, Jimmy and I started going to movies together, eating out, even double dating.

"The next fall, I looked forward to seeing him. We voluntarily roomed together from then on. He quit being a Mexican to me and became human. My best friend. That's when we told each other all our secrets, and confessed our families' shames to each other.

"Jimmy Sanchez's mother and father both came across the Rio Grande one night, back during World War II, and took up residence in Texas, working for half the wages that white cowboys made, something like fifteen dollars a month. All with the hope of a better life.

"Still kids themselves, they wanted their yet to be born children to enter this world in America, to live free and have opportunity. The two of them had left behind the most abject poverty anyone can imagine. People died of starvation. Kids walked around in the dead of winter with no shoes and no coats, and it snows and gets cold in northern Mexico, where they grew up.

"About the time Jimmy turned twelve years old, his father got busted up really bad by this renegade paint stallion they called Big Baldy. He worked breaking horses and gathering range cattle for this rancher, who let the Sanchez family live in one of his dilapidated fence-line shacks. Right off, the old gringo took a liking to Jimmy's dad. You see, his father was quite a good horse wrangler and vaquero, and the rancher admired those skills. Mister Sanchez could spin that sixty-foot Mexican lariat full circle around both him and his horse at a full run, and catch a calf on the fly thirty feet away with it.

"After Big Baldy gave him a stomping, Mister Sanchez laid in that shack for a week, his wife nursing the fever that set in, and then he finally died. He had convinced Jimmy's mother that he just needed to lay in the bed for a few days. They didn't have any money anyway, not even for a doctor, and he thought he'd mend on his own.

"Kind of like he treated his range stock, the old rancher just figured the Mexicans that got hurt working for him could tough out their injuries with what they had at hand. Survival of the fittest, so to speak. Calling a doctor never crossed his mind. That fellow was about as prejudiced against Mexicans as me and my dad were, too, and I think we were pretty typical of most white people in Texas.

"When his dad died, Jimmy had two younger sisters and three younger brothers. Damned beaners, you know, they breed like cockroaches. So this old prejudiced, son-of-a-bitch *patrón*, seeing this twelve-year-old boy quitting school and taking up the work of his dead father, trying to support this raft of little ones and his mother, who washed and ironed laundry, cooked and cleaned house for this guy for something like two dollars a week, I guess the bastard finally got bit by his own conscience seeing them struggle so hard.

"He took the Sanchez family to his bosom, and moved them up to a pretty nice house, just below his own grand castle, where his late mother had lived, and it had then sat vacant for several years after she died. Jimmy's mother kept on cleaning and cooking and doing the laundry for the rancher, but he started paying her a good deal more money for her work, and he fed the family, kept the kids and mother in good clothes, and he sent Jimmy back to school. He said he owed Jimmy's dad at least that much.

"My buddy Jim graduated from high school with a 4.0 grade point average. He got an academic scholarship to the University of Texas, which paid for his tuition and books for four years. That gringo rancher shelled out for Jimmy's room and board, even bought him a pretty nice, used pickup truck to drive, and gave him a hundred dollars a month to spend. The man said he owed Jimmy's father at least that much, too. Him dying on his ranch with broken ribs and whatever else that bronc busted up on his insides, as he did, and not seeing a doctor at all. So the man paid penance by raising Jimmy as a son.

"I never heard Jimmy Sanchez speak with bitterness about the way anybody treated him, his mother, his father, or even how I treated him when we first met. Instead he focused on what we could accomplish, and how he looked forward to going back home and teaching school. He wanted to teach school where he grew up.

"Between my junior and senior years in college I spent the summer with Jimmy at his home on that old man's ranch. I got to know his mother, his sisters, and his brothers very well. They're a wonderful family. Even that old fart gringo rancher, he loves every one of those Sanchez children like his own kids.

"Jimmy Sanchez showed me a lot about myself and my shortcomings. From his example, I learned to take people one person at a time. He taught me to respect poor folks, not pity them, but admire the people for their courage and their strength of character to struggle against an unfair tide, and not quit. Jimmy gave me a charitable heart and an open mind, and showed me how to accept people, even a dumb fuckhead like Michael Carter, who sneaks in the shadows and eavesdrops."

The gangly captain nearly fell, tripping around the wall lockers, and almost turned one of them on its side when he caught himself off balance. Carter sniffed his nose, and then offered a sheepish smile at the two men sitting by the wall and open window.

T. D. McKay picked up the writing paper and turned it over, and pointing to it, said, "This is a letter to Jimmy's mother. It's my fault he died. I can't find the words to tell her. To tell her I am sorry. How do you tell a mother you are sorry that you caused her son to die?"

Jon Kirkwood blinked and looked at Michael Carter. Then he looked back at McKay.

"Your fault?" Kirkwood said.

"When Jimmy got shot, we had to carry him to the rally point and the LZ," McKay explained. "There were four of us: Jimmy, me, the radioman, and the corpsman. Communications were shitty, so we couldn't make contact with anyone outside the platoon until we got to higher ground near the RP.

"Halfway there, we came to this big open space. To go around it would add half an hour to us getting him to a place where the medevac chopper could land. I saw where Jimmy had the clearing marked as a danger area on his map, and the corpsman and radioman warned me about it, too. But I'm mister touchdown, mister Saturday afternoon hero. So I sent Doc and Sneed around, and I put Jimmy on my shoulders and cut across.

"Just like Doc had warned, the NVA spotted me and started shooting. Somehow I dodged their bullets and got across, but they circled around and didn't charge across after me. I later learned they had the field heavily mined. So with Charlie now running over the top of them, trying to catch me, Doc and Sneed had to take cover and sit it out.

"I got to the rally point with Jimmy, but I had left his medical aid and our only source of communications to the outside world stuck behind. My shortcut cost Jimmy the critical time he needed to live. He bled to death in the landing zone just as the choppers finally set down.

"He was so shot up he couldn't talk but in gasps. He suffered unnecessarily for three long hours, fighting for air and battling for his life. All because I left the radio guy and the corpsman behind.

"Had I gone around, I would have avoided the enemy spotting me and pursuing us, we would have gotten to the rally point half an hour later with the doc to help Jimmy, and we could have called for a med-evac as soon as we got there. My fault? Yes! My heroics cost my best friend his life."

Carter started to speak, but Jon Kirkwood, knowing that Tommy McKay would not take very well the sweet pap doled out by the Boston-bluenose bleeding heart, put up his hand just as the gangling captain began to sputter, silencing the no-doubt ill-thought but well-meaning words.

"You're probably right, Tommy," Kirkwood then said. "Your intentions were for your friend, but I see your point. It's valid. No matter what any of us will try to tell you about it, you're going to believe what's in your heart. You were there, we weren't. Now you have to figure out a way to live with it."

"Wait a minute! He was saving his buddy's life!" Carter interjected, his natural instincts to defend the downtrodden kicking into gear.

"Michael, go to your room," Kirkwood said and pointed to the cubicle exit.

"This lieutenant happens to be under my counsel," Carter then proclaimed, crossing his bony, flaky arms.

"What the fuck are you talking about?" Kirkwood growled at the stick-man captain.

"Major Dickinson has written a charge sheet on me," McKay said, now defending Michael Carter's continued presence. "The blond palm tree standing there is my defense counsel."

"He *what*?" Kirkwood then bellowed, and looked straight at Carter.

"Major Dickinson has charged Lieutenant McKay with unauthorized absence, disobedience of a lawful written order, dereliction of duty, and conduct unbecoming an officer and a gentleman," Carter then said, stepping back inside the cubicle.

"The dirty son of a bitch," Kirkwood growled, and kicked Wayne Ebberhardt's wall locker with his nearly bare foot, losing his shower shoe off it and stubbing his right toe. Hopping and limping, the captain continued his rant. "Damn that wasted fuck! That drip down a whore's thigh! He chews my ass out this afternoon for me getting the charges dismissed against my client, doing a fucking fantastic job, I think, and then to top off the insanity, he files a charge sheet on a Marine for heroism under fire. I'm never going to make it through a year of his bullshit! I can see it now! We're not in Vietnam. We've all really died and gone to hell!"

Chapter 7

THE JUDAS KISS

"MAU MAU. YO, Mau Mau, that you, man?" a voice called from down the street. James Harris sat in the driver's seat of a jeep, and turned his head to see a familiar character from the Da Nang Air Base flight line, Lance Corporal James Elmore, ditty-bopping carelessly across the bustling roadway toward him.

His utility blouse unbuttoned, flapping as he bounced on his toes, exposing the clenched-black-fist design printed on the front of his green T-shirt, Elmore sauntered mindlessly between passing cyclo-taxis as he ambled his way across the busy boulevard. From the belt up, his body looked like that of a man who stood more than six feet tall, but below the waist, his stubby, out-of-proportion legs held him to an elevation of just less than five feet, eight inches in height. His long arms swinging as he strode with his hat perched on the back of his wooly, puffed-out Afro-style hair, the cover's bill pressed perfectly flat, the jaunty Marine seemed to openly insult gravity as well as the Corps' dress standards.

"Brother Bear," Harris said, stepping from the open vehicle and walking around it to greet the culprit who had introduced him to dope peddling in Da Nang shortly after his arrival in Vietnam, and had then kept him supplied with ample stocks to sell.

"Look at you now, soul," Elmore said, rapping his knuckles with Harris's. "Done lost that I-want-a-be-just-like-Jimi Hendrix look. Got yourself all high and tight. Starched and squared away. Got sergeant chevrons on your collar. Ain't you the pretty picture of what's right all right."

"Hey, man, just getting by," Harris said, looking up and down the busy boulevard that followed the river. "Keeping cool. You know. What you doing wandering back here, off the air base in the middle of the day?"

"My off-day, bro," Elmore said. "Got a meeting with my main man. You know, business."

"That dude?" Harris said, and nodded toward the open front of the bar where Brian T. Pitts stood inside the shadowed entrance, dressed as a Marine first lieutenant and talking to a heavyset policeman with a cluster of diamond-shaped brass buttons on his epaulettes, and two helmeted bodyguards lurking behind him. Pitts glanced out the doorway, took note of Elmore, and then shifted his eyes back to the high-ranking cop.

"Could be," Elmore said and smiled. "You connected with the Snowman?"

"Yeah, man," Harris said. "Pitts and me, we tight, three, four months now."

"I can see you be tight with the man," Elmore said, eyeballing the backseat of the jeep where he noticed an open canvas bag with two cameras and several lenses. "Got you chauffeuring his ass around all day. Probably shining his boots, too. Kissing his pearly white ass. Seeing how you done changed and all, you probably like that dark-brown taste in your mouth now."

"Fuck you, monkey-looking motherfucker," Harris snarled, putting his hand on the U.S. Government model .45-caliber Colt pistol he wore. "I ain't gotta put up with your tired bullshit no more."

"Be cool, man," Elmore said, flashing his gold front tooth as he smiled. "I'm just fucking with you, man. You know me. I fuck with everybody."

"You don't fuck with me, motherfucker," Harris warned, looking cold-eyed at his former supplier. "Shit happen to your flaky bag ass you keep fucking around. I don't put up with that kind of shit no more, for nobody."

"Hey, yo, I apologize, man," Elmore said, seeing Harris still angry at the insult. "Come on, brother, chill out. I'm just passing time with an old friend. No offense."

"Okay, cool, but I ain't your fucking friend," Harris said, looking again down the street. "Not even peas. I ain't forgetting how you rode my ass when I be selling your shit. Fucking ripping me off, and I have to take it. No more. Not anymore, motherfucker. I'm on top of you now, man. You best remember that, too."

"So you got all spiffy and shiny, man," Elmore said, and put his fingers on the sergeant chevrons pinned to the collars on the crisp, neatly ironed utility blouse that Harris wore. "Wearing jump boots, spit-shined. Got yourself promoted to sergeant. Last I hear about you, they say you took a dive out the backseat of a brig jeep four months ago and disappeared down in Dogpatch. You still owe me for that shit you done lost then, too."

"Why don't you talk to Snowman about that, motherfucker. You can see what the fuck's going on," Harris said, now more irritated than ever. "Just go ahead on and ditty-bop your jive ass down the block and leave me alone."

"I gots business with your boss, man," Elmore said, now reaching in the drab-green canvas satchel and pulling out a new Canon F1. "This got a government property tag on the back, man. You done ripped off Uncle Sam. You in deep shit now."

Elmore laughed as he spoke, and put the camera to his eye and snapped a picture of Mau Mau Harris with it.

"Leave the shit alone, man," Harris said, taking the camera and dropping it back in the bag. "Anybody asks, we're with the public information office."

"Cool, man," Elmore said, now looking at another, but much larger canvas bag in the jeep's front floorboard. "I seen him playing that PIO act before, and his lawyer act, too. So now he got you out showing you the collection route. Things must be going good for my man Mau Mau then. That what I think it is down there?"

"It ain't dope, if that's what you're asking," Harris said, "but you go fucking around with it, and those three cowboys you see standing up the sidewalk, they'll hustle your weak ass down an ally and your mama won't ever see you no more."

"Got cash in there, huh," Elmore said, backing away from the jeep, looking at the Vietnamese gunslingers who had their eyes trained on him.

"Yeah, man," Harris said. "American green. More than you ever see in your life. We pick it up two and three days a week. You're here to drop off your payment. I know that all along. You come up here all jive ass acting like you on top of me still. Brian be dealing with you in a few minutes, and I'm gonna laugh watching you dance for the Snowman."

"Word tell he got suitcases full of greenback Americans over at his ranch in the Patch," Elmore said, still eyeing the drab-green canvas valise.

"You ever think about grabbing some of all that money he got stashed there?"

"Never cross my mind," Harris said. "First place, Pitts don't fuck over his people. So I don't want to fucking rip him off. He make it worth my time to play straight with the dude. All his cowboys know that, too. They kill your lame ass for just thinking about copping any of that money. That's cause Pitts give us all a good share of the wealth. When I go home, I go a rich man."

"I don't do bad my own self," Elmore said, holding open his front pocket to let Harris see the wad of cash he had folded there. That's just my walking-around money. You know, for tips and drinks and pussy and shit. Got Snowman's money here in this paper sack, his cut of what I make last month. I be sitting fat, too, you know. You not the only nigger here be gettin' rich."

Brian Pitts shook hands with the policeman, passed him a small, brown paper bag that he took from a briefcase, and then turned back to look at the street where Harris and Elmore stood talking.

"So where'd you get the jeep?" Elmore said, running his hand down the vehicle's front fender and picking at the white painted numbers across the side of the hood. "Steal it? MPs keep a list of stole vehicle numbers. They nail your ass they see you."

"Ain't stole," Harris said. "Snowman's people down in the Patch made this jeep."

"Fuck you, no way," Elmore said, eyeing the vehicle front to rear. "This ain't no homemade jeep."

"Fender here, bumper there, seat here, hood there, all come together one piece at a time," Harris said. "Jeeps all the time getting fucked up over here. South Vietnamese Army or Americans, they be junking out the shit, and the Vietnamese be scarfing it up fast as they junk it out. We got parts floating in all hours. They be building a six-by truck for Pitts right now."

"Fuck no, you shitting me, man," Elmore said, smiling his gold tooth at Harris and looking at the jeep with admiration. "So these numbers ain't on nobody's list, and it ain't no stole jeep, so nobody be looking for it. You clean, man. You real clean!"

Harris smiled proudly, seeing his old dope boss from the flight line now sincerely impressed. Then he caught the eye of Brian Pitts, standing in the shadows of the bar's doorway, and nudged Elmore to take note. Pitts then motioned with his index finger for the gold-toothed Marine to come inside.

"Who's the asshole watching us across the street?" Pitts said to Elmore as soon as the Marine walked through the doorway.

"Nobody, man," Elmore said, looking over his shoulder to see a sandy-haired enlisted Marine with his hat cocked to the back of his head now walking across the street to where Harris again sat in the jeep's driver's seat.

"Looks to me like he followed your ass," Pitts said, seeing the Marine shake a cigarette from a Marlboro pack as he sauntered to where Harris sat.

"You got a light?" the sandy-haired stranger said to Harris.

"Sure, here," Harris said nervously, and pulled out a cigarette, too, after he had handed the fellow his Zippo lighter.

"Where you from?" the Marine asked as he lit his cigarette.

"Chicago," Harris said, taking the lighter back and touching off his cigarette, too.

"I mean your unit here," the sandy-haired man who seemed just a bit too old for a corporal said.

"Oh, man, sure," Harris said. "I work over at the Da Nang Press Center. I shoot pictures and shit."

"Wow, hey, that's something else, man," the curious stranger said, sucking smoke from the cigarette and looking at Harris, the jeep numbers, and the canvas bags in the backseat and on the front floor. "You want to take my picture and write a story about me for the *Sea Tiger*?"

"Not right now, man," Harris said, acting cool. "I got my lieutenant doing shit today, and I got to drive his ass around all over Da Nang. Give me your name, and I'll get one of the guys to check you out."

"Naw, that's okay, man," the Marine said, "I'm just bullshitting you. I don't do nothing but type shit and make coffee."

"Fuck, that's cool, man," Harris said, relaxing back in his seat.

"Hey, you working over at the press center, you gotta know Staff Sergeant Jordan, and Corporal Dye and Thurman, and what's that other dude over there?"

"Fast Eddie?" Harris said.

"Yeah, that's the guy," the stranger said.

"We all peas," Harris said. He had no idea who Fast Eddie was, but Brian Pitts had given him several press center names to remember, and that was the one the suspicious fellow did not say.

"You see them, say that Gustav said hi," the Marine said.

"I'll be sure to tell them," Harris said, and watched the man walk down the block and disappear down a side street.

"That a CID tail?" Pitts said to Elmore, watching the Marine talk to Harris.

"You know me, Snowman," Elmore pled, his eyes darting in all directions, "I always make sure nobody follow me when I see you. That dude just needed a light and shot the shit a minute."

"That turn out to be a narc, and you know what I will personally do to you?" Pitts said, locking his eyes on Elmore's shifting peepers.

"He ain't no tail, man," Elmore whined. "Here, man. This what you after. Just don't fuck with me no more."

"My guys dropped your shit at the laundry this morning, so you can pick it up anytime. Its all wrapped and ready. Here's your receipt. Just give it to the clerk, and don't open the package until you get someplace you can unpack six kilos," Pitts said, handing the green paper slip to Elmore.

"Snowman, when you open that bag, don't get all pissed off and shit," Elmore said, seeing Pitts now looking inside the paper sack he had just handed to him.

"What the fuck is this shit?" Pitts said, pulling out a handful of South Vietnamese piaster notes mixed with government script.

"Hey, that shit's money, too," Elmore said. "You got thirty-five hundred in cool green American, and another twelve-hundred-fifty bucks in funny money. It still spend."

"You spend the shit then," Pitts growled. "I don't have time nor do I want to go through the hassle of fucking with this Monopoly money. We've been doing this shit a long time, fuck-stick, and you know the rule. No funny money. Just cold American green. You got until Friday to bring me fifteen hundred in Stateside cash. You got that?"

"Man it's only twelve-fifty," Elmore pled.

"That's two hundred fifty bucks worth of penalty," Pitts said, stuffing the sack under his arm and handing Elmore the piasters and script. "After Friday, its another five hundred dollars interest, on top of the fifteen hundred. You got that?"

"Fuck man, that's gonna break my ass to pay you that kind of interest," Elmore whined. "I get this shit change to American green right now, get you pay off now. I bring you twelve-fifty today. How 'bout that?"

"You're already late. Fifteen hundred by Friday," Pitts said.

"Why you do that to me, man?" Elmore pled. "I treat you right for damned near a year now, and you fuck me like this."

"You don't pay me, my cowboys will come and get you. No matter where you try to hide, they'll find you, and drag your worthless ass to the Dogpatch," Pitts said cooly. "Then, while you piss your pants and cry, I will personally carve you a second smile under your nasty little chin and pull your tongue out the hole. Understand?"

"Don't fucking worry, Snowman," Elmore said, backing out of the shadows in the doorway, stepping into the sunshine, and fighting the urge to run. "You'll have that fifteen hundred on Friday. Just like you say. American green cash money. I promise."

"I ain't worried," Pitts said. "You need to worry."

"GET YOUR ASS in here now, dipshit," the sandy-haired Criminal Investigative Division narcotics officer disguised as an enlisted Marine told James Elmore after the dope-dealer-turned-snitch had ditty-bopped down the street and around the corner following his encounter with Brian Thomas Pitts and James Harris.

"Hand over that flash roll, and that green paper that this character gave you," a uniformed Marine gunnery sergeant wearing a gold policeman's badge said. "He really a first lieutenant, or did he just dress the part?"

"He no officer," Elmore said, climbing into the backseat of a white passenger van.

"What's the story?" the sandy-haired narc said, looking at the laundry receipt.

"That's the drop," Elmore said. "We go down that laundry and pick up the dope. That's how it works."

"How come you didn't tell us about this place right off, when we arrested you last night and you wanted to make a deal? We could have had it staked out this morning and nailed him red-handed at the drop," the narc said.

"Every few weeks a different place, mostly laundries. The Snowman, he like laundries for drops. But the last six times, I go at six new places. The Snowman, I think he gettin' paranoy," Elmore said, relaxing in the van's backseat and lighting a cigarette. "I go where the receipt say. Hand the paper to the gook 'hind the counter, and he give me the dope, all wrap like laundry."

"Other people pick up dope when you get yours?" the narc asked.

"Could be," Elmore said, stretching out his squatty legs and leaning his head back as he sucked smoke. "Could be laundry, could be dope. It all wrapped in brown paper, so how's I gonna know?"

"You talked about seabags full of heroin getting shipped out in air force cargo planes, dope crammed in tires, body bags, and camera lenses, how do you know all this? I mean, you don't even know most of the drop zones, so how do you know all this?" the Marine gunny said, slapping Elmore in the back of his head and making him sit up.

"He got that street name, Snowman, don't he? Sure's shit not 'cause he like Christmas. He call Snowman 'cause he sellin' smack. Mostly Burma white, ain't hardly got cut, neither. Snow by the ton. Nearly all it go Stateside, too. I know where the dude live, man. I show you," Elmore said, rubbing his head and picking up his hat that the gunny had knocked to the van's floor.

"He got a ranch in Dogpatch, a whole string of fine-ass whores," Elmore continued. "I go there for a luau a few months back, and this fat American dude he tell me all about this shit and that shit, how he and Snowman tight. He tole me the dude's got suitcases full of American cash stacked in his closets. Snowman give free dope and pussy at that party for anyone wants it. Bowls full of smack, you like that shit. Weed, too. Lots of weed. Ain't no back-street hustle got shit like that, man. Dude called Snowman 'cause he deal shit big time."

"Where's this fat American now? Think he'll talk?" the CID narc asked.

"Fuck if I know," Elmore said, pulling a drag off his cigarette. "I just got invite that one time, and seen the dude then. They lots of fat white dudes in the ville if you open your eyes. One fat white guy look like any other. Take your pick. He a contract dude, though, I know that much. He build shit for the government."

"You think Harris will talk to us if we cut him a deal?" the gunny asked.

"Fuck, that nigger ain't talkin' nobody," Elmore said, sucking more smoke. "Mau Mau have his little club of Blackstone Rangers going on. They don't talk. They kill."

"Harris killed a dude?" the gunny said.

"Fuck if I know he kill somebody. Probably. He kill a dude, fuck him over, that for sure," Elmore said, and then looked at the sandy-haired narc. "You give me immunity on this shit, but now I think about it, I need something more."

"What's that?" the narc said, looking over a clipboard filled with pages of notes he had taken.

"I needs protection, man," Elmore said. "Snowman, he a Marine deserter just like Mau Mau. Brian Pitts his real name. He tole me today he kill me I don't pay up on that funny money I try to hand him. He waste me for that, I know he kill me for sure I rat him out. Harris kill me, too. They got cowboys, and dudes go hunt me down. Snowman say he gonna cut my throat, pull my tongue out the hole."

The sandy-haired CID narcotics investigator and the military police gunny sat quietly in the van. Then the officer who had disguised himself as an enlisted Marine and had gotten the light off Harris and talked with him spoke.

"Here's the deal. Go to court, and testify, and we'll make sure that Pitts and Harris get nowhere near you. Connect them to all the dope traffic and racketeering that you described to us, and for that we will give you immunity in the case we have against you now, and no jail time," the narc said, not taking his eyes off his notes.

Then he looked at Elmore. "What you gave us today, this bullshit, eyeballing these two guys, doesn't do a thing."

The narc glanced at the gunny. "Did your dick get hard with any of this, Jack? You even get a tingle? Mine sure didn't."

Then he stared straight back at Elmore. "What have we got? A couple of deserters joyriding in a jeep, a couple of stolen cameras, and a sack of money. That ain't shit. You talk about murders of local civilians and military personnel. You talk about heavy dope traffic, and I don't mean the lightweight bullshit in the bars and on the flight line you do, but the major tonnage that flies out of here. You make all that shit good, go to court as witness to those crimes, and we will take care of you."

The narc shifted his eyes down at his clipboard, pausing for his prisoner turned star witness to consider what he said. Then he looked back at the snitch.

"You don't testify," the narc then added, staring straight at James Elmore's eyes, "you go to the brig. Case closed.

"Rest assured that we will toss Brian Pitts and James Harris in that same brig. They may not get much time on the petty charges we manage to prove without your testimony, but they will go to jail. Same jail with you. Think about that for a moment. Cooperate, and you go home alive, administrative discharge from the Marine Corps, free as a breeze. We have a deal?"

"CAPTAIN O'CONNOR, SIR!" Staff Sergeant Pride shouted anxiously, stepping through the doorway of the small office space assigned to the five defense section lawyers. "Major Dickinson wants you to drop what you're doing and get over to the cop shop pronto. CID has a prisoner, and they want to make a deal in exchange for his testimony. They want to make the bust on his supplier in the next few days, and can't do anything until you meet with the prisoner and advise him accordingly."

"He just now getting counsel? How long have they had him?"

O'Connor asked, putting on his starched, green utility hat and grabbing his briefcase.

"They arrested him last night," Pride said, grabbing his cover, too. "You'll probably need me to record any depositions or statements, so I'll drive, if you don't mind."

"Be my guest," O'Connor said, walking toward the legal center's two jeeps parked side by side in front of the office complex.

"Apparently this character is the main distributor for most of the dope sold along the flight line," Pride continued, climbing in the driver's side of the general-use vehicle parked next to Lieutenant Colonel Prunella's jeep. When he pressed the starter, the engine lay quiet, and only a clicking noise came from under the hood.

"Doggone it. I think maybe the starter's gone bad or the battery's dead, sir," the staff sergeant groaned. "We can maybe push it and get it going, or I can run inside and call the base taxi to pick us up."

"Forget that," O'Connor said, tossing his briefcase in the backseat of the colonel's jeep.

"Sir! Major Dickinson will write us up for violating his written order!" Pride said, his face quickly draining of color. "Look what he did with Lieutenant McKay for going off with his friend on that disastrous patrol at Con Thien."

"His fucking do's on the wall of his office do not constitute a written order," O'Connor said, honking the horn. "Besides, nearly four months and McKay's charge sheet's growing mold at the bottom of the colonel's in-box. Dicky Doo wants to burn me, I will supply him the matches. Besides, I am the one taking the colonel's jeep and driver, not you. So sit your ass in the backseat and let me worry about Major Dickinson and the colonel."

Then the unblushing lawyer cupped his hands around his mouth and shouted toward the hooch where he knew that Lance Corporal James Dean most likely lay with his hand in his pants and his eyes on the latest *Penthouse* centerfold.

"Movie Star! Get your ass out here now!" O'Connor bellowed, his voice echoing among the buildings.

In a moment the blond-headed lance corporal came dashing from his quarters, buckling his trousers as he ran. In the doorway of the staff judge advocate's office, Lieutenant Colonel Lewis Prunella stood and casually waved at O'Connor.

"Battery's dead on the office jeep, and I've got to get to CID right now, so I'm taking yours," O'Connor called to the colonel.

"By all means, Captain," the colonel answered. "I have an appointment at seventeen hundred, so please make sure that Lance Corporal Dean has it back to me before then."

"Not a problem at all, sir. I'll make sure he gets back well ahead of that time," O'Connor shouted, sitting in the passenger seat while James Dean climbed behind the steering wheel. Then he looked over his shoulder at Staff Sergeant Pride. "See Derek, no problem at all. The colonel's a reasonable man."

"Sir, Colonel Prunella never says no to anything reasonable," Pride said, and then sighed. "It's Major Dickinson. He will still rip you and me both for whatever he can dream up. Now he'll be doubly pissed off because we went around him and got permission from the boss."

"Fuck him and his *dinky-dao* Dicky Doo don'ts," O'Connor snarled, resting his right foot in the door well and motioning for James Dean to hit the gas.

"Right on, sir," Movie Star said, happily tromping the throttle and sending gravel flying from under his rear wheels.

"Keep your opinions to yourself, Dean," Pride said, crossing his arms. "Sir, looks to me like after the past few months that you've been here you'd know by now that Major Dickinson will stick the knife in you any way that he can. Sir, I know that you're not staying in the Marine Corps, so you don't care what he writes on your fitness report, but I care what he does to mine. You've got a career waiting for you back in New York. My career is right here, sir. Dicky Doo has my future on the tip of his ink pen."

"You think Colonel Prunella would ever let him get away with slamming you with the velvet hammer?" O'Connor said, looking over his shoulder at the staff sergeant. "You know he has to review anything that Major Dickinson writes on the fitness reports. You're A-J-squared-away, Johnny on the spot. I bet you even iron your boxer shorts. You think the colonel would let him write anything less than outstanding on you?"

"We'll have to see, won't we," Derek Pride said, sighing again as he tipped his hat back and stretched his arm across the back of the seat.

"Speaking of wait and see, any news on that notorious charge sheet that Dicky Doo wrote on Lieutenant McKay?" O'Connor said, again looking over his shoulder at the staff sergeant.

"Sir, you know I am not supposed to discuss personal matters like that with anyone except authorized personnel," Pride said.

"Bet you talk to Major Dickinson about it," O'Connor said, and let out a sarcastic chuckle.

"I only talk about it to Captain Carter, the defense attorney in fact, or Lieutenant McKay himself," the staff sergeant countered.

"Well, I heard some scuttlebutt," O'Connor said, smiling at Derek Pride. "I thought you might be smiling about it, too."

"Sir, nothing has changed yet," Pride said. "You know that the charge sheet went to Colonel Prunella the day after Lieutenant McKay refused nonjudicial punishment, three months ago. That's as far as it has ever gone, at the moment."

"I heard the colonel tell General Cushman that he was damned proud of Lieutenant McKay, and that he had commended him for his heroism," Lance Corporal Dean said as he wheeled the jeep to a stop in front of the military police headquarters. "He said he'd like to see more of his staff out with the fleet Marines, sharing their meals and seeing how they live. I also heard tell that Lieutenant McKay has got the Bronze Star with Combat V awarded to him for what he did up there by Con Thien, back when his buddy got killed on that patrol he went on. First sergeant told the guys at formation this morning that we're going to have a MAF ceremony and General Cushman will pin it on him Friday afternoon during the wing parade."

O'Connor looked at Pride in the backseat.

"I heard exactly the same news, and that Lieutenant Colonel Prunella has the Officers' Club locked on for a luau in McKay's honor, day after tomorrow, right after the ceremonies," the lawyer beamed, taking his briefcase and stepping out of the jeep. "Bet Dicky Doo is choking on that charge sheet about now. Like to see how the motherfucker two-faces his way with Colonel Prunella on this one."

"Sir," Pride said, climbing out of the jeep, "I suspect that Major Dickinson has choked on the charge sheet ever since he got the telephone call from the squadron office last week that Lieutenant McKay would get the Bronze Star with Combat V. I think he choked on it for several days before he finally addressed the colonel with it. Probably choked even worse when the colonel told him he already knew all about it days ago from General Cushman."

"Like I told you," Movie Star said, smiling as he slouched back in the driver's seat, relaxing for the wait, "the colonel's cool with things. So don't sweat the small shit, man. He knows what's happening."

"Even still," Pride sighed, walking toward the building at the left of the captain, "it doesn't stop the major from exacting his revenge in other ways. The major may well drop his disciplinary action against Lieutenant McKay, but nothing else has changed. Except maybe, after today, after this stunt, you moving to the top of Major Dickinson's shit list."

"Hey, Derek," O'Connor said cheerily, swinging open the door to the provost marshal's office, "think about it this way: We're on top now. Number one, man. Number one!"

"WE GOTTA KEEP driving, Snowman, don't even want to fucking slow down," James Harris groaned to Brian Pitts as they sped down the narrow street that ran behind their villa in Dogpatch in the early afternoon two days following their suspicious meeting with James Elmore, and a day after the seedy lance corporal had picked up his shipment of dope at the laundry. He had missed their noontime appointment today, when he was supposed to make good on the cash he owed. When Pitts noticed the Marine who had gotten the light off Harris on Wednesday, watching them from down the street, they left fast.

"Fucking rat Elmore, I knew it," Pitts said, looking over his shoulder and seeing a shaggy-haired white man standing casually on the corner wearing brown slacks and a yellow, square-tailed sport shirt untucked over his belt with a poorly hidden pistol under it.

"That's the dude that busted me on the flight line," Harris said, making a sharp right turn and speeding out of Dogpatch.

"They've got the ranch covered, too, then," Pitts said, slinking down in his seat. "Can't go back. I got a stash of money down south of town, we can go there. I'll give you half. Then we split up. What we got in this bag won't last long, so we need the stash. Couple two, maybe three hundred grand. It'll get us out of the country. Set us up. You like Bangkok?"

"Yeah, man," Harris said, cracking a nervous smile as he drove. "Good pussy there."

"Like there was ever any bad? Easy to get lost in Bangkok, too," Pitts added. "Benny Lam and Major Toan, they'll fuck us over soon as they know we're running, so we can't depend on anyone outside you, me, and my cowboys. Come to think of it, that fat son of a bitch Major Toan acted awfully sweet when I paid him his cut Wednesday. Guaranteed he and his cops helped CID stake us out. Benny Lam's probably backing him, too. Both those assholes would love to see me gone."

"Let's go kill the motherfuckers then," Harris said, steering the jeep through the back streets of Da Nang, weaving his way south to Pitts's emergency stash.

"Tell you what, I'll give you your split, and you stick around here and kill the motherfuckers," Pitts said, lighting a cigarette. "While you're at it, you can kill that waste of skin Elmore, too. Shit, kill him first, the fucking rat."

"He a dead man now," Harris said, biting his lip and steering the jeep along the winding, narrow roads. "I ain't going no place till I drop the cocksucker to his knees, make him beg, and then I put a round from my .45 through the top of his head."

"We get down here, you keep your cool," Pitts said, watching the homes along the roadsides change from block buildings to shacks and huts. "Got this stash with some Viet Cong. They'll take two hundred grand as commission. That leaves us with about three hundred thousand. One-fifty each."

"They ain't spent it all and not tole you?" Harris said, wondering at Pitt's trust in the VC.

"It's there, believe me," Pitts said. "These are Huong's family."

"Fucker slapped me with his gun first time he see me," Harris said, and rubbed the side of his head. "He never tole me sorry or shit after it, either."

"You pissed about it? I'll let you settle it with Huong if you are," Pitts said and laughed. "He'd probably kill you, but you'd have your chance at satisfaction."

"Naw, I ain't pissed," Harris said, turning the jeep onto a dirt road that led along an irrigation canal toward a small village of thatched huts. "Huong did his job. All the time serious. He think your shit don't stink, too. He's okay."

"I treated him and all the others fair and square, just like you," Pitts said, lighting another smoke. "Give what's right, do what's right, loyalty automatically goes with it if you pick right guys."

"You sure you picked right guys?" Harris asked, slowing the jeep to a crawl as he entered the village that looked deserted of life.

"Yes, I am," Pitts said, relaxed in the passenger seat, smoking his cigarette. "Loyalty goes two ways, my friend. Those not right, we killed. Huong saw to it. He believes in loyalty and trust. Just like I do."

"So he got your six covered in case the bust came down," Harris said.

"Exactly," Pitts said, looking at the end hut, where he saw a familiar-looking dog. "We knew this day would come, so we prepared. Every few weeks Huong took cash to hide here, in case of emergency. In case we have to run. Huong and all the others scattered their stashes down in this ville, too. Our money is here, don't worry. So is Huong."

"How you know he here, man?" Harris said, pulling the jeep to a halt behind a large wooden house with a thatched roof and a wide porch.

"Look at that mutt coming to greet you," Pitts said, laughing.

"Turd!" Harris said, and jumped from the jeep and wrapped his arms around his ugly brown dog. "I figured CID done shot my boy, Turd, cause he not about to leave the ranch for nothing. I had heartache the whole time driving down here, my dog getting left back. Huong got you out with him, didn't he, boy."

In the edge of the trees, Huong stood and nodded at Harris, and cracked a fleeting smile.

"TOMMY! HEY, BOY, you about dressed? Hell, they've got a photographer from the Associated Press and another one from *Time* magazine out there, wanting to take your picture. General Cushman's already cooling his heels in General Anderson's office, and they want you front and center before the two of them come outside. Tommy? Yo, T. D. McKay!" Terry O'Connor shouted as he stormed into the barracks with three enlisted Marines from Third Reconnaissance Battalion striding at his heels.

"Leave me the fuck alone," McKay slurred from behind his cubicle. Still wearing his skivvy shorts and T-shirt, he lay on his bunk, swigging a canteen filled with Wayne Ebberhardt's old North Carolina family recipe.

"Oh, fuck, Tommy," O'Connor said, seeing the lieutenant lying on his bed and stinking of the homemade booze. "I'm sorry, you guys, Lieutenant McKay isn't quite ready. You want to wait outside until he gets dressed?"

"Sir, if you don't mind," Staff Sergeant Paul Rhodes told Terry O'Connor, and stepped past the captain, along with Sergeant Lionel McCoy and Hospital Corpsman First Class Ted Hamilton. The three quickly swarmed the drunk lieutenant, flung open his wall locker, and began rummaging for materials to make some hasty repairs on the officer.

"Captain," Rhodes said, looking over his shoulder, "we'll have him outside, squared away in ten minutes. You need to go let Colonel Blanchard know what we're doing. He's an old salt and has walked many a snake-infested trail. He'll make sure we're covered."

Terry O'Connor shrugged, smiled, and then headed out the door to intercept Doc Blanchard, the Third Reconnaissance Battalion commanding officer, and pass the message that today's recipient of the Bronze Star Medal with Combat V device for valor, had gotten himself drunk early: A full two hours ahead of the Hawaiian-style party and pig roast that Lieutenant Colonel Prunella had arranged to celebrate the occasion with the commanding general of Third Marine Amphibious Force.

With no witnesses now present, the wiry staff sergeant threw the 225-pound lieutenant across his shoulders and route-stepped to the showers.

"Sir," Rhodes said as he walked with Doc Hamilton and Lionel McCoy, carrying soap and a towel, "I don't know what got into you to get yourself all fucked up today, but you'll not embarrass me and my entire platoon in front of my commanding officer, all of whom flew down here today from Dong Ha to see you get decorated."

"Hey, Doc," McCoy said half joking, looking at the corpsman, "you think the dispensary down the block might have some vitamin B-twelve or something you can inject in McKay's ass that will straighten him out?"

"From what I'm told, that's mostly a myth," Doc Hamilton said, watching the staff sergeant strip off the lieutenant and push him under a shower of cold water. "Time and metabolism are mostly what remove the alcohol. I might have a pick-me-upper in my kit, though. Could help to perk him a little bit so that he at least stands still while he gets the medal."

"We'll douche him in cologne to hide the booze stink," Rhodes said, now stripped off, too, neatly laying his solid green, jungle utility uniform on a dry bench. He helped the lieutenant soap off his body and then rinsed him, and pushed him into the arms of Hamilton and McCoy, who dried and dressed the officer.

"What the fuck got into you in the first place?" the staff sergeant said, putting on his clothes. "You having some kind of pity party because your buddy didn't get out alive and you did? Shit, sir, I've seen a dozen pity parties just like yours. I know what I'm looking at. We've all had our turns."

"You don't understand, Staff Sergeant Rhodes," Tommy McKay wept as he snugged his field scarf around the tight-fitting eighteen-inch collar on his khaki uniform shirt. "Jimmy Sanchez was my best friend. My college roommate. And he's dead because I fucked up. I had to be the hero, and run across that open field, trying to save thirty minutes, and cost us three hours, because I dumped off the platoon doc and the radioman. He could have made it to Dong Ha had I not done that stunt."

"The man died on his own, Lieutenant," Rhodes said, buffing off his boots with McKay's towel. "Nothing you did caused him to die."

"Sir," Doc Hamilton then interjected, "do you know anything about how damaged Lieutenant Sanchez's lungs were? The bullets clipped through the tops of both organs, destroyed most of the branches of his bronchial tubes. He never had a chance."

"Doc, he'd of had at least a shot at a chance if I had gotten him to the rally point with you and Sneed aboard," McKay said. "I cannot accept a medal when I am responsible for my best friend dying. Responsible for your platoon commander, your friend, too, dying!"

"Fuck it, man," Sergeant McCoy finally said, and looked at the lieutenant. "We love old Jimmy Sanchez like he's one of our snuffies. Don't you know that if any of us believed you had anything to do with him dying, we'd be someplace else than right here going to watch your lily ass get a medal."

McKay stood still for a few seconds, still feeling the glow of the moonshine, and then put his hands out to the black sergeant, who gave him a strong hug.

"Sir," McCoy said, holding on to the officer as Doc Hamilton shot a syringe filled with a yellow liquid into the man's arm, "you don't know it, but you saved at least three lives with what you did that night, running across that minefield like you done."

"That's right," Paul Rhodes said, pulling a pipe from his pocket and putting it in his mouth, and then finding a paper towel and wiping the fog off his black-framed glasses, still fixed with the green tape over the bridge of the nose. "You have to take the word of our experience. You, Doc Hamilton here, and Bobby Sneed, who's waiting outside with the rest of Lieutenant Sanchez's platoon, all made it out alive because you drew the enemy's focus.

"Think about that night. The lieutenant got shot, waving at the NVA like a schoolkid on the playground. He slacked off for only a second, but that's all it takes. Like I said, shit happens when you go slack. He did, and he got shot for it. I don't blame him for getting killed. I miss the shit out of him. He was about the best I ever saw. But he went slack at the wrong time.

"Those NVA that you took down, they fucked up, too. They're dead because they didn't watch where they were going.

"The gunfire, shit, sir, that drew every Communist soldier within a five-click arc. They focused on that site and came barreling down your throats. We saw more than fifty alone when they hit RP Tango, remember?

"These particular North Vietnamese on our asses out there, they had commando training. A lot like our reconnaissance scouts. They know the woods. They're sharp.

"When they gave chase to you, right when the lieutenant got shot, you have to believe that they came full bore, throttle down. They wanted to kill whoever got in the firefight with their team. They were hot on your ass when you hit that clearing. What was it, thirty seconds or so after you jumped into the open that they started shooting?"

McKay sat on the end of his bunk, listening, and nodded. "Yes, I cleared the open area in less than a minute, and they started firing at me when I still had a hundred yards to cover," the lieutenant agreed.

"Now let's do a little supposing, shall we?" Rhodes said.

"Okay," McKay nodded.

"Let's suppose that you did what Lieutenant Sanchez instructed you to do. You stuck with Doc and Baby Huey, and made the circle around that minefield.

"Shit, the NVA weren't about to tramp across their own minefield in the dark. They circled, too. Even with you running across the clearing, they went around it. Whether or not they saw you running across that open ground, they had already begun pursuit of you. They would have caught up with you at about the point that they ran over the top of Baby Huey and Doc.

"One important thing to consider, though, when you would have gone into hiding with the enemy walking on top of you: What do you suppose Lieutenant Sanchez would have been doing? Holding his wind, too?

"Hell, man, the lieutenant was gasping for every breath. His wheezing carried half a mile that night. The air still as it was. You laying in the bush with Doc and Baby Huey, with the lieutenant hacking like a foghorn, the NVA would have been down on you like stink on shit.

"Now, don't you suppose that when they caught you they would have had blood in their eyes?"

"It would have been the shits," McKay agreed, giving himself a look in the full-length mirror fastened to the wall as the three Marines escorted him toward the front door.

"Those pissed-off NVA would have shot your young ass dead," Rhodes said, pulling open the screen door for the officer. "They would have killed you, Baby Huey, and Doc here.

"Sir, you did not cost Lieutenant Sanchez his life. His bad luck and a brain fart cost him. The fact is, sir, you saved Doc's life, and Baby Huey's life for sure, and probably saved my life, too, and every man in this platoon.

"We got out of the shit with every man intact. Not one man wounded. Nobody killed except the lieutenant. That's damned good, considering where we started.

"My opinion, sir, you getting a Bronze Star with V is a cheap medal for what you did for us. Lieutenant Sanchez is proud of you, sir. So am I."

Thirty minutes later, the bright midday sunlight blinded Tommy McKay as he stepped from the ranks of his fellow officers when the Headquarters Squadron commanding officer bellowed, "Persons to be decorated, front and center!"

When T. D. McKay stepped forward, and marched toward the empty space between guide-on flags where Lieutenant General Robert E. Cushman Jr. stood waiting, Terry O' Connor and Jon Kirkwood walked in step with him. When they reached the front-and-center point, they stood at McKay's left. His award was senior to theirs.

From the public address system an announcer read the Bronze Star citation that included the phrase "for conspicuous gallantry." In three brief paragraphs it told the story of Tommy McKay's heroism.

Then General Cushman pinned the medal on his shirt, and stepped down to Terry O' Connor. The announcer then read the citation for his Navy Commendation Medal with Combat V device for gallantry under fire. In three brief paragraphs it told of that night at Fire Support Base Ross, and his running under fire, pulling a machine gun from a destroyed bunker, and employing it against the enemy, repelling them.

After General Cushman pinned the medal on O'Connor's shirt he stepped in front of Jon Kirkwood, who also received the Navy Commendation Medal with Combat V device for valor. His citation told of his undaunted leadership and tenacity, holding the line with an M14 while his partner retrieved the machine gun, and how together the lawyers demonstrated uncommon valor and dedication.

As they saluted, and then returned to their places in the ranks, they saw Major Jack Hembee smiling and clapping in the grandstand, standing next to Goose, King Rat, and Elvis.

POTTED PALM TREES and Hawaiian music set the tone for the afternoon all-hands reception, luau, and pig roast on the lawn behind the Da Nang Air Base Officers' Club. A deck of several dozen freshly cut pineapples, shipped the day before from Okinawa and grown on one of the plantations on the northern end of the island, rested in layers atop a shelf of ice.

For the Marines who spent most of their time sleeping in holes at Con Thien or Fire Support Base Ross, the sight of the ice seemed amazing. Many of them, used to drinking hot beer, when they could get beer at all, did not realize that the precious cold stuff even existed in Vietnam. Nearly to a man, the entire platoon from Third Reconnaissance Battalion systematically slipped past the pineapple-covered counter time and again, and rather than gobbling cold slices of the sweet tropical fruit, they crammed their mouths with ice. Several of the men even got plastic cocktail cups, and rather than filling the multicolored sixteen-ounce containers with free booze, they stuffed them with chipped ice.

Tommy McKay smiled happily, watching his recon blood brothers delighting themselves with the ice and the cold pineapples, which they soon began to devour by the plateful. Just having them here, knowing they held no grudges, and even applauded him for what he did in combat, made him feel as though half the weight of the world had suddenly lifted from his chest.

Still, the other half of the world, occupied by Jimmy Sanchez's mother, sisters, and brothers, remained pressing on his conscience. But now it seemed less troubling to him than it had before Paul Rhodes had talked to him. September still loomed dark for him, though. Time to pack up and go back to Texas, and face his family, and talk to his best pal's mom about how her son died.

Watching the recon Marines celebrate the existence of ice in Vietnam, however, made the stocky first lieutenant feel good overall, for the first time in four months. His emotions had gone so low that even during the heavy rocket attacks of January 29 and 30, kicking off the Tet Offensive, he didn't get excited or at all afraid. When everyone at Marine Aircraft Group Eleven went underground from the massive barrages of 122-millimeter rockets the North Vietnamese launched against them, T. D. McKay remained outside and watched the chaos.

He even went flying with Lobo when they got news that Hue City had momentarily fallen to the NVA, and the enemy had taken prisoner the Marine lieutenant who commanded the American Forces Vietnam Radio station there in the ancient capital. Stocked with hand grenades and an M60 machine gun, T. D. McKay and Lobo went flying over Hai Van Pass, determined to wreak havoc on the enemy. They got grounded for two days at Phu Bai.

Thinking of his and Archie Gunn's stupidity, Tommy McKay chuckled out loud. Paul Rhodes, puffing intellectually on his English briar calabash pipe, enjoying the taste and smell of a fresh pouch of Borkum Riff black cavendish tobacco he had bought that morning at the Da Nang Air Base PX, just after they had landed, stood next to the lieutenant, watching his platoon, and laughed, too.

"Lieutenant McKay, congratulations. Good show, chum," a voice from behind spoke.

"Oh, thanks," Tommy McKay said as he turned to see Captain Charlie Heyster with Stanley and Manley Tufts close at his side.

"Have you met my brother?" Stanley said, introducing Manley to the lieutenant.

"I saw him at the First Marine Division command post a couple of weeks ago, I think," McKay said, putting out his hand. "Good to meet you face-to-face, though."

"Hell of a party, stud," Manley Tufts said, shaking hands with the lieutenant and then reaching up to take a close look at the Bronze Star Medal hanging on McKay's pocket. "I spent three months with a grunt platoon before joining division legal, living in the shit, and I never got more than a letter of commendation from the battalion commander. Then you wingers go out for a day, just tagging along with some grunts, and you get all kinds of decorations."

"Shit, man, I'd trade you this medal and my buddy's life for you a moment in the sun, stud. How's that?" McKay snapped.

"Oh, don't take me wrong, old sport," Manley Tufts said through his teeth, the words ringing in his ample nasal cavities, "I don't begrudge you the medal, or those other two theirs. My whole point is that it seems that ten men can do the same jobs and no one notices, but in the right place at the right time a man could pick up a Silver Star or Navy Cross doing the same thing. No offense."

Paul Rhodes puffed his smoke and casually eyed the two brothers standing there with their arms held high from their sides, avoiding spoiling the creases in their shirts, and looking like two hot seagulls on a summer day. The silver Scuba head badge and gold jump wings glistening on the staff sergeant's green utility shirt caught Stanley Tufts' eye and he put a finger toward them for a touch.

"Sorry, sir," Rhodes said, and caught Stanley Tufts's approaching digit, and stopped it before it made contact. "You can look, but please don't touch. I hate fingerprints on my shit. I might lose my mind and cut off your hand."

Charlie Heyster laughed, looking haughtily at the enlisted Marine fending off his pal Stanley's envious fingers. Then he looked at McKay.

"Don't worry about Stanley, he's like a greedy little magpie when it comes to shiny objects. Haven't seen you in court for a while, T. D.," Heyster said to the lieutenant, fingering the Bronze Star hanging on his shirt, and then glanced at Staff Sergeant Rhodes to see if he had anything smart to say to him.

"Doing mostly research," McKay said, "helping Terry O'Connor and Wayne Ebberhardt with their murder case, coming up in two weeks."

"Supposedly, they're talking about shipping this ax-wielding maniac to Okinawa for trial, or maybe even Kaneohe Bay or Pendleton," Stanley Tufts said, smiling. "The Brothers B have gotten that word directly from the Fleet Marine Force Pacific judge advocate's shop. The idea of some of you turds getting a trip like that has Dicky Doo going crazy. He's already talked to Colonel Prunella about reassigning himself as the lead defense counsel."

"Lead defense counsel?" McKay said, surprised. "Pretty far-fetched, isn't it?"

"He can do it," Heyster said.

"You know, Kirkwood's wife teaches school in Okinawa," Stanley Tufts said smugly. "Bet he's already promising his Siamese twin O'Connor extra blow jobs to let him join the defense. With Ebberhardt's wife flying in and out of here, he could give a shit about stepping aside for Kirkwood."

"Ebberhardt's wife? Where do you pick up this shit?" McKay said.

"You think he has a gook whore in the ville, spending his off-duty with her?" Heyster said. "Lots of scuttlebutt going on about our man Wayne and some mystery woman."

"Where he goes is his business," McKay said, defending his buddy.

"Don't tell me you don't know about his wife, working as a stewardess on the freedom bird," Heyster said, arching his eyebrows. "Whenever the plane gets grounded, which is almost every week now, our busy bootlegger lieutenant from North Carolina disappears for the overnight. Don't tell me you don't know that, either?"

"I wouldn't tell you shit if I did know," McKay said, and looked at Paul Rhodes, who stood there, trying to ignore the insulting cuts by the prosecutor captain.

"Dicky Doo is gunning to catch them," Stanley Tufts said, spreading a wide smile and watching McKay's face as he did it.

"Catch them at what?" McKay snarled, throwing the glass of ice water he had nursed into the trash can, shattering the tumbler with a loud crash. "They're married. If she's working here legally, and he's on his own time, not out of bounds, then what the hell does Dicky Doo expect to do?"

"You know Major Dickinson," Heyster said, smiling, satisfied he had finally uncorked McKay's anger. "He doesn't have to have any actual violations to get the guy. He plays by jungle rules, didn't you hear?"

"Gentlemen, sorry to break up such fine company and warm conversation, but the staff sergeant and I have some business to attend," McKay said, taking Rhodes by the arm and leading him away.

"What business?" Rhodes said, and caught the eyes of Doc Hamilton, Lionel McCoy, and Baby Huey, who now followed him and the lieutenant.

"I need to get out of here," McKay said, heading toward the barracks. "I've got a couple of canteens of some pretty good homemade whiskey in my locker, if you want a drink. We can come back out here later, once the pig is done."

"Hey, Doc," Rhodes said, looking over his shoulder at his comrades, "maybe you and Sneed ought to grab a few of those pineapples and some beers and bring them, too."

"Sounds good, we'll be right behind you," Hamilton said, making a quick stop at the pineapple counter, and another at a trash can filled with ice, water, and cans of beer.

"Sir, what a surprise!" Jon Kirkwood told Major Danger, seeing him and his three enlisted cohorts from LZ Ross standing near the pig turning on the spit. Already, hungry bystanders had snatched small chunks of juicy pork off the loin and hams.

"I told you I was mentioning you in my dispatches," Hembee said, laughing, pinching a chunk of golden crisp meat off the pig's shoulder. "When did you guys find out that you were getting medals?"

"We had no idea at all, until this morning, when the squadron first sergeant more or less ordered us out on the parade deck and had us walk through the ceremony while the troops rehearsed," Terry O'Connor told the major, shaking his free hand and looking past his right shoulder where Goose, Rat, and Elvis stood smiling, each holding a cold beer.

"Glad to see that you guys made the party, too," O'Connor added, putting out his hand to the trio of enlisted Marines. "Any word on Henry?"

"He's recovered some vision in his right eye, but they ended up taking out the left one," Hembee said. "He's back home in Knoxville, out of the Corps, of course, but he still keeps in touch. We get a letter from him every week. He said to tell you guys thanks for coming out to the hospital ship and visiting him while he was still here."

"Hey, you know us, Marines first," Kirkwood said, and put his arm around King Rat. "We're a team, right?"

"How's your brain-housing-group these days?" O'Connor asked Rat, holding the rapidly dwindling remains of a six-pack of beer under his arm.

"Still get some pretty wicked headaches, but at least I didn't go blind," Rat said, and glanced at Elvis, who still wore a patch on his injured eye. "A few stitches across the side of my head, and a mangled ear, but that ain't shit."

"Funny how you seemed worse off at the time, and came out best," O'Connor said, slapping King Rat across the shoulder.

"Anyone see McKay?" First Lieutenant Wayne Ebberhardt asked, joining the cluster of Marines.

"Wasn't he with that bunch from Third Recon?" Kirkwood said, looking at the growing multitude of faces filling the lawn behind the Officers' Club, eating fresh pineapple and sipping cold beer while awaiting the roast pig.

"He had a snootful this morning," O'Connor said, looking at the crowd, trying to see any of the reconnaissance Marines or navy corpsman who had accompanied him in the barracks earlier. "I see that recon colonel over there with General Cushman and General Anderson, along with Colonel Prunella and Dicky Doo, and I see some of the recon platoon here and there, but I don't see McKay or the two sergeants and the corpsman, either. If I had to look for him, I think I might try the barracks. Ten to one that motley crew went back to his cube to sample some of your white lightning that he's got stacked in the bottom of his wall locker. Besides, from what I saw of our boy Tommy, he probably ducked from sight to stay out of trouble. A few belts, and no telling what he might say to our favorite major, and he'd do it in front of all that heavy brass, too."

"Probably for the best that he's not here," Ebberhardt agreed, looking at the cluster of senior officers glad-handing with the Third Marine Amphibious Force commanding general, Lieutenant General Robert E. Cushman Jr., and the commanding general of the First Marine Aircraft Wing, and Deputy Commander for Air, III MAF, Major General Norman J. Anderson. Among the circle of colonels and two generals, Major Dudley L. Dickinson beamed with excessive animation, and now hastily beckoned Kirkwood, O'Connor, and Ebberhardt to join the conversation of the elite group of officers.

"Maybe we should have ducked out with McKay to the barracks," O'Connor said, waving back at Major Dickinson and nodding, acknowledging the summons. "This ought to be good."

"What ought to be good?" Kirkwood said, walking toward the group of Marines where Major Dickinson busily licked boots and kissed ass.

"I want to hear what that son of a bitch has to say about Tommy and us in front of General Cushman and General Anderson," O'Connor muttered as he walked to the circle, beer in hand. Then he gave Dicky Doo a loud slap between the shoulder blades and asked, "How's my favorite mojo?"

"Terry, my boy," Dickinson heartily bellowed, clapped O'Connor across the back, and then pulled Kirkwood into the circle by his arm. "Great here. How are my favorite two defense lawyers?"

"Where's Lieutenant McKay?" Lieutenant Colonel Prunella asked happily.

"I think he's having a few private drinks with some of the boys from that reconnaissance platoon," Kirkwood said, and then looked at the two commanding generals. "General Cushman, General Anderson, gentlemen, I have to say, honestly, I am overwhelmed. I know I can speak for Terry when I say that today's ceremony will be a high point in both our lives. I know that Lieutenant McKay is equally honored at your presence here today."

The big-shouldered, square-jawed three-star general who commanded all Marines in Vietnam, offered the two captains a wide smile and put out his hand to them. "I enjoyed reading in the report from Seventh Marines how you two fellows gave up your helicopter for their wounded, and then when the enemy attacked, you pitched in the fight out on the perimeter. I know officers who you couldn't blast out of the bunker with a stick of dynamite."

"Marines first, sir," O'Connor offered, and put his arm over the shoulders of Major Dickinson.

"Damned right," Major Dickinson said, putting on a proud-faced show. "As I told both you and General Anderson, I am encouraged to see initiative like some of my attorneys have shown, getting out in the bush when they can, eating grub with our men on the front lines."

Lieutenant Colonel Prunella sipped his beer and tried to hide any appearance of incredulity that might creep across his face, hearing his deputy lie so boldly, and in front of him, too.

"Well, Major Dickinson," the staff judge advocate then said, looking cooly at the military justice officer, "I take it then, based on these expressions of yours, that little bit of paperwork sitting on my desk that I have thankfully neglected to forward to headquarters squadron for processing needs to come back to you?"

Dicky Doo flushed red. Terry O'Connor and Jon Kirkwood did their best to hide grins that wanted to burst out in laughter. Wayne Ebberhardt, who stood on the fringe of the circle, did begin laughing, and quickly walked away.

"Oh, sir," Dickinson stammered, blinking and smiling at the two general officers who smiled back, oblivious to the meaning of Prunella's comment. "Oh, that. Yes, it's just some routine garbage, and it's already been overtaken by events. Just toss it in the can, sir. You know how things get sometimes, so busy and all. It's just some meaningless forms, already replaced, and there are no problems. No problems at all with it, sir."

Both generals now looked more confused, but resisted asking any questions that delved into matters best handled well below their pay grades.

Prunella smiled at Kirkwood and O'Connor and then turned to the generals. "Gentlemen, let me escort you to our table. I think that pig ought to be roasted by now pretty close to perfection," the lieutenant colonel said, leading the two commanders, followed in trace by a gaggle of colonels. Several steps away he glanced back at the major and two captains and smiled again.

"Don't you fucking laugh at me. Don't you dare!" Major Dickinson hissed between his clenched teeth, and smiled and waved back at Lieutenant Colonel Prunella. Then he snapped his face toward the two captains and seethed, "Go ahead and gloat at my humiliation today, gentlemen. I know you will. All I can say right now is, wear those medals proudly. My turn will come. You're going to fucking pay. Believe me, you're going to pay. Both of you, McKay, Ebberhardt, and that idiot Carter, just stand the fuck by. I may have had to tear up McKay's charge sheet, but it doesn't mean that the shitbird's gotten away with anything. I'll still have his ass, and yours too. Your latest stunt, O'Connor, taking the colonel's jeep, usurping my authority, I have some special plans for you. Enjoy the day, gentlemen. Have fun at your luau. Drink up! Because payback is coming, and it is a motherfucker."

Dickinson hurled his half-full beer at a trash barrel three steps from him and missed. Michael Carter, who had skulked nearby, watching the show, dutifully picked up the can and dropped it in the waste bin. The major shook his head at the gangly captain's pitiful gesture and walked away, stopping momentarily at the bar, where he picked up a six-pack of beer, and then tromped, heavy-footed, toward his office.

Buck Taylor and Archie Gunn stepped quickly past the array of flower-festooned tables draped with white and red cloths set beneath a line of general-purpose tents with the sides rolled up, rigged as awnings for the party. Wayne Ebberhardt chased close behind them, all three of the men laughing.

"I see the asshole left your little shindig," Taylor said, popping open a beer and handing it to Kirkwood, and then giving one to O'Connor.

"I guess Ebberhardt already filled you in," Kirkwood said, taking a gulp from the can.

"Wayne, you left too soon," O'Connor added, guzzling several swallows of beer. "The funniest part came when the colonel left us alone with the son of a bitch. Oh, and Wayne, he included your name in his tirade, too. Consider yourself mentioned in dispatches."

"My name? What did I do?" Ebberhardt asked, and then laughed. "Like I give a shit."

"Speaking of not giving a shit, where's McKay?" Taylor asked, opening himself a beer.

"Drunk, no doubt, by now. He got an early start," O'Connor said, and then looked at Ebberhardt. "You didn't happen to look in the barracks for him?"

"Yeah, he's there," Ebberhardt said, and then frowned. "He and those recon guys. They threw me out of my own cube. They weren't drunk or anything. No booze. Nothing. Just talking. Sitting on my rack, shooting the shit. Personal stuff, I guess."

Archie Gunn sucked down three beers without saying a word and then belched as he said, "Ole T. D.'s got the bugaboo."

"Bugaboo?" O'Connor asked.

"Yeah, he hates living," Gunn added. "Maybe those recon boys that was with him in the shit can help him shake it off. Hope so. Two weeks ago, he went flying over Charlie Ridge with me, and we dropped half a box of grenades on some gooners running down a trail. Dumb motherfucker tried to jump out the door on top of one of them. Like Gene Autry or something. He's got that bugaboo bad."

"He did come out and get his medal today, that's something," Ebberhardt said, pulling a beer from a six-pack that Gunn held under his arm.

Kirkwood, O'Connor, Buck Taylor, and Lobo sipped beer in their circle of friends and said nothing.

"COME, LET ME tell you what that dog you name shit do for you," Huong told Brian Pitts and James Harris as he led them to the back of the house. When he pushed open the door, the two Marine deserters saw half a dozen four-foot-long, olive-drab duffel bags stuffed tight with American greenbacks: The same six canvas satchels filled with the majority of their nearly three-million-dollar fortune that Brian Pitts had thought they had lost to the CID raiders who invaded the ranch.

"All the cash!" Pitts sang out and hugged Huong. "You got the money out!"

"This dog name shit make it so," Huong said, kneeling by the mangy beast and putting his arm around him.

"He have some kind of CID radar?" Pitts said, still laughing at the sight of their loot.

"You make joke, but he do," Huong said, putting a pan of roasted pork ribs on the floor for the mutt. "We owe him plenty ribs, rest of his life."

"If he's responsible for getting our money out, I say treat him like one of the family," Pitts said, and then looked at James Harris, who now sat on the floor smiling at his dog.

"I tole you he's good to keep around," Harris said, watching Turd chomp on the bones as he gobbled the cherry-colored, fire-roasted meat.

"That our dinner you feeding him?" Pitts then said, looking for more roast pork on the wood-burning stove that stood in the back corner of the thatched-roof farm home.

"We eat rice and bean," Huong said, walking to a pot. "This Turd, he need to have the meat."

"Well, that's a lot of meat. Four whole racks of ribs," Pitts said, studying the dog's rapidly expanding belly.

"He eat his fill now," Huong said, "then he come back later for more. We save for him. You okay with this, boss?"

"Oh, sure!" Pitts answered, walking to the pot and taking a bowl from the shelf and filling it with the rice, beans, and some variety of seasoned meat dinner that sat steaming on the stove. "You got some *nuc-mom* and chili peppers to throw on this?"

"Take cover off that dish, you see *nuc-mom*," Huong said, pointing to a red and white ceramic bowl with a yellow ceramic lid, and a small ceramic ladle inside it. "It plenty hot, boss. I no think you want more chili with it."

James Harris, famished, had thought of stealing one of Turd's giant helping of pork ribs, but when he reached for an untouched rack of the meat, the dog snapped at his hand, and raised the hair on his back at him, showing his teeth.

All three cowboys in the room and Brian Pitts laughed watching Mau Mau scoot across the floor, dodging the dog's slashing choppers.

"You better get a bowl of this shit, my man," Pitts said, and looked at Huong. "With three million bucks laying on the floor, I hope we can afford something to drink."

"Chung got some 33 Beer, but we no have ice," Huong said, pointing to his brother, who took the lid off a tub of water and pulled out two bottles of the Vietnamese brew. "It taste best when you drink like this anyway. American make taste bad with too much cold."

"Fuck, this piss?" Harris said, taking a bottle and knocking the lid off on the edge of the counter. "You can't get it cold enough to make it taste good."

Huong glared at the black Marine deserter and then walked back to the dog, whose belly now took on the appearance of a dirigible, hanging beneath his bony but now wide-spread hips and ribs. When he knelt by the ugly brown mutt, instead of it growling at the Vietnamese cowboy as he had done to Mau Mau, the beast wagged his tail, and welcomed the man stroking him on the head.

"We take Turd to Saigon with us I think. Okay, boss?" Huong said to Pitts, and then smiled at Harris, who frowned at his pet, who seemed to have betrayed his loyalty to another man. "He still love you, Mau Mau. Turd just no like to share his food. He starve too much his life."

"Yeah, I know how he feels," Harris said, and sucked down more Vietnamese beer as he filled a bowl with rice.

"So tell me how Turd saved the day," Brian Pitts said, taking a wicker-bottomed, straight-back chair from a row of them set against the wall, and sat on it while he ate his dinner.

"This morning, maybe thirty minutes after you go to meet that no-good shitbird Elmo," Huong began, "Turd, he start cry and whine like he need go ca-ca bad outside. So I hurry open door, and he run to gate, look out, run back, and go hide. Then he start bark and bark like he always do when rocket attack come. You know, he no like thunder or rocket."

"That all he did?" Pitts asked, shrugging. "From how you described it at first, it sounded like he told you the spooks were on their way."

"He do tell me that," Huong insisted. "I close door, he run to it again, cry, cry, cry, I open door, he run to gate, bark and run go hide, and bark, bark, bark. Then he run door again. Pretty quick I go take look at what make him bark. No thunder, no rocket. But I see white van down street. Then I see Benny Lam and Major Toan standing on rooftop. They watch us with what you call these thing?"

"Binoculars," Pitts said, helping his top cowboy find the words as he held his hands around his eyes, mimicking the field glasses.

"I know we got set up. That no-good shitbird Elmo," Huong hissed, and then spit on the floor after saying James Elmore's name.

"I tell Chung to take Ty and Bao, get in black Mercedes, and go where you meet Elmo," Huong said, and then spit on the floor again. "We know CID watch us, so we take suitcase, valise, box, all pack full of junk, clothes, what we can find, and we put in backseat and boot of car. That way they maybe follow them so I can get out with our money."

"Good thinking, Huong," Pitts said, scraping the last of his rice from the bowl.

"We lucky that old man Tran Giap Nguyen come today and clean courtyard for party you plan tomorrow, you know?" Huong said, smiling.

"Oh, yeah, I almost forgot about that," Pitts said. "Should be interesting when the guests start arriving."

"Yeah," Huong said and laughed. "Maybe Nanna and some girls still be there. Benny Lam, he probably already put them working for him."

"So old man Tran is there with his boys?" Pitts said, putting his empty bowl in a pan, and then fishing out another 33 Beer from the tub of water.

"He there with his two boys," Huong said, now getting himself one of the beers. "They cut bush along outside wall and patio. I tell Tran to back his three-wheel truck onto porch and then start cut leaf off palm tree."

"Yeah, that big date palm by the back door, sure," Pitts said, sitting back in the chair and sipping the beer.

"While he have that little truck park by door, I go inside and get cash and lay in back of truck," Huong said, squatting on his heels and sipping the beer. "I put in all six seabags, and then we pile dirt and trash, and palm leaf on top. Hide money good. I give Tran ten thousand American cash so he help good. No talk, nobody.

"While CID go follow Chung in Mercedes, maybe take look at your laundry," Huong laughed, "I put on work clothes, straw hat, and get in truck with old Tran. His two boys get in back with this dog, Turd, and sit on top palm leaf and trash. We drive out like we go dump. We look like worker no matter much. Two Marine MP and two cop belong Major Toan they stop us at corner. We no talk English, just Vietnamese. We play dumb, good. Look at truck. Look at me. Look at two boy and Turd in back, then wave past."

Huong smiled and shrugged, "That dog you name shit, he do good. I no see CID before too late. This way we get out, get money, and all okay now."

"Yeah," Harris grumbled, crouched in the corner, looking at his spit-shined boot toes.

"What you be piss about?" Huong scowled at Mau Mau. "You always piss off. Why? We got money, we okay."

"James Elmore got me pissed, man," Harris said, looking up at Pitts.

"When I said you stay here and take care of him, I was only kidding," Brian Pitts said, looking at Harris scowl. "Benny Lam has already taken over the house, and like Huong said, probably got the girls and Nanna working for him now, too. I guarantee you that as soon as CID went through the place, he moved in. He's wanted the ranch ever since I killed Tommy Nguyen. Meanwhile, I guarantee Major Toan and Benny already had our business split between them last Wednesday, when they knew CID was taking us down. We don't have a fucking thing to prove by killing James Elmore, that sack of worthless scum. No way I'm going back there."

"Like I done tole you," Harris glared, throwing his beer bottle, shattering it in a sack of trash, "I want to put that motherfucker on his knees while I drill a .45 through the top of his head. I don't want to go to Saigon or Bangkok or anyplace else until I kill that son of a bitch."

Brian Pitts stared at the floor and looked into the top of his beer bottle, as though the answer to how to handle his cohort's anger floated in the suds drifting across the top of the yellow brew. Then he looked at Huong.

"What if Harris stayed back with you, helped you take care of that business we talked about, should I need to disappear," Pitts said to Huong.

"Sure, he stay," Huong said, and looked at the dog. "Turd stay, too. We ride Saigon, the three of us. I think this dog be happy that way. Ride Saigon with his friend."

"Tell you what, Mau Mau," Pitts said, and looked cold-eyed at the angry man, "you go to fucking up, and Huong or Bao will kill your ass. My orders. Discipline, my man. That's how to win. Discipline. The Marines taught me that much, and I believe it. You go off half-cocked, running on a rampage, slinging lead in the ville, killing people all sloppy and shit, then you become a liability. Understand?

"I want you, Huong, and Bao all three in Saigon with me in two weeks. Got it? Two weeks. You can help them take care of this business. I'll explain what we aim to do. You can kill Elmore if you get the opportunity. That's if you get the opportunity. We will not compromise what we have going to Saigon by some blind hunt for rabid vengeance. Fuck, man, he only ratted us out. We're sitting on nearly three million in cash right here, plus that small change we got stashed. Huong and the boys got their stash down here, too. All that in Saigon, man, we'll take over down there."

Harris looked at Brian Pitts, smiled, and nodded his head, agreeing.

"You right, boss," Harris said, and then looked at Huong. "Just tell me what we need to do. I get it done. Me and old Turd here."

"Discipline, Mau Mau," Pitts said. "Anytime you feel the urge to rebel, you just remember, discipline. And Huong with his .45 in your ear."

"I got that, man," Harris said, rubbing the side of his head where the Vietnamese cowboy had slapped him with the pistol nearly four months ago.

"So you leave to Saigon tomorrow, yes," Huong said, looking at Pitts and his brother, Chung.

"Say," Harris asked, clearing his throat and looking at the six seabags full of money, "how you going to haul that much cash down there without some inspection finding it?"

The light-skinned Marine deserter laughed and tilted his head sideways, giving Harris a smug glance.

"After all we've done here, you wonder how we can haul six seabags of money to Saigon?" Pitts asked, still chuckling. "We've shipped hundreds of pounds of heroin to the States, and never a hitch. Getting this money down south is nothing."

Harris looked at the floor, feeling stupid.

"I'm sorry, Mau Mau," Pitts said, seeing the man's embarrassment for asking the question. "Look, I keep forgetting that you have no scope of what kind of business we did. You just got a glimpse at the very surface when we had to yank up the stakes. You saw that old blue dump truck outside?"

Harris, feeling a bit of his pride returning, looked up and nodded, "Yeah, I saw it out there."

"It has a three-yard bed," Pitts said, raising his eyebrows to emphasize the capacity of the dump truck. "That's a lot of topsoil if you don't know how big three square yards of dirt is. We lay the duffels full of money on the bottom of the bed, zipped inside some rubber body bags we have stashed, and then pile pig shit on top of it. A few square yards of pig shit on top will stop about any cop from digging to the bottom of that truckbed.

"We get to Huong's family out west of Saigon, and we dump the shit, and the money lands on top. Unzip the body bags and take it to the hooch.

"I've got a bank in Bangkok, set up the account a year or so ago. I got a friend, who owes me a big, big favor, and he flies a puddle jumper for Bird Airways in Cambodia. You know, they're what Air America is over here. Anyway, when we get going in Saigon, we will ship a large part of our capital on his plane to Bangkok. There, my bank will wire it to a Swiss account in Zurich.

"We get tired of Saigon, we can go where we want. New identities. Everything. Rich as a motherfucker."

Turd, with his belly almost ready to burst, walked to James Harris and laid his head across the knees of the young man, who sat cross-legged on the floor. Mau Mau looked at Brian and Huong and smiled happily at the two men.

"That be real cool, man," Harris said, leaning over to the tub of water and fishing out another 33 Beer, knocking off its top on the rim of the tub. "Maybe I go back to Chicago in a while, too. Rich as a motherfucker. Got me a nice suit. Nice car. Have me a nice house. All that shit."

While the world grew dark outside the Vietnamese peasant farmhouse and the surrounding village that lay quiet in the night, the light from small fires flickered from the windows as noisy insects and frogs chirped beneath a drizzle that began to fall. Inside, warmed by the glow of the cooking stove and a kerosene lamp, the two Americans with six Vietnamese cowboys made their beds. While they casually dreamed of the wonders that their fortunes might soon buy them, they considered with reverence the hard tasks that lay ahead of them in the coming few days.

Chapter 8

THE BODY

DESPITE THE GROWING shadows and deepening orange light cast from the setting sun, marking the end to another blistering day, sweltering heat still boiled off the pavement and concrete sidewalks that ran next to the wide river that slashes through the heart of Da Nang, forcing three Marines strolling there, stifling in the humidity, to look for shade and cold beer. The short cyclo-taxi ride they had taken from outside the air base gates had left sweat dripping from their faces. At the first sight of pleasurable refuge, the trio of fun-seeking lads ducked inside an open-fronted bar that blared from cathedral-sized loudspeakers Tommy James singing, "My Baby Does the Hanky-Panky." Deep inside the saloon's dark and smoky cavern, the evening's feature entertainment sported a lineup of mostly naked dancing girls go-going on a red-lit stage.

Perching their butts on three open bar stools and drying out under the cool breezes stirred by a quartet of ceiling fans spinning above their heads, the Leatherneck trio ordered a round of 33s from a well filled with water, chipped ice, and submerged brown bottles with the infamous Vietnamese beer's red and yellow paper labels soaking off their sides. Two swigs of the dirty-sock-tasting brew and the boys had their heads turning like swivels as their eyes searched the joint for what quality snatch might troll there.

"Buy me drink, GI?" came the familiar mating call from one hungry old shark that swam by them, smelling the fresh blood and hoping for a bite.

"Take a hike, *mama-san*," the first Marine growled, a corporal who wore sunglasses and a dark mustache above his lip. He had gotten a good look at the hooker when the outside sunlight had caught her hard face that sprouted makeup-filled deep lines around her eyes and mouth. She wore a bad-fitting wig, phony lashes, and dark red lipstick.

"She'd make a freight train take a dirt road," the second Marine scowled as she passed the trio.

"What you name, GI?" came a soft voice from the other side of the third Marine, a blond-haired lad with a baby face and swimmer's build tied to a six-foot tall, 180-pound frame.

"Mike," the young man said, and smiled at the pretty face that had asked him. "What's yours?"

"Wild Thing," the girl said, shaking her long, black hair over her front, bending forward so it touched the floor, and then in a furious cloud tossing it back again, behind her shoulders. "My friend, they call me Wild Thing 'cause I so wild."

"Wild Thing!" the American with the dark glasses and mustache then bellowed, and clapped his hands as he began to sing the 1966 rock and roll hit. The second Marine clapped his hands, too, and rumbled out the bass side of the song, mimicking the hard-edged guitar riff between lyric phrases.

"You make my heart sing!" the first man wailed as his partner kept pace with the bottom side of the music. "You make everything groovy. Wild Thing."

The girl snapped her fingers to their impromptu song and began dancing and gyrating, tossing her hair to the rhythm as she moved.

"Wild Thing! I think I love you! But I want to know for sure," the blond Marine then howled, joining the little barroom choir. "Come on and hold me tight. I love you."

In a moment, seeing the action, the bartender slipped the original recording by the Troggs on the turntable, and then let the full rock and roll blast of "Wild Thing" jam the club. With the booming bass and amplified stereophonic sound shaking the walls and floor, the girl stepped away from the bar and let go with her show.

While she moved, and mesmerized the trio of Marines with her storm of tossed black hair, two of her friends, wearing g-strings and nothing else, dashed from the stage and joined her. The girls flung their waist-length manes fore and aft, and shook their bodies to the hard rock beat, capturing the full attention of the three young Americans.

When the song finally ended, the hookers then moved close to set their barbs in the three GIs while music of The Lovin' Spoonful seguéd into the sound system, "What a day for a daydream, what a day for a daydreamin' boy. And I'm lost in a daydream; dreamin' 'bout my bundle of joy."

"You buy me drink?" the girl then asked the blond Marine as the pair of nearly naked dancers hustled glasses of watered-down fake champagne from his two friends.

Seeing the stemware sliding down the bar, the young blond fellow shrugged his shoulders and said, "Okay, why not?"

"Come, we go sit over there," the young hooker said, pointing to a shadowy table that sat well outside the light that streamed in from the saloon's open front. She took the young man by the hand and discreetly led him from the bar and away from the close attention of his two friends, who now busily ran their hands over the bare skin of the dancers, trying to fast-talk the youthful but experienced bordello veterans.

Seating the young American at the dark table with his back turned to his friends, the young hooker wearing the high, tight, black miniskirt, her nickname, Wild Thing, written in silver sequins on the sleeveless blue knit top that covered her perky, braless, hard-nipple breasts, pulled her chair by his and angled it facing toward him.

"Hey, boy, you like make boom-boom? Me show you plenty good time. All night fuckie-suckie, twenty-dollar," she then blurted to the Marine lance corporal whose look reminded the girl of her former boss, Brian Pitts, especially from behind.

Hunched in a dark corner booth in the bar that opened onto the street that ran along the Han River, in the heart of Da Nang, near the American consulate and the press center, Huong Van Nguyen, his youngest brother, Bao, and James Mau Mau Harris sat quietly and watched their one-night-stand employee work her craft on the unsuspecting young Leatherneck. They had targeted the blond lad the moment they had spotted the trio of GIs as they strolled on the boulevard. With Wild Thing in tow, Harris, Huong, and Bao had followed the three Marines inside the bar.

They could not believe their luck when they first saw the lad. They had hoped at best to find a medium-built American who had a body that when disfigured enough could pass for the Snowman. Such a close match, however, seemed too good to be true. No matter what, they could not afford to let this fellow who could pass for Brian Pitts's brother slip away.

Although Pitts had personally broken in the whore he nicknamed Wild

Thing two years ago at his ranch, when her uncle sold the teenage waif to him for a hundred dollars cash American, she fell under the employ of Benny Lam as of a day and a half ago, when the Snowman's empire fell. That night, rather than trying to fly on her own wings, the Snowman's lead whore, Madam Nanna, had gone straight to Lam and pledged him her and the girls' allegiances. She had wisely calculated that the maneuver would avoid his deadly wrath against her independent competition, or a worse yet fate, her and the girls working for the fat, heavily perfumed, and often sexually cruel Major Toan.

Thus, this afternoon, when Huong found Wild Thing lurking on the street, he had to bribe Benny Lam's watchdog two hundred dollars to let her go with them, and then had to pay the whore fifty more for the one evening's work.

Now seventeen years old, Wild Thing still kept a childish, innocent look about her that attracted men who liked sex with prepubescent girls. When Brian Pitts first saw her, just shy of her fifteenth birthday, he considered the child well worth the five Andrew Jackson bills he paid her uncle when he brought her to Dogpatch. Homesick at first, she quickly forgot about life on the farm after enjoying the luxury that her new profession rewarded her. Nanna had seen great potential in the pretty girl with the raven hair that hung a full twelve inches past her waist when unfurled. For nearly any skirt-sniffing GI or horn dog American contractor, she proved impossible to resist.

"So what's your real name?" the Marine asked the girl as she slid her hand across his lap. "I know your mama didn't name you Wild Thing."

"That my working-girl name, Wild Thing," the childlike whore said, and then lied, "my real name Song, like water that flow from mountain."

"Song. That's a real pretty name," the American said, feeling himself grow hard at the touch of her hand massaging his groin. "Wild Thing. That's not a good name for a pretty girl like you. But Song, I like that a lot. Anyway, your mama know you're working in a dive like this?"

"My mama know, she no care. My daddy, he dead. VC kill him when I maybe ten year old. American GI kill VC, so I like see American GI. You be my boyfriend, maybe you take me Stateside?" she said, unbuttoning his pants with quick, nimble fingers and sliding her hand inside.

"Oh, wait!" the young Marine said, rocking back in his chair. "You can't do that in here!"

"They no care," the girl said, urging him to slide the chair close to her again. Then she slipped her hand back inside his fly. "Nobody see. No sweat, GI. I make you feel too good."

As she began to massage him, she put her left leg across his lap and slipped out his stiff penis so that it rubbed against the hot, bare flesh along the inside of her thigh. Then she took his hand and put it where his fingers rested across the heart of her silk panties, pulled tight into the slit of her hairless mound, soaked wet. As he touched her there, the girl gasped and shuddered.

"You make me oh, so horny, baby," she moaned in his ear, pulling herself tight to him, pressing her small, firm breasts against his bare arm. "Me get beaucoup hot for you. Come. Go my room. Stay all night. Twenty-dollar. Five dollar go one hour. We fuck all way you like. Okay?"

Just as the hooker felt the young Marine nearly succumb to an orgasm, she quickly took her hand from his groin, slid it under his T-shirt, and began massaging his stomach.

"What you say you name? Mike?" she whispered.

"Yeah, Mike Scott," he panted, and took a hard pull on the bottle of beer he had setting on the table. Then he glanced at the bar to make sure that his two buddies from the air wing still sat there, looking out for him. Both of them had six months in country, while he had just checked in a few days ago, and today enjoyed his first excursion off the base.

Taking a pledge not to abandon him for any reason, they had taken the cyclo-taxi to the wide boulevard that ran along the river because this part of town had a low-risk reputation. The new guy felt safe here. Many Americans on the streets. Never any trouble. And the hookers all clean. Nothing worse than a rare case of plain old clap.

Barracks tales of the black syphilis, an incurable, deadly strain of venereal disease, had made all three of them fearful. The saltiest of the trio, the man with dark glasses and mustache, who had the most time on the shitter in Vietnam, reassured his two cohorts, though, that black syph did not occur among the girls who worked the boulevard along the Han River.

"The government has these whores checked," he told the other two while the cyclo driver peddled. Now, while he and his one bud kept busy with the two nearly naked dancers at the bar, the blond Marine drifted toward oblivion with the baby-faced whore, relaxing his caution while her seasoned, professional seduction took hold of his mind.

"You so good-looking man," she breathed, putting the tip of her tongue inside his ear. Then she felt a slight ooze of seminal fluid bead onto her hand from his penis, and with the tip of her index digit she smeared it around the head. Then she took that finger and put it on her tongue.

"Mmmmm, you taste so good," she sighed. "I want taste more."

Suddenly she ducked her head under the table and took him into her mouth. Then she quickly rose up again, and kissed him, darting her tongue between his lips.

"We go now," she breathed and then swirled the tip of her tongue in his ear.

For twenty-one-year-old Mike Scott from Orchard Park, New York, a village just south of Buffalo, this girl named Song who hustled on the streets of Da Nang and stripped in the bars as Wild Thing burst open a whole new vista of life for him that he had never before encountered. His first afternoon off the air base, and he was suddenly in love.

"Where you live?" the blond Marine asked, kissing the girl, his breath racing and his face feeling on fire.

"Down hall next door," Wild Thing lied, standing up and taking the young man by the arm. "I show you. I live just here."

"I need to tell my buddies," Mike Scott said, looking at the two of them still busy at the bar with the naked girls now perched on their knees.

"You stay all night?" the girl said, hoping for the twenty-dollar commission that he would pay up front.

"Naw, we got to get back pretty soon," the lad said, looking at his watch.

With her clinging to his arm, he walked to the dark-haired Marine wearing the sunglasses and mustache and pointed to his watch.

"I'll be back here in thirty minutes, tops," he said.

The salty leader grinned at the blond and said, "No sweat, GI. You go boom-boom. No more Da Nang cherry boy. We'll be right here, unless we go fuck these two hogs first."

"I'm not leaving anyplace without you guys," the blond Marine said, and then looked at Wild Thing wrapped on his arm.

Seeing doubt start to show on his face, the hooker then pressed her groin against his leg and pulled his arm hard.

"We go do short time," Wild Thing said, and then pointed to the two girls, "they no let your friends leave without you. I promise. You be okay. Come, we go my room now."

"Don't sweat about it, Mike," the dark-haired Marine said, reassuring his newbee pal. "We won't leave here without you, man. I promise."

James Harris sat, sipping his beer, watching the show, and shook his head at the trio of fools. Huong and Bao slipped away from the table and walked to the back of the saloon, past the red-lit stage and the bar's one, stinking restroom used by both sexes, and pushed through a doorway that led them into a dark hall that emptied into another passage along which half a dozen single-room apartment doors opened.

Still wearing his uniform and sergeant chevrons, Mau Mau Harris ambled to the front of the bar and elbowed his way to the counter next to the
Marine with the dark glasses and mustache.

"You guys with the wing?" Harris asked the man.

"Yeah, we're with MAG-Eleven," the dark-haired Marine answered.
"You with the wing, too?"

"Naw," Harris said, purposefully killing time, keeping the two buddies
occupied. "I work over at the press center. You know, the PIO? I take pictures and shit."

"You got stuff in the *Sea Tiger*?" the second Marine said, smiling while
holding on to his naked playmate.

"Yeah, that and *Stars and Stripes*," Harris said, making himself feel
important.

"You going to do that for a living when you get out? Take pictures and
shit?" the dark-glasses Marine asked, cupping his hands on his dancer's
breasts as she straddled his leg and ground herself on his increasingly
damp thigh.

"Yeah," Harris lied, enjoying the role, "I've got a job offer already with
the *Chicago Tribune*, man. I rotate out of this hole, and I go back home and
live a good life. Taking pictures of all the shit that goes on in Chicago."

"Fuck, man, I wish I had a job like that," the second Marine said,
grabbing a pull off a fresh bottle of 33 Beer that Harris had the bartender
set up with a snap and point of his fingers. "What's your name? So I can
say I knew the dude back when."

"Rufus Potter," Harris said, almost choking on the beer that he gulped
after saying it. He saw both men fighting back laughs, and then narrowed
his eyes at them. "You got a problem with what my mother gave me?"

"Sergeant Potter, oh, shit, no, man," the dark-haired Marine said, and
took off his sunglasses to show the sincerity in his eyes.

Harris laughed and drank more beer. Then he looked at the two men
and scowled.

"That's my father's name, too," Harris frowned. "So I go by Junior.
My nick. Junior Potter."

He had just thought of it, and Junior had a much better ring to him
than Rufus, which he had typed on the green identification card in his wallet and stamped on the two metal dog tags hanging around his neck.

"When I go to taking pictures for the *Chicago Tribune*, you want to
see my name in that paper, you need to look for Junior Potter," Harris said,
and then gulped down his beer when he saw Bao step into the daylight outside the saloon's front door and give him a nod.

"Hey, check it out, I got to get back to the press center," Mau Mau said in a hurry, making an exaggerated glance at his gold Rolex wristwatch and stepping away from the bar. Then, as an afterthought, he reached in his pocket and laid a five-dollar bill on the counter. "Let me catch another round for you guys, and for your buddy, too, when he gets back."

As the deserter nervously walked to the saloon's entrance, and then jogged to the street corner where the black Mercedes sat with its engine running, waiting for him, he cursed under his breath. His abrupt departure from the newfound friends, and his clumsy exit raised a host of red flags in his mind. He realized that the conversation with the two Marines had never mentioned their third friend. The blond had already left the saloon when Harris had joined the two playboys at the bar. Another thought, too: buying two complete strangers a second round of beers went overboard. Picking up the tab on the first serving seemed a little odd to him, now that he thought about it. When their buddy would eventually fail to return, and their search for him would turn up nothing, they might smell the rat and connect Mau Mau to his disappearance.

Speeding down a back street, Harris thought, "Why should I give a shit? I'm out of here anyway. Soon as I kill that rat bastard Elmore." With a new life and fresh identity, and his share of three million dollars, why should he ever worry?

However, as the car whisked out of the heart of Da Nang, the bumping and kicking from the automobile's trunk troubled him.

A COOL BREEZE stirred from the South China Sea brought the marine layer ashore and shrouded the low-lying lands and river bottoms with fog south of Da Nang. Huong switched on the yellow lamps mounted on the front bumper, near the center of the Mercedes-Benz's grill, as he followed a narrow dirt road westward alongside the Cau Do River.

Hidden by the fog and the night, at a spot where the road branched north, a quarter of a mile east from its intersection with Highway One, Huong shut off the lights and stopped the car. He said nothing to James Harris, who sat in the backseat, smoking a cigarette, but simply looked at his brother, Bao, who got out of the car and opened the trunk.

Huong lifted the latch on the driver-side door and stepped out of the car when Bao dragged the first victim to the road's edge, atop a steep bank, ten feet above the Song Cau Do's low-tide water. James Harris looked at the foggy silhouette of the person the two cowboys had bound with communications wire and gagged with a knot tied in an old T-shirt.

While Bao held the short man by the wrists, Huong put his .45 Colt to the back of the fellow's head and sent a bullet out his face. Just as the gunshot popped, Bao let go of the dying cowboy's hands and he splashed into the mud at the water's edge.

The younger Nguyen brother returned to the trunk and pulled the young whore from it. Seeing her, James Harris jumped out of the car.

"Oh, now, wait, man," Mau Mau pled with Huong. "That's Wild Thing, man! She one of us!"

"She Benny Lam whore now," Huong said, putting his .45-caliber pistol at the back of the girl's head as Bao held her by the hands, and quickly pulled the trigger before the frantic black deserter could do anything. Then the cool older brother shrugged at the terrified American as he slipped his pistol back in its waistband scabbard. "She talk too much. She tell anybody, all this be no good then. No work. Not buy any time. CID keep looking. Benny Lam cowboy, he talk, too. We no need anybody talking. You understand?"

"Yeah, man, I understand," James Harris said, looking at the muddy edge of the river where the girl and her watchdog lay dead, their hands and feet bound, and the rags tied around their mouths. "It's just, I liked that chick, you know? She's sweet."

"Sweet like bamboo snake," Huong said, taking a pearl-handled straight razor from the dead girl's black velvet clutch purse with the long, thin gold chain shoulder strap. He flipped open the weapon under James Harris's nose and made a quick swipe with it in front of his face. He snapped the blade shut and then dropped it in Mau Mau's shirt pocket as a souvenir. Then he found the fifty dollars along with two more American twenty-dollar bills and a ten plus three fives, and folded the cash into the two hundred dollars he had recovered from Benny Lam's watchdog. Turning the small handbag inside out, spilling the whore's wallet, compact, and makeup onto the road, Huong dropped it over the side where it landed in the mud next to the two bodies.

Harris followed Huong to the back of the car, where Bao now pulled the bound feet of the unconscious blond Marine out of the trunk and waited for his two cohorts to take the young man by the shoulders.

"No, not here," Huong told Bao in Vietnamese, and pushed Harris's hand away from their barely breathing victim. "We no do here. Him dead someplace else much better."

"You don't want the cops to tie those two with this guy, right?" Harris said, realizing that authorities finding the three corpses together would naturally investigate the homicides as connected, and eventually tie the identity of the blond Marine with the missing man from the bar. As he climbed in the backseat and Huong slammed the trunk shut, with their captive safely inside it, Harris reminded himself that he had to think matters through better.

"GUNNY JACKSON," THE sandy-haired CID lieutenant called as he walked through the doorway of the III MAF Criminal Investigation Division work quarters where the gunnery sergeant with the gold badge pinned on his green utility uniform sat behind one of three desks crowded into the small office space. "Somebody took out the Snowman."

"Oh, really?" the seasoned veteran criminal investigator said, and leaned back in his chair, taking a sip of hot coffee from a white mug with a gold Marine Corps emblem and the name "Jack" painted on one side and gunnery sergeant chevrons painted on the other. "You sure, sir, or are you just supposing?"

"Supposing, I guess. We won't be sure until they confirm the ID on the body at Hickam Air Force Base, in Hawaii," the lieutenant said, pouring a cup of coffee and then walking to his desk. "Graves and registration are packing him out today. We may know something in a few weeks.

"Chief Toan claims it's Brian Pitts for sure, though. And you know, he knew him better than we ever did. A pair of his patrolmen found the body this morning on the edge of Dogpatch, not two blocks from the Snowman's villa. Staff Sergeant Lyons and Sergeant Knight got the call on it, about five o'clock this morning. We're going out to investigate the scene in the daylight, as soon as they get in. Probably around noon. I let them catch forty winks this morning, since they got hauled out of the rack last night.

"Toan thinks that Benny Lam's boys took out Pitts last night after somebody, most likely the Snowman's crew, whacked one of Lam's best whores and her watchdog. A patrol from Seventh Marines found the two bodies in the tidal wash of the Cau Do River this morning, near that big, green, iron bridge on Highway One.

"So the chief concluded that Lam's boys must have caught Pitts trying to sneak back to his ranch, sometime after one or two this morning, some six to eight hours after the whore and the cowboy bought it, based on the time-of-death estimates, and shotgunned our man Pitts in reprisal. Blew his face off with a couple of blasts of twelve-gauge, ought-two man-stoppers."

"You know, Lieutenant Biggs, Hickam will take a hell of a lot longer than a few weeks. We could be sitting here three or four months. Can't we just run his fingerprints and make an ID? The FBI can turn it around in two weeks flat," the gunny said, running his index finger down an incident report as he read through its data.

"Be nice, Jack," the sandy-haired CID lieutenant named Melvin Biggs said, leaning back in his chair and sipping coffee. "Apparently Pitts saw it coming, and put his hands in front of his face. You know the typical defensive wound. Turned both his mitts into hamburger."

"Convenient if you're Brian Pitts and want the world to think you're dead," the gunny called Jack Jackson said, drinking more coffee and tossing the report he had just read across to the lieutenant's desk. "Check out the description of this lost soul, a newbee from MAG Eleven, one Lance Corporal Michael Jerome Scott, age twenty-one, six-feet-nothing tall and 180 pounds. My last sighting of our infamous Snowman, Corporal Brian T. Pitts, matches this boy top to bottom."

"That certainly casts a new light on the discovery of Pitts's dead body, doesn't it," Biggs said, picking up the report passed to CID from the military police watch commander from the previous night.

"You know, sir," Gunny Jackson added, "we were damned lucky to get that report you've got there in your hot little hands. We wouldn't have had a clue about this kid, otherwise, had Scott's two buddies not raised holy hell with the night watch, demanding that they call out the cavalry because their newbee lance corporal had gotten himself snatched.

"After these guys spent a couple of hours scouring the area around that bar, searching for Lance Corporal Scott, they beat feet to the MP shack and reported him kidnapped. That's right, kidnapped, right off the bat. No missing-person bullshit. And they stuck to their guns about it being a snatch job, too, not just another Marine in love suddenly gone native, like we see more often than not.

"Given that this was the lance corporal's first trip to the ville, and that he was nervous about being out of sight of his two buddies, the watch commander ordered a full sweep of that area. Of course he turned up zip-zilch, but because the incident involves a possible kidnapping, it landed the report and Scott's description right in our hands this morning.

"Talk about dumb luck. If these guys would have just gone back to the barracks, like so many other people would have done, and let their buddy just get listed as absent, failing to return from liberty, we wouldn't know a damned thing other than a body fitting the description of Pitts turned up dead."

"Hmm, maybe our luck has changed," the lieutenant said and cracked a smile. "Any hope of getting our hands on some physical records telling us a little more about Pitts?"

"I doubt it. I'd sure like to see his SRB, medical and dental files, but most likely they got shipped to St. Louis many moons ago, him being a longtime deserter and all," Gunny Jackson said. "Ten to one they're not here, if our luck lately holds true to course."

"The body they found in Dogpatch this morning had Pitts's dog tags and ID card on it," the lieutenant said, reading the report on the corpse and then looking up with a big smile at his noncommissioned officer in charge. "Besides religion, service number, and name, a man's dog tag has his blood type imprinted on it, like his ID card."

"Bingo!" the gunny said, and laughed. "I guess even a blind hog finds an acorn now and then, doesn't he? Maybe our luck has changed! Be a hell of a note if the blood type of the body is not the same as the blood type listed on Pitts's ID card and dog tags."

"Tell you what I'm going to do," the lieutenant said, snatching the telephone on his desk and putting it to his ear. "I'm having a copy of this Lance Corporal M. J. Scott's medical and dental files sent to Hawaii with that body. We may not have Pitts's records right now, but we do have this missing lad's. At least they can bounce the physical data they collect from the body to what this boy has on his medical and dental charts. If it matches, then we've located our missing soul, and it answers the Pitts identity question, doesn't it."

BY NOONTIME, THE March heat in Da Nang had both the lieutenant's and the gunny's uniforms soaked with perspiration. Staff Sergeant Tommy Lyons and Sergeant Billy Knight also sweated in their civilian clothes as they walked behind the uniformed officer and senior NCO. Two Vietnamese policemen stood watch over the section of Dogpatch dirt alley while a Naval Investigative Service detective who had arrived ahead of the four CID Marines squatted next to a dried blood puddle, poking the ground with his pocket knife.

"Mister Walters, I see you're hard at it," Lieutenant Biggs called to the man as he ducked under the ropes strung across the alley, barricading the crime scene.

Special Agent Bill Walters looked up and smiled. "Good job here by your sergeants. They roped off the area immediately, and preserved the scene intact before Major Toan's hamsters could fuck it up beyond value."

"Gunny Jack taught them well," Lieutenant Biggs said, and then knelt by the NIS investigator. "What you digging up?"

"Blast particles from the shotgun," Walters said, and then showed the

Marine officer the speck of black residue he had plucked from the ground. "Our man was shot lying down. Check out the splatter pattern. We have body materials spread in a twelve-foot circle. Right here, we have spent powder and other debris from the shotgun blasts. Definitely, our guy died lying on his back right here."

"Could he have been dead beforehand, and just shotgunned here?" the lieutenant suggested, and then looked around at the many windows that viewed the alley. "Of course, no witnesses, right?"

"Nobody's talking, and I don't expect any of the good citizens of Dogpatch to step forward either," the forty-year-old naval investigator grumbled. "I guess it is possible that he died elsewhere, but judging from the massive volume of blood puddled here, it leads me to believe that his heart pumped for a while after he took the two blasts to the face and hands."

"Unconscious then," the lieutenant said, surveying the bloody scene as the three sergeants stood above him.

"Could be that he got hit from behind, knocked to the ground, and then shotgunned," Walters said, standing and giving Gunny Jack a smile and a handshake. "Probably the most likely scenario. Then, too, just about as likely, someone could have clubbed the guy elsewhere, kept him alive, and brought him here to kill him. A lot of trouble to go through to stage a pretty scene for us."

"My thoughts from the get-go," Gunnery Sergeant Jackson said. "This ain't Brian Pitts we're talking got clipped here. We're talking about a kid named Michael Scott who looks a lot like Brian Pitts, and they killed him here to throw us off Pitts's trail so he can beat feet out of the area."

Bill Walters slapped the gunny on the shoulder and smiled at the lieutenant. "The man has a point. It also explains a hell of a lot more than that dirt-bag Toan's hare-brained theory of a reprisal over a dead whore and a cowboy."

"We never turned up even a shoebox of money stashed in that villa of Pitts's, either," Jackson said, looking at the lieutenant. "Elmore the magnificent claimed the Snowman had a room full of seabags stuffed with American cash. How many seabags is yet to be seen, but I think the snitch may have a basis of truth underlying his bullshit. Pitts did have a major corner in Dogpatch, and did a lot of dope business, so we've come to learn. We check his hooch and find no dope and no money. Just a nervous old broad with a string of whores. My point is this: he saw us coming and got his shit out of Dodge. He killed this poor kid to try to throw us off his trail. Somewhere, he's out there with a shitload of cash, and maybe a bunch of dope, too, and he needs to get someplace where it can do him some good."

*   *   *

BRIAN PITTS CLOSED his eyes, pulling the rice-straw conical hat over his face, shielding it from the afternoon sun as he bounced in the center of the bench seat inside the cab of the baby-blue dump truck loaded with pig manure atop the half-dozen duffel bags stuffed with three million dollars in American cash, zipped inside nylon-reinforced, black polyurethane body bags. Once the truck had made its way past Duc Pho and Phu Cat, the fugitive crime lord relaxed and began to doze off, sitting between Chung, who drove the old diesel, and Ty, who rode shotgun. The Snowman felt much safer once they had entered the central military region of South Vietnam, overseen by U.S. Army forces and ARVN units from its Second Army Corps headquartered at Pleiku. Here, these soldiers didn't know him, weren't looking for him, and cared nothing about Brian Pitts.

When the blue diesel finally rolled through Nha Trang and turned southwestward toward Saigon, the Marine deserter felt euphoric. Seeing a seafood restaurant on the outskirts, he had Chung pull to the roadside, and the trio strolled inside the establishment and casually ate a magnificent dinner of broiled prawns and fish stew. A few more hours down Highway One, and they would make the turn westward toward a village near Cu Chi and their new home where Huong, Chung, and Bao's grandparents and his two uncles awaited their arrival.

While Brian Pitts, Chung, and Ty enjoyed their seafood dinner with ample cold beer to wash it down, James Harris, Huong, and Bao ate warmed-over rice with salt pork for flavoring.

"This shit, hangin' out in the hooch ain't cuttin' it, man," Harris complained, choking down the rice dinner. "Why we ain't got some beer and real food?"

Huong looked at Mau Mau and then tossed a hunk of salt pork from his bowl to Turd. Bao took a kettle of hot tea from the stove and refilled Huong's cup and then his own. He took a step toward James Harris, to refill his cup, but the black man glared at him so he stopped, and set the kettle back on the stove.

"This tastes like your sister washed her hair in it," Mau Mau said, sipping the last of his tea, and then setting his cup on the floor next to where he sat in one of the straight-back chairs. He fought back his inclination to throw the cup across the floor, along with his bowl of rice. His memory of the day he saw Huong kill the cowboy for cheating at mah-jongg kept him from any excessive belligerency.

Turd wagged his tail, and James Harris fed him his piece of salt pork, too. Huong smiled at the gesture as he scraped his rice bowl clean.

"When we goin' to find that rat fuck Elmore?" Harris then said to Huong.

"We do soon," Huong said, sipping his tea and going to the wooden porch across the front of the frame house with the thatched roof. "We need know where Elmo stay now. Then we see if we can make good plan. We kill him then."

"What if they got him protected?" Harris said, walking outside, too. "I ain't gonna just walk off."

"We kill Elmo if we can do," Huong said, and then looked cooly at James Harris. "We no kill him if no can do."

"Fucking double-talking motherfucker!" Harris exclaimed, and glared at Huong. "Why ain't you talkin' English that makes some sense? We kill if we can do it, we no kill if we no can do it. That's just bullshit. We gonna kill that motherfucker. I make sure of that!"

"No do if no can do," Huong said and walked away from Harris.

"There ain't any no can do, motherfucker," Harris snarled.

Huong wheeled at Mau Mau and pulled his .45 Colt semiautomatic pistol as he moved. He had it cocked and pointed under Harris's chin before the deserter could take another step.

"We no fucking kill Elmo if we no get fucking chance, motherfucker!" Huong snarled, pausing between each word so that his American cohort could clearly understand him. "Pitts say we no take chance. We kill Elmo if we can do okay, but not if it make us big trouble. You no like? Then maybe I kill you, motherfucker."

The pistol's barrel left a circular imprint under Harris's chin as the Vietnamese cowboy took it away from the man.

"Hey, man, you shoot me and Turd won't have a daddy," Harris said, offering a smile with his attempt at humoring the cowboy. He knew that Huong would kill him in a heartbeat.

"LANCE CORPORAL ELMORE!" Gunny Jackson shouted as he walked inside the hooch in the Marine Aircraft Group Eleven compound where James Elmore lived. The frightened dope dealer turned snitch had erected barricades of footlockers, wall lockers, and wooden freight boxes around his cubicle and bunk. When he peeked around the corner, he smiled his gold front tooth at the two men he saw approaching.

"Yo, gunny," Elmore said, and stepped from behind the wall of wooden boxes. Then he recognized the Marine captain who entered with the CID gunnery sergeant.

"You remember your lawyer, Captain O'Connor," Gunny Jackson said, pointing to Terry O'Connor.

"Sho, man," Elmore said and put out his hand. "How's it hangin', Skipper?"

Terry O'Connor looked at the gunny. "You mind if we have some private time?"

"Sure, sir, take your time," Jackson said, "I'll just have a smoke outside. However, sir, please remember we have a chopper flight to catch."

"Where you goin'?" Elmore asked, ushering Terry O'Connor inside his rabbit-warren cubicle.

The smell of the stagnant air within the confined space and the stench of the man's pile of filthy clothes left the lawyer wanting to talk outside the rancid den. O'Connor tried to stomach the odor but finally broke down.

"Tell you what, let's step outside, too," O'Connor said, and led James Elmore out the back of the hooch, where the two men then stood on a gravel walkway.

"Now to answer your question a moment ago," O'Connor said, looking around to see who watched them, "I'm not going anyplace. You are moving to Chu Lai."

"Ho, man, whoa! No I ain't goin' down at Chu Lai," Elmore squalled.

"We think that Brian Pitts may be dead, or he may have committed a murder to make it appear that he is dead, all in the aftermath of your informing on him," O'Connor said to the lance corporal who flicked out a Kool cigarette from a flip-top box and popped it between his lips.

"What else is new?" Elmore quipped, flipping open the top of a Zippo lighter and igniting a four-inch-high flame that made the smart-talking snitch flinch back from it as he lit his smoke.

"If Pitts is not dead, but has murdered a Marine in an attempt to make us believe the corpse is his, then it is highly likely he will be looking for you," O'Connor said, and finally snatched Elmore's chin with his hand so he could lock eyes with the man.

"Yo, man, I heard you!" Elmore shouted, and pulled away from O'Connor's grip. "I know he be lookin' for me the day I give his ass up."

"If Pitts is not dead, he could be anywhere, just waiting for the chance to kill you. Does that make sense to you?" O'Connor said, stepping in front of the elusive lance corporal.

"Yeah, man, I heard that," Elmore said, and then looked at the captain. "No word on Mau Mau?"

"You mean James Harris?" O'Connor said.

"Yeah, man, Harris," Elmore said, sucking on his cigarette.

"No word on him or the several cowboys loyal to Pitts," O'Connor answered, fighting back his frustration.

"See, I told these motherfuckers," Elmore said, looking in every direction, wondering who might watch him without his knowledge. "Pitts might try to kill me if I step in the open while he still loose. That Mau Mau, he one crazy motherfucker, though. He might try comin' on base, lookin' for my young ass."

"That's why we want to move you to Chu Lai. No one will know you've gone there," O'Connor said, now holding the man's attention. "Are you high or something?"

James Elmore laughed, and looked at the captain.

"You too cool, man," Elmore said, and laughed more. "Fuck, yeah, I'm high. How you think I deal with this shit? Fuck yeah, I be stayin' high, too. I got my peas and my bros here, man. They cover my ass. I stay here."

"No, you have to go to Chu Lai, because Pitts and Harris both know where you live. You cannot stay here because they will kill you," O'Connor snapped back. "Pack your shit, now! That's an order, lance corporal."

Chapter 9

CHINA BEACH PARTY

A FLASH OF daylight alerted the three Marine lawyers leaning against the bar inside the Da Nang Officers' Club that someone had just walked through the outside door. Celestine "Ax Man" Anderson's defense team suspended their Friday afternoon conversation about the trial slated to begin on Tuesday and that would likely end by next Friday, and turned their heads to identify the new arrival. The sight of a woman, a Western woman, a tall and shapely woman, stopped them cold.

The flickering yellow glow cast from her gold butane lighter as she lit a cigarette illuminated her pretty face while she looked toward the bar and the trio of officers drinking beer there. She smiled at the men as their eyes met hers, and casually she slipped off her jacket and draped it over her arm. Then she looped the carrying straps of a large, blue canvas flight bag and her black leather purse back over her shoulder as she cut across the lounge area and dance floor. When she walked close to her small audience, she set down her luggage, opened the top two buttons of her white blouse, and fanned the exposed skin of her throat, upper chest, and bulging cleavage. The smell of the woman's perfume, enhanced by the glow of her perspiration, filled the rush of air that her presence stirred.

When the voluptuous female eased herself next to Wayne Ebberhardt, he gulped several swallows of Budweiser draft from his drippy mug. Then he began gathering his change from the round of beers he had bought for himself, Terry O'Connor, and Jon Kirkwood. Shoving two quarters toward the bartender for a tip, he began stuffing the rest of the money in his pocket.

"Where are you going in such a hurry, sailor? I hope that I'm not scaring you away," the tall redhead said, blowing a mouthful of cigarette smoke at the first lieutenant's face as he fumbled with the few coins left that he hurriedly gathered from the countertop. Brushing her ample breasts against the young lawyer's arm as she slid atop the bar stool next to him, she crossed her legs, causing her tight, short-fitting, flight attendant uniform skirt to ride high on her legs. The hem rose well past the tops of her stockings, and exposed the white garter-belt snaps holding her nylons taut.

To get a better view, Jon Kirkwood and Terry O'Connor both took two steps back from the bar. They stood on the side of their fellow Marine lawyer opposite from the woman, and now the two heroes looked wide-eyed at the sexy vision dressed in Flying Tiger Airlines blue, taking in the full view of her long and shapely body and her fully exposed legs. She smiled warmly at the awestruck pair of onlookers, took another pull from the cigarette she held delicately between her fingers, and then looked back at Wayne Ebberhardt.

"Oh, sorry, ma'am, I just stopped for a beer and was on my way out to grab a bite," the lieutenant said with a distinct nervous quiver in his voice.

The airline stewardess shrugged and smiled at the Marine, and let the smoke flow from her mouth, riding on a gentle breeze that she blew with a seductive pucker toward Lieutenant Ebberhardt's face.

The two captains stood speechless, looking at the woman's perfect and beautifully long legs, at her large, upwardly lifted breasts that peeked from beneath her partially opened white blouse, and at her gorgeous milk-white face framed by pageboy-cut, dark red hair, and accented by her sparkling blue eyes. Then Kirkwood and O'Connor drilled their stares at the shrinking lieutenant, who hurriedly gulped the last of his beer from its mug, and slid the dripping glass across the bar and tried to stand.

Jon Kirkwood immediately caught Wayne Ebberhardt on the shoulder, pushed him back atop the stool, and motioned to the bartender to bring another round of beers for the men, and a martini cocktail for the lady.

"Oh, he's not that hungry, ma'am," O'Connor said, beaming his up-curled, Irish eyes and dimpled smile at the woman, and then glaring at

Ebberhardt with wild amazement for his attempt to leave such an inviting opportunity.

"I'll be right back," Ebberhardt said defensively, trying again to stand, but being held in place by Jon Kirkwood's locked-down grip over his shoulder. "I just wanted to get something quick and easy."

The red-haired beauty smiled at all three Marines and then looked at Ebberhardt squarely in his eyes.

"I'm not at all that quick, I have to admit," she said, broadening her smile and letting a wisp of cigarette smoke drift from her lips, "but for you, cutie-pie, I could be very easy."

Terry O'Connor choked on his beer and bent over, coughing.

Wayne Ebberhardt's face flushed, but not nearly the shade of deep crimson that Jon Kirkwood's complexion turned.

"Terrence Boyd O'Connor, ma'am, at your service," O'Connor quickly spoke, putting out his hand for the lady to shake.

"Gwendolyn Crookshank," the redhead replied, and took the captain's hand with both of hers and held it, "but call me Gwen."

"Wayne Ebberhardt, ma'am," the lieutenant then followed, and took her hands from O'Connor. "The speechless gentleman next to Captain O'Connor is a fellow attorney and defense team colleague of ours, Captain Jonathan C. Kirkwood."

"Lawyers three. Defense team colleagues. Indeed. Well, it seems I have fallen in with some bad company, haven't I," the flight attendant said, letting her mellow voice flow with her cigarette smoke.

"We're the world's worst," O'Connor bubbled. "We're the bad boys of First MAW Law. Just ask our mojo if you don't believe us."

"Captain O'Connor," the woman said, smiling warmly at the cheery officer, "I have a feeling that you're a very bad boy indeed."

Jon Kirkwood said nothing. The smell of the attractive stewardess's perfume had gotten him to thinking more about his wife, Katherine Layne Kirkwood, whose latest letter he carried in his back pocket and had just finished reading when Terry O'Connor had dragged him to the Officers' Club to meet with Wayne Ebberhardt for a beer and a relaxed talk about Tuesday's opening arguments in the Anderson trial: more of a formality now that the presiding judge had thrown out the charge of first-degree murder, ruling that the prosecution failed to show any evidence of premeditation. Their client had openly confessed to killing Buster Rein, backed by a hundred eyewitnesses, so a conviction of second-degree murder seemed automatic. The only arguments now involved length of sentence based on the mitigating circumstances.

The fragrance of Chanel Number Five took Kirkwood's mind to thoughts of Okinawa, where Katie patiently waited for Jon to get a chance to catch an R & R hop on a ninety-six-hour pass. They had hoped that a trial or legal conference also might get him there, but Dicky Doo had vowed to never let it happen.

In the Anderson case, Dickinson had expressly forbade Kirkwood from assisting O'Connor and Ebberhardt, should the trial move from Da Nang. When it looked like it might convene at Camp Courtney, Okinawa, Dicky Doo began making overtures of taking charge. Based on some advice from the Brothers B, the major had even prepared to formally ask in writing that Lieutenant Colonel Prunella grant him direct cognizance of Anderson's defense. His letter had stated a plethora of phony rationale.

Lucky for him that Staff Sergeant Pride read the mojo's letter first, and then tactfully cut him off from certain embarrassment, just in the nick of time, showing Dickinson the backup file copy of a week-old message from the staff judge advocate in charge of Fleet Marine Force Pacific legal affairs directing that the court-martial remain in Da Nang, as a matter of convenience and economy for the many witnesses and the command. Someone had pulled the original message from the daily read-board, circulated each morning among all the law center's officers, before Dicky Doo had a chance to see it. Apparently ripped it off as the board passed from Lieutenant Colonel Prunella's desk to the major's. With this revelation, which eliminated hope of anyone on his shit list going to Okinawa, Dickinson laid Anderson's defense back in O'Connor's and Ebberhardt's laps and gave Kirkwood the green light to help them.

Even though he knew he had no hope of getting on the team if it went to Okinawa, Kirkwood still felt hurt by the major's meanness by depriving him simply out of spite. With each week that passed while his wife waited only a three-hour plane ride away, and no hope of getting a ninety-six-hour pass, R and R, or any kind of official business trip to Okinawa, Jon Kirkwood's resentment toward the mojo major grew bitter.

"Cat got your tongue, cowboy?" the redhead said, putting her fingertip with its dark-red-painted nail under Kirkwood's chin.

The captain responded by holding up his left hand and showing the woman the gold ring on his finger.

She smiled, and then kissed him on his cheek.

"Wayne," she said, looking at the lieutenant, "your little friend here: I don't think he's a bad boy at all."

"They're both really pretty good boys, Gwen," Ebberhardt answered.

"But you, Wayne," the woman said, "you are bad. Aren't you?"

"Oh he's bad, all right," O'Connor said, and slapped Ebberhardt on the back. "He's shy, but a very bad boy."

"Indeed?" the stewardess said and smiled, dashing out her cigarette and sipping the martini.

"Ma'am, don't believe anything he says," Ebberhardt retorted, and stood from the bar.

"So you're going to leave anyway," the pretty woman sighed, sucking an olive from her cocktail off its toothpick skewer. "I'm a little hungry, too. Mind if I tag along?"

"Anything special in mind?" Ebberhardt said, picking up his cap and then shouldering her purse and flight bag.

"Oh, I rented the cutest little duplex cabana at China Beach, for the weekend. Do you like seafood? We can have dinner there," the redhead said to the lieutenant, and then smiled at Kirkwood and O'Connor as Wayne Ebberhardt helped her on with her blue uniform jacket.

"Ta-ta, boys," she cooed as they walked away.

"Holy Mother Mary and Joseph!" O'Connor said, looking at Jon Kirkwood as Wayne Ebberhardt and the beautiful red-haired flight attendant left. "He's headed to China Beach with that fox."

"Hope he gets back before Tuesday," Kirkwood said, turning toward the bar and drinking his beer.

"GWENDOLYN CROOKSHANK!" WAYNE Ebberhardt laughed as he climbed aboard the shuttle van to China Beach recreational area with the red-headed woman. "Crookshank? What kind of name is that, honey?"

"Oh, something that just popped in my head. Heaven knows where I heard it," she said, laughing, and then looked at the lieutenant with her eyes twinkling. "Now, if you know what's good for you, bub, you'll shut up and kiss your wife like the man I married!"

While she spoke, she grabbed the lieutenant by both of his shoulders and then kissed him hard as the van pulled from the curb and sped down the road, heading to other stops for passengers riding to China Beach for the weekend.

"I've got until 6:00 AM Tuesday," Gwen Ebberhardt then told her husband. "You have that trial that starts then, too, so we can have Saturday and Sunday on the beach. My crew is at the hotel by the American consulate, and you can stay there with me Monday night, after you do your office boy thing all day. Oh, by the way, I saw that strange captain again. You know, the tall one with the wild blond hair and bad breath?"

"Michael Carter," the lieutenant said, lighting two cigarettes and handing one to his wife.

"Yes, that's the one," she answered, drawing in a breath full of smoke. "He helped me pack a few of your things, you know, some of your underwear and socks, your bathing suit, toiletries, and other stuff for the weekend. I've got it here in my crew bag."

"He's a nice guy, just eccentric," Ebberhardt commented.

"He also told me that you were in the club with your little friends, so I thought I would have a go at you," Gwen said and laughed. "Thanks so much for acting sweet and not letting on. I had such fun!"

"I don't think I had to do much acting," Ebberhardt said, smiling at his wife. "You had me honestly stuttering and blushing."

"Oh, poo, Wayne," Gwen laughed as the small bus pulled to the curb and the side door slid open for more passengers, "you're always so bad. Putting on that little lost choir boy act. I know you better than that, my bad little boy. Don't forget, I know just how bad you like to be. You bad, bad little boy."

As she spoke, she rolled on top of her husband's lap, bringing her face close to his, and passionately kissed her captive Marine just as two air force captains dressed in drab green flight suits and blue garrison caps climbed aboard the China Beach shuttle. They gawked while stumbling to their seats, and then one of the men offered Wayne Ebberhardt a thumbs-up when the lieutenant finally raised his head for air.

"HI, GUYS!" MICHAEL Carter called to Jon Kirkwood and Terry O'Connor as he strolled inside the Da Nang Officers' Club. "I guess I missed them, darn it."

"Missed who, stick man?" O'Connor said, looking at their colleague, who now perched himself on a bar stool next to them. "You talking about Wayne Ebberhardt and that red bombshell who came in here and picked him up? In the end, I think he picked her up."

"Yeah," Kirkwood said, peeling the label off his beer bottle. "The way Wayne just got up and decided to leave, and she hooked right on him. He did the picking. She was trolling, but he landed the fish."

"What are you talking about?" Carter said, getting the bartender's attention and ordering a sloe gin fizz.

"Ebberhardt, fuck nuts," O'Connor said, taking a pull off his beer. "He left here with this gorgeous, red-haired stewardess from the freedom bird not five minutes ago. She was hot to trot, wanting a bad boy to go play with her, and she snatched up Wayne like a Seventh Avenue pro."

"It's arguable who did the snatching," Kirkwood added, "but she was definitely hot to trot. Had her skirt way up past her thighs and her boobs just jumping out."

Michael Carter laughed and snorted, and then sucked sloe gin fizz up the red swizzle stick straw jutting from his highball glass.

"I shouldn't tell you then," he said, honking as he laughed. "This is too good. Telling you would spoil it."

"Spill it, ass wipe," O'Connor growled, and spun Michael Carter on his bar stool toward him, still snickering.

"That was Gwen, stupid," Carter said, and laughed more.

"I know it was Gwen," Kirkwood answered. "She introduced herself to us."

"She tell you her last name?" Carter teased.

"Yeah, Crook something," O'Connor said, and then began to smile, realizing he had fallen prey to a rich joke.

"Crookshank, Gwendolyn Crookshank," Kirkwood added, and then smiled, too. "Come to think of it, that's an awfully stupid name."

"Oh, that's too funny," Carter said, hacking as he laughed. "Gwen Ebberhardt! You guys were had. She came by the barracks looking for Wayne, picked up some of his stuff for the weekend, and I told her that he was over here with you two."

"Fucking Ebberhardt," O'Connor said and laughed. "Damn, he's got a fox of a wife, though."

Jon Kirkwood felt in his back pocket and pulled out the letter from Katie. He smelled the paper, still faintly scented with the Chanel Number Five she had sprinkled on the stationery. Her favorite perfume. The same fragrance that Gwen Ebberhardt wore.

Another flash of daylight drew the three lawyers' attention back to the alcove that led to the front door. Silhouetted by the glow from the jukebox and the cigarette machine, they saw Dicky Doo's unmistakable semiportly frame topped by his salt-and-pepper flattop head. He stood there for a moment, letting his eyes adjust to the darkness, and then strolled to the bar, smiling like he had encountered old friends.

"I should have figured that you three hogs would not stray far from the well," Major Dickinson said, laughing at his own condescending humor. "Stanley, Charlie, and the Brothers B have gone to PT, but I see you fellows have more sensible business here at the bar."

"Talking defense strategy, Major," O'Connor said, sliding his beer mug across the counter to the barkeep for a refill. Jon Kirkwood still toyed with the label on his half-drank bottle of beer, and paid no attention to the mojo.

"And a cocktail to relax after a trying day," Michael Carter added, holding up his nearly empty sloe gin fizz sloshing in the bottom of a glassful of pink ice cubes.

"Looks like you're ready for another Shirley Temple there, sweetie," Dickinson said, looking at Carter smiling pink teeth at him.

"You offering to buy, sir?" Carter asked, pushing his glass to the bartender.

"You're not my idea of a date, but I think I'll spring for a round all around," Dicky Doo said, motioning for beers for himself, O'Connor, and Kirkwood. "And give the lady whatever pink shit that she's drinking today," he added, pointing at Michael Carter.

"What's the special occasion?" O'Connor said, taking his fresh mug of draft beer and pushing another bottle of Olympia to Jon Kirkwood, who sat silent on his stool and stuffed his wife's letter back in his pocket.

"Stanley and I fly to Okinawa on Tuesday morning," Dickinson said, and then looked directly at Kirkwood.

"Oh, really?" Jon said and forced a smile. "Business or pleasure?"

"A bit of both, I'm afraid," Dickinson answered, taking a sip from a fresh mug of Budweiser draft.

"That's too bad, sir," O'Connor offered. "Damned but they're always fucking up a good business trip with pleasure, aren't they."

Dicky Doo laughed.

"I guess I had that coming," he said and smiled. "After nearly nine months here, I have to admit some reluctance at enjoying myself for a week while you chaps hold down the fort."

"First R and R then, sir?" Kirkwood asked, finishing his earlier bottle of beer and then sliding it across the bar. "I heard that everyone rates it after four months. What happened?"

"Just never had time, you know, work, work, work," Dicky Doo said, drinking his beer.

"So our man Stanley will carry your bags for this business and pleasure trip," O'Connor said, reaching for a bowl of peanuts that the bartender had just filled and slid in front of the men.

"He and Charlie flipped for it, and Stanley won the toss," Dickinson said, taking a handful of peanuts and popping one in his mouth.

"Why weren't we included in the coin toss, sir?" Kirkwood then blurted.

"Well, this is the Fleet Marine Force Pacific legal conference, and I am representing the wing's defense side of the house," Dickinson said in an almost taunting voice to Kirkwood. "The only competition for the other representative slot logically had to go to the prosecution team. I'm afraid we can afford to send only two people. Sorry, Jon, I know how you want to see your wife."

"Stick it up your ass, sir," Kirkwood said, and then walked away from the bar toward the restroom, not waiting for a reply.

"Did you hear that?" Dickinson fumed, and looked at Michael Carter and Terry O'Connor.

"Hear what, sir?" Carter said, smiling his pink teeth.

O'Connor smiled, too, and shrugged.

"Look here," Dickinson then scowled, "that's insubordination and disrespect."

"Sorry, sir, I missed it," O'Connor said, drinking his beer. "Did Jon say something insubordinate? That's awfully out of character for him. Now, me? I wouldn't be surprised at anything I said."

"Where're the other two trolls from the defense section?" Dickinson snapped, shifting the conversation's subject to an area where he held better control.

"Trolls, sir?" O'Connor asked and then laughed. "No one has ever called me a troll that I can recall. I guess I need to grow out my hair and take up residence under the Han River Bridge."

"Keep it up, and you'll have to stand tall before the colonel," Dickinson cautioned the smart-aleck captain.

"Sir, if you want Lieutenant McKay and Lieutenant Ebberhardt, I think they've gone already," O'Connor said, and relaxed back on his bar stool.

"Where, Captain?" Dickinson said, relaxing on his bar stool, too.

"You know those two, they're always busy prowling around every weekend that they don't pull duty," O'Connor said, and then patted Jon Kirkwood on his shoulder as he came back to his seat. "Jon, Mike, and me, well, as you said, sir, you can always count on us hogs not straying too far from the well."

"I wanted to hold a meeting in my office at zero seven hundred tomorrow," Dicky Doo said, and then smiled a mean grin at the three captains. "The lieutenants skated again, but I know you'll be there. In my office at seven, gentlemen."

"Sir, can't it wait until Monday?" Carter said, trying to take up for his team and fulfill his role as senior defense section officer.

"No, Miss Carter, it cannot," Dickinson snapped back, "I have many things to attend on Monday, since I catch the freedom bird first thing Tuesday morning. We have to have our weekly conference Saturday morning, if that's okay with you, Captain."

"I guess the only saving grace of having a seven-o'clock meeting is knowing that you have to get to the office early on Saturday morning, too, sir," Kirkwood said, and turned up his bottle of Olympia.

Dickinson sat and thought a moment and then looked at Kirkwood.

"Okay, Jon," Dicky Doo said, "how about nine o'clock? I'll cut you a little slack."

"Seven, nine, it's okay, sir, whenever," Kirkwood replied.

"Nine o'clock, gentlemen," Dickinson said, and stood to leave. Then he looked back and laughed. "I nearly forgot to pass along the good news."

"I could use a bit of good news, sir. What is it?" Carter bubbled, and sucked on the swizzle stick straw of his sloe gin fizz.

"Couple of things, and I know that they will make all three of you happy," Dickinson said, smiling. "Promotion board published the selections for major today. Charlie Heyster made the list. He'll pin on his oak leaves within six months."

"Well, hell, sir," O'Connor chirped, "why isn't he here buying us beer?"

"You'll have ample opportunity to congratulate him, gentlemen," Dickinson said, nearly laughing. "He has agreed to extend in country another three months beyond the end of his regular tour, along with me."

"You extended too, sir?" Kirkwood asked.

"I had to," Dickinson said, offering a serious frown. "Colonel Prunella rotates home after the thirtieth of June. So he's out of here on the first freedom bird in July. As of today, Headquarters Marine Corps has not designated a replacement for him. Therefore, beginning July first, I will assume interim duties as staff judge advocate, until the new colonel arrives, mid-September at the earliest. Major-select Heyster will move up to my old job as military justice officer and deputy staff judge advocate. This plan also assures continuity of our office until most of us rotate in November and December."

"That's wonderful news, sir," O'Connor said, and then looked at Kirkwood and crossed his eyes. Jon Kirkwood laughed, seeing the face his buddy made, and then looked at Dicky Doo.

"You know, sir," Kirkwood said, still smiling, "I'm happy for you both. I am sure your family, and Major-select Heyster's are thrilled to no end at hearing this news."

"Nine o'clock, tomorrow, my office, gentlemen," Dickinson said as he left the bar, and then stopped halfway across the dance floor. "Oh, Kirkwood. Anything you want me to pass along to your wife while I am at Okinawa, just let me know."

"Thanks, sir. I'll think it over," Jon Kirkwood said, holding up his beer toward the major, mocking a toast, and extending his middle finger from the bottle.

A ROTUND, GRAY-BEARDED, retired master chief who had survived Pearl Harbor, piloted a Higgins boat at Iwo Jima, and landed Marines at Inchon smiled at Gwen Ebberhardt when she walked through the double glass doors that led into the lobby at the China Beach special services recreational area cabana check-in lobby and fast-food grill.

The stone-faced building that served as the beach headquarters, Laundromat, general store, gift shop, and café opened onto an earth-filled, concrete, and stone-fronted deck elevated above the sand and surrounded by a circular walkway. Colorful parasols shading picnic tables scattered across the patio and storefront that overlooked the broad stretch of sand and surf on the north side of the peninsula that jutted into the South China Sea like an outstretched arm reaching east from Da Nang.

A stone's throw west and slightly inland from the American forces R and R resort, Charlie Med bustled with saving lives of wounded from central I Corps' battlefields. Another kilometer south, on the opposite side of the strip of land, trees, and rocks, the Marble Mountain air facility rumbled day and night with hundreds of helicopters racing support to Marines scattered from Phu Bai to Chu Lai. East from the recreation area, near the tip of the peninsula, beneath the shadow of Monkey Mountain, U.S. Navy swift boats sailed to and from their mooring stations morning and night while merchant freighters and navy replenishment vessels landed thousands of tons of new equipment, supplies, and munitions on the half-dozen long concrete docks that stretched into the sea from the China Beach logistics wharf and cargo terminal.

"Hi, I'm Gwen Ebberhardt. I called from Da Nang this morning, and reserved a beach house for the weekend," the redheaded flight attendant said to the grizzled old sailor who stood behind the counter wearing a sky blue tank top shirt and blue, green, yellow, and white flower-covered Bermuda shorts. The skin on his barrel chest and thick, gray-hair-covered arms spoke of the sun. The green ink of his many tattoos lay nearly hidden beneath the dark-tanned color of his skin.

"Got ya right here, ma'am," the shaggy, silver-haired chief said, shoving a white registration card in front of her to fill out and sign. "Cabana 22B. Just back up that path, into those trees and the first duplex on the left. Your front window looks right out at the beach, just like you wanted."

"Oh, thanks so much," Gwen Ebberhardt said, and pointed to the smiling lieutenant standing behind her. "This is my husband, Lieutenant Wayne Ebberhardt."

"Glad to meet you, sir," the chief said, and put out his meaty paw for a shake. "I hope you enjoy your weekend with the pretty missus. You're a lucky fella getting to have your wife visit like this. Mostly we just get singles. Once in a while a contractor or embassy employee gets out here with his lady, but not many military folks. Yes, sir, you're a lucky one."

"I truly appreciate it, sir," Ebberhardt said, smiling while he filled out and signed the registration card.

"Oh, don't call me 'sir,' " the chief laughed, "I work for a living. Name's Master Chief Clinton Sparks, U.S. Navy, retired. Call me Chief or Sparky. Whichever suits your tongue best, sir."

"Well, Chief, I like the name Sparky," Ebberhardt said, picking up Gwen's flight bag and throwing the strap over his shoulder.

"You folks need anything, just hoist that little hailing flag by your front door and I'll send a houseboy running to your service," Chief Sparks said.

EARLIER THAT AFTERNOON, Rabbi Arthur Zimmerman had rented cabana 22A at the China Beach special services recreational area. When he heard the footsteps outside he thought it might be some of the five Jewish officers, two army captains, two air force captains, and a Marine lieutenant who had made plans to devote their weekend R and R together as a religious retreat, and use the time for personal meditation, prayer, and religious discussions with the navy chaplain.

However, when he heard the voices of the man and the woman in the room next door, the rabbi returned his attention to the Book of Tehillim (Psalms). Even as a boy, growing up in the Bronx, he had memorized many of its verses, and learned to sing the songs in the old Hebrew language, which made them even more beautiful to hear. The words that David had originally used when he sang them first gave their meaning a special significance for the rabbi.

As he read he sang to himself, waiting for the other officers to arrive. His voice carried out the open window and disappeared into the sounds of the crashing surf and the wind.

Now completing his second consecutive year in Vietnam as a lieutenant commander in the navy chaplain corps, Rabbi Zimmerman had heard God's voice speak to his heart three years ago, when President Lyndon Johnson ordered ground forces ashore at Da Nang. Until then he had shepherded a small congregation near the botanical gardens and Fordham University, just a few minutes by subway from Yankee Stadium, where outside his life in the synagogue he had devoted himself to raising his two sons as faithful Bronx Bomber fans, just like him.

Troubled after hearing the news of the Marines' landing at Da Nang's Red Beach in March 1965, he found himself unable to concentrate. Even with his sons, Ishmael and Ruben, at his side, cheering their beloved Yankees, Arthur Zimmerman's mind left the game and listened to his heart as it ached for the boys who left home and went to war in that place that most people then still called Indochina. Finally he told his wife, Ruth, that he had to go over to that place, too. There were good Jewish boys who needed a rabbi near them, to help them pray, to reassure them that God remained with them, especially in battle.

Assigned to Marines, he found himself praying a lot not only with the Jewish members of the Corps, but also with Baptists and Catholics and Presbyterians and Methodists, and one night he even prayed with a Muslim lad, just nineteen years old, who died as they spoke to Allah. As the boy faded, Arthur Zimmerman had recited Psalm 121 with the Christian brothers of the dying Marine from Los Angeles, whose mother and father had immigrated to California from Casa Blanca, Morocco, and named their son, born in Van Nuys in August 1948, Muhammad.

"*I will lift up mine eyes unto the hills, from whence cometh my help,*" the rabbi began reciting.

A Baptist boy from Oklahoma followed his opening phrase, saying with a trembling voice, "*My help cometh from the Lord, which made heaven and earth.*"

"*He will not suffer thy foot to be moved: he that keepeth thee will not slumber,*" the rabbi continued. "*Behold, he that keepeth Israel shall neither slumber nor sleep.*

"*The Lord is thy keeper: the Lord is thy shade upon thy right hand.*

"*The sun shall not smite thee by day, nor the moon by night.*

"*The Lord shall preserve thee from all evil: He shall preserve thy soul.*

"*The Lord shall preserve thy going out and thy coming in from this time forth, and even for evermore.*"

Rabbi Zimmerman wiped tears from his eyes as he remembered that night, nearly a year ago. Sitting on the wicker-bottom, ladder-back chair by the small dining table near the window, he sang a song that David had first played as a simple shepherd, long before he became king of Israel, a song that rejoiced over God's personal care. "*O Lord thou hast searched me, and known me. Thou knowest my downsitting and mine uprising, thou understandest my thought afar off."*

He closed his eyes as he sang to himself, waiting, and his voice carried into the evening and the setting sun as he heard the man and woman from next door leave their room. He opened his eyes to see them, and watched the couple walking, holding hands, meandering across the sand toward the beach and the crashing water, with the lowering afternoon sun beginning to tint the clouds orange.

He thought of Ruth and home, his two boys, and the Yankees, now finishing their last week of spring training in Florida.

"Commander Zimmerman," a voice called from outside.

"Oh, Frank, in here. Come in, please," the rabbi answered, and went to the door to greet the lieutenant named Frank Alexander from the Seventh Marine Regiment.

"I saw Captain Fine and Captain Jacobs up at the gedunk," the lieutenant said. "You want to go up there and grab a hamburger and beer with them?"

"Oh, that sounds good," the rabbi said, picking up his cap and walking out the door with the Marine. "I thought that Michael and Eric probably went shopping or sightseeing, since I had not yet seen them and the shuttle from the air base came through here an hour ago. I think that they may have arrived with the couple who have the room next door.

"Our two army friends from Chu Lai have a long journey, so I expect that they will arrive late, but hopefully before the Sabbath begins this evening. They will likely get here while we're at the restaurant. Do you think we ought to wait for them before we eat? You may be too hungry to wait, though."

"No, Rabbi, I am fine. Let's wait for them. We can grab a beer first, and then order our food once their bus gets here. It's due at any minute anyway," the lieutenant said, glancing at his watch while walking with the chaplain. Casually, the two men strolled to the bar and grill, where a growing crowd of servicemen, and a few women, nearly all of them clad in beachwear, stood in small clusters, drinking beer or cocktails, or sat at the picnic tables beneath the rainbow of parasols as the outdoor lights and the Tiki torches brightened and the evening faded toward darkness.

The two air force captains who had ridden the shuttle with Wayne and Gwen Ebberhardt sat at a picnic table and waved when they saw the rabbi and the Marine. With the pair of air force officers sat an army captain named Raymond Segal, and another named Joel Stein, who waved, too. Their bus had just arrived.

*   *   *

"HONEY! YOU CAN'T go in there," Gwen Ebberhardt said as her husband ducked around the partition that divided cabana 22B's front porch and patio from that of cabana 22A's. "They'll think you're trying to steal something."

"Nobody's here," Wayne Ebberhardt answered as he looked through the screen of the open front window of the quarters next to his in the beach-house duplex. "I don't think they rented it to anyone."

"How could you come to that conclusion by just looking in the window?" Gwen asked, standing by the low hedge in front of cabana 22A's small patio, watching Wayne search the interior from outside.

"They have a rollaway bed and three cots stacked by the wall," he answered, walking away from the window and stepping over the shrubbery. "You know, a bunch of spare stuff. They're using this room for storage. It probably has plumbing problems or something."

"Why on earth should you care whether or not anyone lives in that room?" Gwen said, putting her arm around Wayne's waist and walking with him to their patio.

"First of all, honey," the lieutenant told his wife, "I like my privacy. Did you see how thin the walls are in this cabana? A layer of plaster over a few laths, and that's it. Somebody in there could hear everything."

"You're such a prude," Gwen laughed. "You're afraid someone will hear us fucking? Come on, Wayne, the walls aren't that thin. And so what if they are. We're married and I love my husband. If anyone hears us making love, then it's their problem, certainly not mine. They don't have to listen, you know."

Wayne smiled and cocked his eyes to a devilish slant.

"Oh, you want to be bad, don't you!" Gwen said, and returned the mischievous glance.

"Me want play Tarzan," the lieutenant said, and beat his chest with his fists. "Tarzan want get naked and hump like monkey in tree with Jane."

Then Wayne Ebberhardt scooped his wife off her feet and carried her into their cabana, and with his foot, slammed the front door shut.

EARLIER THAT EVENING, while eating their hamburgers and drinking cold beer, the air force captain named Michael Fine had pointed out to his four Jewish brothers and the rabbi the beautiful redhead in the pink bikini bathing suit eating fish and fried potatoes with the man in the red T-shirt and baggy, flower-print surfer shorts.

"They rode the shuttle with us this afternoon," Captain Fine whispered across the table to his comrades. "He's a Marine and she's a stewardess."

"You know, I bet they're married," Rabbi Zimmerman commented. "Look at how they love each other. He's a very lucky fellow to have his wife here for a weekend."

The army captain named Ray Segal laughed and looked at the other officers, who smiled and agreed with his skepticism.

"Rabbi, I mean no disrespect, but do you honestly believe what you just said?" Segal said, raising his dark eyebrows at the group's religious mentor.

"I know what you're thinking, and given the laws of probability, you're more likely right than wrong," Arthur Zimmerman said, looking at the half-eaten hamburger resting on his plate. "I say what I hope is the truth. I want to believe the best about people, not the worst. I think that is important for all of us to try to do."

"Rabbi, this is Vietnam, don't forget. A combat zone," Joel Stein said, echoing his army colleague's skepticism at the couple. "Eric and Michael rode the shuttle with them, and said that the man is a Marine and the woman an airline stewardess. Those two might be married, but not to each other."

"I have to agree with Joel and the others, Rabbi," Marine Lieutenant Frank Alexander said. "After all, that man's a Marine, and I know Marines, don't forget. And look how the woman flaunts her nakedness. The bathing suit hardly covers her lower regions, and she might as well take off the top. It hides nothing. Would a faithful married woman dress like that at all? Would a husband allow his wife to dress like that?"

Rabbi Zimmerman shrugged as he picked up the hamburger from his plate and took a large bite.

After several rounds of beer following their hamburgers, the Jewish officers headed down the gravel walkway to their cabana. The couple had long ago left the restaurant patio, and the evening twilight had descended into night. Tiki torches lit the way to their room, and the six men laughed as they stumbled along the path.

Realizing that they had allowed their beer and fellowship to take them well into the time when many people had gone to sleep or had retired to quiet contentment before sleep, they silently made their way into cabana 22A. The six men had seen a dim light from the neighboring room, so they did their best not to disturb the people next door as they prepared their beds, drawing names from the rabbi's hat to determine who slept where.

Since it was already late, they quietly decided not to have any further Sabbath discussions tonight, but would go to sleep and start fresh in the morning.

In the dark silence all six men soon realized that the purring and groaning sounds they heard from next door did not come from anyone's slumber. Then the voices spoke.

"Oh, Tarzan!" the female sighed, and moaned. "Oh, oh, please, oh! Tarzan so bad. Bad to Jane. Oh, oh, oh, so bad."

Then came a bang on the wall, and a thud on the floor.

"Jane, bad girl. Jane need spanking," the man spoke, and the sound of a hand slapping skin followed.

"Ouch, Wayne! That's too hard, honey," the woman said.

"*Umgawa!*" the man answered, and the sound of a hand slapping skin came again.

"Damn it, Tarzan! Jane not going to play if you spank so hard!" the woman's voice cried back.

"Okay, okay, honey! Come back, please. I won't spank you so hard," the man's playful voice then pled.

"For Pete sake, Wayne," the woman's voice said, "don't you ever run down? I've got to pee anyway."

Then came a bang and a crash, and the man cried out a nearly flaw-less imitation of Johnny Weissmuller's Tarzan jungle yell.

"What was that, Wayne?" the woman's voice called from the bath-room. "Did Tarzan break something again?"

A few seconds later she cried out, "Oh, Tarzan! Bad boy! Just look what you've done. How on earth did you manage to knock the bed flat to the floor?"

"*Umgawa,*" the man's voice answered. "Cheetah break bed, blame Tarzan; jump out window."

Then the man let out another jungle yell, and the woman laughed.

WHEN DAYLIGHT SHONE through the front window, Rabbi Zimmerman still had the pillow over his head. No matter what he tried, he could not cease from hearing the couple's lovemaking and romping. When the door slammed from the neighboring room, the chaplain opened his eyes and sat up.

"How on earth can those two do that all night and get up so early?" Eric Jacobs said, sitting up from one of the folding cots.

"Love is a wonderful thing," the rabbi answered, rubbing his aching eyes. "It fills our spirits with energy. It brightens the whole world. If my Ruth were here, we would have already been on the beach this morning."

"Rabbi," Joel Stein said, walking to the bathroom, "I believe if your Ruth or my Ellen were here, they would have knocked on those people's door last night and told them one or two things."

"Joel, you're a stick-in-the-mud," the rabbi said.

BOTH JON KIRKWOOD and Terry O'Connor waited until five minutes past nine Saturday morning before they walked inside Major Dickinson's office. Michael Carter had arrived fifteen minutes early and sat on the couch with his knee bouncing, glancing at his watch every few seconds as he and Dicky Doo waited for the two captains to come in and sit down.

When the pair finally walked into the room and took their seats, Dudley Dickinson didn't look up from the papers he read for another ten minutes. Then he glared at the two men for a full thirty seconds before he spoke.

"I saw you standing behind the building ten minutes before nine, gentlemen," Dickinson spat. "Keep up this disrespect and insubordination, and you'll catch every duty quota that comes to headquarters squadron."

"Each of us in the defense section already stands duty three and four times a month, sir," Kirkwood said, opening a stenographer pad and clicking the point out on his pen, ready to take notes. "I didn't know that the law center could get tasked with any more extra-duty quotas than we already stand now."

"I am sure that other work sections will gladly pass along their quotas for us to fill, Captain," Dickinson answered, "so don't press the issue. Your fellow defense team members will regret it. Now, what about Ebberhardt and McKay? Anyone see them since yesterday evening when we had our drinks at the bar?"

"They must have slept over someplace else," Carter offered.

"No one from our section has seen them, sir," Kirkwood interjected before Michael Carter could say too much.

"They'd better not be out flying with that idiot Captain Gunn," Dickinson growled. "That man is a menace to anyone's sanity. Throwing hand grenades from the window of his plane. What if one fell back in the cockpit? My God!"

"I can't say, sir," Kirkwood answered before Michael Carter could open his mouth and put his foot in it.

"Well, to business then, gentlemen," Dickinson said, and then began passing manila folders to the three captains. "You can brief the two wayward lieutenants when you see them, hopefully before Monday, when I want them both standing tall in front of my desk at zero seven hundred."

Jon Kirkwood flipped open the folder that the mojo had handed to him, and began reading the charge sheet and supporting statements.

"That boy's a real bad egg," Dickinson said, watching Kirkwood read. "Sergeant Donald T. Wilson, soon to be private, I would say: calling his platoon commander a coward, in front of the entire platoon and the company commander."

"He really say all this shit?" Kirkwood said, looking up. Then the captain looked down and read aloud:

"*The men don't like you because you're an asshole-fucking coward, Lieutenant. I'll bet that you even squat to pee. You have to because you sure the fuck don't have any balls. You fucking pussy!*"

"I think we met him at Fire Base Ross," O'Connor laughed.

"He's from up north, with the light antiaircraft missile battalion," Kirkwood said, looking at O'Connor. "Definitely a healthy grunt mentality though."

"Captain Kirkwood," Major Dickinson said, looking at a list of notes scribbled on a yellow legal pad, "you may want to joke about him, but I would not get too close to this man. When you talk to him it is advisable that you have a guard present with you. Sergeant Wilson remains deeply agitated with anyone who tries to talk to him, and he is especially pissed at officers."

"I'll feel him out. See how he acts," Kirkwood said, discounting what the major had warned because the officers and enlisted men who had talked to Wilson until now represented the prosecution and jailers.

"A bit of background then, Captain," Dickinson said, leaning back in his chair. "Maybe a week, or ten days ago, Wilson's lieutenant had sat down on his cot and when he bent over to untie his boots he noticed a can under his cot. He also smelled gasoline. When he looked more closely at the can, he saw that someone had placed a hand grenade in it.

"Of course, this sent the lieutenant flying out of his hooch, and outside he encountered Sergeant Wilson and several of his men, who began laughing.

"The company commander called an explosive ordnance technician to come deal with the booby trap. He had to crawl under the cot and tip the can to one side to see if the grenade was a frag or an illume. It was a frag. Someone had pulled the pin and wrapped the spoon with masking tape, and dropped it in the can of gasoline. Theoretically, the gas would dissolve the glue on the tape and release the spoon. However, due to poor planning on the perpetrator's part, he got too small of a can, so the spoon still did not release.

"Our EOD guy had to tie a long cotton string to the can and gently drag it outside. Then he had to carry it to the burn barrels. Using the string again, the explosive specialist pulled the can onto its side so that the grenade fell out.

"Gentlemen, when it detonated, it put a definite fear factor into all the officers at that missile battery up on the Hai Van Pass. Both the company and platoon commanders concur that they believe that Sergeant Wilson planted that grenade.

"A few evenings later, someone tossed a live grenade on the tin roof of the officers' hooch. It clattered down, bounced on the ground, and exploded. Luckily, no one got hurt here either. It did tear a hole in the wall and peppered the hooch with fragments.

"Since then, we have had repeated instances of troops throwing rocks on the tin roof of the officers' hooch, sending the Marines inside scrambling out. This gives the enlisted men there no end to entertainment.

"We have to make an example of Sergeant Wilson, gentlemen. I hope that you can appreciate why."

"Sir, we're the defense attorneys," O'Connor said, tilting his head to one side and narrowing his eyes. "That sounds like something you need to tell the prosecution."

"Don't you worry about the prosecution, Captain," Dicky Doo snapped back, "Major-Select Heyster will make sure that Sergeant Donald T. Wilson is made a lasting example. You just need to do what is right, too, and make sure that this man gets what he deserves."

"Sir," Kirkwood said, cutting off Terry O'Connor's hot temper, "rest assured we will seek justice for Sergeant Wilson. I can assure you we will strive to ensure that this Marine gets what he deserves."

Dicky Doo sat back in his swivel chair and scowled.

"No judge will allow Charlie to introduce any of this fragging business as evidence against Sergeant Wilson," O'Connor said, fidgeting in his chair, unable to keep the voice of his passion for justice in check. "I know that's what Major-Select Shyster has up his sleeve or you guys wouldn't—"

"It's my case, Terry," Kirkwood interrupted. "I'll take care of it. We will make sure this Marine gets what he deserves!"

Terry O'Connor clamped his jaws tight and took a deep breath.

"Captain Carter," Dickinson said, looking at the disheveled lawyer with his knees under his chin, sitting on the couch, "your client, the Magnificent Kilgore, has done it again."

"Escaped, sir," Carter said, smiling and blushing.

"Oh, and I know that Captains Kirkwood and O'Connor will have a good laugh with this one, so let me entertain you with another amusing story," the mojo said.

"Our illustrious Private Thomas Kilgore, incarcerated last November, probably a week before you two arrived here, has flown the coop for the third time. I can't prove it, but our good Captain Michael Carter, sitting there so dumb and innocent, probably knows much more about Kilgore's escape than he will ever let on.

"I know you knew he had this planned," Dicky Doo snapped at Carter.

"Anyway," the mojo sighed, and again leaned back in his chair, "Thomas Kilgore is a thief. Not just your ordinary, run-of-the-mill petty criminal, but a man who will steal anything not nailed or chained or padlocked. We locked him up for unauthorized absence and grand theft. He stole a truck full of utility uniforms and boots and drove it to Hill 55, and started passing them out to all the Marines there.

"This mental-midget friend of yours, First Lieutenant Michael Schuller, the duty brig officer at the time of the escape, decided that Private Kilgore deserved to go outside the wire on a working party. The chasers no sooner had unloaded the prisoners to start work than the Magnificent Kilgore made like a rabbit straight into this Vietnamese village.

"Two MPs responded to the chaser's radio call and pursued Kilgore into the village. When they parked their jeep to search the back of a hooch, Kilgore slipped around the other side and stole the damned jeep.

"So he's gone again!"

Jon Kirkwood started to laugh, and fought back the urge, but then broke down. Seeing their pal crumble, Terry O'Connor and Michael Carter both let go, too.

"Gentlemen!" Dicky Doo said, at first trying to rein in his lawyers, but then he started to laugh, too. "Oh, shit. You're right. It is funny."

"Can you see those MPs? Kilgore waving good-bye to them as he heads to town?" Carter said, laughing hysterically now.

"One more item and we'll call it a day," Dickinson said, wiping his eyes. "Carter, you have the con on this case. One Corporal James Gillette, spelled like the razor blades, shot a hooker a week ago Wednesday night. He's assigned to the information services office, along with two other corporals we charged with him, although Gillette pulled the trigger. The specifications include assault with a deadly weapon, battery, attempted murder.

"Lieutenant McKay has already met with the two accomplices, and they have agreed to plea out for lesser charges, settling for restriction, a fine, and reduction to lance corporal. We'll take this lad Gillette to trial next Wednesday, after I get back from Okinawa.

"It's open and shut. We have statements from the two lance corporals, and the statement from the hooker, who is fully recovering and is already back on the street."

"Must not have been that bad then," O'Connor said.

"Naw, the bullet just grazed her ear, took off a piece of it," Dickinson said and laughed. "The corporal was lucky he was a lousy shot. However, the illustrious Major Tran Van Toan, one of the local constabulary's hardhead district chiefs, demanded that we prosecute this lad for clipping the girl's ear. So we gotta do it."

Dickinson stood behind his desk and crossed his arms.

"Any questions, comments, or concerns?" he asked.

"See you Monday, then, sir," Kirkwood said, grabbing his notebook and hat, and then headed out the door. Terry O'Connor and Michael Carter fell in step behind him.

"We'll make sure to get the word to the lieutenants, sir," Carter called over his shoulder as the trio left.

Terry O'Connor slugged the thoughtless captain on the arm when they got past Dicky Doo's door.

SHORTLY AFTER TEN o'clock Saturday morning, Wayne Ebberhardt trudged up the sandy slope from the beach to the cabana that he and Gwen had rented. While she lay facedown on a blanket with her bikini top unfastened and pulled off her shoulders, her husband went to get a bucket of ice, some sandwiches, chips, and a six-pack of Cokes. He stopped by their room to use the toilet on his way to the gedunk.

Rabbi Zimmerman waved when he saw Wayne Ebberhardt, and the lieutenant waved back. The chaplain and five officers sat in a circle on the patio, discussing ethics while the rabbi guided them with passages he read from the Torah.

Seeing the chaplain with a tallith draped over his shoulders and all six officers wearing yarmulkes on their heads stopped Lieutenant Ebberhardt for a moment. Then the rabbi motioned for him to come close and talk.

"Don't worry, sir, you're not interrupting a thing," Zimmerman said, smiling as he stood and then put out his hand. "I am Lieutenant Commander Arthur Zimmerman, one of the many navy chaplains assigned to you Marines here in I Corps."

"Wayne Ebberhardt, sir," the lieutenant said. "I'm a lawyer with the First Marine Aircraft Wing. That's my wife, Gwen, down at the beach. She's with Flying Tigers."

"Wonderful!" Zimmerman said, and then smiled a quick look of great satisfaction at the five men who had also risen to their feet, and uncomfortably smiled back. "You and your wife. What a lucky man you are. I saw my wife one year ago, when I took leave. Oh, if I could see her and my two sons now. If they could see this beautiful beach."

"I feel embarrassed that I interrupted your worship," Wayne Ebberhardt said, still feeling that he had intruded on something private and sacred.

"No, no, don't feel that way, please," Arthur Zimmerman said. "We celebrate the Sabbath with prayer, of course, but also with friendship, lively discussions, and love of our families. You disturbed nothing. Please join us if you wish. We were talking about ethics and divine will. The battlefield, you well know, puts our ethics and our faith to a great test."

"I would love to join you, believe me. The discussion sounds fascinating," Ebberhardt said, and then turned toward the beach and pointed. "However, the time that my wife and I have together is very precious to us. I hope you understand."

"Think nothing about it!" the chaplain said, waving his hand as he spoke. "In your shoes, I would be there on that blanket with my Ruth right now."

The chaplain looked back at the five men still standing and saying nothing.

"Well, at least let me introduce my friends here," the rabbi said, stepping to one side and laying his hand back in a sweeping gesture. "Starting from the left, I would like you to meet Captain Joel Stein and Captain Raymond Segal, both from the army's American Division at Chu Lai. Then we have your fellow Marine First Lieutenant Frank Alexander from the Seventh Marines based on Hill 55, southwest of Da Nang. From your own Da Nang Air Base, please meet Captain Michael Fine and Captain Eric Jacobs, both from the U.S. Air Force."

As the rabbi introduced each man, Wayne Ebberhardt shook his hand.

"Well, it is good to meet all of you," the lawyer said, and began to walk toward the patio of cabana 22B. "I do need to get back with my wife, though."

"Oh, sure, please don't let us keep you," the rabbi answered.

Then as Wayne Ebberhardt stepped through the low hedge that fronted his cabana's patio, he looked back at the group. One question had troubled him from the moment he saw the six men sitting next door. He had to ask.

"You guys checked in this morning, right?" Ebberhardt queried, hoping for a yes answer.

Rabbi Zimmerman lowered his face and shook his head while the lieutenant and all but one captain just gave Wayne Ebberhardt a wide-eyed, blank look.

"*Umgawa*, Tarzan," Joel Stein said and spread a wide grin across his face. "We checked in yesterday."

Chapter 10

THE SETUP

"WHEN I GET back from the brig, want to have lunch?" Jon Kirkwood asked Terry O'Connor as he put on his starched utility cover and headed toward the barracks doors.

"I may not get back that soon," O'Connor answered, leaning back and looking around his wall locker door to see his buddy. "I finally got hold of that staff sergeant. You remember, with the Huey? Toby Dixon."

"Yeah, nice guy," Kirkwood said, stopping at the door. "Was he worried about the rifles and headsets? Bet he wondered if we just ripped him off."

"He wasn't too worried since they have shit fall out of the helicopters all the time, and he was never signed out with the rifles in the first place," O'Connor said and smirked. "He admitted that was how he came across the two M14s; in the confusion of the moment somebody left them behind. Dixon said that hauling people scrambling to just get out of a hot LZ alive, piling in whatever gear that got dropped by others during their hasty departures, the choppers end up with lots of extra stuff, believe it or not. I guess the battalions just mark it up to lost in action."

"Yeah, and write up the poor schmuck who dropped his weapon, unless he got seriously wounded or killed," Kirkwood added. "The brig's full of guys who couldn't shit a helmet, flak jacket or, heaven forbid, a rifle when the first sergeant held inspection."

"Hey, you know, that's the Marine Corps," O'Connor chuckled, shaking his head, shouldering the two rifles. "Hell, the guys who lost these peashooters probably already did six months in the can for it."

"What's the deal with lunch, though? It's only ten-thirty," Kirkwood said, looking at his watch.

"Yeah, I know," O'Connor said, joining his partner at the door, "but Staff Sergeant Dixon's squadron moved from the base, here, over to Marble Mountain. I'm catching a chopper there now. Don't you want to come? You can see your renegade sergeant this afternoon or tomorrow. What the hell's the rush?"

"I know," Kirkwood said, walking out the door with O'Connor, "but I can't stop thinking about how this sergeant must feel, getting interrogated for three days in the brig, and not having anyone on his side. You know Charlie Heyster has given him the shits by now. No telling what the son of a bitch told the kid. Probably sat there pretending to defend him while the guy got the third degree by Dicky Doo himself, no doubt. No, the sooner I talk to Sergeant Donald T. Wilson, the better."

"You sure the fuck aren't going to let that mojo SOB get that fragging bullshit introduced as evidence," O'Connor snarled. "One part of me stands fully shocked and amazed, but deep in my heart I know that's what Dicky Doo will push. Look, we're talking about a matter of simple disrespect: an offense they should have handled with office hours, for crying out loud. Article fifteen, nonjudicial punishment by the man's company commander, maybe boot it up to the missile battery commanding officer. They've got this case already elevated to special court-martial status, and I'll bet they'd love to pretend it's murder and boot it on up to a general court-martial if they can. Don't count that out."

"That's why I've got to get to the brig and dig into Sergeant Wilson's skull," Kirkwood said. "This stinks of railroading. I'll bet you next month's pay they did their dead level best to try to pin a charge of attempted murder on this guy but just had no evidence. We've definitely got a fight on our hands. I only hope that this kid will open up and talk to me. Otherwise he's dead meat."

"Hopefully, Wayne and I can get the Celestine Anderson trial put to bed this week," O'Connor said, walking with Kirkwood to the staff jeep. "Then I can pitch in with you on this one. I've got a head of steam worked up for this Sergeant Wilson. I'd love to have the combination to the lock for the inside of his head. Bet that would be an eye-opener."

"I'll keep you posted on what develops," Kirkwood said, getting into the jeep. "What time you think you'll be back? Maybe we can catch evening chow."

"Sure, probably three or four o'clock," O'Connor said, getting in the jeep's passenger seat. "Give me a lift to the flight line, if you don't mind."

"Yeah, no sweat," Kirkwood said, backing the vehicle into the street and heading down the roadway to the apron, where rows of helicopters sat. "You just going there and back?"

"I might swing over to China Beach and try to grab lunch with Wayne and his wife," O'Connor said, and flashed a toothy grin at Kirkwood. "Might get a good look at how she trims out in beachwear, if you know what I mean."

"You're a degenerate, you know that?" Kirkwood scoffed. "She's a man's wife, for Pete's sake. You'd look up her dress if she uncrossed her legs, wouldn't you."

"Damned right I would," O'Connor hooted. "Nothing wrong with a little sightseeing."

"I'm going to tell Wayne you're lusting after his wife, you perverted sack of shit," Kirkwood huffed with a halfhearted laugh.

"That's right, me and every hard dick between here and wherever her freedom bird lands," O'Connor smirked, blowing off his pal's idle threat. "Wayne had to learn to live with that fact of life long ago, my friend. You recall what they did to us in the O Club, don't forget. He seems pretty comfortable with it, if you ask me."

"You've got a point," Kirkwood said, pulling the jeep to a stop in front of a Quonset hut where several Marines in helicopter flight gear milled around. "Just don't get any bright ideas about leering at Katie that way when we get home."

Terry O'Connor jumped out of the jeep, grabbed the two rifles and pairs of headsets, and jogged toward the hut.

"Your wife is a fox, Jon," he shouted back, looking over his shoulder and jeering. "I have wet dreams about her."

SITTING IN THE door of the Huey, Terry O'Connor could see Toby Dixon standing on the tarmac outside the ready room door as the chopper set down at the Marble Mountain air facility. Another man, dressed in a green flight suit, stood next to the staff sergeant, and waved when Dixon raised his hand to signal the captain.

"How's it going, sir?" Dixon said, greeting O'Connor on the flight line. "I wanted to catch you before you went inside with those rifles. So we didn't get asked questions."

"Sure, whatever you like," O'Connor said. "Where do you want to put them?"

"Right over here," Dixon said, walking down the asphalt apron past a row of UH1H Hueys and several AH1J Cobra helicopter gunships. "We'll stick them back in the cargo box on my plane."

"Terry O'Connor," the captain said, putting out his hand to Dixon's friend, who had a rank insignia with three inverted chevrons under an eagle pinned on the leather name patch of his flight suit, and "HN1 Doc Adams" stamped below it in gold lettering.

"Sorry about that, sir," Dixon said, pointing to the man. "That's my home boy, Bobby Adams. We call him Doc. Of course, we call all corpsmen Doc."

"Doc Adams, just like on TV, you know, *Gunsmoke*," O'Connor said, shaking the hospital corpsman's hand. "You get any Matt Dillon, Chester, or Festus jokes?"

"No, sir," Bobby Adams answered, shrugging. "I think you're the first to ever make that observation. Besides, I thought that was Doc Holliday. You know, Dodge City and all."

"He was Wyatt Earp's partner," O'Connor said, walking to the side of Dixon's helicopter and handing the crew chief the headsets and rifles. "Doc Adams was on with Matt Dillon and Miss Kitty."

"My grandmother always watched *Gunsmoke*," Dixon said, shutting the lid on the helicopter's cargo box. "I was like ten years old when I saw it with her. That was when Chester was still on the show. We always thought it was Doc Holliday."

"Now they got Festus, and that new kid that's the gunsmith, Newly what's his name," O'Connor said.

"So, where you headed now, sir?" Dixon asked, walking back toward the ready room.

"Thought I might catch a shuttle to China Beach and have lunch with a buddy and his wife," the captain answered.

"Going to be about forty-five minutes or so wait," Dixon said, looking at his wristwatch. "Want to grab some coffee with Bobby and me?"

"Hey, thanks," O'Connor said, looking at his watch, too, and following the two men inside the crew lounge where a silver, two-gallon coffee urn sat with its black-handled spigot hanging over the edge of the table, enabling a person to fill one of the oversized mugs from the stack of glassware that sat by the big pot.

"Where're you guys from?" O'Connor said, taking a seat on one of the brown vinyl-covered lounge chairs ringed around a coffee table.

"Me and Toby grew up together in Artesia, New Mexico," Bobby Adams said, sitting in a chair across from the captain.

"Yes, sir, we went through grade school, junior high, and high school together," Dixon said, sitting next to the navy corpsman. "We played football, basketball, and baseball. Won state championship in football our senior year, 1965. I played halfback on the offense, and Bobby played end on defense. We was good."

Then the staff sergeant pushed up the sleeve of his flight suit, exposing the dark brown skin of his forearm for the captain to see.

"Sir, take a look at this bulldog I got tattooed here. That's not a Marine Corps bulldog, that's an Artesia bulldog."

"You guys graduated in 1965 and you're a staff sergeant and Bobby's a first-class petty officer?" O'Connor said, quickly calculating their time in service. "That's quite impressive, both of you making E6 in about half the time it normally takes a person."

"People come from where we do," Dixon said, looking at his hometown pal. "We're raised that way. Put out one hundred and ten percent. Our coach back home, he'd take off our heads if we didn't. Coach, he even had these Vince Lombardi signs all over the locker room. Winning is the only thing. Operating on Lombardi time, ten minutes early. All that stuff. So we learned only one way to do anything. That's nothing less than our best. Rank just kinda happens for us both. I guess natural, given where we come from, and how we were raised."

Bobby Adams smiled and added, "Also, our occupations have a lot more opportunity for advancement. Aviation and medicine, both high demand and you can't be a rock."

"Still impressive, Doc," O'Connor said, and took a sip from his coffee. "Me, I graduated high school in Philadelphia in 1958. Born and raised there. I was too small to play football. I love the game, though."

"You live where we grew up," Adams said, smiling, "even you would have played football. If a guy didn't at least go out for football, he had to put on a dress and pick up pom-poms."

"Hey, look at me," the captain said, standing and turning around. "Five-foot-ten if I stretch. I'm all of what, a hundred fifty-six pounds, dripping wet with my stomach full. Not your standard state football champion material. Back in high school, I couldn't get my weight beyond a hundred thirty-five pounds."

"Philadelphia's probably a lot different than Artesia, too," Dixon added. "We had a hundred fifty, maybe two hundred students in our class. Hell, the whole high school wasn't more than five or six hundred kids total. Where you grew up, you most likely had six hundred in your class."

"We had eight hundred fifty graduates in my senior class," O'Connor said, nodding at the two men. "That's after half the population dropped out when they turned fifteen. Big, inner-city school. Predominantly black. Tough as hell, too."

"So, your old man a steelworker or coal miner?" Dixon asked and smiled.

"You're thinking of western Pennsylvania and places like Pittsburgh," O'Connor said, putting his feet on the coffee table when he saw the two enlisted men do it. "My dad is a college professor. Teaches history at the University of Pennsylvania. I joined the Marines to please him, one of the reasons. He fought on Iwo Jima, and I admired him for it, so I thought he'd like me joining the Marine Corps, too. I got a rude awakening when I told him what I had done."

"Why's that, sir?" Bobby Adams said, raising his eyebrows.

"He's dead set against this war, right from the get-go," O'Connor said and shrugged. "He never really talked about it with me, nothing serious, just mixed with all the other political garbage he'd spew while reading the newspaper. I should have figured it out, though, when he pushed me to enroll at Columbia University in New York rather than Pennsylvania. I just assumed that he considered Columbia Law School top drawer. Me and my blinders, I can't see the forest for the trees. So I graduated college in '62, law school in '64, and then joined the Marines.

"Columbia, as you may know, is to the East Coast liberal community what the University of California at Berkeley is to the West Coast left wing.

"I knew my dad was an old school Democrat, and I took his comments about the war to be simply that of a history professor. I never really understood the depth of his passion against this war until I came home and surprised him with my contract and orders to OCS, TBS, and Naval Justice School at Bridgeport, Connecticut, after I finished law school."

"Shit, sir, being a lawyer beats hell out of being a private in the army, which is what you would have gotten had you hung out for the draft to get you," Bobby Adams commented, and took a sip of his coffee.

"Absolutely right, but my dad would have rather seen me drafted in the army, or better yet, ducked out to Canada," O'Connor said, and laughed. "You should have seen him when I voted for Barry Goldwater that same year, on top of joining the Marines, and then told him about that, too. The little rusty-headed Irishman was on his toes and in my face, screaming how I betrayed everything he had ever taught me to believe. He's a couple of inches shorter than me and has a firecracker temper, if you can picture it. I thought his head would explode. Me in the Marine Corps, and then voting for Goldwater. He blew his gaskets.

"He's pissed off at President Johnson, says he won't vote for Humphrey either, since he's Johnson's man and probably crooked. He doesn't trust Bobby Kennedy, and sure as hell won't vote for Nixon or *any* Republican, for that matter. So now he's preaching Eugene McCarthy since he came out against the war with that book of his, *Limits of Power*, which lambastes Johnson's foreign policy and the war. McCarthy damned near beat Johnson in the New Hampshire primary with forty-two percent of the vote, probably the biggest reason Johnson decided to bow out of the race, but still I don't think Clean Gene's got a prayer, despite his victory over Bobby Kennedy in the Oregon primary. At any rate, my dad told me if I voted for anybody other than his man McCarthy, I should consider moving to Arizona, where Republican lawyers are welcome."

"So your ole man's a peacenik, huh," Dixon said and laughed. "So's my mama, except she loves Bobby Kennedy. My dad, he got killed driving an asphalt truck when I was in junior high, so my mama raised me, put me through high school, my brother now, too, and she's just like your daddy, can't stand Johnson or Humphrey. Man, I'd like to see those two start talking."

"I got something to top that," O'Connor said, taking a sip of his coffee and looking at the two men. "I got a Swedish girlfriend the FBI investigated when I got my commission and they did the background check on me. She's a corker, and puts my dad to shame with his social conscience. Vibeke, that's her name, Vibeke Ahlquist, she used to keep me in trouble with the crap she wrote, getting it published in the *Daily Worker* newspaper, a propaganda rag that the Communists distribute there at Columbia University. Still, I get clipped because of her. She preaches against the war, and I get blamed for it. I'm a fucking Republican, damn it!"

The two enlisted men laughed with the captain.

"I checked in, and got the third degree from the military justice officer, right off the bat," O'Connor added. "Dicky fucking Doo and his don'ts, the motherfucker. He's got a poster put up in his office with his long list of don'ts written on it. Don't do this and don't do that. Now you want to talk about the exact opposite end of the spectrum from where your mother, my dad, and Vibeke sit, just take a look at Major Dudley L. Dickinson."

"Shit, sir, the woods are full of assholes like that around here," Dixon offered. "We're top-heavy with radical fanatical lifers with concrete for brains. Then, I guess to balance out things, we got guys like you, my skipper, Captain Oliver, and some other pretty good officers with hearts and brains. Like ol' Major Danger over at LZ Ross. Now, there's a good guy.

"By the way, sir, he told us about you and the other captain getting medals for valor over at Ross when we dumped your asses there last fall."

"Yeah, the medals surprised Captain Kirkwood and me both," O'Connor said and laughed. "Just another Cracker Jack prize, though. Navy Commendation medals get passed out for keeping the files straight these days."

"Big difference between the admin medal, that Cracker Jack prize, and what you got, sir," Adams interrupted, sitting up and giving the captain a serious frown. "Check that ribbon and see if it doesn't have that little bronze V stuck in the middle. That's the important part. Bronze Star gets passed out for showing up for meals on time if you're in the army these days, but that little V on the ribbon separates the wheat from the chaff."

"Right on, sir," Dixon added, "that little V says you earned the medal committing heroic action while under fire against a hostile enemy. Major Hembee, he told us all about you and your buddy holding the line that night. You two being officers but manning that fighting hole like a couple of snuffies. That's shit-hot, sir. Major Danger, he's proud of you guys. Best lawyers he ever saw in a fight, that's what he told Captain Oliver and me just the other day."

"Another thing, sir, and I'll shut up about it," Bobby Adams said, leaning back in his chair and crossing his legs. "To have a grunt battalion operations officer write up a couple of straphangers and horse-holders for medals makes what you got even more significant. That battalion has an allotment of awards to issue to its Marines. The squadrons and so forth do, too. Guys like us, you know, detached support folks, straphangers, we don't fit into the equation most times when they go to passing out the medals. Sir, for you two guys to pick up Navy Com's with V's from a grunt battalion, and you're just visiting, tells me that you did something pretty special."

"I think Major Hembee is just a fair-minded officer and did what he felt was right," O'Connor said, feeling humbled at the two enlisted men's praise.

"Oh, he's one of the best, sir," Dixon said, nodding in agreement.

"You should have seen ol' Dicky Doo, though, when Jon and I got awarded those medals," the captain said, leaning back in his chair and laughing. "Talk about one pissed-off mojo. He hates Captain Kirkwood and me. Hell, he hates anybody who defends enlisted Marines, for that matter."

"Lots of them do, sir," Dixon added.

"Oh, but not like Dicky Doo," O'Connor said, shaking his head. "I have heard him say that we should just lock in the brig everyone who gets written up. They're all guilty of something, he will say. No such thing as an innocent enlisted man."

"So how do you handle living with that guy?" Adams asked.

"We try to get in our licks when we can," O'Connor replied. "My buddy, Captain Kirkwood, for instance, he sneaks in Dicky Doo's office when the major leaves the building, and he loosens the bolts on the office furniture, so that it rocks around and crap. Drives the major crazy. Best of all, every time he loosens up the furniture, Jon takes another screw out of Dicky Doo's swivel chair and throws it away. Pretty soon, Major Dickinson will sit down and that chair will fall apart right out from under him. I only hope that I'm there to get a look at him when his seat collapses under his chubby little ass."

"Why not slip a dose of phosphate of soda into his coffeepot?" Adams asked, and laughed after thinking about it a second. "Stuff will give him the screaming shits. Big time! The more he drinks the worse it gets."

"What is that again?" O'Connor asked, and picked up a notepad off the coffee table and pulled a pen from Staff Sergeant Dixon's sleeve pocket to write down the name of the chemical.

"Sodium phosphate," Doc Adams said. "It comes in a variety of forms. Even pills. We have a yellowish granulated powder that we mix with a couple of liters of water, and have a patient drink it to lavage, or in other words, wash out his bowels before we do surgery or anything else that involves the colon, or lower intestines. The compound supposedly irritates the lining of the bowels so that the colon shuts down absorption. Any water the person consumes then goes straight down the pipe. There is one form of this stuff that is really wicked and combines sodium phosphate with polyethylene glycol and some other electrolyte salts. A dose of that stuff and your guy drinks a quart or two of liquids, he will start shitting diarrhea like a fire hose. The more water he has in his system, the more he squirts. He can hardly control it, either. As you can imagine, a guy will get massive gas, too, if he's got any food in his stomach. In short, it will leave him helpless as a puppy."

Terry O'Connor slid out of his chair, laughing.

"Oh, shit, that is perfect," he said to the corpsman. "I wish I could get my hands on some of it. I'd dump it in his private coffee mess as soon as our duty admin clerk turned on the pot first thing Monday morning."

"No sweat, sir," Adams said, helping O'Connor off the floor. "We're heading by Charlie Med when the shuttle gets here. Tag along and I'll get you a specimen cup full of it. More than enough to give him a rip-roaring case of everlasting squirts. Him and a couple of other people, if you use the whole cupful. A little bit of the stuff goes a long way."

"WAKE UP, SLICK, your lawyer's here," the stocky, bald staff sergeant shouted as he rapped Donald T. Wilson's cage door with the heel of his boot.

The sergeant sat up from the plywood bunk with no mattress, and kneaded his eyes with his knuckles. After yawning and rubbing his face, he looked at Jon Kirkwood. Then he lay back down on the plank for a bed and rolled his back toward the cell door.

"Fuck you, go away," Wilson grumbled.

"Sergeant, that's exactly how you got in here," Kirkwood said, standing at the jail door with the staff sergeant next to his side, his arms folded and scowling.

"See, Skipper," the jailer said, "this bum's not worth your breath. Don't waste your energy, sir. He's not talking."

"Sergeant Wilson," the captain called again, "my name is Captain Kirkwood. I am a defense lawyer. I want to help you. I think I can, if you'll talk to me."

Wilson lay motionless on the bunk, and said nothing.

"Staff Sergeant, will you open his door and let me inside?" Kirkwood asked the jailer.

"Sir, I'm not sure if that's a good idea, given this man's attitude," the staff sergeant said, frowning at the captain.

"I've dealt with prisoners, Staff Sergeant," Kirkwood said, putting his hand on the cage door. "Unlock it and take a walk. I need to talk to my client privately."

"Sir, I'm not too sure about letting you in there, and I'm supposed to stay close to you while you interrogate the prisoner," the staff sergeant said.

Kirkwood wheeled at the brig NCO and looked down at the stocky man who stood three inches shorter than the captain's six-foot height.

"First, I am not interrogating anyone," the lawyer snarled at the jailer. "This is my client. He has a right to see me, his attorney, in private. You may not observe me, nor may you listen to our conversation, Staff Sergeant. That is the law. If anyone ordered you to eavesdrop on the interviews, conversations, or any other interactions I have with my client, I want to know who issued such unlawful orders to you. Now open this fucking door!"

"Sir, your boss did," the staff sergeant said, pulling the handle that released the lock on the cell.

"Lieutenant Colonel Prunella?" Kirkwood asked, swinging the door open.

"No, sir," the staff sergeant replied, closing the door behind the lawyer. "That major and the captain that was with him a few days ago."

"They interviewed my client without giving him the benefit of legal representation?" Kirkwood asked, frowning.

"Sir, they were both lawyers," the jailer said, pulling down the latch, closing the lock. "I just keep the prisoners, sir. You officers make the rules. They told me when you came here that I should stick right by you for your safety, and report to the captain anything the prisoner told you."

"That didn't seem out of place to you, Staff Sergeant?" Kirkwood said, hissing through his clenched teeth.

"Sir, like I said, you officers make the rules," the staff sergeant answered, walking away.

"Staff Sergeant, one more thing," Kirkwood called to the NCO as he stepped from the cell. "Did you hear what my client told the major and the captain?"

"Sure," the staff sergeant said and laughed. "Your client told them to fuck themselves. Several times."

"You're my lawyer?" Donald Wilson said, rolling onto his back and then looking at Kirkwood, who still stood by the cell door.

"Yes, I am," Kirkwood said, looking at the Marine lying on the bare wood in the darkness of the cell.

"You really give a shit what they do to me?" Wilson said, sitting up, rubbing his hands over the burred stubble of hair covering his head.

"Sergeant Wilson, I care a great deal," Kirkwood said, walking to the bunk. "Mind if I sit down?"

"Sure, go ahead, have a seat," Wilson said, leaning back against the wall. "You smoke?"

"No, I don't, Sergeant," Kirkwood said, sitting on the wooden bed next to his client.

"Just my luck," the sergeant said, rubbing his face with his hands. "I guess I quit smoking, too. No cigarettes for nearly a week now."

"I thought they brought you in here on Wednesday," Kirkwood said, raising his eyebrows.

"Last Sunday, sir," Wilson said, shaking his head. "I got pissed off and called the lieutenant a pussy on Sunday morning. That night, I got that door slammed shut on me here, and I haven't been out of it since. I shit and piss in that bucket, and sit on the floor to eat my chow. What little of it I get. C rations on a paper plate and a cup of water."

"You're not marched to chow with the other prisoners?" Kirkwood said, taking out a notebook from the cargo pocket on his utility trousers and clicking out the point on the black pen that he took from his shirt pocket.

"No, sir," the sergeant said. "I ain't been out that cell door since I got here on Sunday afternoon."

"Who have you talked to about what happened?" Kirkwood asked, jotting notes on the pad.

"I ain't said shit to anybody," the sergeant said, and then smiled.

"Not a word to anyone?" Kirkwood asked, and smiled back at the Marine.

"I only told them to go fuck themselves," the sergeant said, still smiling.

"Well, that's not too good," Kirkwood said, writing in the notebook. "Remember, you must still operate under the rules and discipline of the armed forces. Therefore, when you tell an officer to go fuck himself, that is a violation of disrespect to an officer. I think it would be best if next time any of them try to talk to you that you respectfully decline their invitation. Just say, 'No, sir, upon advice of my counsel, I prefer to only talk to you with my attorney present.' "

"It's too late, sir, I'm fucked. What difference does it make now?" Wilson muttered, resting his elbows on his knees and hanging his head.

"You're charged with one violation of the UCMJ, from what I have read on the charge sheet," Kirkwood said. "Disrespect. Nothing else. We do not want to add to it, not even at this late date."

"Okay, sir," Sergeant Wilson said, sitting up.

"I think they have you in here because they believe you planted that grenade under your platoon commander's bunk," Kirkwood said, looking up from his notebook.

"Fuck an A!" Wilson shouted, and jumped to his feet and stomped to the cage door, where he clutched his fingers through the crosshatched steel. "I know all about that fragging bullshit, sir. I don't know who's trying to kill the lieutenant, or the other officers, but it sure as shit isn't me.

"I can't blame who the fuck is trying to frag that sniveling little coward, though. He's got six of our guys killed, him running any time the enemy opens fire on us during our security patrols. Shit, the little pussy falls apart under fire. A platoon's got to have a leader with balls. That way the platoon holds tight. Shit, Lieutenant March goes to pieces, hiding and crying when we get bushwhacked, and it's all I can do to hold the platoon together and get us out alive.

"Sir, isn't there a law or something about cowards under fire?"

"Cowardice in the face of the enemy," Kirkwood said, jotting notes. "A serious charge, especially against an officer."

"I want to burn that little queer bastard, then," Wilson said, turning from the cell door, streaks from tears glistening on his dark tan cheeks.

"So you called him a coward in front of the company commander, I gather, reading from your charge sheet," Kirkwood said, taking the paper from the manila folder he carried.

"What they wrote down on that charge sheet," Wilson grumbled, "I said every word, and meant it. They got that part right."

"You're guilty of that charge then?" Kirkwood asked, looking up at the sergeant.

"Yes, I am," Wilson replied, looking down at the lawyer, "if it's wrong to be disrespectful of a certified coward."

"What about all this grenade business?" Kirkwood asked, turning a page in his notepad.

"I guess I know as much as anyone," Wilson said, coming back to the bunk and sitting down. "Sir, I never rolled any grenade off the roof of the officers' hooch. I never put one under the lieutenant's rack either. I never even threw a rock on the roof. Anytime I saw a troop picking up anything to throw up there, I chewed his ass. I don't go for that kind of crap. I'm a good Marine."

Jon Kirkwood sat for a moment and then let out a deep breath. Then he stood up. Sergeant Wilson followed him to his feet.

"Thank you for talking with me," he said to the sergeant, and put out his hand.

The sergeant took it and then hugged the captain. When he stepped back, tears rolled down the man's face.

"Sir, I am a good Marine," Wilson repeated. "I love the Corps. I love my men. That's why I got so pissed off when we started losing people, getting boys wounded, because our platoon leader runs from any fight."

"To be honest with you, Sergeant Wilson," Kirkwood said, tucking the notebook in the pocket on the leg of his trousers, "I don't know how much of this cowardice business we will be able to use for defense. The judge may prohibit us from saying anything unless the lieutenant is charged.

"I do promise you one thing, though, I will do everything in my power to see that none of this fragging business is brought into the court either. If they open that door, then we may use that same shallow reasoning to introduce the cowardice as evidence, too."

AT STRAIGHT UP one o'clock, Terry O'Connor stepped out of the shuttle van at China Beach recreation area, carrying a white and blue, six-ounce Dixie cup with a paper lid held on it by a rubber band. He walked to a group of six men dressed in T-shirts and Bermuda shorts, but had the telltale sign of being officers from the white socks they all wore with their tire-tread-sole sandals.

"Hey, guys," he said as he drew near the sock-clad crew seated around a picnic table on the gedunk patio, drinking beer.

"What's up, Skipper?" one of the men answered, and stood, putting out his hand. "First Lieutenant Frank Alexander, Seventh Marines."

"Captain Terry O'Connor, First MAW Law," O'Connor said, shaking hands with the fellow Marine.

The older gentleman who sat with a slight stoop in his shoulders wagged his finger at the lawyer.

"Your friend has the cabana next to ours," Rabbi Zimmerman said, then stood and put out his hand. "Lieutenant Commander Arthur Zimmerman, chaplains' corps."

"Glad to know you, chaplain," O'Connor said. "As a matter of fact, I'm looking for my friend Wayne Ebberhardt and his pretty wife, Gwen."

"*Oy vey!*" the rabbi exclaimed, slapping his hands on the sides of his cheeks and rolling his eyes. "Such a beautiful woman indeed! This lieutenant friend of yours, such a lucky man."

"Yeah, that's right, Captain," Joel Stein said, laughing. "Tarzan and Jane, they're just down there by the beach on that big red blanket. Tarzan and Jane, that is."

"Joel!" the rabbi snapped, scolding the mischievous officer and then turning back to O'Connor. "Please forget this Tarzan and Jane business. It will only embarrass your friend and his wife. I beg of you, Captain."

"Oh, I'll forget all about it, chaplain," O'Connor said, a twinkle flashing in his eyes as he lied. "I won't embarrass them. Relax."

"Thank you," the rabbi said, shaking his head. "We overheard some things from their room last night that left a lasting impression with all of us, and I would not want your friend to feel mortified any more about it than he already is."

"Rabbi," Eric Jacobs said, smiling at the other officers and the chaplain, "I think that Captain O'Connor understands perfectly well now."

"I do, chaplain," O'Connor said, fighting back his urge to laugh. "You said they were on the beach, right?"

"Yes, just down there. See? On the red blanket," Joel Stein said, pointing and grinning, noticing the sly sparkle in the Marine captain's eyes.

"YOU KNOW, THERE'S a damned chimpanzee running around, back up there by the cabanas," Terry O'Connor said, pointing his thumb over his shoulder as he walked to the blanket where Gwen Ebberhardt lay on her stomach, sunning her bare back, next to a portable radio, turned down low, and Wayne Ebberhardt sat with black plastic sunglasses riding the bridge of his nose and his back propped against a mound of sand, reading Joseph Conrad's masterpiece novel *Nostromo*.

"Excuse me?" the lieutenant said, laying the book in his lap and looking up to see his colleague standing above him. "What the fuck are you talking about, Terry? What are you doing here, anyway?"

"I returned those two M14 rifles that Jon and I had stashed in our wall lockers since last fall, and because the helicopter crew had moved to Marble Mountain and I landed in your neighborhood, I caught the shuttle over here to see if you guys wanted to grab a late lunch," O'Connor answered and took a deep breath.

"There's a chimpanzee where?" Gwen Ebberhardt said, rolling onto her back and as she sat up, scooping her unfastened pink bikini top under her breasts, clutching it in place with her hand and forearm. Wayne reached behind her and latched the clasp, allowing his wife to release her grip.

"Oh, yes, that must be Cheetah," O'Connor said, and laughed. "They say that Tarzan and Jane have come here for the weekend, you know."

Wayne Ebberhardt shut his eyes and fell backward, holding his head and moaning.

"Oh, fuck, that's all I need," he groaned, pulling off his sunglasses and looking up at the smiling captain. "Why don't we call AFVN and have them broadcast it to all the American forces serving in Vietnam. How the fuck did you? Oh, never mind."

"Yeah, I met your next-door neighbors and asked directions," O'Connor said, still laughing.

"I know it's a waste of breath to ask you, but could you please keep it to yourself?" the lieutenant begged.

"You kidding me?" the captain chirped. "Now, as your lawyer, once you told me all the steamy details, the attorney-client privilege would then prevent me from disclosing any specifics of our conversation to anyone you did not approve."

"Oh, come on, you guys, it's no big deal, we're married. You're acting like schoolboys at a peephole to the girls' locker room," Gwen said, standing up from the blanket and brushing sand off her legs. As she bent over, Terry O'Connor widened his eyes, exaggerating his facial expressions as he leered at her jiggling breasts and then at the four rows of pink fringe sewn across the back of the bathing suit, dancing across the seat of her bikini bottoms.

"Don't fuck with me like that, Terry," Wayne Ebberhardt said, standing from the blanket, too, and dusting the sand off his legs. "I'm not some pervert who gets his kicks watching other guys groping my wife. I have my limits, you know."

"Captain O'Connor," Gwen said, shaking her finger at him, "you need to know that Wayne likes to get naked, jump on the bed, and beat his chest like Tarzan. In fact, the bed is still flat on the floor from his romping last night. Now, you can imagine the pictures to fill in the blanks, I'm not telling you those parts. But you have the general idea. The six Jewish gentlemen had apparently rented the duplex apartment next to ours for their weekend religious retreat, and Wayne thought it was empty, so he felt free to play Tarzan with all the sound effects. There, you have it. No more questions. Let's go get something to eat. I'm starved."

Then, without waiting for a response from either man, Gwen Ebberhardt started up the slope of sand toward the gedunk and cascade of rainbow-colored parasols.

"You see! Do you see?" Rabbi Zimmerman said, wringing his hands and walking from the picnic table where he and his colleagues sat. The chaplain hurried through the sand to intercept the woman who stomped toward him.

"I am so sorry, I asked him to not say anything," the rabbi pled to Gwen Ebberhardt as she approached.

"Chaplain, forget about it," the redhead snapped, and walked straight past the anxious clergyman.

When she came abreast of the table where the five others sat, snickering, and Joel Stein laughed out loud, she turned at them and put her hands on her hips.

"You little boys need your butts warmed up," she snapped at the men. "Didn't your mothers teach you any manners at all? You ought to be ashamed of yourselves."

Then she stomped inside the gedunk, where she met the burly old chief named Sparky standing by the double glass doors.

"Those men bothering you, ma'am?" he growled.

"Oh, it's nothing," she said with a smile. "You see that Marine captain there, with my husband?"

"Yes ma'am," Sparky said, unfolding his thick arms and putting his fists on his hips, glaring through the glass as Terry O'Connor, Dixie cup in hand, smiled his way past the six Jewish officers and headed toward the gedunk entrance, with Wayne Ebberhardt struggling close at his heels, carrying the red blanket, a canvas bag filled with Gwen's odds and ends, his book, and the portable radio.

"He's buying us lunch," the stewardess said, smiling. "I want you to bring out the most expensive setting of food and drink that you can dream up, plus all the trimmings. If you have French wine, serve that, too. In fact, he's going to buy drinks all round, even for those six guys at that table."

"You sure, ma'am?" the chief said, raising his bushy white eyebrows.

"Terry, you're picking up the tab, aren't you?" Gwen said as the captain came through the doorway.

"Sure, my pleasure," the captain answered, and gave a thumbs up to the chief.

"You got it, hotshot," Sparky said, and then disappeared to the kitchen, where he began barking orders in Vietnamese.

"What's in the Dixie cup, Captain O'Connor?" Gwen asked as she slid in the booth, followed by her husband, and as Terry O'Connor sat down across the table from them. "To be honest with you, it looks like you're wandering around with a urine specimen in your hand. You are okay, aren't you?"

Wayne Ebberhardt laughed, and looked at the lawyer captain sliding the white and blue paper cup back and forth between his hands on the marbleized gray and white Formica tabletop.

"Don't even try to get into a cutting-remarks contest with Gwen," he said, then glancing at his wife as she lit a cigarette. "You won't win."

"I'm fine, Gwen, thanks for asking," Terry said, and smiled a sly look at them both. "Revenge. That's what's in the cup. Revenge."

"It's for Major Dickinson, I gather by the way you're smiling," Wayne said, raising his eyebrows and looking at the container with blue floral trim printed on the outside of it near the top. "What is it, some kind of itching powder or laxative?"

"Very perceptive," O'Connor answered, and released the rubber band off the paper lid, uncovering the cup, full to the brim with a granulated substance that looked like pale yellow sugar.

"That's not cyanide or some other kind of poison, I hope," the lieutenant said, looking at the powder.

"No, nothing harmful. At least not fatal," the captain said, taking the slip of notepaper from his pocket and reading what he had written on it. "A compound of electrolytic salts, polyethylene glycol, but primarily sodium phosphate. The doctors at Charlie Med use it to clear a patient's bowels before they do abdominal surgery. They give him this and half a gallon of water, and his shit chute gets washed squeaky clean."

"Oh, crap, I hope you're not planning to spike the hail and farewell punch with that stuff, are you?" Wayne said, rolling his eyes and then shutting them as he shook his head.

Terry O'Connor stopped and tapped his temple with his index finger, frowned, and then looked back at Wayne Ebberhardt.

"Not a bad idea," he said, arching his eyebrows nonchalantly. "We could take out Dicky Doo and all the prosecution assholes in one fell swoop. But no. All of this is for our favorite mojo, in his private coffee mess."

"You know, Colonel Prunella drinks out of that pot, too," the lieutenant reminded the captain.

"I know, but like I said, it's not fatal," O'Connor said with a shrug. "If the colonel happens to drink a cup, well, as the great white father Westmoreland says down at the MAC-V five-o'clock follies, sending the B52s out dropping their arc-light tonnage on the Ho Chi Minh Trail, taking out a village full of *mama-sans* here, and *baby-sans* there, we have to accept some negligible collateral damage in order to accomplish the greater mission."

"What if someone sees you dumping that crap in the major's coffeepot?" Wayne said, looking at his wife and shaking his head. "Terry, personally, as much as I would love to see Dicky Doo shitting his pants, I think it's a bad idea. They could put you in jail for something like that, seriously. Colonel Prunella, as nice a guy as he is, would turn the lock, too."

"Not if you guard Dicky Doo's door while I do it," O'Connor said, still smiling.

"No way," Ebberhardt answered, shaking his head and shutting his eyes. "Besides, in order for you to even attempt it, you have to get in the office at about six o'clock Monday morning, right after the duty makes coffee for the general mess and the one in Dickinson's office. I won't be around. The first shuttle Monday leaves here at seven. I had planned on slipping in the back door about eight-thirty or nine."

"Oh, you'll be there, pal," the captain said, tilting his head to one side as he smiled, and then rolling his eyes and batting his lashes.

"I will?" the lieutenant said, unconsciously blinking back.

"Yes, because Dicky Doo and Stanley Tufts take the freedom bird to Okinawa on Tuesday," O'Connor began. "News flash. Dot, dot, dot. They're representing us at the Fleet Marine Force Pacific law conference."

"Why am I not surprised, but that's Tuesday, and so what about it? We're talking Monday morning's coffee," Ebberhardt said, and then looked at O'Connor shaking his head. "I'm sure he rubbed it in good for Jon Kirkwood, too, his wife being in Okinawa and all, didn't he."

"Yes, he did," O'Connor purred, and then smiled at the lieutenant, "but Dicky Doo also expressed his regrets at missing you and Tommy Touchdown at the O Club yesterday evening, too. He came in, right after you and this redheaded babe in the showy stewardess outfit left. Oh, and by the way, Gwen, that was a stunning performance at the bar. Sizzling. It's a movie scene that I know I'll be replaying in my mind for many nights while I lie in my rack and dream about you."

"What about Dicky Doo, asshole?" Wayne said, snapping his fingers at Terry O'Connor raising his eyebrows and blinking his eyes at Gwen, who blew a big cloud of smoke back in the captain's face.

"Oh, he came to the club to tell all of us trolls in the defense section, and he did call us trolls, by the way," O'Connor said, leaning back in the booth, "that we had a meeting in his office this morning at zero seven, bright and early. Jon said something about it being nice that he had to get up with the chickens, too, on Saturday, along with the rest of us, and so Dickinson changed it to nine o'clock this morning. By the way, he missed you and T. D. there, too."

"Shit, that's got him nosing even deeper in my private affairs now," the lieutenant said, taking his wife's hand on the tabletop. "He's been snooping around my shit a lot lately. I figure he suspects that I have something going on out in the ville."

"Yeah, I'm pretty sure of that, based on a conversation that McKay had with the Tufts brothers and Charlie Heyster a couple of weeks ago," O'Connor said, and then slapped himself on the cheeks. "Oh, yes, I didn't tell you the good news, too. Dicky Doo said it was good news, so it must be. Anyway, Charlie the Shyster got selected for major. Furthermore, when the colonel leaves the first of July, Dicky Doo takes over as the SJA, and Major-Select Shyster will fill his old billet as mojo until the new boss gets here, like in mid-September."

"Oh, that's dandy, I've got Dicky Doo to contend with until I rotate, the middle of September," Ebberhardt said, bowing his head as he spoke.

"Think of Jon and me, ass wipe," O'Connor said. "Dicky Doo extended through November. We rotate in December, if we're lucky."

"See, Daddy, not everything's all bad," Gwen cooed in her husband's ear, and kissed his neck.

Then Wayne looked across the table at the captain, still showing a Cheshire cat smile.

"What?" the lieutenant snapped, frustrated at his colleague's game.

"You never heard why I know you will be in the office early Monday morning to guard the door while I doctor Dicky Doo's coffee mess," O'Connor said, bobbing his eyebrows up and down like Groucho Marx.

"What!" Wayne Ebberhardt spat at the captain.

"The mojo got pissed because you and Tommy-poo missed the meeting this morning," O'Connor said and shrugged. "So he wants you and T. D. in his office Monday morning, standing tall at zero seven hundred. Sorry to ruin your holiday, pal."

"Ah, fuck," the lieutenant sighed and hung his head.

"Wayne, we can't get there by then!" Gwen whined. Then she frowned and looked at the two officers. "That means we have to leave tomorrow afternoon, doesn't it."

"Afraid so, honey," the lieutenant said, putting his arm around his wife and hugging her head to his shoulder.

"Don't fucking do that," Gwen snapped, pulling away from her husband. "I'm not a poor baby girl. I'm a pissed-off redheaded woman right now."

"I know, honey, I'm sorry," Wayne said, and again tried to hug his wife, but she shot her elbow into his chest, leaving him momentarily stunned and gasping for breath.

Terry O'Connor sank in his seat and felt glad that he had not popped off with a me-too-honey wisecrack. Clearly the woman's temper had boiled to a dangerous point. He rightly considered that she might break his nose with an ashtray if he said anything.

"We'll just have to check out tomorrow afternoon, instead of Monday morning," she sighed, and tears trickled from her eyes. "I hate this war, I hate my job, and I hate having to sneak! Oh, God, September cannot come soon enough. I can quit this Flying Tiger nightmare with the filching hands and smart-ass remarks, from the pilots to the damned ground crew, and go back to my old job at Delta, and you can get out of the damned Marine Corps and be a lawyer in Atlanta, like we planned."

She fought back her tears, and lit a fresh cigarette as she snuffed out one.

"You okay, ma'am?" the scruffy navy chief in Bermuda shorts said, walking to the table with a platter stacked with several big lobsters, and a large bowl filled with boiled jumbo prawns.

"I think I got a hundred bucks in my wallet, Chief," O'Connor said, looking at the service trolley loaded with side dishes that a waiter wheeled behind his American boss.

"Let's see, with the French wine and the drinks for the guys outside, that comes to eighty-seven dollars and ninety cents, Chief Sparks said, and then winked at Gwen Ebberhardt, who now began to laugh.

"Here's five twenties," O'Connor said, handing the chief the hundred dollars. Then he looked inside his wallet. "Wait a minute, there's a five and three ones in here, too."

"That's okay, Skipper," the chief said, and grinned, "I'll just take what's left from the hundred for our tips."

"I fucking got you back, you smart-ass," Gwen said, laughing at Terry O'Connor.

"I concede victory to you, Missus Ebberhardt," the captain said, and put out his hand for her to shake, which she took and ceremoniously shook.

Then the redhead reached across the table and snatched the Dixie cup full of supercharged laxative.

"Wait!" O'Connor said, grabbing her hand.

"I want it, Captain," she hissed, and then pulled her hand and the cup away from his grip. "I have a right to get even with him, putting up with all this nonsense of having to avoid his catching me visiting my husband, and now he's ruined my weekend, too. Besides, I have a foolproof way to pull it off. You two idiots would just get caught Monday, dumping this in his coffee. You think you're slick, but you're just an accident waiting to happen. Both of you. Anyway, I'm good at this sort of thing. Subterfuge is my middle name."

"Your mother named you subterfuge?" Terry O'Connor said, his eyes sparkling.

"Yes, she did," Gwen said, holding her head up, dashing out her cigarette, and lighting a fresh one. Then she looked at her husband and at the captain. "Major Dickinson and Stan the Man take my flight Tuesday morning, right?"

Both men nodded yes and smiled.

"What's the worst that can happen to me if I got caught putting this in his drinks?" she asked and looked at Wayne.

"I don't know, get fired I guess," the lieutenant said.

"Dicky Doo would sue the airline, too," O'Connor offered.

"They deserve it," Gwen said, and shrugged. "Besides, who said I would get caught? You two, on the other hand, would definitely get nabbed. He'll figure out his coffee got sabotaged, blame the enlisted guys, who will then put two and two together and let your little secret slip out, if he doesn't catch you red-handed dumping that shit in the pot in the first place.

"On the other hand, I can put this on my serving cart, and when I fix his coffee, juice, and whatever else he wants to drink, I can simply spoon it in as I pour. He's sitting down and can't see what I'm doing, since I'll park the cart behind his shoulder when I serve him. It will be perfect."

"Sounds like a plan," O'Connor said, breaking a claw off a lobster and pulling out a hunk of meat. "You know what Dicky Doo looks like?"

"I've seen him a couple of times when I went walking past the law center looking for Wayne. I think I can pick him out of a crowd," Gwen said, smiling at her husband and taking a boiled prawn from the bowl and dipping it in cocktail sauce. "Besides, I can look on the passenger manifest and locate him by his seat assignment."

"Just look for the potbellied major with three chins and a black and white flattop haircut," Wayne Ebberhardt said and laughed.

"Yeah, Gwen," O'Connor chuckled, pulling lobster meat from the claw, "he'll be with this sawed-off captain walking with his arms out like a seagull on a hot day."

"How could I miss them then?" Gwen said, and laughed with the two Marines as they ate.

"Hey, Sparky," Wayne Ebberhardt called to the chief, "why don't you tell those guys out there sucking on their beer bottles to come inside and enjoy the air conditioning and help us with all this food."

YAMAGUCHI AND HIS Five-Star Country All-Stars mimicked George Jones while four nearly naked girls go-go danced on round pedestals at each end of the stage. Terry O'Connor and Jon Kirkwood had finished their dinner late, and now drank beer at the Da Nang Air Base Officers' Club bar.

"Where's Stanley?" O'Connor said to his partner. "I've got a little plan up my sleeve that fell in my lap by accident while reading *Time* magazine on the shuttle this afternoon. It's perfect."

"Hey, don't fuck things up, Terry," Kirkwood warned. "You start saying shit to Stanley and he'll figure out you're tied into this prank and tip the whole thing off."

"No, no, no," O'Connor said, shaking his head as he spoke. "I'll be cool with it. Very subtle."

"Like a grenade down the shitter," Kirkwood followed. "Okay, there he is, sitting with his brother and no less than Charlie Heyster."

"That makes it even better," O'Connor said, grabbing his beer from the bar. "Come on, you can help."

"I don't know about this," Kirkwood said, picking up his bottle of Olympia and following his buddy to the table where the three prosecutors sat.

"Congratulations, Charlie," O'Connor said, putting out his hand for the new major-select.

"Thanks, Captain O'Connor," Heyster said, feeling the power of his newly realized, soon-to-be field-grade status, and already separating himself socially from the company-grade scum.

"Oh, you're quite welcome, Major-Select Heyster, sir," O'Connor said, and pulled out a chair and sat with the trio while Jon Kirkwood remained standing and silent.

"Say, Stanley, I hear you're flying to Okinawa on Tuesday with the mojo," O'Connor said, taking a pull off his mug of beer.

"Yeah, and what's it to you, wiseguy?" Tufts snorted, sipping from the top of a glass of ice, scotch, and water.

"Hey, nothing I guess," O'Connor said, shrugging. "I just wanted to pass on a little good scoop to you, that's all. If you don't care to hear it, I'll go back to the bar."

"That's okay. What scoop?" Stanley Tufts said, his curiosity always at a peak when teased with the right question.

"I had to chop over to Marble Mountain today, to take back those rifles that Jon and I ended up with when we got stuck out at Fire Base Ross last November," O'Connor began, and leaned back in his chair, sipping his beer. "Once I got done, I had to take the shuttle back to base, so I had some time to kill. Anyway, I picked up a copy of *Time* magazine that somebody had left over at the chopper ready room, and took it with me to read. You know, the long ride and all. So I open up the magazine and low and behold they've got this article on flight fatigue and how to beat it. I thought of you, since you and the mojo are flying out on Tuesday. I got the magazine in the hooch, if you want to read it."

"No, I don't have time, but thanks," Stanley said, and sipped his scotch. "Anything good that I could use?"

"Oh, sure, lots of tips," O'Connor said, and then looked at Kirkwood and smiled. "Best thing you and the major can do before you fly Tuesday morning is to drink lots and lots of water Monday night. You know, at high altitude there is no moisture in the air. You dry out really bad on a plane, so lots of water in your system before you fly keeps you fresh. Like a rose. Take it out of the water, it wilts. People work the same way."

"Sure, that makes sense," Stanley said, looking seriously at O'Connor. "How much water should I drink, did it say?"

"Yeah," O'Connor said, and shrugged. "They gave it in liters. Two liters the night before, and a couple more liters an hour or so before the flight, if you can handle that much water. Sounds like a lot to me."

"Two liters?" Stanley said and wrinkled his brow. "That's like half a gallon or so, right?"

"Yeah, about that," Charlie Heyster said, taking out a briar pipe and lighting it.

Jon Kirkwood motioned with his head and eyebrows at Terry O'Connor to look at the pretentious man assuming the mantle of a field-grade Marine. Both defense lawyers smiled.

"So I drink half a gallon of water the night before I fly, and then another half a gallon that morning, too?" Stanley said, shaking his head. "Sounds like a hell of a lot of water."

"Ah, you know these magazines," O'Connor said, shrugging and drinking his beer. "I bet if you just drank all you could hold, that would be plenty. Hell, any is better than nothing, you know."

"I could make sure that the major and I drink plenty on the plane, too," Stanley said, smiling.

"You sure could, Stanley. You sure could," O'Connor said, and grinned at Kirkwood, who rolled his eyes and walked away from the table.

Chapter 11

TROLLS' REVENGE

"THAT'S US, STANLEY, scoop it up and let's go," Major Dudley L. Dickinson said to Captain Stanley Tufts, pushing his chair away from the café table in the passenger terminal snack bar at Da Nang Air Base. A voice over the public address system had just echoed through the waiting area the first call for boarding the Tuesday morning Flying Tigers freedom bird flight to Okinawa and then to Norton Air Force Base at San Bernardino, California.

The five-foot, eight-inch-tall captain took his fork and raked the last of his scrambled eggs onto a triangle of buttered toast, and shoved it in his mouth. Then he finished his fourth twelve-ounce tumbler of water that morning, and took a last gulp of coffee before getting out of his seat.

"Sir, I think if you'd drank just one more glassful of water," Tufts said, hurrying behind the major before Dicky Doo cut him off.

"Stanley, if I finished one more glass of water, I would have it leaking out my ears," Dickinson snarled back, shoving his way past a jam of enlisted Marines and soldiers waiting their turns to board the aircraft. "I drank two canteens full of water last night, and then a big glass of water when I got out of the rack this morning, and two more with breakfast."

"Wouldn't you like to hit the head first, sir?" Tufts said, scrambling behind the major, pushing to the front of a line of junior officers who scowled at the captain for breaking through their ranks.

"They have a head on the plane," Dickinson said, barging his way to the aircraft.

"Fucking field-grade and his asshole cleaner," a voice grumbled from behind the pair of lawyers, stopping Dickinson in his tracks.

"Who said that!" Dicky Doo hissed, spinning on his toes and eyeing a line of a dozen or more lieutenants and captains with a few collegially minded majors and a lieutenant colonel mixed with them, choosing to board the plane with the crowd rather than using their ranks to jump ahead in the line. Behind the officers, staff noncommissioned officers waited, then mostly sergeants and corporals, and at the tail end of the queue, the majority of passengers for the flight, the nonrated enlisted soldiers, sailors, airmen, and Marines. Scattered among these lowest-ranking servicemen, a sprinkling of field- and company-grade officers waited with them, holding out to board last, a subtle show of respect for the lower ranks. Hustling tight on Dickinson's heels, his arms held out slightly from his body, keeping the inside creases of his khaki shirt wrinkle-free, Stanley Tufts dutifully emulated the major by also turning back and glaring at the congregation of pissed-off servicemen behind them.

"Come, Stanley," the major snapped, wheeling on his toes and stepping onto the silvery stairway parked against the front passenger portal of the Boeing 707 jetliner.

"Yeah, come, Stanley, kiss my ass," the voice called again. "Major Lard-Bottom and his boy."

Dicky Doo grabbed the rail of the stairway and whipped his head around, trying to see who said the blatantly disrespectful remark. Stanley Tufts, trying to stay close, slammed against the major's backside and caused both men to stumble. The Laurel and Hardy wreck sent a shock of laughter rippling through the approximately two hundred servicemen who watched the clumsy duo fumbling at the foot of the gangway.

Noticing the increasing gap in the line of officers boarding the aircraft, Gwen Ebberhardt stepped out of the doorway and looked down the stairs, where she saw Dicky Doo glaring up at her, his teeth clenched and his face boiling, as he trundled up the steps. Stanley Tufts hurried behind the mojo with his nose nearly touching Dickinson's back pockets.

The shapely, six-foot-tall, red-haired flight attendant smiled and waved at the sea of mostly homebound men from her perch at the stairway's top deck, and then took Major Dickinson by the arm and led him inside the plane, with the captain hot on his heels. Seeing the eye-fetching woman, the laughter immediately changed to a chorus of cheers and wolf-calling whistles, mostly from the lower ranks of veterans who had survived their thirteen-months-long tours of combat duty and now headed Stateside to their waiting families.

"Major Dickinson and Captain Tufts here, shouldn't we be up front someplace?" the mojo told Gwen Ebberhardt.

"What does that card with your seat assignment say, sir?" she asked Dicky Doo, pointing to the tickets he held clutched in his fist, issued to the two men when they checked in for the flight that morning.

"They put us back there on row nineteen," Dickinson spoke in a quick and angry tone. "I think that's where the enlisted men sit. Field-grade and their companion officers should sit at the front accordingly."

"That's not how we do it on this flight, sir," Gwen said, still smiling, and then taking the two boarding passes that the senior lawyer held and reading the information printed on them. "You have assignments on an exit row, just above the forward edge of the wing. Those are excellent seats, sir; extra legroom."

"Okay then," Dickinson grumbled, snatched the two tickets from her hand, and rumbled down the aisle, with Stanley Tufts glued to his back. Gwen Ebberhardt shrugged and walked toward the aircraft entrance where other servicemen now hurried aboard.

"I think First Lieutenant Ebberhardt's wife is named Gwen," Stanley Tufts said, following Dicky Doo to the aisle and middle seats on row nineteen, where a captain by the window sat with his eyes closed and his head resting against the bulkhead.

"Woman like her wouldn't marry some lowlife Marine," Dickinson told Tufts as he settled onto his chair, letting out a condescending chuckle as he spoke. "A guy's got to have a pretty big stack of cash in the bank to get inside that babe's bloomers, I'll bet you. Besides, that broad's got higher sights than to settle on some lowlife troll like Wayne The-Hick-from-North-Carolina Ebberhardt."

Both Marines laughed at the major's degrading comment, and as Gwen Ebberhardt walked past the two lawyers, Stanley Tufts waved to her.

"Yes, sir, may I help you?" she asked, leaning over Dickinson to talk to Tufts, the fragrance of her Chanel Number Five filling their nostrils. Both men's eyes focused inside the open top of her white blouse, catching a glimpse of the bulging porcelain flesh of the upper area of her generous breasts peeking from beneath.

"I see that your name tag says Gwen," Stanley Tufts said and then blushed. "Is that Ebberhardt?"

Gwen blinked but kept smiling, and never let any shock of the question show on her face, even though inside herself she felt panic wanting to leap out.

"Oh, no," she shrugged, closing her open neckline with her right hand, "Crookshank. Gwendolyn Crookshank. I know who you're talking about, though, but she's on another crew. Her husband's a lawyer in Da Nang, I hear."

"Yeah, he's a buddy of ours," Tufts said, smiling.

"That's nice. Gentlemen, I need to get back to my chores," Gwen said, standing straight and then heading toward the front of the plane.

"See, what did I tell you?" Dicky Doo said, watching the stewardess walk away, enjoying the sight of her legs and derriere moving beneath her short, tight-fitting blue skirt. "That's some high-priced snatch, my friend, way outside that troll Ebberhardt's league."

In ten minutes, the last passengers to embark the aircraft buckled themselves in their seats while the ground crew continued loading the baggage. While airmen outside hurried to get the plane launched, and Gwen and three other stewardesses latched doors, closed overhead bins, and made sure that they had everything inside secured for taxi and takeoff, the pilot began firing engines and turned up the air conditioning.

"Damn you, Stanley, and your goofy water project, now I've got to take a leak," Dickinson said, unlatching his lap belt and stepping away from his seat.

The Marine captain by the window looked at Tufts, crowded in the middle, fidgeting with his safety belt, and at the major, now stomping down the aisle toward the lavatory by the plane's front door.

"Hey, sport," the captain by the window growled at the junior partner of the law firm seated by him on row nineteen, "we can't taxi if you're out of your seat. If you go take a piss, too, we'll sit here all fucking day."

Stanley Tufts smirked and started to say something cutting to the rude officer, but then he saw the gold jump wings and silver Scuba head badges pinned above his uniform's left breast pocket.

"Yeah, you're right, Skipper," Tufts gulped, and smiled with a meek shrug at the recon Marine. Then he retightened his seat belt, and concentrated on holding his bladder.

"Sir, you'll have to return to your seat," Gwen Ebberhardt told Major Dickinson as he closed on the airplane's toilet. "The pilot is ready to taxi. We cannot move until you sit down and strap in."

"Soon as I take a leak, lady," Dicky Doo grumbled, pointing at the lavatory door a few rows of seats ahead of him, and then pushed his way past the stewardess.

Gwen looked for help from the air force colonel seated in the sixth row, but he simply shrugged and put his nose back in the newspaper he had unfolded across his lap.

"Captain, we have a Marine major who has gone to the lavatory, despite my order for him to return to his seat," Gwen spoke in the telephone handset just outside the restroom door, talking over the intercom to the plane's pilot in command.

"Tell me when he gets back in his seat so we can get rolling," the pilot responded. "If he gives you any further heartburn, let me know."

"I can handle it, Captain," Gwen answered. "I just needed to make you aware so you didn't get under way with him in the john."

"Thanks, Gwen," the captain replied. "Ground has already cleared us to taxi to the active, and tower has traffic holding for us to roll for immediate takeoff, if we can get out of the blocks. I hope this guy can take care of business within the next sixty seconds, or we may have to delay for no telling how long if we miss our departure bubble."

"Sir!" Gwen shouted, knocking on the lavatory door. "Please return to your seat. The tower is holding traffic for us to take off right now."

"Stuff it, lady!" Dickinson shouted back.

After another full minute had passed, the major finally shoved open the restroom door, wiping the water from his hands with a paper towel. Glaring at Gwen as he stepped out of the lavatory, Dicky Doo grabbed her wrist and slapped the damp napkin onto her outstretched palm, and then huffed as he pushed his way past her.

"You're clear to taxi, Captain," Gwen called on the intercom to the pilot. Then she hurled the wet paper towel into the galley's rubbish bin, next to the refreshment cart that she had withdrawn from its slot in the galley bulkhead earlier, to check its supply and restock any shortages of refreshments or service items.

While watching the rude man trundle to his seat and finally sit down, the flight attendant pulled open the foldaway door to a small closet opposite the forward lavatory. In it she found her flight bag, and unzipped the top. The Dixie cup with the paper lid and rubber band holding it closed lay nestled among her clothes. Casually, she took out the container, stowed her bag, and carried the cupful of laxative granules back to the galley, where she set it in the condiment tray, on top of the beverage trolley. Then she shoved the metal cart back inside its wall compartment and secured its latches for takeoff.

As the plane began to move along the taxiway, Gwen started down the aisle to make her final check of her assigned passengers, ensuring that they all had their tray tables up, seats forward, and safety belts fastened. When she glanced down at the air force colonel on the sixth row, he took his nose out of the newspaper and looked up at her, and again just shrugged his shoulders and shook his head.

GLASS IN THE window shook as the Flying Tigers Boeing 707 jetliner roared over the two-story-high apartment building where Mau Mau Harris and Bao sat waiting for Huong to return with news of James Elmore. Seeing the gray airplane with the blue tail and red and blue trim turning east made the Chicago native homesick.

"When I be working on the flight line, I see that freedom bird taking off on Friday and Tuesday, and I'd think about how glad those boys going back home must feel," Harris said to Bao, staring through the glass, watching the plane grow smaller at the end of a dark streak of exhaust smoke in the distant sky. The younger brother of Chung and Huong smiled sympathetically at the American but understood little of what he had just said.

Harris looked at the Vietnamese cowboy smiling and then shook his head and returned his gaze out the window.

"Your brother sure taking his sweet-ass time getting back here with the skinny on where we going to get Elmore," Mau Mau spoke without taking his eyes from the view outside.

"Elmo number ten," Bao said, and spit on the floor.

James Harris laughed and looked at Bao. "You sure the fuck understand that much, don't you."

The cowboy smiled and nodded in reply.

Steps from the hallway, outside the apartment door, hushed Mau Mau and Bao. Both men drew their pistols as they waited for whoever turned the doorknob to step through the entrance.

"It me," Huong said before he eased open the door, knowing well that anyone else would get shot.

"Come on in," Harris answered, both he and Bao still holding their Colt .45s ready to fire, just in case someone else came using Huong as a talking shield.

Huong stepped through the entrance first and then brought in a uniformed police officer with him.

"It okay, this Inspector Nguyen," Huong said, motioning for his two cohorts to lower their weapons. "He work CID for Major Toan."

Harris frowned at the cop, but slid his pistol back in its scabbard. Bao dutifully put his .45 back in the holster clipped to the inside waistband of his trousers, under his square-tailed shirt.

"I ask Inspector Nguyen to come say you what he say me," Huong told Harris. "No good news on Elmo. He go Chu Lai. So forget about it. We go back Hue City tomorrow then."

"What the fuck you mean, go Hue City tomorrow! What's the story on that shitbird Elmore?" Harris snarled, and looked at the policeman for his answer.

"I work CID so I know about Elmore," the police inspector said, taking off his tan cap and wiping sweat from his forehead with his bare arm. "I find out last night that Marine CID send Elmore to Chu Lai two, maybe three weeks ago. Keep him safe. Pretty soon they send him Stateside unless they first catch you and Snowman."

"We go to fucking Chu Lai, then," Harris snapped, and looked at Huong.

"No," Huong said calmly. "Pitts say we must leave and come Hue City, where he stay if no can get Elmo. You hear him say it, too. We no can get Elmo. Three week all go by now. Too much bad place they keep him Chu Lai. So we go now."

"I can fucking get in there and get him," Harris said, now pacing back and forth by the window. "I know exactly where they be keeping him, too. That hangar down off the end of the flight line, down there where they got the fuel dump and all them barrels stacked way up high."

"Too many guard Chu Lai," Huong said, still keeping his voice relaxed, and sitting on a sofa chair, lighting a cigarette. "Jeep patrol, foot patrol, watchtower, all see you when you try go through fence. No good. I think about it. No way you do. You be caught."

"I won't fucking get caught, man," Harris now pled. "They see a Marine in uniform out for a little PT, they don't think nothing about it. Lots of guys be out jogging and shit. I be cool."

"No, we need go now like boss tell us do. Time pass, no get Elmo. So we go Hue City, first thing," Huong said, and took a long drag from the cigarette. Then as he sighed and let out the smoke he looked at Mau Mau and shook his head at him. "I tell you something more, but I have Inspector Nguyen say for you. That way you know it true."

The policeman lit a cigarette and looked at James Harris eye to eye and did not blink as he spoke.

"Benny Lam put out contract kill you, Pitts, Huong, Bao, Chung, all Snowman cowboy crew," Nguyen said, taking a pull off his cigarette, letting the smoke drift out of his mouth, then inhaling it back through his nose. "That boy you kill with that whore, he Benny Lam's nephew. His sister boy. Benny very angry. He want blood for blood. Best you go long way from Vietnam. Even Hue City not safe from Benny Lam."

James Harris said nothing, and wondered if the cop really bought the misdirection to Hue City. He concluded very quickly that Huong had brought the policeman to their apartment only to feed him the ruse, but still he could not get the idea of James Elmore so easily escaping their retribution from the forefront of his increasing anger. So he stewed silently while he watched Huong walk to a rolltop desk and open a green metal box, where he withdrew a handful of American bills. After he put them in the policeman's hand, he went to the apartment door and opened it.

When the inspector walked into the hall and began stepping down the main stairwell, Huong hurried back to the box, emptied out the cash that remained, and stuffed it into his pants pockets. Then he looked around the room, giving it one last visual inspection, ensuring that he had missed nothing, and headed out the door, with Bao and Mau Mau walking fast behind him.

"We go *didi mao*," Huong said, jogging to a closed door that led to a set of stairs housed in a concrete shaft on the outside of the building. "Take fire escape out before Inspector Nguyen have time to get to street and send people after us. I think he like get pay Benny Lam money for kill us."

"Why ain't we just kill that motherfucker when he in the room then?" Harris blurted as the three men rushed down the concrete steps.

"Because he policeman," Huong said, running out of the alley onto a nearby back street that led to the place where they had parked the black Mercedes-Benz, well away from their Da Nang apartment that he anticipated would get surrounded as soon as he surfaced in the city asking questions.

"Just like in Chicago," Harris said, breathing hard behind the two brothers. "Bushwhack a cop, and they knock down the buildings until they get your ass. Kill anybody else, and it's just another homicide in the big city."

"Now you think smart," Huong said, pulling open the driver's side door and slipping inside. James Harris jumped in the backseat, and Bao rode shotgun in front.

"I still got to kill Elmore, that rat-dog motherfucker," Harris grumbled in the backseat. "He keep his mouth shut, we still be sitting pretty in Dogpatch, man. Wild Thing, she still be alive, too. That white boy you shot off his face, he be alive. So would Benny Lam's nephew."

"You keep smart, Mau Mau," Huong warned, looking at the man in the rearview mirror. "No good try kill Elmo now. Best we wait. I know. I want kill him bad, too. First, we need go Saigon, *didi mao*. Major Toan, Marine CID, Benny Lam, they all come look for us big time when that shit Nguyen tell he see us. Already now, I bet. We go tomorrow morning. Early, early. Maybe we still get Elmo someday. Okay?"

"Yeah, man," Harris grumbled, "someday."

A FINE GLOW of perspiration beaded on Gwen Ebberhardt's forehead as she stood in the galley, out of sight of the passengers, and lit a cigarette. Her nerves felt totally wrecked. She had nearly called the game for rain, having second thoughts about spiking Dicky Doo's coffee and orange juice with the laxative, but then the way he had bullied everyone on the plane gave her the courage to do the job. She heaped a teaspoon full of the yellow granules and stirred it in his coffee, along with the cream and sugar, and then stirred in an ample amount in the two glasses of orange juice he ordered from her, too. She had stirred it in Stanley Tuft's coffee and apple cider as well.

Now the flight attendant worried that she had put in so much that the two lawyers would taste it, and start asking questions when it began to work. The worry made her sweat, so she grabbed a quick smoke to relax.

As always, a few minutes after the crew finished serving drinks and snacks, one by one, passengers began to swarm by the doors of all three lavatories on the airplane, two in the rear and one up front, opposite the galley. Gwen kept her eye on row nineteen, waiting for the major and the captain to start feeling discomfort.

Both men had finished their coffee and juice, and now began to stir in their seats. She could tell that their bowels had already built up a head of methane gas.

"Damn, I think that breakfast we got may have had something gone bad in it," Stanley Tufts said, wallowing in his chair and unlatching his safety belt.

"You, too?" Dudley Dickinson said, releasing himself from the seat and stepping into the aisle. Tufts scooted out after him, and both men then ambled toward the aft restrooms, which appeared to have fewer people waiting to use them.

Standing in line, the stomach bubbling descended into their lower abdomens and Dicky Doo suddenly farted without realizing he had done it until it was too late. Stanley jumped one step back and smiled while he sought air away from the major's gas.

"Gee whiz, sir, cut us a little slack," a gray-headed sergeant major growled, stepping away from the senior lawyer and waving his hand in front of his face to breeze away the rank odor.

"Sorry, Sergeant Major," Dickinson said, blushing. "I think the captain and I ate something that went bad that they put in our breakfast from that greasy snack bar in the passenger terminal."

"Fucking Viet Cong," the sergeant major said. "They damned sure will sabotage your food, you go eating in a gook gedunk like that one."

Stanley Tufts felt his gut rumble hard, and then he fought with all his will to keep the rapidly building gas and excrement from creeping out, standing stiffly with his legs pressed together and clenching his butt cheeks tight.

"Oh, please help me," he sighed, his face growing ashen and sweat beading across his forehead. He felt rivulets of perspiration starting to run along the valley of flesh that followed his backbone and down the middle of his chest. Even with his arms held out from his sides, his pits became soaked, spreading large wet circles in his khaki shirt.

"Look, pal, I can wait, you need to get on inside the head," a lieutenant colonel who stood next in line told Stanley, and pulled the captain ahead of the men waiting, and shoved him through the open lavatory door.

"Can I please go too, sir?" Major Dickinson begged with a timid voice. The colonel then pushed the other Marines aside to allow the visibly sick man to get into the opposite restroom.

"What do you want? Those two assholes shitting all over you guys?" the lieutenant colonel said to the crowd standing in line after the pair of lawyers had gone inside the two rear heads.

Gwen dashed out her second cigarette and made her way back toward row nineteen, when she saw the captain and the major walking back to their seats.

"You two don't look so good," she said to the lawyers as they sat down. "Can I get you anything? Some water, perhaps?"

"We got some bad chow at that gedunk in the passenger terminal," Dickinson grumbled, already feeling more gas boiling in his gut. "My insides feel like a volcano churning and about to erupt."

"Mine, too!" Stanley groaned. "We got food poisoning or something worse."

"How about some Bromo-Seltzer in a big glass of cold water?" Gwen offered. "Does that sound like something that might help you to feel better?"

"Yeah, lady," Dicky Doo growled, gritting his teeth. "Bring us a couple of glasses apiece."

"Yes, ma'am, please," Stanley Tufts whined, offering Gwen a meek smile.

"You don't say 'ma'am' to the hired help, stupid," Dickinson snapped at the captain as the flight attendant turned and left.

Walking back to the galley and filling four tumblers with water, Gwen had almost felt sorry for Dicky Doo. She did feel sorry for Stanley Tufts. The redhead had started to bring them both Bromo-Seltzer and water, to perhaps help settle their stomachs. Seeing them struggle to the restrooms had made her feel that the prank had fulfilled its objective. However, the remark she overheard Dickinson say as she had left them, after she had genuinely wanted to help the two men, left her pissed off all over again.

As she stirred the seltzer into the glasses of water, she divided what remained of the granulated laxative among the four containers.

"There, that ought to do it," she said as she set the glasses on a serving tray and walked back to the pair of lawyers.

At first the bubbling water felt soothing, neutralizing the acid in the two men's stomachs. Major Dickinson sighed, let his seat back, and closed his eyes to relax.

"Viet Cong in the snack bar," he said to Stanley, who also let his seat back. "It damned sure was something in the food there. I'm going to have a visit with the health inspector or somebody, and have that place shut down."

"Did you see any of the other lawyers going to the conference on this flight?" Stanley said, feeling momentary relief.

"Nobody I know," Dickinson said, still keeping his eyes closed. "If they're on the flight, I don't recognize them."

"My brother wanted to go on this trip, too, but he had a case. I'm not sure who his office sent, if anyone. They're shorthanded still, you know," Stanley said, and then sat up, his eyes peeled wide open. "Oh, no!"

"What?" Dickinson said, sitting up, too.

"I've got to go shit, sir, bad!" Tufts said, panic filling his voice and raising his words into a rapid, high-pitched staccato. "Right now!"

The captain unbuckled his seat belt, leaped to his feet, and began trying to climb across the major's legs.

"Now that you mention it," Dickinson said, feeling his bowels coming alive with new thunder. The gas had left his stomach, which momentarily made him feel better, but the additional dose of phosphoric soda, polyethylene glycol, and electrolytic salts now went to work with a vengeance as it surged through his intestines.

He stood between Stanley Tufts' legs and knocked the captain backward. The junior lawyer fell across the now dozing recon Marine's lap and slammed his head against the airplane's window. The sleepy-eyed captain angrily pitched the lawyer off his legs and onto the floor.

"Oh, God!" Stanley cried as he struggled to his feet, the strain causing him to release a wet fart that he immediately pinched off for fear of filling his shorts.

"I'm heading up front," the major yammered, stepping into the aisle and fast-walking toward the nose of the plane with his butt cheeks clenched. "You can have the back, Stanley," he called over his shoulder.

MICHAEL CARTER COULD not get to his cubicle fast enough. At the foot of his bed he dropped to his knees and began praying while tears gushed from his eyes.

"There you are," Terry O'Connor called as he walked through the barracks door and saw the captain he called Stickman crouched over his footlocker.

"What?" Carter said, sobbing.

"We're getting ready to head to the courtroom, and I thought you wanted to come, too," O'Connor said, walking to where Michael Carter knelt. "Wayne's already there with our client. I've still got a couple of things to go over with our three defense witnesses. Only one of them worth a shit, though, this fellow, Private First Class Wendell Carter, apparently PFC Celestine Anderson's hometown buddy and only real friend.

"Meanwhile, Charlie Heyster has this sideshow of good ol' down-home peckerheads he's going to parade through, led off by this darling of rebel pride and eternal prejudice Private Leonard Cross, who Charlie the shyster has come to lovingly call Laddie-my-boy. This clown seriously believes that wearing a white sheet and a peaked hat is something noble. He thinks the Ku Klux Klan is a benevolent service club like Lions and Kiwanis."

"Of course, Dicky Doo took Stanley Tufts to Okinawa with him so he could get him off the case and put that shark Charlie in charge of the prosecution. He had to throw in his best gun considering how you and Wayne outplayed their hand and got the judge to reduce the charges from first-degree murder and all," Carter said, standing and wiping his nose on his arm.

"Oh, hell, I know that," O'Connor said, and then laughed. "I'm looking forward to seeing the circus that Charlie will want to unleash. However, we'll concede those facts and jump right to mitigating circumstances, which will park most of his long train of witnesses on the siding, and leave him only these three bigots to confront our ax murderer, who has his own racial issues. Then we do have our straight-arrow kid from Houston, this young Marine, Wendell Carter. By the way, he any relation to you?"

"Of course not! The young man is a Negro," Michael Carter exclaimed and frowned.

"He's half Cherokee, from his full-blood mother, and his father's grandfather was Irish, a railroad terrier named Carter who took a slave girl as his wife," O'Connor said, spreading a big smile. "So if only a third or fourth of this guy's heritage comes from African lines, what does that make him? I think more Cherokee than anything."

"He regards himself, as do his friends consider him, a Negro," Carter said, unconsciously raising his nose, showing his strong Boston elitist, limousine-liberal side.

"I just thought that since you've got Irish ancestry, and had the same last name, you might be kin," O'Connor said, checking his uniform in the full-length mirror fastened to the barracks wall. "Also, when you're around Wendell or Celestine, or any of the other defense witnesses, try using the term 'black' instead of 'Negro.' I think these guys prefer it. I know I do."

"Well, excuse me, but I said 'Negro,' not 'nigger,' " Carter huffed.

"These days, 'Negro' is not cool. Kind of reminds me of 'Mick,' if you know what I mean," O'Connor said with a sharp edge to his voice and no smile.

Michael Carter put up his hands and conceded the point to Terry O'Connor.

"Now, tell me why you were on your knees, Michael," O'Connor said, and put his arm across the gangly man's shoulder.

"As you know, Lieutenant McKay and I have to face Major-Select Heyster and Major Dickinson next week in the trial of this boy who shot the prostitute in the ear," Carter said, putting on his cover.

"So I hear," O'Connor answered, walking toward the door with Carter. "They mean to humiliate you."

"Hard to humiliate a person like me," Carter said, hanging his head. "My client deserves better, though, and I am such a loser."

"What the fuck happened, Mike?" O'Connor said, stopping on the barracks' front porch and looking Carter in the eye.

"Dicky Doo is a pervert," Carter said, and fought back tears. "I believe that he wants to make a spectacle of this trial because the hooker, well, the prostitute, she is not at all what we think."

"What is she, Mata Hari?" O'Connor quipped, letting his growing impatience get the best of him. "Michael, spit it out. I don't have but a minute to waste here."

"Well, I interviewed Corporal James Gillette, finally," Carter began and sighed. "I had to get over to the brig at six this morning because they had him going on a working party at seven o'clock."

"Mike, the point!" O'Connor snapped.

"The reason he shot that hooker is because she has a dick!" Carter said, and then sighed and moaned.

"A dick?" O'Connor squawked, and then laughed.

"Yes! She's one of those, you know, like the Benny boys in the Philippines," Carter said, closing his eyes, embarrassed.

"Yeah, a horse of a different color, so to speak," O'Connor chuckled. "Feminine housing but masculine plumbing. I've heard of them, you know, big tits and a dick, but never saw one. I thought that the police report said they had gotten into a lovers' spat, he lost his temper, and blew off her ear."

"It does," Carter croaked, and let out another deep sigh. "This morning I asked what they had fought about, and Gillette whispered the answer to me. He said that instead of a blow job, he had changed his mind and wanted to have, you know, intercourse. The girl refused, so he pushed her down and pulled off her panties, and found, well—"

"So at the sight of her dick he lost it and started shooting," O'Connor said with a laugh. "Hers was probably bigger than his, which pissed him off doubly bad."

"I don't know what to do," Carter said, snuffing his nose and wiping away tears. "Dicky Doo and Charlie Heyster will have a riot with a transsexual whore. You think this morning will be a circus when the Ku Klux Klan meets the Black Panthers? Just wait!"

"Hold on, Michael, let's consider this for a moment," O'Connor said, taking the dejected captain by the arm. "Don't you see that this Miss Dick represents your ace in the hole? Hell, no Marine juror with a set of balls can blame this Gillette kid for blowing off this fruitcake's ear. In the same pair of shoes, even Dicky Doo would have wanted to kill him or her or whatever you call this cocksucker."

"You think so?" Carter said, smiling.

"What about the two guys McKay represented in this?" O'Connor said, cutting across the lawn toward the law center.

"McKay is another issue," Carter said, biting his lower lip thoughtfully. "He's got me concerned."

"Yeah, you don't even have to say it," O'Connor answered, frowning and shaking his head. "He spends more time these days throwing grenades out Lobo's airplane window than he does in the office. Tommy's got a real short-timer attitude along with that baggage about his buddy's death that he's dragging around."

"McKay bought a plea deal right off the bat for his two clients tied to Jim Gillette's case. In this instance I think that even I could have gotten them off clean," Carter said, still nibbling his lip. "My client said that his buddies knew nothing. They waited outside and had no idea of anything going on with him and this prostitute inside the apartment. Understandably, he never told them about the dick issue, either. These two guys just came running when they heard the gunshot. They only tried to help. Did everything they could, and even offered to get a doctor. However, the hooker called the cops, so they got scared and ran."

"You can't get the thing dropped?" O'Connor said, pulling open the law center's main door.

"Everything has gone through," Carter said, following O'Connor through the entrance. "These two guys accepted a bust to lance corporal and a month's pay fine. What's done is done."

"So what about your guy?" O'Connor said, waving hello at Wendell Carter, who sat in the hallway across from Laddie Cross and the late Buster Rein's two other cohorts. "Will he plea out?"

"He tried as soon as McKay got the papers on his buddies processed," Carter said, waving at the black Marine, too. "He figured a bust to lance corporal and a fine seemed acceptable, considering that he did shoot the hooker's ear off."

"I think it's fair," O'Connor said, smiling, "even though the shooting was justifiable from the perspectives of most Marines."

"Major Dickinson says that since it's a high-profile incident, a case of attempted murder and assault with a deadly weapon, and the command wants to satisfy the public outrage, it must at least go to a summary or special courts-martial. They are hellbent to put my client in the brig for a good long while," Carter said, sighing.

Something about the whole story kept itching Terry O'Connor's brain. He stopped in the hallway outside the courtroom and pondered: Why hadn't anyone from the other side mentioned that the whore was a transsexual? Not even the police report detailed anything about it. It only listed the victim with a female name, when it should have shown a male name with a feminine alias. A gunshot wound to her ear apparently required no medical inspection of her plumbing. Then the lawyer's eyes began to twinkle and he started laughing.

"Michael, have you told anyone else about this? You know, the true nature of the beast, so to speak?" O'Connor asked, taking his colleague by the arm and leading him away from earshot of the crowd.

"No," Carter blinked. "Corporal Gillette only told me about it this morning. He's terribly embarrassed, you know, going for sex with another man and all. When Charlie Heyster parades that in court, poor Corporal Gillette will be a laughingstock. That's why I got so upset. Why I had to pray about it."

"Cheer up, pal. Gillette will be fine with it, believe me. This isn't bad at all. It's really pretty good. The chick with a dick drops an atom bomb on the prosecution and thus becomes a big plus for your defense. You know what's really funny? I'll bet you anything that Dicky Doo and Charlie the shyster don't have a clue that their little bimbo is really a guy," O'Connor said in a low voice, and then spread a wide smile at Carter.

"GANGWAY! COMING THROUGH! Emergency. Sorry, fellows," Dudley Dickinson roared as he rumbled his way past two lieutenants standing outside the forward lavatory on the Flying Tigers flight to Okinawa. Then when he got to the restroom's closed entrance, its "occupied" sign showing above the latch, he began pounding.

"Hey, you inside the head! Hurry the fuck up!" the major bellowed, slamming his palm against the closed door. "You hear me? Break it off, and make way. I've got to get in there right now!"

In a moment the air force colonel from row six pushed the folding hatch open and stepped out with his *Stars and Stripes* newspaper clutched under his arm.

"Major, you don't have to be rude," the colonel said, shaking his head and walking past the two lieutenants, who now stood smiling at Dicky Doo.

Dickinson leaped inside the cramped lavatory and slammed the door shut. Gwen Ebberhardt stood in the forward galley area, smoking a cigarette, and laughed.

"Oh, God, please, God! Please help me!" Stanley Tufts whined, dancing on his toes as he finally reached the line for the two rear heads, joining three other Marines who waited their turns. A full bird colonel stood patiently ahead of two sergeants, so the captain dared not just barge his way to the front despite his emergency.

The senior officer and two enlisted men looked back at Tufts.

"Are you okay, Skipper?" the colonel asked, immediately concerned about the obviously distressed man.

The lawyer gasped for air and suddenly locked his heels while his arms levitated to their natural, hot-seagull stance. Gas pressure in Tufts' bowels sent lightning-bolt pain through his gut, pushing him beyond his limits of internal control. Frozen in place, Stanley desperately pressed his legs and butt cheeks together as hard as he could hold them, hoping to keep anything from escaping. Nonetheless, as his gut rumbled again, his sphincter let go.

"Oh, God!" he shrieked, looking straight in the concerned colonel's pale blue eyes while a flood of diarrhea exploded out of his ass with the force of a fire hose. The foul smell from it moved through the air inside the plane like a shock wave from an artillery round. Horrified passengers, mostly Marines, fled for cover.

Watery, brown excrement ran onto the floor after gushing along both legs of Stanley Tufts' trousers, leaking down his socks and over his shoes as well as loading the seat of his drawers.

"Oh, God," the lawyer whimpered as he stood with his arms out, his legs now spread wide, his lower regions covered in shit, and two brown puddles surrounding his feet, creeping across the airliner's light blue carpet.

Just as his bowels rumbled again, and another bubbling eruption gushed into his boxer shorts, the Marine colonel grabbed Captain Tufts by the shoulder and shoved him inside the now open lavatory, where an army specialist fourth class had just escaped and leaped past them like a deer fleeing a lion.

Several more thunderous downpours struck the captain as he perched on the throne, feeling as though the violent contractions would turn him inside out. Then, after stripping off everything below his waist, Stanley Tufts spent nearly half an hour trying to wash out his boxer shorts in the lavatory's tiny sink, holding the spring-loaded water valve open with his thumb while trying to scrub with the fingertips of his one free hand. Finally he simply tossed the soiled underwear into the trash bin under the bathroom counter.

He took off his shoes and socks, rinsed them in a small puddle of water in the little stainless steel basin, and hung his socks over the counter to dry while he ran a paper towel over his shoes. The reeking khaki trousers presented the greatest challenge, since the seat and inside of both legs had gotten soaked with his diarrhea.

While sitting on the toilet, emptying what remained in his bowels, the captain scrubbed and rubbed the fabric, using the liquid soap from the dispenser above the sink. Finally he just gave up and began to moan and stare at the floor.

"I think he may have died in there," the Marine colonel said to the brunette flight attendant who with her blond partner oversaw the rear cabin area. After waiting so long, the officer had finally sat down on the armrest of an aisle seat on the last row, waiting to see if he could help the captain.

"Are you okay, sir?" the blond woman called, tapping on the lavatory door.

"Oh, probably," Stanley answered, sighing. Like all the other passengers, he had checked his valise to the baggage compartment before boarding the plane. The airline allowed only briefcases and small satchels in the passenger area, stored under the seats or in the overhead luggage bins. On a Stateside flight he would have had a folding suit bag stuffed in the hold above his seat, and someone could have gotten him a fresh pair of pants from it. Now he had no choice but to put on the wet, stained, foul-smelling khaki trousers.

"Look, Captain," the colonel finally said, rapping his knuckles on the door. "Want me to come in there and see if I can help you get squared away?"

"No, thank you, sir," Tufts called back. "I'll come out in a minute."

"Take your time, cowboy," the colonel said, "but at some point you'll just have to suck it up and walk among the living."

"Thank you, sir," Stanley said, and finally opened the door.

"Well, that ain't so bad," the colonel said, looking at the captain with his trousers soaked front and back and throughout the inseam area.

Then the colonel put his arm across the captain's shoulders and started walking him back up the aisle, daring anyone to make a remark or even laugh at the humiliated Marine.

"I shit my pants on a date once, when I was in high school," he told Stanley Tufts. "It made such an impression with the girl, she married me a few years later. She's home waiting with my four boys. They'll be at Norton when we finally get there. Shitting your pants just makes you human, like the rest of us."

"Thank you, sir," Tufts sighed, feeling better about the whole ordeal as he came abreast of Major Dickinson, who finally glanced up to see his protégé waiting to sit down.

"Thanks for taking care of my man, Colonel," Dickinson said as he stepped into the aisle and let the captain get back into his seat.

As Stanley slid into the row, the recon Marine captain by the window laid his *Stars and Stripes* newspaper on the lawyer's chair bottom, to absorb the wetness. Then he leaned back and offered poor Tufts a friendly smile.

"Anytime, Marine," the colonel said, and then walked toward the rear of the airplane, returning to his own seat.

"I don't think I will be in the mood for that Kobe beefsteak and mai tai we had planned on tonight at Sam's Anchor Inn," Major Dickinson said as he fastened his seat belt.

"Oh, good, sir," Stanley Tufts sighed. "Honestly, I had begun to really dread having to go there for dinner this evening."

"You know, Stanley, I think I lost ten pounds today," Dicky Doo said and smiled at the captain. "When I hitched up my britches after shitting my brains out, they were loose as a goose."

"YOU'RE A PRIVATE in the Marine Corps, that is correct isn't it, Mister Cross?" Terry O'Connor said to Leonard Cross.

"Yes, sir," the witness responded, and then looked at Captain Charles Heyster for approval with his answer. The prosecutor only smiled, trying to hide his concern.

"Let's see," O'Connor continued, thumbing through pages of Private Cross's Service Record Book as he walked to a tabletop lectern set in the center of the room between the tables for the prosecution and the defense. "When you return to the States, you'll go to Camp Pendleton for release from active duty, it says here. You've been in Vietnam now eighteen months, five months on legal hold. Is that correct?"

"Yes, sir," the skinny, darkly tanned, dark-haired Marine answered. "Me and Buster was suppose to rotate back in November, only a week before that. Uh, before he got his self killed."

"Yes, Private Cross," O'Connor said with a smile, "only a week before Private Harold Rein got his self killed."

"That's right, sir," Cross responded, and looked at Charlie Heyster, who had his face turned toward a yellow legal pad, where he busily jotted notes.

"As Captain Heyster had you testify earlier," O'Connor continued, "you and Private Harold Rein were very close friends."

"Yes, sir," Cross said and nodded, and then quickly wiped his eye with his fist, just as Heyster had told him to do, to gain sympathy from the jury. "We joined up on the buddy system."

"Right!" O'Connor said, and picked up a legal pad. "You testified that you and Harold Rein joined the Marine Corps together, went to boot camp together. You even went to the brig together, didn't you."

"Sir, Captain Heyster told me I didn't need to answer anything about me and Buster going to the brig any of those times," Cross said, and looked at Charlie Heyster, who leaped to his feet.

"Objection, Your Honor," Heyster said, looking at his witness, whom he had instructed to say nothing if asked about his two times in the brig with Buster Rein. "The witness's service record is not relevant to this case. What he observed has nothing to do with whether he ever served time in the brig."

Colonel Richard Swanson, who flew to Da Nang from Fleet Marine Force, Pacific Headquarters, in Hawaii, to preside over the murder trial of Private First Class Celestine Anderson, put up his hand when he saw Terry O'Connor about to counter Charlie Heyster's objection.

"Captain Heyster, I am overruling your objection because I allowed you to open that very door with your witness's combat record," the judge said, and nodded at the defense counsel to proceed.

"You and Private Rein did serve time in the brig, right here in Vietnam, isn't that correct, Private Cross?" O'Connor said, leaning over the lectern and looking coldly at the witness.

"Yes, sir," Cross mumbled, but then looked up, curling his lip at the captain. "We didn't start none of those fights. They just stuck us in the brig because they didn't like us boys from Alabama. Them damned niggers started all those fights. Just like this time."

"Damned niggers. Right. They got you and your pal, Buster Rein, thrown in the brig both times. Right?" O'Connor said, and walked in front of the lectern, crossed his arms, and looked at the six jurors, one of whom was a black Marine staff sergeant.

"Your Honor!" Heyster shouted. "The defense counsel is leading the witness, and goading him to express these unacceptable racial epithets."

"Is this an objection, Captain?" Judge Swanson said, looking over the top of his tortoiseshell-framed half-glasses.

"Ah, yes, sir!" Heyster responded.

"Overruled," the judge said with a smile, and then looked at Terry O'Connor. "Captain O'Connor, you are also opening some dangerous doors for your client. I understand the nature of your questioning, but racial tension is an area of deep concern for the Marine Corps today. So be cautious on where you may tread."

Terry O'Connor nodded, stepped back behind the lectern, and read his notes. Then he looked up at Leonard Cross.

"Private Cross," the defense lawyer said, "you had just gotten promoted to lance corporal when you came to Vietnam, and your friend Private Rein was a private first class. You have no page eleven entries prior to coming to Vietnam either. What happened?"

"We got put on shit detail," Cross answered, now slouching down in the witness chair. "We had this gunny that didn't like us."

"Was he black?" O'Connor asked, looking at his notes.

"Yes, sir," Cross answered, and then narrowed his eyes and looked hard at the defense lawyer.

"Why do you suppose a black gunny would have it in for you two?" O'Connor asked, looking back at the witness and not blinking.

" 'Cause of this," Cross snarled, and then pulled up the sleeve of his shirt, exposing the stars-and-bars rebel flag tattooed on his shoulder.

"That's the flag of the Confederacy, correct?" O'Connor asked Cross.

"Yes, sir, it is," Cross answered, letting down his sleeve.

"It expresses your southern roots, does it not?" O'Connor said, looking at the jury.

"Yes, sir," Cross answered.

"You're proud of the fact that you're a southern boy," O'Connor said, smiling at the witness.

"Damn right, sir," Cross said, holding his head high and pitching his shoulders back as he now scooted upright in the witness chair.

"I'm from Philadelphia, the city where our Constitution was born," O'Connor said, smiling. "I fully understand what you mean."

"Yes, sir," Cross said, taking a deep breath.

"That black gunny you worked for, he didn't understand though, did he," O'Connor said, leaning over the lectern and looking at Cross sympathetically.

"No, sir," Cross said, shaking his head. "He called me and Buster and Duke and Ray white trash, and put us on shit detail because we was proud of who we was."

"That made you mad, right?" O'Connor said, still leaning over the lectern.

"Made me feel like it wasn't no use," Cross said, looking down at his hands.

"So you didn't take shit off anybody then, did you?" O'Connor asked.

"No, sir, we didn't," Cross said.

"I think we all understand, and greatly appreciate your frustration with racial bias," O'Connor said, looking back at his notes.

"Thank you, sir," Cross said, and then reached for a glass of water set on a side table for the witness.

"You ever hear of the Grand Knights of the Ku Klux Klan, or any variation of that name, the Klan or the K-K-K?" O'Connor asked, and looked at Charlie Heyster for an objection but got none.

"Of course I have, sir," Cross said, and frowned. "Everybody's heard of the Klan."

"Down in Dothan, Alabama, where you and Harold Rein were both born and raised, did you ever see anybody from the Ku Klux Klan, or ever know anybody in the Klan?" O'Connor asked.

"No sir, not me," Cross said, and smiled at Charlie Heyster.

"You and your buddy Buster never went to any Klan meetings, and certainly never joined it," O'Connor said, looking at the witness, who kept smiling.

"That's a secret club, sir," Cross said, leaning back in his chair. "Nobody knows anybody in it, unless they's in it, too."

"What do you think of the Grand Knights of the Ku Klux Klan, Private Cross?" O'Connor asked, leaning on the lectern again, clasping his hands.

"They just some old outfit from the Civil War," Cross said, wrinkling his lips, trying to outguess the questions now.

"So they're just historic. Not around anymore?" O'Connor said, still clasping his hands.

"Not exactly," Cross said, shrugging. "Everybody's seen the stuff on television about the race protests and such down in Mississippi and back home, too. They got some guys I seen wearing the Klan robes."

"So all you know about the Klan is what you saw on television news of the racial protesters," the defense lawyer said. "Who's right in that mess?"

"Now, sir, the Ku Klux Klan did good for the South, back when the Yankees took over everything. They run out the carpetbaggers and whatnot. We learned all that in school," Cross said, defending his heritage.

"So the Ku Klux Klan is not a racist hate group then," O'Connor then said, looking at the jury.

"Sir, not like you Yankees think," Cross said.

"Your Honor," Charlie Heyster stood, and then looked at Terry O'Connor, "we are supposed to be examining the murder of Harold Rein, not trying him and the prosecution's witness. Many southern people regard the Ku Klux Klan much differently than we from other regions. It has no bearing on the death of Private Rein, though. I object to this continued trial of the Ku Klux Klan and beg Your Honor to bring us back to the subject of the murder."

"Point well taken, Captain Heyster," the judge said, and then looked at O'Connor. "Captain, we are clear on the witness's perspective or racial prejudices and the Ku Klux Klan. Can we now move on to something more directly relevant to the events that led to the death of Private Rein? If you please."

The defense counsel looked at his notes and then looked up at Leonard Cross.

"Laddie. That's your nickname, is it not?" O'Connor continued.

"They call me Laddie instead of Leonard, yes, sir," Cross said, folding his arms.

"What about that other tattoo?" the defense lawyer said, tapping himself on his right shoulder. "The one above your rebel flag."

Leonard Cross pushed up his sleeve and turned his shoulder toward the jury.

"That's a Maltese Cross above your flag tattoo, is it not?" O'Connor said.

"I don't know about Maltese, but it's a cross," Leonard said, letting down his sleeve.

"What does it represent?" O'Connor asked.

"Nothing, just a cross. I'm a Christian, you know," the private said, looking at Heyster for help but getting none.

"Buster, and your other buddies, Duke and Ray, they all have that same tattoo, do they not?" O'Connor asked, and smiled at Charlie Heyster.

"Yes, sir. We're all southern boys. You know that," Cross said, wrinkling his lips and narrowing his eyes at the defense lawyer.

"What about the circle around the cross, is that a Christian symbol, too?" O'Connor asked, and looked at Heyster, but he now only looked at his notepad.

"That's just part of the cross, sir," the private said, shrugging.

"It looks just like this cross, does it not?" O'Connor said, and held up an eight-inch-by-ten-inch photograph of a man wearing a white peaked hood and a white robe with a circled Maltese cross on the left breast, identical to the tattoo on Leonard Cross's shoulder.

"That's the symbol of the Ku Klux Klan," the private said, and then curled his lips at the jury, and stared straight at the black sergeant seated there.

"Correct!" O'Connor said, and took the photograph to the presiding judge and laid it on his desk. "Sir, we ask that the court enter the photograph of the Ku Klux Klan costume as defense exhibit twelve."

Walking to the edge of the witness stand, leaning on the rail, and looking hard into Laddie Cross's eyes, O'Connor then asked, "Is there or has there been a brotherhood of you good southern boys here in Da Nang who espoused the teachings and philosophies of the Ku Klux Klan?"

"I can't say," Cross snapped back, and scowled at the lawyer.

"That's right, it's a secret society," O'Connor said, and looked at the jury. "The Marine Corps would put you and anyone else in it back in the brig for having such a group. Right?"

"It's just a tattoo, sir," Cross answered, and clenched his teeth.

"That's all I have for this witness, sir," O'Connor said, and walked back to the defense table, where Wayne Ebberhardt sat next to Celestine Anderson, his wrists clapped in manacles chained to a belt he wore around his chest, and his legs chained to the chair.

"Any redirect questions, Captain Heyster?" Colonel Swanson asked.

"Yes, sir, Your Honor," Heyster answered without standing. Then he looked at Leonard Cross, who sat in the witness chair wiping sweat from his face with his hands.

"Who killed Private Harold Rein?" the prosecutor then asked the witness.

"That man there," Laddie Cross answered, pointing to Celestine Anderson.

"You saw him do it, correct?" Heyster asked.

"Yes, sir, I did," Cross answered.

"What did you see Private Rein do before he was so brutally murdered?" Heyster asked.

"He just asked that guy there for a light," Cross said, pointing at Celestine Anderson. "He just wanted him to light his cigarette. That guy hit Buster in the head with his hatchet, and killed him right there on the spot. They weren't no fight. He just killed him when Buster stood there getting a light."

"That it?" the judge asked Charlie Heyster.

The prosecutor nodded, and the colonel excused Leonard Cross from the stand.

"Sir, before the prosecution calls his next witness, the defense will stipulate that Private First Class Celestine Anderson did in fact kill Private Buster Rein by striking him in the head with his field ax," Terry O'Connor said, standing behind the defense table. "The prosecution has listed seventy-six witnesses, and in the consideration of time and expedience, the defense will stipulate those matters of evidence."

"Thank you, Captain O'Connor," Colonel Swanson said as he took a brief that Staff Sergeant Pride handed to him, expressing in detail the stipulations. Then he handed a copy of the statement to the prosecution, who quietly read the document.

"Your Honor, the remainder of my witnesses simply support these stipulations; therefore, the prosecution rests its case," Heyster said, and dropped the brief on a neatly laid pile of manila folders that Captain Philip Edward Bailey-Brown had tried to keep organized in several equally distant rows, but that Charlie Heyster kept scattering anytime he looked in one.

"Good," the judge said, looking at his watch. "How about we quit early today, and get started with the defense arguments first thing tomorrow."

Terry O'Connor stood and smiled as he watched the presiding judge leave, and the jury file out the door.

"You're a motherfucker, O'Connor," Heyster whispered to him as he stepped from the prosecution table. "That race shit will bite your client squarely in the ass come tomorrow. I hope you're not thinking of putting him on the stand. I will rip him to shreds."

"He's leading off, Charlie." O'Connor smiled and shrugged happily, and watched Major-Select Heyster stomp out of the courtroom.

Philip Edward Bailey-Brown finished stacking his manila folders back in a dark brown accordion file and tied it shut with the brown silk ribbons wrapped around the container. Tucking it under his left arm, above his briefcase, he walked to where Wayne Ebberhardt and Terry O'Connor busily put away their papers.

"Captain O'Connor, nice job," the New England aristocrat said, and put out his right hand that the defense lawyer immediately took and shook.

"Thanks, Philip," O'Connor said, surprised by the gesture from a man who until now had not said two words to him in the five months he had served in Vietnam.

"Tomorrow is another day, after all," Bailey-Brown said, and smiled. "However, you are the first to ever get the shyster's goat. The first I have seen. You beat him down to his bootstraps today, sir. My compliments."

Chapter 12

THE MEASURE OF A FOOL

SILENCE AWAKENED HUONG Van Nguyen. He sat up in the pitch darkness from the mat where he had lain, covered by a thin wool blanket. Bao sat up, too. The sudden lack of sound outdoors had stirred him from his sleep as well. The elder Nguyen brother snapped his fingers for the dog to come to him, but Turd had long since gone from the thatched-roof house, following Mau Mau Harris as he had slipped away while the two cowboys slept.

The American tried to make the motley pooch go back to the farm, but the rotten cur would have none of it. He chose James Harris the day he met him in Dogpatch, and he stubbornly stuck by his friend. While the mutt liked Huong well enough, he devoted himself to Harris. The black man could not make the animal return to the dwelling without risking that the noise he made urging the mongrel to stay home would awaken his two Vietnamese cohorts. So with a shrug, he allowed the pet to tag along.

Mau Mau knew that if he had awakened Huong, and the cowboy saw him trying to slip out, he might put a bullet in his head. On the other hand, if he returned from his mission holding an ear or finger along with James Elmore's gold front tooth, proof that he had killed the traitor, Huong might very well scold him for his disobedience, but would likely congratulate him, too, for his success in exacting revenge.

With Turd sniffing the ground close at his heels, James Harris had sneaked out of the farmhouse, down the two steps to the bare-earth front yard, and slipped into the forest. However, as he stepped through the tall grass and into the trees, the incessant, loud croaking and buzzing of the thousands of frogs that lurked there went silent, spooked by his motion. The sudden quietness made the Marine deserter jump. He knew that as lightly as Huong slept, he might notice the change in the night sound and awaken. Anxiety sent Harris running, with Turd loping at his side.

After awakening and finding the dog and his master missing, Huong walked outside, leaned against one of the front porch's four support columns, and lit a cigarette.

"He's gone after that rat Elmo," Bao said in Vietnamese to his brother, spitting as he said the traitor James Elmore's name, and then lighting a cigarette. "Will you try to stop him?"

"What do you think?" Huong asked, looking at Bao.

"I say let the fool go," Bao said, blowing out a breath of smoke. "Maybe he can kill Elmo."

Both men stood on the front porch, saying nothing and thinking as they looked into the morning darkness and listened as the voices of the frogs slowly returned.

"I think maybe the Marines that patrol the fences at Chu Lai may very likely kill our foolish friend," Huong said, clenching his cigarette in his lips as he spoke to his brother in their native language. "If Mau Mau remains lucky, though, the Americans may only capture him. That troubles me. I worry that he may talk of our plans and our money."

"Then we should go after him," Bao said, flicking his spent butt onto the ground in front of the two steps that led onto the wooden porch where he stood by his older brother.

"We have no hurry," Huong said, and flicked his cigarette onto the barren yard, too. "I know where he is going. He told us yesterday, you may recall. Even if he runs the entire distance it will take him several hours to travel forty kilometers. We can drive near that place in thirty minutes, and maybe get a shot at the fool before the guards capture him. For now, I think I would like to drink some tea and eat a nice breakfast. It will take us a good while to drive to Saigon, once we finish our business here."

Nearly an hour had passed before James Harris ever slowed his fast jog to a more comfortable shuffle. The sense that Huong may pursue him only moments away left his anxiety level high.

Finally the Chicago native stopped to catch his breath, and took several short chugs from a flat, round canteen of water that he had filled from the farm's well and had thrown across his shoulder after he found it in the tool shack that morning. As he left the house, he had sneaked into the shed to retrieve a bolo knife with a foot-long inwardly curved blade that he had spotted several days earlier. When he had first examined the razor-sharp weapon, he considered that with one deft whack he could lob off James Elmore's head with it. So as he departed that morning, he grabbed the canteen along with the knife and slipped it through his belt opposite the .45-caliber Colt pistol he had hanging on his other hip.

While in the shed, Harris had noticed a dusty, oil-stained, olive green tarpaulin covering what he had thought were only machine parts and other junk belonging to a dilapidated mechanical rice thrasher that sat next to the pile. At first he started not to look under the canvas, but then he thought that Huong's Viet Cong relatives who lived there might have hidden some worthwhile weaponry there, too. As he folded back the cover he found a grit-caked gallon can of thirty-weight motor oil and a large wooden box filled with greasy parts to the thrashing machine. Next to them, however, he also discovered two dusty cases of sixty-millimeter mortar rounds and a wooden box with half a dozen dirt-covered fragmentation hand grenades nestled on a heap of corroded .30-caliber rifle rounds, their dingy brass casings turned green with age. Mau Mau had smiled as he grabbed one of the fist-size green bomblets and dropped it in the cargo pocket on the right leg of his utility trousers.

"Why you always on my ass?" Harris whispered to the dog as he knelt on the narrow trail that he followed south toward Chu Lai, and poured water in his cupped hand for the mutt to drink. Turd lapped the liquid with great thirst, and then shook a shower of slobber onto Mau Mau's face.

"Damn, you dumb motherfucker," the deserter said, wiping the splatter off his brow and cheeks with his upper sleeve and shoulder. "That's some nasty shit, Turd."

Screwing the lid back on the canteen, James Harris let it drop again to the rear part of his hip, where it rode suspended by its green webbed-canvas shoulder strap. Then he gave the bolo knife a tug to make sure it still held tight beneath his belt, patted the hand grenade in his cargo pocket, and set off jogging again as the new day's gray light began to show color and expose form where moments earlier shadows and blackness had surrounded him. Ahead, he could now see a greater distance of the trail he followed.

While he ran, he tried not to think of the Viet Cong and North Vietnamese patrols that haunted this stretch of countryside north of Chu Lai. Would they shoot a lone American deserter and his dog should he cross the kill zone of their ambush? Why waste all that on one man and a mutt? He considered the logic and pressed onward, gambling his safety on his Chicago street instincts and Turd's innate sense of avoiding danger.

"FOR THE RECORD, please state your name," Terry O'Connor said, standing behind the lectern between the defense and prosecution tables in the courtroom.

"Lance Corporal Wendell Carter," the witness recited, speaking with a clear voice, just as the defense lawyer had instructed him to do.

"I see that you have recently been promoted from private first class to lance corporal. Congratulations," O'Connor said, smiling at his leadoff witness.

"Yes, sir, thank you," Carter answered, and beamed a smile, too. "My squadron CO pinned it on me the day before yesterday."

"How long have you been on legal hold, Lance Corporal Carter?" O'Connor asked, stepping from behind the lectern to allow a barrier-free discourse of conversation to develop between him and the star defense witness.

"Three months now, sir," Carter answered, and frowned.

"You miss your family, too, don't you?" O'Connor asked.

"Oh, sir, I miss them real bad," Carter said, shaking his head. "My mama, she pray for me every day, and just about everyone else I know in Houston, too. They all wanting me home."

"So these three months on legal hold have taken their toll," O'Connor said, shaking his head, too.

"I want to go home, sir, but I keep my attitude squared away. You know, I do what I got to do," Carter said, and nodded at the captain to put emphasis to his words.

"It's easy to let go and have your attitude slide downhill at times like this, isn't it," O'Connor said, nodding, too.

"Well, sir, my mama taught me to do my best, always, and let the good Lord sort out the difficulties," Carter said and smiled.

"You got yourself promoted, even on legal hold," O'Connor said, and walked back to the defense table and picked up his notepad, glancing at the top page. "Says here that your proficiency and conduct marks are 4.7 and 4.9 out of a possible 5.0, so you're a pretty good Marine."

"Sir, I pride myself at being a good Marine," Carter said, puffing out his chest.

"I think if the prosecution wanted to investigate your record they would only find exemplary conduct, would they not?" O'Connor said, laying his legal pad back on the table. Then he walked back to the witness stand and put his hands on the rail surrounding the plywood platform.

"How many security patrols have you gone on during your tour?" O'Connor asked, and turned toward the jury as he spoke.

"More than I care to count, sir," Carter answered, his eyes following the captain as he now stepped so that the witness's face looked at the six men seated in the side gallery deciding the case.

"One a month?" O'Connor asked, crossing his arms.

"No, sir, more like five, sometimes six a month," Carter answered.

"These patrols last how long?" O'Connor asked, holding the witness's face toward the jury.

"Mostly overnight, but sometimes we get tagged with patrols that stay out for a week," Carter said.

"You stand fire watch and guard duty, too?" O'Connor asked, now leaning his hand on the rail that surrounded the jury box.

"Yes, sir, that and perimeter watch, too," Carter said, nodding at the captain.

"Oh, yes, that, too," O'Connor said, glancing back at the jury.

"You're a skilled radio repairman as well as a communicator, are you not?" the captain then asked.

"Yes, sir, me and PFC Anderson, we work together in the same shop over at Group Seventeen," Carter answered.

"Well, if you're on guard duty, fire watch, perimeter watch, and half a dozen security patrols a month, when do you work on radios?" O'Connor asked, and looked at the jury.

"I don't get to do a whole lot of radio work, sir," Carter said, shaking his head.

"Do the white Marines pull the extra duty that you do?" O'Connor asked, crossing his arms and frowning at the witness.

"Sir, I don't worry about what the white Marines do. That's how a guy ends up with a bad attitude," Carter said, and shook his head. "It's tough enough just pulling the tour and getting home. I don't need to get my head all messed up thinking about what the other Marines get."

"Your mama taught you that, too?" O'Connor asked, and smiled.

"Yes, sir, she did, as a matter of fact," Carter said, and held his head up. "We live pretty poor. Just about everybody got lots more than we got. Times be I didn't have shoes. Never had them in summer anyway. Save them for school. Then they be too little for my big old feet, so I take out the laces and try to get a few more miles out of them. Anyhow, my mama taught all us kids not to look at what other folks got, but thank God and my Lord Jesus that we got what we do. We had food, and we had a house. Not much more, but we did get by."

"How well do you know the defendant, Private First Class Celestine Anderson?" O'Connor asked, walking toward the defense table where his client sat bound by chains.

"He my pea," Carter said, looking at his buddy.

"Pea?" O'Connor asked and shrugged.

"Like peas in a pod, you know what folks say," Carter said, trying to explain the colloquial term. "We close. Always do stuff together, live in the same hooch, come from the same hometown and all."

"Buddies," O'Connor offered.

"Yes, sir," Carter nodded.

"So you know the defendant as well as anyone could know him?" O'Connor asked, walking behind Anderson and putting his hands on Celestine's shoulders.

"He's my brother," Carter said and sighed.

"Not by blood but by friendship," O'Connor said, offering clarification.

"In the larger sense we have the same blood," Carter said, nodding his head. "Our African blood. Our slave blood. So we have a term we call each other, Blood. For that reason."

"Right," O'Connor said, walking from behind the defense table and approaching the witness stand as he spoke. "Pride in your heritage. Your common roots."

"The struggle of our people to overcome oppression," Carter followed.

"Do you feel oppressed?" O'Connor asked, and looked at the jury, focusing on the black staff sergeant seated on the end.

"You can't be black and not feel oppressed," Carter said, and looked at the staff sergeant, too, who nodded back at the witness. Then Carter looked at the captain. "Sir, we fight a war here to save these South Vietnamese people from oppression by the Communists, yet we brothers fighting in this war have to deal with oppression from our own country. You read the newspapers. You know what's going on back home."

"Yes, I do, Lance Corporal Carter," O'Connor said, and looked at Charlie Heyster, who had his head down, writing furiously on his yellow legal pad.

"How often did PFC Anderson stand the same duties you described earlier to us?" the captain then asked, walking back toward the jury so they could see Carter's face as he answered the question.

"I don't think he ever get off duty," Carter said, and laughed. "He stood more than me or any of the other black Marines in our unit."

"Why did he stand more duty?" O'Connor asked.

"Objection!" Heyster spat, kicking his chair back as he jumped to his feet. "Your Honor, he is asking the witness to speculate."

"Your Honor, I will rephrase my question," O'Connor said before the judge could overrule him.

"Lance Corporal Carter, did your work section assign duty in an even distribution among all Marines?" O'Connor asked.

"No, sir," Carter said, and looked at Charlie Heyster, "the gunny and I think the captain, too, they assign duty as punishment. A guy mouth off, he get shit detail for a week. Stuff like that."

"Did Private Anderson have a problem mouthing off?" O'Connor asked, walking back toward the defense table.

"No problem at all," Carter said, and laughed. "Celestine, he mouth off just about anytime he want. He never had a problem mouthing off. Controlling his mouth, well, sir, he did have a problem there."

"As a result, he got every duty quota that came through the door," O'Connor said, looking at the jury.

"Objection, your honor, speculation," Heyster said, slamming his hand on the table where he sat.

"The witness can have firsthand knowledge of why Anderson was assigned duties, so I will allow it. As long as he testifies to what he has witnessed firsthand, then it is not speculation," the judge said in his ruling. Then he took off his glasses and looked at Captain Heyster. "Could you please come here, Captain? I have a question."

Charlie Heyster scowled at Terry O'Connor and walked to the judge's bench, where he joined the defense lawyer in a private conversation with Colonel Richard Swanson.

"I've had enough of your surly attitude this morning, Captain Heyster. When you voice an objection, a clearly spoken word not shouted will suffice. We happen to be in the same room, and my hearing is excellent," Swanson whispered to the prosecutor. "What's going on with you?"

"Sir, I apologize," Heyster said, and then curled his lips at Terry O'Connor. "The defense informed me yesterday that he would lead off with Private Anderson's testimony, and I had prepared for his appearance this morning. The defense counsel's trickery has left me somewhat unprepared for the current witness."

"So you're pissed off at the defense?" Swanson said, looking at Terry O'Connor, who fought to keep a smile off his face.

"Deceitful trickery!" Heyster hissed.

The judge looked at the papers on his desk, and then back at Heyster. "According to the witness list that the defense has provided, Lance Corporal Carter's name appears with two other witnesses before Private Anderson. Captain, you had ample notice. If you based your preparations on the order that the defense presents its witnesses, I think you should revisit your methodology," the judge said, chiding the prosecutor.

"Sir, he told me yesterday that Private Anderson would lead off this morning," Heyster pled, now leaning toward the judge for help.

"As far as I know, Private Anderson may or may not testify," Swanson said, and looked at O'Connor.

"Sir," the defense lawyer said, "I apologize for misleading Captain Heyster. He spoke to me after you adjourned yesterday's session, and said some unkind remarks, using very brutal language. I have to admit that I responded in anger to his challenge against my client and what he would do to him once he got on the stand. I do apologize, sir."

"Gentlemen," the judge said, frowning at both captains, "as difficult as this may seem for you to understand, this is no game. We have no prize for the winner, no points or pennant to award. We only have losers if you let your petty, personal differences interfere with the justice we must strive to achieve in this man's trial. Captain Heyster, I know your reputation, so don't act so innocently violated. Captain O'Connor, I admonish you for lying to the prosecution, even in an unofficial manner through casual conversation. From here forward, you both will conduct yourselves with civility in my court. You will present your cases in a professional manner, respectful of all parties present. Is that clear?"

"Yes, sir," Heyster said, and turned his eyes downward.

"Sorry, Charlie," O'Connor said, and offered his hand for the prosecutor to shake. After a hesitation and a cool glance from the judge, Heyster accepted the defense lawyer's gesture and then returned to his seat.

Terry O'Connor walked back to the jury and then looked at Wendell Carter.

"Private Anderson stood the majority of duty because he vocalized his frustrations?" the lawyer asked the witness.

"Yes, sir, to put it one way, he did," Carter answered.

"Put it your way then," O'Connor said, shrugging.

"Celestine he mouthed off at the gunny every time a brother caught shit," Carter said, and looked at Anderson. "Most times it was none of his business, but he'd make it his business because most times a brother caught shit was because of his blackness."

"Your Honor," Captain Heyster said, standing from his seat, "the witness is speculating as to the reason why a brother caught shit, specifically because of his blackness. It's clearly his opinion, and not a statement of what he witnessed."

"Captain, I disagree and will allow the question and answer to stand," the judge said, leaning forward and looking at the prosecutor. "The witness is testifying as to his perception of what occurred. Our truths are based on what we perceive to be true. Granted, the gunny's motivations for dealing the extra duty to black Marines may have been different from what the witness perceived, but his own perceptions are what constitute the witness's reality. What the witness represents as honest beliefs commonly held among himself and his peers as to his gunny's motivations behind assigning the extra duty to black Marines are relevant."

During the objection and ruling, Terry O'Connor had returned to the defense table and scanned his notes. Then he walked back to where Wendell Carter sat.

"Lance Corporal Carter, did you at any time believe that Celestine Anderson intended to kill Harold Rein?" the defense attorney asked, and stepped toward the jury box.

"No, sir," the witness responded, following the captain with his eyes.

"The prosecution would like us to believe that you knew that Private Anderson meant to kill Private Rein, thereby using your actions to imply a sense of premeditation on the part of the defendant. They have presented several witnesses who say that you tried to stop Private Anderson from killing Private Rein. Why did you step in front of Private Anderson then, if you did not believe that he intended to kill Private Rein?" O'Connor asked, leaning against the jury box rail, waiting for another objection from Major-Select Heyster, this time for leading the witness with his question, but no objection came. Charlie the shyster busily scribbled notes on his legal pad and let the question stand.

"Those boys, Buster Rein, Laddie Cross, and the other two white Marines, they was trying to pick a fight with us," Lance Corporal Carter said, glancing at each juror's face. "I knew Celestine's temper, and he would not back off a fight if somebody threw down on him. I figure that Buster going to walk up and sock Celestine in the nose, and that start a big fight. So I try to get Celestine to just ignore those boys. I step in front of him, so I can turn him around. Stop it from being a fight. I never dream he kill that boy."

"What did Private Rein and the others do to try to start the fight?"

O'Connor then asked, still leaning against the rail that surrounded the jury box.

"They be calling us niggers, and porch monkeys, and coons, and stuff like that," Carter responded, still looking at the defense lawyer and the jury. "They say they ain't afraid of black power, and that when Buster Rein put that cigarette in his teeth and walk at us hollering, 'Any you niggers got a light?' "

"What is your attitude about racial epithets and such slurs as they were using?" O'Connor asked, walking toward the witness stand.

"I don't like hearing none of that stuff," Wendell Carter said, shaking his head.

"Do you use any of those words?" O'Connor asked, resting his hands on the rail surrounding the witness stand.

"Some black people, they say them," Carter said, shaking his head and looking at the jury, "especially the word, 'nigger.' I hate that coming out anybody's mouth, black or white. I never say them names. The sooner people forget words like that life be getting a whole lot better for everybody."

"What about Private Anderson?" O'Connor said, and walked toward the defense table. "He ever use those words?"

"Not as I recall, sir, no, sir," Carter said, looking at his pal seated next to Wayne Ebberhardt.

"Before the incident, you and Private Anderson had made some plans, had you not?" O'Connor said, picking up his yellow legal pad and looking at notes he had written on it.

"Yes, sir," Carter said, turning his face, following the defense lawyer as he walked back to the jury. "We supposed to get released from active duty a couple of months after we go Stateside. That was before that day at the chow hall last November. Anyway, we was going to take our bus fare home, and pool our pay and go join the Reverend Doctor Martin Luther King and his crusade for civil rights."

"You were going to just show up on Doctor King's doorstep?" O'Connor asked, resting his hand on the jury box rail.

"No, sir," Carter answered, looking at the jury. "One of Doctor King's assistants, a preacher named Andrew Young, he wrote me back a letter after I wrote to them last summer when Celestine and I first talked about doing something for civil rights. Reverend Young said that we be welcome to join up. He said they could sure use a couple of good Vietnam veteran Marines."

"So today, had this unfortunate event not occurred, you and Private Anderson would be with Doctor King's campaign on this very Wednesday morning, isn't that correct?" O'Connor said, wagging his legal pad in his hand as he spoke.

"Yes, sir," Carter said, smiling. "We was supposed to get released from active duty on March first, so today being April third, we would have been with him at least a couple of weeks by now."

"Do you dislike white people?" O'Connor asked, walking toward the witness stand.

"No, sir," Carter said and smiled. "I know lots of white guys that's real decent. I don't dislike nobody unless they give me a reason."

"What did you think of Private Harold Rein and Private Leonard Cross?" O'Connor asked, crossing his arms.

"I didn't think much of those boys at all," Carter said, frowning.

"You did know them before the incident," O'Connor said, still holding his arms crossed, the yellow legal pad dangling from his hand.

"We seen them around, and heard plenty from them," Carter said, still frowning.

"Care to explain that?" O'Connor asked, and walked back toward the jury.

"They always making trouble around black Marines," Carter said and shook his head. "They see black Marines talking, dapping, or what have you, and they always looking to start some trouble."

"Dapping?" O'Connor asked, looking back at the jury. "Please explain dapping."

"That's just a greeting, like when white people shake hands," Carter said and looked at the jury. "It symbolizes friendship and unity among black brothers."

"So it is not a symbolism of black power, meant to degrade white people, as the prosecution has asserted with its witnesses yesterday," O'Connor said, smiling at Charlie Heyster and then at Wendell Carter.

"If it meant to degrade anybody, I wouldn't do it," Carter answered.

"So you would dap with a white Marine, too?" O'Connor asked, and walked to the witness stand.

"If he want to dap with me, sure I do it," Carter said and smiled. "It's a symbol of friendship, like I said."

"Would you show the court by dapping with me?" the captain then said, putting out his fist for the witness.

"Yes, sir," Carter said, and then put his closed hand above the lawyer's. "My knuckles up here means that you're not above me. Then when I put my fist under yours, it means that I'm not above you either. Then we rap on this side and that side, like this, and that means we are equal. We bang our knuckles like this, says we brothers. Then we put our fists across our hearts, pledging our friendship to each other."

"What about when you put your fists in the air?" O'Connor said, raising his clenched hand above his head.

"We are brothers, united," Carter said, raising his fist, too.

"Would you recommend that all Marines dap?" O'Connor asked, lowering his hand and walking back toward the jury.

Wendell Carter smiled.

"Yes, sir, I certainly would recommend it," the witness said, and looked at the jury. "Marines are warriors. Great warriors. This salute come from the Masai, who are great warriors, too, in Africa. They kill a lion with a spear. This how they greet each other. I think it be a good thing for Marines to have something like that to use, too."

"Thank you, Lance Corporal Carter," O'Connor said, and walked back to the defense table.

"Do you have any questions for this witness, Captain Heyster?" Judge Swanson said, looking at the prosecutor flipping through several pages of notes he had taken during the defense examination.

"Yes, Your Honor," Heyster said, and walked to the tabletop lectern, where he leaned across it and stared coldly at the witness.

" 'Chuck,' 'honky,' 'white bread,' 'cracker,' " Heyster began, "these terms mean anything?"

"I hear some guys say them, yes, sir," Carter said, gripping the rail around the witness stand.

"What would you say if I told you I had witnesses who heard you and Private Anderson saying some of these very words," Heyster said, still gripping the lectern and leaning over it.

"I don't use those words, sir," Carter answered, and then looked down. "They bad as saying 'nigger.' "

"Yes, they are," Heyster said, and stepped from behind the lectern. "Equally offensive. Now, will you categorically state for the record that you have never uttered these offensive racial slurs?"

"No, sir, because I have said some of them a time or two," Carter said, still looking down. "Maybe when I got mad."

"So what makes you different than Private Rein, when he called you a nigger?" the prosecutor asked, walking toward the witness.

"When I call him a Chuck, I guess nothing, sir," Carter shrugged and shook his head.

"Did you see Private Celestine Anderson kill Private Harold Rein?" Heyster said, folding his arms. "Just a yes or no answer please."

"Yes, sir," Carter said, squinting his eyes closed.

"No more questions," Heyster said, and walked back to the prosecution table and sat down behind it.

MIDMORNING SUN COOKED the ground brick hard where James Harris jogged, raising a cloud of dust around his feet. He had drank the last of his water, tossing the canteen in the weeds just before he crossed through the layers of fencing, tanglefoot, German tape and razor wire that ran along the perimeter of the American military compound and air facility at Chu Lai. Now he wished that he had refilled the can when he had the chance as he jogged past a well at a farm he crossed. However, the stop might have cost him his life had Huong caught up with him there. So he ran on, and made it clean through the fence at Chu Lai, but he was still very thirsty.

While Harris had fretted much of his journey, worrying about how he could sneak through the wire at Chu Lai, the task proved almost too easy for him. Spring rains had washed a low place along the ground, just deep enough so he slid on his belly beneath much of the barrier, out of sight of the bunkers and guard stations keeping watch. While Mau Mau crawled through the fencing, Turd sat in the weeds, watching him. Then when his master stood, and dusted off his clothes, the dog bounded under the barrier, carefree and his tail wagging happily.

Ahead, through the dancing mirage, the deserter could see the white hangar at the far end of the flight line where he felt certain that James Elmore now secretly worked, fabricating metal parts for airplanes. He knew this hangar well. Late last summer, while a newbee in Da Nang, Mau Mau's gunny had sent him and three other airframe mechanics to Chu Lai to work for three weeks, helping out a shorthanded friend. Harris knew from that brief stint that this was the only maintenance hangar outside the main stream of traffic where CID could keep James Elmore working secretly. He smiled confidently, looking at the red and white checkerboard roof on the building, knowing well that the traitor worked inside.

As he ran, Mau Mau saw a familiar black Mercedes-Benz pull through an opening in the trees less than five hundred yards away, drive along a dirt road outside the fence line, and then park, hidden behind some tall bushes. Turd saw the car, too, and stopped to look at it. As the driver stepped out and walked to the front of the automobile, wading through the underbrush, the dog wagged his tail. He thought nothing of the rifle that Huong carried in his hands.

Behind and ahead of where Mau Mau Harris ran along the perimeter road, skirting the far end of the base's runways and taxiways, red signs eight feet tall stood at the edge of the dirt track that ran parallel to the airfield's boundary and read in great white letters, *Restricted Area—Keep Out*, in both English and Vietnamese. Maybe Huong would think twice before opening fire, the deserter hoped. Surely his old comrade knew that the shooting would draw attention from the guard posts overseeing this remote part of the compound. At the sound of rifle fire, they would come rolling like gangbusters, their guns blazing.

Then Harris considered that Huong could easily shoot him anyway and still make a run for it. Whether or not the reaction force that would doubtless pursue the pair ever caught Huong and Bao, he would still suffer the brunt of the bullets that the cowboy managed to launch at him. With no place to take cover, Harris leaned forward and ran hard.

From the corner of his right eye, Mau Mau saw Huong raise the rifle to his shoulder and aim at him. He clenched his jaws as he pumped his legs, waiting for the first bullet to strike. Then he noticed that the cowboy had taken the rifle out of his shoulder and now hurried back behind the weeds and bushes where he had hidden the car. A second later, he heard the whine of a GMC pickup truck's engine and the clanking and banging of its body against its frame as it bounced across the ends of the runways and open terrain between them.

The deserter smiled as he saw the dirty green M880 truck with a three-foot-wide orange and white checkered flag flapping on a stick mounted to the rear corner of its cargo bed, an M2 .50-caliber machine gun stationed above its cab and a Marine wearing goggles holding on for dear life behind the gun. When the truck bounced onto the well-traveled dirt trail that ran along the airfield's fence, it slid sideways and raised a cloud of calcium-rich dust from the crushed oyster shells packed onto the road's surface.

At first sight of the pickup truck speeding cross-country toward them, Turd wheeled on his tail and made a mad scramble for the place in the fence where he and his master had crossed a few moments ago.

As the truck slid to a stop ten feet from where Mau Mau Harris stood, the Marine behind the big machine gun opened fire at the fleeing dog, sending geysers of dirt twenty feet in the air all around the mutt but nowhere near him.

"Cease fire, motherfucker!" a staff sergeant dressed in a jungle utility uniform screamed as he leaped from the passenger side of the M880 truck.

"Why you want to waste a fucking dog anyway, you stupid son of a bitch?! Besides, you shoot like Little Stevie Wonder. You ain't ever hit Jack shit!"

"Now, I like Little Stevie Wonder," Mau Mau Harris said, smiling and wiping sweat off his face with a blue bandana that he pulled from his pocket and then tied around his head like a sweatband. "Don't be insulting my favorite singer just cause he blind and your man can't shoot worth shit, Sergeant."

"What the fuck do you think you are doing out here?" the staff sergeant said to Harris, who kept smiling at him. "What part of *Restricted Area—Keep Out* do you not understand?"

"Hey, chill out, man," Harris said, walking to the truck and pushing his thumb on the silver button at the base of a green water canister strapped to the side of the pickup bed, sending out a stream into his mouth and over his face. "I thought that meant people outside the base. Military is cool, isn't it?"

"You're lucky those guys over in that bunker between the parallel runways didn't blow you away," the staff sergeant said, walking to the water can and squirting out a drink, too. "Let's see some identification."

"Hey, man, I'm new here, I didn't know," Harris said, smiling and shrugging his best act, pulling his fake identification card from his wallet and handing it to the staff sergeant while the staff NCO examined his dog tags. "My name's Sergeant Rufus Potter. I just got transferred down here from Da Nang Air Base. I'm over at Group Seventeen, working up yonder in that hangar in the fabrication shop. I came out for a little morning run, keep myself fit for the commandant, you know, and this looked like a pretty good spot for PT, so I went jogging up here. I didn't mean nothing. Sorry to get anybody upset."

"We can maybe let you slide, Sergeant Potter, since you're new," the staff sergeant said, wiping his mouth with his sleeve. "Just let me hold on to your pistol and that knife you got in your belt while we haul your ass up to that hangar and check you out. I want you to introduce me to your gunny, and let me talk to him."

"That's cool, man," Mau Mau said, handing the weapons to the staff sergeant and then climbing in the back of the pickup next to the errant machine gunner.

"That your dog?" the Marine asked Harris as he saddled up next to him.

"Shit no, man," Harris lied. "He probably belong to some gooners living outside the wire, and he just wanted to come run along with me, I guess."

Suddenly Mau Mau slammed his hands on the roof of the truck's cab just as the driver had pulled forward.

"Stop! We got Viet Cong over there!" Harris screamed, and began pushing the barrel of the machine gun toward the bushes where Huong and Bao had hidden in their black car.

"How you know they VC?!" the Marine lance corporal behind the machine gun screamed back, pulling Harris's hands off the weapon's barrel. "We can't just go shooting at people outside the wire."

"The dude got a rifle, man! You didn't see it?" Harris said, looking down at the staff sergeant, who jumped out of the truck with an M16 rifle, raised it to his shoulder, and took aim at the bushes where Huong and Bao hid.

"I ain't seen shit, Sergeant Potter!" the staff sergeant shouted, looking for the enemy.

"Two dudes over there!" Harris screamed, pointing at the bushes. "I seen one of them with a rifle. They VC, man. Open fire with this machine gun. We find that rifle when you kill the motherfuckers!"

Mau Mau then tried to push the lance corporal from behind the machine gun and open fire with it. The young Marine, with his goggles now askew, fought back, trying to hold control of the heavy weapon.

"Back the fuck off, ass wipe!" the staff sergeant screamed, climbing in the back of the truck and pulling Harris's hands off the tailpiece of the machine gun before he could release a burst of fire.

"Look, motherfucker, now they getting away!" Harris whined in a loud voice as he watched Huong tromp the gas on the Mercedes and speed down the dirt road.

"Radio the reaction squad, Corporal O'Brien!" the staff sergeant shouted, leaning over the truck cab and looking inside the driver's window.

"Shit, man, they be long gone now," Harris said, shaking his head and seeing the black car disappear.

HUONG AND BAO had lain in the bushes, watching the guard vehicle stop Mau Mau Harris. In a few seconds Turd had jumped in the brush with them. When the two cowboys saw their former cohort swing the machine gun their way, Bao leaped inside the car as Huong threw Turd in the backseat and then jumped behind the steering wheel, stomping the accelerator pedal to the floorboard, and punctuating their departure from the scene with a rooster tail of dirt flying through the air.

They had packed ample food and water, and all of their belongings and

money, but to Huong's dismay he had badly underestimated Mau Mau
Harris's ability to traverse forty kilometers of countryside crosshatched
with rice canals, fields, hedges, and fence lines, not to mention dodging
Communist and American patrols. The cowboy had hoped to ambush
Mau Mau as he crossed the road outside the military base, and then speed
off to Saigon with his brother.

Although disappointed that he had missed killing his former comrade,
Huong felt good that the dog had escaped. He liked Turd, and seeing him
again flee well ahead of danger, outrunning the erratic bullets, he regarded
him as a powerful carrier of good fortune. However, with Harris now a
matter of the past, Huong decided to change the name of this good dog to
something better. Even for a no-account cur, the cowboy certainly would
not insult him by calling him a name like shit.

ALREADY, THE MIDMORNING heat sent a mirage boiling up from the tarmac
outside the hangar where Lance Corporal James Elmore stood near a window, working on a thick, flat square of metal. A man-sized electric fan
mounted on a five-foot-tall stand droned in the heat, blowing hot air
toward the building's massive, open doorway.

While he fashioned the hunk of steel, the slack-minded Marine gazed
across the runways at the flight line where A-4 attack jets sat, parked between high stacks of oil barrels that protected the planes from enemy rockets and mortar shells. Their bird-shaped bodies shimmered, taking on an
almost liquid appearance in the distorting mirage generated by the scorch-
ing sun. As Elmore dreamily watched the heat waves dance across the runway matting, asphalt, and concrete that covered the ground, he noticed a
speck of a person and a dog plodding along the perimeter road toward the
aircraft maintenance and fabrication hangar where he worked.

Elmore had begun boring holes in the flat metal plate for a helicopter
gun mount when he first noticed the ambling gait of the Marine and the
mangy brown mutt lumbering at his side. Even at more than a quarter of
a mile distance, the jogger had a haunting look about him that made the
tattletale nervous.

His heart started to beat more quickly as his mind began to place this
gangly black Marine who drew closer and closer. Could it be him? James
Mau Mau Harris?

Then, when the guard vehicle slid to a stop by the running man, and
the men had their brief conversation, followed by the runner casually getting a drink of water and then climbing inside the back of the guard vehi-

cle, hitching himself a ride, all of the Marines acting friendly to each other, Elmore relaxed. He focused his attention back to the square hunk of metal and bored more holes where he had drawn red ink marks, laid out from a master template. To him these days, nearly everyone at first looked like James Mau Mau Harris, or worse yet, Brian Snowman Pitts.

Anymore, with so many weeks of worrying about the two notorious deserters finding him, and each time he thought that he saw one of the deadly duo and it always turned out to be just another Marine, he began to more easily discount his fears. He reassured himself as he bored the hole in the steel that had Mau Mau Harris shown his face on the flight line—or at any other American base in the Da Nang and Chu Lai areas, for that matter—military police would have descended on him like a cloud of locusts and clapped him in chains. They certainly would not have had a casual conversation on the flight line with the fugitive, nor would they have offered the scoundrel a ride, much less given him a drink of their water.

"JUMP OUT, SERGEANT Potter, let's go and get your gunny," the staff sergeant said, walking into the shade just inside the hangar door.

As James Harris jumped from the back of the truck, he held his hand firmly against his cargo pocket to keep the hand grenade from bouncing out. Then as he walked through the entrance, too, he shoved his hand inside the pouch on his leg and wrapped his fingers around the small fragmentation bomb.

James Elmore stood at the drill press, next to one of the hangar's large, multipane side windows, the light streaming on him. Mau Mau Harris saw the traitor's eyes grow wide and his mouth drop open, a high-pitched scream echoing through the high building.

"Grenade!" a voice behind Mau Mau shouted, and Marines everywhere dove for cover. All except James Elmore, who stood wide-eyed, his mouth agape and still screaming.

Mau Mau Harris laughed as he yanked the pin from the hand grenade and threw it like a fast-pitched baseball straight at the pigeon who had ratted him and Brian Pitts out, and had caused the death of Wild Thing.

Instinctively, James Elmore put up his right hand just as the green, explosive ball hurtled at him. The smooth metal stung the palm of his hand as he caught the object, and the sharp edge of the fuse end of the grenade cut two of his fingers as he closed them around it.

For several seconds the shocked Marine stood paralyzed in fear with the explosive device wrapped by his hand. Then his senses came to him and he shrieked.

"Motherfucker!" Elmore screamed, and threw the hand grenade through a glass windowpane behind the drill press and dove flat on the concrete floor.

Seconds passed and nothing happened. Then Marines in the hangar began to stand up and dust off their trousers. The staff sergeant ran full force at Mau Mau Harris, who now fled toward the open door, and knocked the fugitive to the ground while his two assistants wrestled the deserter's hands behind him.

"Tie this goofy motherfucker up, and somebody call the provost marshal!" the staff sergeant growled.

"Don't you know who that son of a bitch is?" James Elmore cried, dancing on his toes, pointing at the prisoner.

"He says his name is Sergeant Rufus Potter, and so do his dog tags and ID card," the staff sergeant said, and looked at Elmore. "What do you know that I don't?"

"That's Mau Mau Harris, man," Elmore wailed. "He come here to murder my ass. Throw that grenade at me. CID look all over Da Nang for him and a dude name Brian Pitts. Pitts be the Snowman, and kill people and sell dope and shit. This guy here, that his main man. He want kill me to shut me the fuck up."

"Fucking dud grenade," Harris grumbled with his cheek pressed against the concrete floor. "Someday I still kill your ass, you rat weasel motherfucker. If I don't do it, Snowman, he do it. Maybe even one his cowboys. You ain't safe no more, nowhere, Elmore."

"How you know I be here, man?" James Elmore squealed, still dancing on his toes. "They rat me out?"

"Yeah, man," Harris laughed. "They tole me you down here in da Chu Lai, fabricating metal. What else they be doing with your rat ass no way?"

"Who tole you that, man? Who they?" Elmore cried.

"Cops, man, they tole it all," Harris said with a laugh, the side of his face against the concrete and the staff sergeant's boot standing squarely between his shoulder blades. "They take payoff like anybody else. Money open doors, show the way. I got me this nice Viet Cong bolo knife that this staff sergeant done took. I sharpen it all up to cut me some pigeon. I guess now Snowman or his buddy Huong be cuttin' that pigeon. Pigeon name Elmore. Give you what they tole you they do, pull your traitor tongue out your throat. Ain't no place anybody keep you that we ain't gonna find your rat ass, you turncoat motherfucker."

Suddenly a deafening boom erupted outside and blew the entire frame of panes inward from the big window behind the drill press, sending glass shards spraying across the concrete floor. The staff sergeant dove on top of Mau Mau Harris, while everyone else jumped for cover where they could find it.

"Shit, man," Harris grumbled. "Slow-ass, greasy, nonworking, Viet Cong fuse on that grenade, I guess. You one lucky motherfucker, Elmore, you know that? Only that luck run just so deep. Nobody be forgetting what you done. Ever."

"Mau Mau!" James Elmore now pled, rising from the concrete to his hands and knees and spreading a wide smile at his prostrate nemesis, his gold front tooth sparkling as his lips quivered around it. "I ain't saying shit, man. Not now, not no more. You gots to tell Snowman I ain't saying shit."

With the culprit's hands tightly bound with nylon parachute cord, the staff sergeant yanked James Harris to his feet and shoved him at the two Marine guards, who each took an arm. As they led him out the hangar door, Mau Mau looked back at James Elmore and laughed.

"You one dead-rat-motherfucker," the deserter snarled, and then he hawked a mouthful of spit at the cowering snitch. The glob sailed in a high arc but fell short of the target, splattering on the floor.

For a while, James Elmore only stared at the wet splotch on the concrete. Then his stomach turned from the shock of the morning's ordeal, and he raced to the head to upchuck his breakfast.

Chapter 13

I GIVES THE BEAST A LIGHT

BY THREE O'CLOCK Thursday afternoon, Terry O'Connor had finally completed his examination of all but one defense witness in the Celestine Anderson murder trial, with only a begrudging wave coming from Charlie Heyster that he had no questions for the last man in the chair. O'Connor asked the judge to recall one of the prosecution's early witnesses he had reserved to possibly return to testify for the defense, and now wanted him, Gunnery Sergeant Ray Glickman, the noncommissioned officer in charge of the work section that employed Celestine Anderson and Wendell Carter.

Since the gunny had to commute to Da Nang from Chu Lai, Judge Swanson adjourned the court-martial until eight o'clock Friday morning, April 5, 1968. Captain O'Connor had promised the judge that he would have the defense's case wrapped up by ten o'clock, and they could begin closing arguments.

"I know that you're a busy man, so thank you for returning to the court this morning, Gunny Glickman," Terry O'Connor said to the Marine from Binghamton, New York, after the presiding judge reminded the witness that he had earlier sworn to tell the truth and that his affirmation from that time still held effect. "I just have a few questions, and the prosecution may have some to follow mine. I promise to have you off the stand as quickly as possible.

"Do you recognize these documents?" O'Connor said, holding up a black, three-ring binder filled with lists of names and job assignments noted by them.

"Yes, sir, that's my duty rosters," the gunny answered. "You guys had them confiscated a couple of days ago."

"Correct, gunny, we had them subpoenaed, and taken as evidence," O'Connor answered, and laid the black binder on the judge's desk. "Your Honor, please enter this black notebook containing the duty assignments as exhibit twenty-six, and this other binder as exhibit twenty-seven."

"That green one's my personnel roster," the gunny said, seeing the olive binder that the captain had entered as exhibit twenty-seven.

"Thank you, gunny," O'Connor said, turning and smiling at the Marine. "I was about to have you identify it, and you saved me the trouble. For the record, exhibit twenty-seven is the corresponding personnel roster. Now, how many Marines work in your section?"

"Not counting Private Anderson and the three men on legal hold, seventeen," the gunny said.

"So minus Private Anderson, who has been in the brig since November, but counting the three men on legal hold, you currently have twenty Marines working in your communications electronics repair facility. Correct?" the defense lawyer asked.

"That's right, sir," the gunny said, shifting in his seat.

"How many black Marines make up the shop?" O'Connor asked.

"I'm not sure, I never counted noses like that," the gunny said, shaking his head.

"Seven, gunny," O'Connor said, opening the personnel roster and showing him the names he had underlined in red ink. "You see how I have marked each name of a black Marine?"

"Yes, sir, I'll go along with what you say. It sounds about right to me. We have a few, I guess," the gunny said with a shrug.

"Seven out of twenty is more than just a few," O'Connor said. "That's thirty percent of your shop."

"I guess so, sir," the gunny smiled.

"My associate and our staff went through your duty rosters and found that these seven Marines, this thirty-percent minority, have stood more than seventy-six percent of all the extra-duty quotas that your squadron and your group have tasked your work section, including those on legal hold. In fact, the three legal hold guys stand twice the number of duty that the others do. How do you account for those figures?" O'Connor said, laying in the gunny's hands a stack of papers with columns of statistics typed on them.

The Marine staff NCO shook his head as he looked at the sheets and the columns and then looked at the presiding judge and shook his head some more.

"Your Honor, these statistics are exhibit twenty-eight," O'Connor said, and took the papers from the gunnery sergeant and laid them atop the two binders as Wayne Ebberhardt passed copies to Charlie Heyster, who then frowned as he read the data.

"You do not dispute these numbers then," O'Connor said, walking toward the jury so that the gunny's face turned toward the six men.

"I guess I could do the math, too, but then we'd be here until next week," the gunny shrugged and smiled. "I trust that you're telling the truth, sir."

"Oh, they're true, Gunny Glickman," O'Connor said, folding his arms. "Why do the black Marines stand so much duty and the white Marines stand so little?"

"Sir, when a guy messes up, I put him on a detail," the gunny began, now beading sweat. "I never thought about what color the man was who messed up."

" 'Messed up' meaning what?" O'Connor said, walking toward the gunny.

"We fix communications gear, and a guy doesn't fix it right, it can cost a pilot or a Marine in the field his life," the gunny answered and then swallowed hard. "I keep my best men on the job, the guys who fix radios right the first time and don't mess them up. Men who can't fix a radio right, I put on the duties, so the good workers keep on the job."

"I guess that's one way to look at it, Gunny Glickman," O'Connor said. "Troublemakers, you put them on duty, too. Right?"

"Absolutely, them more than anyone else," the gunny said and pursed his lips while nodding. "They don't just mess up a piece of equipment, but they mess up the shop, too."

"Private Anderson a troublemaker?" O'Connor asked, walking to the jury.

"Worst in the shop," Glickman said, shaking his head. "Any of his black brotherhood gets in the slightest difficulty with me, and I can count on Anderson to be right there to tell me all about why I am wrong. So, if for only my peace of mind, I keep him out of the shop as much as I can. He stands a hell of a lot of duty, Captain, and that's why. Not because he's black."

"And these others that stand seventy-six percent of the watches, they troublemakers, too?" O'Connor asked, picking up the pages of statistics.

"No. Take Lance Corporal Carter, for example," Glickman said, holding his head up proudly. "He's a good man. He represents colored people well."

"He stands a lot of duty," O'Connor countered, holding up the statistics for the jury.

"Sir, he's not exactly the sharpest tack in the box," Glickman said and smiled. "Like I said, I keep the qualified technicians in the shop working while the less qualified stand the duties. It's a matter of life and death, not necessarily what we find politically acceptable. However, I remind the captain that we are at war and do not enjoy the luxuries of some levels of kindness to the inferior races."

Terry O'Connor blinked and looked at the jury, still blinking, showing his amazement at the gunny's answer.

" 'Inferior races'? 'Kindness to the inferior races'? Did I hear you correctly, Gunny Glickman?" O'Connor said, walking toward the witness stand and looking at the Marine eye to eye.

"Sir, I don't mean it to sound like that," Glickman said, choking on his words. "I'm from New York State. I'm not some southern bigot."

"No, I agree you are not some southern bigot," O'Connor said, and smiled, and then looked at Celestine Anderson, who now glared at his former noncommissioned officer in charge. "Binghamton, New York, is truly a far piece from Birmingham or Atlanta. Certainly not in the South."

BY NINE O'CLOCK Friday morning, Lance Corporal James "Movie Star" Dean had finished two sets of tennis with Lieutenant Colonel Lewis Prunella, had caught a cockroach that measured nearly three inches long while returning from his shower, saved the lively bug inside an envelope that he took from his stationery kit, had then driven the staff judge advocate to a morning-long meeting with the chief of staff at wing headquarters, and now worked at stuffing the frantic insect inside the leather tobacco pouch of Major-Select Charles Heyster, which he had left atop his desk with his pipe. Movie Star had the critter scrambling in the Cherry Blend, kicking shredded leaves out of the bag as the Marine struggled to zip the top of the pouch shut when Staff Sergeant Derek Pride walked through the door and caught him in the act.

"I don't want to know," the legal chief said, seeing the lance corporal finally pull the zipper shut and then noticing the soft leather sides of the tobacco container bouncing from the bug trying to dig its way out.

"Hey, Staff Sergeant, its just a joke on the asshole," Dean said and laughed. "You'll have to keep watch on Heyster when he goes to load his pipe. Shit, I wish you had a camera, so you could get a picture."

"No!" Pride said, and grabbed the lance corporal by the arm, leaving the wiggling tobacco pouch on the desk and leading the tan, blond lad out of the prosecutor's office. "I don't want any part of any more of this insanity. I see that you have now buddied up with Captain Kirkwood, and you're helping him loosen the bolts on Major Dickinson's desk, his chair, his credenza, his side table, and unscrew the lightbulbs in his lamps so that they flicker on and off anytime someone walks past them. The major pesters me now to order him a whole office of new furniture, and his is perfectly good except for what you idiots do to it. I end up dealing with base maintenance here at least once a week, checking the wiring and outlets because of Major Dickinson's chronic electrical problems. Then Corporal Farmer and Sergeant Amos, always sabotaging the major's coffee mess. Did you know I caught Lance Corporal Pounds washing the officers' pot in the toilet with the john brush? And you guys keep dumping your snuff and tobacco spit cups in it, too. The colonel drank some of it the other day and asked me if we had gotten a Louisiana blend because of the unusual flavor. He loved the taste and wants more of it. What am I supposed to do now? Let him drink shit and tell him it's chicory?

"I've had it, Lance Corporal Dean! Do you hear me?"

"Lighten up, man," Movie Star said, walking out the door and heading back to his barracks. "You better be glad that we like you so we tell you most of the bad shit. Think about drinking the wrong coffee."

"Oh, I think about it daily," Pride said, standing in the doorway, watching the colonel's driver cut across the grass. "I nearly gag when I see the prosecutors drink their coffee or anyone else get a cup from the major's pot. I am running out of excuses when I have to cut off Colonel Prunella from pouring his own coffee, so I can fill his cup from the enlisted mess. Is it still safe?"

"Fuck yeah, man," Movie Star said, walking away. "Best rule is that if you see any of us snuffies getting some of it, most likely it's safe for consumption."

Then the lance corporal laughed and turned toward the staff sergeant while still ambling his way to his hooch.

"Oh, I dropped off mail in the barracks," Pride said, standing on the steps. "I put your new *Penthouse* on your rack."

"Fresh jack-off material," Dean said with a laugh, walking backward. "Thanks."

"I can't get over how you just beat your meat right there in the barracks in front of everybody. Doesn't it ever bother you to be so gross?" Pride said as the driver walked backward, smiling at him and grabbing his crotch.

"Everybody beats off, except you, maybe," Movie Star said and laughed again. "I just don't make any secret of it. What the fuck, right?"

"You're strange, Corporal Dean, you know that? If you're not goofing off, you're jacking off," Pride said, shaking his head. "Why not go out in the ville and spend five bucks on a bar girl, like most of the other guys do?"

"Man, you know, the black syph. It abounds!" the lance corporal said and shrugged. "I ain't catching any shit that will keep me from getting home. Besides, old Rosy Palm and her five sisters don't charge five bucks, and they never say no."

"Black syphilis! Nonsense! There's no such thing!" Pride said, throwing his head back in frustration and shutting his eyes.

"Not from what I hear," James Dean called back, and then turned and began jogging toward his quarters.

"The man is plagued by stupidity," Derek Pride said to himself and walked back to his office, where he turned on the radio and began sorting through his own mail. He looked forward to some peaceful time to himself, alone in the office while everyone else had duties outside the building, mostly in the courtroom. Corporal Jerry Farmer worked as bailiff, and Sergeant Dick Amos had relieved Pride as recorder for today's and tomorrow's sessions. As the staff sergeant walked back to his work space, holding a freshly poured cup of coffee from the enlisted men's mess, where all the defense lawyers got their coffee, too, he glanced in the prosecution section's door and studied the brown leather pouch lying next to Charlie Heyster's pipe. It now lay still.

TERRY O'CONNOR WALKED back to the jury and looked at the witness.

"Tell me then, Gunny Glickman," the defense lawyer said, folding his arms, "when you say 'inferior races,' you mean the black Marines are like when we refer to the lower echelon of enlisted men as inferior ranks."

"Yes, sir, something like that," Glickman said. "I don't mean anything prejudice by it, but just a way of categorizing those people, I guess."

"No, nothing prejudiced at all," O'Connor nodded. "Does intellect have anything to do with their inferior status?"

"Probably, sir," Glickman said, swallowing hard. "I'm no sociologist, but we all know that colored folks don't have the intelligence of white people."

"So that's why you give the black Marines the lion's share of duty then, generally speaking," O'Connor said quickly, before Charlie Heyster could raise an objection.

"Yes, sir, one of the reasons," Glickman said. "That and their conduct, and the Q-A numbers."

"Q-A numbers, meaning quality assurance," O'Connor added.

"Yes, sir, quality assurance," Glickman said, nodding. "We test everything that gets repaired, to be sure it goes to the field working at a hundred percent."

"We don't seem to be able to find any data on that, gunny. Can you help us there?" O'Connor said, walking to the defense table.

"Well, sir, I keep track of that stuff in my head," Glickman answered, smiling.

"You don't commit to writing a running tally on performance, then?" O'Connor said, walking back to the jury.

"I've been leading Marines and evaluating their performance for better than nineteen years, sir," Glickman said. "I keep track, but not on paper. I just don't have time to do that sort of thing."

"Oh, I understand," O'Connor said, walking toward the witness. "So from your insight and experience, you just know which of your Marines make mistakes and which ones consistently effect repairs without flaws in their work? Is that it?"

"Pretty much, sir, yes, sir," Glickman said, nodding.

"What is the minimum general-clerical-technical score for a Marine to achieve in order to get to work in your occupational field?" O'Connor asked, walking to the defense table and picking up a stack of papers fastened together in the upper right corner.

"Sir, you probably have it in your hand," Glickman said, shaking his head. "You have to be pretty smart, I know that much."

"Yes, you do, gunny," O'Connor said, looking at one of the pages from the handful of papers. "According to the Marine Corps' *Military Occupational Specialty Manual,* a person has to have a general-clerical-technical score of at least one hundred ten points. For example, your GCT score is one hundred eighteen. So is Celestine Anderson's, one-eighteen. Did you know what Lance Corporal Wendell Carter attained for his GCT score?"

"Not a clue, sir," Glickman said, shaking his head. "One hundred eighteen?"

"Guess again, gunny," O'Connor said, and laid the pages of data on the witness's outstretched hand. "According to a survey my office did of all your workers, Wendell Carter ranks the highest, with a general-clerical-technical score of one hundred forty-two. To put that in perspective, we require a warrant officer to have at least a one hundred ten GCT, and a commissioned officer to have a minimum score of one hundred twenty."

"I didn't know that, sir," Glickman said.

"Your Honor, this document with the citation from the Marine Corps' *MOS* Manual, and the listing of personnel in Private Anderson's section with their GCT scores and other individual personnel data for each man, is exhibit twenty-nine," O'Connor said, laying the stack of paper stapled in the corner on the judge's bench. Then he turned to the gunny.

"This survey that we just entered into evidence shows that there is little difference in the intellect among your work section's Marines, whether black or white. Those scores are color-blind," O'Connor said, walking back to the jury and facing the witness. "In fact, the man with the highest GCT in your section is black, Lance Corporal Wendell Carter. Now, how do you suppose those Marines feel, standing the majority of watch because you consider that they have inferior intelligence?"

"Sir, with all due respect," Glickman said, now showing anger in his face, "those numbers you just reeled off are just numbers. They may use them to choose how a guy gets in my occupational field, but they don't reflect work performance and dependability. And they sure don't say a thing about a bad attitude. I know my shop, and I base the duty assignments on performance, not color."

"I know you believe that, gunny," O'Connor said, walking to the witness stand and smiling. "I don't think you mean to let prejudice influence how you manage your men, but I suggest that you need to take a closer look at it. Could be that your treatment of these men instills their bad attitudes. Could be that your subconscious bias does not allow them the time on the job they need to gain the necessary experience to perform their work flawlessly. Would you agree that perhaps your treatment of Celestine Anderson could help account for his anger, and burst of passion that led to the death of Private Harold Rein?"

The gunny turned his eyes down and he sighed while wringing his hands.

"Yes, sir," the gunny said, and looked up, his voice cracking as he spoke. "I've thought of that quite a bit. I just try to run my shop as best as I can, and maybe I was unfair to Anderson, but he brought it on. We just never got along. I wish things could have been different for him, sir."

While Terry O'Connor finished his last question, Staff Sergeant Derek Pride slipped in the courtroom's back door and handed a note written on a slip of paper to Captain Michael Carter, who had sat in the gallery throughout the week-long trial.

"Oh, my God!" Captain Carter blurted as O'Connor walked back to the defense table after telling the judge he had no more questions of the witness.

Colonel Swanson rapped his gavel and glared over his half-glasses at the distraught captain seated in the audience, now whispering anxiously at the staff sergeant.

"Captain Carter, is that something for the court?" the presiding judge grumbled.

"Yes and no, sir," Carter answered, coming to his feet, his face and blond hair emitting a deep red glow.

"Let's send the jury out of the court and take a fifteen-minute recess so you can tell me all about it," Swanson said, motioning for Corporal Farmer to move the six jurors outside earshot to the next room while also allowing them the freedom to use the restroom and get drinks of water.

"Sir, I've just been given news that the Reverend Doctor Martin Luther King has been shot and killed in Memphis," Carter said, announcing the headline to everyone left in the courtroom. "Just before six PM on Thursday, April fourth, Stateside time in Memphis, only about three hours ago, the reverend was shot while standing on the balcony of the Lorraine Motel. President Johnson has ordered four thousand National Guardsmen to keep order in Memphis, to avoid rioting. He has also ordered that flags shall fly at half staff until Doctor King's interment. I might add that Robert Kennedy has made a most passionate speech in Indianapolis. Sir, we have lost a great American this morning."

Judge Swanson shook his head.

"I fail to see the bearing on the case at hand, Captain Carter, but I appreciate your announcement during our recess. We all share your grief at Doctor King's loss," the colonel said, rising to leave the court and noticing Celestine Anderson, who had his forehead laid on the defense table, his shackled hands cupped around his shaved head, and his shoulders trembling as he absorbed the news of Martin Luther King's death.

As the judge closed the door to his chambers behind him, Terry O'Connor jumped from his chair and dashed at Michael Carter, who looked down at his chair as he postured to return to his seat.

"Outside! Now!" O'Connor growled, snagging the wiry palm tree of a man by the arm and yanking him out the courtroom door.

"What?" Carter gasped, stumbling as the defense lawyer pulled him outside.

"That couldn't wait a couple of hours?" O'Connor hissed, staring wild-eyed at the bewildered man. "At least until we got out of court?"

"Why? It's important news!" Carter said, defending his actions.

"Yes, and totally disruptive of what I am trying to accomplish," O'Connor fumed.

"Which is?" Carter blinked.

"To get the jury to find for a lesser charge of manslaughter, and give my client five years instead of the full-blown second-degree murder term of thirty-five years!" O'Connor snapped. "Did you see Private Anderson's reaction? I have no idea what he may do now. He's a hothead! And you, Captain, with your Harvard Law degree? You're a fucking idiot!"

"I'm sorry!" Carter said and started to cry. "Please, Terry, I didn't mean to do something bad."

"Just go away, Michael," O'Connor said, turning and walking back inside the courtroom. "Why not go and pray for us now."

RAY GLICKMAN HURRIED back to the witness chair and remained standing while Judge Swanson and the jury returned to their seats. During the fifteen-minute break he had sucked down two cigarettes, the second of which had left him somewhat light-headed, but his nerves felt much more relaxed. He liked the prosecutor, and that helped settle his emotions, too.

When Charlie Heyster stood and approached the witness stand, he left his legal pad lying on the prosecution table. He offered the gunny a warm smile and casually rested his hand on the railing in front of the gaunt, narrow-faced man with the gray and brown flat-top haircut and nicotine-stained fingers. Gunny Glickman could use a shower, Heyster thought; the smell of stale tobacco and rank armpits had a definite repulsion factor that ranged high on the prosecutor's personal radar, but he smiled anyway and tried to avoid a full nose of the odor.

"Well, I guess you had hoped to see the last of me, but the defense had other plans for you, didn't they? Instead of trying a man for murder, it seems we have the Marine Corps on trial for its racial policies. So I hope you'll bear with us and our bleeding-heart defense lawyers," Heyster said and laughed. The gunny laughed, too, and then coughed a raspy rattle of phlegm from his tar-clogged bronchia and swallowed the glob without an excuse me or even bothering to cover his mouth. He had truly relaxed.

"You've got a few years in the Corps under your belt," the captain began, walking away from the gunny. "When we talked to you the first time, you told us about your first taste of combat. Korea, was it not? Fox Company, Seventh Marines, correct?"

"Yes, sir, I wound up assigned to them," Glickman said, and coughed again. "I started out with First Marine Division, the Fifth Regimental Combat Team, and got sent over to the Seventh Regiment after we landed at Inchon on September 15, 1950. The Seventh Regiment were mostly reactivated Marine reserves, quite a few World War Two veterans, but lots of others, young guys like me. Some of them never even went to boot camp. Lots of them came from New York and New Jersey, so I got sent to Fox Company, Seventh Marines, since I came from New York, too."

"You fought at the Chosin Reservoir, and earned your Silver Star Medal during the breakout from the frozen Chosin, fighting the Chinese yard by yard from Hagaru to Koto-ri during the early weeks of December with subzero temperatures so cold that frostbite became as big a risk factor as Chinese bullets, and the snow so thick that our airplanes could not get through to support you," Charlie Heyster said, walking toward the jury and looking at each of the six men, locking eye contact with them as he spoke. "You fought the Chinese hand-to-hand, didn't you, gunny?"

"Yes, sir, it was a rough time," the gunny said, speaking in such a quiet voice that Sergeant Dick Amos, the court reporter, had to look up.

"You said it was a rough time, gunny?" the recorder asked, and the judge nodded with Gunny Glickman.

"I said it was a rough time," the old veteran repeated.

"A guy in your outfit, a big kid from New Jersey, a Marine reserve, one of those boys who didn't even go to boot camp, he got the Medal of Honor for his heroism, didn't he, Gunny Glickman?" Heyster asked, turning back at the witness.

"That was Private Hector Cafferata," the gunny said with a smile. "There at the Chosin, he held a big gap in the line, single-handed. We fought them for six nights and five days before they backed off of us. When it was done, there were dead Chinese soldiers on the ground for as far as you could see. At one point I saw Hector batting Chinese grenades back at the enemy with his entrenching tool! Swinging that little shovel in one hand and shooting his firing rifle with the other hand. That first night, when the Chinese attacked, he jumped up out of his sleeping bag and fought all night, standing there in his skivvy shorts, barefooted. He got shot several times but still held his position. That inspired everyone. I think he still has a bum wing from those wounds. Grenade or bullet messed up his right arm. What I hear."

"That's correct, gunny," Heyster said, and walked midway between the witness and the jury. "Were you a radioman back then, too?"

"No, sir, I was a grunt," Glickman said, nodding. "When I reenlisted, I got promoted to corporal, and they gave me a lateral transfer from the infantry to the radio battalion. I wanted to develop a skill so I could make a living when I left the Marine Corps."

"When did you begin working on communications electronics?" Heyster asked, his arms folded.

"Right after I got home from Korea and reenlisted, ten November 1953," the gunny said, smiling.

"That's more than fifteen years," Heyster said, looking at the jury. "So with all your experience in communications and your time in the infantry, serving in Korea, you have a pretty good fix on the way things are done in the Marine Corps."

"I think so, Captain," the gunny said, smiling again.

"Well, correct me if I am wrong, but a noncommissioned officer earns certain privileges, and usually isn't the guy on the business end of a shovel when it comes to filling sandbags or the fellow dragging the honey bucket when it comes time to burn the dewdrops out of the privy," Heyster said with a grin at the jury.

"No, sir, a sergeant or a corporal should not be the man filling sandbags or burning the shitters," Gunny Glickman said and laughed.

"Excuse me, but how many black noncommissioned officers did you say you had in your work section?" the prosecutor said, and then looked at Terry O'Connor, smiling confidently at the defense lawyer.

"None, sir. We have no blacks above the rank of lance corporal in my section," Glickman said, and looked at O'Connor, too.

"So seven black Marines in a section of twenty men, including the three fellows on legal hold, leaves thirteen white Marines, correct?" the prosecutor said, and walked back to his table and picked up the sheets of statistics and personnel listed per individual, showing each man's rank, GCT score, and highest level of education.

"Yes, sir, that sounds about right," Glickman said, nodding and watching the captain as he scanned the personnel data.

"One staff sergeant, your assistant NCO in charge, I gather," Heyster said, looking at the top sheet.

"Yes, sir," Glickman said. "That's Staff Sergeant Kenneth Dunn."

"You have three buck sergeants and four corporals, too," Heyster said, and looked at the defense team and Celestine Anderson, who now sat slumped in his seat, staring at his hands. "Eight men out of fourteen who are noncommissioned officers, including one staff noncommissioned officer besides yourself."

"That's correct, sir." The gunny smiled, seeing the direction the prosecutor had taken. "That leaves six, and three of them are lance corporals."

"So three lance corporals and three privates first class?" Heyster answered and looked at the jury. "You have no slick sleeve privates."

"No, sir, no buck privates," Glickman said, nodding. "Most of the boys get private first class when they graduate basic repair school."

"Ever hear the term 'rank hath its privileges'?" Heyster asked, shrugging at the jury.

"Yes, sir," the gunny answered.

"Care to explain that, just so we have it on the record, because I know that the four officers and two staff noncommissioned officers serving on the jury know its meaning quite well," Heyster said, smiling at the six men.

"As a Marine rises in rank, he gains privileges," Glickman said, looking at the jury.

"One big privilege an enlisted Marine gains is that he no longer has to burn the honey pot from the privy, nor does he have to fill sandbags," Heyster said, walking back to the center of the court.

"Correct, sir," Glickman said, following the captain with his eyes. "Staff Sergeant Dunn and myself, we stand staff duty NCO once or twice a month, at the group. The sergeants and the corporals stand duty NCO at the squadron a couple or three times a month, but the working details, fire watch, security details, guard duty and so forth, that falls to the nonrated Marines. Once in a while I have to supply a corporal or a sergeant for guard duty, but mostly nonrates."

"So would you say that the lion's share, probably even more than seventy-six percent of the extra duty falls to the lance corporals and below?" Heyster said, tossing the statistical sheets on the prosecution table.

"That's about right, sir," Glickman said, nodding.

"You've already said you do not assign duty based on race," Heyster said, walking back to the witness. "You do assign the working details to Marines whose technical quality lacks, and to troublemakers. Correct?"

"Yes, sir, that's what I said," Glickman nodded.

"I'll bet you're the only work section in the Marine Corps who does that or ever has done that, aren't you!" Heyster said, and laughed.

"No, sir," Glickman said with a smile. "I'd be surprised to run across a work section that doesn't operate that way."

"Attitudes toward black Marines, gunny. Are your concepts toward these men out of line with everyone else in the Marine Corps today?" Heyster asked, looking at Terry O'Connor and daring him to object.

"Not from my experience, sir," Glickman said, and shook his head, and then looked at the defense team and Private Anderson, who still stared into his lap.

"What about quality assurance and your record-keeping? Does the Marine Corps require you keep these kinds of statistics?" Heyster asked, picking up the data sheets.

"No, sir," Glickman answered, and cleared his throat. "I know when a man fixes equipment right and when a man keeps making mistakes with the gear. The stuff that doesn't work goes back to the bench, and he gets one of the more experienced technicians to show him where he messed up. I don't need a bunch of numbers on a page to tell me who gets it right most of the time and who needs help most of the time."

"Kind of a commonsense thing, when you think about it," Heyster said, walking toward the jury. "How about education levels in your shop?"

"I never really looked that close at them, but Staff Sergeant Dunn has an associate's degree, and some of the others have a year or two of college, too," Glickman said, looking at the jury.

"Helps get a guy promoted, doesn't it?" Heyster added, looking at the witness from the jury box.

"Yes, sir," Glickman said, nodding. "Off-duty education helps, as well as military education, such as NCO school and correspondence courses from the Marine Corps Institute."

"So let's talk promotions. Any problems there?" Heyster asked, folding his arms and looking at the gunny. "Bias problems?"

"No, sir, we do it fair and square by the orders," Glickman said, nodding.

"Thank you, gunny," Heyster said, and returned to his seat.

"Any redirect questions, Captain O'Connor?" Judge Swanson asked, looking over his half-glasses at the defense counsel.

"Yes, sir," O'Connor said, looking at Charlie Heyster.

"No objections from the prosecution?" the judge asked, looking at Heyster.

"None, Your Honor," the captain answered.

"Gunny Glickman, speaking of promotions and the fact that no black Marines have risen in rank above lance corporal in your section, does that strike you as out of the ordinary?" O'Connor asked, walking to the lectern on top of the table.

"No, sir, the black Marines in my shop just haven't earned anything higher," Glickman said, shrugging his shoulders. "Most have little time in grade, and just a short time in the occupational field. We did promote Wendell Carter a few days ago."

"Yes, I want to talk about Wendell Carter," O'Connor said, smiling. "Thanks for mentioning him. He is a Marine who has now served beyond his four-year enlistment and has an excellent record, yet he just now got promoted to lance corporal."

"Sir, that's not anything to do with what I do in my shop," Glickman said and frowned.

"You've had him in your shop, along with Private Anderson, since you arrived here last August," O'Connor said, picking up the statistical data and turning to the page with Wendell Carter's background written on it. "Says here he graduated high school with a three point six grade point average, joined the Marine Corps, got private first class out of basic radio school. Never got a quota for a follow-on school, but he has taken college courses at night when he was stationed at Twenty-nine Palms, just before coming to Vietnam. He has consistently good proficiency and conduct scores, average about four point seven pro and four point nine con. He had more than a high enough cutting score for promotion when he checked in at Group Seventeen a year and a half ago. Yet he only got recommended for promotion last month. How come?"

"Just because a Marine has the cutting score does not get him a promotion, not in my shop. Some places do it, but not in my shop, no, sir," Gunny Glickman said, shaking his head. "He has to go before the captain and me, and then we recommend him to appear before the squadron promotion board. He's got to pass those promotion boards, too."

"So he failed the boards?" O'Connor asked, looking at Lance Corporal Carter's data sheet. "Nothing in his record indicating he failed any promotion boards."

"I have to recommend a Marine appear before the board," Glickman said, clenching his jaws.

"Based on what?" O'Connor asked, leaning on the lectern.

"Based on my judgment of his performance and conduct," Glickman said, glaring at O'Connor.

"I thought that's what his proficiency and conduct marks indicated, gunny," the defense lawyer said.

"My judgment call, too," the gunny added and shook his head.

"So it's subjective, based on how you see the man's fitness?" O'Connor asked, still leaning on the lectern and staring cold-eyed at the gunny.

"I'm not sure what you mean by subjective, but when it comes down to where the boot heel hits the grinder, my word goes," the gunny growled, jutting out his jaw. "The captain will back me up, too."

"Thank you, gunny," O'Connor said, and sat down.

"Does racial prejudice ever play a part in whether or not you recommend a Marine for promotion, gunny?" Charlie Heyster asked, remaining seated.

"Certainly not! Sir!" Gunny Glickman said, and then he looked at the jury and nodded his head once, hard.

"No more questions?" Judge Swanson asked, looking at both the prosecution and the defense.

"None sir," Heyster said, leaning back in his chair. Terry O'Connor shook his head no.

"Does the defense rest, then?" Judge Swanson asked, taking off his half-glasses.

"Yes, Your Honor," Terry O'Connor said, nodding his head.

"Hold on just a minute!" Celestine Anderson cried in a loud voice, straightening up in his chair and looking at the judge. "I ain't got no say? Nobody asking me nothing!"

"Your counsel indicated to me this morning that you would not testify," Judge Swanson said.

"That's correct, Your Honor," Terry O'Connor said, standing while Wayne Ebberhardt held Celestine Anderson by the arm, keeping him seated.

"White man's law gonna lock me up, and I ain't got no say?" Anderson then bellowed, pulling away from Lieutenant Ebberhardt's grip. "Doctor King got killed today 'cause of your white oppression, and I got my rights to say my say!"

"Corporal Farmer, please escort the jury to the anteroom and close the door," Colonel Swanson snapped, and then glared at Terry O'Connor. "Captain, I expect you to control your client until we can at least get the jury outside earshot of the defendant's outburst."

"That's right, motherfucker! Get them where they can't hear me, 'cause I know I'm going down. I ain't going down quiet! Like that Irish dude said, I won't go gentle into nobody's night. Yeah, I read a book or two, motherfucker! I ain't just somebody's dumb-ass house nigger you can shuffle off gentle into the night," Anderson said, glaring at Charlie Heyster and fighting both Terry O'Connor and Wayne Ebberhardt.

"I will not go gentle into the night either, Private Anderson!" Colonel Swanson boomed, rapping his gavel and the palm of his hand on his bench. "Captain O'Connor, you have five minutes to discuss with your client the good, the bad, and the ugly about his choices of testifying or not testifying. Hopefully by that time I will have cooled my temper as well."

Charlie Heyster laughed, holding a file folder in front of his face to keep the judge from seeing his glee. He could not have asked for a greater gift than his opponent's client poisoning any sympathy the jurors may have held for him. When the judge left the court, Heyster turned to Philip Edward Bailey-Brown and slapped him on the shoulder.

"Well, I guess we bagged and tagged this one, didn't we!" the prosecutor said and laughed, turning his back to Terry O'Connor, who now had Celestine Anderson by the shirtfront.

"You have to be totally out of your mind!" O'Connor said, hissing in his client's face. "How dare you put me to shame in front of this judge. This judge who has gone way beyond the fifty-yard line to give you every break humanly possible, and you spit in his face just now! How dare you! You insolent fool!"

"I gots my rights!" Anderson sobbed, and tears flowed from his eyes.

"Private Anderson, get a grip," O'Connor said, taking a deep breath. "We agreed yesterday afternoon that we did not need your testimony. That captain sitting over there now laughing at us has prepared for one and only one thing in this trial, and that is to rip you to ribbons in front of that jury. Until two minutes ago, you had them on your side. Doctor King's assassination put their sympathies directly in your favor. Those closing words of Gunny Glickman reinforced his bias, too. Before you shot off your mouth, you looked at five years, worst case, I am certain. Now I think you just added five years to it. However, the flip side has them finding you guilty of second-degree murder and giving you thirty-five years. Thirty-five years, Private Anderson!"

"They give me that anyway. That Oreo cookie on the end, staff sergeant black-like-me-but-white-in-the-middle, I seen it in his face. He looking at me like I some stinking piece of shit. I see that look. Them officers, they tie me down and whip me if they could."

"You got it wrong, Private Anderson," Wayne Ebberhardt added, getting a nod from O'Connor. "Agreed, the black staff sergeant probably would lock you up for life. You'd think it would work the other way around, but in most cases, a black juror is hardest on a black defendant. On the other hand, white officers tend to show great leniency to black defendants. Please take our advice and do not get on that stand. At least four of the six jurors will remain understanding. They know the stress you've faced, and with the death of Doctor King, they're sympathetic. Don't blow it, man."

"You don't know," Anderson said, looking at the lieutenant. "I'm going down, so I want my say. That's what I want. My rights."

Terry O'Connor slumped in his chair and looked at Corporal Jerry Farmer, who stood by the judge's chamber door. After a deep sigh of resignation, the captain nodded his head at the bailiff to notify the judge that court could resume.

PRIVATE FIRST CLASS Celestine Anderson sat on the edge of the straight-back chair centered on the plywood platform that served as the witness stand, surrounded by a four-inch-wide handrail set on wooden columns three feet high. His khaki shirt showed large streaks of wetness where the accused killer had perspired heavily listening to his gunny try to rationalize his bigotry. Then the news of Martin Luther King's death left him soaked in angry sweat. The shackles on his hands and feet, tied together by a chain laced through steel rings on a wide leather belt padlocked around his middle, rattled against the small platform's deck each time he moved, and deepened his resentment of all white authority.

Each day that the court began, Terry O'Connor had beseeched the judge to remove the hardware from his client. Each day the judge denied his request, citing that Celestine Anderson had a history of uncontrolled anger. Seeing the chains and manacles left the jury uneasy when they regarded the defendant.

"Where did you grow up?" O'Connor asked, walking to the witness stand and leaning on the rail, glancing at the jurors as he spoke.

"Houston," Anderson replied in a sticky click that let every person in the court know his throat had gone dry from dehydrating nervousness. The shackled prisoner blinked as sweat dripped into his eyes, and when he wiped the stinging stuff away, chains clanking, he swallowed hard and answered again in a more bold voice that carried through the room. "Houston, Texas, sir. I was born and raised in Houston. On the north side, off Jensen Drive."

"What does your mother do?" O'Connor asked, now easing his way back toward the jury.

"What she can. Work for white folks. Clean. Cook. We mostly got welfare," the defendant said, keeping his hands in his lap.

"And your father?" O'Connor followed.

"I never knew him. He left afore I's born," Anderson answered, licking his cracked lips.

"Is it tough being a Negro and living in Houston?" O'Connor said, and then flushed, suddenly realizing the word he had used, hoping it might slide unnoticed.

"I ain't no Neeegro, sir. I'm black!" Anderson said, trying to contain his hostile feelings.

O'Connor blushed at his obvious blunder. He knew better, yet the blind habit from his youth had unconsciously slipped past his brain. News of Doctor King's death and the chaos it set off with his client had left him unnerved, and his mind still reeled from it. Even so, he could not believe how he had made such an embarrassing mistake with his own client. For months he had concentrated on always using the term 'black.' He felt angry at himself now.

"Excuse me, Private Anderson," the defense lawyer said, still flushed. "I apologize for my thoughtless misstatement. Is it tough being a black person and living in Houston?"

Anderson smiled, and then narrowed his eyes as he spoke slowly. "Yes, sir. It is very tough. White folks there treat blacks like dogs. I grew up feeling all poor and ugly 'cause of that. It's very tough to be a black person and live in just about any city back in the world. I can tell you that!"

O'Connor looked at the jury while Anderson spoke. He turned back toward the stand and asked, "Have you ever been in trouble before now?"

"No, sir," Anderson said, "not until I done what I did."

"You're a good Marine, then," O'Connor said, looking at the jury.

"Yes, sir!" Anderson snapped and smiled.

"Did you know Private Rein before that day?" O'Connor said, walking toward the witness stand.

"I seen him here and there, but I didn't know him. I know of him. I don't hang with the likes of that bunch," Anderson said, shaking his head.

"What bunch is that, Private Anderson?" O'Connor asked, leaning his hand on the witness stand rail and looking back at the jury.

"The Klan, sir, folks like that," Anderson said, curling his lips as he spoke.

"Folks like that?" O'Connor asked, looking back at his client.

"Yes, sir. Bigots," Anderson said, and swallowed hard against his dry throat. "Can I get some water?"

"Sure," O'Connor said, and took a glass from the defense table and brought it to him.

Celestine Anderson drained the entire tumbler, and nodded his head in a gesture of thanks as he handed the glass back to his lawyer.

"Did you kill Private Rein?" O'Connor said, walking to the defense table, refilling the empty glass with water, and walking back to the witness stand, where he set it on the four-inch-wide handrail for his client.

"Yes, sir. I did. I killed him," Anderson said, taking the glass and sipping more water.

"Why? What did Private Rein do to provoke such anger?" O'Connor asked, walking toward the jury box.

"Me and my peas—" Anderson began.

"Peas?" O'Connor asked, shrugging at the witness.

"Yes, sir. You know, my brothers. Bloods," Anderson answered.

"Friends," O'Connor offered.

"Yes, sir. Peas. You know," Anderson repeated and blinked sweat from his eyes. "We's all standing out front of the chow hall, dapping. You know, like we do?"

"We're clear on dapping, Private Anderson. Go on," O'Connor said, waving his hand for his client to continue.

"We's waitin' to go in the chow hall, and we hear this group of chucks talkin' tough," Anderson said, and wiped the sweat from his eyes with his chained wrists.

O'Connor swallowed at the sound of the word "chucks" and started to interrupt Anderson for a definition, but decided to hope that the racial epithet did not cue anyone. Anderson stopped talking, seeing O'Connor's reaction, and waited for the captain to ask his question. In the silence, Charlie Heyster scrawled a note on his pad.

"Go on," O'Connor said calmly, hoping none of the jurors had focused on the word "chucks."

Feeling as though he had to explain himself more clearly, Anderson began again. "We's all standing there and hears these honky motherfuckers callin' us niggers, and other names like it."

The defendant's voice rose angrily as he spoke, recounting the day.

O'Connor quickly interrupted his client.

"You regarded these whites as bigots?" the lawyer asked, glancing at the jury to see if he could assess the damage made by the slur.

"Yes, sir!" Anderson said loudly, his voice still sparking with an angry tone. His chest heaved as he told how the white Marines had approached his small group of friends, taunting and jeering at them. Sweat dripped from the defendant's face, and his shaved head sparkled with wetness.

"I was real mad at hearin' what they's sayin'. I wasn't scared of no honky motherfucker neither. I's scared of what might happen. But I weren't scared of any white trash crackers like those boys was!" Anderson strained in an increasing pitch. His voice wavered from the surge of anger that pulsed within him as he recalled the moment.

O'Connor looked at his client and took his chained hand. "We understand. Take a minute and get your breath."

Anderson swallowed the remaining two gulps left in his glass. It felt like a wad of cotton going down his throat.

"Can I have some more water, sir?" he asked, holding up the empty container.

Terry O'Connor took the pitcher of water from the defense table and filled the glass.

"Here. Continue once you've cleared your voice," the lawyer said, putting the nearly empty pitcher back.

"My peas. They all nervous and soundin' scared," Anderson continued, sweat dripping from his forehead. "They talk about gettin' away from there. My hometown boy, Wendell Carter, he try to make me cower away. These boys my bloods, but they didn't want no truck with no trashy redneck chucks.

"So I tole 'em. I says, you ain't nothin' but nigger slaves. That's all you ever be! You talk freedom, fightin' oppression, but you won't make a stand against no white-bread white trash.

"Then I walks down toward them loud-talkin' honky motherfuckers and I waits. I'm proud. I don't run."

O'Connor saw Anderson's anger again boiling hot, and cut the story short.

"That's when you killed Private Rein? When he approached you?" the lawyer said, blocking eye contact from his client with the jury.

"Yes, sir," Anderson said, nodding.

"Were you frightened? You felt the white Marines may hurt you or your friends?" O'Connor added, nodding back.

"If you mean, I scared? Yes, sir, I scared all right," Anderson nodded. "They a whole mess of them, and only one of me. I scared, but I ain't backin' off. No, sir. I stand and I fight. I don't tuck tail an' run like some whipped dog. I stand like a proud black man!"

"Were you in control when you killed the man who taunted you?" O'Connor asked while silently praying that Anderson would say no.

"Sir?" Anderson blinked.

"In control of yourself?" O'Connor repeated. "Were you in control of your emotions?"

"Hell, no!" Anderson snapped at his lawyer. "I mean, no, sir. I felt real mad right then. I guess I lost control. I couldn't think. Everthing kinda blur, crazy-like—"

Hearing the words he wanted the jury to appreciate and remember, O'Connor quickly cut off Anderson in midsentence. "Thank you, Private Anderson. I think that we have the picture clearly now."

Charlie Heyster stood, smiling after Terry O'Connor sat down. He had waited the entire trial for this moment. Like a matador in the bull ring, his verbal sword lay hidden, sparkling sharp behind his red cape, ready to drive home through the animal's hump, straight into his heart.

Calmly, the prosecutor walked to the lectern atop the table in the center of the court and spoke across the room at Anderson. Keeping his eyes on his notes that lay in front of him, the major-select asked, "Do you like white people?"

"Some," Anderson answered.

"But not all?" Heyster responded, looking directly at the defendant.

"No, sir," Anderson answered, hoping that he had spoken correctly. "I don't know that many. I don't know, sir."

"Why do you call them 'crackers,' 'chucks,' and 'honkies'?" Heyster said, frowning so the jury could see him.

"That's street talk, sir," Anderson replied. "You know. Slang."

"Slang, like 'nigger'?" Heyster countered.

"No, sir!" Anderson snapped, his voice just short of a shout. "It's different. Lots different."

" 'Nigger' is bad, but 'cracker' is all right," Heyster said. "Cracker isn't meant to be insulting? Is that it, Private?"

"Yes, sir," Anderson said, and wiped his sweaty forehead on his shoulder as he spoke. " 'Cracker' don't mean nothing."

"Are you a bigot, Private Anderson?" the prosecutor asked, looking at a sheet of paper on the lectern and then nailing eye contact with the defendant.

"No, sir!" Anderson snapped back. "Black people can't be no bigots. Only whites is bigots."

"I wasn't aware that bigotry was exclusively for white people," Heyster said, and smiled at the jury.

"Tell us about how you killed Private Rein," Heyster then said, still smiling and now leaning over the lectern and looking at the defendant. "It seems that you had that story going along so well, and then the defense counsel quickly finished it for you. Tell us?"

"I told it, sir," Anderson said in a pleading voice.

"What about the details after you stood out by yourself?" Heyster asked, remaining behind the center table to keep his intimidation factor for the witness strong. "What about the details of when Private Rein approached you? Did he run at you, brandishing a weapon, or did he merely walk toward you, casually? Tell us, Private Anderson."

Charlie Heyster walked back to his chair and sat behind the prosecution's table, leaned back, lacing his hands behind his head, and waited for the man in the hot seat to finally respond to his question.

"What do you want to know?" Anderson asked, confused.

Captain Heyster leaped to his feet, slammed his fist on the table, and shouted, "I want to know how you killed Private Rein! I want you to tell the jury the same thing that you said in your statement following your apprehension! Do you understand now, mister?"

Celestine Anderson felt his rage surge past its limits and explode toward this white Marine captain who shouted from behind the table. In a booming voice the private first class bellowed at the prosecutor, "Yes, sir!"

Quietly, Charlie Heyster sat back down and waved his hand at the defendant in a motion to continue.

"I'm standin' there and this chuck walks up and says real loud, 'Hey! Hey! Any you niggers gots a light?' " Anderson roared, his chest heaving as he shouted at the prosecutor. "So I says to him, and I'm smilin' like I don't give a shit, 'Sho! I gots a light.'

"So I reaches down in my pocket with my left hand and I pulls out my Zippo. Then, as I gives the beast a light, I reaches around with my right hand, pulls out my hand ax, and I splits the motherfucker's skull!"

Anderson shouted his testimony in a tear-filled cry, spittle and sweat flying from his lips with every syllable.

Charlie Heyster stood, walked to the lectern, crossed his arms, and bowed his head.

" 'I gives the beast a light.' Private Rein, the beast. Right. Where were your friends, Private Anderson?" the prosecutor asked, walking slowly toward the jury.

"Behind me," the defendant sobbed. "Just watchin'. Behind me."

Charlie Heyster then looked at the jury, shook his head, walked back to the prosecutor's table, sat, and asked no more questions.

Terry O'Connor stood, his face drained of its color. The bristle of rust-colored hair on top of his head sparkled with perspiration. He looked at the judge and asked, "May I redirect, Your Honor?"

Charlie Heyster nodded his approval, and Colonel Swanson shook his head yes.

O'Connor cleared his throat and in a low voice asked, "Private Anderson, why did you have that hatchet?"

"Sir," Anderson said, still shaken, "we bush Marines all carries them to cut through the close jungle out there."

Walking toward the witness stand, O'Connor calmly asked his last question of his client. "When you killed Private Rein, when did you last sleep?"

Anderson cleared his voice and in cool composure said, "Not all night. I stood listening post, and I patrolled all day before that, too. I ain't had no chance to sleep since two days before. When I killed that white boy, I had wore myself right down to my boots, dog tired."

"Thank you, Private Anderson. That is all," O'Connor said and returned to his seat.

After another brief recess, Terry O'Connor began his closing statement to the jury. He sought their sympathy toward the black Marine's difficult struggle throughout his life. He told how Anderson was a victim, too, because of his growing up without a father, living on welfare, suffering from racial bias all his life.

O'Connor closed his plea to the jury, saying, "Private First Class Anderson struck out against a lifetime of cruelty that manifested itself in the body of a bigoted white Marine one evening in front of the chow hall at Chu Lai. Yes, he killed Private Harold Rein, but after provocation, driven by physical exhaustion, and committed the slaying in a mindless blur. He had no premeditation but acted in blind passion. A fight, intentionally provoked by the victim. A lost temper that resulted in death.

"You have a choice to find my client not guilty of the charges, or you can find him guilty of manslaughter, the lesser offense. He is certainly not guilty of murder in any degree."

Charlie Heyster spent less than ten minutes making his summation to the jury.

"Private Anderson has said he was guilty," the prosecutor began, walking to the jury box and looking at the face of each man seated there. "He freely admits to killing Private Rein, yet he pleads not guilty. Not guilty! How incredulous!

"The defense wants you to believe that the brutal ax murder of Private Harold Rein was an act of passion. A sudden fit of rage in what he envisions a two-sided fight by an exhausted Marine who had been the victim of abuse all his life. An act that was unthought. A reaction to a provocation. A moment of insanity brought on by a life of neglect.

"I do not dispute that Private Anderson has had a life filled with the disgust of racial bias. So did his best friend, Wendell Carter, and he tried to stop the violence. But when Private Anderson spoke to us, did he once say he felt remorse for killing Harold Rein? Did he ever express anything but satisfaction in his own words? His descriptions of whites moments ago in his testimony says much about Private Anderson. 'Chucks!' 'Crackers!' 'Honky motherfuckers'!

"These are not the words of the late Doctor Martin Luther King, God rest his soul, who the defense wishes us to associate with their client and his cohort. Would men of peace utter such profanity? Such verbal hatred? These are not the words of any equality-seeking crusader for righteousness that the defense would like you to believe is Private First Class Celestine Anderson.

"These words, uttered in your presence only moments ago by the defendant—"honky," "cracker," "chuck"—are as ugly as "coon," "spade," or "nigger." I submit to you that these are not the words of a just man, but the words of a murdering bigot.

"Bigotry is just as wrong, black or white. In this case, the bigotry and hatred expressed by Private First Class Celestine Anderson claimed the life of a fellow Marine.

"Private Anderson killed for hatred of a race, not to right an injustice. Hatred, gentlemen. Hatred. Logically, such a crime demands that you find for the maximum charge and seek its penalty, ridding free society of this hatemonger."

The jury deliberated less than an hour. They brought back a verdict of guilty of second-degree murder and recommended that Celestine Anderson receive reduction to the lowest rank and a dishonorable discharge, and that he serve the maximum penalty that the judge had provided them in their instructions, thirty-five years in prison. Judge Swanson sentenced him to reduction to private, a dishonorable discharge, and twenty years at hard labor.

That night Private Anderson returned to the III MAF brig on Freedom Hill, where he began his wait for the commanding general to review his case and approve the sentence, before he would finally transfer to the Naval Disciplinary Barracks at Portsmouth, New Hampshire. The process would take several more months.

MOVIE STAR AND three other lance corporals from his barracks lay on a quartet of nylon-webbed chaise lounge chairs by the tennis court watching the law center's front doors while sipping cold sodas from an ice chest, telling lies, and improving their suntans.

The final session of the Anderson trial had lasted far longer than any of them had considered possible, and they were about to give up and get dressed when people finally began pouring from the building. As soon as the crew of snuffies saw Charlie Heyster emerge with Philip Edward Bailey-Brown, lugging the files while the major-select strutted ahead of him, the four lance corporals made a mad dash for the wing's legal office headquarters and piled on Movie Star's desk, where they had a clear view through the doorway of the prosecutor's office.

"Hello, boys!" Heyster chirped as he brushed past the four nonrates who pretended to pour over Movie Star's new edition of *Penthouse*. "Half a buck to the first man to bring me a hot cup of Java!"

Lance Corporal Bobby Pounds, who sat at his desk in the administrative section and had the nickname "Happy," jumped first, grabbed Heyster's cup, and dashed into Major Dickinson's office, where he had just dumped his spit cup full of Copenhagen snuff juice into the pot, and dashed a pinch of the fresh-ground tobacco into the brew, just for good measure. He wondered how much he and his low-ranking colleagues could doctor the officers' coffee before someone finally got sick on the stuff. As of yet the watch-standers who formulated the morning brew only got compliments on its often zesty gourmet flavor.

For the snuffies in the office, it felt good to see the officers slurping down the rotten crap and complimenting the chef who stood the previous night's office duty and mixed the concoction of odds and ends. Pounds had even suggested putting a turd in the pot, but Movie Star shot down the idea, citing that diseases like hepatitis came from shit, and they might catch it, too, if they got it started in the office.

"Here you are, sir," Happy Pounds said, offering a freckle-faced grin at the triumphant prosecutor, handing the hot cup to the captain and watching as he kicked back in his swivel chair and took a big sip.

"Damned fine stuff, Happy!" Heyster sighed contentedly and then flipped half a dollar in the air toward the sandy-haired Marine, whose skin was spotted from head to toe with big, brown freckles, like the mottled skin on a salamander. "You had the duty last night, so I guess I owe you the compliment for another great pot of coffee."

Movie Star and his three buddies from the motor pool crowded around Heyster's door and looked in with Happy Pounds in front of them.

"I guess you won, sir," Lance Cool James Dean said from behind the group.

"Am I smiling that much?" Heyster said, and grabbed the pipe off his desk.

"Afraid so, sir," Movie Star chimed back. "Guess you'll be celebrating another scalp on your lodgepole."

"Correct again," the major-select said, knocking out burned tobacco crumbs from the briarwood pipe and then unfolding his pocket knife to dig out the tar-soaked chunks stuck to the bottom. After scraping the bowl well, he put the stem of the device in his teeth and blew through it as he picked up his pigskin pouch and gave the leather bag a good shake, stirring up the Cherry Blend tobacco mix inside it.

Movie Star started laughing as he saw the walls of the pouch bounce from the lively bug kicking after the good shaking he got. The other Marines held their breath as they watched the captain take hold of the zipper and pull.

"Ahhh!!" Heyster screamed as the big brown cockroach jumped from the pouch and ran up his arm, finally spreading his wings and taking flight off the captain's neck. "Holy shit!"

The prosecutor fell backward in his chair and flung pipe tobacco to the ceiling, showering his desk and both of the Brothers B, who sat blinking wide-eyed at the startled lead attorney.

"Motherfucker!" Heyster bellowed and jumped to his feet. He immediately began searching the room for the cockroach, and then found him clinging to the top of the wall at the edge of the ceiling, swiveling his head a full circle to the right and then a full circle to the left, sizing up the chaotic situation.

"That has to be the largest roach I've ever seen!" Captain Miles Bushwick commented, brushing tobacco off his shoulders and standing to get a better look at the reddish-brown bug that followed his movements with his turning head and flicking his long antennae with nervous snaps back and forth.

"Why he's as big as a CH-fifty-three helicopter!" Philip Edward Bailey-Brown exclaimed as he, too, stood to look at the massive insect and watched in awe as it again took flight, buzzing the crowd of hysterically laughing enlisted Marines and lighting on the wall in the administration office, then darting to hide in the shadow behind an overhead pipe.

"McKay! Carter! Kirkwood! You motherfuckers!" Heyster yelled, and shoved his way through the crowd of lance corporals who cackled and howled with no remorse nor showed any kind of reservation for fear that the officer might blame them for the prank.

Derek Pride stood behind his desk and smiled, offering an innocent shrug at the enraged prosecutor as he stormed through the administration office and then broke into a full-out run toward the defense section.

"You motherfuckers! You rotten motherfuckers!" Heyster kept screaming as he kicked open the opposing lawyers' door and tromped his way into their office.

From his shadowy hiding place behind the pipe, the cockroach swiveled his head, looking for anything that might again threaten him. Then he zeroed on the open door of Dicky Doo's office, and flew into the unoccupied room to find better refuge.

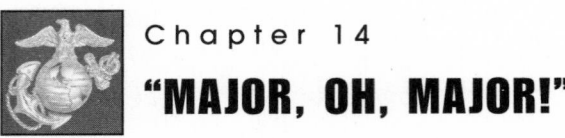

Chapter 14

"MAJOR, OH, MAJOR!"

JON KIRKWOOD LAY with his head at the foot of his rack so that he could see the barracks door and not miss T. D. McKay when he came to get ready for this evening's bash that would celebrate the lawyer lieutenant's going back to the world, home, and Texas, along with the departure of the staff judge advocate. Lieutenant Colonel Prunella had planned an especially festive hail-and-farewell party for Tommy Touchdown and himself, and had combined it with their Fourth of July celebration. Monsoon rain had washed out the last Friday night in June, their regular hail-and-farewell date, so the colonel had moved the soiree to the first week in July and doubled it with their observance of Independence Day.

Even though duty in Vietnam had little respect for the Monday-through-Friday workweek typical of life "back in the world," a slang expression for civilization in America that even Jon Kirkwood found himself frequently using as he passed the midway point of his thirteen-month combat tour, Lieutenant Colonel Prunella had made great efforts to make duty in his shop as much as possible like the weekly routines Stateside. He believed that the more things he could keep consistent with those at home, the Marines under his supervision would encounter less stress in their lives and duties.

This week, since the Fourth of July fell on a Thursday, the colonel had closed shop on Friday, too, and gave all hands four days off, like most people back home in America would enjoy. Kirkwood thought about how much he really liked Colonel Prunella, even though he kept himself removed from the daily grind of First MAW Law, and spent the last several weeks mostly on the tennis court with Movie Star or the wing adjutant, who had won a national tennis championship in college and whom Prunella had only beaten in the game once in six months.

The captain sighed as he thought of the good boss leaving in days, and Dicky Doo with Charlie Heyster at his side taking over. As Kirkwood rolled on his back, he could hear Michael Carter snoring below his self-styled altar to his martyred political heroes, who now included black-bunting-draped photographs of Martin Luther King and Robert F. Kennedy alongside those of Pope Paul VI and Bobby's big brother President John F. Kennedy.

Carter had barely finished his wall of martyrs rearrangement and gotten the objects balanced with the addition of Martin Luther King's photograph, and had finally stopped crying every time he knelt at his footlocker to pray, when word of Bobby Kennedy's assassination flashed on American Forces Vietnam Radio. The devout stick man began a prayer marathon on the morning of June 6, Vietnam time, as soon as news of the younger Kennedy brother's early-morning shooting on June 5 in a Los Angeles hotel by an Arab terrorist had reached that side of the world. The Boston defense lawyer held a rosary in his hand, chanting constant prayers, until the next day, when word finally came that Bobby had at last died without regaining consciousness. The lawyer refused to eat, sleep, or work while Kennedy clung to life, devoting his full attention to prayer for the mortally wounded presidential candidate and his family.

As Kirkwood lay on his back, looking at the wall of smiling, dead politicians looming beneath Carter's wooden crucifix, across the barracks from him, where the stick man snored below the garish scene, and as Terry O'Connor busily scratched a fountain pen across stationery with a light-blue map of Vietnam in the upper right corner and a gold Marine Corps emblem centered at the top, seated at the little desk by the window, writing a letter to Vibeke Ahlquist, the slamming of the front doors startled the daydreaming lawyer from his daze.

"Carter, you maggot! I've got the goods on you now!" Charlie Heyster shouted as he stomped down the aisle, where the blond man now sat up on his bunk and rubbed his sleepy eyes.

Jon Kirkwood swung his stocking feet to the floor and cut off the major-select before he could lay his hands on stick man.

"Whoa!" Kirkwood said, putting out his arm, stopping the enraged lead prosecutor and soon-to-be interim military justice officer for the wing. "What goods? As this Marine's attorney, I advise him to remain on his rack and keep his mouth shut."

"Oh, get out of my way!" Heyster snapped, and pushed Jon Kirkwood backward.

"That's assault," Kirkwood said, and looked at Terry O'Connor, who stood and walked to the side of his pal. "I have witnesses. You've had it now."

"You'll feel like joking when Major Dickinson writes Miss Carter up for robbing marijuana from the evidence locker, and you two join him in the brig for your complicity," Heyster said, and scowled at the trio.

"What are you talking about, Captain?" Michael Carter said, combing his tangle of unruly blond hair with his fingers as he spoke, and yawned out a breeze of bad-smelling sleep breath when he finished asking his question.

"Major Dickinson has launched an internal investigation after he discovered a large number of kilogram-sized bags of marijuana missing from the evidence locker," Heyster said, looking directly at Carter. "We know that someone from inside took the dope, because the only evidence taken were those bundles associated with cases that we have completed, and were now awaiting disposal by the provost marshal. The major has focused his search on the enlisted troops working in the office, such as the colonel's driver. However, I suspect culprits elsewhere."

"Namely us?" O'Connor said, smiling. "You sure Dicky Doo didn't peddle the stuff on the side, and now wants to pin blame on someone unknown so he can clear the books with CID? Sounds mighty suspicious and very convenient to me."

"It would take a low-life scum like you to suggest that a regular Marine officer might commit such an act, Captain O'Connor," Heyster said, and then looked at Michael Carter, who had reclined on his bunk and blinked lazily up at the men. "Look at him. He's all dulled out on reefer right now. How much you smoke of it, Michael, and how much did you sell?"

"You have no idea how stupid you sound, Charlie, do you," Jon Kirkwood said, looking at Carter and then back at the belligerent lead prosecutor.

Heyster glared at the dark-haired captain.

"What motivates a person to sell dope?" Kirkwood asked, raising his eyebrows.

"Money, of course," Heyster responded, and then looked at Terry O'Connor, who stood next to his taller friend and cast a sarcastic smirk at the prosecutor.

"Michael Carter's family owns half of the office buildings in downtown Boston, and several more on Park Avenue in New York City," O'Connor bubbled, blinking his eyes and smiling at Heyster. "Stick man counts his money by the millions of dollars. His butler makes more than the three of us put together."

"So maybe he rips off the evidence to get high, and gives the rest of it away to those lunatic friends of yours," Heyster said, jutting out his jaw. "That character Lobo, I'll bet he would smoke a joint. Even Buck Taylor, too. He's pretty radical, now that I think about him. Oh, yes, and let's not leave out that bleeding-heart sister, Mike Schuller, trying to reform inmate life at the brig."

"You're reaching way out of bounds with your stupid accusations on this one, Charlie," Kirkwood said, and took the major-select by the arm and began leading him toward the barracks door. "Now, crawl back under your rock. Oh, and say hello to Chopper if you see him."

"Fucking assholes! I'll get you, Kirkwood, for that cockroach trick. Don't think that I've let it slip from my mind," Heyster said, stomping out of the barracks.

Jon Kirkwood smiled and shrugged at the two captains.

"Well, with that comment, I guarantee you that he believes you're the one who put the roach in his tobacco," O'Connor said, walking to the foot of his rack and sitting down.

"He's never gotten over it, has he," Kirkwood said. "Even Dicky Doo eventually gets past the harassment. The day he got back from Okinawa and sat in his chair, and the arms fell off on the floor, I thought he would explode. He got over it."

"Well, I think that the drawers crashing out of his desk, and the one entire pedestal collapsing to the floor under it had a lot to do with him getting past the chair," O'Connor said and laughed. "He still hasn't figured out the electrical problem! Lights flicker in his lamps and he yells at poor Derek Pride to call base maintenance."

"Dicky Doo as staff judge advocate and Charlie Heyster at his left hip is really scary, gentlemen, all joking aside," Michael Carter said, standing up and putting on his pants. "I think I will go to the club and have a few drinks before the party, just to get myself in a better mood now, and try to get this internal investigation off my mind. I find it deeply disturbing."

"Hold on and we'll tag along," O'Connor said, walking to his wall locker.

"I'd still like to catch Tommy McKay before tonight, so we can have that last good talk," Kirkwood said, looking at his watch.

"You know, Jon, he may not show up at all. Not even for his own going-away party," O'Connor said, shrugging as he buttoned his shirt. "You've always got tomorrow, the weekend, and all day Monday to catch him and have that talk before he flies out Tuesday. Besides, we may see our buddy Wayne and that sweet-looking Gwen Ebberhardt at the club. He said he had to meet her in town, at the hotel by the consulate, and that they would probably drop by the Officers' Club before the luau."

"True," Kirkwood said, and picked up his shirt off the corner of his wall locker door. "I had almost forgotten that she had lain over here this week, and will fly out with McKay and the colonel. Will Tarzan and Jane be back at China Beach this weekend?"

"They're committed to the party tonight, but with Friday, Saturday, and Sunday wide open, my bet's with yours and China Beach," O'Connor said and then laughed. "I want to see Dicky Doo and Stanley when she shows up."

Michael Carter frowned and bit his fingernail, thinking.

"What's wrong?" O'Connor asked the tall, skinny man, putting his arm over his shoulder.

"I know it's been a few months ago, but didn't Wayne say that his wife had told the major and Stanley on that flight to Okinawa that her name was Crookshank, and that Gwen Ebberhardt worked on another crew?" Carter said, still gnawing on his finger.

"Oh, my! That's right!" O'Connor said and laughed. "Wayne had his weekly MARS [Military Affiliate Radio System] telephone call with her right after that shitty flight, and said then that he hoped she and Dicky Doo never met in a social setting, because she had lied to the major about who she was."

"Well, you know he has always blamed the old *papa-san* in the coffee shop at the passenger terminal for his and Stanley's shitty ordeal," Kirkwood said, and shrugged, chuckling. "Suspecting a flight attendant of intentionally giving him the trots would be a reach for him, I think, especially when Dicky Doo has the local Vietnamese so convenient to persecute. He'll probably just blow off the identity thing to female fickleness, and her not wanting to get familiar with him and Stanley while she was working. You know, guys like those two have built-in rejection acceptance when it comes to attractive women."

"That's right, he still insists that the old guy that does the cooking over there is a Viet Cong spy," O'Connor said with a laugh, walking toward the door with his two friends. "I think he still has the counterintelligence guys pestering that poor fellow at least once a week."

"Stinky sure has it in for that unfortunate old fart at the gedunk," Kirkwood said, pulling open the screen door. "I thought I would bust a gut laughing when Buck Taylor relayed what his buddy who made that same flight had told him about Tufts squirting his drawers full and smelling up the entire airplane. Halfway to Okinawa, and he shits all over himself. Couldn't have happened to a nicer guy."

"Stinky Stanley Tufts," Carter said, laughing. "I like that nickname almost as much as the one the troops gave that cockroach that flew out of Heyster's tobacco, and they now keep fed and protected in Major Dickinson's office. Holy cow! I thought Charlie would uncork one and sock you when you told him to say hello to Chopper."

NO ONE EVER questioned Sergeant Michael Fryer's toughness until Major Sidney Rich took charge of Second Battalion and put him to the test. Captain Jesse Holt stood up for Fryer and the other men of Echo Company, but when Major Rich pressed the subordinate commander, he always folded. This pissed off the black sergeant, who led First Platoon without benefit of a lieutenant to command the small unit and keep peace with the brass. So Fryer, desperate for his men, went to general quarters, finally vocalizing his frustrations, after the forty-second man in his company had died in combat, with no sense of concern for the losses expressed by the major.

"Press on, men," he would say. "Suck it up. That's what Marines do. Come home carrying your shield or lying on it. We live by the Spartan ethic."

"Fuck the Spartans," Fryer had said to Captain Holt one evening after he overheard four of the men in his second squad plotting to frag the captain and Major Rich. "We don't operate as a team no more. We zombies now days. He keep going to the head of the line for every operation that nobody else want. Shit too dangerous, so leave it to Major Rich to volunteer us. We ain't seen a day off in three months. Not one day off!"

Then two days ago, twelve men in his platoon died in an ambush that left Echo Company in total disarray, bringing the unit's body count to fifty-four brothers killed in action. Then this morning two more from his platoon died after the major had ordered the company back into the same area the same day they had bugged out, facing an enemy regiment with vastly superior numbers, and taking them on again within hours of their retreat, with no improved firepower or additional supporting arms. Michael Fryer and Captain Holt both agreed that Major Rich had decided to put them right back in the meat grinder, without rest or even a meal, as a harsh lesson for their previous failure. He had looked bad at regiment, and was determined to wipe out that blot before anyone could write the score in the book.

This time Echo Company killed seventy-six North Vietnamese soldiers in the regiment that they took on, surprising the enemy in an insane counterattack while licking their wounds, and Sergeant Fryer lost two friends from his platoon.

Staggering from fatigue after so many days in battle, the black sergeant wearily marched his Marines through the wire at Fire Base Ryder: the last platoon from Echo Company to reach home. The sergeant felt certain they would find a hot meal welcoming them back, and a congratulatory greeting from the battalion commander for kicking serious ass. Yet what he found was Captain Holt standing atop a bunker with the first sergeant, going over a list of housekeeping items, and the men hard at work with picks, shovels, and hundreds of empty sandbags. Several cases of C rations sat on a pallet by the skipper's command post tent: Echo Company's dinner.

"What the fuck, sir?" Fryer said, dropping his pack by the bunker where the captain stood.

"Division and Three-MAF got the commanding generals heading our way first thing in the morning," Holt said, shaking his head at the tired sergeant. "Major Rich has everybody turned to improving positions, policing the area, polishing brass. You name it and we got to do it."

"This ain't right, sir," Fryer said to the captain, and then looked at First Sergeant Eddie Lyle, who shared in the sergeant's frustration but agreed with Captain Jesse Holt that arguing with the battalion commander would only leave them having their virility put to question by Major Sidney Rich.

Along with his hardness on the men, Rich allowed himself no slack either. He hardly slept, and had no qualms of walking out to the forward listening posts in the middle of the night, just to see if he could catch a Marine dozing off. He would march and never lose step, even with blood oozing out the air vents in the sides of his jungle boots.

"Spartans recognize no pain. We block it from our consciousness. We endure, and we win," he would boast with his blistered feet soaking in a pot of salt water turned pink with his blood from the long march.

"Sergeant Fryer, I know what you feel," First Sergeant Lyle told the Marine NCO, wrapping an arm around his neck and walking him back to his platoon area. "The skipper and I talk about that insane fuck all the time. There's nothing we can do."

"I can talk to the major," Fryer said, stopping and then looking back at Captain Holt.

"He'll humiliate you and make you feel worse," Holt said, jumping off the bunker and walking to where the first sergeant and the platoon sergeant stood.

"So be it, then," Fryer said, taking off his helmet and wiping his forehead with his bare arm. "Two-thirds of my platoon is way past due for some R and R, and the rest are coming due now. I know the whole company ain't much different."

"We're all due for a trip to China Beach at least," Holt said and shook his head. "No way he gonna stand us down for even a day. Hell, man! He ain't even giving us a break this afternoon for the Fourth of July!"

"I want to just ask him, sir, anyway," Fryer said, taking a deep breath. "I owe my men to at least see me going to bat for them."

"If you're willing to take an ass-whipping so your troops feel better, then more power to you," the captain said, and put his arm around Fryer. "I admire your spirit. Give it a shot, but don't count on a damned thing but bitter disappointment."

Michael Fryer walked back to his platoon area with a renewed spring in his step, carrying his pack and his rifle in his hands. After he delegated the housekeeping duties to his three squad leaders, he washed the dirt off his face and trudged with his rifle slung on his shoulder to the battalion commander's tent, with Captain Holt at his side.

"Sir, I have a Marine who wishes to speak to you," the company commander said as he stepped inside the major's command post tent, where Rich busily drew a new battle plan on a plastic overlay he had spread atop a tactical map.

"Make it quick, Captain Holt," the major said, looking up from his work. "Head-shed brass coming down tomorrow to take a look at us. We're the hottest battalion in either division. We got more body count than some regiments, in fact."

"Does that mean we have some relief in sight?" the captain asked, hoping that the answer might negate Sergeant Fryer's request.

"We have a war to fight, sir," the major said with a frown. "No rest for the wicked, I'm afraid."

"Our men, they've been in the bush too long, Major. They have more grass time than most guys with six months edge on them. They need some R and R now. At least a day or two off," Fryer said, stepping in front of his captain, who gladly faded back through the tent's doorway and disappeared down the hill. The black Marine sergeant looked at the major's expressionless face and waited for a response.

"That it?" the major asked. "I thought you had something that was different to convince me that your men deserved more than any other platoon in the battalion. Look around, Sergeant Fryer. Tell me if I'm wrong, but do you see any squad that isn't bone skinny and dogged to death? We've been the meat hanging on the end of the stick, and there's no relief in sight.

"If I had my way, I'd move this whole battalion off the line and down to China Beach for two weeks, or a month. Every man deserves it. Not just your men.

"Remember this, Sergeant. We're Marines. As Marines it's the mission. The mission and only the mission. Men die. Privates and lance corporals die first and most often. That's the way it is. We spend their lives to accomplish the mission. We don't ask why. We just do it.

"Until regiment changes our mission, we will keep on here. We will patrol and we will bust our asses, and your buddies and my Marines will die. We don't have time to send people off to get drunk and screwed. As long as I'm in command, we will fight this war my way. The Marine Corps way. All of us together and with every ounce of muscle we have.

"I'm not letting up on you or anyone in this battalion. Got that? There will be no R and R. There will be no free time. We have a mission, and that's all that should concern you. Now get out of here. I know that you have more important matters to attend."

Fryer stood at attention while fine beads of sweat glittered on his face like diamonds on black satin. It was as though he spoke to a rock wall. Nothing seemed to daunt the major. Nothing seemed to clue him in that the men were near the end of their ropes. Didn't he know that he can push men only so far? Didn't he realize that to accomplish the mission the team had to work together? Didn't he know that for the team to work, they had to be motivated, and not just hung out like meat on a stick?

Fryer started to excuse himself and leave, but his frustration kept him in front of the major.

"Sir," Fryer managed to summon up from his dry throat, "can I ask you something, and not have you go off on me like I mean disrespect or something?"

"If it's disrespectful, don't say it, Sergeant Fryer," the major cautioned. "Just because you excuse yourself by saying no disrespect intended doesn't mean it isn't disrespectful. You be the judge. I'll listen, but maintain your bearing."

"Yes, sir," Fryer said firmly. "Sir, I wonder if the major is not aware of the great deal of frustration and bad morale among the men?"

"We're Marines, Sergeant," the major growled through clenched teeth in a voice that rose in both firmness and volume. "We don't quit. Discipline. Remember, it is discipline that keeps us tough. Keeps us alive. Discipline! Spartan discipline!"

The major's face became flushed red as he glared at Fryer, who stood locked at attention, afraid even to blink. The tension made every muscle in the major's face and arms stand out hard, and as he spoke, he tightened both of his fists bloodless white, pressing them down on the tabletop, where he worked on the tactical map and overlay that placed battalion positions, lines of departure, and points of coordination for a battle he had planned.

"If there is a morale problem among your troops," the major said, continuing his angry volley of words, "I would suggest disciplining the crybabies who cause the problem. That's leadership, Sergeant Fryer. Reward those who deserve rewards. Discipline those who do not hack it. Make them tough. Marines, Sergeant. Marines! Think tough. Get tough. We're at war!

"Now, I've heard what you have to say. You know my thoughts on the subject. The men will get R and R when we stand down from this position. It may take weeks or months, but I expect every man to pull the load, do his work here, and keep the patrols sharp."

"Yes, sir," Fryer said, feeling hopelessly frustrated. He knew that R and R was normally handled on an individual rotation, not unit by unit. He knew that there would be no R and R.

He wanted to tell the major what he really thought. What he knew to be true. What the men were all saying. He felt like telling the major, "Fuck your success. Fuck your promotions. Fuck the body count. Fuck the mission!"

Fryer knew that the major was making big points at regimental headquarters and at division. He knew because his men did not live in a vacuum. They heard the talk that filtered in with the couriers who made the run to LZ Ryder from Da Nang, where the commanding generals watched this battalion and bragged about Major Sidney Rich. His Second Battalion registered more kills and more enemy contact than any other battalion in either division, or in the entire American contingent of ground forces in Vietnam, for all he knew. The sergeant understood that could only mean big points for the major, and Fryer also knew that those points cost lives and the sanity of his men.

He felt like saying, "Fuck you, Major. Fuck this war and all the fucking brass and ribbons that go with it."

However, Michael Fryer did not say a word. He briskly wished the major good day, followed with a "By your leave, sir," a crisp about-face, and a rapid departure while the battalion sergeant major stood next to the tent flap, holding it open.

The frustrated sergeant had walked nearly all the way back to his platoon's position when he stopped dead in his tracks. He could not go on. He could not see another day of the major's hell. How could he face his men? How could he tell them that the major had points to make at division? How could he say, as the major had said, "We're Marines. We're tough. The mission, men. The mission! Suck it up. Be like the Spartans."

"Cheap-ass talk. That's all he is. Cheap-ass talk," Fryer shouted as he wheeled about and unslung his M16 rifle. "Fuck the mission. Fuck the major."

Reaching into a pouch that hung on his web belt, Michael Fryer pulled out a magazine loaded with eighteen 5.56-millimeter shells taped to another equally loaded magazine. He jammed it into the rifle and slammed its bolt home behind the first round.

"Major, oh, Major," he began to say as he briskly marched across the compound to where the small command post tent stood, its flaps dropped shut.

"Major, oh, Major," he chanted rhythmically with each step. "Major, oh, Major. Major, oh, Major."

As the angry sergeant walked, he gained momentum. Each time his boot heel struck the dusty ground, he picked up speed in his march. Longer and longer strides. Louder and louder he called out, "Major, oh, Major!"

Several Marines down the hill from the battalion commander's tent had worked most of the day digging a bunker. They stopped filling sandbags when they heard Fryer shouting, "Major, oh, Major!"

When they saw him raise his M16 to his shoulder, they wasted no time diving deep into the hole they had spent the better part of the day digging.

The first burst of gunfire sent Marines scrambling for cover at nearly every corner of the combat base. By the time anyone realized that the loud commotion came from Fryer shooting into the battalion commander's tent, the angry Marine had emptied the first magazine and quickly turned it over, sent the bolt home on the next round, and began to fire again, flipping the rifle's selector switch to full automatic.

"Major, oh, Major!" Fryer cried out, shouting and sobbing as he shot into the tent. "Why do you fuck with the troops like you do?"

Billowing dust shrouded Sidney Rich's command post tent. The crash of breaking glass and flying metal accompanied the crack of Michael Fryer's rifle report as he unloaded his weapon into the battalion commander's dusty green shelter.

Before the angry sergeant could jam another full magazine into his rifle, First Sergeant Eddie Lyle tackled Michael Fryer and sent him tumbling headlong into the hard-packed earth outside the major's tent. The first sergeant took Fryer's rifle and left the sobbing Marine lying on the ground, flat on his back, completely broken.

"Boy!" Lyle said to Fryer, "you're damned lucky that nobody was in that tent!"

An ashen pale battalion commander stepped through the crowd of Marines who now circled Sergeant Fryer, who still lay on the ground, crying in deep distress.

"I went to take a shit!" the major exclaimed. "That crazy bastard would have killed me!"

Major Rich looked at the sergeant major, the first sergeant, and then at Captain Jesse Holt, who had run back up the hill at the sound of the first rounds fired. The distraught battalion commander then shouted his orders at the dumbfounded captain.

"Get that black son of a bitch out of here tonight. I want him in the Da Nang brig immediately!" Rich bellowed.

WHEN GWEN EBBERHARDT stepped around the corner of the Officers' Club and headed across the lawn toward Lieutenant Colonel Prunella's and T. D. McKay's hail-and-farewell party and First MAW Law's Independence Day celebration luau, a hush rapidly spread through the all-ranks crowd of Marines. Movie Star Dean and Happy Pounds stood speechless as the fine-smelling woman brushed past them, turning heads with each sway of her hips and bounce of her breasts.

She had told Wayne to go ahead with the boys when they finished their drinks in the club. Gwen had to powder her nose while her husband, Terry

O'Connor, Jon Kirkwood, and Michael Carter sauntered out back to join the festivities.

The six-foot-tall redhead loved to make an entrance. Wayne knew it, so he didn't wait to escort her to the backyard, where the crowd of nearly two hundred hungry, thirsty, and horny Marines mingled and sipped booze while their luau pig roasted in a pall of thick white smoke inside the O Club's barbeque grill, made of two fifty-five-gallon drums welded together.

"She ain't wearing any bra, man!" Happy Pounds crowed as the woman swung past him and Movie Star. "Got them perky nips jumping right through that sweater! You see that grillwork? Like a '57 Cadillac."

"Shut up, Happy, she heard everything you just said," Movie Star snapped, stamping his foot. "Now she's gonna think we're all fucked-up perverted and shit, like you. That's Lieutenant Ebberhardt's wife, you dip."

Hearing both lance corporals' words, Gwen looked over her shoulder and gave the two young jerks a big smile. Then she sashayed a beeline straight to the small circle of officers where Major Dudley L. Dickinson stood, holding court with Charlie Heyster, Stanley and Manley Tufts, and the Brothers B.

Special for the occasion, Gwen had slipped on a thin, white, tight-fitting, midthigh-length miniskirt, a bright yellow, lightweight cotton-knit tank top with a deep plunging back and strings for straps over her shoulders, and white sandals that had crisscrossed leather thongs that laced up her calves, well past her ankles. Gold-rimmed sunglasses covered her emerald eyes, but she took the sunglasses off when she said hello to Dicky Doo and the boys, whose speech she stopped cold as soon as they saw her.

"Major Dickinson, so good to see you!" Gwen said, flashing her smile at the portly Marine with his salt-and-pepper flattop hair. "Captain Tufts, so nice to see you again, too."

"Why, Miss Crookshank," the mojo said, putting out his hand for her to shake, "what a pleasure to see you. Which one of these animals persuaded you to come slumming in our little garden party?"

"Oh, my husband, of course," Gwen said, and pointed to the group of men where Wayne Ebberhardt stood, smiling.

While Dicky Doo furrowed his brow and squinted to see which man had brought the beautiful woman to the legal office's luau, Stanley Tufts slipped away from his group and found an obscure spot at the end of the bar where he could avoid the woman who had seen him shit his pants.

"You mean, one of those goons?" Dickinson said, pointing at the group and then looking back at the tall, shapely redhead.

"Yes, that good-looking goon right there in the middle, waving back at me," Gwen said, smiling and waving her hand at Wayne.

"Why, you told me that Lieutenant Ebberhardt's wife worked on another flight crew," Dickinson said, frowning at the woman.

"Yes, and I am sorry for lying to you, Major," Gwen said, hooking her arm in his and giving him a squeeze. "I hope you'll understand that I had so many people to attend, and I just didn't have the luxury to spend any time chatting with passengers. So I fibbed a white lie, and I am sorry. You're such a nice man, too."

"Oh, I understand how things can be," Dickinson said with a smile, puffing his chest and holding in his round stomach.

"That poor captain, where did he go?" Gwen said, looking for Stanley, who now hid at the bar.

The shorter Tufts brother had no desire to speak to the woman. He felt too ashamed to endure the humiliation of talking to her while knowing she had seen him at the worst moment of his life. He downed two fast beers while he watched his brother bouncing on his toes and bobbing his head, talking to the flirtatious stewardess.

"I am so happy to meet you!" Gwen said to Manley Tufts, shaking his hand and holding on to it while she talked to him. "Why, I would never have guessed that Stanley is your brother. You sure you have the same mothers?"

Manley laughed, and Stanley fumed as he watched the embarrassing show. He knew they talked about him. He could see his name on his brother's lips, and then the finger came up and pointed right at him.

"There you are! Come here!" Gwen shouted at Stanley, who now blushed beet red.

At first he tried to pretend he didn't see her, but she kept shouting at him, so he had to look. Then he smiled and halfheartedly waved back at her.

"What's the matter with your brother, Captain?" the redhead asked Manley Tufts and looked back at Stanley, who kept leaning against the bar and now fumbled with a napkin.

"Let me check," the taller Tufts said, leaving Gwen with Dicky Doo and walking to the bar, where his brother lurked.

With the afternoon sun disappearing beyond the western mountains, and bright orange beginning to bleed across the sky, Yamaguchi Ritter and his Angeles City Cowboys mounted their plywood stage and opened their show with the Bob Wills classic, "A Maiden's Prayer." Gwen Ebberhardt smiled at Major Dickinson and took his hand.

"I love this song!" she said, and began dragging the mojo to the center of the lawn in front of the band, where wide slabs of Masonite covered the grass as a makeshift dance floor. "Surely you know how to waltz."

"Oh, barely," Dickinson said as he proudly took the breathtaking flight attendant in his arms and began to count one-two-three as he stepped the waltz with her. As they circled, Gwen flashed a glance and triumphant smile at Wayne and the boys.

"You know, I would make her take a bath tonight, Wayne," Terry O'Connor said with a laugh while looking at Gwen dancing with Dicky Doo.

"She's out there dancing with that ape because of you, Captain O'Connor," Wayne Ebberhardt said, shaking his head at the sight of his wife with the mojo. "Keep that in mind. The last thing all of us need is for that bubble-butt tub of shit to guess that she might have something to do with his and Stanley's little brown blowout on the freedom bird."

Stanley Tufts edged his way over to the group of defense lawyers and moved close to Wayne Ebberhardt.

"So this is your wife?" Tufts said, pulling a beer from the six-pack he had carried under his arm from the bar and handing the six-pack to the lieutenant.

"Why, Stinky, how nice of you to join us," Terry O'Connor said, taking a beer from the shorter captain, too.

"Fuck you, O'Connor," Stanley hissed, and grabbed the can back from the Marine. "Get your own beer. You have no heart, you know that?"

"Lighten up, Stanley," Jon Kirkwood said, handing a beer to Terry O'Connor from his own six-pack.

"Wayne, she told you all about my accident, didn't she," Tufts said, looking at the lieutenant.

"No, Stanley," Ebberhardt lied, "Gwen's not that kind of person. Buck Taylor had a friend on that flight, and he told me. If anything, she felt very sorry for you. But as far as your accident on her flight goes, she has never said a word about it to anyone."

Stanley Tufts smiled.

"Thanks, Wayne," he said, and walked back to where Charlie Heyster stood, sucking on his pipe next to Manley and the Brothers B, watching Dicky Doo dancing a second Bob Wills number, "Faded Love," with Gwen.

"Well, if it isn't the jailer himself, Michael Schuller," Terry O'Connor said, seeing the lieutenant from the brig walking across the grass with a fresh six-pack of Budweiser in one hand and chugging a just-opened extra he had gotten at the bar in his other paw.

"Seven beers at once, plan on a little combat drinking tonight, Mikie?" Jon Kirkwood said, slapping the newly arrived lieutenant across the back.

"This three-two shit takes a lot more than I can carry to do the job," Schuller said, laughing. "Sure does make a fellow piss good, though."

"Kind of a late start. What happened?" Kirkwood said, tapping the crystal of his wristwatch to emphasize the Marine's tardiness to the festivities. "Your boss is over there drinking beside our boss. Has been for the better part of an hour. Lieutenant Colonel Charles Dewitt Webster, doesn't that name just roll off your tongue like peanut butter fudge?"

"He's not a bad sort," Schuller said, looking at the provost marshal sipping mai tai cocktails with the staff judge advocate. "Got a late arrival and had to get him squared away. Scary tale with this one. A platoon sergeant, division Marine from down south, went over the edge, opened fire on his battalion commander's tent."

"I take it the tent was unoccupied at the time, since the word 'murder' didn't creep into your commentary," Kirkwood said, taking a sip from his beer.

"The CO had gone down to the privy, lucky for him," Schuller said, crushing his empty beer can with his hand and opening a second one. "Still, they charged him with attempted murder, clapped him in irons, and fragged a helicopter to ferry him straight to Freedom Hill. The man's first sergeant and captain came with him, and turned him over to our jailer. I say sad story because these guys all hugged like family when they said their good-byes."

"Wow, that's interesting," O'Connor said, putting his arm around Mike Schuller's shoulders and giving him a hug, too. "So a sergeant tries to murder the battalion commander and has his company CO and first shirt hugging him good-bye. Wonder if they would hug the guy their sergeant wanted to kill?"

"We just lock them in storage," Schuller shrugged. "I wouldn't know."

"Speaking of locking men in storage," Kirkwood said, narrowing his eyebrows at the lieutenant as he spoke, "I have a serious bone to pick with you. My client Donald T. Wilson, whom you have in pretrial confinement, has apparently joined the gang of convicted prisoners out in the yard these days. You know that is a major no-no, don't you?"

"We only have so many monkey cages, Jon," the brig officer said, defending his actions. "First you complained that we held him in solitary confinement, now you complain because he's out in the general population."

"It's against regulations, first of all, Mikie, and secondly, it violates his constitutional rights, technically," Kirkwood said, shaking his head at the lieutenant. "I've said it in the past and I will say it again: you guys need to set up a minimum-security compound for low-risk, pretrial inmates separate from the regular brig. Same goes for inmates convicted of these cockamamy infractions like disrespect and tardy to formation. Put these otherwise good Marines to work, and get them away from the really bad apples."

"From your lips to God's ear," Schuller said, shaking his head and shrugging. "That makes too much sense! Colonel Webster even supports that notion, and so does Colonel Prunella. However, we have a chief of staff, and a bunch of wing and division colonels who subscribe to the same code of discipline that Dicky Doo espouses. Burn them all and let God sort them out."

"You know I will complain about this situation at trial," Kirkwood said, furrowing his brow and pressing his lips thin.

"Maybe the judge will order Three-MAF to do what you suggested with the minimum-security work compounds," Schuller said, nodding at the captain. "We have correctional custody platoons at the recruit depots for similar low-risk personnel. Why not do it here?"

"I see talking to you about it is about as useful as me talking to O'Connor," Kirkwood said, putting his hand on his buddy's shoulder.

"Like I told you," Schuller said and sighed, "Colonel Webster, Colonel Prunella, all of us who deal with criminal justice, we agree. Right now that brig is a powder keg, ready to blow. It just needs the right kind of spark to set off a disaster. We are doing our best, putting the high-risk, most dangerous people in the layered confinement areas and allowing the low-risk inmates, whether pretrial or posttrial, to mingle in the general population. Still, we have an increase in fights among the men, especially those provoked by racial tension. We break up the polarized groups when we see them form, but we're busting at the seams and we can only do so much."

While Michael Schuller talked about the worsening conditions at Freedom Hill, Charles Heyster and his shadow, Stanley Tufts, joined the circle of defense lawyers.

Seeing the lead prosecutor and his Sancho sidekick sliding quietly into the defense section's discussion group, Terry O'Connor raised the red flag for his mates, making a comment about the pipe that Heyster held clamped in his teeth, sucking with an irritating whistle.

"You know, it must be that we're going to get a flood of a rainstorm," O'Connor proclaimed, craning his neck and surveying the evening sky.

"What makes you believe that?" Michael Carter said, looking at the sky, too, and seeing only the purple and orange of a midsummer sunset, with no clue of rain in sight.

"Observe, if you will, my dear man," O'Connor then said, pointing at Charles Heyster. "The pigs have put sticks in their mouths. A clear indication of heavy rain."

"Heavy bullshit is more like it," Charlie Heyster snapped back, taking the pipe from his teeth and shoving it in his pocket.

"A word with you, Miss Carter," Heyster then said, taking Michael Carter by the arm and causing him to slosh sloe gin fizz out of his glass.

"Hold on," Kirkwood said, taking Heyster's hand away from Carter's arm. "Anything you say to Mikie, you say in front of his attorney: me."

"This isn't about anything important," Heyster said, grabbing Carter by the arm again.

"Wait, damn it," Carter said, and pulled away from the major-select's grip. "You say what you need to tell me in front of my friends and colleagues. I keep no secrets from them."

Charlie Heyster rolled his eyes and looked at the circle of Wayne Ebberhardt, Mike Schuller, Terry O'Connor, and Jon Kirkwood. Then in the corner of his eye he also caught a glimpse of T. D. McKay ambling across the grass toward them, with Buck Taylor and Lobo at his sides.

"Captain Carter, congratulations, you've finally won a case," Heyster said and shook his head. Stanley Tufts shook his head, too, mirroring his senior partner.

"I have?" Carter exclaimed and spread a smile across his pink-tinted yellow teeth.

"Well, yes, in a way. Yes, you've won a case," Heyster sighed, and then took a deep breath. "The Corporal James Gillette case."

"But I lost that hands down," Carter said, frowning. "The jury found him guilty, unanimously."

"Right," Heyster said with a laugh. "Your defense of momentary insanity because the chick had a dick did not quite fly. However, powers greater than ours have intervened and have acquitted Corporal Gillette."

"The bomb dump fire, right?" O'Connor said and laughed. "Michael, the bomb dump over by First Division CP. When it took a rocket attack last week, the fire burned the legal admin office at division, too. Major Dickinson must have sent our overflow transcription work to division legal. Your court record went up in smoke, right, Charlie?"

Heyster bowed his head and shrugged.

"Yes, that and a deposition we took from this rat fink down at Chu Lai who rolled over on some dope dealers," Heyster said, shaking his head. "We can get a new deposition from the fink as soon as he decides to cooperate again."

"Isn't that my client James Elmore?" O'Connor then exclaimed. "You weren't going to tell me, were you!"

"Look, we would have told you," Heyster said, looking at the suddenly angry Irish defense lawyer.

"But not just yet!" O'Connor snapped, glaring at the prosecutor. "Not until after you and your interrogators had regained your lost testimony, plus a little extra, I imagine. After you had sweated a few more miles of life out of my client, without benefit of counsel."

"Your client is sitting in a cell as we speak at Freedom Hill, for his own protection," Heyster snapped back at O'Connor.

"Oh, you've locked him up, have you?" Terry O'Connor bellowed, throwing his half-full beer into a nearby garbage can. "You lost his deposition, so now you lock him up to sweat another one out of him."

"It's for his protection!" Heyster shouted back. "We locked up the guy who tried to kill him, but we believe that this character Pitts may now have him in his sights."

"That was April, Charlie!" O'Connor snarled, stepping close to the major-select and still yelling. "Today is July Fourth! Nothing's changed except you got your deposition burned, and now you think you can sweat a new one out of my client without making good on the original promises you made him."

"Oh, we kept our promises," the prosecutor fired back.

"He's still in Vietnam, you shyster!" O'Connor retorted. "You've held him in custody here since February, March, whenever it was you first arrested him. You were going to nail his suppliers and send him packing home. What happened to that deal?"

"We just now got Harris," Heyster said, wide-eyed and backing away from the red-haired, irate captain.

"Just now last April!" O'Connor hissed. "Check your calendar, Charlie!"

"Can we discuss this later?" Heyster said, lowering his voice after seeing Major Dickinson frowning at them because of the noise. He had taken Gwen Ebberhardt to meet Lieutenant Colonels Prunella and Webster, and First Wing's commander, Major General Norman Anderson, who had gathered under the fly tent by the table covered with platters of fresh pineapple, cheeses, and fondu pans filled with pigs-in-a-blanket. The shouting had drawn everyone's attention.

"What about Mikie's win?" T. D. McKay shouted at Heyster just as he and Stanley started to step away from the unwelcome group.

"Oh, yes," Heyster said. "General Cushman agreed with Colonel Prunella that as far as the Vietnamese know, we took care of the matter. We cannot re-create the transcripts and all the other trial documents that burned in the fire. We would have to reinvestigate, and retry the whole case from scratch. So he said to just let it slide."

"So no conviction, no record at all?" McKay asked, smiling.

"That's how it has to go down, I guess," Heyster said, smiling back.

"What about Gillette's page eleven?" O'Connor chirped, jutting out his jaw at the prosecutor.

"What about it?" Heyster answered, raising his eyebrows at the still-angry Irishman.

"Corporal Gillette should have no reference to any of this matter in his military record, if the command is just going to let it slide, as you say," O'Connor said, pointing his finger at the major-select as he spoke. "You think about it, and you know I am right."

"I thought it would go in the record as an acquittal," Heyster said, frowning.

"No," O'Connor said, shaking his head. "With no record of trial, and no due process taken, then it is as though the event never took place. No record whatsoever."

"Well, Miss Carter will have to follow up at the Marines' command section then, and ensure that everything gets expunged from his record," Heyster said, walking away.

"We'll expect a letter from you supporting it, so we can get the record expunged!" O'Connor shouted, and looked at Michael Carter, who now hung his head and sucked on the red swizzle-stick straw sticking out of his crimson-colored cocktail.

"Mikie, you won!" Wayne Ebberhardt said, slapping the captain on his back. "What's wrong with you?"

"Oh, that's not a win, and you know it," Carter said, still sucking sloe gin fizz through the plastic tube.

"Your man is free!" Kirkwood said, laughing and shaking the skinny, tall captain by his shoulders.

"Oh, my stars, that's right!" Carter said and then smiled wide. "We need to get him out of the brig! Mike, can we do that?"

"I will take you there myself, tonight," Schuller said, smiling and putting his arm around the stick man.

"Hold on," T. D. McKay said, looking at the happy crowd. "I've got two clients who took a bust, a fine, and did a little confinement to quarters. They get expunged, too?"

Jon Kirkwood looked at Terry O'Connor and then at Wayne Ebberhardt. Both men shook their heads.

"Of course, it's always up to General Cushman, but I am confident that your two guys won't get any relief," Kirkwood said, shaking his head, too. "It's already gone down the river. They pled guilty, took the punishment. The trigger puller walks free, and the guys standing outside, who happened to be at the wrong place at the wrong time, they get their dicks and balls cut off. That's how it goes sometimes. Jungle Rules, man."

T. D. McKay shrugged and then smiled, looking across the lawn at the dance floor, where Gwen Ebberhardt now skipped a lively two-step with Lieutenant Colonel Prunella.

"She's quite a number, Wayne. How do you stand it?" McKay laughed.

Lobo had stood silent behind the group of lawyers during the exchange with Charlie Heyster, and now bobbed his head watching the tall, sexy redhead stretching her legs on the dance floor. Buck Taylor had his arm looped inside Archie Gunn's, just in case the lumbering ox decided he needed a turn with the flight attendant.

"I don't know," Wayne Ebberhardt sighed. "Life with her sometimes, well, its sort of like wearing somebody else's shoes. Some things you can never get used to."

"That lady loves you, though, cowboy," Buck Taylor said, and nudged Archie Gunn to stop drooling at her.

The lieutenant smiled at the two pilots.

"Enjoy the sight while you can, gentlemen," Ebberhardt said, turning toward the half circle of men, all looking at his wife dance with the staff judge advocate. "Tuesday, when she flies out, she's gone for good. She's headed to Atlanta, and her old job with Delta Airlines. I rotate in September, and get out of the crotch in October, so this is it."

"You're headed to Atlanta for sure?" Kirkwood asked the lieutenant.

"Contract law," Ebberhardt answered, smiling. "No criminals, just negotiations. I'm joining a firm that represents Delta, as a matter of fact. Thanks to that long-legged redhead out there who is the master of saying the phrase that pays to the ears that count."

"Tuesday, the colonel and I hit the ville in Okinawa," McKay said, spreading a rare smile on his face. "Then on to Norton, a bus to Pendleton for outprocessing, and after that I fly from Los Angeles to Dallas, where my mom and dad promised to pick me up a week from this Thursday night."

Tears began to fill the lieutenant's eyes as he looked at his buddies and thought of his home and family.

"I got to go see Jimmy's mom, you know," McKay choked, and then took a big drink of beer.

"Yeah," Kirkwood said, shrugging and bowing his head. "We know."

"Do me a favor, Tommy," Buck Taylor said, walking to the lieutenant and putting his arm around his shoulders. "Don't try to kill all the demons at once when you get home. Take them on one at a time, and don't try to do it alone. Don't shut people out, either, when you need to let go of some of that grief you've got all bottled up. Wounds have to air out to heal. Give it some time and you'll be fine. When you talk to Mrs. Sanchez, and Jimmy's brothers and sisters, try listening a little bit. Hey, and you stay in touch with us back here, too. That's an order."

Tommy McKay nodded and wiped his eyes.

"I never thought it would be hard to say good-bye to you bums, but it is," he said, and smiled again.

"Tommy Touchdown, we will all see you back in the world," O'Connor chirped and raised his can of Budweiser in a toast.

"How about a year from today?" McKay said, looking at his pals. "What about Denver? Fourth of July 1969 in Denver, Colorado!"

"The middle of the country," Kirkwood said, raising his beer, too. "No excuses why we all can't get there."

Archie Gunn smiled, too, and raised his glass, making the commitment to join their first annual reunion in Denver. So did Buck Taylor, Terry O'Connor, Wayne Ebberhardt, and Michael Carter.

"ANOTHER SEVEN-AND-SEVEN, Tam," Bruce Olsen called to the Vietnamese bartender at the Continental Hotel in Saigon. While most members of the U.S. Embassy staff celebrated Independence Day with the poolside barbecue in the American compound, several of the CIA field operators opted to relax away from the flagpole.

Olsen had served for nearly a year under the umbrella of a highly secret unit designated, Intelligence Coordination and Exploitation, better known among company circles as ICEX. This clandestine Central Intelligence Agency spin-off group, overseen by veteran CIA field officer Evan Parker, officially the director of ICEX, did the jobs rumored by Marines who talked to a guy who knew a guy who told wild stories of ninjas in black suits stalking the enemy's leaders and sympathizers, putting bullets in their brains, or sawing through their necks with piano wire. They code-named it Phoenix.

Before picking up the tour in Saigon, Bruce Olsen had lived his navy

life aboard small ships, riding in submarines, swimming in a frog suit during the night, doing all those sorts of things that members of the U.S.
Navy's two Sea-Air-Land Teams, SEALs, like best. He had excelled
through his training at Coronado, and pulled one and a half tours in Vietnam before Evan Parker and his boss, Robert Komer, handpicked him for
the Phoenix program.

Komer, a well-respected and powerful agent in the CIA, got the job of
putting the wheels on the idea of Phoenix. He went to Saigon and opened
shop as the head of the CIA's Civil Operations and Revolutionary Devel-
opment, which funded and sheltered ICEX and Phoenix.

Black-suited commandos, handpicked from the Army Special Forces,
the Navy SEALs, Marine Corps Reconnaissance, Force Reconnaissance,
and Scout/Sniper units, and Special Weapons and Tactics units in the air
force, stalked through the cities and the countryside, not just in Vietnam
but also in neighboring Laos and Cambodia, and assassinated enemy leaders, and suspected leaders who sympathized with the Communists and
caused harm to American and South Vietnamese forces.

They terminated targets without prejudice, meaning the poor sap just
got in the way; with prejudice which meant they had put the hit on the
man, and with extreme prejudice, which meant die now, motherfucker, die
immediately.

In many covert operations that went beyond any concepts of legality,
and simply amounted to outright murder, blatantly violating the Geneva
Conventions, Olsen and his black ninja cohorts recruited, trained, and
oversaw field agents who often did the actual trigger-pulling or neck-
sawing, or they set up the victims so he and his Phoenix team associates
could do it. Then, after the mission, they terminated these torpedoes, too,
cleaning up all loose ends. They left no living witnesses or participants to
the deeds who might betray their secret with a nudge or a buck or two.
Killing the friendly, unsuspecting local shills after their use ran out, that was
the ugly part of the job that Bruce Olsen detested. That was one reason why
he liked his seven-and-seven with more Seagram's Seven than Seven-Up.

"Hey, pal, got a light?" a voice behind Bruce Olsen said, surprising the
SEAL.

"Wow, where'd you come from, Marine?" Olsen said, seeing the trim
cut of the blond man with the clean smile and definite look of one of Uncle
Sam's misguided children.

"How did you know I'm a Marine?" Brian Pitts said, taking a stool
next to Olsen and pointing to a beer tap that said San Miguel on the plastic handle.

"I knew you weren't a SEAL," Olsen said, and laughed. "We know each other personally, here in 'Nam. You don't have a dog face, and your hair does not say 'wild blue yonder' or 'anchors aweigh,' so that just leaves Marines."

"You're good, man," Pitts said, grabbing a book of matches off the bar and lighting his cigarette. "I take it you don't smoke, then."

"No, sorry," Olsen said, finishing his drink and pointing to the bartender named Tam to bring him another.

Sam Madison, a CIA field supervisor close to ICEX director Evan Parker, sat at the other end of the bar with a colleague of Olsen's named Bart Johnson, a SEAL, too, and a Phoenix man as well. A third associate, Mike Hammond, a Force Recon Marine, made up their close-knit, hand-picked team. Sam and Bart watched Bruce and the stranger with short glances in the mirror behind the bar.

They, too, saw the short haircut, and knew all the military operators in the Saigon area. He looked the part but did not have a face that matched a known commodity.

"Hey, I just checked in down here, and tonight got my first chance to scope out the ville," Pitts offered, since the American who was obviously a serviceman said nothing. "Say, you're not an officer, are you?"

"Aw, no," Olsen said and shrugged. "I'm a regular navy enlisted guy—you know, the Donald Duck suit and 'ships ahoy.' "

"Same here, only Marines. Sergeant Franklin's the name, Jesse Franklin," Pitts lied, even though the identification card in his wallet read First Lieutenant Joseph A. Russell, matching the dog tags around his neck. The real Jesse Franklin, an old black man, swept the floors and shined shoes in Robbie's Pool Hall back in Kansas City, and had given Brian his street name, Small Change. Next to his Uncle Joe Russell, he liked Jesse best.

"Bruce Olsen, petty officer second class," the Phoenix hit man said, and shook Brian Pitts's outstretched hand. "Glad to know you, Sergeant Franklin."

Pitts smiled at the stranger as they exchanged introductions, curious to know if this guy was really a deserter in disguise, like himself. When he first ventured into the city of Saigon, just getting his legs back on the ground, he had encountered others such as himself, deserters on the run, mingling in bars along Tudo Street, in the city's tenderloin, wearing civilian clothes, trying to blend with scores of others who looked like them. With their stoic, out-of-place faces, though, they often presented easy targets for the CID rat dogs who scouted the watering holes now and then, looking for deserters gone native, trying to get lost in the crowds of round-eyed, Western contractors and civilian adventurers who migrated to Saigon from Australia, New Zealand, and the U.S.A. for big money made easy.

Pitts envisioned developing a small circle of American-born confidants to work with him in his Asian empire, operating throughout the Indochina region with home base in Bangkok, where he planned to live like a sultan. However, he needed trusted people in South Vietnam both in the northern provinces as well as in Saigon and its lucrative surroundings. He concluded that deserters on the run would be more than glad to find a fellow countryman who would lend them a hand. They would naturally cooperate and keep their mouths shut.

That's how he had recruited his two colleagues, Tommy Joyner and Robert Matthews, a pair of division Marines from northern I Corps who stowed away on a C-130 Hercules cargo plane that landed at Tan Son Nhut Airport in Saigon instead of the Marines' El Toro air station in California. The pair looked worse than Mau Mau Harris when Chung and Bao found them and took the two men to their big brother Huong to either shoot or present to the Snowman for disposition. Talking to the anxious duo who only wanted to go home from the war, Brian Pitts devised his brainstorm for an Asian empire with American deserters as his most trusted associates.

In the few months that he had lain low, clothing, feeding, and educating Matthews and Joyner to the ways and opportunities of the Snowman and his well-paying business, he also had made fresh contacts with Viet Cong and North Vietnamese agents who supplied him with pure heroin and Buddha at cut-rate prices. He had taken a million dollars and invested it in a massive dope inventory, and now looked to move product not only in South Vietnam, but also ship truckloads of it back to America. He needed trusted hands to do the work. Deserters had everything to gain, and if they failed him he could kill them with no questions or concerns coming from anyone. Deserters were disposable.

Tonight, while the Snowman went looking for potential recruits, and took the opportunity to wet his whistle in a setting more sociable than the stucco plantation house with the red tile roof that he and his cowboys had procured in the countryside west of Saigon, just off the highway that led to Cu Chi, Chung, Joyner, Matthews, and Turd held down the fort.

"So, what do you do here in Saigon?" Pitts asked, sipping the suds off the top of his beer.

Bruce Olsen looked at the Marine, who wore an expensive white-on-white brocaded silk shirt and black silk pants with canvas deck shoes.

"Stuff," he shrugged, and then thought about the prying question and decided to put the dog off his scent. "Logistics, you know, supply stuff."

"Oh!" Pitts smiled, and then sipped more beer. He could use a man who knew how to get stuff shipped.

"What's your story?" Olsen smiled at the newfound friend.

"I got reassigned down here to work for, let's just say part of the embassy," Pitts lied, feeling like making himself sound exotic and mysterious to the potential recruit.

"CIA?" Olsen shrugged, taking a sip of his whiskey cocktail. "I know guys who got assigned there. Marine Recon guys, SEALs, green beanies. They got special operations, you know. At least that's what I heard from the guy on the second shitter."

Pitts laughed at the term for scuttlebutt, unfounded rumor.

"If I told you I'd have to kill you," Pitts smiled and took a long drag off his smoke.

"I'm not asking what you do now," Olsen said, putting up his hands, pretending to fend off any sense from Pitts that he wanted to pry into anything he had no business knowing. "What did you do up north?"

"Sniper," Pitts lied, and took a big drink of his beer. His ego had led him over a line that he knew better than crossing. His subconscious haughtiness and need to inflate his esteem wanted this no-name stranger, who worked some dead-end job on a supply barge trapped in the doldrums, to be impressed with him. To admire his heroic masculinity and dash.

"Oh, wow, Murder, Incorporated!" Olsen beamed, and smiled at his boss, who watched him with increased interest.

"Hey, man, not so loud," Pitts said, and looked at the two men huddled at the end of the bar who apparently paid him no mind.

"I heard of those scout/snipers up there in I Corps. Who's that sergeant that's got all those kills? What's his name, Hathcock? Yeah, that's the guy. I read about him in the *Sea Tiger*. You work with him at all?"

"Sure, Hathcock. Yeah, I've done a turn or two with the guy. He's back at Da Nang last I saw," Pitts said, taking another drink of beer and now breaking a sweat. He had no idea about this sergeant named Hathcock. Then he thought about something that this sailor said early in their conversation. "I thought you said you were a SEAL when I sat down."

"Oh, no. Sorry if I misled you," Olsen shrugged, and offered a sheepish smile while in the back of his mind he pondered the Hathcock answer, and knew for sure that his new friend was a phony. Olsen had worked with Carlos Hathcock and a corporal named John Burke back when he first began the Phoenix program in early 1967. Hathcock had rotated home after that, about a year ago, and Burke had died this spring at Khe Sanh. No way this clown was a sniper and didn't know that common scoop among the close-knit special operations crowd.

"I work at supply with the SEAL teams," Olsen finally said, lowering his head as though embarrassed, "so I guess I was vague about my job. I make that mistake sometimes. I'm not a SEAL. I guess just wishful thinking on my part. I'm a storekeeper. Sounds dull when you put it up against a SEAL, so I'm sometimes a little misleading about it, maybe subconsciously trying to impress people. That's a bad thing to do, considering my friends and what they went through to earn the right to call themselves SEALs. A supply clerk just doesn't excite anyone, so I'm sometimes vague about it."

Brian Pitts patted Bruce Olsen on the shoulder.

"Everybody's job is important," Pitts said, consoling the storekeeper caught exaggerating about being a SEAL. "You work with the SEAL teams, so that's pretty cool. They're your buddies, too. You work inside their circle."

"Yeah, that's true. I guess it's pretty cool what I do," Olsen said, and smiled. "So, what unit you work with up north?"

"I started with Seventh Marines, then got shipped up to Ninth Marines," Pitts said, waving to Tam to bring him a fresh beer. "Then I got orders here."

"You're not one of those Phoenix guys, are you?" Olsen whispered, widening his eyes, showing his enthusiasm toward the exciting unit that American servicemen mostly knew only by way of rumor and sea story.

"Like I said, I can't really say," Pitts said in a hushed voice, and then smiled and gave the man a wink as if to confirm the suspicion.

"Yeah, I knew it," Olsen said, and drank more seven-and-seven. "Shit, I bet that's wild-ass work. Damn!"

"How long you been in the navy?" Pitts asked the new admirer, gloating with his phony nonchalance.

"Six years come September," Olsen said, telling the truth. He had learned in his training to tell as much truth with lies as possible, making the whole story more believable.

"You're not a deserter, are you?" Pitts then asked, and his face flushed as he asked the hard question. He had to finally ask, though, to get down to business. "I mean, most military guys don't hang in a fancy bar like this, and dress in nice civilian clothes. It's cool if you are. I'm no cop or anything. Like I said, I have my own kettle of fish to cook."

Olsen looked down both directions of the bar and then leaned close to Brian Pitts and whispered, "What if I am?"

"It's cool," Pitts whispered back. "If you are, I have a good-paying job. If you're not, and you do supply like you say, I still have a good-paying job. Maybe."

"Doing what?" Olsen asked, looking both ways down the bar.

"Stuff," Pitts said, sipping his beer and then lighting a cigarette.

"I got to take a piss," Olsen said, and got off his stool and walked to the back of the bar.

Brian Pitts watched him disappear behind the restroom door. When the older of the two men sitting at the bar also got up and went to the toilet, the Snowman got nervous. He left a twenty-dollar bill on the bar, gave Tam a nod to keep the change, and ducked out the main doorway.

As he left the Continental Hotel bar, a middle-aged Vietnamese woman wearing a black cocktail dress walked out the door behind him after the bartender gave her a nod.

"I told Tam to have him followed, just in case," Sam Madison said to Bruce Olsen in the bathroom as they stood over the urinals.

"If he's still there when I walk back to the bar, he may be just another jarhead out shooting off his lying mouth," Olsen said with a laugh, zipping his pants. "He's got something definitely dirty going on, though, asking me if I was a deserter, and then offering me a well-paying job because of my supply connections. Ten to one the guy's tied to dope."

"Dope's tied to the Viet Cong," Madison said, washing his hands. "Effective weapon. We have more and more of our guys using it. We'll find out what this cat's all about. Tam put his hit team on this guy. Their people will tie a can on his tail he can't shake. We'll pass the lowdown on this bum to DIA, or kick it over to General Cushman. Let his folks sort it out. If he's tied to the Cong, which is a good bet, if he's dealing serious dope, we might just whack this turd."

Olsen laughed and dried his hands.

"Man, if this idiot only knew who sat at the same bar with him tonight when he breezed out his line of bullshit," the SEAL said, shaking his head. "He wore expensive threads, a Rolex watch—not standard Marine Corps issue, my friend. His look spoke of dope loud and clear."

Brian Pitts kept looking over his shoulder, and the woman in the black cocktail dress finally disappeared in a hotel door. He stopped and turned, and saw no one on the street, so he doubled back up the block and made a right, where Huong and Bao waited for him in the black Mercedes-Benz.

As he settled in the backseat he lit a cigarette and then pounded his fist on his knee, blowing out a big sigh. He had stepped way over the line tonight, and felt sick at knowing how badly he had allowed his ego to brag and jeopardize everything. That so-called SEAL supply guy could easily have been CID stalking a bar, looking for deserters or dope peddlers. He felt stupid for allowing his vanity, greed, and anxiousness to hurry the job of recruiting soldiers for his new army overwhelm his more characteristic good sense of caution and attention to detail.

Sometimes his vision got to pushing too hard, and he knew he had to keep that drive under control, working more methodically and carefully.

"No more fuckups like tonight," he told himself as he sucked on his cigarette. He watched Huong and Bao both checking the mirrors and glancing in every direction, looking for anyone who might follow them.

"See anyone back there?" Pitts asked his senior cowboy as he steered the car westward toward the edge of the city.

"No, sir, just Vespa, but it turn left back by that last hotel," Huong said. "One car come now, but it just pull from curb. No follow."

"Good," Pitts sighed, and took a relaxing drag off the smoke. "Let's go home."

Chapter 15

THE CHU LAI HIPPIE

CHOPPER CREPT FROM the hole in the wall where the water pipe came through and ran overhead in the mojo's office, across the hall, into the prosecution section, where it bent ninety degrees to the right, and then branched off to feed a deep sink in the utility room and traveled next door to supply water in the all-hands head. The roach flicked his antennae and then pulled them down, one at a time, using his front feet, and ran the wirelike appendages along his mouth, cleaning the dust particles from them. Then he tilted his knobby brown head and caught sight of the dry coffee creamer that Charlie Heyster had spilled on the black lacquer tray that held the jars of sugar, Carnation Coffeemate, and a stack of clean, white ceramic mugs next to the officers' coffeepot.

The giant, northern Florida variety palmetto bug opened his wings, ready to fly down to partake of the inviting meal, but then caught sight of the man sitting at the desk below him. Chopper recognized the all-too-familiar bald spot on the back of the human's head. Instead of just watching him eat the dry creamer and sugar, as the others always did, the ones who came in and cleaned the office, dumped the trash, and made the coffee, and talked to him like a house pet as he ate, this man and the fat fellow with the black and silver hair from the office next to this one, would scream and swat at him with manila folders or a rolled-up magazine. So the big roach eased back inside the hole, leaving his head poking out so he could watch, and waited for the obnoxious creature below him to leave. Then he could fly down to the tray and eat at his leisure.

Three years ago, the insect's great-great-great-great-great grandmother, along with several of her closest friends and relatives, had set up house-keeping in the bottom of a case of toilet paper in a Jacksonville, Florida, warehouse. Someone had knocked a small hole through the cardboard near a bottom corner, giving the roaches free run in and out of the container, allowing them access to forage for grub outside the box while developing their colony among the rolls of soft paper. Then one day the case got trucked up to Warner Robins Air Force Base in Georgia, where a C-141 Starlifter carried the box of toilet tissue and the nest of North Florida palmetto bugs to Da Nang Air Force Base in South Vietnam.

After a few days in this new country, where night and day seemed backward to the bugs, a small man put the big box in the back of a panel truck and drove it to the enlisted men's head next to the First Marine Aircraft Wing legal office, and stacked the box with some others in a storage room lighted by the glow from the gas burner beneath a water heater. Chopper's great-grandmother and her growing family ventured out and made their home inside the walls of this damp building. They found food plentiful and the climate ideal for their species, so they proliferated.

When Chopper hatched from his egg case, his great-grandmother had long since disappeared from the transplanted community of palmetto bugs. However, her hearty genetics in such a supportive and welcome environment produced a roach race that dwarfed any of their two-inch kin that remained in Florida. While among most communities of cockroaches, a three-inch-long male might seem rare, such size was now common among Chopper's South Vietnamese kin.

The big roach watched as this man took a package wrapped in brown paper from inside a white laundry bag. He shook it and listened to its side, then he sniffed it like he might take a bite from the bread-loaf-size item. Seeing the human now absorbed with the object he held in his hands and shook again and smelled, Chopper eased himself out of the pipe hole and spread his wings, launching in a low, fluttering buzz a few feet above the desk, and then landed with a thud on the black lacquer tray. He managed to swallow three good mouthfuls of the dry creamer before the man leaped from his chair, shoved the paper-wrapped package back in the white cotton bag, and bellowed while grabbing a manila folder and running to the side table, where the cockroach dined on Coffeemate and sugar spillage.

As the shouting human swung the file folder, Chopper launched himself skyward, lit on the wall, took one look back, and flew to his pipe-hole nest.

"Staff Sergeant Pride!" Charlie Heyster screamed, trying to kill the elusive roach. "I thought base maintenance was supposed to spray this place last week! That damned cockroach is still here!"

"Sir," Staff Sergeant Pride said breathlessly, "they did all they could."

"This fucking roach probably thrives on Malathion, then," Heyster said, now looking around for the bug. "He'll be feeding on cats and small children before long, unless we kill the bastard. That asshole Kirkwood brought it in here, you know. Put it in my pipe tobacco, and now the fucking bug lives in my office."

"Sir, Major Dickinson had his bouts with that roach, too, when he had your office," Derek Pride said, reminding the new military justice officer about the screaming and furniture throwing that Dicky Doo had done before he moved into Colonel Prunella's old office.

"Surely the damned thing will finally die from old age then," Heyster said, spinning on his toes and swiveling his head 360 degrees, still looking for the roach that the enlisted Marines had come to call Chopper because of his enormous size and vague similarity to a helicopter. "How long do these bugs live, anyway?"

Pride shrugged his shoulders and looked at the major-select as he tied the drawstrings on the top of his dirty-clothes bag.

"Someone told me that big roaches like that can live for several years," the staff sergeant said. "By the way, sir, I am heading to the laundry myself. Would you like me to drop that off for you?"

"Thanks, but no, Sergeant," Heyster said, and blushed as he laid the white cotton bag on the floor by his chair. "I have to go out anyway. I'll drop it myself."

"HELLO, CAN YOU put me in touch with Bill Walters, please?" First Lieutenant Melvin Biggs said on the telephone, calling the Naval Investigative Service special agent who investigated the Brian Pitts look-alike murder. Gunnery Sergeant Jack Jackson sat in the Criminal Investigation Division office with his feet propped on his desk and a wide smile on his face as he read a copy of the message that had just come from Hickam Air Force Base in Hawaii.

"Bill?" the lieutenant said after waiting for the investigator to answer the call. "Mel Biggs here at Three-MAF CID. We just got a message from the forensics lab at Hickam regarding the identification of the body we shipped to them a few months back, supposedly that of a Marine deserter named Pitts."

The lieutenant nodded and listened as Agent Walters spoke.

"Right. Right, Pitts and Scott both had the same blood types, go figure the odds," the lieutenant said. "Look here, they finally dug up an X-ray from Pitts's dental records in boot camp. One of those wraparound films. According to the X-ray, Pitts had an impacted wisdom tooth on his lower left side. This tooth grew sideways into the roots of the molar next to it. The lad's dental records show they extracted that tooth and another wisdom tooth at San Diego back in 1963, while he was in boot camp. This body has all its wisdom teeth, while Pitts had his pulled. Based on that and a perfectly healthy second upper molar on the right side of this body, compared to Pitts's dental record showing he had a filling in that same tooth, the folks in the lab at Hickam say this body obviously is not that of Corporal Brian T. Pitts."

Gunny Jackson laughed and slapped his leg.

"I told you so," he said, and took a big drink of coffee.

Lieutenant Biggs waved at him and smiled.

"That's correct, sir," Biggs said. "They compared dental records of Michael Jerome Scott with those of the body and they have a pretty conclusive match. So the body is that of our missing lance corporal. It just took time to get the dental records in the hands of the forensics people in Hawaii. Didn't take them fifteen minutes after they ran their comparisons. So, like you guys, we're focusing our investigation on Pitts and his people as the primary suspects in Scott's murder."

Lieutenant Biggs sat up in his chair and looked at the gunnery sergeant seated at the desk across from him.

"Agent Walters, I want to put you on the speakerphone so that Gunny Jackson can hear what you just told me," the lieutenant said, and flipped a switch on the front panel of a six-inch-wide, slotted, gray plastic box that sat next to the telephone on the corner of his desk.

"Right, Mel," Walters said over the speaker. "This news of yours, as far as I'm concerned, confirms the identity of a character that the CIA put a tag on in Saigon. Defense Intelligence Agency passed the information through channels, and I got it this morning. This person of interest that they're watching matches the Snowman's description to a tee. It seems that our friend Brian Pitts has tried to masquerade as an ICEX operator. Unfortunately for him, Pitts picked the wrong guy to shine on: an actual Phoenix ninja, a navy SEAL. Get this: Pitts tried to recruit the guy."

"What did they do?" Gunny Jackson said in a loud voice so it would carry on the squawk box. "The CIA folks?"

"One of the senior supervisors of ICEX happened to sit just down the bar at the time, watching the curious meeting unfold, so he put a covert surveillance team on our wayward friend's ass," Walters said and laughed. "Pitts is royally screwed, sports fans. Our NIS bureau in Saigon has people going out there now, with a company of soldiers from the Tenth Infantry Division. The surveillance team has indicated that Pitts and a couple of other deserters have linked up with Viet Cong elements, probably dope connections. So forces down south in coordination with our naval investigative people and this Phoenix team will pull a full-out special-operations raid on the location and surrounding area. If the Snowman survives the onslaught, you should have him in custody up here within the week."

WHEN TERRY O'CONNOR saw Charlie Heyster stroll down the sidewalk toward the wing legal office's general-use jeep, swinging the laundry bag in his hand, he dashed out the building's side door and ran as hard as he could to the enlisted barracks, where Movie Star Dean lay on his rack talking to a pair of his buddies from the wing and two divisions' joint public information office.

"I need a jeep that Captain Heyster won't recognize if it follows him!" O'Connor said, gasping for breath as he looked at the driver.

"Yo, sir, what's up?" Movie Star answered, jumping to his feet and grabbing his hat.

"Captain Heyster, I want to follow him, but I don't want him to see me," O'Connor said, and looked at the two Marines from the information office.

"Bruce and Russ, they have a jeep out back," Dean said, pointing to his friends.

"You've got a camera, too!" O'Connor said, seeing the green canvas bag piled on the floor by one of the young men's feet. "What luck! Come on, grab your gear and let's go!"

"Where, sir?" Movie Star said, running behind the captain, along with his two buddies, who wrote stories and took pictures for the local Marine Corps newspaper, the *Sea Tiger*.

"Follow Captain Heyster! Like I said," O'Connor squawked, jumping in the backseat of the jeep, and grabbing Movie Star by the arm and helping him into the rear compartment with him.

"I know that, but where?" Lance Corporal Bruce Dobbs said as he started the vehicle and put it in gear.

"Laundry! Head for the laundry. He had a laundry bag," O'Connor said, looking and not seeing Charlie anywhere. "Let's go! Step on it!"

"What's going on with Captain Shithead?" Movie Star shouted as Lance Corporal Dobbs wheeled the utility vehicle around a corner, sliding against the curb, and nearly flipping the jeep over. "Hey, watch it, man! We about fell out!"

Terry O'Connor gripped the back of the passenger seat where Lance Corporal Russ Sherman rode, holding on to the handlebar on the jeep's dash with both of his hands and keeping his feet on top of his camera bag to prevent it from flying out.

"Just get us there alive, Dobbs," O'Connor said to the freewheeling driver, who maneuvered the jeep like a stock car on a figure-eight track.

"That missing dope, right?" Movie Star then said, and smiled at the captain. "Major Dickhead's trying to blame the office snuffies for ripping it off. He's been on our case for weeks."

"Right," O'Connor said, shaking his head at the lance corporal. "The shyster has accused everybody, including you guys and all of us in the defense section. He's screamed just a little too loud, though. You know, the guilty dog barking. His hue and cry have got my suspicions up. Just suspicions, mind you."

"Hell, sir," Movie Star said and laughed. "Why don't you just ask the snuffies in the office? Can't you smell that shit in his pipe? Not even Cherry Blend can cover up burning weed, man. He's been sampling the reefer you guys keep in that locked closet all fucking year. Happy Pounds said he even saw Heyster loading some of the shit in his tobacco pouch one morning when my man had the duty and got back early from turning off the night lights and unlocking the side hatches. Old Shithead still had the evidence room unlocked and the door standing wide open when Happy walked in the admin office, and caught a quick peek inside the prosecution section before the captain noticed him. So Hap goes out to his desk and starts rattling crap around, to let Shithead know he was back. He said that Heyster threw some kind of box in his bottom drawer and locked everything up real quick when he heard Happy rumbling around."

Terry O'Connor looked at the lance corporal and blinked.

"Sounds interesting," the lawyer said, and then looked at the parking area by the laundry. "However, Lance Corporal Pounds did not see dope. He saw the captain putting something in his tobacco pouch, throw something in his bottom drawer, and the evidence locker was standing open at the time. Very suspicious, but not conclusive. Plus what you guys smell him smoking may only be pipe tobacco. I've smelled a Canadian blend that has a very distinct aroma, much like reefer. I can't say that I've noticed any scent of it in Heyster's Cherry Blend when he's smoked his pipe around me."

"Well, sir, you're the lawyer," Movie Star said, looking for the captain that the enlisted Marines called Shithead. "As far as any of us low-life non-rates are concerned, Captain Heyster's been ripping off the evidence locker all year long and smoking the shit. Now with a truckload of dope gone missing from the evidence locker, my bet's that he's selling it, too."

"He's not at the laundry," O'Connor finally said after surveying the parking lot. "We either missed him or he didn't come here."

"He didn't come here," Russ Sherman said, and then pointed through a gap between buildings where he could see the roadway outside the base. "Because he went out the front gate, and looks like he's headed to the ville."

"Shit!" O'Connor said, seeing Charlie Heyster driving the jeep eastward toward the bridge that crossed the Han River.

"Ten to one he's going down to the bar district," Bruce Dobbs said as he tromped the gas and headed toward the front gate at Da Nang Air Force Base.

"Can we get off base in your jeep?" O'Connor said, grabbing the driver by the shoulder.

Lance Corporal Sherman then reached by his seat and pulled out a clipboard with a white form attached to it, and pointed to the top of the page where in bold, black letters it had stamped on it: "Off-Base Operation Authorized."

As Bruce wheeled the jeep through the main gate, his pal Russ held up the clipboard for the sentry to see, who, in turn, noticing the captain in the backseat, waved the vehicle through without even asking them to stop. Halfway into a sliding right turn, Lance Corporal Dobbs floorboarded the gas and sped down the main drag where they had last seen Charlie Heyster driving toward Da Nang's popular section of bars, tourist shops, and restaurants that lined the boulevard that ran along the Han River.

After crossing the bridge and making a left turn, merging into the thoroughfare jammed with bicycles, cyclo-taxis, pushcarts, pedestrians, and little, multicolored taxicabs honking to get through the crush of people and traffic, Movie Star managed to pick out the top of Captain Heyster's head three blocks away from them.

"Got him, sir," James Dean said, and pointed at the prosecutor creeping slowly in front of the four Marines.

"Right, I see him, too," O'Connor nodded, and then stood in the back of the jeep to see his target better. "It looks like he is trying to pull to the curb and park up there. Dobbs, find a spot anywhere along here and we can slip closer on foot."

Bruce Dobbs sat in the jeep while the captain, Movie Star, and Russ Sherman, with his camera bag on his shoulder, made their way to an open-front restaurant with white wrought-iron tables set out on the sidewalk.

"This will work beautifully," Terry O'Connor said, pulling out a chair and sitting down. "Grab a seat and get your camera ready."

A smiling waiter immediately descended on the trio of Marines. While Lance Corporal Sherman focused his Nikon F with an 85-to-250-millimeter f/4 Nikkor zoom lens on Charlie Heyster, who now stood on the sidewalk next to a building, obviously waiting for someone, Terry O'Connor ordered four dishes of stir-fried noodles with pork and vegetables mixed in it, and Cokes all around.

While the three men waited for the meals, Lance Corporal Dobbs managed to pull the jeep to the curb in front of the restaurant, and then joined his cohorts at their outdoor table.

"The way he keeps checking his watch and looking around, I hope he doesn't see us," O'Connor said, slouching low in his chair as the prosecutor's glance turned in their direction, obviously searching for someone. "Clearly, whoever he was supposed to meet is running behind schedule. That has to have old Charlie pissed off. He's waited, what, more than fifteen minutes now?"

"Something like that, sir," Movie Star said, scarfing down the fried noodles after he doctored them with a healthy dose of catsup.

"Hold on!" Dobbs said, looking across the street and seeing a familiar person weaving his way through traffic, and whistling to get Heyster's attention. "That's fucking Sergeant Randal Carnegie! You know who he is, don't you, guys?"

"The Chu Lai Hippie!" Movie Star said and laughed. "Now, there's a dude that crawled out of one flaky bag!"

Russ Sherman began snapping pictures as the captain and the Chu Lai Hippie exchanged greetings. Charlie Heyster walked to his jeep and took a brown package out of his laundry bag in the backseat and handed it to Carnegie. Then the sergeant gave the prosecutor a white envelope. They shook hands again, and Heyster got in his jeep and pulled back into the jam of traffic.

"Do we follow him, sir?" Dobbs said, pushing back his chair.

Terry O'Connor sat silent for a full minute, looking up the street and watching the man Movie Star had called the Chu Lai Hippie now pulling T-shirts off a display from a street vendor's stand and stuffing them in a large shopping bag that the merchant handed to him. Then he took the package that Heyster had passed to him, dropped it in the sack, and shoved more shirts on top of it.

"I've seen enough," O'Connor said, pushing his half-eaten dish of noodles to the center of the table and then taking a big drink of Coke.

"You not going to eat that, sir?" Movie Star said, grabbing the captain's meal and raking the noodles and pork on top of what was left of his own dish.

"Go ahead, I lost my appetite," O'Connor said, taking another sip of the Coke. Then he looked at the three lance corporals. "Tell me about that character."

"Who, Sergeant Carnegie?" Dobbs said, finishing his food and then lighting a cigarette. "Everybody knows him. He peddles dope. Him and most of his flight crew out of Marble Mountain."

"How come you call him the Chu Lai Hippie then, if he's from Marble Mountain?" O'Connor said, watching the man now weaving his way back across the street with the big shopping bag in his hand.

"Hell if I know, sir," Movie Star said, shrugging and talking with his mouth full. "I suppose he worked out of Chu Lai at some point and got the name there. I guess it just stuck with him. It sounds better than the Marble Mountain Hippie."

"How about these pictures, sir?" Russ Sherman said, winding the roll of film in his camera and taking it out.

"Can you develop them and make me some eight-by-ten blowups?" O'Connor asked, laying a dollar bill on the table as a tip for the waiter.

"Sure thing, sir," the lance corporal said. "I'll knock it out this afternoon and tonight, and bring them by your office first thing tomorrow morning."

"How about I pick them up from you in the barracks, at Movie Star's rack, say, seven-thirty in the morning," O'Connor said, considering that he didn't want the photographs seen by any unwelcome eyes. "Be sure to put them inside a big envelope, too, and don't show them to anyone."

"Got you covered, sir," Sherman said, and finished his drink.

"Whenever you're ready, gentlemen," O'Connor said, and looked at his wristwatch and then at Lance Corporal Dean. "I never thought about it when we left, but won't Major Dickinson be looking for you, Movie Star?"

"Let him look, sir," Dean laughed, getting the last forkful of fried noodles off his dish and downing a final gulp of his drink. "It'll be good for him."

"He'll give you a hard time if he can't find you," O'Connor said, walking to the back of the jeep and climbing in.

"He does that anyway," Dean said, climbing in the vehicle next to the captain. "Besides, I'm too short to give a shit. Forty-six days and a wake-up."

"Oh, fuck, if I had that much time I'd jump off a cliff. You call that short?" Dobbs said from the driver's seat as he pulled into traffic. "I've got twenty-seven days and a wake-up, and my pal Russ here, he's down to twenty."

"Yeah, man," Russ Sherman said, looking over his shoulder at the two Marines. "I'm so short that I have to look up to see down."

"You think that's short," Movie Star cackled, not to be outdone. "I'm so short I can walk under a snake's belly wearing a top hat. Oh, and I'm so short I've got to use a stepladder to get out of my rack."

"Yes, sir, all three of us are two-digit midgets," Dobbs said, making a right turn and moving down a side street back toward the air base. "We can stack BBs while standing on our heads. There's no amount of grief that anybody can hand to us these days that will make us lose a minute of sleep."

"That's right, sir," Movie Star said, leaning back in the seat and slipping on his black plastic-rimmed sunglasses. "Dicky Doo don't mean shit. In a little over a month, I'll be back at Malibu looking at all the chicks with big tits and tight asses and living large, man. Living large."

"Sir, how much time you got left?" Sherman asked the captain, leaning his arm over the back of the passenger seat and looking toward the rear of the jeep at the officer.

"I'm still a three-digit midget," O'Connor said, and shook his head. "Something like a hundred and fifty-five days, and a wake-up, of course."

"Oh, my God, sir!" Dobbs hooted as he drew near the air base. "If I had that much time left, I think I would slash my wrists!"

"MY, MY, IF it isn't Sergeant Randal Carnegie if I live and breathe," Melvin Biggs said, stepping in front of the Marine with a black leather thong tied around his wrist and another one with a brass peace symbol hanging on it tied around his neck.

Just as the Chu Lai Hippie tried to turn and go in the opposite direction, Gunnery Sergeant Jack Jackson cut him off and stopped him in his tracks.

"Not so fast, sweetpea," the gunny said, taking the Marine by the arm and reaching for the big shopping bag he carried.

"You don't mind if we take a peek inside, do you?" the CID lieutenant said, grabbing the sack as Randal Carnegie pulled it from the gunny's hands.

"Man, you can't do that," Carnegie pled, and reached to take back the shopping bag from the sandy-haired officer. "You got to have a warrant to search my shit, man."

"Maybe back in the world," Gunny Jackson said, pulling out a handful of T-shirts and dropping them on the sidewalk. "Not here, pal."

"Look, man, I know my rights, and you can't search me without cause," the sergeant protested, picking up the T-shirts and trying to put them back in the sack. "Besides, you're fucking up my clothes. You're going to have to pay for them that you ruined. I've got lawyers that will see to that. I got friends in high places, too, that will fix you guys. You wait."

"No, you wait, shit-for-brains!" Gunny Jackson snarled. "You don't fucking threaten me or my lieutenant. We can strip you naked right here on the street and I can shove my flashlight up your ass looking for dope if I want to. You're under military rules over here, smart-ass! Now, kiss the pavement for me while I take a look in this sack of crap you're holding."

"What are you doing in Da Nang?" Lieutenant Biggs said while the gunny dumped the contents of the shopping bag on the sidewalk.

"I'm on flight crew this week," Carnegie said, lying spread-eagled on the sidewalk with his cheek against the concrete. "We broke down at the air base, so I slipped in the ville to buy my buds back at the mountain some T-shirts and shit."

"Well, Lieutenant, looks like he's telling the truth," Gunny Jackson smiled, holding in one hand a wad of tie-died T-shirts with various designs printed on their fronts, and in the other hand a bread-loaf-size package wrapped in brown paper. "Here's all those T-shirts he bought, and here's the shit he mentioned."

"What's wrapped in this package, asshole?" Lieutenant Biggs growled, pushing his hand against the side of Carnegie's head, pressing it against the pavement.

"Ow, man! That hurts!" the Chu Lai Hippie whined.

"Let me guess," Gunny Jackson said, tearing the paper off the loaf. "Your mama sent you a fruitcake, or is it a loaf of banana nut bread?"

"Oops!" Lieutenant Biggs said, lifting the loaf of opiated marijuana from the torn paper and cardboard. "This looks like shit, all right! Ain't that what you hippies call it? Shit? Some real good shit, I'll bet."

"Looks like you just wasted what, a thousand dollars? That's at least what a five-pound brick of Buddha goes for wholesale these days, isn't it, fuckwad? Got your ass busted, too," Gunny Jackson laughed, and pulled the hippie to his feet.

"Funny how we just run into your ass on the street like this," Lieutenant Biggs said, taking handcuffs off his belt and snapping them on Randal Carnegie's wrists. "Damn! We are getting awfully lucky these days, Jack."

"I'd say so, sir," Gunny Jackson said, leading the Chu Lai Hippie to the white panel truck they had parked on the side street when they happened to spot the infamous Randal Carnegie wandering down the boulevard with the big shopping bag in his hands. "Funny though, sir. This loaf of Buddha looks just like some of that load of stuff we confiscated off of dipshit James Elmore six months ago."

"Yeah, I noticed that, too," Biggs said, turning the brick of opiated marijuana over in his hands. "Hell, anymore it all looks alike. That stuff from the Elmore bust should have got burned at least three months back."

A GENTLE SEA breeze blew off the South China Sea and helped clear away the afternoon heat as the sun set and Privates Clarence Jones and Samuel Martin stood the road guard duty on a perimeter trail along the fence at Chu Lai. They heard the sound of the jeep before it rounded the turn, and stepped off the roadway to avoid getting hit.

Private Martin put out his hand and waved his flashlight to signal the jeep to slow down. As the vehicle passed the two Marines they heard a voice shout at them.

"Don't you soldiers know how to salute?" army captain Charles Edwards bellowed at the two black Marines from the front passenger seat. He and two of his subordinate officers, First Lieutenant Philip Ziegler and Second Lieutenant Franklin Webster, had spent the afternoon at an Americal Division field meet and beach party. The three company-grade soldiers, their bellies full of grog and barbecue and their heads swimming from too much booze, now headed toward the visiting officers' quarters at the infantry compound and air facility.

The trio had come to Chu Lai a week ago to answer questions about a mishap that had occurred in March at a Vietnamese hamlet they nick-

named Pinkville. They called it Pinkville because of the Communist presence there, and the constant trouble they encountered with its nearly one
thousand inhabitants, more than half of whom had now disappeared.

Investigations of such matters happened now and then, usually after
some newspaper reporter wrote a pack of lies about American soldiers and
brutality on the innocent civilian populace. Innocent? They've got to be
kidding. These people are the Cong. They shoot a man in the dark and kiss
his hand in the daylight. However, the army has to appease the concerned
citizens back home. Back in the world, where few have the stomach for
this war, or any war, given what crap the news media use to poison their
minds. Throw them a bone, and a head if you can lob one off. That'll shut
the bastards up for a while.

"We ain't soldiers, asshole!" Clarence Jones shouted back as the jeep
blew past them in the dim evening light, blowing dust in his and Sam Martin's faces.

Frank Webster, the junior man aboard the vehicle, drove the jeep, and
hit the brakes when he heard the smart retort coming from the two enlisted
bodies at the roadside they had just passed. He ground the gears to reverse
and tromped the gas, nearly losing control of the open-top car.

"You smart-mouth motherfuckers, which one of you called me an asshole?!" Captain Edwards screamed, leaping from the jeep and confronting
Sam Martin, getting his mouth six inches from the Marine's nose. Then the
officer shoved the road guard backward. "I'll teach your black ass not to
salute when an officer passes you!"

One problem that had always caused Sam Martin no end to grief, one
reason he had remained a career private, he possessed a very bad temper.
Growing up in St. Louis, just him and his dad, who drove a truck for a
brewery, Sam had learned at a very early age to stand up for himself in
order to survive on the tough streets of the Gateway City. He didn't take
shit off anybody.

"You'll teach my black ass nothing, you son of a bitch," Private Martin exploded, and gave the captain a hard shove back.

"Wait, wait, sir," Clarence Jones shouted, jumping between his buddy
and the Americal captain. "First of all, I'm the one that said 'We ain't soldiers, asshole!' " We didn't see you was officers. Second of all, they taught
us not to salute in the field. Some Viet Cong sniper might take you out, sir,
we salute you."

"That man pushed me!" Captain Edwards yelled, trying to step
around Private Jones and get at Sam Martin.

When the Marine shoved the captain, Phil Ziegler bailed out the back of the jeep and ran to aid his company commander, with Frank Webster hot on his heels. Just as Clarence Jones moved to hold the angry Charles Edwards at bay, the first lieutenant jumped past them both with his Colt .45 pistol drawn and slapped it against the side of Sam Martin's face. Frank Webster then grabbed Private Jones and hit him, too.

Corporal Jimmy Seals of Seymour, Texas, Jones's and Martin's security patrol leader, saw the scuffle erupt. Reacting to the emergency and intent on rescuing his two men, Seals launched his squad of a dozen Marines into action. When the fight broke out, the squad lay resting in an ambush formation, two men at a time taking one-hour turns at road guard duty. Seals' radioman called for help, and the military police rolled two units.

"Get off my Marines!" the angry corporal yelled as he leaped on Phil Ziegler, knocking the first lieutenant backward. Then the squad leader laid a full roundhouse right hook square against the officer's jaw and sent him tumbling.

The sight of Seals pummeling the lieutenant who had slapped their pal with his pistol essentially popped a green star cluster for the squad to assault the remaining two soldiers.

With fifteen Marines swarming them, in seconds the three army officers lay flat on the ground. That's when Corporal Seals realized that the three men they had accosted wore brass on their collars.

"Get the fuck out of here, now!" he ordered his Marines, who ran back to their security ambush site, and waited in the dark as the military police swarmed the scene.

ON FRIDAY MORNING Terry O'Connor met Russ Sherman in the enlisted men's barracks and looked at the photographs. The lance corporal handed him a dozen beautifully exposed prints clearly showing Charlie Heyster extracting the package from his laundry bag in the backseat of the jeep and then handing it to the Chu Lai Hippie. The series of pictures also showed Randal Carnegie handing the prosecutor a white envelope that the captain folded and put in his trousers pocket. The last two photos showed the hippie stuffing tie-died T-shirts in the shopping bag, along with the package that Heyster had given to him.

Revisiting each scene with such vivid black-and-white detail put Terry O'Connor's stomach in a knot. He told Movie Star, Bruce Dobbs, and Russ Sherman that until he advised them otherwise they would not breathe a word to anyone about the pictures or what they had all seen Charlie Heyster do.

"We don't know what he gave this guy. It could all be legal," the captain reminded the three lance corporals.

"Right, sir," Movie Star scoffed, "and I believe in Santa Claus and the Easter Bunny, too. That's the Chu Lai Hippie; he deals more shit than anyone these days. Why would our good Captain Shithead even be talking to this piece of crap? He may be the prosecutor, but even I know he ain't any cop. So this isn't a case of him working a snitch. He's dealing, sir. Face it."

"You heard what I said, Corporal Dean," O'Connor snapped. "It's important. You say nothing. None of you three. You got that?"

"I got it, sir," Movie Star grumbled. "Meanwhile, Major Dicky Dickhead is dead in our shit, thinking we got that grass. What about that, sir?"

"Like you said yesterday," O'Connor reminded the lance corporal, "Dicky Doo is dead in all our shit anyway. So fuck him."

The three lance corporals laughed with the captain's comment.

Instead of taking the photographs to the office, Terry O'Connor made a side trip to the barracks and put the pictures on the top shelf of his wall locker, under his hats and shaving gear. Then he reported to work.

"You're late," Jon Kirkwood said as Captain O'Connor slipped through the side door that led into the defense section.

"I had a little something to attend to, nothing important," O'Connor said, and sat at his desk and began looking at a folder that Major-Select Charles Heyster, the interim military justice officer, had left for him ten minutes earlier.

"I got one just like it," Kirkwood said, looking up from the military police incident report and charge sheets. "I talked to this army officer, Captain Charles Edwards, this morning and he's going to drop the charges against Corporal Seals, since he agrees that the Marine only acted when he saw his men in danger, and he did not realize that Edwards and these other two jamokes were officers."

"So we split a pair of privates, I take it," O'Connor said, reading the charge sheet and police report. "Good of this captain to let the corporal go."

"He admitted that he and his two lieutenants were drinking, going to the Q after an American field meet, beer bust, and barbecue," Kirkwood said, closing his folder. "However, he claims that none of his men or himself were drunk. He says that the blacker of the two privates, which I take is Samuel Martin, hit him first, and he struck back."

"Of course, it's the word of three officers against that of two privates," O'Connor said and laughed. "These guys are bacon sizzling on the grill."

"Our clients, God help them, both claim that Edwards started the fight by pushing Martin, and Private Clarence Jones tried to stop the fight," Kirkwood said, leaning back in his chair and lacing his hands behind his head. "This is where it gets interesting. Both Jones and Martin say that First Lieutenant Philip Ziegler slapped Private Martin on the side of the head with his pistol."

"The lieutenant had a pistol drawn?" O'Connor said, now flipping through the pages of statements. "Then he hits our guy with it? That's assault with a deadly weapon!"

"Good luck getting that to fly," Kirkwood said, getting up from his chair and grabbing his and O'Connor's cups and heading for the enlisted coffee mess.

"Look at this, our two Marines whipped the holy shit out of three Americal infantry officers. They beat them to a pulp," O'Connor said, reading the report of the medical examination on the three soldiers and two Marines. "Corporal Seals didn't have a scratch. Private Jones, a few bumps and some busted knuckles. Private Martin, severe bruising to the side of his head, and a broken tooth? Wait a minute, Jon—this supports getting pistol-whipped."

"Hey, Terry, I believe our guys," Kirkwood said, walking down the hallway toward the table that held the coffeepot for the general public and enlisted Marines.

"Why can't we file a complaint? We can charge this jerk Ziegler with assault with a deadly weapon," O'Connor said, trailing after his partner.

"Heyster, Dicky Doo, nobody in the command, including General Anderson and General Cushman, will let it fly," Kirkwood shrugged, stopping at the pot and handing O'Connor his cup. "Something's funky about these three Americal bums, and they have the command anxious to make this incident go away with as few ripples as possible."

"I still don't understand," O'Connor said, filling his mug.

"Me either," Kirkwood said, taking a sip and heading back to the defense section. "Dickinson let me call the chief of staff about it, and I got told in no uncertain terms that we would not have an incident where a drunken army officer pistol-whipped any Marine on road guard duty. Walter Cronkite would have that one on the evening news. I happen to agree. It would make a headline or two."

"So these doggies lie, say they only went back to correct the misconduct of our Marines, and that our guys jumped them out of the blue, and they're going to get away with it," O'Connor said, slamming his chair against the wall and sitting down.

"It was dark, our clients didn't know these guys were officers, and considering that the motive for jumping these soldiers is thin at best, I think we have a shot," Kirkwood said, sitting at his desk and drinking coffee.

"Meanwhile, our Marines rot in the brig for defending themselves," O'Connor grumbled, and set his coffee mug down hard, causing it to slosh over the sides. "No wonder our enlisted people have attitudes."

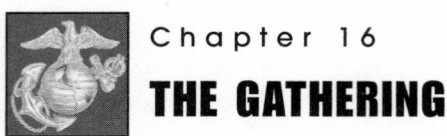

Chapter 16

THE GATHERING

"YO, SNOWMAN! THAT you, man?" Mau Mau Harris called from his cell when he saw the brig guards escort Brian Pitts to the cage next to his. "Hey, you got your wing in a sling, man. They clip you?"

Brian Pitts cleared his throat and spit on the floor. Then he walked to the cold shelf of steel with a thin mattress laid on it that served as his bed and sat down. Heartsick thoughts of home and Aunt Winnie Russell pressed on his mind at the moment. He didn't answer his old friend. He just stared out, across the aisle at the wild eyes of the black man clinging to the crosshatched steel of his cell door, flashing a gold front tooth through his trembling lips.

"Snowman, yo!" Harris shouted, pressing his face against the steel front of his cage, trying to see inside the dark cell next door. Then he looked across the narrow passage of concrete floor bordered by red-painted lines on each side. Any prisoner crossing the red line without permission left himself open to a beating or worse.

James Elmore ran to his toilet and pulled out his already urinating penis, sending the stream into the can.

"You see who come?" Harris called to the man he had tormented daily for several weeks now. "We gonna get yo rat ass now, motherfucker. Say your prayers."

Then Mau Mau pressed his cheek against his cell door and tried to see his silent friend.

"Brian, man, talk to me, my blue-eyed brother," Harris said, now in a quiet voice. "What happen with you? We still good with that stuff in them seabags? You know what I mean?"

"You are one stupid waste of skin, you know that, Harris?" Pitts finally said, still sitting on his bunk.

"What I do, man?" Mau Mau called back, his feelings hurt.

"Just don't fucking talk. Okay?" Pitts said, and then laid back on his hard bed, resting his wounded shoulder by laying his arm across his chest.

No matter how hard he tried, Brian Pitts could not shake the vivid flashback of seeing Tommy Joyner suddenly looking up with surprise at his buddy Robert Matthews after a .30-caliber sniper round knocked him to the floor, flat on his back, where he died after a few blinks and a gasp for air that never came. That's when Huong's younger brother, Chung, blindly opened fire out the front door of the white stucco plantation house with the red tile roof. A second sniper shot put the middle Nguyen brother on the floor, too, dead with a pencil-size hole in his forehead and a fist-size cavity out the back where the round emptied his pulverized brains.

Horrified at seeing their brother die, Huong and Bao lay in the front windows with Chinese SKS rifles sold to Pitts by the Viet Cong and began to shoot at movement in the tree line. This brought a volley of machine gun fire that swept across the front porch, and wounded Bao in the calf when a .30-caliber bullet slashed through the muscle, laying it open two inches deep.

"We go, now!" Huong said, and made a run for the back door with his brother's arm over his shoulders, not waiting to see if Pitts and Matthews followed him. When the two Vietnamese cowboys ran toward the trees, only twenty yards away, the machine guns from the Tenth Division company turned after them. Huong and Bao didn't go down, but there was no way that Brian Pitts could tell if they had survived the gunfire and made it to the series of trenches, rabbit holes, and tunnels that led away from the house and opened near others that networked for miles. He didn't know for sure that his friends had made it until he overheard the comments of the captain who commanded the company of soldiers that the two gooks had gotten away.

At least Huong and Bao had evaded capture. Turd, the lucky beast, must have sensed it coming. He disappeared from the plantation early that morning, and would likely sit hidden in a tunnel until his troubled feelings passed. He had begun doing that stunt quite often during the past week or so, and it gave Huong fits of anxiety. When the top-hand cowboy couldn't find the mutt this particular morning, he became more worried than ever, and suggested that everyone should go to the tunnels. At least until these uneasy feelings passed, and Turd returned to his regular spot, resting on the red tile porch by the front door. Then, just before noon, when the three American outlaws talked about grilling some steaks that Brian had purchased in Saigon two evenings earlier, the sniper round caught Tommy Joyner square in the chest.

Seeing Huong and Bao abandon their stand, Robert Matthews gave up, too. He threw his hands in the air and stepped out on the porch. Then, realizing the attackers had the house now fully surrounded, Brian Pitts put his arms above his head and walked outside.

He saw someone stand up, waving his hands and blowing a whistle, but that did not stop Bruce Olsen from letting one go at the Snowman. The only thing that saved Brian Pitts was the movement that he saw, and he turned just as the Phoenix sniper dropped the hammer on him.

"I should have killed you in the hotel bar," Olsen hissed at Pitts as he stood over the wounded Snowman, who lay on the porch while a Tenth Division medical corpsman did his best to patch the wound. The shot broke both the deserter's shoulder joint and his collarbone.

"It'll never heal right," the doc said as he worked to stop the bleeding and felt the shattered bones crunching under the pressure of his bandage.

"Small price, the fucking traitor!" Olsen snapped, and stomped off the porch.

After ten days under guard in the army hospital in Saigon, two Marine Corps chasers from the Freedom Hill brig watched Brian Pitts get dressed in a fluff-dried green utility uniform with black canvas, high-top Bata Bullet tennis shoes on his feet. They handed him a white laundry bag with another uniform inside it, along with three sets of white skivvies and three pairs of olive-drab woolen socks. Then they hauled him to Da Nang in the belly of a C-130 airplane.

Robert Matthews came to Freedom Hill two weeks ago, and now enjoyed life in the yard with the general population. He caused no trouble, and kept his mouth shut, so First Lieutenant Michael Schuller released him from the block of holding cells and let the kid breathe outdoors. It freed up the space that he needed to keep Brian Pitts locked up.

Given Matthews' Saigon history with the Snowman, Schuller had wisely decided to not allow the new prisoner contact with any of Pitts's Da Nang associates, namely Harris and Elmore. So the two men had no clue who the new man was.

"Tell me, Mau Mau, how you making it?" the Snowman finally asked, sitting up on the hard bunk, finally breaking his hour-long silence, and now wishing that he had a cigarette.

AUGUST HEAT PUSHED Terry O'Connor's temper to the edge, so it took very little to cause the Philadelphia Irishman to blow his top. After a short meeting with Major Dickinson, the lawyer walked into his office and kicked his swivel chair across the room.

"Now sit down and spill it," Jon Kirkwood said, taking the angry captain by the shoulder and pushing him into his seat. "You've been stomping around this office for the past two weeks like a cat with a fish bone stuck in his throat. You need to tell me what has got you so pissed off."

"This morning, it just takes the cake," O'Connor said, and let out a deep breath in disgust. "First Charlie Heyster cuts a sweet pretrial deal for this character, Sergeant Randal Carnegie, a sack of shit that our troops here in this office call the Chu Lai Hippie, because even they know he's the biggest doper around I Corps. Then yesterday, Charlie the shyster, with the blessings of Dicky Doo, lets four of this bum's dope-dealing cohorts walk free."

Jon Kirkwood shook his head and squinted his eyes shut. Then he looked at his partner with an expression of amazement. He walked to the office door, looked at the crimson placard with yellow lettering on it, and then went back to his desk and sat down.

"The sign on this office's door says Defense Section," Kirkwood said, raising both hands in an exaggerated shrug. "You'll find people down the hall, in the office labeled Prosecution Section, who will readily sympathize with your frustration of defendants finally getting a break."

"Jon, these guys are guilty as sin," O'Connor exclaimed, standing up and kicking his chair again. "CID busted these four bums, people from the same unit as Carnegie, his buddies, when the drug dogs alerted on the uniforms that these characters wore. They had Buddha sewn in the sleeves of their shirts and inside the legs of their trousers. Big lumps of reefer!

"So Charlie gets a message from this piece of shit Carnegie that says he sold these four-star citizens his old utility uniforms, because he is getting out of the Marine Corps in a month, when he exits the brig. He claims that he sewed the dope in his clothes and that these guys knew nothing about it being in their sleeves and trouser legs when they bought the used uniforms.

"Tell me how anyone can put on a shirt and pants and not feel pillow-size lumps of dope sewn in them?"

"Hey, it worked and the guys got free," Kirkwood said and smiled. "Chalk four pluses on the defense section's tote board."

"Jon, they're guilty," O'Connor said, throwing his head back. "There is something patently wrong when we let guilty people slide. This character Carnegie got only thirty days and no bad time. Thirty days! And it doesn't even count! None of it will appear in his service record, so he gets out of the Marine Corps with a clean discharge. He had a five-pound loaf of Buddha, and he only got a month in the brig for it, none of it bad time, and he kept his rank! Now, in this latest turn of events, he even gets his buddies off, scot-free!"

"That's why we have a prosecution section, my friend," Kirkwood said and walked to the door. "I can see something else boiling under that red Irish head of yours, and I'm going to leave you alone, in peace, until you decide to let me in on what's really bothering you."

Terry O'Connor shook his head and slouched in his chair as he watched his buddy walk away. He wanted to tell him about the photographs. That's what really bothered him. However, he still felt uncomfortable with the idea of showing anyone the pictures. Not even his best friend. Besides, would Kirkwood or anyone else even believe what the images showed?

O'Connor felt certain that Heyster must have a fail-safe plan, just in case Carnegie got busted and sang. Would the pictures showing the exchange of dope, coupled with the later arrest of the Chu Lai Hippie, and Charlie the shyster cutting him a sweet deal, would that be enough to slam shut an iron door on the interim mojo?

"Not yet. I need a better smoking gun than some photographs taken from an unauthorized surveillance," O'Connor said to himself as he leaned over and twisted the power and volume control knob on his leather-clad, portable AM-FM-shortwave radio that rested against the wall on the side of his desk and had its silver stick antenna extended all the way out. American Forces Vietnam broadcast network played his favorite song, a hit from 1967 written by Mick Jagger and Keith Richards, and performed by Jagger and the Rolling Stones. As the mellow tune drifted from the small speaker, the captain closed his eyes and tried to let his troubled soul take a ride with the sweet melody.

She would never say where she came from. Yesterday don't matter if it's gone. While the sun is bright. Or in the darkest night. No one knows. She comes and goes.

Good-bye, Ruby Tuesday. Who could hang a name on you? When you change with every new day. Still I'm gonna miss you.

Don't question why she needs to be so free. She'll tell you it's the only way to be. She just can't be chained. To a life where nothing's gained. And nothing's lost. At such a cost.

Good-bye, Ruby Tuesday. Who could hang a name on you? When you change with every new day. Still I'm gonna miss you.

"Still I'm gonna miss you!" the lawyer captain sang in a loud voice that carried down the hallway to the administration office where Staff Sergeant Pride raised his head from a page full of budget numbers he was studying.

"GOOD-BYE, RUBY TUESDAY. Who could hang a name on you?" Corporal Nathan L. Todd sang as he walked out of the control center at the Freedom Hill brig, singing with the music that played on the radio in the glass-walled room that ran the switches that locked or released all doors into and out of the central cell block that housed all the high-risk prisoners.

"Why you singing that fag song, butthead?" Sergeant Mike Turner said, heckling the corporal while leaning back in a swivel chair with his feet propped on a desk secured behind a row of bars that overlooked the cells where Celestine Anderson, Brian Pitts, James Harris, Michael Fryer, and James Elmore counted time by the day.

Turner had earned the nickname Iron Balls from both the prisoners and his fellow guards. Seated on a stool at the other end of the hall of cells, Lance Corporal Kenny Brookman sat with his heels hooked over the wooden spindles connected between the legs that braced his seat and held it rigid while he slapped the palm of his hand with a truncheon that he and Iron Balls had drilled down the center and filled with lead. Usually, when a person saw Iron Balls, the sadistic Lance Corporal Brookman, who had picked up the nickname Bad John, wasn't far behind.

"What makes 'Ruby Tuesday' a fag song, Sergeant Turner?" Corporal Todd asked as he stepped through the barred door when Gunnery Sergeant Ted MacMillan released the latch from the control center. "The Rolling Stones fags? Is that it?"

"Yeah," Iron Balls said and laughed. "They're from England, and that makes them queer. The whole fucking country's full of fruitcakes. The men all wear lace, and the women smoke cigars."

Todd said nothing back, but kept humming the song as he walked down the rows of cells, checking each inmate and making a corresponding note on a clipboard he carried. Then he walked back to the port where

Iron Balls now stood, his nightstick withdrawn from the silver ring on his Sam Browne belt, and spinning it like a yo-yo with the leather thong on its handle. The corporal gave the gunny a thumbs-up signal, and he pulled a handle that released all cell doors and slid them open.

"Stand up and step out!" Corporal Todd ordered. "Put your toes on the red line and come to the position of attention. Prisoner Elmore, you will remain in your cell."

All fourteen prisoners on the row stepped to the red line except for James Elmore, who stood in the back of his small space, glad to remain behind.

"Right face!" Todd shouted at the two lines of inmates from the center of the hallway. "Forward march!"

Iron Balls used to herd the prisoners to their meals and the recreation yard until two days ago, when he and Bad John got relieved for cause by Chief Warrant Officer Frank Holden, the deputy brig officer under First Lieutenant Schuller. While in the recreation yard, Mau Mau Harris and Ax Man Anderson, along with several other members of the secretly organized Freedom Hill chapter of the Black Stone Rangers, had cornered Iron Balls and Bad John and laid hands on the two guards, triggering a full lockdown of the entire brig.

When Holden questioned Harris and his yahoo buddies, they lied and said that Turner and Brookman had gotten into a card game with the inmates, and when they lost they refused to pay up. In retaliation, the wronged prisoners turned on the two Marines.

While Nathan Todd and Gunny MacMillan both stood up for their two fellow guards, claiming that the prisoners flat-out lied, and that in no way had Turner and Brookman played cards or in any other way fraternized with the inmates, the deputy brig officer relieved the pair anyway. It staved off trouble.

Seeing the two men relieved of their principal duties of handling prisoners and reduced to watching the hallways put Mau Mau Harris and his right-hand man, Ax Man Anderson, at the top of the food chain in the hierarchy of who's who inside Freedom Hill.

"So they let us out every day like this?" Brian Pitts asked James Harris as the two men set their meal trays on a long bench table and sat down. Mau Mau had faithfully carried his wounded friend's drink with his own and helped the one-handed Snowman get seated without spilling anything. Celestine Anderson glared at the white man from the other side of the seating arrangement until Harris frowned at him.

"Yeah, man. We get lunch and then three, four hours rec time in the yard," Harris said, and then gave Anderson a hard look. "Yo, Ax Man, this my blue-eyed soul brother. Call the dude Snowman. He cool, so lighten up. He one of us, bro. A ranger."

"Ain't no white dude no Black Stone Ranger," Anderson grumbled, digging his spoon in a pile of mashed potatoes.

"I say what go and what don't go," Harris barked back at the insolent gang brother. "In Chicago, we got white dudes not in just the rangers, but Black Panthers, too. Pitts and me, we go way back. He one smart motherfucker. You hang with him, life get good. I know. We have it good, right, brother?"

James Harris put his arm around Brian Pitts's neck and gave him a good squeeze.

"We play it cool and smart, my men, and we can have it good once again, too," Brian Pitts said with a smile, looking cold at Celestine Anderson, and with his good arm giving James Harris a hug back.

"So, my man the Snowman, he one of us," Harris said, spooning meatloaf and potatoes in his mouth. "I got two more white dudes we need in our brotherhood. Word come around that this Chu Lai Hippie he have people on the outside that can get shit done. So he's in."

"Fucking Randy Carnegie? You talking about him? He's in here?" Brian Pitts said, surprised and smiling.

"You know the dude?" Harris said, smiling at Pitts.

"I know of him," the Snowman answered and shrugged. "He bought shit from me, but I could never get him into my regular program. He was always sort of a maverick. Independent. He's okay, though. If he's got somebody hooked up outside, he's worthwhile having in the club."

"Glad you approve, 'cause I already sent word to tell him he's a ranger," Harris said, stuffing his mouth while talking.

"Who this other cracker motherfucker you want with us?" Anderson said, wiping up gravy with a slice of bread.

"Dude named Watts, Kevin Watts," Harris said, drinking red Kool-Aid from a paper cup. "He got three years for trying to hijack a plane to fly him out of 'Nam."

All three prisoners laughed.

"I ain't totally sure about the dude, but I say okay when Jones and Martin tell me about him," Harris said and shrugged. "Only thing I don't like about this turd, he ain't never told the truth in his life. He always trying to say shit just happen, and he fall in it."

The three prisoners laughed again.

"We need a fall guy, then he's our man," Pitts said, and smiled at Anderson, who simply glared back at him. Then he looked around and watched the guards talking with each other, relaxing.

"So tell me, Mau Mau," Pitts said in a low voice, looking at his food as he spoke, "when we go in the yard, after we eat, we can just mingle?"

"We ain't supposed to, but we do," Harris said, looking back at Pitts. "Guards is cool for the most part except for Iron Balls and Bad John. They two genuine pieces of shit. When me and the Ax Man do the job on that rat-shit motherfucker Elmore, we figure we take down Turner and Brookman, too. We go down, we gonna do it all. They write about our black struggle back home when we do it."

"Do what?" Pitts asked, frowning.

"Bust up this place, man," Harris said with a smile, eating his black-eyed peas and the last of his bread.

"We gonna take it down, man," Celestine Anderson offered and then smiled, thinking about the day he could lash out in open rebellion.

"Whoa," Brian Pitts said and raised his eyebrows. "Taking the place down might work for the short term, but in the end we got to have an objective. Not just a bunch of newspaper headlines, but something that will pay us a few dividends, for our old age."

He smiled at Harris and winked, and then shook his head that Mau Mau should say nothing more.

"I got another man I want to recommend for our brotherhood, if I may," Pitts said to Harris and then looked at Celestine Anderson.

"Hey, fuck you," Anderson snapped at Pitts.

"Man, we gonna get along," Harris commanded with clenched teeth, and scowled at his lieutenant, the Ax Man. Then he looked at Pitts. "Who you want in the rangers?"

"Guy I had working with me in Saigon," Pitts said, and smiled at Anderson, who glared back at him. "Dude named Matthews. He's here someplace. His buddy, Tom Joyner, got whacked when they took us down. Mau Mau, he's one of our brothers and we're gonna take care of him."

"Anything you say, man," Harris said, wiping his mouth and getting his tray in his hands. He looked up and nodded at Nathan Todd, who nodded back at him, giving him approval to stand and take his dirty dishes to the brig scullery. "I'll pass the word to Martin and Jones. They working back there washing trays and shit."

When Mau Mau returned to the table, Pitts and Anderson followed suit, turning in their dirty trays and dumping their paper trash. Once the prisoners had finished their meals, Todd blew a whistle and then marched them into the prison yard for their daily afternoon recreation.

*   *   *

SHORTLY AFTER THREE o'clock, Terry O'Connor and Jon Kirkwood sat down in the warden's office at Freedom Hill brig and sipped coffee with their friend First Lieutenant Michael Schuller.

"We've got some formal complaints to issue, Mike, and I hate doing it," Kirkwood began, shaking his head as he laid the written objections on the lieutenant's desk.

"Why do you have my client James Elmore locked in a cell directly across the aisle from the man who tried to kill him?" O'Connor said, setting his coffee on the table and frowning at the lieutenant. "Now I hear that the man who probably orchestrated the attempted murder, and the key person against whom my client has agreed to testify, also resides across the aisle from Elmore."

"I've got no choice," Schuller said, leaning back in his chair. "I can release Pitts and Harris into the main population, or I keep them where they sit now, in our highest-security cell block. We can trust them to live in the hooches with the general population, or we can keep them under lock and key. You tell me."

"You mix them most of the day anyway, what difference does it make where they sleep?" Kirkwood said, sipping coffee. "That leads me to my complaint. You already know what it is."

"Your client Wilson?" Schuller asked, raising his eyebrows.

"Yes, my client Wilson," Kirkwood said. "He has not yet gone to trial and he is with the general population. Mixed with convicted felons. Also, written in those formal complaints, we have concerns about two new clients here awaiting trial, and you have them both working in the kitchen like convicts, too."

"They're all three low-risk confinees, so we keep them in the low-risk area with other low-risk people," Schuller said and sighed. "Like I told you at Colonel Prunella's party, I wish we had better facilities. Appropriate facilities. We don't, and both the wing and the two divisions keep shipping more prisoners in here every day.

"Now, what I am about to say, you did not hear it from anyone in this brig. Do I have your words?"

Both Kirkwood and O'Connor nodded their agreement.

"We not only have prisoners who await trial mixed with convicted inmates," Schuller said, and then leaned over his desk and whispered, "we have Marines locked in this brig who have not even been formally charged with a crime! At least a dozen of them right now, and more coming each day. One or two at a time. They pissed off a captain, major, or colonel, and he ships them to Freedom Hill, using our prison facility like a correctional custody platoon or motivation squad in boot camp. No charge sheet. At his discretion, the commander just locks them in jail. They may have mouthed off, embarrassed the command, or failed to show up for chow on time. Maybe they just pissed in the wrong shitter. Who knows?

"These no-trial Marines get slammed in jail for the flimsiest of reasons, and then their units move on without them. They send no one to visit these men. No one to counsel them, or see if they need anything. No one to offer them any sense of hope. The troops call it getting shit-canned.

"In my opinion, these are innocent men inappropriately incarcerated at this level, and abandoned. They were basically branded as shitbirds by their units, and got dumped here because most of our line officers have the decency not to poison anyone else's unit with what they consider human waste. All I can do is turn the key and try to keep them warehoused until they get flushed on down the pipe. Yeah, I have convicts mixed with pre-trial confinees. I also have no-trial confinees mixed with them, too. What about these men? You going to stand up for them?"

"Eventually they have to get a charge sheet," Kirkwood started to say and then Schuller stopped him in midsentence.

"I have a Marine private first class here who we've had locked in general population for more than six months," Schuller said and slammed his hand on his desk. "He's due to rotate! He's supposed to go home and get out of the Marine Corps in a couple of weeks. He's never been charged! His unit forgot him."

"What are you going to do?" O'Connor asked, narrowing his eyebrows and feeling his heart pound as anger surged in his chest.

"I'm going to let him out, and ship him over to headquarters battalion at Third Marine Division with a letter signed by my boss, Lieutenant Colonel Webster, stating that the Marine has finished his tour in Vietnam and is due to go home and be released from active duty," Schuller said, and then blew out a deep breath.

"Think it will work? Shouldn't he have some kind of orders?" Kirkwood asked, now feeling a sense of the frustration that Schuller lived with daily.

"He's a nonrate Marine," Schuller shrugged, and took a drink of coffee. "Lucky for him the battalion can cut orders to Pendleton for the kid and assign him to RELAD. They'll have to fish out his service record book, if they can find it, or just rebuild a new one once he gets to Pendleton. I think the officer who sent him here long ago rotated. The poor kid will wind up in limbo at RELAD until the personnel division at headquarters Marine Corps ferrets out some paperwork on him and documents his release date. But that's a damned sight better than rotting in this brig."

"How can this happen?" O'Connor sighed, and slouched down in his chair.

"The freewheeling way commanders can arbitrarily toss these kids around, with little to no accountability to higher authority," Schuller said, leaning his elbows on his desk. "Field commanders do what works, bend the rules, break them, make them up as they go along. We're at war, and units do what they have to do to succeed with their missions. I understand it, but I don't like it. It's a throwback to the almighty ship's captain, when we operated on the rocks and shoals system. Still alive and well. Like a jungle rules basketball game. Only we gamble with lives and play for keeps."

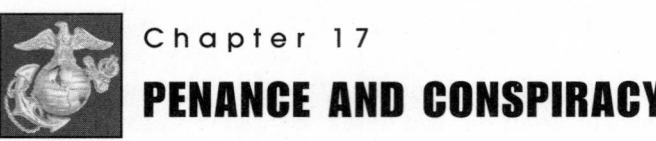

Chapter 17

PENANCE AND CONSPIRACY

A TRAIL OF white dust boiled behind T. D. McKay's brand-new, blue-and-white two-tone 1969 Chevrolet pickup truck with a genuine 327 power-pack Corvette engine blowing hot smoke through dual-tuned exhaust pipes. He had written his dad back home in Dumas, while he was still in Vietnam, and told him of his dream pickup truck: a blue-and-white Chevy with chrome bumpers, trim, and grill; a tucked and rolled interior of blue-and-white leather; and a Corvette engine with tuned exhaust. A short bed. Had to be a short bed. Tommy told his dad that long beds looked out of proportion, even though they hauled more bales of hay.

With the letter in hand to show the Chevrolet dealer, Tommy's dad drove to Amarillo and ordered the truck. Then with the money his son had sent home all year, to help out with the bills at the ranch, his dad paid for the vehicle in advance. That way the boy could not argue with his father, and had to either take the pickup or park it.

McKay's parents, his cousin Bill, his aunt and uncle, and his ninety-one-year-old grandmother all drove from Dumas, down U.S. Highway 287, through Amarillo, Childress, Wichita Falls, and Fort Worth to the international airport in Dallas the day before Tommy's plane landed. The crowd gathered around Granny McKay, who sat in a wheelchair, and greeted their Marine as he walked down the ramp from the plane in the fancy, new Dallas-Fort Worth air terminal.

When all of them got their hugs in on the boy, and wiped their eyes, Tommy's dad handed him the keys hanging on a ball chain with a clear plastic tag encasing a small, new-vehicle identification card, and on the owner's line of the yellow slip of stiff paper inside the plastic carrier it read Thomas Gaylord McKay.

Dressed in his green serge uniform with his rows of ribbons pinned above his glistening silver rifle and pistol shooting badges, silver bars shining on his collar and blouse's epaulettes, his football player's physique bulging against the fabric, the look of her son took his mother's breath away.

"Stand right there!" she ordered her young man. "Daddy, get that Kodak out and take a picture of this boy! I swear if he ain't the prettiest thing I ever did see. My Lord! He looks awfully smart in that uniform. Tommy, won't you wear that to church for us Sunday?"

"Mama, I got out of the Marine Corps so I didn't have to put this uniform on anymore, and now you want me to wear it to church?" McKay said, frowning at his mother. She always did love to show off her good-looking son, especially at the First Baptist Church of Dumas, Texas, a place where even in July of 1968 people appreciated a man in a Marine Corps uniform.

He finally agreed to her begging, and he dressed for the last time in his green serge uniform, for his mother, so she could show him off at church. People at the First Baptist Church of Dumas took pictures of the young man. Old veterans there slapped him on the back and talked about landing at Normandy and Iwo Jima. High school girls who knew of Tommy McKay as the star Demon of Dumas's football team, and now a Marine lieutenant with medals, all swooned and giggled when he caught them staring at him.

The preacher had the young veteran stand up in the congregation, and he openly thanked the lad for serving his country. Vietnam War protesters were never welcome in Dumas, Texas. However, at the Dallas airport, while getting his baggage on the newfangled carousel where suitcases came falling down a metal slide and landed on the big metal turntable, some people did shout rude remarks at him. Big-city people with no sense, his dad called them, and told Tommy to never mind the idiots. They all smoked dope and were probably Communists, too.

That's how homecoming went for T. D. McKay. Flashcubes popping and family hugging him, his mama in love with how her son looked, and his father, who had gone to war himself twenty-five years earlier, just glad to have his boy home alive.

Mid-August temperatures in West Texas boiled the tops out of most thermometers. One place outside Big Spring, where he stopped to buy gas, the big dial in the shade of the filling station awning read 114 degrees. T. D. drank a Coke and bought two more that he set in a little Styrofoam ice chest he kept on the front seat in which his mother had put a plastic bowl full of fried chicken and several dill pickles sliced in quarters, so the boy would not die of hunger on the eight-hour trip from Dumas down to the Lyle Langtree Ranch near Fort Stockton, Texas, where Jimmy Sanchez's mother, two sisters, and three brothers still lived.

He turned off the pavement a few minutes past four o'clock, and finally at ten minutes before five, he saw the sprawling brown stucco and stone ranch headquarters and below it the white stucco house with the wide, stone-faced front porch and white shingled roof where Jimmy's family lived.

The rutted road needed a good bulldozing at the bottom of the draw he had to cross to get to the houses. He slowed his new truck to a crawl, but still the rocks jumped underneath, and banged against the frame and the oil pan. Once up the other side, he pulled to the side and got out of the truck and crawled on his knees and looked for oil or transmission fluid leaks. Nothing wet. Just dust. He worried too much, fearful of a scratch on the paint.

Near the house he saw the old windmill that he and Jimmy had fixed before they shipped out to Vietnam, Tommy going just a week ahead of Jimmy. It spun in the stiff, hot breeze and kept a trickle of water overflowing from the holding tank where a dozen white-face heifers had flopped after taking their fill. The small herd of young cows looked at the blue-and-white pickup as it eased past them and drove on up the hill to the white stucco house where a gang of people, all smiling, stood inside a wire-mesh fence tied to steel oil well pipe that emerged out of a low concrete and stone wall.

Beyond the house, on the low hills covered in soapweed and sage, Tommy saw a whirlwind towering in the distance, sweeping across the dry country, churning up the white dust into a column that must have gone a thousand feet in the air. He and Jimmy had ridden horses across those hills, chasing Lyle Langtree's cattle to a set of pens where the three younger Sanchez brothers and two more ranch hands waited to cut and brand the strays that the Diamond-L crew had missed working in the spring roundup.

Everyplace he looked, Tommy saw reminders of what he and Jimmy had done here. Too few summers and not nearly enough Christmases. McKay could have used a lot more time with his best friend, riding and romping on this place he loved.

As he rumbled over the cattle guard and passed under the archway that connected the front gate to the exterior welded-pipe fence line that surrounded the Sanchez home and ranch headquarters compound, Tommy noticed a new brand painted on the metal arch by the Diamond-L. A J-bar-S brand. Something new since he went to Vietnam.

McKay had not even shut down his rumbling engine before the three Sanchez boys and one of their two sisters had pulled open both doors and clambered inside, taking a look at the next-year's model Chevy.

"Aw, she's a beaut, Tommy!" Henry Sanchez, the brother next to Jimmy in age, said as he jumped in the truck. He would graduate from the University of Texas next spring, just ahead of Marguerite, the younger of the two girls, named for her mother. She stood by the driver's side and smiled, lowering her eyes, showing her shyness. Hector, the next younger brother, had finished his freshman year at Texas and now felt himself a man as a sophomore. José would finish high school this year, at Fort Stockton, where he played football. Maria Sanchez-Ochoa, the elder daughter, was the only sibling of Jimmy's not home to greet his best friend. She taught elementary school in Dexter, New Mexico, where her husband, Robert Ochoa, worked as the New Mexico State University extension agent, helping Pecos Valley farmers develop more efficient ways of cultivating and growing alfalfa and feedlot cattle.

She had sent her love and kisses to Tommy McKay, though, and Marguerite Sanchez told him over and over how badly Maria wanted to be there to see him.

"Maybe she and Roberto will drive down here this weekend," the mother said, walking Tommy to the house while the boys carried his suitcase. "You will stay through the weekend. You must, you know. Señor Lyle told the boys to butcher one of the steer calves and make a big barbecue in your honor. Many of our neighbors will come, and most of the people from church, too. I'm not supposed to tell you, but I know you will stay if you know all the trouble they have gone to, and what they have planned."

"Oh, I can do that, for you, Mama," Tommy said, and then gave the Mexican woman a long and tearful hug.

Tears now streamed from her face, too. They stood on the porch both looking at each other, and not able to speak, because they knew it would mean talking about Jimmy, and that hurt too much right now. So they hugged some more and wept.

"It makes me feel so good that you call me Mama, too, like my Jimmy," she finally said, still holding her arms around Tommy's neck. "I hope your own mother will not mind it."

Tommy said nothing, because he did not tell his mother that years ago he had begun calling Mrs. Sanchez Mama, too. Everyone there at the Diamond-L Ranch called her Mama, and he felt uncomfortable calling her anything else. Only Señor Lyle called her Marguerite, and sometimes he even called her Mama Sanchez.

"You split the room with Henry, just like before, when you came here with Jimmy, only it's Henry in there now," Mama Sanchez said, leading Tommy through the house to one of the three big bedrooms. "With everyone here all at once, we have to sleep two people in a room. Before, when the boys were much younger, they could all sleep together. Now you're men, so men need more space than boys."

"*Hola,* Marguerite," Tommy said, turning around and seeing the younger sister walking quietly behind him, still smiling. Her creamy, tan skin glowed in contrast to her jet black hair and dark brown eyes. She had high cheekbones like her mother, and a beautiful, slightly upturned nose that gave her almost a pixie look. The girl stood only five feet tall, if that, and wore pumps with a good lift in the heels so she didn't appear so short. However, Tommy liked her smallness because it became her quiet and gentle personality.

Maria, on the other hand, stood a full two inches taller than her mother, and had the anger of a lioness that exploded easily. Like Jimmy, she sought to achieve greatness by addressing the best of her talents to the people with the least. It made perfect sense to Tommy that she would marry an extension agent after graduating at the top of her class at Texas, and going to teach school in a rural classroom with mostly Hispanic children whose parents came to America one night when they waded across the Rio Grande.

"*Hola,* Thomas, Marguerite answered, and smiled her perfect teeth at him. All of the Sanchez children had perfect teeth. They hardly saw a dentist, yet even the mother had perfect teeth, strong enough to chew through screen wire.

Most of Tommy's molars held large fillings, caused from too many sweets as a lad and not enough time over the sink with a toothbrush in his mouth. Jimmy, on the other hand, always liked having a toothpick or matchstick in his mouth. Once in a while he chewed a stick of Spearmint chewing gum, but he seemed to always prefer a small piece of wood.

"We must go see Señor Lyle pronto," Mama Sanchez said, and looked at her daughter, frowning and shaking her head, as though the girl were bothering their guest. Tommy noticed the gesture, and then smiled and took Marguerite's hand.

"I sure would like you to come, too, if Mama doesn't mind," McKay said, and caused the young woman's face to flush deep red.

"If Mama does not mind, I would like that, too," Marguerite said, still holding Tommy's hand.

"Oh, I suppose," Mama Sanchez said, and then smiled at the attraction that both of the two young people seemed to have sparked toward each other. "Marguerite, you know how bad Señor Lyle can talk, so do not be offended if he says too much. You know he is old, and men of his time think different than men today."

"Yes, Mama, I know Mister Langtree can say awful things," Marguerite said, and then walked alongside Tommy McKay and her mother as they crossed the broad patio behind the ranch headquarters and entered the big house through the sliding glass doors.

The old man sat inside, feeling the cool breezes off the air conditioner as he reclined in a wooden rocking chair draped with a red-and-blue Navajo blanket. He had his hats hanging on a set of deer antlers just inside the door. Just like Tommy's father, his favorite one hung on the outside of the rack, nearest the door, handy to grab. The tattered gray Stetson had a sweat stain that reached halfway up the crown and halfway out the brim, with its nose rolled almost to a point and polished slick from years of handling.

His bald head was pink and pale, surrounded by snow-white hair. From the tops of his ears downward, the skin on his neck and face shone a dark tan color, weathered tough from a lifetime of outdoor work. Tommy thought how his father looked the same way but had twenty-five years less time on his watch.

Old Lyle Langtree took his first breath of life on this ranch eighty-two years ago, when his mother gave birth to him in a dugout cabin with a sagebrush and dirt roof that his parents had hacked into the ground the winter before his birth in 1886. They carried water in wooden barrels, hauled twice a week in a wagon they drove fourteen miles each way, until Lyle's father managed to hand-dig a well deep enough to finally strike a trickle of ground water outside their dugout. Although rank with gypsum, leaving white chalk in their clothes, they survived on it until a driller came along with a cable-tool rig and put down a decent, deep well that sprang fresh water even in the driest summers.

He never forgot his hard beginnings, and reminded anyone who admired his fine home today that it all began in a single-room hut with a roof that dropped dirt, scorpions, and big, black centipedes with yellow legs into a person's bed or the stew pot, if someone forgot to put the lid back on it.

"I hope you'll stay a spell," the old man said, smiling and chewing on a cigar that he would never light. "Maybe we'll kill the fatted calf for the prodigal son, if you're a mind to visit a day or two."

"Sir, I am honored to stand in your home and in your presence, and thank you for your kind hospitality," McKay said, and bowed slightly for the old gentleman. "I am glad to stay a day or two, but insist that you allow me to pitch in with the chores so I am not such a burden."

"Hell, son, we got a tribe of wetbacks that take care of the chores," the old man said with a laugh, and coughed a wad out of his throat that he held in his mouth until he could amble to the back door and launch it into the flower bed by the patio.

Tommy rolled his eyes at the thoughtless remark, and looked at Mama and Marguerite Sanchez, who smiled back at him and shook their heads as the three of them watched the old cowboy totter his way back to his rocking chair and sit down.

"Now, for supper, I want you girls to fix us a mess of those flat enchiladas with the chili meat, hot sauce, and salad between the tortillas that you stack up like pancakes," Lyle said, rocking the chair and his knobby knees bobbing back and forth as he pushed with his long, skinny legs. "This boy ain't ate good over in that Vietnam, so I expect a plate of decent food would set right with him. Ain't that right, boy?"

"A plate of Mama's enchiladas sets right with me anytime," McKay said with a smile, and looked at the two Sanchez women. "I think I could eat them for breakfast, dinner, and supper seven days a week and never get tired of them."

"Spoke like a true Texas gentleman, Mister McKay," the old man said and laughed, and cleared his throat again and took another trip to the patio door for a spit.

"You all be over here by six o'clock sharp," Lyle Langtree said, rocking in his chair. "I don't want to have to wait supper on them wild kids of yours, either. Mama Langtree, my boy, Sonny, and his wife, Vanessa, with their tribe of younguns, they'll all be back shortly. I expect Mama and Vanessa and her two girls will help in the kitchen, too. So I guess I'll see you back here in a little bit, unless the good Lord takes me first."

Then the old man returned his stare out the patio doors, gazing across the hills where the whirlwinds twisted up dust in the afternoon heat, and once in a while, if a person had extra-good eyes, he could spot a mule deer that might have strayed up from the mountains in the Big Bend country.

"Not much time," Tommy McKay said, walking back across the patio with the two Sanchez women and glancing at his wristwatch.

"We already have most of the meal cooked," Mama said, and put her arm inside the crook of Tommy's. Marguerite walked close at his other side.

"Mama, I need to talk about Jimmy. I need all of you to hear me. Not just you, but Henry and Hector and José and Marguerite," Tommy said, stopping on the white stucco house's long front porch where a glider and several other metal chairs sat.

"I know what you want to tell me," Mama Sanchez said, putting up her hands, and then taking both of Tommy's in hers. Tears immediately filled her eyes. "My boys and my girls, they all read the letters. Your letters, and the letters from the colonel, Jimmy's commanding officer, and from his sergeant, that good man named Rhodes. Why must you torture yourself so much, my good boy? It breaks my heart to see you grieve so deeply for my son."

Then the woman walked to the metal glider and sat and patted her hand on a spot next to her.

"Sentarse, por favor," she said in Spanish, asking the young man to please sit with her.

Tommy settled on the swinging chair next to the woman and swallowed against a hard lump that grew big as a baseball in his throat.

"Marguerite, you tell the boys to come out here and listen, too," she said to her daughter, and then took Tommy's hand. "They may want to say something as well."

"I have to explain myself, and ask for you to forgive me," Tommy said, and tears flowed from his eyes when he spoke.

"You did nothing but risk your life to save my son!" Mama Sanchez said as her three boys and daughter returned to the porch and sat down. "Why must you need forgiveness? I read the letters, and what you did saved all those men, too. Jimmy is proud of you! Can't you understand?"

"If I had not gone on patrol with him, he would have been more careful," Tommy said, swallowing against the lump and choking out his words.

"If you had not gone on patrol my son would have died without his best friend, the boy he called his brother, by his side," Mama Sanchez said, crying as she spoke. "He would have died whether you had gone or not. God put you with him, so he could die with someone who loved him close to him. Tommy, we love you like our own. We love you more because you were with our Jimmy, and you cared for him so much that you risked your own life for him."

Tommy McKay put his face in his hands and he cried. Mama Sanchez held him close to her, tucking his head under her chin, and she cried, too. Henry knelt by them both, with Hector and José standing behind him, tears flowing down their cheeks as well. Marguerite sat quietly by her mother, her hands folded in her lap, sobbing, too, in short, silent breaths.

As the family held each other close, Tommy remembered what Buck Taylor had told him: "Don't go trying to kill all those demons at once, and share the grief with the people you love."

"WHAT'S THIS, VIP seating?" Brian Pitts asked James Harris as the two men sat on a bench in the brig's recreation yard where the guards showed movies on the cell block wall, and purposefully left a wide gap between Mau Mau and Celestine Anderson. Harris had ordered his lieutenant to keep long noses and pointed ears away from his and the Snowman's private conference. He added that he would include the others at the appropriate time.

In the dim light cast from the projector, the Ax Man glared at Brian Pitts, feeling pangs of jealousy as he watched the commander of the Freedom Hill chapter of the Black Stone Rangers confiding secrets with a new man. A white man!

"We high-risk, so the guards they keep us up front where the light shine good on us," Harris said with a chuckle, and glanced over his shoulder where he saw Iron Balls and Bad John leaning against a hooch wall, absorbed in a cartoon featuring Yosemite Sam trying to blow Bugs Bunny to smithereens.

"Look here," Pitts whispered, taking advantage of his first real opportunity to talk to his old partner about their very secret matter of two million dollars in cash and the stash of dope that the other million dollars had bought. "You did good, getting this gang started and putting this notion of a prison riot in the heads of these dudes."

"We gonna make national headlines back in the world, you wait and see," Harris said with a smile, still focused on the idea of standing in the limelight and bringing attention to the black cause.

"I know, and that's cool, but Mau Mau, we got our money and our dope to think about," Pitts whispered, looking to see that no one eavesdropped. "I took a million dollars and bought enough heroin and Buddha that we can roll it into fifty million bucks, man!"

"What about that other two million we gonna split?" Harris said, whispering in a panicked voice.

"You didn't hear me?" Pitts strained, clenching his teeth. "Listen closely to me. Fifty million dollars, man! It's just sitting in a tunnel out west of Saigon. Our two million in cash, too, right there with it."

"You bury our money out west of Saigon?" Harris said, his voice rising loud enough that Celestine Anderson turned his head when he heard the word "money."

"Shhhh!" Pitts hissed, putting his hand over Harris's mouth. "Not so fucking loud!"

"Huong and Bao they got away, and I know that they went straight to the stash and have it under their control," Pitts said, and looked at Harris's eyes. "You remember what I said about loyalty, and why it was important? This is why. I know Huong will stick with us. Our stuff will be there when we can break out of this hole."

"So you wants to get this riot going so we can bust loose and go south, right?" Harris said, smiling.

"Fuck an A, man," Pitts said, smiling back. "I mean civil rights is cool and all, but fifty million dollars is a whole lot more cool."

"You got that right, Jack," Harris said, and looked over his shoulder and nodded to Celestine Anderson to wait just one more minute. "So we bring down this house, and you and me, we splits out the back door."

"You and me, and Bobby Matthews," Pitts said, giving the Ax Man a friendly wink and getting a snarl in return.

"Who that?" Harris said, twisting his neck as though he might see him in the crowd of dark faces watching the cartoon. "Oh, yeah, that dude we let in the rangers. Why he so special?"

"Like I said, his partner, Tommy Joyner, got popped when the army took us down," Pitts said, and pointed to his shoulder. "Same asshole that nailed me, killed Tommy and Chung. I ever see that motherfucker again, I'll park a .45-caliber hardball straight up his tailpipe. I want to put the muzzle of my pistol up his asshole and empty the magazine."

"So this kid Matthews, he thrown in with you down there at Saigon," Harris whispered.

"Yeah," Pitts answered, and smiled at Anderson, now taunting the angry man. "What I said about loyalty goes deep. I ain't never cut you out, and I won't cut this man out either. Fifty million goes a long way among friends."

"So, what we need to do?" Harris said, looking at Anderson and three other rangers all staring at him and Pitts.

"Go ahead and bring in the boys, and we'll lay out our plan for them, but when we head south, Mau Mau, it's just you, me, and Matthews," Pitts said, and waved at Anderson to bring the others close.

Harris looked at Ax Man, too, and motioned for him to come near.

"Snowman, he got a plan on how we bring this motherfucker down," Harris smiled at the four rangers who slid close to him on the bench. "Once they get this piece-of-shit movie rolling, we talk about what we gonna do."

All hands, including the guards' day shift and the brig's two officers, came for the evening's showing of Stanley Kubrick's blockbuster science-fiction hit *2001: A Space Odyssey.* Even on the white-painted concrete block wall, the picture didn't look all that bad. However, halfway through the feature, most of the audience dozed off with boredom.

Chief Warrant Officer Frank Holden and First Lieutenant Michael Schuller surveyed the disappointed crowd and decided that they would stick to action films, Westerns, and comedies in the future. They had *Eight on the Lam,* starring Bob Hope, Phyllis Diller, and Jonathan Winters slated for the next movie night, August 16, 1968, and decided that shows like it would suit the prisoners best.

"I figure there be two times of the day when we can bust things open here, when everybody in the brig gets put in one place, all together," Harris told his cohorts. "One time is when we eat and go out in the rec yard, and the other time is like tonight, at the movies."

"We want to launch this happening on August 16, when everyone's out here in the rec yard, at the movies," Pitts said, looking to his right and left as he talked, and glancing at Iron Balls and Bad John, who had begun looking at the suspicious group talking. Then they looked around at other prisoners and saw that many of them now idly chatted instead of watching the picture, so they shrugged off the confab and focused back on the man in the space suit growing really old and then becoming a baby at the same time. "The advantage that movie night has is that it's dark."

"See, when it dark, the guards they might not want to drop gas on our ass," Harris added. "We got the advantage at night. None of these dudes want to put on a gas mask in the daylight. They can't see shit. At night, they sure as hell can't see shit out those goggle eyes, so they ain't going to want to pop the CS."

"So when the movie ends, and the projector gets shut off, when we have that window of darkness, before they turn on the yard lights, we kick off the riot," Pitts said, and nodded at Harris.

"See," Harris added without consulting Brian Pitts, but thinking on his own to cover their escape, "when everybody in the yard gets busy burning this motherfucker down, we gonna take our Black Stone Rangers and go out the fence."

"We gonna escape?" Anderson said and smiled.

"Fuck an A, bro," Harris said and put out his fist for Anderson to dap. "We going out and join up with the Viet Cong. Then we come back and kill these motherfuckers."

"Fuck yeah," Anderson said, and looked at Bad John and Iron Balls watching him. "I gonna come back and commit special duty on those two motherfuckers for sure."

Brian Pitts leaned over and whispered to Anderson, "Be cool, man. When the time comes, we gonna let you go straight at those two dudes. You gonna start the fight we need to set this whole thing off."

"I like that," Anderson said, still looking at Iron Balls and Bad John.

"Mau Mau, he's going to get into a pushing match with me while the film is still rolling," Pitts said, looking at Harris. "The guards will take him up to control, to see the duty warden. Once they get him inside, then Ax Man, you can do what you like to Bad John. I want you to take him down hard. The rest of us will deal with Iron Balls."

"What I do up in control?" Harris said, puzzled at how he could help up there.

"Everybody's gonna be running down here, because of the fight, and that's when you just hang back and pull down all the switches, opening the gates," Pitts said with a wide grin. "You just stay quiet and keep out of the way when the shit goes down, and our little hoorah will give you all the time you're gonna need. Just a second or two to grab those gate handles and pull them down."

"Cool, man," Harris said and smiled. "Then, with everybody raising hell, I can take command of my rangers and we hit the gates and go free, right?"

"Yeah," Pitts said and frowned.

Chapter 18

"ONE BLACK MOTHERFUCKER"

"LOOK AT THIS," Clarence Jones whispered to Samuel Martin as the two men stood in the library over a two-week-old Sunday edition of the *New York Times*. "That article's right here where my sister Brenda said in her letter. This one about Captain Charles Edwards gettin' his ass put on general court-martial for killing a bunch of gooks down south of Chu Lai last March. See here? That piece of shit First Lieutenant Philip Ziegler got charged, too. The newspaper say that the army trying to cover it up, but that some of the enlisted men in the company wrote letters home about killing those people and how bad they feeling about it."

"Army's all fucked up anyway, they got hopheads and shit out there just shootin' in the rice paddies," Sam Martin said as he ran his finger down the article, reading the paragraphs that Clarence Jones showed him.

"See this?" Jones said, pointing to a paragraph. "This say the army counted twenty-one dead people down there, but letters from the soldiers say they shot like two hundred folks."

"Bullshit," Martin said, and looked toward the front desk of the library to see if the senior trustee paid any attention to them. "I can see maybe a unit blowin' away a couple dozen gooks, but not two hundred. Man, the whole world find out about that shit. I mean, people be talkin'."

"That what it say, man," Jones shrugged, looked at the librarian's desk, quietly ripped the article from the page, folded it, and tucked the news story inside his back pocket. "We need to call Captain Kirkwood and Captain O'Connor and show this to them. This prove that we didn't start any fight with these shitbird army officers. Anybody get wrote up on charges murderin' a bunch of women and children, they sure as hell lie about startin' a fight with some snuffy dudes."

"They damn sure lie about whackin' me with that gun, too!" Martin said, falling in step alongside Jones as they walked out of the library and into the lower hallway of the main cell block. They headed toward the sally port so the two pretrial confinees could then cut across the recreation yard to the prison administration building, where they planned to request permission to use the telephone to call their attorneys.

Since the two men worked diligently and cooperated with everyone in authority, Lieutenant Schuller had granted Jones and Martin trustee status in the brig, allowing them greater freedom. He also moved them from the scullery to the library, as Kirkwood and O'Connor had requested, where they now worked putting away books and keeping the place clean. The two men enjoyed a great deal of free time and no sweat.

Sergeant Mike "Iron Balls" Turner did not hear Jones and Martin as they came down the hallway and turned the corner toward the sally port, where he and Lance Corporal Kenny "Bad John" Brookman sat talking, and keeping watch over the main entrance that housed the maximum-security cell block and the library.

Two nights earlier, a pair of prisoners had escaped through a hole in the fence they had cut in a dark area behind a restroom and shower facility built between two of the minimum-security prisoner hooches.

"Limp-dick Lieutenant Schuller screwed the pooch this time, because Gunny MacMillan told him and Gunner Holden both about that area behind the head," Sergeant Turner said, taking a cigarette that Lance Corporal Brookman offered him when he pulled one out for himself.

"You think Colonel Charles Dimwit Webster will do anything, though?" Bad John said, lighting his smoke and then holding the match so Iron Balls could get his cigarette going, too. "He ain't done shit for the last three escapes, so what makes this time different?"

"Fucking Colonel Dimwit gonna yank him by the stacking swivel this time, take my word for it," the sergeant said with a smile. "Those other escapes, they just happened. Bad luck mostly. This time, Gunny MacMillan got on the rag, because he told those two yahoo brig officers a bunch of times about needing to get a light down there between that head and the hooch, where the fence makes that turn, and those boys cut that hole and slipped out."

"I ain't looked at it that way," Bad John said, sucking on his cigarette and looking over his shoulder as Clarence Jones and Sam Martin approached them after they turned the corner in the hall.

"Well, all I got to say is that's one black motherfucker back there," Iron Balls said.

"Yip, that's one black motherfucker," Bad John echoed, looking at Sam Martin and noticing that the darker of the two black prisoners glared at him.

"What you say about me?" Sam Martin shouted. "That's one black motherfucker? I'm one black motherfucker! That it?"

"Hold on, stud," Sergeant Turner commanded, stepping in front of the two prisoners. "Nobody said anything about you being a black motherfucker. We were talking about the two dudes that escaped the night before last, how that area behind the head is a black motherfucker. No lights on back there."

"Yeah, I believe you, all right," Sam Martin sassed. "We see what the warden say about your prejudice remark on my color."

"Private, you do what you got to do," Turner said, and shrugged, watching the two prisoners step out the doorway into the recreation yard, where the high-risk prisoners sat at several picnic tables watching a basketball game. "I told you the truth."

"Yo, what's shakin', bro?" James Harris called from the table next to the basketball court, seeing the two rangers walking out the main cellblock door and hearing Iron Balls calling after them.

"Fucking asshole guard talkin about me, sayin', that's one black motherfucker," Martin said, walking toward the picnic table where Mau Mau sat with Brian Pitts and Celestine Anderson. " 'Course, when I call him down, he deny sayin' shit. Iron Balls say they talkin' about that dark area behind the head where them two dudes escape a couple of nights ago."

"They ain't caught them brothers either," Harris said with a laugh. "They be long gone now. Joined up with the Cong most likely. So what you gonna do about Iron Balls callin' you a black motherfucker, you black motherfucker?"

All three prisoners at the picnic table laughed.

"Me and Clarence, we headed to the admin office now, so we can call our lawyers," Martin said, half lying because he let Harris think they intended to call their attorneys about the insult instead of about the newspaper article.

"Well, you two black motherfuckers, have fun then," Harris said and laughed. Then he turned to Pitts, who nudged him.

"You know, Mau Mau," the Snowman said in a low voice, "we can use that incident to convert the remaining prisoners who aren't with us to come aboard. Tomorrow night's the big show."

EVEN THE BREEZE that the window fan stirred seemed hot enough to bake bread. Jon Kirkwood stood up from his desk and took off his shirt.

"Oh, I'm telling," O'Connor chirped. "That's don't number seven, isn't it? Don't take off your shirt in the office, no matter how hot it gets in here."

Kirkwood then unfastened his belt and pulled off his pants, too, and stood in the defense section office wearing his shoes and socks, white boxers, and T-shirt.

"It doesn't say a fucking thing about pants, does it," the captain snapped at O'Connor, and then sat back in his swivel chair much more comfortable with the mid-August heat.

"Well, two can play this game," Terry O'Connor said, laughing, and then shucked off his shirt and pants, too.

"Does Major Dickinson know that you're working in your underwear?" Michael Carter said straight-faced as he walked through the door and stopped cold after seeing the two officers seated at their desks in their skivvies.

"No, Mikie, we want it to be a surprise," Kirkwood said with a smile.

"If it gets much hotter, I think I will strip off these drawers, too, and start working in my altogether," O'Connor said, smiling at Carter. "Au naturel."

"I'm not sure what to think of your unprofessional conduct," the tall, thin captain said, blushing and trying not to look at the two underwear-clad lawyers.

"Looks like a great idea," Wayne Ebberhardt said, nudging his way past Michael Carter, who had not moved from the doorway. He quickly unbuttoned his shirt, slipped off his trousers, and flopped in his swivel chair, where he took off his shoes, too.

"Well, I cannot work here with you men undressed," Carter said, walking to his desk, picking up a briefcase, and heading for the door. "If anyone wants me, I will be at the barracks, where casual undress seems more appropriate."

As the gangly, disheveled attorney ambled toward the door, he stopped and looked back at O'Connor.

"Oh, I know what it was that I meant to ask you," Carter said, putting his finger in his mouth and starting to gnaw on the cuticle. "Those secret photographs. Can I see them, too?"

"What?" O'Connor said, sitting up and slamming his feet on the floor, his heart skipping a beat. As he looked up at stick man, he tried his best to show a deadpan face. "I'm not sure I catch your drift, Mikie."

"The ones that the troops keep mentioning," Carter said, now unconsciously biting his knuckles. When Movie Star had told him about the surveillance of Heyster in town, and them not only seeing him passing off dope from the evidence locker to the Chu Lai Hippie, but also that Captain O'Connor had photographs of it, he also had emphasized to the senior defense section attorney that he should keep the news to himself, and above all things not talk about it to anyone, especially someone with brass on his collar. "Pictures of Captain, er, Major-Select Heyster selling drugs to some hippie! They're all talking about it."

"Fucking Movie Star, he spilled his guts to you didn't he!" O'Connor said, throwing his head back and squeezing his eyes shut, feeling suddenly overwhelmed with frustration. "Come inside, sit down, and shut the damned door."

"I'm not sure I like your tone," Carter said, still standing in the entrance with his briefcase clutched under his arm.

"Michael, please," Kirkwood said, and then looked at O'Connor. "This may shed a glimmer of light on why you're pissed off at any little thing."

"Shut the fucking hatch, Mike, please! Damn it!" Terry O'Connor shouted, and jumped from his chair, walked to his palm-tree-looking colleague, yanked him inside the office, and slammed the door shut with a bang.

"Look, if you're going to accost me, I will definitely not stay," Carter said, pulling away from the angry Philadelphia Irishman.

"I don't want stray ears listening to what I am about to tell you three gentlemen, Mike. Please sit down and listen," O'Connor said, and led Carter to his chair.

"Jon, you're right, this thing has eaten me alive the past few weeks," O'Connor confessed, and flopped in his chair. "All I have so far is suspicion and circumstantial evidence, including photographs. Very circumstantial, since we did not keep either man under surveillance after the exchange of whatever articles they passed to each other.

"Yes, I have photographs of Charlie Heyster taking a package from his laundry bag and passing the article to a Sergeant Randal Carnegie, also known as the Chu Lai Hippie. I have a photograph of this so-called Chu

Lai Hippie then handing our illustrious interim mojo a white envelope. One could speculate that the envelope contained money and the package contained Buddha absconded from the evidence locker."

"This may sound simpleminded of me, but how on earth did you find yourself in a position to photograph this curious exchange of items?" Jon Kirkwood said, leaning over his desk and frowning at his best friend. "I guess a better question is this: If you were so suspicious of Captain Heyster ripping off the evidence locker, why didn't you go to CID about your suspicions? Also, please bear in mind that there is this newfangled concept called reasonable cause, you know."

"Jon, you're exactly right," O'Connor said, and waved both his hands in the air as he spoke. "Rules of evidence, reasonable cause, privacy issues, they all bit me in the ass when I looked at the pictures and thought about what I had done. In my own defense, the photographs are admissible evidence because we took them on a public thoroughfare, and Charlie performed these deeds in that public arena, and we used no extraordinary measures to obtain the photographs. So, for what they're worth, they could support other, more damning evidence, if we had it."

"Terry, I'm surprised at you," Wayne Ebberhardt said, and then smiled. "You didn't even invite Jon or me along when you went spying on the shyster."

"You remember that day he came in the barracks and accused Mikie of ripping off the dope in the evidence locker?" O'Connor said, looking at Kirkwood and then at Michael Carter.

"Sure, it pissed off everyone," Kirkwood said, and Carter nodded.

"Heyster seemed so hell-bent to pin it on Michael, and he did his best as well to keep Dicky Doo stirred up, accusing the troops," O'Connor said, cradling his fingers under his chin. "He ranted and fumed, but you know what he and Dickinson didn't do? They never reported the missing shit to CID."

Jon Kirkwood sat up and smiled.

"Interesting point," he said, and looked at Ebberhardt and Carter. "Had the troops really stolen the marijuana, or had Carter done it, Charlie would have had the criminal investigators digging in our lockers and desks. Obviously Heyster knew who took the dope and didn't want the cops nosing into it. He had to raise hell, because Dicky Doo took inventory and found the stuff missing with no burn receipts. Ten to one, the shyster gambled that Dickinson would move on to other challenges once he saw his man Charlie firmly in the driver's seat of their so-called internal investigation. I would also venture a wager that if Dicky Doo had suggested calling in CID, Heyster convinced him that they should handle the problem in house. Why put yourself on the skyline? That's something Dickinson certainly doesn't want."

"Right," O'Connor said, shifting his look to each of his three colleagues. "That's why Heyster made such a show of having Stanley Tufts supervise a surprise wall-locker inspection with our enlisted people on a Sunday morning, hoping to catch some of the troops with dope and perhaps claim that the stuff was part of the missing contraband. You remember how pissed he got when nothing showed up? Not even a pin joint! I thought that Movie Star and Happy Pounds would have had dope if any of our troops did, but they were all clean as a whistle. No dope anywhere."

"So you started tailing Heyster, because he had virtually eliminated the enlisted Marines from this office, and you know very well that Carter nor anyone else in our barracks took the dope," Ebberhardt said, and looked at Kirkwood, who was nodding.

"Terry, that's certainly reasonable suspicion, but I think it falls short of probable cause," Kirkwood added and shrugged.

"That's why I followed him myself, and didn't call CID or anyone," O'Connor said. "The reasonable-cause thing, but more significantly, he is a senior officer here, and a prosecuting attorney. That's a giant leap of faith to accuse someone like Heyster. Thus my caution."

"So, how did Movie Star and the troops get involved with your private investigation?" Kirkwood said, and frowned at his pal.

"I fucked up," O'Connor said, shrugging and shaking his head. "When I saw Charlie take off, swinging his laundry bag, headed for the office jeep, I got an overwhelming feeling that I needed to follow him and see what he was doing. I needed wheels, and I couldn't take the other office jeep: one, because Dicky Doo would raise hell, and two, because it sticks out like a sore thumb with the shiny paint and the red license plate that looks like a flag officer rolling down the road. So I ran to the enlisted barracks where I knew Movie Star and his asshole buddies would most likely be wasting time and staying out of sight. Two guys from the information office were there, and they had a jeep, and one had a camera, so we went after Charlie. The rest is history."

"Where are the pictures now?" Kirkwood asked, resting his chin on his hands with his elbows propped on his desk.

"In the barracks, in my locker, on the top shelf," O'Connor said, and let out a deep sigh. "You know, I feel a lot better."

"So, Charlie the shyster is ripping off the evidence locker and selling it?" Ebberhardt said, wrinkling his lips and thinking.

"His primary customer got busted, though," O'Connor said, shaking his head.

"What about those other assholes?" Kirkwood said, raising his eyebrows. "The ones that had you so pissed the other day."

"Oh, yeah, the Hippie's buddies that he got Charlie to let off the hook," O'Connor said and smiled. "You know, one of them might be picking up where Sergeant Randal Carnegie left off."

"Ten to one Charlie has cooled his jets," Kirkwood said and frowned, shaking his head. "The man would have to be a complete idiot to keep selling dope from the evidence locker after all the bullshit that has gone on about it."

"Well, according to Movie Star," O'Connor said, raising his eyebrows, "Charlie has a taste for the stuff. Apparently Happy Pounds saw him loading his tobacco pouch with Buddha."

"Mixing it with that dog-shit Cherry Blend?" Ebberhardt said, sticking out his tongue and mimicking a gag. "Yuck! That would fuck up good dope, wouldn't it?"

"I wouldn't know, Wayne," O'Connor said, and looked sidelong at his colleague.

"We just need to get Charlie busted with his pipe tobacco then," Kirkwood said, smiling and looking at his fellow defense lawyers. Then he looked at Michael Carter, who sat quietly but beaming a snaggy yellow smile.

"Stick man," Kirkwood scowled, "what we have said here cannot leave this room. No talking to anyone outside our small circle about this, is that clear?"

"Who could I talk to about it?" Carter said, shaking his head so hard that his blond palm-tree mop wagged like pampas grass in the wind.

"God knows," Kirkwood said, now thinking about the lawyer's next-to-nonexistent list of friends, all of whom sat in the room with him at that moment. "Just keep it in mind, should you have the opportunity to chat outside our circle and need something hot to discuss."

"I'm not a gossip," Carter said, standing up and still clutching his briefcase. Then he smiled his jack-o'-lantern teeth at the group. "So are we going to bust Charlie?"

A RED PAINTED line cut down the center of the concrete porch and step of the brig administration building, and ran the length of the concrete sidewalk that ran across the prison yard to the cell block. All inmates stayed on the left side of that red line. If a confinee, whether pretrial or convict, crossed the red line anywhere in the brig, he could be shot.

Chief Warrant Officer Frank Holden stood the duty as warden that day, when Samuel Martin complained that Iron Balls Mike Turner and Bad John Kenny Brookman had called him one black motherfucker. Now he strolled down the right side of that red line to the middle of the recreation yard and then stepped across it and stood on top of one of the picnic tables by the basketball court.

Earlier that afternoon, after he had sent Sam Martin and Clarence Jones back to the library, and forwarded a message to the wing legal office that Kirkwood's and O'Connor's clients wanted to see them as soon as they could find time, the gunner radioed the duty watch commander, Gunnery Sergeant Ted MacMillan, across the yard in the cellblock control station. At first he wanted Turner and Brookman relieved, but after a short conversation with the gunny, who had already talked to the pair of guards after they had come to him, concerned about any misunderstanding, he convinced the warden that the two men on duty at the sally port had not directed an insult at the black prisoner but simply commented on the dark area behind the head next to the minimum-security hooches.

However, for several weeks now, Chief Warrant Officer Holden and First Lieutenant Schuller had discussed the dire possibilities that the increasingly overcrowded conditions and stifling August temperatures could present in the Freedom Hill brig. They both agreed that one small spark could set off a riot that might result in injury and death to both inmates and guards. Something like a misplaced comment, taken as a racial insult, "That's one black motherfucker," could ignite disaster.

Believing that it is better to eat crow than wrap bodies, Gunner Holden called Gunny MacMillan and had him send Turner and Brookman out to meet him in the yard, and stand at his side while he addressed the prisoners.

"Why apologize to these knuckleheads when Turner and Brookman did nothing wrong?" MacMillan had pled, trying to persuade the chief warrant officer that expressing regrets for the misunderstanding would only elevate the incident in the inmates' minds. "No matter what you tell them, they will believe the worst. They don't call Turner and Brookman Iron Balls and Bad John for no reason. Gunner, I think you ought to just let it go."

Holden disagreed, and mounted the picnic tabletop while Turner and Brookman stood on the bench seats below him, holding their arms crossed and clenching their jaws. They could see the satisfaction spread in the cynical smiles on the prisoners' faces.

"I deeply regret the injured feelings of Privates Martin and Jones after they heard Sergeant Holden and Lance Corporal Brookman say, 'That's one black motherfucker,' " Holden began, speaking with his arms crossed over the front of his chest. "Such a comment uttered by any member of the brig staff, whether intentional or, as in this case, accidental, nonetheless can cause unjust pain. For that, these two guards are sorry. While Sergeant Turner and Lance Corporal Brookman were discussing a dark area of the fence line, the misunderstood meaning of their thoughtless phrase still caused damage. I want all of you to know that the brig staff regards each of you as human beings who require a level of respect and decent treatment."

Then he had Turner and Brookman each step on the tabletop with him and express their personally felt regrets about the incident. After apologizing to the prison population, the two guards stepped off the table and returned to the sally port to finish their shifts, and the deputy warden strode along the right side of the red line, back up the sidewalk to the administration building.

While the minimum-security prisoners trickled back to their hooches, Corporal Nathan L. Todd and two other guards marched the high-risk prisoners back to their cells.

"Ol' Gunner Holden, he sure like to kiss our ass," James Harris said to Brian Pitts, who marched ahead of him. "You believe any that shit?"

"It doesn't matter what we believe," Pitts said as he walked in the line of men whom Nathan Todd herded back to the cell block. "What do the inmates in the yard think? Do they buy Holden's bullshit apology? I hope not."

"I already pass word that old Iron Balls and Bad John be lyin' to the boss, trying to backpedal out the mess they in right now," Harris said, smiling as they entered the sally port, where Brookman and Turner stood on each side of the main entrance. "Ain't nobody gonna believe their cop-out story that they was talkin' about that place in the fence behind the head. People in the yard, they too pissed off now. With Holden coming out and kissing ass, that just make it better."

"That's kind of how I see it, too," Pitts said, smiling at Turner and Brookman as he passed them in the entrance. Then he glanced over his shoulder, showing his smile to Mau Mau Harris. "I am really looking forward to the movies tomorrow night."

Chapter 19

THE RIOT

BY SUNSET ON August 16, most of Freedom Hill's crew of prison guards had gathered in the rear of the recreation yard, near the back doors to the administration building that they called the blockhouse, which also served as the main entrance to the brig from the outside world. At this vantage they could oversee the entire inmate population that now gathered to watch the regular Friday evening movie, except for James Elmore, who chose to remain in his cell, where he took all of his meals these days. His free time in the exercise yard came only when the guards had Pitts and Harris locked down, per Lieutenant Schuller's instructions.

Earlier that afternoon, the warden and his deputy, Chief Warrant Officer Holden, had drawn high card to see who stood the Friday night duty and who could go have fun at the Da Nang Officers' Club, where First Lieutenant Wayne Ebberhardt threw a wetting-down party in celebration of his promotion to captain that day. The gunner had drawn the trey of clubs while the lieutenant pulled out the nine of diamonds. Even winning, Schuller still offered to stand the watch and let Holden go to the party, to which the chief warrant officer put up his hands like a good sport, refusing the offer, and urged the lieutenant to go have fun with his friends. He reassured Mike Schuller that all would go well tonight in his absence.

Normally, the warden would watch the regular weekly film seated in a lawn chair on the blockhouse back porch, with other members of his staff, directly behind the minimum-risk prisoners, who made up the vast majority of the men who resided inside the brig. These less-dangerous confinees lived in two lines of tin-roofed, screen-walled, wooden hooches that surrounded the recreation yard and main cell block, a two-story concrete building that housed the high-risk inmates, the library, and the chow hall. The rows of hooches sat between the cell block and the prison's twelve-foot-tall security fence. Spaced among every few hooches, engineers had erected sea-hut-style shower and toilet facilities for the low-risk inmates. Water came from a small, silver-painted tower built next to the blockhouse, which controlled its flow into the brig, as well as the main circuit for the prison's electrical power.

Tonight, Chief Warrant Officer Holden, still concerned about the potential of the "one black motherfucker" remark setting off trouble, decided to spend the evening in the cell block's control center with Gunnery Sergeant MacMillan. To him it seemed a more entertaining choice than suffering through *Eight on the Lam*, a year-old comedy about a bank teller played by Bob Hope with seven children and a crazy housekeeper, Phyllis Diller, who finds a sackful of loot, gets accused by his employer of embezzlement, and goes on the lam with the money, his kids, and their nanny while a nitwit police detective played by Jonathan Winters pursues them. Since he had liked last week's movie choice, *2001: A Space Odyssey*, and the prisoners seemed dulled to boredom by the Kubrick blockbuster, he felt confident that tonight's weak comedy more appropriately addressed the intellects of most inmates.

While the recreation yard bustled with confinees yammering and grab-assing, waiting for the sky to finally go dark so that the projectionist could spread the Technicolor entertainment across the main cell block's white concrete wall, kicking things off with a Woody Woodpecker cartoon, Celestine Anderson took his seat at the end of the picnic bench closest to the sidewalk that led to the sally port where Bad John and Iron Balls stood duty.

Brian Pitts took a seat at the opposite end of the bench next to James Harris while Randal Carnegie, Sam Martin, and Clarence Jones sat between him and the Ax Man. Robert Matthews and five other Black Stone Rangers sat on the bench across the table.

"As soon as you pop open the gates, up in control, I want you to beat feet back down here," Pitts reminded Harris, whispering so that no one could overhear their conversation. "All hell's gonna break loose, so I don't want you getting caught up in the confusion and other bullshit. Me and

Bobby Matthews will shoot the gap down to that head, right over there by the fence. He grabbed a pair of diagonal cutters in the tool shop yesterday, and stuck them in his mattress. He has them in his pocket tonight. We'll start chopping through the wire as soon as we get down to the fence, whether you're with us or not. Once shit starts happening, we won't have but a few minutes to bust out before the guards start lighting up the fences and putting out the dogs. So you better cut a trail as soon as you pull those handles."

Harris nodded and then laughed with excitement, pounding his right fist in his left palm. "We gonna bring down this motherfucker! Rangers gonna put it to the man! First thing we gotta do, we kill that piece of shit Elmore!"

"You ain't heard shit I just said!" Pitts snapped, grabbing Harris by the sleeve. "Fuck Elmore, man. We got two million in cash and fifty million dollars worth of dope tucked in a tunnel out west of Saigon. Focus on that, motherfucker!"

"Shit, man," Harris said, "I thought we kill Elmore, then go. It take me no time to waste that rat-bag pile of dogshit."

"Mau Mau," Pitts said, and then turned the man's face with his hand so he could see his eyes and his seriousness, "forget Elmore. We kill him, they come after us for murder. They'd have us dead to rights. Us murdering Elmore now would be stupid. My lawyer, Lieutenant Ebberhardt, told me that Elmore's statement got burned up a few weeks ago, and now he ain't talkin'. So CID's out of luck. That's why they stuck him in the cell across from us. So we'd scare him into cooperating. Right now all they got on me is desertion, and they're trying to say I collaborated with the enemy because my cowboys opened fire on them. They ain't got shit."

"My lawyer, some cracker look like a zombie with white hair and pasty skin, Captain Carter," Harris said, and laughed. "Man, the dude got breath that peel paint off the shithouse wall. He feedin' me that same line, too. Say all they got on me is dope and sellin' the shit, but they lost the evidence now. So they ain't got much more than desertion and escape. That captain say I probably walk out here with six-six and a kick. 'Course, that don't mean shit, 'cause tonight we gonna bring this motherfucker down."

"Yeah, that's about what Ebberhardt told me, and that's what Matthew's lawyer told him, too. I think six-six and a kick's a standard package for turds like us," Pitts nodded. Then again he took Harris by the chin. "We're getting out of here tonight, though. Six-six and a kick doesn't cut much against two million in cash and fifty million in dope."

"No shit, man," Harris agreed, now locking eyes with Pitts.

"So you need to get all this riot nonsense out of your head. Don't get sidetracked in it, and don't fuck with Elmore," Pitts said, narrowing his eyes so that Harris understood him. "We leave him alone, he keeps his mouth shut. Since they ain't got squat on us, nobody will really care that we escaped. They might look a little while up here, but they won't look that hard for us. With this war, the Marine Corps got more important fish to fry. We just quietly disappear, and slip on down to Saigon. We pull out the cash and the stash, close the deals to get our dope on the market, then shoot on over to Cambodia, where my man with Bird Airways will haul us out to Bangkok. When we get there, we'll start living a life so rich you can wipe your ass on hundred-dollar bills if that's what tickles your fancy. So don't fuck up, Mau Mau! You do, and you'll stay here while me and Bobby go south. You might have a few kicks bringing down this mother-fucker, but you'll always be poor."

"I ain't fuckin' up, man," Harris said, and pulled Brian Pitts's hand off his chin.

"Okay, then," Pitts said and stood up. "Let's do it."

Lance Corporal Kenny Brookman and Sergeant Mike Turner had just walked to the edge of the prison yard so they could watch the movie. When Brian Pitts stood up and James Harris began yelling obscenities at him, the two men backed away and let Corporal Nathan L. Todd and Lance Corporal Paul Fletcher take charge of the disturbance.

"Fuck getting my head bashed in," Iron Balls said to his sidekick. "The Chief and Fletch need a few lumps, after what you and me got the other day."

"What if they get a hoorah going?" Bad John asked, watching Paul Fletcher, a twenty-year-old kid who stood six-foot-three and tipped the scales at 219 pounds, all muscle.

The lance corporal whom fellow guards and prisoners alike called Fletch had grown up in Ardmore, Oklahoma, where he played high school football and spent his summers harvesting wheat from North Texas to Canada, working seven days a week from the day after school let out in May until the end of August, just before Labor Day weekend and the be-ginning of a new school year. Most boys didn't last the summer. Fletch did it every year since junior high, when his mother relented and let her thirteen-year-old child travel that long, hard road with his big brother, sixteen-year-old Raymond.

Then, right in the middle of the 1966 wheat harvest, six weeks after Paul had graduated from high school, the dutiful lad called home on a Sun-day night and his mother told him that he had a letter from the draft board waiting in the mailbox. The next day, in North Platt, Nebraska, he found a Marine Corps recruiter and joined up, rather than landing as a draftee in the army and taking the same kind of abuse his drafted brother had endured. After boot camp and a tour in Vietnam, Ray Fletcher told Paul to join the air force or run to Canada, but don't get drafted. It ain't worth it.

Not one to take advice well, Paul enlisted in the Marines and then told his brother, fresh out of the army, who howled laughing.

"You'd been better off getting drafted!" Ray said on the telephone after the lad had told his mother the news.

However, Paul Fletcher breezed through recruit training and graduated as platoon guide and meritorious private first class. He drew the occupational specialty of 5800, military policeman, and out of boot camp went to the U.S. Army Military Police and Criminal Investigation schools at Fort Gordon, Georgia. When he got to Da Nang, four months ago, he volunteered to work in the brig. He told Lieutenant Colonel Webster that he hoped to become an officer and a provost marshal, and that working in corrections would round him out. The colonel agreed. He needed good men in the brig, especially an intimidating, muscled hulk with a brain.

Seeing Paul Fletcher come at him and then clamp a death grip on the nape of his neck made Mau Mau Harris immediately cooperative.

"Yo, Fletch, man, hey, I'm cool, man," Harris whined, dancing on his tiptoes as the lance corporal led him from the table.

Then Corporal Todd got in Mau Mau's face.

"What is your major malfunction, Mister Harris?" Todd growled while Fletch still held the prisoner dangling like a marionette.

"That motherfucker, Pitts, he pinch my ass while I waitin' to see the flick, man," Harris said, pointing at Brian Pitts, who smiled innocently. "Piss me the fuck off, man."

"Keep you hands to yourself, Mister Pitts," Todd called to the prisoner seated at the picnic table.

"Hey, Chief, I ain't done nothing," Pitts said, shrugging and smiling at the corporal the inmates and guards alike called Chief because of his Cheyenne heritage.

"You two will sit down, and keep your hands and your remarks to yourselves, or you will go to your cells. Clear?" Todd said in a strong voice.

"I ain't sittin' by that motherfucker," Harris said, crossing his arms and shaking his head after Fletch had let him go. "I want to see Gunny MacMillan, let him straighten that cracker motherfucker Pitts out, since you won't. You white boys be stickin' together, I know."

"Fletch, haul Mister Harris up to control and let the gunny talk to him, and then lock him in his cell," Todd said, and cast a menacing look at Brian Pitts.

"What?" Pitts retorted, holding his hands up in innocence. "I ain't done shit. Harris just fucking with you, Chief."

"He's gone, Mister Pitts. One more word from you and I will take you to your cell as well," Todd said, walking back to his post at the front of the recreation yard, standing among the left bank of picnic tables filled with prisoners. Lance Corporal Fletcher would watch the right grouping of tables once he returned from upstairs.

Brian Pitts smiled and slouched back against the table, watching the empty wall, waiting for the cartoon to begin, and the fight that would set off the riot.

Celestine Anderson kept smiling more and more as the sky darkened. He knew that as soon as Bad John and Iron Balls stepped to their usual spots where they could see the cartoon projected on the wall, he could attack them. The Ax Man relished the idea of putting the hurt on Iron Balls, a guard he had hated more than others since the day Turner arrived last December.

His partner, Bad John, came on the scene in May, but had served in Vietnam since February. One day in April he dumped a peasant woman on her can who had stopped to pee on the side of the road, right next to the spot where Lance Corporal Brookman stood sentry duty at the main entrance of Three-MAF headquarters compound. The woman, squatting low and pissing down her splayed fingers, sending the yellow stream out her rolled-up pants leg, fell in the puddle of urine when the Marine shoved her on her shoulders and told her to get the fuck out of the area.

A Vietnamese policeman saw the incident, and took offense at the belligerent lance corporal's assault on some poor old lady whose only crime was to stop and take a leak in front of the Marine headquarters gate. The cop complained to his boss, who shared in the patrolman's anger and sent the incident up the flagpole. The local constabulary demanded that the offending military policeman should get run up the target carriage and disked.

In turn, Colonel Webster received a call from the Three-MAF chief of staff, who angrily advised him that the commanding general did not want Bad John any longer standing sentry duty at anybody's gate. So the provost marshal shit-canned Brookman to brig duty.

Iron Balls got dumped on Freedom Hill after continually loafing at all his other military police assignments, and soon no staff NCO in the provost marshal's office wanted him working in his duty section.

"Look at that splib smiling at me like I might suck his dick," Iron Balls said, and nodded toward Celestine Anderson, who grinned even more now.

"Think he might want to start a hoorah?" Bad John said nervously, seeing the excited look that the Ax Man had in his eyes.

"Just let him try," Iron Balls said, grinning back at the prisoner. "I passed word to the guys up in the watch posts on top of the blockhouse and at the fence corners that anybody start a hoorah, they needed to open fire in the air."

"Fuck nuts Holden or the gunny buy that?" Brookman said, raising his eyebrows and blinking at the sergeant.

"No. You think I'm gonna tell those two pansy-asses something like that?" Turner sneered. "What they don't know won't hurt them. Meantime, any of these knuckleheads go to throw down on me or you, and my boys in the towers gonna start shooting."

"In the air, though," Bad John affirmed, wanting reassurance that he would not get connected to any incident that led to bloodshed.

"Fuck, yeah," Iron Balls said, and wrinkled his lip. "Be nice, though, if somebody slipped up and shot that Looney Tunes spook over there that keeps smiling at me like a queer in a boys' camp."

Brian Pitts had wanted to wait until Paul Fletcher had returned to his post in the recreation yard before he sent Celestine Anderson after Iron Balls and Bad John, but he had overheard Corporal Todd's instruction to lock Harris in his cell once he had talked to Gunny MacMillan. Mau Mau couldn't pull the control center's handles from his cell. So the Snowman had to improvise, and estimate that his partner had time enough to get upstairs, but not enough time to finish his informal request mast with the gunny.

"Go ahead, Ax Man," Pitts said, taking a chance based on his instincts, and then nudged Sam Martin to give Anderson a hand.

Celestine Anderson let out a war cry and sprang to his feet, bouncing on his toes as he dashed toward the sally port where Bad John and Iron Balls stood outside, far enough to see the movie and too far from the cubicle to take advantage of its iron-barred shelter. Both Martin and Jones joined the Ax Man in his pursuit of the two guards, who had now turned and tried to run to the reinforced concrete booth where they had truncheons and tear-gas grenades, and where, despite orders against weapons in the yard, Sergeant Turner had stashed a Remington model 870 folding-stock shotgun loaded with ought-two man-killers.

When the Ax Man and his two accomplices started at the pair of loafing guards, all fifty-seven members of the Freedom Hill Chapter of Black Stone Rangers jumped to their feet and began shouting, "That's one black motherfucker!"

Raising their fists and chanting, the rangers spread among the three hundred other prisoners, encouraging them to join the harangue. If an inmate did not voluntarily get up and start participating in the hoorah, they yanked him to his feet and slapped him around until he changed his mind.

Despite the threats and abuse, several prisoners who had too much to lose by rioting, getting months added to a sentence that might end in days, slipped under the picnic tables. Others, such as Donald T. Wilson and Michael Fryer, tough and intimidating even to a crowd of rioting inmates, openly defied the rangers' orders and remained seated. The two men sat quietly, watching and daring anyone to try something with either man.

Kenny Brookman screamed when he saw the three black men running at him. He tried to wave to the Marines in the towers to open fire, but Ax Man Anderson took him down with an outstretched right arm, as he ran past the guard, clotheslining Bad John across the throat, lifting him off his feet, and slamming him to the ground, flat on his back. As Brookman rolled on his stomach and tried to get back to his feet, Sam Martin kicked his size twelve, extra-wide Bata Bullet tennis shoe hard into the downed lance corporal's ribs, knocking the air out of the crumpled man's lungs.

"Call me one black motherfucker, motherfucker!" Martin yelled as he kicked Bad John again. "Say it, motherfucker. I want to hear how tough you get now with my boot in your ass!"

Clarence Jones looked over his shoulder and noticed a Marine standing on the catwalk outside the guard tower overhead the blockhouse and saw the man raising a rifle to his shoulder.

"He gonna shoot!" Jones yelled and grabbed Martin by the back of his shirt collar and pulled him to the ground with him.

Suddenly several gunshots cracked overhead, and Brian Pitts jumped under the picnic table with Randal Carnegie and Bobby Matthews. All three men looked toward the sally port and saw Celestine Anderson on top of Iron Balls Mike Turner, beating his head against the hard-packed ground.

More than a dozen single-shot reports of the tower guards' rifles echoed across the prison yard, and rapidly sent the hoorah into full-blown chaos. While some men ran for cover, many others, angered by the shooting, rose in rebellion, and now sought to destroy everything in sight. Prior to the shooting, the company of guards rallying in the blockhouse had a chance at regaining control of the inmates, but not now. Not after the shooting had served to ratchet up so many prisoners' emotions to such a high frenzy that they now vented their anger with unbridled outrage and showed no thoughts about danger or consequence.

"That sounded like gunfire!" Chief Warrant Officer Frank Holden exclaimed, and then dashed into the upstairs hallway of the main cell block when a second volley echoed through the brig. "We've got big trouble outside!"

James Harris casually stepped to the side of Gunny Ted MacMillan's desk, where he had begun telling the watch commander a bullshit story about Brian Pitts organizing a gang of white supremacists, and that was why he had lost his temper with the man. While he spun his yarn, Mau Mau spied the gunny's infamous Babe Ruth signature model Louisville Slugger baseball bat leaned in the corner of the control unit, behind the senior guard's desk.

"Sit your ass on the floor, now!" MacMillan ordered Harris, and then looked at Paul Fletcher. "You stay in here with this maggot while I go out to the sally port with the gunner and check this shit out."

Holden had already started down the stairs when MacMillan ran after him.

"Ten to one they got into it with Turner and Brookman again," the gunny said, running after the chief warrant officer as the two men hurried down the concrete steps to the lower deck.

"What's going on, man?" Harris said, sitting on the floor, easing his feet underneath his body so he could spring for the bat before Fletcher realized he made his move.

"Prisoner Harris, keep your mouth shut and remain on the floor," Fletcher said, and took the nightstick from the silver ring on his Sam Browne belt.

"Why you be down on me, man? I ain't done shit," Harris said, putting his hands over the top of his head so Fletcher would realize that the prisoner meant him no harm.

Staff Sergeant Orlando Abduleses, a dark-skinned Marine from Sacramento, California, whom everyone had nicknamed Abdul the Butcher, had charge of the guards in the exterior posts and in the blockhouse. When the fight began, he immediately sent six men rushing toward the trouble. They made it only halfway through the crowd of inmates before scores of prisoners took them down, and sent the Marines running back to the administration building. Then the tide of excited prisoners turned toward the cell block and pushed forward, surrounding Celestine Anderson, Sam Martin, and Clarence Jones as they pummeled Bad John Brookman and Iron Balls Turner.

"Control! Control! Blockhouse, over," Staff Sergeant Abduleses shouted over his handheld walkie-talkie and squawked through the radio speaker of the unit resting in its battery charger on Gunny MacMillan's desk.

"Stay put," Lance Corporal Fletcher said, and walked to the gunny's desk and picked up the radio. "Staff Sergeant Abdul, Lance Corporal Fletcher here. The gunny's gone down in the yard with the deputy warden. Anything I can—"

Mau Mau Harris cut the lance corporal's sentence short with Gunny MacMillan's Louisville Slugger.

When the guard turned to answer the radio, Harris had quietly slid across the slick-waxed tile floor, grabbed the baseball bat, and sprang to his feet with a roundhouse swing, catching the lance corporal behind the ear and sending him tumbling over the desk, unconscious and badly injured but still breathing.

"You big-ass motherfucker," Harris said, looking at the crumpled Marine and then taking another swing through the air with the yard-long, flame-treated ash wood club. He wiped a spot of blood off the bat against his trousers leg and then yanked down all the handles in the control unit.

Mau Mau danced into the hallway and started to jog downstairs, but then looked at the bat once again, and turned toward the gate that led into the maximum-security section of the cell block.

"Yo, Elmore," Harris said with laugh. "Maybe you be wondering why your cell door just slide open. Elmo! Here I come, baby!"

When the doors to the sally port sprang open, Celestine Anderson led a wave of prisoners inside and met Chief Warrant Officer Holden and Gunnery Sergeant MacMillan head-on. Other prisoners had surrounded and taken down Nathan L. Todd, and now sat with him trapped under a picnic table.

"Bobby, I think Harris has fucked up," Brian Pitts said to Robert Matthews, looking around him and realizing that Mau Mau had already spent more than enough time to get down to the yard once the interior gates had sprung open, and he still had not emerged from the building. "He's gone after Elmore, that dumb sack of shit. We've wasted way too much time waiting on that fucked-up asshole. Let's run on down to the fence before the guards get their floodlights set up and put a reaction team in here. I guess Harris would rather be stupid and poor."

Just as the two conspirators headed across the chaotic prison yard where some inmates crouched under picnic tables, trying to avoid injury from the crowd of several hundred men gone wild, now trying to destroy everything in sight, James Harris called to them, clutching James Elmore by the back of his shirt while the terrified man wiggled and danced in urine-soaked pants. When his captive would not move fast enough to suit him, Mau Mau gave him a rap across the legs with the bat, causing the snitch to let go a harsh scream.

"I told you not to fuck with that piece of shit!" Brian Pitts bellowed when he saw James Elmore and the crazy, smiling Mau Mau Harris.

"Shit, Snowman, I thought you like to see what this motherfucker do when I shove this bat up his ass," Harris said, laughing. "Come on, man, don't you want to watch me fuck this bitch with Gunny MacMillan's big stick?"

"Were you born this stupid or did you have to work at it?" Pitts said to Mau Mau Harris while looking at the pitiful James Elmore with his pissed pants and gold front tooth.

"He killed Wild Thing, so he ought to pay somethin' for it," Harris said, shaking the frightened bag of wet rags as he spoke.

"No, he ratted us out!" Pitts argued, looking at Harris and realizing that it was useless trying to reason with the man. Then he shook his head and turned his back on Mau Mau, heading toward the fence. "Come on, Bobby, this stupid motherfucker wants to get us all hung out to dry with him."

James Harris released Elmore, and the scared man dashed toward the cell block, hoping to find a good hiding place.

"Look, I let him go!" Harris said, following Pitts and Matthews.

"Huong and Bao killed Wild Thing and some other people, too," Pitts snarled at Mau Mau. "You watched. Blaming that poor, stupid bastard. Fucking Elmore. That's why you and guys like you end up in places like this, or dead. You have no balls to take responsibility. We all killed Wild Thing, damn you!"

Then Brian Pitts broke into a run toward the toilet facility and the fence line that now lay obscured in the darkness. Bobby Matthews and Mau Mau Harris double-timed close behind him.

"Get those cutters going, man," Pitts said to Bobby Matthews, breathing hard and looking to see if anyone watched them.

Matthews began working the sharp blades of the ten-inch-long diagonal cutters into the fence wire one link at a time, using both hands to snap the pliers' jaws together. His weak grip frustrated James Harris, who tossed the baseball bat aside and then yanked the tool from the man's hands and went to snipping a hole with one hand and pulling apart the chain-link fabric with the other.

"Help me push this shit apart so we can get out this motherfucker," Harris grumbled, struggling with the fence, trying to pry open a hole big enough for the three of them to climb through.

While Pitts and Matthews strained to enlarge the hole, Harris snipped against the heavy-mesh steel fencing and slowly spread open a widening gap. However, beyond the fence, Lieutenant Schuller had engineers lay down three rows of German tape stacked as an additional barrier outside the twelve-foot-high fence, after the two inmates had escaped the prior week.

Harris looked at the coiled wire with the razorlike barbs on it and then glanced back at Pitts.

"We ain't cuttin' through that shit," he said, still snipping at the chain-link, but now thinking about the next barrier.

"Low crawl under it, just like in boot camp. It ain't tied down," Pitts said, looking at the coils and noticing that the engineers had not yet driven stakes to hold the wire in place against the ground. "We'll get a few cuts, and rip our clothes to shit, but we can slide under it. Just take a little time."

"What the fuck, man, you leaving without saying good-bye?" Randal Carnegie said, coughing after running across the prison yard when he noticed in the low light cast from the end lamps on the nearby hooches the three men cutting the fence.

"Who that flaky-Jake with you, Randy?" Harris said, looking over his shoulder as he worked on the fence and seeing the Chu Lai Hippie accompanied by the slimeball Kevin Watts.

"My bunkmate, he's cool," Carnegie said, putting his arm around the dark-haired and pale-skinned Watts.

Brian Pitts looked at the unwelcome company. Neither man comprehended even the basic notion of loyalty. The Hippie had allegiance only to himself, and Watts would be a turncoat in a heartbeat and lie with a straight face. While he didn't like James Elmore one bit, Brian Pitts thought even that sorry bag of worms had more redeeming qualities than Kevin Watts.

"That lawyer friend of yours you keep bragging about," Pitts said to Carnegie. "You think he would help us once we get out?"

"I don't know, man," Carnegie said, and looked at the growing hole that Harris managed to get cut in the fence. "I ain't leavin'. I only got two more weeks left and I'm gone home and out of the crotch. Watts here got three years to do, so he might want to tag along with you guys."

"He's welcome to run with us," Pitts said, smiling at the intruder and considering that the skinny, out-of-shape Watts wouldn't put up much of a fight when the time came to dump his scaly ass. They could easily leave him dead in a ditch once they had put a little distance between them and the brig.

Suddenly a flickering yellow glow began to illuminate the fence line where Pitts and his cohorts worked to escape from the brig before the guards got organized, and the inevitable infantry reaction platoon could arrive and secure the surrounding area.

"The dumb motherfuckers are burning the hooches!" Pitts shouted at Harris. "Come on, let's try to get through the fence before the guards see us. It's going to look like broad daylight here once these cracker boxes start flamin' up."

"Fuck, yeah!" Harris yelled, and raised his fist in the air after seeing the rows of prisoner quarters starting to lick flames through their windows and roofs. "Burn this motherfucker down!"

He had no more than shouted when the five prisoners heard the un-mistakable chop of an M60, .30-caliber machine gun opening fire toward them. Outside the fence they saw the splashes of dirt leaping from the ground as the bullets struck twenty feet from them and began to close in their direction, warning the escaping inmates to turn back.

Brian Pitts fell hard against the head wall, gasping for breath, a dozen feet back inside the fence and shouted to Harris, who now worked more frantically than ever trying to open the hole so they could still escape.

"Look at him," he said to Bobby Matthews. "That's what I loved about that guy. He has never considered impossibility. We're fucked, but that dumb bastard thinks that he can still get through this fence, and those bullets will just bounce off his hard head."

"Hey, bro, me and Kev, we're gonna head on back to the picnic tables," the Chu Lai Hippie said, patting Brian Pitts on the shoulder. "Better luck next time."

Pitts said nothing, but just leaned against the side of the head, its opposite wall now starting to burn. He stayed there, watching Mau Mau Harris desperately fighting the fence wire while the guards fired their machine guns down the outer perimeter of the fence until the man finally looked over his shoulder and saw the Snowman shaking his head and motioning to him to give up.

"Yo, man, those guards they only tryin' to scare us back," Harris said, breathing hard as he fell against the head wall next to where Brian and Bobby waited for him. "We climb through the wire, they ain't gonna shoot us."

"I think they would love to shoot us all right now," Brian Pitts said, and smiled, shrugging his shoulders at the ever-optimistic Harris. "Let's go back and sit under a picnic table and figure out what we want to do now."

ORANGE FLAMES FROM the two rows of burning prison hooches lit up the night sky, and the west winds carried the pall of smoke down Freedom Hill and into Da Nang. At the air base, Wayne Ebberhardt had laid out a pineapple and pig spread for all hands on the Officers' Club back lawn, nearly as elaborate as the best of those organized by Lieutenant Colonel Prunella. He even included live dance music by Yamaguchi Ritter and his Angeles City Cowboys, and paid the extra money for the quartet of Filipino LBFM go-go girls, who tonight wore glittering gold bikinis with tassels whirling on their breast cups and fringe bouncing on their butts.

Lobo Gunn had downed a six-pack of beer before sunset and now finished his second one when he smelled the smoke and noticed the glow coming off Hill 327.

"Looks like Charlie rocketed the brig tonight," he casually mumbled to his pal Buck Taylor, who had worked halfway through his second six-pack of Budweiser.

"Someone needs to grab Mike Schuller and tell him his house is on fire!" Taylor shouted through the crowd at a table where Terry O'Connor and Jon Kirkwood had the brig officer cornered, talking shop.

"Fire?" Schuller said and stood up. Then he saw the infernal glow rising on the brig side of the mountain. He quickly shifted his eyes across the gathering, searching for Lieutenant Colonel Webster, who had given him a lift from the provost marshal's office, but the PMO had already gone. Then he looked at Kirkwood and O'Connor. "Hey, guys, you've got to get me up to the brig. Colonel Webster must have gotten word and left already; he probably couldn't find me because we were sitting back here, out of sight."

"Grab your hat and let's fly," O'Connor said, looking to see Wayne Ebberhardt, who came running to them.

"Colonel Webster just left with the chief of staff," the newly promoted captain said. "We'll take the office jeep."

"What about me?" Michael Carter asked, hurrying behind Ebberhardt, Kirkwood, O'Connor, and Schuller. "I don't think we can fit five in the jeep."

"Mikie," Jon Kirkwood said, stopping and taking the captain by the shoulders, "you need to find Movie Star and have him take you and Major Dickinson up to the brig. They will need the staff judge advocate there, and you can ride with him."

"What about Major-Select Heyster and the others?" Carter asked, looking at the group of prosecutors standing in their usual small circle, Charlie with his pipe clenched in this teeth.

"They don't have any clients in the brig, so they would just become curious onlookers, and would most likely get in the way," Kirkwood said, turning Carter back toward him. "Don't worry about those guys. Go get Movie Star and the other jeep."

"Well, where is Lance Corporal Dean, anyway?" Carter asked, wringing his hands and turning again to look in all directions. "I saw Lance Corporal Pounds with Sergeant Amos and Corporal Farmer all talking to Staff Sergeant Pride just a moment ago, but Dean disappeared right after he ate dinner. I haven't seen him for quite a long time. Not in the past hour, anyway."

"Use your head, Skipper," O'Connor said, pointing at his temple and tapping it. "It's Friday night. Bet our horny lance corporal has a date with Rosy Palm back in the barracks. Take a look there."

"Well, he'll just have to send her back to her quarters on her own then," Carter said, putting his nose in the air. "We have an emergency, and no time to spare for running prom dates home. I am sure that Major Dickinson won't even want to know about Movie Star's date. Is she a nurse? The name doesn't sound Vietnamese."

"No, Mike, but she is an American," O'Connor said, and then laughed. "You be nice to her."

"Of course!" Captain Carter huffed, and then took off running toward the enlisted quarters, where Lance Corporal Dean lived in a cubicle wallpapered with centerfold pinups from the past dozen issues of *Penthouse* magazine.

"You asshole!" Wayne Ebberhardt said, laughing as he jogged alongside Terry O'Connor. "Only Michael Carter would not know the true identity of Rosy Palm and her five sisters who never say no. It's almost worth going back to watch!"

Jon Kirkwood had already sat down behind the steering wheel, and Mike Schuller occupied the front passenger seat, leaving the back bench for Ebberhardt and O'Connor. When the two captains jumped aboard, Kirkwood popped the clutch and raced toward the air base main gate.

*   *   *

AN IRRITATING TAPPING sound outside his wall lockers stirred James Dean from his lust-driven daze. He had a red lightbulb screwed in his desk lamp, providing a certain sultry ambience to his cubicle, and a fifteen-watt reading light mounted on the pipe frame of his bunk, focused on the spread-open centerfold of the August issue of his favorite American publication.

"Don't fuck with me right now, man, I'm almost there," Movie Star called out, not taking his eyes off the pair of large breasts and nearly hairless pubic triangle in the centerfold photo that he held up with his left hand while his right worked frantically at his crotch and had his libido racing at ultrahigh speed. His blurring vision shifted continuously from the pinup's muff to her breasts, to her bright-red lips, then back to her muff.

When he reached his slippery right hand toward the night table where he had a large plastic bottle of creamy-pink baby lotion with a handy pump top, trying to quickly reload his palm with the sweet-smelling lubricant and get his sloppy fist back into action, he heard a high-pitched scream that for an instant he thought came from a woman. The lance corporal sat up only to see Captain Michael Carter standing in the cubicle entrance, twittering with his hands over his eyes and vibrating on his toes.

"Oh, my God!" Carter cried, glancing down to see the naked, fully erect Marine. Then he covered his eyes and twittered again like a young, inexperienced girl getting her first look at pornography.

"Holy shit, sir, I'm almost there, can't you give me just about thirty seconds?" Movie Star whined, and then went back to work on his masturbation with furious intensity.

"Oh, I've got to get some air!" Carter squealed, and staggered back into the center aisle of the barracks, holding his hands across his chest and gasping for breath. "Corporal, you have no shame! Oh, my God! Captain O'Connor said you had a girl here with you, a person named Rose something or other."

"Yeah, sir, Rosy Palm, she's right here," Dean called back and began groaning. "Oh, that's it, baby. Take it all. Yeah, ride it hard. Let your daddy come home. Oh, yeah, baby."

"Oh, my God!" Carter gasped, stepping back into the lance corporal's doorway, looking to see if a girl was there and considering that he might not have noticed her at his first glance. However, when he took his second look, he only saw the driver with his hand stroking away and a stream of semen suddenly gushing over the top of his fist.

"Damn, sir," Movie Star said, catching his breath and wiping himself with a towel that he had lain by his side, "what's so fucking important?"

"You've got to drive me and the colonel, or rather the major, to the brig," Carter said in a rapid-fire staccato. "We think that the Viet Cong have attacked it and overrun the place. It's on fire! You can see it burning from down here."

"Why the fuck would Charlie want to rocket the brig?" Dean said, pulling on his utility trousers without putting on any underwear, and then slipping on his blouse without a T-shirt under it. Then he flopped on the side of his bunk, yanked up his socks, stabbed his feet down in his boots, and laced them before Michael Carter could think of a reason why anyone would want to rocket a jail.

"You know, I cannot imagine how I can explain what just happened in your cubicle when I go to confession to the chaplain tomorrow," Carter said, completely flustered and walking with a hurried step alongside the driver as they headed toward the jeep where Major Dudley Dickinson sat in the passenger seat, waiting and trying to make a two-way radio work that Staff Sergeant Pride had given to him so he could communicate with the PMO if needed.

"What do you have to confess, sir?" Dean said, jumping in the driver's seat while Carter climbed over the side and fell onto the back bench.

"Why, your masturbation, of course," Carter replied, straightening himself up.

Dudley Dickinson looked at Lance Corporal Dean and then glanced over his shoulder at Carter.

"What the fuck are you talking about?" Dickinson growled at the captain.

"I saw the lance corporal, sir," Carter stammered, and then blushed so badly that he could not wrestle his voice from his throat.

"What? You walked in on this shitbird jacking off?" Dickinson asked, and then laughed so hard he lost his breath.

"Yes, sir," Carter answered, and took a hard swallow. "Some of the men told me that Movie Star had a date accompany him to his barracks, a girl named Rose or something. So I wandered in, and I did knock, by the way. I fully expected to see him having a nice conversation with a young woman, but what I encountered! Well, sir! Like I tried to tell Lance Corporal Dean, I just have no idea how I will explain it to the chaplain when I go to confession tomorrow."

"You fucking moron, Rosy Palm! Your damned hand! Haven't you ever?" Dickinson shouted, and then laughed as the jeep rolled past the air base's main gate and headed for the brig. "No, I take it back, you probably have never whacked your noodle, have you."

"If you mean masturbation, sir," Carter said, blushing uncontrollably,

"I do not make that a practice in my life. I pray about it when I feel my loins aroused. I certainly do not discuss the matter with anyone."

"Whoever left your cage door unlocked back there in Boston should get the death penalty," Dickinson growled while Movie Star smiled as he drove, holding in his laughter.

Chapter 20

THE RAGE

AS JON KIRKWOOD steered his jeep around the final turn approaching the Freedom Hill brig, two CH-46 Sea Knight helicopters launched from the clearing across the road from the prisoner of war compound next door and downwind from the military prison. Several canvas-topped Marine Corps six-by trucks sat with their diesel engines idling in front of a cluster of hooches across the parking lot from the blockhouse.

Nearly ninety inmates who had earned base-parolee status lived in these quarters. A panel of officers who included the provost marshal and brig warden and three members of the general staff, assigned on a rotating basis, reviewed the case of each man proposed for the parolee program. Envisioned by the provost marshal and Lieutenant Schuller, it served as a halfway house for inmates who neared the end of their sentences and demonstrated potential to return to the operating forces, serving to transition them back to Marine Corps units rather than the men getting shit-canned out of the service with an administrative discharge under less than honorable conditions. It offered Marines a second chance to finish their military obligation and obtain a general discharge under honorable conditions, which also warranted them receiving the full package of veterans' benefits they would have otherwise lost. Putting the men back in the operating units also helped the Marine

Amphibious Force with its manpower shortfalls, which had become an increasing concern.

Staff Sergeant Abduleses had organized the base parolees into working parties that now helped the guard staff erect floodlights all around the brig's perimeter. They had used the trucks to transport the Marines and equipment around the fence line and to tow generator trailers in place.

One by one as the workers started the generators' engines, the banks of floodlights came on and fully illuminated the brig's surroundings as well as the recreation yard and burning hooches.

"My God!" Jon Kirkwood exclaimed as he pulled the jeep in front of the administration building and Mike Schuller leaped out before he had a chance to stop. "This wasn't a rocket attack. It's a riot."

"You think they killed anybody?" O'Connor said, looking at the many fires and seeing the prisoners inside the fence running aimlessly or hiding under the several rows of picnic tables that flanked the basketball court and served as movie seating on Friday nights.

"I'm afraid to even consider it," Kirkwood answered, pausing to take in the view and trying to absorb what had happened.

Michael Schuller had run ahead of the three lawyers and quickly found Staff Sergeant Abduleses talking to Lieutenant Colonel Webster, the MAF chief of staff, and several other officers standing in a group on the walkway between the parking lot and the blockhouse. As the trio of lawyers approached the group, they recognized the familiar face of an old friend.

"Major Danger!" Terry O'Connor called out, seeing Jack Hembee across from the chief of staff and the provost marshal. The former operations officer from Fire Support Base Ross turned his head and smiled, seeing the two defense lawyers with an unfamiliar third man accompanying them. He gave the men a quick wave, and returned his attention to the colonels who conferred with him.

"We've got the prisoners contained for the night," Hembee said to the group as the three lawyers approached and listened. "With our reinforced reaction company covering every foot of that fence line, nobody's going anywhere. I say let them fight among themselves, get good and tired, and we can start clearing them out sometime tomorrow. They'll want to sleep by then."

"I think Jack's right," Colonel Webster said, slapping the major across the shoulders. "I've come to the same conclusion. We start popping gas in the dark and no telling what kind of disaster we can stir up. Besides, we have all those prisoners of war right down the hill, and the smoke has them coughing up a storm as it is. Mix in a bunch of CS and we'll have a riot over there, too."

"Staff Sergeant Abduleses mentioned that we had some shooting from the towers when this thing started," Lieutenant Schuller said, looking at the senior member of his guard staff present with the group.

"Right," Colonel Webster said, and looked up at the towers. "First thing I did when I got here, after the staff sergeant told me what happened, and those jokers were still shooting, I had every man who pulled a trigger brought out of the towers and replaced. Those men are now supervising the working parties among the base parolees. Last thing we need is somebody getting shot. According to Abdul here, our illustrious Sergeant Turner had apparently told those men to start shooting over the prisoners' heads if trouble broke out. Although they were just following Turner's orders, I still replaced the men, just to make sure I don't have any trigger-happy jocks remaining up topside.

"We did have a group of inmates that tried to cut through the fence, but ol' Abdul the Butcher here, had one of the M60s walk a little machine-gun fire in front of them as an attention-getter. Needless to say, it turned them back in short order. So I left a standing order to do that again if anyone else attempts to escape. Major Hembee and the reaction force have orders to do the same. I just don't want anyone opening up on people inside the wire."

"What about our people, sir?" Schuller asked. "What's the count?"

"Abdul says that they took hostage six of our men: Gunner Holden, Gunny MacMillan, Sergeant Turner, Corporal Todd, and Lance Corporals Brookman and Fletcher," the colonel answered. "We have no idea of their status. Last word on Fletcher, he had escorted a prisoner up to control. Turner and Brookman got beaten, but the people in the tower said that they observed them moving inside the cell block with the others, walking on their own, apparently protected by a couple of pretrial prisoners, Fryer and Wilson, who fought back other inmates, keeping them off our guys. I've put people with cameras and long lenses up in the towers. If we shoot anything, let's shoot pictures so we can learn who's in charge down there and who's helping our side. Apparently we have at least two good guys in the crowd."

"Sergeant Donald T. Wilson, sir," Kirkwood said, offering the name of his client after the colonel had finished. "He's my client. A good Marine. Big guy. Tough as a boot. I don't know about Fryer."

"Fryer came to us from division," Schuller said, looking at Captains Kirkwood, O'Connor, and Ebberhardt. "His unit charged him with attempted murder after he shot his battalion commander's tent to ribbons. The major was in the crapper at the time. I talked to Fryer about it, and he volunteered to tell me what happened. He said he saw his major leave the tent, so he shot it all to hell to send the commander a message that the troops had reached the ends of their ropes with him. Apparently this major is a grade-A careerist asshole. I've had my share of dealing with the type. Not fun. While I don't agree with Fryer's methods, he certainly made his point clear. Remember me telling you about him? How his captain and first sergeant hugged him like family when they left him here?"

"Sure, now that you mention it," Ebberhardt said, nodding.

"Yeah, right, I recall the tale," O'Connor said, nodding as well.

"It's right in character that Sergeant Fryer would try to help Sergeant Wilson protect the guards and get this riot settled down," Schuller said, and looked at Colonel Webster and the chief of staff. "They may be able to help us segregate peaceful prisoners and our captive guards away from the troublemakers, so that if we go in there with force we can spare the men who aren't part of the riot."

"You really think we can trust those two?" Colonel Webster asked, and then looked past the blockhouse at the scene of chaos. "It would be nice if they got our guards and a few of the noncombative prisoners out."

"Given what I know about those two men," Schuller said, "and Captain Kirkwood can back me up at least on Wilson, I believe that if we give them the chance to bring people out, they will do it. In fact, sir, I'll wager you that they are already trying to do something like it. Despite incarceration, they just don't strike me as the kind of men to sit back and let things go to hell. I think them pulling Turner and Brookman out of the melee and protecting them demonstrates my point."

"So if we see a group of inmates coming toward the blockhouse, and it looks like Wilson or Fryer have charge of the men, then we should open the doors and let them through?" Colonel Webster said, and looked at Staff Sergeant Abduleses and Lieutenant Schuller.

"Yes, sir, that's my recommendation," Schuller said, and took a deep breath.

"What about you, Abdul?" the colonel asked. "How do you size up this situation? You think those two men might work from the inside to help us?"

"I'm quite leery of just opening the gates for a gaggle of prisoners headed for the blockhouse," the staff sergeant said, shaking his head. "I'd want guards to check the men through as they entered the building. However, the lieutenant is right about Fryer and Wilson. Despite their troubles, they seem like pretty solid Marines to me. I doubt very seriously if either of them had anything to do with this riot.

"My bet goes to that bunch of shitbirds that ganged around prisoners Harris, Pitts, and Anderson just before the movie was supposed to start. That's where my people observed the whole thing starting. Pitts and Harris got in a shoving match, Fletcher took Harris upstairs, and then Anderson and two other inmates jumped Turner and Brookman. Then from right there in that same area, at that same moment, a whole mob of prisoners jumped up and went ballistic. It looked orchestrated. Planned.

"About the same time that some of the rioters set the hooches on fire, we saw Fryer and Wilson push their way into the circle around Turner and Brookman, and they started breaking up the fight. Fryer jumped on Anderson, and it looked like he hurt him pretty good because he backed right off our guards. Then Wilson and Fryer took our men inside the block."

"HOW IT FEEL! Motherfucker!" James Harris ranted as he walked down the line of cells now containing the four guards, the deputy warden, and the watch commander. He carried Gunny MacMillan's baseball bat on his shoulder and strutted, feeling charged on a handful of little white pills that he took when he and Randy Carnegie broke open the dispensary substation in the cell block, going after the supply of psychodrugs kept there. "How it feel, now you's lookin' out from that side of them cage doors? Huh, motherfuckers? Newspaper and TV gonna be here and show the black man in charge. Show him standin' up for his rights and shit."

"Shut up," Michael Fryer yelled from inside the cage with Iron Balls and Bad John curled on the floor in a back corner and Paul Fletcher lying on the bunk, drifting in and out of consciousness. The incarcerated sergeant sat next to the lance corporal and spoke to him in a low voice. "Try to stay awake, man. You need to keep your eyes open and don't let yourself go to sleep. We gonna get you some help soon as we can."

James Harris peered through the steel front of the cell.

"I ain't hit him that hard," Mau Mau said, trying to rationalize the injured Marine into a better state of condition. "Just smacked him upside the head a little bit with gunny's bat. He too big a motherfucker to take down any other way, you know."

Michael Fryer looked out at Harris and shook his head. Then he walked to the cage door and spoke in a quiet voice.

"You know, this man will probably die tonight if he doesn't get over to Charlie Med pretty soon," the sergeant said, locking eyes with Mau Mau. "Let these guards go, so they can carry Lance Corporal Fletcher out and get him some help. Hostages ain't doing a thing for you, and this man die, you're looking at first-degree murder. I hear the feds still hang people for the death penalty. Pretty nasty way to go. Maybe they cut you a break, though, and shoot your sorry ass with a firing squad."

Fryer walked back to the bunk, and sat again with Fletcher, holding his hand and checking his eyes. The injured Marine could say nothing, and his pupils had dilated and wandered in two different directions, uncoordinated and unseeing.

"Fletch, you hear me okay, give me a blink," Fryer said, watching the man's eyelids both slowly close and then reopen. "Good, boy. You stay with me, you hear. I don't think you're seeing right now, but you're awake and responding to my voice. That's real good."

Mike Turner and Kenny Brookman both sat in the corner of the cell, their eyes swollen nearly shut and their faces bloody from the kicking they received. Both men bled from their ears, and Bad John had the crotch of his pants bloody, too. His belly ached worse than he had ever known, and he could hardly breathe due to the pain from his ribs. He felt sure that several of them had broken when Sam Martin kicked him.

"You know these other two boys ain't doing much better than Fletch," Sergeant Fryer said from the bunk, glancing at Harris, who still looked in the cage. "I think old Bad John might have a ruptured spleen, the way he's bleeding out his ass. You see that puddle under him? That ain't pee."

"So what? The motherfucker can stand to lose a little juice," Harris said and laughed.

"Look, a man can bleed to death from a ruptured spleen," Chief Warrant Officer Holden called from the cell across the aisle. "You depriving these injured men medical attention constitutes complicity to murder if any of them die. Oh, and by the way, the armed forces correctional facilities both at Portsmouth and at Fort Leavenworth still do hang men for capital offenses."

"Shut the fuck up, you cracker ass motherfucker!" Harris screamed, and slammed the bat across the front of the cell where the inmates had locked up Holden and Gunny MacMillan along with Nathan L. Todd and Donald T. Wilson. "I ain't said nothing about you openin' your honky-ass mouth. When I ask you something, then you can talk. Otherwise, stay the fuck out of a couple brothers' conversation."

The deputy warden went back and sat on the bunk next to Corporal Todd and Gunny MacMillan. Donald Wilson stood in the front corner of the cell and did not flinch when Mau Mau had swung the baseball bat into the cage door, only inches from his face. The sergeant just stared at Harris and said nothing.

"How come a brother be taking up for white trash like these dudes, man?" Harris asked Michael Fryer. The sergeant tilted his head and shrugged.

"We all children of the Lord, man," the sergeant said, and looked back at Paul Fletcher. "Jesus said to do good to those who spitefully use you. Blessed is the peacemaker. I messed up back at my unit when I shot up my battalion CO's tent. So when they locked me in this jail, I made a promise to the Lord that I'll never pick up a gun again. I'm a peacemaker, man. These men here, they just doing their job. Lance Corporal Fletcher, you busted up his head, broke bones in his skull. I felt them crunch around when I helped him lay down here. He ain't never done nothing but treat you and all these other prisoners right. He even called you mister. How many men call you mister in your life?"

James Harris looked down at the lance corporal and then glanced over at Nathan L. Todd.

"He call me mister, too, ol' Chief over there," Harris said, nodding across the aisle at the corporal. Then he looked back at Fryer. "You done fought my rangers. I think you broke a couple of Ax Man's fingers, and I know you did in his nose, takin' him down and gettin' him and Jones and Martin off ol' Bad John and Iron Balls there. That ain't right."

"What you're doin' ain't right!" Fryer snapped back. "They'd 'a killed Sergeant Turner and Lance Corporal Brookman, had Wilson and me not pulled them off these boys. I don't want no truck with you and your Black Stone Rangers. I just want to get on with my life, what I got left, when I ever get out of prison."

Harris nodded, and looked at the man.

"Tell you what, bro," Mau Mau said, and glanced back at Donald Wilson. "Your white brother over there, Wilson, him and Corporal Todd, they can carry out Lance Corporal Fletcher. I let them slide on out. They can get ol' Fletch to Charlie Med if they want to go."

"Bad John needs to go, too," Wilson said, and nodded toward Kenny Brookman, who now lay on his side, doubled in a fetal ball. "Wouldn't be a bad idea to send him and Iron Balls out together. They paid their dues, man. You got your licks on them."

Harris laughed.

"You got a voice after all!" Mau Mau said, and shook another handful of little white pills from a bottle he had stuffed in his pocket when he and the Chu Lai Hippie had raided the drug locker in the cell block sick bay. Then he popped the tablets in his mouth and looked at Turner and Brookman. "Wilson, you probably right. They done paid dues, and it look like they good Christian souls now. You boys done had a change of heart from your racist ways?"

"I'm sorry, man," Turner mumbled, and then lay Kenny Brookman's head in his lap.

"Okay, Wilson," Harris said, walking over to where the sergeant leaned against the cage door. "They go, too. We keep Gunner Holden and Gunny MacMillan for barter. My bro, Fryer, he stayin' here. I call him the Preacher Man. You like that nickname?"

"Sounds good to me," Wilson shrugged and then gave Fryer a quick smile.

"That ain't all," Harris said, and glanced back at Michael Fryer, noticing the friendly exchange between him and Wilson. "You gonna set up some negotiations with the boss man when you take these peckerheads out. He gonna come in here and meet me and my war council at the sally port."

"What do you want?" Wilson asked, looking at Harris eye to eye.

"They got to send in somebody that can talk for the man," Mau Mau said, nodding at the pretrial imprisoned sergeant. "We gots demands."

"Like what?" Wilson asked, raising his eyebrows.

"Like none of your fuckin' business, cracker," James Harris snapped, and tapped the steel door with the bat as he spoke.

"So your message to whomever is in charge out front is that you need them to send in an officer to the sally port to hear your demands?" Wilson asked, not reacting to the cracker slur.

"Yeah," Harris said, and then blinked with an afterthought. "Him and our lawyers."

"Which lawyers?" Wilson asked, shrugging.

"Not my lawyer, that stupid scarecrow-lookin' motherfucker," Harris said and laughed. "He a scary-lookin' scarecrow, too. No, I want some good lawyers."

"How many you need?" Wilson asked.

"I don't know," Harris said, and looked back at Fryer. "One might be fine, but I think two be better. These be lawyers that's on our side, not no fuckin' prosecutor motherfuckers."

"Defense lawyers," Wilson said, and wrinkled his brow. "The one who has my case is a good one. I'll ask for him. Captain Kirkwood."

Celestine Anderson had walked into the hallway and had sat down on the desk at the barred entrance. Complying with General Mau Mau's orders, he had searched the cell block and surrounding grounds for James Elmore but had not yet discovered where the rat had hidden.

"You just gonna let these motherfuckers waltz out here?" Anderson said, looking at Mau Mau.

"Fletch need a doc, and maybe Bad John, too," Harris said, looking at his cohort and inwardly worrying about how it might feel to swing at the end of a hangman's rope. "We done with them anyway. Elmore, that's the dude I want. You ain't found his raggedy ass yet?"

The Ax Man shook his head from side to side and then slid back on the desk and leaned against the wall.

"We need something back for trade," Anderson said, and glared at Donald Wilson, who had locked eyes with him. Then he shifted his look to Michael Fryer. "I want a piece of that nigger's ass 'fore we get done here. He broke my nose and bust up my hand, stompin' shit out of my fingers when he took me down. When him and white boy here be gettin' me and Jones and Martin off those two assholes layin' in there."

"Tell you what, motherfucker," Harris said and laughed. "We let ol' Preacher Man out this cage and you and him can go at it out in the yard."

"Maybe we do that tomorrow," Anderson said, looking at the big man, who had size, strength, speed, and meanness well above his own abilities.

Harris laughed and then yelled up the hallway to Brian Pitts, who sat at the gunny's desk in the control unit.

"Ax Man he gonna take down the Preacher Man out in the yard tomorrow!" Mau Mau called, his voice echoing in the building. Pitts showed a thumbs-up through the control room window and laughed.

Celestine Anderson spun on the desk to look up the hallway at Pitts, and then snapped back at Harris.

"I'm gonna kill that smart-ass, white-bread motherfucker sittin' up there like he in charge," the Ax Man seethed at Mau Mau.

"He my soul brother, man," Harris snapped back. "You ain't killin' nobody unless I say. I'm general of the Black Stone Rangers, don't forget. You a lieutenant, and Snowman, he my colonel. My chief of staff. Ax Man, you my bro, but I ain't lettin' you mess with my man. We get out this motherfucker, I let you come live with me in Bangkok. How you like that?"

"We ain't goin' noplace, bro," Anderson said, and looked at the men in the cells. "Not unless you talk General Cushman outta the keys to this brig."

"That's what we be negotiating, man," Harris said, and looked back at Wilson. "Our man here gonna set it all up. Bring us lawyers and shit so it be legal. That way they have to give what we say."

"Kirkwood's a good man," Nathan Todd said, now standing next to Wilson. "I know him from back in Chu Lai."

"Who else good, Chief?" Harris asked, looking at Todd.

"Captain O'Connor is a good lawyer," Gunner Holden offered, still sitting on the bunk. "Also Captain Ebberhardt. He just got promoted today."

"Fuck those two flour bag motherfuckers!" Celestine Anderson shouted from the desk where he sat. "They handle my trial, man. Five years all I be lookin' at before those two shitbirds fucked up my case and I end up with twenty-five years. Twenty-five years, motherfucker, and I start out sittin' on just five. No way I want O'Connor or Ebberhardt talkin' 'bout nothin' 'bout me."

"One lawyer work fine then," Harris said, shrugging at Anderson. "Yo, bro, I think that Ebberhardt dude he be Snowman's lawyer."

"Why don't you open these doors and let Wilson get these men out of here so they can go to sick bay?" Michael Fryer said, getting Paul Fletcher to his feet and holding the injured man's arm across his shoulders. "Yo, Don, you handle this big boy okay?"

"Sure can, Mike," Wilson said, and looked at Nathan Todd. "The corporal will have his hands full helping Brookman and Turner, but we'll make it just fine."

"Open them up!" Harris shouted down the hallway, and Brian Pitts pulled down the handle that sent all the cell doors rolling. He looked at Donald Wilson as he carried Paul Fletcher across his shoulders, and Nathan Todd stood between Brookman and Turner, helping both men walk. "Rangers will lead you across the yard, then you go on your own when you deal with the boys in the tower that got those machine guns."

Harris laughed as the four guards and Donald T. Wilson walked down the hallway. "Don't go and get your ass shot!"

"As long as none of your rangers fuck with us, we'll make it out in good shape," Wilson said, walking to the stairwell, now lifting Lance Corporal Fletcher across his shoulders and starting down.

"I FIGURED IT was only a matter of time before I ran into you boys," Jack Hembee said, walking onto the blockhouse front porch where Terry O'Connor, Jon Kirkwood, and Wayne Ebberhardt stood by a table with three five-gallon vacuum jugs of coffee lined up on it and several plastic sleeves of insulated paper cups laid next to them.

"I thought you rotated home back in March," Terry O'Connor said, filling a cup of coffee for the major and handing it to him.

"I did," Hembee said, blowing across the top of his drink and then skimming a sip of the steamy brew. "About six years ago I married this sweet little Texas rose from Tyler. I don't know if you've heard of the place. It's between Dallas and Houston, kind of down in East Texas. Everything went dandy with her, she loved life as an officer's wife until I got sent to Vietnam last year and she had to leave base housing at Camp Pendleton. I sent her home to Tyler when I did my tour here."

Major Danger blew over his cup and took another careful slurp of coffee, then walked to a wooden bench set near the blockhouse front door and sat down. He patted a place next to him, motioning for the lawyers to take a seat, too.

"Well, Dixie, that's her name," Hembee continued, "she caught the itch and needed to do a little traveling. So she and her girlfriend, Beverly, they hopped in my 1967 Corvette Stingray and shot on down to Houston, where they commenced to having a hell of a lot of fun with an old boy they met at the Hilton Hotel named Spencer Kelly.

"Now, good old Spencer and his low-life compadres, who never saw a day of military service in their lives because their oil-rich daddies bought and paid for the local draft board, they wined and dined Dixie and Beverly and apparently a few other West Pac widows on a regular basis. They'd hang out at Trader Vic's and the Warwick Hotel, go to the livestock show and rodeo at the Astrodome, dressed up in their fancy cowboy suits, and generally took up the conjugal slack for the husbands of these women while their men served overseas, here in Vietnam.

"I get home last March, and the first thing Dixie tells me is that she has found a new life in Houston, with her new circle of wealthy friends, and that she no longer feels at home as the wife of a Marine. Especially now that she is against the war and all."

Terry O'Connor laughed and shook his head.

"I'm sorry, Major Hembee," he said. "I don't mean to laugh at what happened to you. It just reminded me of a blond Swedish girl I left in New York. She sort of has a similar attitude."

"She know old Spencer Kelly?" Hembee said with a laugh, and slapped O'Connor across the shoulders. "That boy does get around."

"No, but she sure gives me hell about my joining the Marines and serving in this war," O'Connor said, smiling.

"Well, shit, boys," Hembee said, taking larger gulps of his coffee now that it had cooled. "I got my car back, turned it over to my brother to keep care of it, and I put in an AA form, volunteering for another tour in Vietnam."

"You didn't divorce Dixie?" Kirkwood asked, narrowing his eyebrows at the major.

"No, I didn't," Hembee said with a laugh. "I figure the best way to fuck her back is to stay married to her. She can't file for divorce while I'm over here, so it kind of fouls up her plans of marrying one of those oil-rich Houston boys, or old Spencer himself."

"I'm sorry to hear about your marriage, Major," Kirkwood said, and then clasped his hands. "I guess I am awfully lucky. My wife, Katherine, she got a job teaching school in Okinawa just on the off chance that I might get a hop over there during my tour here. She's back home in California now, and I never got to the rock either. But she did that out of love for me. Just to try to be near me. Lots of wrecked marriages coming out of this war, so I am awfully lucky to have a girl like Kat."

"Well, here's to Katherine Kirkwood then, and all the women like her," Hembee said, raising his coffee cup in a salute.

"So you've gone back to Seventh Marines?" O'Connor asked, and noticed Movie Star dashing out the blockhouse door and looking around in a big hurry.

"No, they put me to work at Three-MAF operations for the time being," Hembee said, finishing his coffee and crushing the cup in his hand. "I'm selected for lieutenant colonel, and next month when I pin it on, I will pick up command of a battalion. Probably one with the Ninth Marine Regiment. General Ray Davis has command up north and he asked for me by name, once I put on my silver oak leaves."

"Congratulations!" O'Connor said, raising his coffee cup along with Kirkwood and Wayne Ebberhardt, saluting the major. "I guess it will be Colonel Danger now."

Hembee laughed, "I guess so, but somehow it doesn't have that ring that Major Danger does."

"Sir!" Lance Corporal Dean said, finally seeing Captain Kirkwood sitting on the bench between the other officers. "Major Dickinson needs you inside like five minutes ago!"

"What's going on?" O'Connor asked, getting up with Kirkwood and the others.

"One of the prisoners, a big guy, he carried out one of the guards on his back and led out three others," Dean said, talking fast from his excitement. "They're all beat to hell. One guy's nearly dead. They got a medevac chopper inbound for them right now. The one guy has a serious head injury. Got brained with a baseball bat."

"What about the prisoner?" Kirkwood asked, curious if it was who he suspected.

"I don't know, sir," Movie Star said, and opened the steel front door to the blockhouse for the captain and the others. "All I know is that he wanted to talk to you, so the chief of staff and Major Dickinson sent me out to find you."

WHILE DONALD T. Wilson carried Paul Fletcher down the stairs, and Nathan L. Todd followed him, helping Kenny Brookman and Mike Turner negotiate the trek without falling, Brian Pitts left his perch in the control unit and walked down the passageway to his cell and laid down. The white-faced wall clock behind the gunny's desk showed two-fifteen in the morning, but to the Snowman it felt much later. So he decided to take a nap.

He had just closed his eyes when James Harris stepped inside his cell.

"Yo, Snowman, what's up?" Mau Mau said, tossing back his head and slapping the bat across his palm.

"Fucking after two o'clock in the morning," Pitts answered, lacing his hands behind his head as he lay on his bunk, looking back at his old partner. "Thought I'd catch me a few z's before the shit comes down in the morning."

"Shit like what?" Harris said, reaching in his pocket and taking the last of the little white pills.

"Probably nothing," Pitts sighed, "but if I had that reaction team, I'd make an assault at about daylight. Catch us sleeping."

"Nobody sleeping, man, except maybe you," Harris answered, taking a swig of water from a green plastic canteen that he picked up from the table in Pitts's cell.

"What's that you taking? Any good?" Pitts asked, changing the subject to avoid any conflict with his drugged-up friend.

"Uppers, man," Harris smiled. "Old Carnegie, he know his shit. He know the name of every pill we got in the sick bay."

"Yeah, he does know his shit," Pitts said and smiled. "So you're wired for the night, then."

"Hey, I feel like King Kong, man," Harris beamed. "Ain't nobody takin' me down tonight, bro."

"You're having lots of fun, aren't you," Pitts said, closing his eyes and yawning.

"Bet that Hippie got some shit that will make you wake right up, man," Harris said, looking at the Snowman trying to sleep.

"Maybe later," Pitts answered, still keeping his eyes closed.

"So what you thinkin' 'bout?" Harris asked, frowning.

"Our money and our dope, man," Pitts said, and sat up and looked at Harris. "You're having the time of your life, lord of the cell block. Meanwhile, I'm thinking about Huong and Bao sitting on two million dollars of our cash, and a million dollars' worth of dope that I can turn into fifty million in two weeks flat."

"Now, how you done that?" Harris asked, and sat on the bunk by Pitts. "I know you sellin' shit in Da Nang, but three million dollars is a lot of cash to just scarf off some dope-smokin' doggies and Marines in I Corps."

"What we sold here didn't amount to jack shit, man," Pitts said, and lay back on his bunk. "The big cash came from the major hauls of heroin and Buddha I put in contractor containers and got loaded on ships that carried it back to San Francisco."

"See, I figure somethin' like that, but you ain't tellin' me shit," Harris said and then frowned. "Why ain't you trust me, man? I thought we bros."

"You didn't need to know," Pitts shrugged. "If it makes you feel any better, I didn't tell Huong, either. He knew what I shipped, because he set it up with the Viet Cong to supply what I needed. He didn't know my contractors or my buyers. Only me. Huong arranged for the deliveries to get trucked down to the port at China Beach, but who brought the money and who made the deals were always a mystery to him. Of course, he didn't really care, because he was living well and getting rich, too."

"For sure, man," Harris smiled. "That little time at the ranch, that's the best I ever live in my life. Man, like millionaires."

"We *are* millionaires, man," Pitts said, and then blew out a deep breath. "We just need to get out of here and get to Saigon."

"So let's slip out now, while everybody sleepin'," Harris said, and then looked around to see if anyone lurked outside who might hear their conversation.

"You didn't see that company of Marines set up outside the wire?" Pitts said, closing his eyes. "We get shot the second we cut through that fence. No way anybody leaving here now. Not unless he can slip through the crowd in the blockhouse."

"How he do that, man?" Harris asked, bewildered at the suggestion of simply walking out the brig's front door.

"They're going to want to segregate the prisoners who aren't part of the riot from the rest of us guilty bastards," Pitts said, now sitting up and whispering to Mau Mau. "Our brother Bobby Matthews, you haven't seen him lately, have you."

"No, I ain't seen the boy since we all took cover under that picnic table, while those bastards was still shootin' up in the towers," Harris said, scratching his head.

"Well, while you were having your heyday as King Run Amuck," Pitts whispered, smiling, "and don't get me wrong, that's okay, it's not hurting a fucking thing for you to have your fun. Anyway, while you raised hell, Bobby and I had a nice talk. I told him to play it cool and stay low. Buddy up with the guys not causing trouble, and when the guards let them out, which they will do, you can count on it, slip out with those boys. Nobody saw him do shit. I don't think they'll recognize any of us from the fence, so I think Bobby's cool."

"So they take him over to them hooches across the road and he just slip off in the trees?" Harris said, spreading a big smile, feeling smart for coming to that conclusion without help.

"No," Pitts said, wrinkling his mouth as he spoke. "I told Bobby to do his time and be the model prisoner. All they got on him is desertion. He surrendered as soon as the shooting started at Saigon, and never fired a gun at anyone, so I think he's okay with that issue. Only thing he's got to deal with is his desertion. Like I said, six-six and a kick, and he's out."

"So he do his time and he get discharged, and then how the fuck you expect that poor, dumb son of a bitch to get to Saigon?" Harris said out loud.

"Bobby may be quiet, and he's not the strongest or the toughest dude on the block, but he's smart," Pitts said, and then added, "he's loyal to a fault, too. Never told me a lie, and never tried any smart-ass shit with me either, like a certain Mau Mau I know."

"Hey, man, I always be true blue, bro," Harris said, puffing his cheeks, feeling hurt.

"Brother, you *are* true blue, absolute," Pitts said and put his hand on Harris's shoulder. "So is Bobby. He's a good guy."

"So how he gonna get to Saigon?" Harris asked, still puzzled. "You know they can him out at Pendleton."

"Exactly," Pitts said and smiled. "My contractor, from Da Nang, he's up in San Francisco. This guy floats back and forth from Da Nang and Saigon to the Bay Area, and Seattle. He's a construction contractor, all the time going and coming. Bobby will catch a bus up to Seattle and make a phone call to my man in Frisco."

"Oh, so the fat man in Da Nang, he your connection to shipping the dope," Harris said, smiling. "Now I know."

"He's one of three, but he's a key man in the operation," Pitts whispered, and sat up to speak close to Mau Mau's ears. "Bobby will let him know about our stash in Saigon. And that I want this guy to put him on the company payroll, and that we will pay him ten cents on every dollar we make shipping the dope."

"Damn, bro!" Harris whispered, opening his eyes wide. "Bet that get his attention. What like five million if we do fifty million?"

"Hey, you're quick," Pitts whispered, and then lay back on his bunk.

"So, Bobby, he know where the dope hid?" Harris asked, kneeling by the bunk and whispering.

"Generally," Pitts said, closing his eyes. "He knows Huong and his people out west of Saigon. They also like him, because he is quiet, does not lie, and he's totally loyal. A lot like Huong. Like I said, Huong and Bao are sitting on our cash and our stash. They have it tucked in a good spot. The Viet Cong, they cool with us, too. They want to do business because the money's good, and they got an endless wholesale supply coming out of China. Everything's gonna be cool. We just got to be patient and work things out with this brig nonsense."

"So what we do? We just go do time, too?" Harris asked, standing up and frowning at the Snowman.

"We'll do what we do," Pitts answered, still keeping his eyes closed. "Once Bobby gets out, and has all the connections made, he's gonna use some of our cash to hire us a no-shit law firm that will get our young asses out of jail."

"What's gonna stop that boy from just gettin' all of a sudden greedy like a motherfucker, and leave our young asses in the can?" Harris asked, sticking out his lower lip like a pouting kid.

"Huong and Bao will stop him," Pitts said, opening one eye.

"What we supposed to do now?" Harris asked, walking toward the cell door, his head jammed with confusing thoughts.

"Mau Mau, why don't you and Ax Man and the Hippie, and all our Black Stone Rangers brotherhood, just do your thing and enjoy the moment," Pitts said, rolling on his side, trying to sleep. "If it looks interesting, I might jump in, too. None of us sure as hell are going anywhere very soon. So we might as well live it up."

"What about that rat's ass Elmore?" Harris said, walking into the passageway.

"Good question," Pitts said and sat up. "We probably ought to get rid of him. After today, he'll probably want to talk about everything, including what all he saw go down in here, or maybe overheard."

Harris smiled a wide grin and took the baseball bat and slapped his palm with a loud smack.

"I find that motherfucker, I'm gonna lay the wood to him," Mau Mau said, and took a full swing through the air.

"Everyone is watching us," Pitts said, and thought for a moment. "While you might enjoy laying the wood to the motherfucker, I think we need to let Ax Man do it. Out in the yard. And we do not want to be anywhere near it when it goes down."

"Shit, man, that ain't no fun," Harris frowned.

"Swinging on a rope ain't no fun, and you sure as hell can't get rich doing it," Pitts reminded his pal.

"WHAT'S THAT CLOWN got in his hands?" Staff Sergeant Orlando Abduleses asked the spotter from one of three scout sniper teams from Seventh Marine Regiment that Major Danger had brought as part of the reaction force. The sniper had set up his rifle on the sandbagged parapet that surrounded a twelve-foot-square room built atop the blockhouse with expansive windows on all four sides so that sentries stationed there could observe the prison yard and its surroundings. Doors opened from each side of the blockhouse observatory, and led to a catwalk that ran the entire length of the administration building's roof. At each end of the gantry that overlooked the prison yard, the guards had set up sandbagged emplacements and manned an M60 machine gun in each of them. The towers at the two back corners of the prison also had similar machine-gun positions.

Terry O'Connor and Wayne Ebberhardt had followed the staff sergeant up the concrete stairs inside the blockhouse that led to the rooftop observation station. They had tried to persuade Michael Carter to come with them, but he refused and seemed frozen in front of a window, looking out into the prison yard. His lips moved rapidly as he whispered to himself, and every so often he made the sign of the cross by pointing the fingers of his right hand from his forehead to the center of his chest, then to his left shoulder and last to his right.

Major Dudley L. Dickinson hovered near the chief of staff, Major Hembee, Lieutenant Schuller, and Colonel Webster who talked with Jon Kirkwood and his client Donald T. Wilson. Since O'Connor and Ebberhardt had nothing to do, they trailed after the staff sergeant when he jogged upstairs.

"Wow, much better view up here," Ebberhardt said as he and O'Connor stepped behind Abduleses, the two snipers, another prison guard, and a photographer from the joint wing and division photo lab who stooped behind a huge gray lens mounted on a tripod with a thirty-five-millimeter single-lens-reflex camera attached to the rear of the foot-and-a-half-long optic.

"That's a fire extinguisher, Sergeant," the photographer said, and clicked a picture of an inmate who had just run out of the back door to the kitchen, which sat at the rear of the chow hall in the lower part of the cell block. "Looks like he's carrying a bucket in the other hand."

"Yeah, that's what he's got," the sniper's partner said as he peered at the man with an M40, twenty-power spotting scope. "What the hell does he want with a bucket and a fire extinguisher?"

Suddenly a loud boom echoed across the prison yard and balls of fire leaped out of the kitchen windows and blew the steel back door off its hinges. Another explosion followed, sending a massive fireball skyward with thick, black smoke. A second prisoner ran from behind the kitchen, carrying a bucket in each hand, and joined the man with the fire extinguisher. As flames roared from the chow hall, the latter inmate took one of his buckets and threw it at one of the chow hall's side windows. Immediately, fire exploded from where he had hurled the bucket.

"Kerosene, I should have guessed," Abdul said, looking back at the two lawyers. "All the cooking and heating equipment in the kitchen runs on kerosene. That must have been the five-hundred-gallon tank out back that they blew up. You wouldn't happen to know either of those two outstanding citizens, would you?"

"The tall guy that had the two buckets and tossed one, that's Sergeant Randal Carnegie, better known among the I Corps herbal society as the Chu Lai Hippie," O'Connor said, immediately recognizing the man as soon as he saw him. "I'd know that bum anywhere."

"Kevin Watts," the prison guard standing on the other side of the sniper team said. "The prisoner with the fire extinguisher. He and Carnegie are tight. Watts is doing three years for a whole host of petty crimes, along with trying to hijack an Air America gooney bird down at Chu Lai and have the pilots fly him out of Vietnam. The crew disarmed him as soon as he pulled the gun, and then he tried to claim that the pilots had framed him, and that he had never had a gun or had even gotten on their plane. He's a real piece of work, Sergeant. I think the man even lies in his dreams. You never get a straight answer out of him, even for the time of day."

"You know this guy pretty well then," Ebberhardt said to the guard.

"He's one of the men in the two hooches that I supervise, sir," the guard answered.

"What the shit is he doing with that fire extinguisher?" O'Connor asked, seeing both Carnegie and Watts pumping the handle up and down in the top of the long cylinder.

"They've filled it with kerosene, sir," Abduleses said, looking at the two men through binoculars. "They probably dumped the soda mixture out of the can, washed it out, and refilled it with kerosene from that big tank we used to have behind the chow hall. You know, the big boom we heard. Those fire extinguishers work just like a garden sprayer. Pressure it up, and it will squirt thirty feet or more. We used to have water fights in the barracks with them all the time. That was fun. I'm afraid this might get ugly. Hot kerosene, lots of fire."

Randy Carnegie had set his bucket down next to the one Kevin Watts had carried out of the kitchen, and ran back toward the picnic tables. Then Watts took the hose off the side of the fire extinguisher, pointed it toward the cell block roof, and opened the valve, sending a geyser of kerosene more than twenty feet in the air. He lowered the spray toward the fire leaping from a nearby kitchen window and then raised it back toward the roof. After he did this several times, the stream caught fire and sent a string of flames onto the roof, igniting the kerosene he had already sprayed there as well as the line of liquid shooting from the fire extinguisher hose.

"Just like a fucking flamethrower!" Watts shouted, looking over his shoulder and laughing at Randy Carnegie.

"Oh, shit, Kev, it has the roof going good now!" Carnegie shouted back, jumping up and down with excitement.

Then Watts swung the flaming stream around and shot it toward the Chu Lai Hippie, who dodged out of the way. The jet of burning fuel splashed fire across the picnic table behind Carnegie, sending prisoners running in every direction.

"How good a shot are you?" Staff Sergeant Abduleses asked the sniper who followed the prisoner with the fire extinguisher with his rifle scope.

"You want me to take this man down?" the sniper asked, not moving from his eyepiece.

"Let me get clearance from the colonel, but I may need you to try to shoot that fire extinguisher, if you can hit it," Abdul said, picking up a field phone and ringing it downstairs. A voice answered, and the staff sergeant asked for Colonel Webster.

After a brief conversation on the telephone, the staff sergeant looked at the sniper and then glanced back at the other guard and two captains in the room with him.

"Any of you guys have an idea of what might happen if this sniper shoots that can?" Abduleses asked.

"It'll blow up," the sniper said, still looking through his rifle scope. "Lots of oxygenated kerosene vapors under pressure, given how those two pumped it up. No question, a big bang. The good news is that the explosion will mostly vent from the hole my bullet makes. Probably rip out that side and make the cylinder take off like a rocket. Sort of like putting a firecracker under a tin can. Might be pretty spectacular."

Terry O'Connor smiled. He liked the idea of shooting the canister and watching the surprise of the idiot who used it like a flamethrower on the other prisoners.

"Either of you captains have any objections if I clear this sniper to shoot that fire extinguisher?" Abdul the Butcher asked.

"See if he sets it down, then shoot it," Ebberhardt suggested.

"We can't wait too long; he may kill someone if he showers them with that burning kerosene," Abduleses said, again looking at the man with his binoculars. "Sniper, take your shot when you see a good opportunity."

"Randy!" Kevin Watts screamed, laughing and shooting the burning fuel toward the fleeing prisoners. "Throw those other two buckets into the cell block!"

Carnegie ran behind Watts, grabbed the first bucket, and hurled it at the window but hit the wall. Fire jumped as the liquid splashed against the concrete. Then he picked up the second bucket and just as he hurled it at the window, he heard what he thought sounded like a single gunshot, but then the fire extinguisher jumped past him and exploded skyward with a deafening boom. So he considered that what he had heard was the fire setting off the kerosene gas inside the pressurized container.

The concussion from the explosion knocked both inmates off their feet and the fire extinguisher hurled across the night sky, leaving a trail of burning vapor in the air behind it.

"Wow, man!" Kevin Watts screamed, looking at the canister sail over the roof of the cell block. "Fucking cool! Fire must have got inside and blew it like a bottle rocket. Fucking outrageous, man!"

The Chu Lai Hippie got on his knees and slapped the hand of Kevin Watts, celebrating their successful destruction of the chow hall, and setting the cell block roof ablaze.

"They don't have a clue!" Staff Sergeant Abduleses said, and turned to the other Marines, laughing. "Those have to be the two dumbest people on this planet tonight."

"Someone running to the wire!" the sniper said, following the fleeing inmate with his rifle scope.

James Elmore had sneaked to the kitchen and crawled in the stainless steel pot cabinet when James Harris had released him, just after the riot began. He had lain in the small space all night. Then when everything around him burst into flames, he ran through the fire and out the opening where the kitchen's back door had blown off its hinges when Kevin Watts had set off the kerosene-fired pot boilers, cooking stove, and ovens. Had Elmore not hidden in the stainless steel cabinet, the violent force of the explosions in the kitchen would have killed him. He hoped that his good luck would still hold true as he made a desperate run for the fence.

"We've got inmates running after him now," the prison guard said, watching with binoculars.

"Mind if I get a closer look?" Terry O'Connor asked, and took a pair of binoculars from the staff sergeant.

"You know that man?" Abduleses asked, looking at the captain.

"That's my client James Harris," O'Connor said, frowning as he handed the binoculars back to the staff sergeant.

"I thought that was him," Abduleses said, watching the prisoners now capturing the fleeing man, knocking him to the ground, and dragging him back toward the cell block by his feet.

"I suppose there is no way to stop them," O'Connor asked, watching Elmore writhing on the ground as the inmates dragged him. His screams echoed through the prison yard. "You know, they'll probably kill him."

"No great loss, if you ask me," Staff Sergeant Abduleses said, looking blankly at O'Connor.

The lawyer looked back at Abdul the Butcher, started to say something, but then shook his head. He agreed that James Elmore offered the world little good, and most likely never would be missed. However, the vision and sounds of the helpless man screaming and struggling as the inmates dragged him by his heels to the sally port as the fire spread across the roof would live in his mind forever.

"WHOA, MAN!" BRIAN Pitts said as he awakened, coughing from the acrid smoke that filled the hallway and upstairs cells. When he opened his eyes he saw fire licking through several holes in the roof, and he leaped to his feet and ran out of his cell.

"Hey! You can't leave us here!" Chief Warrant Officer Frank Holden screamed at him. He, Gunny MacMillan, and Michael Fryer sat in the cell farther down the passageway, coughing.

"Fucking die, motherfuckers! Fucking roast in hell!" Kevin Watts screamed, running from the top of the stairs, dashing toward the entrance to the cell block control room.

"Get out of my way, dirt bag," Brian Pitts growled, and shoved the skinny derelict to one side. Then he ran to the wall and pulled down the control handles, releasing the locks on all the cage doors. "Where the fuck is Mau Mau, and who set the roof on fire?"

"Harris's downstairs, man." Watts smiled his slimy grin at the Snowman, and then proudly pointed to the roof. "Me and Randy got that motherfucker to burning. Ax Man told me to let you and those three assholes burn. Said I should lock your door if you still asleep."

"Fuck-an-A you say!" Pitts snapped, glancing toward the stairwell. "I guess I'm lucky I got out before you had a chance to shut me in then, you slimy little roach."

"No, man, I wouldn't let you burn," Watts said with a smile. "I was gonna wake you up an' get you out. Let them out, too. Honest! Ax Man, he one crazy motherfucker. Wantin' you all dead, man."

"Get the fuck outta my way," Pitts snarled, and wrinkled his nose. "Even in all this smoke you're chokin' me out smellin' bad."

"Snowman, I'm sorry, man," Watts whined and trailed behind Pitts, trying to gain a little favor. "We ain't got no water now. So I can't wash all the kerosene and shit off me. I'm sorry I stink."

"Disappear, you fucking maggot!" Pitts yelled, then he turned and looked at the three men he had just released, who also followed him. "I don't know what I can do for you guys, but I sure as hell don't want you dead. Maybe when we get downstairs you can slip out through the crowd and confusion."

Chapter 21

JAILHOUSE JUSTICE

"YO, MOTHERFUCKERS!" BRIAN Pitts bellowed as he stepped from the stairwell, and threw Kevin Watts down the hallway toward the sally port where Ax Man and Mau Mau had James Elmore hanging from the bars overhead the gateway. They had tied his feet and hands with mattress ticking ripped from beds the inmates had torn apart, and suspended him to the entrance's upper frame with the heavy blue-and-white-striped fabric.

Celestine Anderson hissed and showed his teeth behind curled lips when he saw the worthless body of Kevin Watts slide along the concrete floor after the Snowman had slung him down and sent him skidding.

Frank Holden and Ted MacMillan crouched behind Michael Fryer in the stairwell, staying in the darkest shadows to keep out of sight. The three Marines hoped that Brian Pitts could distract the mob so they could slip out via the sally port. With James Elmore now trussed by his heels like a pig awaiting the knife, screaming and sobbing, the deputy warden and watch commander as well as Fryer quickly realized that they had no realistic chance of escaping through that door right now.

Heavy smoke billowed down the stairwell, leaving the two hostage brig supervisors and their compatriot fighting back the urge to cough, which would draw attention to their presence. Trying to filter the air, the men slipped their noses and mouths under the necks of their T-shirts. The trio knew that unless something dramatic happened soon, they would have to step into the crowd.

"Kill my ass, will you! Burn me in my bed, that right, motherfucker?" Pitts yelled at Celestine Anderson, and then charged full force at the Ax Man.

"Ho!" Mau Mau Harris shouted, and jumped between the Snowman and Anderson, wrapping his arms around Brian Pitts and pushing him backward, away from Ax Man, who now laughed and beckoned the aggressor, taunting him and waving his hands while he danced like Muhammad Ali.

"Come get it, cracker-ass motherfucker!" Anderson jeered, glancing over his shoulders at Clarence Jones and Samuel Martin, who also began to shout their own dares at Brian Pitts.

"He sent that rat maggot upstairs to lock me in my cell!" Pitts said, pointing to the floor where Kevin Watts still lay. "Ax Man told him to let me burn to death with Fryer and the gunny and Gunner Holden. He was running up there to lock my fucking door, but I got out before he made it to control, the motherfucker!"

"Ax Man, you tell Watts to do that shit?" Harris asked, still embracing Pitts and looking at his enraged ranger lieutenant. "You know I told you the Snowman is my main man. Take him down, you take me down, too."

"No, man, I ain't told that shitbird nothing," Anderson said, and then glared at Watts on the floor. "That lyin' sack of shit! If I want to kill a motherfucker, I'd done it myself. You know that about me, bro."

Seeing that he had no allies, Kevin Watts scrambled on his hands and knees to the sally port, and then jumped to his feet and fled outside.

James Harris and Brian Pitts ran after the departing slimeball, boxing James Elmore's head like a punching bag as each man shoved his way past the dangling prisoner. When Harris stepped off the concrete porch, following Watts with his eyes, watching as the creep scrambled under a table next to his buddy, the Chu Lai Hippie, Mau Mau noticed three men starting down the sidewalk from the blockhouse. Pitts saw them, too, and fell in step behind the ranger leader.

Mau Mau watched as one of the three men ran from the other two at about the midpoint in the recreation yard. He quickly recognized the burly shape of the third person's body when he ducked under a picnic table. It was Donald T. Wilson.

"Stupid motherfucker," Harris said, watching Wilson as he talked to inmates and then dashed to the next picnic table. "Fuck him."

"Looks like Lieutenant Schuller and probably that lawyer, Kirkwood," Brian Pitts said, walking behind Mau Mau Harris. Celestine Anderson, Sam Martin, and Clarence Jones now followed on their heels, and then the mass of other Black Stone Rangers flowed out of the sally port behind those three inmates.

As Michael Fryer made his way to the door, he climbed up the sidebars to the gateway and began pulling at the mattress ticking that held James Elmore by his feet.

"Here's my pocketknife," Chief Warrant Officer Frank Holden said, handing the blade to the sergeant.

One swipe and Fryer had the prisoner's feet cut free, and the wriggling, terrified man fell into the arms of Gunny MacMillan.

"Here you go," Michael Fryer said to the gunner as he handed him back his knife and then climbed off the bars.

The deputy warden quickly cut the bonds off the prisoner's wrists, but then grabbed a handful of the man's T-shirt and held tight, so he didn't try to flee through the crowd and draw the mob's attention to them. Gunny MacMillan casually slipped through the sally port behind the distracted prisoners as the last of them jammed behind their leaders in the recreation yard. Then he took a good look outside.

"No way we're going to get through that cluster-fuck right now," he said over his shoulder to Fryer and Holden. "You see anyone down at the library?"

"Looks empty. It might be a good place to take cover," the warrant officer said, and then coughed. "Lots of smoke, though, building up here. I can see lots of fire down at the end of the passageway, in the chow hall, so that exit's blocked. Looks like they piled all the tables in the middle of the dining area and then touched them off."

"We go in the library, there's no way out. I think we're better off waiting out here, near the door, where we can get away from the fire," Fryer said, trying to appraise their options. "No way they're going to let this dirtbag that they just had strung up simply walk through that crowd. I bet that you two guys can get out, though, if you just step through that door and start walking. I don't think they'll do anything out there in the open. Not with all that brass and the whole guard company up in the blockhouse and on the fences watching them. That's your best chance to escape, right now."

"I can't do it, Sergeant Fryer," Chief Warrant Officer Holden answered after thinking about what the sergeant said to him. "Ted, you take a run for it. I have to stay here. They'll kill this man. I can't let that happen."

"Gunner, we're better off sticking together, all four of us," MacMillan said, looking out the sally port at the unruly mob. "Let's fall back near the library door and wait. They may forget about us."

"Not likely when they notice Elmore not hanging where they left him," Holden said and smiled. "They'll eventually come looking, but maybe whatever has their attention right now will buy enough time so that the guard company can storm these assholes. I don't understand why they haven't done it before now. Maybe because of the darkness, but now it's starting to get light."

"They've got two important hostages, sir," Michael Fryer reminded the deputy warden. "If I'm the commander of the reaction force, I'm going to be reluctant to storm the place until I know where you and the gunny are, and that you're okay. I think if you two will make a run for it, then the guard company may go ahead and shut down this riot. Just my opinion, sir."

"Gunner," Gunnery Sergeant MacMillan said, looking out the sally port and seeing the silhouettes of two men approaching and noticing glints of silver flashing off their collars, "here comes the distraction: Two officers approaching. I think it's Lieutenant Schuller and a taller guy with him. Looks like they've finally come to powwow with Harris and his boys."

Frank Holden looked out the door, too.

"That's the lieutenant, all right," he said, and if I'm not mistaken, the other guy's Captain Jon Kirkwood. Just like Harris asked. Looks like our side decided to take advantage of the invitation so they can run recon before assaulting. If we can hold out a little while longer, until the good guys attack, we'll have it made."

NINE MEN CROWDED under the last of the picnic tables that Donald T. Wilson had to visit. While Lieutenant Schuller and Captain Kirkwood listened to Mau Mau Harris's and his Black Stone Rangers' demands, the pretrial confined sergeant had agreed to gather as many peaceable inmates he could find and lead them to the blockhouse while the two officers held their parley. Talking to this final group, in the poor light he did not recognize Kevin Watts and Randal Carnegie, who slouched with their heads down.

"Obviously you're not part of the cause of this disaster, or you'd be over there with those fucked-up individuals," Wilson said to the group. "If you want to get out of this mess, get some chow and a place to sleep, then follow those two officers when they start back to the blockhouse, unless they instruct you otherwise. That's Lieutenant Schuller, and a lawyer named Captain Kirkwood. They're arranging for Harris and his gang to allow you to leave with no trouble."

"You think it's cool?" Robert Matthews said, crouching close to Wilson. "The guards won't open fire on us, will they? I mean, what if they think we're going after the warden and that captain?"

"Don't sweat it, we're cool. I was with the lieutenant when he gave Staff Sergeant Abduleses the instructions. No shooting," Wilson said, and put his hand on the smaller Marine's shoulder. "Lots of guys out here, like you and me, want no part of this shit."

"That's me, Jack," Bobby said and smiled. "I'm probably lookin' at six-six and a kick for desertion, but that's all. I can do six months standing on my head, but these guys rioting, they're looking at a couple of years, aren't they?"

"I don't know, but I bet a couple of years is probably the minimum," Wilson said, looking out from under the table and watching Mau Mau Harris waving his hands with excitement as he talked. He could hear the echo of his voice but couldn't quite make out what he said.

"Look here, motherfucker! I'm the man, now. So listen the fuck up," Harris ranted, and pointed at Mike Schuller as he spoke. "You goin' to do what I say, or we start stringing up hostages. You dig?"

"Settle down, Mister Harris," Kirkwood interrupted. "Things are not nearly as bad as you might believe. So far you and your men have killed no one, and that's good. However, we do have three guards hospitalized, and that's not so good. We'll know more about their conditions later this morning, but they're alive and we're optimistic. Releasing them so that they could get medical attention put you in good stead with the powers that be. You've killed no inmates, have you?"

"Fuck no, man," Harris snapped. "We all bros in here. We tight. We together. This a protest, man. We ain't intendin' to kill nobody. Not unless you make it happen. Anybody die, it's your fault, not mine."

"Some of the men out here in the recreation yard, they may want to go ahead and move out, get a little chow and some rest at the temporary quarters we've established across the road," Schuller said. "It would look good for you if you at least allowed those prisoners who wish to leave, to do so."

"Ain't nobody but you keepin' any man inside this brig," Harris said, and looked over his shoulder at Brian Pitts, who nodded his approval of Mau Mau's assertion. "I seen Wilson come out the door with you, and then jump off in the rec yard. He probably got all the chickenshits told what to do by now anyway. Like I said, they free to go, they want to."

With that comment, Lieutenant Schuller turned toward the recreation yard and shouted, "Listen up! This is the warden! You men who wish to leave the yard, please get out from under the tables and form two lines at the blockhouse doors! You're free to depart at this time!"

Bobby Matthews crawled from under the table first, and then stood and looked with a hint of a smile at Brian Pitts and James Harris, who stood twenty yards away from him. The Snowman watched as his and Mau Mau's silent partner joined more than two hundred other inmates who formed double lines at the blockhouse back door. Then he looked back at the lieutenant and the captain, who continued to explain that even though the Black Stone Rangers had destroyed the brig, it was not as bad a situation as they might imagine. All could be put back in order if they began cooperating. The release of the nonviolent inmates represented a positive step.

AS THE SKY began to brighten with Saturday morning's gray dawn, red coals still glowed in dark piles of debris that at one time stood as prisoner hooches but now lay as smoldering ashes. Overhead, fire roared and crackled from the burning roof of the cell block, and then with a sudden crash part of it fell to the floor of the chow hall. The massive collapse blew out a plume of red and orange sparks that drifted across the prison yard and showered the long, double line of inmates that moved past a gauntlet of guards outside the blockhouse back door.

Michael Carter watched from the window of the prison administration building, where he had kept a vigil, praying most of the night. Every now and then he wandered to the front porch and got a cup of coffee. Once, looking for Wayne Ebberhardt and Terry O'Connor, he climbed the interior stairs to the upper deck and the observation-post and machine-gun positions. The look of the prison from above scared him.

As the devout Catholic man gazed across the field of horror, seeing the men running for their lives, screaming from the ring of burning hooches and the out-of-control fire that engulfed the chow hall and spread farther and farther onto the cell block roof, he thought of how similar Hell must look to this place. It made him start to recall passages from the "Inferno," written in *The Divine Comedy* by the thirteenth-century Florentine poet Dante Alighieri. With the lawyer's fluence in Latin, and his equal understanding of French and Italian, Carter had read and studied the classic work in its unspoiled, original text.

Watching the turmoil below him, he recalled Dante's cantos and imagined how he must have felt descending into the bowels of Satan's kingdom, led by his unassuming guide, Virgil. The smoke, the rain of sparks, the smell of Hades at his feet sent the pale lawyer's head to spinning, and he stumbled most of the way as he finally fled down the stairs and ran outside to throw up.

The gagging and coughing awakened Lance Corporal Dean, who had made himself a bed in the jeep by folding the passenger seat forward and stretching out on the back bench. He asked Captain Carter if he needed some help, but the tall, skinny man only looked at him and shuddered. So Movie Star lay back on his makeshift bed and shut his eyes.

After standing over the brink of Hell, virtually smelling the brimstone as he watched the anguished souls thrashing about, and then seeing Lance Corporal Dean, and having the vision of the man masturbating in the red light, surrounded by pictures of naked women, Michael Carter felt his body shake in disgust. It sent his stomach into another somersault, and he wretched several dry heaves.

Then he noticed a water trailer in the parking lot, hooked behind one of the six-by trucks, and the distraught Michael Carter ran to it and pulled open a valve. Cupping his hands under the flow, he splashed the cool liquid over his face, head, and on the back of his neck. Then, holding his hands under the faucet, he gulped a big drink of it.

Earlier, Carter had tried to listen to Major Hembee talk with Major Dickinson, the chief of staff, the provost marshal, Lieutenant Schuller, and the other three lawyers. He wanted to help, too, but all his mind could see was Dante's Hell. He needed to pray, so while the officers planned their strategy, Michael Carter spoke to God about the disaster, begging His mercy for all the embroiled souls.

Now, as he watched out the window and saw the long double line of prisoners formed, and his friend Jon Kirkwood standing by his friend Michael Schuller, and the prisoner who led the riot had finally quit waving his hands in the air, appearing to have settled upon reason, Michael Carter felt better. Perhaps God had heard his frantic prayers and now finally delivered the men to safety.

"WE AIN'T SHUTTIN' nothin' down till we get news cameras in here, showin' our protest," Harris said, and then looked back at the crowd of sympathetic faces behind him. "People back home got to see the black man standin' up for his cause. Discrimination got to stop."

"Mister Harris," Lieutenant Schuller said, "take a look up in the guard towers. Don't you see the news cameras?"

Both Pitts and Harris shifted their eyes upward and noticed the long lenses set on tripods. At the distance they stood from the towers, all they could recognize were the big gray optics.

"How long they been up there?" Pitts asked, now trying to recall what all he had done in the open, just in case someone had snapped a picture of him.

"The news media got here just after this mess started," Kirkwood lied. "Hell, you can see the fire from the city. We didn't have to call them. They came running when they saw smoke."

In reality, the III MAF commanding general had ordered his staff to keep all news media away from the brig. He knew that the incident would gather smaller headlines and fewer pictures and television coverage if all that the reporters saw were piles of rubble and no riot.

The command information officers told journalists that a faulty fuel storage device had caught fire, and burning kerosene spread through the brig. He assured the newsmen that the command had evacuated all prisoners to a makeshift compound they had established nearby, and cheerfully added that no one had suffered any injuries, and the damage was confined to the buildings inside the prison. Because of security concerns with the prisoners in the unusual circumstances, no one except authorized military personnel could enter the area at this time. He faithfully promised photographers and reporters that once the military police had relocated all the prisoners, the media could take pictures of the damage, sometime later in the day or surely by Sunday morning in the worst case.

Several news photographers and a television crew had tried to drive up Hill 327 despite the commanding general's orders, but South Vietnamese authorities and U.S. military police turned them back well out of sight of the Freedom Hill brig. The information specialties officer at the roadblock dutifully promised the news crews full access to the story as soon as Marines on the scene gave him the green light. For now, however, because of prisoner security, concern for those men's rights, as well as the safety of the journalists, the reporters had to keep away.

"Yo, Ax Man!" Harris yelled over his shoulder, beaming. "We got news cameras up in the towers all night, man. We goin' to get on Walter Cronkite! Folks back home goin' to know all about our protest!"

Then the forty-two disorderly Black Stone Rangers who remained defiant with James Harris began to wave and scream at the cameras.

"I will give the colonel your demands, and Captain Kirkwood is my witness," Schuller said, trying to regain the distracted riot leader's attention.

"Fuck that! The man got to see those demands," Harris countered, focusing back on the two officers. "You ain't got no rank to say what's what, and that colonel, he just a go-between. General Cushman, he got to deal with this shit."

"I assure you," Kirkwood said, looking at both Pitts and Harris, "General Cushman will have a full appraisal of all that has happened, and will address each of your demands. However, I will tell you realistically that some of them we will not even consider. Such as releasing you, and just letting you disappear out of the country, even though you promise to never show your face in the United States or Vietnam again. That's impossible."

"Fuck, man, we got to ask," Harris said and laughed. "Never know, the man might like to see all us shitbirds fly the coop and be shed of us."

"I'm sure he'd love to be shed of you, Mister Harris," Kirkwood said, smiling. "However, you know very well that will not fly. Neither will the demand of no punishment for anyone. You will have to face charges, and you will have to take responsibility for this damage. I guess on the good side, it's mostly property damage, and a few minor injuries, except for the three guards. You and the others will face charges for assaulting those men."

"Fuck you, then," Harris snapped. "I want out of this motherfucker! I only act in self-defense, man. I ain't part that other shit, that assault on Iron Balls and Bad John."

"You'll receive your day in court, and all the evidence will be weighed," Kirkwood said, looking squarely at Harris. "If the guard attacked you, then we will take that into account. As for some of your other demands, I agree with you. We do need to insist that units visit their members in the brig, and that they provide them support, such as new uniforms, health and comfort items, and communications with their families and other members in their units. Also, prisoners should not have to address any enlisted guard as 'sir.' I have already voiced concerns of my own in some of these same areas as well, and I can assure you that we will visit with the commanding general about all of these matters, and some others."

James Harris smiled and looked at Brian Pitts, and then back at Celestine Anderson, Sam Martin, and Clarence Jones.

"Yo," Mau Mau chirped. "We gettin' someplace now."

"What about the hostages you're holding?" Michael Schuller asked, and looked directly at Brian Pitts. "Where are Gunner Holden, Gunny MacMillan, and the inmates you have taken prisoner with them? More importantly, what are their conditions?"

"They all just fine!" Harris snapped, and then looked at Brian Pitts, who nodded. "We got them inside. That dude, James Elmore, he joined up with the rangers. He one of us now. Ain't that right."

"I'd like to see Mister Elmore," Kirkwood said. "His attorney has raised concerns about his safety."

"Fuck his attorney!" Celestine Anderson shouted. "Fuck all you moth-erfuckers."

"Yeah," Harris said, realizing that except for his handful of rangers who remained at his side, the majority of prisoners now made their way through the blockhouse. "We done talkin'. You go see General Cushman and see what he say about what we ask. Then you can come back and maybe we talk about releasin' them hostages and turnin' this brig back to you. We let you see Elmore then, too."

"Very well," Schuller said, looking across the now empty recreation yard. "If you men wish to surrender at this time, we can avoid a great deal of trouble. It would go well for you, if you surrendered. At least release the warrant officer and the gunny."

"Fuck that shit! I ain't stupid. We keepin' those dudes with us for now, so you all don't try nothin'. We sure the fuck ain't surrenderin'. So get that shit out your head, I ain't doin' nothin' until you come back here with General Cushman sayin' that he's willin' to make a deal. Do us right," Harris said, and then turned his back on the officers. He walked toward his gang of Black Stone Rangers and raised his bat in the air, triumphant, while his men shouted in celebration and Jon Kirkwood and Mike Schuller walked quickly back to the blockhouse.

"WHOA, STICKHORSE!" STAFF Sergeant Abduleses said, catching Kevin Watts by the shirt as he tried to slip past him, just ahead of Randal Carnegie. "This man and that other one there, take them to the side for a little one-on-one."

"Fuck this shit," Watts yelped, and then ducked under the hands of the guards who went for him.

Seeing Abdul grabbing at his pal Kevin, the Chu Lai Hippie stepped out of the line of men and dashed away from the blockhouse before any-one could put a hand on him.

"Wait up!" Watts shouted at Carnegie as the two men now beat feet toward the sally port, where their ranger comrades gathered outside and now looked up to see that the entire cell block roof burned out of control.

Several of the Black Stone Rangers began pulling wooden picnic tables and benches into a circle, turning them on their sides and stacking the material to form a makeshift fortress.

Donald T. Wilson helped some of the rangers take the table where he had hidden to the growing pile of outdoor furniture. He fell into line behind the crew, as if he, too, would go back and grab another set of benches and table, but he peeled off at the last moment and jogged to the cell block and fell in with another gang. This new gaggle seemed at a loss of what to do next. They mostly looked up at the roof and watched the fire destroy their last shelter. Some of the men took a seat on the ground or lay down, so the sergeant joined them.

Where he squatted, he could see the sally port and Sergeant Mike Iron-Balls Turner's metal two-pedestal desk. It stood untouched in the open booth, and Celestine Anderson sat in the swivel chair by it with his feet cocked on top. No one had found the Model 870 Remington twelve-gauge folding-stock shotgun loaded with ought-two man-killers that Iron Balls had hidden in the back of the desk, stuffed between the steel rear panel and the two columns of side drawers.

"Pull everything out from both sides and the shotgun will fall to the floor. It's got seven ought-two rounds loaded in it, so if you have to use it, make them count," Turner had whispered to Sergeant Wilson as they approached the blockhouse when the prisoner led them to freedom and saved Lance Corporal Fletcher's and Lance Corporal Brookman's lives. Iron Balls had made a special point of letting the friendly inmate know about the shotgun, because he worried that if the wrong man got his hands on the weapon the blame would eventually fall back in his lap. Lieutenant Colonel Webster and Lieutenant Schuller had specifically forbade guards from carrying any firearms within the interior confines of the brig.

When the medical corpsmen took away Fletch and Bad John, both Nathan Todd and Mike Turner gave Donald Wilson a hug. Todd tried to remain in the blockhouse, but Colonel Webster ordered him to sick bay with the others.

"Good luck," Iron Balls had said, and gave the man another hug and whispered in his ear while he embraced him. "You're going back in, aren't you. That's why I told you about the shotgun. I hope you can get your hands on it before those crazy sons of bitches in there find it. Maybe you won't have to use it, but it'll damned sure be good to have if you do need it."

In some respects, Don Wilson had wished he didn't know about the deadly weapon hidden only inches from the most unstable prisoner on the loose. Just knowing that the shotgun lay in the back of the drawers and could easily fall to the floor put his stomach in a full twist.

Sitting with his head down, resting it on his wrists with his arms wrapped around his knees, the sergeant tried to discreetly look inside the cell block entrance. He had remained behind, after sending out all the non-violent inmates, so he could retrieve the shotgun and help his fellow sergeant and new friend, Michael Fryer, escape the rangers, along with the deputy warden and the gunny.

Inside the cell block he could hear shouting, and he raised his head trying to get a better look.

"How come these motherfuckers ain't dead?" Celestine Anderson bellowed when he saw Mau Mau Harris and the Snowman bringing Gunner Holden, Gunny MacMillan, Michael Fryer, and James Elmore toward the sally port. "They suppose to get cooked in that cell upstairs!"

As the group made their way outside the burning building, Brian Pitts looked at Anderson and smiled.

"So you didn't send anybody to kill us, huh?" Snowman said, touting the Ax Man. "You lying sack of shit!"

"Fuck you!" Anderson screamed and charged after Pitts.

Calmly, in a fluid motion, the Snowman turned toward his assailant, parried off the Ax Man's roundhouse right swing with his left forearm, thrust his knee into Anderson's groin, and slammed his right elbow into the attacker's throat. Pitts held nothing back, and let the full force of his movement carry through with his blows. The counterattack took the man off his feet and sent him to the ground, where he crumpled in a heap, moaning.

"Damn, bro!" Harris exclaimed and laughed. "I don't know why I worry about that nigger wasting your lily ass when you the baddest motherfucker I seen lately. Where you learn that shit?"

"Robbie's Pool Hall on the south side of Kansas City, bro," Pitts said, taking James Elmore by the arm and leading him toward the pile of benches and tables. Gunner Holden, Gunny MacMillan, and Sergeant Fryer followed close behind, with Harris now covering their rear with the baseball bat in his hands.

Once they had escorted their hostages to the picnic table fortress, Mau Mau turned and raised both his empty hand and the fist wrapped around the handle of the bat, waving them over his head.

"We gonna have court, motherfuckers!" Harris shouted to his congregation, and laughed between each of his announcements. "The gunner and Gunny Mac, they gonna observe. My man, the Snowman, he gonna be judge. The honorable Judge Pitts, presiding! Now, ain't that the pitts?"

Mau Mau laughed hard at his little joke and then added, "I'm gonna be the prosecutor, and when the Ax Man catch his breath and swallow his sore balls back down out of his throat, he gonna be the defense lawyer for these two ratbag traitor motherfuckers we got on trial here."

When Mau Mau pointed at Michael Fryer and James Elmore, the entire gathering of forty-four Black Stone Rangers, including the Chu Lai Hippie and Kevin Watts, who had returned to ranger ranks from the blockhouse, cheered. Don Wilson stood, too, and raised his fist like the others, but kept his voice quiet.

ALL OF THE inmates who took advantage of the opportunity to leave the riot and surrender themselves peacefully to the guards at the blockhouse back door now ate a hot breakfast of scrambled eggs, bacon, sausage, toast, apple sauce, orange juice, and coffee. Instead of having more food trucked from the Da Nang Air Base dining facility, Lieutenant Colonel Webster arranged for a detachment from First Force Service Regiment to put together a field kitchen at the temporary prison compound across the road from the brig and cook breakfast there. The light morning breeze carried the smell of the food into the recreation yard and wafted where Mau Mau Harris and his rabble now shouted and jeered behind the haphazard fortress of piled-up picnic tables and wooden benches they had built since they could no longer take shelter inside the burning cell block. The provost marshal theorized that the smell of scrambled eggs, bacon, and coffee on the morning breeze might help to hasten the unruly mob to give up their stand.

Staff Sergeant Orlando Abduleses had just sat down with his plate of scrambled eggs, bacon, and toast, and had put a metal spoon in his cup of coffee when he saw a GMC M880 pickup truck with the canvas top taken off the wooden ribs above its cargo bed and what looked like twenty or thirty lumpy duffel bags piled in it.

"Special Services has finally come through!" Lieutenant Colonel Webster said, sitting across the folding table from Abdul and several other prison guards.

"What's in the bags, sir?" Abduleses asked, while shoving a piece of toast in his mouth, followed by a spoonful of eggs.

"All the baseball and softball gear that wing and division had in Da Nang," Webster said, smiling.

"We going to play baseball?" Abdul said with a laugh, and looked at the other guards eating at the table with him and the provost marshal.

"Bats," Webster said, and winked at Abduleses. "I got the idea watching that asshole Harris swaggering around with the one that Gunny MacMillan kept in control. Along with bases, balls, and mitts, each of those bags from Special Services has half a dozen bats inside."

Abdul the Butcher smiled at his cohorts as Major Jack Hembee came to the table and pointed at the truckload of baseball gear. "I see that the chief of staff worked his magic, and it looks like they brought every sack of equipment in the barn," the major said with a big grin. "My alpha has one of our reinforced rifle platoons headed over here now. Between your guard company and my guys, we should be able to field at least a hundred batters."

"We count about fifty bad guys left inside, so with a two-to-one edge, I think that those inmates who might consider resisting will think again when each of them sees two Marines apiece with baseball bats in their hands," Webster said, smiling confidently.

"BEFORE WE HANG this guilty motherfucker!" James Harris shouted, laughing toward his jury that included Samuel Martin, Clarence Jones, Kevin Watts, and the Chu Lai Hippie along with eight other Black Stone Rangers, handpicked by the Ax Man and Mau Mau together. "We got to have ourselves a fair trial decided by this lyin' dog's peers. Now, you jurors that we selected, you the most lyin' dogs we know!"

All the rangers gathered with their backs toward the burning cell block and laughed at Mau Mau Harris's comedic routine. Then Celestine Anderson stood up and kicked over the bench where he sat next to James Elmore, tumbling the hapless bum to the ground.

"First of all, Mau Mau, I ain't no good at this defense lawyer bullshit, mainly because I not only want to kill this motherfucker, but that one, too," Ax Man said, and pointed at Michael Fryer. "Why don't you let me be prosecutor, and you defend these two shitbags."

"Okay, motherfucker, if that make you happy, then you prosecute and I'll defend," Harris crowed, strutting to the overturned defense bench where James Elmore sat in the dirt, crying.

Brian Pitts had taken a seat on a picnic table he had set upright as the judge's platform. He had a yard-long, two-inch-by-four-inch-thick table leg that someone had broken from one of the piled-up picnic sets, and rapped it across the wooden planks where he sat, calling the court to order.

"How does your client plead?" he asked Harris and laughed, waiting for the ridiculous answer he knew he would get from Mau Mau.

"Before I plead this motherfucker guilty as charged, we need to tell the court what this waste of breath done to deserve havin' his head cut off!" Harris proclaimed, and then laughed at Elmore. "This stupid piece of shit ratted out everybody he ever knew. He stole money from your honor, and got his self busted! To wit!"

Harris laughed at himself, reciting the legal jargon.

"To wit, motherfucker!" Mau Mau said again, and laughed. "Tryin' to get his slimy ass off the hook with C-I-fucking-D, he ratted out his main man and his only living friend, namely me, and his honor, the Snowman."

"Guilty as charged then!" Pitts said, rapping the table leg, and then looking at Celestine Anderson, who glared at Mau Mau Harris. "Does the prosecution have anything to add before we decide what sentence our man Elmore should receive from this court?"

"Wait one motherfucking minute, motherfuckers!" Anderson roared, leaping from his bench, where he sat alone, and walking to the center of the court arena. "What the fuck I suppose to do? The fucking defense done prosecuted and convicted the motherfucker!"

"You win, motherfucker!" Pitts said with a laugh, and then rapped his table-leg gavel. "How about you tell the court how we need to deal with this piece of shit sitting over there."

"That'll work," Ax Man said and then looked at James Elmore, who sat in a pathetic slouch, sobbing, his piss-soiled pants wet again and his gold tooth dripping slobber. "How about we tie the motherfucker on one of these tables and throw his ass in the fire!"

A roar of approval came from the gallery of rangers who edged closer in a tightening semicircle around the freshly condemned prisoner, the up-coming defendant, and two so-called observers.

"I wanted to see him wearing a stool-pigeon necktie myself," Brian Pitts suggested, and looked at Mau Mau Harris.

"What the fuck's that?" Anderson asked, getting the Snowman's attention back on him.

"Cut the motherfucker's throat and pull his tongue out the hole!" Harris called to Anderson. "You ain't never heard of doin' that shit before? I thought you's a tough dude from Houston, man."

"I ain't never seen a dude get his throat cut and his tongue pulled out," Anderson said, looking back at Harris. "We do that and then tie the motherfucker to the table and burn his ass."

"I vote for that!" Harris cheered, and looked at his client, who now fell off the bench, passing out from the terror.

"Bury the motherfucker alive!" Randal Carnegie shouted from the group of rangers who made up the jury. "That's a whole lot worse than anything. Think about layin' underground and bein' alive and you can't move or see or nothin'. Then you start runnin' out of air. It takes hours to die like that!"

"I want to cut this motherfucker's throat and burn his ass," Harris screamed, and then grabbed James Elmore off the ground.

Seeing the attack on the pathetic and nearly helpless man, Michael Fryer leaped to his feet and tackled Mau Mau Harris. Celestine Anderson immediately jumped into the fray, while Sam Martin ran to the "judge's" bench, yanked the two-by-four from Brian Pitts's hands, and clubbed Michael Fryer from behind.

"This guilty motherfucker gonna get his throat cut and burned, too!" Anderson said, giving the injured prisoner a hard kick in the ribs.

"You won't kill anyone with me here!" Chief Warrant Officer Frank Holden screamed and then ran to where Michael Fryer and James Elmore both lay. Gunnery Sergeant Ted MacMillan leaped to his feet, too, and now stood over the deputy warden, ready to fight.

Suddenly from behind the crowd two gunshots echoed across the prison yard, one in close succession after the other.

"Nobody killing anybody except maybe me wasting the first son of a bitch that lays hands on any of those men!" Sergeant Donald T. Wilson shouted, holding the 870 Remington shotgun with its barrel now leveled at the crowd of Black Stone Rangers.

While the prisoners held their kangaroo court, Wilson had slowly moved behind, man after man, until he came even with the sally port. Then he eased his way to the gate, crawled under the desk, and pulled open the drawers. Just as Iron Balls Turner had told him, the shotgun fell to the floor.

"I've got five more rounds in this ally-sweeper. Anybody want a taste of ought-two lead, just make a move," Wilson yelled, walking toward the group, which parted for him like Moses dividing the Red Sea. "Gunny, you and the gunner grab up those two Marines and let's head to the blockhouse."

STAFF SERGEANT ABDULESES had taken his station in the observation tower, preparing for the assault on the prisoners that Major Hembee and Lieutenant Schuller would lead as soon as Lieutenant Colonel Webster had given them the go-ahead to execute the assault.

"Who fired those shots?!" the provost marshal immediately screamed on the field telephone in the lower level of the blockhouse, where he sat with the chief of staff and Dudley Dickinson.

"Shot came from the yard, sir!" Abduleses answered, holding the telephone receiver between his shoulder and his ear and looking at the scene below in the recreation area with his binoculars.

"Who is shooting?" Webster asked, panic in his voice.

"Prisoner Wilson has a shotgun, sir," Abduleses answered, watching the rangers part ways for the group of hostages the sergeant now led toward the blockhouse. "I have no idea how he got his hands on the weapon, but he's got the gunner and Gunny MacMillan carrying two prisoners toward the blockhouse, and he's guarding their rear."

"What about Harris and that bunch?" Webster asked, now starting to smile.

"They're just standing behind that pile of tables, watching Wilson point that shotgun at them," Abduleses said and laughed.

"Let's take the sons of bitches down then!" Webster growled and smiled at the chief of staff as he set the telephone receiver back in its pouch.

In seconds, more than a hundred helmeted Marines wearing flak jackets and wielding baseball bats poured through the back door of the blockhouse and quickly formed an assault line facing the mob of rioters, who now crouched behind their wall of picnic tables. Jack Hembee blew a single blast on his police whistle, and the reaction force and brig guard company let out a loud growl and began rapping the ends of their bats on the ground.

"You men behind that wall, step out with your hands on top of your heads!" Mike Schuller shouted through a bullhorn. "Those who remain behind that wall will face these Marines and their bats!"

Brian Pitts stepped out first, then came Mau Mau Harris, Sam Martin, and Clarence Jones. After seeing no place else to run, Kevin Watts followed, too, and so did Randal Carnegie. Gradually, more and more of the now defunct Black Stone Ranger rebellion surrendered. Finally, Celestine Anderson, the last man out, walked to the center of the recreation yard.

A FINE RAIN fell across Da Nang and Freedom Hill on Sunday morning. It cooled the smoldering ashes of the burned hooches and the now fire-gutted cell block. The guard company still used the blockhouse for their administrative offices and the prison sick bay, overseeing the temporary compound across the road, now encircled by several high rolls of concertina wire and German tape.

They really didn't need to put up the fence, since all the inmates contained in the makeshift brig posed little threat of violence or escape. They all had short times to do and wanted no trouble.

On another slope of Freedom Hill, the military police had trained and housed a company of working dogs. Mostly German shepherds, but a few Labrador retrievers and a couple of Belgian shepherds filled the ranks of canines used by the American military to run down spider holes and ferret out Viet Cong soldiers hiding there, or to find bombs or to now sniff out dope stashes in the barracks and at the airport in the inbound and outbound baggage.

With all the usable jail facilities now destroyed, Lieutenant Colonel Webster found it somehow poetic that he put the high-risk inmates and the nearly fifty former Black Stone Rangers in the working dogs' kennels. He had the military canines temporarily housed in hooches with their handlers. While the secure dog facility offered metal-covered, chain-link pens with uncomfortably cramped quarters for the inmates, Major Dudley L. Dickinson assured the provost marshal that nothing in the *Manual for Courts-Martial, Staff Judge Advocate Manual,* or the Uniform Code of Military Justice prohibited him from keeping these prisoners there.

Brian Pitts had the kennel next to Celestine Anderson, so the two men spent the rainy Sunday either glaring at each other or watching the water drip off the corrugated steel roof that slanted over their heads. The brig guards put Kevin Watts and Randal Carnegie in a run together, which the two men didn't mind at all.

"Hey, that's cool, the Hippie had said, crawling through the three-foot-high door that led inside the roomy, plywood doghouse and lying down on a thin mattress spread over the concrete floor. Kevin Watts sat outside, under the tin roof fastened over the chain-link dog run, watching the rain drip into growing puddles that surrounded the kennel's cement slab floor.

Mau Mau Harris drew a solitary cell next to Sam Martin on one side, and Clarence Jones on the other. Mau Mau lay on his stomach, gazing out the kennel, watching the raindrops splash in the puddles.

Chapter 22

GACA

A FLUTTERING, NOT quite buzzing sound rattled down the law center's main hallway, and Jon Kirkwood ducked his head just in time as Chopper, the errant cockroach, made a low pass at him, winging his way back to the nest he had built in the hole where the water pipe came through Charlie Heyster's office wall. Michael Carter had flattened himself against the bulkhead, banging his back against the photographs of President Lyndon B. Johnson, the commandant of the Marine Corps, General Leonard F. Chapman Jr., and the commanding general, III Marine Amphibious Force, Lieutenant General Robert E. Cushman Jr. When he stepped away after the dive-bombing roach had made his pass, the three pictures fell to the floor, shattering the glass from their frames.

"Now look what that bug has caused!" Carter wailed, and knelt to collect the broken shards while Staff Sergeant Pride sought out the office broom and dustpan in the utility room.

Chopper had gotten fat on granules of Carnation Coffeemate dry creamer, and today had a hard time launching from the open shoe box full of oatmeal-raison-walnut cookies that Vibeke Ahlquist had sent to Terry O'Connor, which he in turn set out at the enlisted coffee mess for everyone to enjoy. The now overweight North Florida palmetto bug especially appreciated the captain's gesture.

When Sergeants Michael Fryer and Donald T. Wilson stepped through the door at the end of the hallway, it had surprised the insect as he grazed on the sugary treat. Fearing a swat from the two strangers, he jumped skyward and spread his sails, beating his way to shelter and safety.

Kirkwood and Carter had just finished a short talk with Derek Pride when they saw the two free Marines step through the back door and start down the passageway toward them when the big roach flew by, causing stick man to wreck the photographs.

"Damn, that bug's as big as a helicopter!" Wilson exclaimed, seeing the flying monster dip past Kirkwood and Carter.

"Everybody says that," Terry O'Connor said with a laugh as he and Wayne Ebberhardt stepped out of the defense section's office and welcomed the pair of visitors.

Just as the five men finished shaking hands, Major Dudley Dickinson, First Lieutenant Melvin Biggs from the provost marshal's Criminal Investigation Division, and a military policeman with a yellow Labrador retriever burst through the front door.

"Everyone stand up and step away from your desks and then stay put!" Dicky Doo shouted in a deep, drill-instructor-style growl to show he meant business. "Stanley, you and Captain Bailey-Brown step out of your office, too!"

Then he looked down the hall at the defense section.

"All of you men, come on up here!" Dickinson bellowed. "Is there anyone left inside your office?"

"No, sir," Jon Kirkwood said, walking slowly toward the administration section and law center's front entrance, followed by the two sergeants, who only came to say hello and thank you, and the three captains.

Terry O'Connor laughed when he saw Charlie Heyster bound through the front door and try to go to his office, but had the CID officer cut him off.

"Skipper, you'll have to wait out here with the other men," Lieutenant Biggs said, noticing that the narcotics-sniffing dog had focused his attention on the former prosecutor and now temporary military justice officer, and had sat down on point in front of the major-select.

"That's okay, lieutenant," Dicky Doo said, and put his hand on Heyster's shoulder. "He's not part of this investigation. This is our deputy staff judge advocate and military justice officer, Major-Select Charles Heyster. I think it's fine if he goes to his office."

"Sir, if you please," Biggs answered, still looking at the dope dog, and then glancing up at his handler, who shrugged and smiled. Then he looked at Charlie Heyster and Major Dickinson. "Just to do this thing right, if you gentlemen don't mind, it would really work best if you both joined the other officers and enlisted Marines standing over there. That way no one can say we singled anyone out. It'll make our investigation much more compliant with Marine Corps guidance regarding search and seizure, and inspections of this nature."

"Oh, certainly," Dickinson said and smiled. Then he took Charlie Heyster by the arm and led him next to Stanley Tufts and Philip Edward Bailey-Brown.

"Is this your entire staff?" Lieutenant Biggs asked, looking at Staff Sergeant Pride and Lance Corporal Happy Pounds standing by him, both men smiling so much they nearly laughed.

"Well, Captain Bushwick is in Okinawa, about three weeks past due from when I wanted him back here," Dicky Doo said, and flushed red when he thought of how the Brothers B had rooked him into taking turns on rotating duty at Camp Butler. Dickinson had devised a way to see his wife by taking a turn at the temporary assignment, split three ways. Captain Bailey-Brown had gone first, but when Miles Bushwick went for his week-long turn, he managed to convince the Fleet Marine Force Pacific staff judge advocate that to preserve continuity in the work, one attorney should take care of the entire assignment. Bushwick managed to stay on the rock, and would rotate home from there. Rightfully, Dicky Doo felt used.

"Anyone else not here that we didn't see in the barracks?" Lieutenant Biggs said, writing down Bushwick's name in his notebook.

"All of our enlisted people, except these two and our visitors, you saw when you went through the barracks," Dickinson said, nodding at the investigator.

"Gentlemen, Sergeant Jim Reilly and his partner there, Manfred, will conduct a narcotics inspection of your working area," Biggs announced. "All quarters will be searched equally. No one has been singled out, nor do we have anyone who is a specific suspect at this time. If you have any contraband in your possession, or wish to surrender any contraband in your working space, please do so at this time. Surrendering such contraband will not exonerate you from any charges for possession of narcotics or any other controlled substances, but it may help reduce some charges that may be brought against you. If you do fall under suspicion for possession during this inspection, you will immediately be informed of your rights and then taken into custody. Is that clear?"

"Knock yourself out, Lieutenant," Terry O'Connor said, and cracked a wide smile at Charlie Heyster. "Help yourself to any and all quarters. We have nothing to hide."

"Come, Manfred!" the handler called at the dog and pulled hard on his lead. The Lab got up, turned, and then looked back at Charlie Heyster and sat down.

"Search!" the handler ordered again, and pulled the dog away from the captain.

The first office he let the retriever sniff out was the prosecution section.

"Lieutenant Biggs, we have the evidence locker in that room, so the dog will alert on the dope that we keep in there," Dickinson called to the investigator and dog handler as the Lab sniffed the desks, and then sat down in front of Heyster's old workplace.

"Do they keep evidence in this desk?" the handler asked, pulling open the side drawers, looking for anything that might have set off the dog.

"Of course, they work on cases and handle evidence at those desks, so you're probably going to get false positive readings," Dickinson suggested, seeing the canine detective sitting stubbornly at Heyster's old desk.

"He didn't alert on any of the other desks, just this one," Lieutenant Biggs said, now concerned that he may have an officer who dealt in dope.

"That's the lead prosecutor's desk, so he may have spilled some in the drawers when he handled the evidence," Dickinson offered, and then looked at Heyster, who had now broken a sweat.

"Why don't we come back to this one later," Lieutenant Biggs suggested, and then led the handler down the hallway, where they checked the head and the utility room, and then went to the defense section. The dog walked straight past the cookies on the side table and never gave them a second thought.

"Now, that's impressive!" Wayne Ebberhardt said, looking at Terry O'Connor. "Old Manfred has his shit wired for sound. My dad's black Lab, Captain Morgan, he would have gobbled up those cookies before you could have pulled his head back."

"These dogs are well trained," Dickinson said, and put his hand over Terry O'Connor's and Wayne Ebberhardt's shoulder, and then looked at the two sergeants and smiled. "Congratulations on your good work, Sergeant Fryer and Sergeant Wilson. General Cushman told me that he fully agreed that you two deserved a second chance. Glad to see you're free and clear."

"Thank you, sir," Fryer said and put out his hand for Major Dickinson to shake.

Donald Wilson extended his hand, too, and shook the major's in turn after Fryer.

"Your recommendations to the general really helped us, sir," Wilson said, and then glanced back to see the wide-eyed expressions on the faces of all the officers, except for Heyster, who still seemed distracted and watched the doorway of the defense section, waiting for the dog and investigators to emerge.

"You spoke up for our boys?" Jon Kirkwood said to Dicky Doo. "I knew that several people went to bat for them, but you, sir? You did that? I'm impressed, and grateful on behalf of my client."

"Yes I did, and why not?" Dickinson answered, and then put his arms around the shoulders of the two sergeants. "You know, in Korea, I made it to sergeant. Then I went home, put myself through college and law school, using my G.I. Bill, and then returned to the Marine Corps with a commission. I knew a few good men in my time. I know one when I see one. These two fellows set a fine example for any Marine, officer or enlisted."

"Thank you, sir," Jon Kirkwood said, and with a big smile put out his hand for the major to shake.

"Right on, Major!" Terry O'Connor followed, and shook Dickinson's hand, too. So did Wayne Ebberhardt and Mike Carter.

"All clear down here, Major Dickinson," Melvin Biggs called through the hallway. "Since we didn't find anything stashed in that desk in the prosecutor's office, I'll write it up as the dog alerting on residue left behind from handling evidence."

"Well, I guess that wraps it up, then," Charlie Heyster said, and then sighed happily.

"We still need to check those two front spaces," Biggs replied, pointing at Major Dickinson's office and Captain Heyster's.

"Oh, that's my office and the one next to it is my deputy's," Dickinson said, and walked to the front door of the law center. "There's nothing there."

Then he put his arm over Melvin Biggs's shoulder and began walking the lieutenant toward the door.

"Like you said, it is possible that we lost some evidence receipts along the way when we turned the dope over to your people to destroy," the major said, shaking his head. "Staff Sergeant Pride is so meticulous, though, keeping track of everything right down to the gnat's ass, I felt certain that someone had ripped off the evidence locker. Nobody's perfect, not even our man Pride. We'll have to be more careful with our accounting. I guess it's my bust. Sorry to have wasted your time."

"Sir," Lieutenant Biggs said, stopping short of the front door, and then looking back at the dog handler, who frowned at him. "To do this inspection by the book, we really ought to cover the entire building. We still ought to check those two offices. No one could complain or raise any suspicions then, saying that we conducted our inspection improperly or favored anyone."

"Major Dickinson, sir," Terry O'Connor said, and stepped close to the lieutenant by the front door, "I think it would make the troops feel better if you checked the whole building, too. They wouldn't feel as though you singled them out and then excluded yourselves. You and Major-Select Heyster, that is."

"Damn it, O'Connor, you're wearing my patience thin," Dickinson growled, and then had Charlie Heyster interrupt him.

"This officer has a busy schedule, and you'd require him to waste his time on a wild goose chase just to make the enlisted people feel better," Heyster said, taking his pipe from his pocket and slapping it across the palm of his hand.

Manfred immediately sat down and looked at the captain.

Dicky Doo noticed the dog pointing on alert this time, and his face drained pale as he looked at Terry O'Connor, who stepped back to the side of Jon Kirkwood and beamed a wide smile at him and nodded.

"Go ahead, Lieutenant," Major Dickinson said, and then took Charlie Heyster by the arm. "Why don't you and I go sit in my office until these people finish."

"Right after we check your office, Major Dickinson, then you can go in and have a seat, both of you," the lieutenant said, and accompanied the dog handler as he searched the major's workspace.

No one spoke for the five minutes it took for the dog to clear Dicky Doo's office. The lieutenant waved at the major, and allowed him and Captain Heyster to go inside and have a seat. Then they went into the shyster's workspace.

Terry O'Connor looked at Michael Carter, who leaned against the wall and had tears dripping from his eyes.

"They're going to bust Charlie, aren't they," Carter whispered, his voice quivering as he spoke.

"It's okay, Mikie," Jon Kirkwood said, and put his arm around the sad palm tree of a man.

"Good boy!" a voice from inside Heyster's office spoke. Then in a moment the lieutenant walked out carrying the captain's leather pouch filled with pipe tobacco and went into Dicky Doo's office.

"Look here! You cannot arrest me! Those assholes out there in the hall planted that in my tobacco pouch," Heyster protested, and then hurried out to the hallway and pointed at Jon Kirkwood. "He did it! He put that in there! He put that fucking cockroach in my tobacco, too, and now he's trying to frame me!"

Lieutenant Biggs hurried after the captain and took him by the hand.

"Sir, I need to advise you of your rights," Biggs said, and then led Charlie Heyster to the chair by Derek Pride's desk and sat him there.

"I know my fucking rights, Lieutenant!" Heyster snapped. "I'm a fucking lawyer, for Pete's sake! The damned lead prosecutor!"

"Sir, I must charge you with possession," the CID investigator said, and took out handcuffs and put them on the captain's wrists. "We will go to the provost marshal and book you. Then I imagine that the chief of staff and the commanding general will take action on the charges. Typically, you will be confined to your quarters. It's just a possession charge, sir."

When Michael Carter heard the lieutenant's comment that it was just a possession charge, he thought about Raymond the Weasel. That was just a case of simple possession, too, and Charlie Heyster railroaded the man.

"Lieutenant," Terry O'Connor said, and walked to the investigator, "I think it will be more than simple possession. I have some photographs you will want to see, and you will want to take statements from me and the men who accompanied me when we took those photographs."

"Pictures of what, sir?" Lieutenant Biggs asked, and then looked back at Heyster, who now looked wild-eyed at Terry O'Connor.

"We observed and photographed Captain Heyster exchanging a package that looked like narcotics for an envelope that appeared to contain money," O'Connor said, and shook his head at the former prosecutor.

"Do you know who he made the exchange with, sir?" Biggs asked, and motioned for the dog handler to stand by the handcuffed captain.

"Yeah," O'Connor said, and frowned at Heyster. "A man who's sitting in one of your dog kennels right now. Randal Carnegie. My troops call him the Chu Lai Hippie."

"Do you recall the date and time of that exchange by any chance?" Biggs asked, jotting notes on the pad he took out of his pocket when O'Connor started talking. "Yes, Lieutenant, I wrote a detailed report the evening that we took the pictures, and I put it in the envelope with the photos. They're also stamped on the reverse side of each print with the date and time that the shots were taken, along with the signature and service number of the photographer."

"Wouldn't have been back in July, would it?" Biggs now smiled. "Gunny Jackson and I personally busted Carnegie with a package of Buddha that looked awfully like the wrappings on some we turned in as evidence last spring."

"I think that we can safely say the packages are one and the same," O'Connor said, and then smiled at Charlie Heyster.

Happy Pounds eased close to Staff Sergeant Pride, looking at the disgraced officer slouched in the chair by the admin chief's desk, his hands clamped in steel cuffs.

"Gaca, man," he said, and shook his head. "Gaca!"

"Yeah," Pride answered. "That's gaca all right. Big-time gaca. Just goes to show. Damned sure happens, doesn't it."

Pounds nodded and looked at Terry O'Connor and Jon Kirkwood, who frowned at the two enlisted Marines and blinked their eyes, confused.

"Gaca?" O'Connor said, shrugging his shoulders and then glancing at his best friend.

"What's that?" Kirkwood asked, completely puzzled by the strange word.

"Gaca," Pride nodded. "You've heard people say what goes around, comes around. Right? Get it? Goes around, comes around. It's an acronym. We say, gaca."

"SO THE LONG good-bye has finally arrived for you two!" Terry O'Connor said to Movie Star and Wayne Ebberhardt as the two men stood by the office jeep, their seabags and the captain's Marine Corps-issued, green, rubberized nylon, Valpac suitcase piled in the backseat. All their buddies from the law center had come to the curb to say farewell to the two homeward-bound Marines.

"You know why I'm glad to see you guys go? Because that makes peckerhead O'Connor and me next!" Jon Kirkwood said, laughing and standing by Michael Carter and Happy Pounds, and the new office driver, a kid named George Mason from Vicksburg, Mississippi. The enlisted Marines had already christened the new man College Boy, because of his name being the same as the university in Fairfax, Virginia.

Corporal Jerry Farmer and Sergeant Dick Amos, the wing law center's two other enlisted legal specialists, stood on the opposite side of the jeep and shook hands with the two departing friends.

"Excuse me, Captain Kirkwood, but I'm next!" Carter beamed. "I rotate in October, and you two have to wait until December."

"Okay, I'm glad to see you two go because Mikie's next, and then it's peckerhead and me!" Kirkwood said with a laugh.

"We made a promise to Tommy McKay," Terry O'Connor said, and looked at all the Marines present, enlisted and officer alike. "July Fourth in Denver! We'll all be home by then. No excuses! We're going to meet up at the bar at the Hilton Hotel at five o'clock in the afternoon, Mountain Standard Time. If you're not there, you'd better have a good excuse! That includes you, Sergeant Pride, and you guys, too, Sergeant Amos, Corporal Farmer and Corporal Pounds. And especially you, Movie Star. Where would we be without you there?"

Wayne Ebberhardt hugged his buddies hard. Then they all hugged Movie Star. Even Michael Carter, who still had not gotten past the event in the barracks. His confession about it with Father Flannigan, the wing Catholic chaplain, had gone badly, so that added to the stick man's guilt.

"I think that you need to find a new girlfriend, and you should let Rosie Palm rest with her five sisters for a while," Carter said, and then laughed at his own joke.

"Oh, good one, Mikie!" Ebberhardt said and laughed, wrapping his arm around James Dean and rapping his knuckles on the man's head.

"They never say no!" Movie Star said with a laugh, and then put on his black-plastic-rimmed Foster Grant sunglasses. "Captain Carter, believe me, when I get home, and back on the beach at Malibu, Rosie Palm will be hard pressed to take me out on a date."

"You're one fucked-up individual, you know that, Movie Star?" Archie Gunn said, walking up to the group with Buck Taylor at his side, and Mike Schuller shutting off the engine to the jeep in which he gave the two men a lift when he saw them walking toward the law center.

"Wayne, you and Movie Star know we couldn't let you two catch that freedom bird without a proper farewell from us flyboys, and, of course, the brig warden, too," Taylor said with a laugh, and put out his hand for the two Marines to shake.

"Damn, I'm glad you guys came over to say so long," Ebberhardt said, and then hugged both pilots and the warden.

"Wouldn't have missed it for the world," Lobo said, and wrapped his arm around Lance Corporal Dean and gave him a hard squeeze. "We're kind of like family. After all we've seen together."

Mike Schuller looked at Wayne Ebberhardt and smiled.

"I got orders back to the division," the lieutenant said and then sighed.

"I don't know if it's a move up or a step down. I'm getting command of a company, though, so I think it's probably a move upward."

"You did good at the brig," Wayne said. "It's their loss and the division's gain. Where're you going?"

"Up to Ninth Marines, with Lieutenant Colonel Jack Hembee!" Schuller said and then laughed. "I got you good! I am so happy I could bust! Colonel Hembee put in the word to General Davis that he wanted me commanding one of his companies. So I got the blessings from on high!"

"Super news!" Ebberhardt said, and hugged the lieutenant.

"I had to extend my tour for another six months, but shit, I got a company!" Schuller said.

"You know, they didn't call Jack Hembee Major Danger for nothing," Terry O'Connor reminded his happy friend.

"Yeah," Wayne Ebberhardt said. "That's Colonel Danger now, so you better keep your head down. The incoming rounds will probably get a lot bigger. I'm serious. You watch your ass. You hear me?"

"Loud and clear my friend, loud and clear," Schuller said, beaming at his friends.

"Hey! How about a picture, guys?" Staff Sergeant Pride shouted, and stepped back with his camera to get a snapshot of his pals.

"College Boy," O'Connor called to the new driver who sat behind the wheel of the major's jeep, "do us a favor and shoot the flick for us, so Staff Sergeant Pride gets in it, too. That way we have the whole gang!"

"Okay, you guys," George Mason said, and then took the twin-lens Roleflex camera from the staff sergeant and hung it around his neck. He looked down into the ground-glass viewfinder and then slowly released the shutter, capturing the faces of Dick Amos, Jerry Farmer, Happy Pounds, James Dean, Derek Pride, Buck Taylor, Archie Gunn, Michael Schuller, Jon Kirkwood, Terry O'Connor, Michael Carter, and Wayne Ebberhardt.

"Just one guy missing from the shot," Ebberhardt said, thinking about his pal, T.D. McKay.

"Hey, wing photo took that picture of me, Jon, and Tommy when we got our medals last spring. Nice big color print, too," Terry O'Connor said with a smile. "I'll get copies made and send one to everybody here. That way we have the whole fucking crew immortalized!"

"Okay, I'll look for it," Wayne Ebberhardt said, sitting in the front seat of the jeep while Movie Star piled on top of the baggage in the back. Then as George Mason backed the vehicle from the group and pulled into the street to get his passengers to the freedom bird, the captain shouted to his friends, "Denver, guys! Don't forget! The Hilton Hotel bar, July Fourth at five o'clock. Be there or you better be dead!"

Terry O'Connor waved as the jeep rolled slowly down the block, and sang with his loudest voice: "Good-bye, Ruby Tuesday. Who could hang a name on you? When you change with every new day. Still I'm gonna miss you!"

Chapter 23

"GOOD-BYE, RUBY TUESDAY"

A GREEN FERN flowed over the sides of a wicker-covered planter that hung by wires from the ceiling in front of one of three massive plate-glass windows in Terry O'Connor's corner office on the fifteenth floor of the Third Avenue high-rise business complex owned by the law firm where he now worked as one of its senior partners. In the nearly thirty-seven years since the brig riot, the Philadelphia Irishman had lost a good third of the hair on his head, only to have it replaced by mysterious stray fibers that grew from his back, making him look like the part-human fly monster in the old 1950s horror movie. Now, whatever once rusty-red foliage that had graced his crown in those bygone years had in the recent past turned silvery-white.

He hated looking in a mirror these days, because the youthful kid with dimples and twinkling eyes and magnetic smile now stared back at him with furrows for dimples and sagging jaws where the smile went. The eyes still sparkled, though, when he told his jokes, and his voice sounded much the same. Just a little deeper, and he had to clear his throat quite often these days, too.

"Got to see a doctor about that scratchy feeling down the gullet," he told himself as he put his fingers between the blinds and looked down at the corner of Fifty-fourth Street and Third Avenue, on Manhattan's East

Side, where he hoped to see his pals Wayne Ebberhardt and Gwen emerge from a taxi at any minute.

He married Vibeke Ahlquist three months after he got home from Vietnam. He had no job then, nor did he have any prospects of finding one soon. However, Vibeke was happy to live in Philadelphia with Terry's mom and dad. She and the old man talked politics most evenings and weekends. They had it all figured out. Eliminate state sovereignty and put everything into a centralized federal government that ensured that all people's needs found equal and sufficient fulfillment. Terry thanked God that he belonged to the Republican Party.

The couple celebrated thirty-six years together on March 17, 2005. That's right, St. Patrick's Day. Any good Irishman would do likewise. Terry had surprised himself when he asked her to marry him, Christmas morning, 1968. Just home from the war a few days, and suddenly very much in love with the Swedish girl who tortured his Republican nerves with her left-wing social conscience. He didn't want to wait for November 10, the Marine Corps birthday, the other date that seemed appropriate. Besides, with Vibeke's attitude about the American military at the time, St. Patrick's Day worked best all the way round.

Terrence Otto O'Connor came to live on planet Earth May 28, 1970, and owed his name to each of his grandfathers. Then Jonathan Wayne O'Connor joined his big brother at play on the fourth day of June 1971. After his second son's birth, Terry loved to joke with people that he was John Wayne's dad.

Six years later, Christiana Marie O'Connor came to live at their house, and the two boys had to clean up their acts so their baby sister did not grow up a hooligan like them.

Each of Terry's and Vibeke's children had two offspring of their own now, and Grandpa, as the little ones now called him, had that to think about as he looked at his gray hair and ever more ruddy, wrinkled complexion.

His dad died in March 2000, well in his eighties. Prostate cancer had claimed him in a heartbreaking battle. Terry promised his pop that he would never neglect seeing the doctor at least once a year, and getting checked. Last October, as the doctor had the third joint of his right hand's middle finger planted deep in the lawyer's ass, the joking Irishman asked the physician, "Which is worse, getting it or giving it?"

When the doctor finished and yanked off the rubber glove, he laughed. "Thanks for asking," he said, tossing the K-Y-drenched surgical mitt in the trash. "Giving the prostate exam is much worse."

Terry O'Connor laughed, thinking about his friend Doctor Ken Silverman, who had his office in the medical tower two blocks down the street. Then he saw the taxi stop and three people got out: Wayne, Gwen, and Vibeke. They carried bags from Bloomingdale's.

"That explains it," he said to himself as he walked to the sitting area in the corner of his office and picked up his canvas briefcase and checked to be sure he had packed all the folders he needed to keep up with the work he had to complete before the middle of next week.

Corporate contracts had paid him well. It afforded him a spacious Third Avenue condominium six blocks uptown from his office, and a Long Island summer cottage near the beach at Southampton. After he left the Marine Corps, he never defended another criminal case. Contract litigation and negotiations kept him at peace with himself.

"Mister O'Connor," the voice of Cynthia Marvel, his personal assistant, said on the intercom. "Your wife and friends have just cleared security and should be up in a few minutes."

"Thanks, Cyn," he answered, and lay his briefcase on the corner of his desk. "Any word from Mister Gunn or Mister Taylor?"

"Nothing yet," Cynthia answered, and clicked off the speaker.

Terry sat down in his brown leather swivel chair and swung around toward the black walnut credenza and hutch that stood against the wall behind his desk. He took from the shelf the framed picture of him and his buddies at First MAW Law that George Mason had snapped the day Wayne and Movie Star had flown home from Vietnam, and laid it in his lap. A tear splashed on the glass, and he wiped it away with his thumb.

He did that every time he looked at the photograph now.

A black, compact-disc player sat on the middle shelf, above his Vietnam pictures and memorabilia. He leaned forward in his chair and pushed the center button on the machine. Instantly Mick Jagger's young voice came flowing through the speakers that sat in all four corners of his office.

"She would never say where she came from," Terry sang with Mick, setting the group photograph next to the miniature Marine Corps and American flags that stood in the small stand by a shadow box of his medals. Then he picked up the picture of him, Tommy McKay, and Jon Kirkwood that the wing photographer had snapped of the three Marines just after they had pinned on their awards for valor.

"Yesterday don't matter if it's gone," he sang, looking at the smiling faces of two of the best men he had ever known in his life.

"While the sun is bright," Terry sang through a broken voice, and tears came again. "Or in the darkest night. No one knows. She comes and goes."

"Good-bye, Ruby Tuesday. Who could hang a name on you? When you change with every new day," the music drifted from the four speakers.

"Still I'm gonna miss you!" O'Connor choked, and then broke down and sobbed, looking at the two photographs.

He cried because he thought of the empty seats at this year's reunion. Two new ones because of a tragic plane crash at Aspen this past Christmas.

The first vacant chair that he and his buddies leaned against the table before an undrunk glass of beer belonged to First Lieutenant Michael Schuller. It was their inaugural get-together in Denver on July 4, 1969.

On January 20, 1969, Colonel Robert Barrow launched all three battalions of his Ninth Marine Regiment against the North Vietnamese Army ensconced deep in the A Shau Valley, in the western mountains of northern I Corps, near the combat outpost that Marines knew as Khe Sanh. The Marines called the massive strike Operation Dewey Canyon. It lasted until March 18, 1969, and it exacted a heavy toll on the Ninth Marine Regiment, nearly decimating its First Battalion, nicknamed the Walking Dead.

Midway through the operation, while February snows blew down the streets of Philadelphia, Lieutenant Colonel Hembee led his battalion on a sweep, trying to push the enemy into the other two battalions, which waited in ambush. Mike Schuller, now selected as captain, led his company at the point of the assault.

While they moved at the head of the sweep, the North Vietnamese sprang their trap and attacked Schuller and his men from both sides. He never knew what hit him. The lieutenant, who insisted at walking near the point, fell first.

Nearby, that same day, a fellow first lieutenant who commanded a company in First Battalion, had his hands full with the enemy regiment that swept upon his positions. The young officer, who had seen his first combat action in Korea as a corporal, dug in his heels and despite the overwhelming force he and his men faced, suffering heavy casualties, including the death of his executive officer, turned the tide against the relentless enemy. For his valor, the young mustang lieutenant, Wes Fox, received the Medal of Honor.

That empty chair that leaned against the table haunted Terry O'Connor. It seemed to add a somber color that at first came into conflict with the original intent of the annual gathering of friends. Then it became the reason why they got together, because new chairs leaned against the table. Now, two more chairs.

So as he listened to his favorite song, Terry O'Connor cried.

"Oh no!" Cynthia Marvel sighed as she stood next to her boss's closed door and looked back at Vibeke, Gwen, and Wayne, who had just walked in the O'Connor office reception area. "He put on that damned music again. I knew I should have had him come out here to wait for you guys. I'm so sorry. Do you want to go in there, Vibeke? Last time I did, I felt so bad seeing him like that. You know, with Mister Kirkwood and Mister Dean and all."

"Why, they died last Christmas," Wayne said, wrinkling his eyebrows, concerned about Terry. "He's still grieving about it? I feel bad, too, but this is July third. It's been seven months now."

"I think we can sit out here and talk while he gets through this little bump," Vibeke said, and smiled at Wayne and Gwen. "He's always kept those pictures there in his office. I suggested that he should put them away for a while, at least until he can look at them without getting so upset. Oh, he won't hear of it. He says that he has to see them every day."

"Look, none of us is in any kind of hurry, Vib," Gwen said and put her arm around O'Connor's wife, who now took a napkin from her purse and dabbed her eyes. "Lobo and Buck, they said they would come here in a limo and take us to lunch and then out to LaGuardia, where Archie parked his plane. What is it, Wayne? A Gulfstream Three?"

"Yeah, Gwen," Wayne said, nodding and still frowning. "Totally re-fitted. Looks like a pimp's Cadillac inside now, but that's Lobo's style."

Both women laughed, and Cynthia chuckled, too, as she sat in the chair across from Gwen and Vibeke.

"Mister Gunn is too funny," she said, smiling at the ladies and then noticing that Wayne Ebberhardt smiled, too.

"We had just got back to Atlanta from Wayne visiting his mother and dad, four brothers, two sisters, and ten thousand cousins in North Carolina when we got that call that Jon and Movie Star had crashed, flying to Aspen," Gwen said and sighed. "Yes, James Dean, the ever-powerful motion picture agent, had deals to swing at the Telluride Film Festival and made that poor pilot wait until the weather was just too bad to fly. Then our dear know-it-all and the forces be damned, Movie Star, demanded that the pilot put that plane in the air that foggy afternoon. Lucky for Katherine and the grandkids, and James's wife, Helen, and their grandchildren that they had gone ahead to Aspen that morning. Let me tell you from experience, eveningtime in the winter in Colorado, trying to land at a place like Aspen, is pure stupidity."

"People who had talked to those two before they flew said that Jon had expressed some serious reservations about flying because of the cloudy and foggy conditions that he heard reported on the television at the hotel," Cynthia offered, getting up and going to Terry O'Connor's office door and listening. "The music's still playing, so I guess he's in his funk."

"Katherine Kirkwood and Helen Dean had just gotten back to Movie Star's lodge on Woody Creek Road when they actually heard the plane crash," Vibeke said and shook her head. "Kat told me that when she heard the loud explosion and then saw the glow toward the Aspen airport that she knew Jon and James had died just then."

"Didn't Katherine tell Terry that she and the boys were coming this year on Jon's behalf?" Gwen asked, wiping a tear from her eyes, too.

"Yes, and Helen and their children, too. They have remained in Aspen the whole year," Vibeke said, dabbing her eyes. "Now, this year's weekend trip, we're supposed to go to the Stanley Hotel in Estes Park. You know, the hotel from that movie *The Shining*? I hate to say this, but you know why Terry wants to go there?"

"Oh, I don't know, but given Terry's moods these days, I imagine it's probably a creepy reason," Gwen said and shuddered.

"Well, if you consider ghosts creepy, then yes, it is," Vibeke said, and then leaned forward to whisper. "Terry read that the Stanley Hotel is really haunted. He thinks that Jon and Movie Star will want to contact the group, and this hotel, because of its spiritual allure for the departed, would offer the best opportunity for Jon's and James's spirits to make contact with us."

"Oh, that is too creepy!" Gwen said, putting her hands over her mouth.

"Don't you women ever get tired of dragging around the dead?" Wayne Ebberhardt growled, got up from the sofa, and walked to Terry O'Connor's door, and knocked.

"Careful, Wayne," Vibeke said, standing, too, and walking to the office door. "This is the first Independence Day reunion without Jon and Movie Star."

"I know," Wayne said, and then looked at Gwen. "Don't forget, I was with those two in Vietnam. We were all close. I cried for a week when I got the news about Mike Schuller getting killed in action. Happy Pounds died in a car wreck in 1973, and Sergeant Amos got shot and killed by a drive-by gang-banger on the one-oh-one outside Santa Monica in '89. Then, two years ago, I felt devastated when I learned that Derek Pride dropped dead at his desk in the Sears Tower in Chicago. The man never quit trying to get ahead and died at the ripe old age of fifty-nine. Hell, we're all over sixty now. Pretty soon we're all gonna start dropping like flies."

"Hush, Wayne!" Gwen snapped, and looked at Vibeke, who raised her eyebrows at the brashness of the Atlanta-based airline lawyer.

"I'll just step inside," Vibeke said softly to Wayne Ebberhardt, who now went back to the sofa and sat down.

Terry O'Connor leaned over the two photographs in their polished mahogany frames, adjusting them equally distant from the small Marine Corps and U.S. flags stapled to ten-inch-long standards and mounted in a black plastic disc. He kept singing in a soft voice, even though the Rolling Stones had long ago finished "Good-bye, Ruby Tuesday."

"Still I'm going to miss you," he whispered as his wife put her arm around his shoulders and gave him a squeeze.

"You know, Captain O'Connor, I loved you the first moment I saw you," Vibeke said and kissed his forehead. "I never stopped, not even after you told me that you voted for Barry Goldwater. Nor when you voted for Richard Nixon."

"I know," Terry said, and patted her hand where she rested it on his shoulder. "I loved you, too, in spite of you being a Communist, and having the FBI digging into everything I ever did, and talking to every person who ever knew me. I loved you very much last April, too, at the Marine Corps-Law Enforcement Foundation gala, at the Plaza Hotel, because you put your passion and your politics aside and treated Vice President Cheney so elegantly, after he made his address to our gathering and then greeted us in the crowd."

"Well, I do have some decorum, you know," Vibeke said, smiling at her husband. "Also, I never joined the Communist Party. I am a socialist. I believe all humanity should care for his neighbor. There should be no homeless people, nor hungry people, or old people and children without someone to care for them."

"Well, I'm old, and I only have you to care for me," Terry said, smiling up at the sixty-year-old woman who radiated timeless beauty and absolute grace.

"You have two sons and a daughter who will never let you need a thing," Vibeke said, and pointed to the shelf filled with photographs of their children and six grandchildren.

Terry took the picture of the group gathered by the jeep and smiled at his wife.

"I was a handsome devil then, wasn't I," he said, pointing at his smiling face.

"Yes, you still are quite a handsome devil, too," Vibeke said, and touched him on the tip of his nose with her finger.

"Sometimes I wish I could go back," Terry said, looking at the photograph. "You know, just step through time and go back to those days. God, I miss Jon!"

"I know you do," Vibeke said, and then put her arms around her husband, took the picture from his hands, and set it back on the shelf by the flags.

"Any word from Lobo and Buck?" Terry asked, wiping his eyes with his hand and looking back once more at the photographs of him and his buddies in Vietnam nearly thirty-seven years ago.

"The phone rang just as I came in your door, so that may be them," Vibeke said, straightening her husband's pale green polo shirt and giving him a quick glance to make sure he had on the right slacks to contrast with his sport jacket, and to be sure he had not sneaked out his comfortable old shoes that looked so tacky but that he always insisted on wearing because they felt so good on his feet.

"We can go downstairs," Terry offered. "Catch them when they pull to the curb."

"No," Vibeke said, taking his canvas briefcase and leading him to the door. "I have my standards. I do not wait at curbs. Now, before we leave this room, you must promise me that I will not hear you arguing with any of your friends about this awful war in Iraq."

"You mean that nitwit Carter," Terry said, and shook his head. "He's more fucked up than ever, now that he's become the great Boston political activist. Those people are out to lunch, and you know it. Even you agree that we have no choice but to see this thing through in Iraq. The eggs are broken! Damn!"

"Now, you watch your language, too," Vibeke scolded her husband. "That word you like to use, I don't approve. It makes you appear ignorant. People who use such profanity have no imagination.

"As for the war, you and I do agree about that issue. It was wrong to go in the way we did, without more consideration about the cost in American lives as opposed to the benefit. However, as you say, the eggs were broken the day the bombs fell in Baghdad. Yes, Michael Carter and his bunch are, as you say, out to lunch.

"Now that we have those issues settled, and I hope out of your system, we will hear no more talk about it."

"I promise, no war arguments," Terry O'Connor said, walking out his office door and smiling at Gwen. Wayne had slouched back in the sofa and closed his eyes.

Cynthia Marvel smiled at Terry O'Connor and Vibeke. She loved how they looked together. She hoped that when she reached sixty years of age that she and her husband looked as good, and as in tune with each other.

"Of course you know my friends, Cyn," Terry said, pointing to Wayne and Gwen.

"Well, yes, Mister O'Connor," Cynthia said, "I met them last year and the year before that, too."

"Oh, that's right," Terry said, and looked at his wife, who smiled at him.

"You've had your mind elsewhere," she said, hooking her arm through his as they walked into the reception area.

"Wayne, did you know that Cynthia's husband, Ken, is a Marine Corps Reserve pilot?" O'Connor said, looking down at his pal, who kept his eyes shut.

"I think so, yes," Wayne answered, still slouched with his head laid back and his eyes closed.

"Do you know what his rank is?" Terry said and laughed, looking at Cynthia, who shook her head and walked back to her desk and sat on its corner.

"Oh, don't tell me," Wayne said and laughed, still trying not to look up. "Since his last name is Marvel, he's got to be a captain."

"Right!" Terry said with a laugh. "My assistant is married to none other than Captain Marvel! I love it!"

"You have a sick and twisted mind, Terry O'Connor," Wayne Ebberhardt said, and then opened his eyes. "You know, Stanley Tufts called me yesterday."

"No, I didn't!" Terry said, and then looked at Gwen who shrugged and shook her head. "I haven't heard anything about him since he left Vietnam."

"He has a law practice in Seattle and just called me out of the blue, looking for buddies who served with him in Vietnam," Ebberhardt said, and took a drink from a glass of tea he had sitting on the coffee table. "I told him to come to Denver and join up with us at the Hilton. That's okay, isn't it?"

"Of course!" Terry said, smiling. "Why, he wasn't such a bad fellow. A kiss-ass, but not a bad fellow."

"Yeah, that's how I felt about it, so I invited him," Wayne said and opened his eyes. "We can see if he still walks with his arms out like a sea-gull on a hot day."

Terry laughed and sat down on the couch in his office's reception area. "How did he find you?"

"Marine Corps Association," Ebberhardt answered, and took another sip of iced tea. "He joined the MCA and got a copy of the membership directory and looked me up. I'm surprised he hasn't tried to call you, too. You got one this year, didn't you?"

"Sure, it's on a shelf behind my desk," Terry said, and pointed with his thumb toward his office door. "I never thought to look to see if Stanley or anyone else was listed in it. I guess all the people I want to know, I have their addresses and numbers in my Rolodex."

"He told me that Dicky Doo is still with the living," Wayne said and smiled. "Thought that would make you smile."

"Oh, he wasn't such an enormous asshole," Terry said, and laughed. "Just a moderate-sized one. Don't forget, he went to bat for Sergeant Fryer and Sergeant Wilson after the brig riot, and got the charges dropped on both of them. They spent the rest of their tours at special services, but that beat hell out of the brig and bad time on their records."

"He's down at Hilton Head, South Carolina," Wayne said, and smiled. "Pushing eighty years old, I guess, and Stanley tells me the old fart plays golf every day."

"Good for Dicky Doo!" Terry said and looked at Gwen and laughed. "He and Stanley never figured out what gave them the shits, did they."

"Terry, I have borne the guilt of doing that to those poor men like a millstone tied to my neck!" Gwen said, and then laughed, too. "Thank God they didn't figure it out. I might have gone to jail! I certainly would have had no chance of ever working at any airline either."

"Might be fun to tell Stanley now," Terry said with a laugh.

"No, it might not," Wayne said, and then sighed. "I called Dicky Doo, and invited him, too. He said he'd have to think it over and talk to his ball and chain—his words, not mine."

"Ball and chain?" Gwen laughed. "Oh, I might find some more of that magic powder then and fix him another drink! Can you imagine a man these days calling his wife a ball and chain?"

"So, he's listed in the directory, too?" Terry asked, and then looked at his watch, wondering what kept Lobo and Buck.

"Yeah," Wayne said and smiled. "After Stanley called me, I got to looking and found our favorite mojo. It lists his home address, telephone number, and electronic mail. Want a good laugh? Guess what he has for an Internet address."

"I wouldn't have a clue," Terry said, not wanting to think too hard about the man who tormented him during most of his tour in Vietnam.

"Believe it or not, its Dicky Doo at Earthlink dot com," Wayne said and howled laughing.

"I don't believe you!" O'Connor said with a laugh, and looked at Gwen and Vibeke, who laughed, too. "I wonder who told him?"

"I asked Colonel Dickinson about it and he laughed," Ebberhardt said. "Charlie Heyster told him. Kept him filled in on all our dirty deeds."

"He never figured out that Jon and Movie Star loosened the bolts on his furniture though, did he," O'Connor said with a smile and nodded confidently. "Not even after he moved into Colonel Prunella's old office. The stuff kept wobbling and the lamps kept flashing, and he never had a clue, did he."

"I don't know, he might surprise you," Wayne said and noticed the lights above the elevators outside the double glass doors that led into the reception area flash across the numbers and stop on fifteen. "I didn't think to ask him about the furniture, but I did inquire about his fair-haired boy Charlie Heyster."

"All I ever knew about the shyster was that General Cushman didn't even let him spend the night in Da Nang after Lieutenant Biggs arrested him. They put him on a gooney bird to the rock, and that's the last anybody saw of him," O'Connor said, looking out at the elevators, too. "Jon said that they kept him overnight in Okinawa, then flew him to Camp Pendleton, where they tossed him in the brig."

"Matches pretty close to what Dickinson told me," Ebberhardt said, nodding in agreement. "You ever wonder why nobody asked for those photographs, or none of us had to ever testify? It just all disappeared like fog?"

"Yeah!" Terry O'Connor said, sitting up. "I stayed pissed off for a couple of years. I figured they let him slide and reassigned him someplace, or worst case, let him resign."

"Dicky Doo told me that Charlie bought a plea deal in exchange for all the names of the people he supplied with dope," Wayne said and shook his head. "Of course, the Marine Corps yanked his commission, busted him to private, dismissed him from the service, and put him on ice for two years of hard labor at Portsmouth. However, he avoided serving ten. Got disbarred, though, thank goodness. The three deadly D's—disgraced, dismissed, and disbarred."

"So the dirty bastard did time after all," O'Connor said, and let out a deep sigh. "Wonder what he's doing now? Hell, I wonder what just about anyone we tried to keep out of the brig is doing these days."

"Dickinson said that Heyster managed to put together enough money to open a used-car dealership in Oakland," Ebberhardt said, noticing a familiar hulk stepping out of the elevator. "He's been in touch with him off and on. I guess Heyster's doing okay selling cars. It broke Dicky Doo's heart, though, when Charlie went down in flames."

"Kind of disproved his theory about the good guys and the bad guys," O'Connor shrugged, and looked at the mass of humanity that ambled toward his reception area.

"Hey, shit for brains!" Archie Gunn bellowed at Terry O'Connor as he pushed open the double glass doors that led to his suite of offices. "You know, we need to get rocking and rolling if we're going to swoop down to Dallas and pick up that jockstrap McKay and his little Mexican-cutie wife, Marguerite, and still get to Denver in time to have dinner tonight at Stockman's Steakhouse."

"Where's Buck?" Terry said, grabbing his briefcase, and luggage he had staged in the corner of the reception area.

"Down there keeping that fruitcake company that's driving our limo," Lobo said, grabbing two handfuls of suitcases and helping the four people get to the elevator. "Good thing this is just for the holiday weekend, or I'd have to hire a truck for your extra shit."

"Speaking of fruitcakes," Wayne Ebberhardt said, pushing the down button on the elevator, "I take it that we're not taking a jag to Boston to pick up Mikie and his life companion, Tab?"

"Fuck, no," Lobo said, and then looked at the ladies. "Oh, sorry. Shit, no! The twirp has some kind of rally tonight. Something to do with gay marriage and taking it before the Supreme Court. He and Tab will fly tomorrow. I've got a car picking them up at DIA about noon."

"Oh, yes, he called me about wanting to hire one of our partners at this firm to argue the gay marriage case before the Supreme Court, if they can get it heard by the Court, of course," Terry said, and smiled. "Mikie's their lead man in pressing the issue before the courts."

"As long as they have that nitwit Carter in charge," Lobo said, shoving the double armloads of luggage onto the elevator as the doors opened, "we won't have to worry about gay marriage anytime soon."

"So Archie, how's business with that chain of sporting goods stores you have, Lobo Sports?" Wayne Ebberhardt said, getting on the elevator.

"We're opening a super center in Atlanta," Lobo said, putting his arm around Gwen's shoulders and giving her a lusty squeeze. "That makes me coast to coast. One hundred seventeen stores. Amazing what a guy can do with a handful of fishing reels and hunting rifles."

"Buck's still your chief financial officer and vice chairman of the board?" Terry said, and slapped his old friend across the back.

"Yeah, but the shithead's talking about wanting to retire and go fishing every day at Corpus Christi," Lobo said and laughed. "Shit, he doesn't have to retire to do that!"

A FINE MIST lay over Bangkok and formed a halo of light above the Normandy Restaurant, which sat atop the main tower of the famous, old Oriental Hotel. Its luminance caught the eye of Brian Pitts, who stood dressed in black silk pajamas and matching velvet slippers at one of the ten cathedral widows that lined one side of his five-thousand-square-foot penthouse atop the skyscraper owned by his construction company. He gazed into the lonely wet night and at the lifeless lights below, and he watched the endless traffic of barges pushing their loads down the river, past the grand, five-star hotel set at the water's edge, and its restaurant with its circle of light.

For the past several years he found himself sleeping less and less as he spent night after night alone with only his thoughts, his memories, and his regrets for company as he looked out the big windows of his palace, gazing upon the city that waited at his feet. While he stood his solitary vigil, night after monotonous night, he often thought of his Aunt Winnie Russell, now ninety-two years old, stubbornly living in her modest frame house in Olathe, Kansas, despite his incessant invitations to come reside with him in Thailand. Never giving up on the boy she loved as a son, she had the housekeepers and home health nurse, whose wages her dear nephew paid, keep the room above the garage tidy, in case Brian ever decided to come home.

INDEX